THE ROUTLEDGE COMPANION TO CRIME FICTION

The Routledge Companion to Crime Fiction is a comprehensive introduction to crime fiction and crime fiction scholarship today. Across forty-five original chapters, specialists in the field offer innovative approaches to the classics of the genre as well as groundbreaking mappings of emerging themes and trends.

The volume is divided into three parts. Part I, *Approaches*, rearticulates the key theoretical questions posed by the crime genre. Part II, *Devices*, examines the textual characteristics of the genre. Part III, *Interfaces*, investigates the complex ways in which crime fiction engages with the defining issues of its context – from policing and forensic science through war, migration and narcotics to digital media and the environment.

Engagingly written and drawing on examples from around the world, this volume is indispensable to both students and scholars of crime fiction.

Janice Allan is Associate Dean in the School of Arts and Media at the University of Salford, UK.

Jesper Gulddal is Associate Professor in Literary Studies at the University of Newcastle, Australia.

Stewart King is Senior Lecturer in the School of Languages, Literatures, Cultures and Linguistics at Monash University, Australia.

Andrew Pepper is Senior Lecturer in English and American Literature at Queen's University, Belfast.

ROUTLEDGE COMPANIONS TO LITERATURE

Also available in this series:

The Routledge Companion to International Children's Literature
Edited by John Stephens, with Celia Abicalil Belmiro, Alice Curry, Li Lifang and Yasmine S. Motawy

The Routledge Companion to Picturebooks
Edited by Bettina Kümmerling-Meibauer

The Routledge Companion to World Literature and World History
Edited by May Hawas

The Routledge Companion to Pakistani Anglophone Writing
Edited by Aroosa Kanwal and Saiyma Aslam

The Routledge Companion to Literature and Economics
Edited by Matt Seybold and Michelle Chihara

The Routledge Companion to Twenty-First Century Literature
Edited by Daniel O'Gorman and Robert Eaglestone

The Routledge Companion to Transnational American Studies
Edited by Nina Morgan, Alfred Hornung and Takayuki Tatsumi

The Routledge Companion to Victorian Literature
Edited by Dennis Denisoff and Talia Schaffer

The Routledge Companion to Health Humanities
Edited by Paul Crawford, Brian Brown and Andrea Charise

The Routledge Companion to Crime Fiction
Edited by Janice Allan, Jesper Gulddal, Stewart King and Andrew Pepper

The Routledge Companion to Literature and Trauma
Edited by Hanna Meretoja and Colin Davis

The Routledge Companion to Literature and Disability
Edited by Alice Hall

THE ROUTLEDGE COMPANION TO CRIME FICTION

*Edited by Janice Allan, Jesper Gulddal, Stewart King
and Andrew Pepper*

LONDON AND NEW YORK

First published 2020
by Routledge
2 Park Square, Milton Park, Abingdon, Oxon OX14 4RN

and by Routledge
52 Vanderbilt Avenue, New York, NY 10017

Routledge is an imprint of the Taylor & Francis Group, an informa business

© 2020 selection and editorial matter, Janice Allan, Jesper Gulddal, Stewart King and Andrew Pepper; individual chapters, the contributors

The right of Janice Allan, Jesper Gulddal, Stewart King and Andrew Pepper to be identifi ed as the authors of the editorial material, and of the authors for their individual chapters, has been asserted in accordance with sections 77 and 78 of the Copyright, Designs and Patents Act 1988.

All rights reserved. No part of this book may be reprinted or reproduced or utilised in any form or by any electronic, mechanical, or other means, now known or hereafter invented, including photocopying and recording, or in any information storage or retrieval system, without permission in writing from the publishers.

Trademark notice: Product or corporate names may be trademarks or registered trademarks, and are used only for identific ation and explanation without intent to infringe.

British Library Cataloguing-in-Publication Data
A catalogue record for this book is available from the British Library

Library of Congress Cataloging-in-Publication Data
Names: Allan, Janice M., 1966– editor. | Gulddal, Jesper, editor. |
King, Stewart, 1968– editor. | Pepper, Andrew, 1969– editor.
Title: The Routledge companion to crime fi ction / edited by Janice Allan, Jesper Gulddal, Stewart King and Andrew Pepper.
Description: Abingdon, Oxon; New York, NY: Routledge, 2020. |
Includes bibliographical references and index.
Identifiers: LCCN 2019055758 | ISBN 9781138320352 (hardback) |
ISBN 9780429453342 (ebook)
Subjects: LCSH: Detective and mystery stories–History and criticism. |
Crime in literature.
Classification:L CC PN3448.D4 R68 2020 | DDC 809.3/872–dc23
LC record available at https://lccn.loc.gov/2019055758

ISBN: 978-1-138-32035-2 (hbk)
ISBN: 978-1-032-57052-5 (pbk)
ISBN: 978-0-429-45334-2 (ebk)

CONTENTS

List of contributors	ix
Acknowledgements	xviii

Introduction: New directions in crime fiction scholarship *Janice Allan, Jesper Gulddal, Stewart King and Andrew Pepper*	1

PART I
Approaches

		11
1	Genre *Jesper Gulddal and Stewart King*	13
2	Counterhistories and prehistories *Maurizio Ascari*	22
3	The crime fiction series *Ruth Mayer*	31
4	Crime fiction in the marketplace *Emmett Stinson*	39
5	Adaptations *Neil McCaw*	48
6	Hybridisation *Heather Duerre Humann*	57

Contents

7 Graphic crime novels   65
   Robert Prickett and Casey A. Cothran

8 World literature   76
   Jakob Stougaard-Nielsen

9 Translation   85
   Karen Seago and Victoria Lei

10 Transnationality   94
   Barbara Pezzotti

11 Gender and sexuality   102
   Gill Plain

12 Race and ethnicity   111
   Sam Naidu

13 Coloniality and decoloniality   120
   Shampa Roy

14 Psychoanalysis   129
   Heta Pyrhönen

PART II
Devices   139

15 Murders   141
   Michael Harris-Peyton

16 Victims   149
   Rebecca Mills

17 Detectives   159
   David Geherin

18 Criminals   168
   Christiana Gregoriou

19 Beginnings and endings   177
   Alistair Rolls

20 Plotting   185
   Martin Edwards

Contents

21 Clues 194
Jesper Gulddal

22 Realism 202
Paul Cobley

23 Place 211
Stewart King

24 Time and space 219
Thomas Heise

25 Self-referentiality and metafiction 227
J.C. Bernthal

26 Paratextuality 236
Louise Nilsson

27 Affect 244
Christopher Breu

28 Alterity and the Other 252
Jean Anderson

29 Digital technology 261
Nicole Kenley

PART III
Interfaces 271

30 Crime fiction and criminology 273
Matthew Levay

31 Crime fiction and theories of justice 282
Susanna Lee

32 Crime fiction and modern science 291
Andrea Goulet

33 Crime fiction and the police 301
Andrew Nestingen

34 Crime fiction and memory 310
Kate M. Quinn

Contents

35	Crime fiction and trauma	318
	Cynthia S. Hamilton	
36	Crime fiction and politics	327
	José V. Saval	
37	Crime fiction and the city	335
	Eric Sandberg	
38	Crime fiction and war	343
	Patrick Deer	
39	Crime fiction and global capital	353
	Andrew Pepper	
40	Crime fiction and the environment	362
	Marta Puxan-Oliva	
41	Crime fiction and narcotics	371
	Andrew Pepper	
42	Crime fiction and migration	379
	Charlotte Beyer	
43	Crime fiction and authoritarianism	388
	Carlos Uxó	
44	Crime fiction and digital media	397
	Tanja Välisalo, Maarit Piipponen, Helen Mäntymäki and Aino-Kaisa Koistinen	
45	Crime fiction and the future	406
	Nicoletta Vallorani	

Index 414

CONTRIBUTORS

Janice Allan is Associate Dean in the School of Arts and Media at the University of Salford. Her research focuses on nineteenth-century crime and sensation fiction and constructions of literary value. She is the Executive Editor of *Clues: A Journal of Detection* and the co-editor of *The Cambridge Companion to Sherlock Holmes* (2019, with Christopher Pittard). Recent publications explore Gothic topographies in *The Hound of the Baskervilles*, the representation of private investigators in sensation fiction, the use of false hair in the construction of nineteenth-century femininity, and the relationship between realism and sensation in the periodical press. She is currently working on a new Oxford World Classics edition of *The Case-Book of Sherlock Holmes* (2022).

Jean Anderson is Associate Professor of French at Victoria University of Wellington, where she founded the New Zealand Centre for Literary Translation in 2007. Her research interests include translation theory and practice, late nineteenth-century fiction and francophone writing. With Barbara Pezzotti and Carolina Miranda, she has co-edited three collections of essays, *The Foreign in International Crime Fiction: Transcultural Representations* (Bloomsbury, 2012), *Serial Crime Fiction: Dying for More* (Palgrave, 2015) and *Blood on the Table: Essays on Food in International Crime Fiction* (McFarland, 2018). She is currently working on intercultural aspects of French crime fiction, particularly the work of Charles Exbrayat and Maurice-Bernard Endrèbe.

Maurizio Ascari teaches English Literature at the University of Bologna (Italy). He has published books and essays on crime fiction (*A Counter-History of Crime Fiction*, Palgrave, 2007, nominated for the Edgar Awards), transcultural literature (*Literature of the Global Age*, McFarland, 2011) and inter-art exchanges (*Cinema and the Imagination in Katherine Mansfield's Writing*, Palgrave, 2014). His edited collections include "Crime Narratives: Crossing Cultures" (*European Journal of English Studies*, 2010), with Heather Worthington, and *From the Sublime to City Crime* (2015), with Stephen Knight. He has also edited and translated works by Henry James, Katherine Mansfield, William Faulkner, Jack London and William Wilkie Collins.

J.C. Bernthal is a panel tutor at the University of Cambridge and Visiting Lecturer at Middlesex University. His interests are in crime fiction and queer theory, separately and in combination. He is the author of *Queering Agatha Christie: Rethinking the Golden Age of Detective Fiction* (Palgrave, 2016) and *Agatha Christie: A Companion to the Mystery Fiction* (McFarland, 2021). Bernthal has edited or co-edited multiple books on Christie, including, with Rebecca Mills, *Agatha Christie Goes to War* (Routledge, 2019). He founded the annual international Agatha Christie conferences in 2014 and co-founded the Golden Age of Crime Network in 2019.

Charlotte Beyer is Senior Lecturer in English Studies at the University of Gloucestershire, UK. She has published widely on crime fiction and contemporary literature. She edited the 2017 special issue on contemporary crime fiction for *American, British and Canadian Studies*, and the 2019 special issue on "Feminism and Motherhood in the 21st Century" for *Feminist Encounters*. She published *Teaching Crime Fiction* (ed., Palgrave) in 2018, *Mothers Without Their Children* (ed., Demeter Press) and *Travelling Mama: Mothers, Mothering, and Travel* (ed., Demeter Press) in 2019. She is currently writing a monograph on crime fiction for McFarland. Charlotte serves on the editorial boards for the journals *Feminist Encounters*, *The New Americanist* and *American, British and Canadian Studies*.

Christopher Breu is Professor of English at Illinois State University. He is the author of *Insistence of the Material: Literature in the Age of Biopolitics* (Minnesota, 2014) and *Hard-Boiled Masculinities* (Minnesota, 2005). He is co-editor of the forthcoming *Noir Affect* (Fordham, 2020) and is the guest editor of the special issue of *Symploke* on "Materialisms". He is currently working on two monographs, *In Defense of Sex* and *Infrastructure and Biopolitics*.

Paul Cobley is Professor in Language and Media in the Faculty of Arts and Creative Industries at Middlesex University. His research focuses on the thriller genre, including crime fiction. He is the author of *The American Thriller: Generic Innovation and Social Change in the 1970s* (Palgrave, 2000) as well as three other books and fifteen edited collections. Recent articles on the genre include "Geopolitical Reality: The Thriller, Global Power, and the Logic of Revelation" and "The Reactionary Art of Murder". He is currently working on a volume titled *Semiotics of Paranoia: Anxiety, Subjectivity and Geopolitics in the Post-9/11 Thriller*.

Casey A. Cothran is Associate Professor and Chair of the Department of English at Winthrop University in Rock Hill, South Carolina. Her research interests include both nineteenth-century literature and mystery fiction, as well as work by women writers. She is the co-editor of *New Perspectives on Detective Fiction: Mystery Magnified* (Taylor and Francis, 2016) and has published on nineteenth-century detective novelist Wilkie Collins in the *Victorians Institute Journal* and in the *Wilkie Collins Society Journal*. Other publications address New Woman writers and YA fantasy fiction. With Robert Prickett, she is currently beginning work focused on graphic novel mysteries.

Patrick Deer is Associate Professor of English at New York University. His research and teaching focus on modernism and contemporary British, American and postcolonial literature, war literature, film and music. He is the author of *Culture in Camouflage: War, Empire and Modern British Literature* (Oxford University Press, 2009, paperback edition 2016). His recent articles on war writing, film and war culture have been published in *Modern Fiction Studies*, *College Literature* and *Modernism/modernity Print+* online. He is currently working on two book projects, *We Are All Embedded: Understanding American War Culture Since 9/11* and *Deep England: Forging National Culture After Empire, 1945–1982*. He is also faculty coordinator of the NYU Cultures

Contributors

of War and the Postwar research group, which offers public programming with scholars, veterans, organisers, writers and artists.

Martin Edwards is the author of eighteen crime novels and has received numerous awards in the UK and the US for his fiction and non-fiction. He has edited forty anthologies, and is President of the Detection Club, consultant to the British Library's Crime Classics and former Chair of the Crime Writers' Association (CWA). As archivist of the CWA and the Detection Club, he established the British Crime Writing Archives in 2015. *The Golden Age of Murder* (2015) is a study of the Detection Club during the 1930s, while *The Story of Classic Crime in 100 Books* (2017) surveys crime fiction in the first half of the twentieth century.

David Geherin is Professor Emeritus of English at Eastern Michigan University, where he taught courses in modern and contemporary literature and in crime and mystery fiction for forty years. He is the author of nine books on a wide range of crime writing, including the first book on Elmore Leonard (1989) and two others – *The American Private Eye: The Image in Fiction* (1985) and *Scene of the Crime: The Importance of Place in Crime and Mystery Fiction* (2008) – that were finalists for the Mystery Writers of America's Edgar Allan Poe Award. Among his other books are *The Dragon Tattoo and its Long Tail: The New Wave of European Crime Fiction in America* (2012) and *Carl Hiaasen: Sunshine State Satirist* (2019).

Andrea Goulet is Professor of French and Francophone Studies at the University of Pennsylvania and co-chair of the Nineteenth-Century French Studies (NCFS) Association. She is the author of *Optiques: The Science of the Eye and the Birth of Modern French Fiction* (2006) and *Legacies of the Rue Morgue: Space and Science in French Crime Fiction* (2016). She has also co-edited journal issues on "Visual Culture" (*Contemporary French Civilization*) and "Crime Fictions" (*Yale French Studies*), as well as a volume on the cloning science and reproductive politics of the BBC television series *Orphan Black* titled *Orphan Black: Performance, Gender, Biopolitics* (Intellect Press, 2018).

Christiana Gregoriou is Associate Professor in English Language at the University of Leeds. She researches (critical) stylistics and crime writing. Most notable are her three monographs: *Crime Fiction Migration: Crossing Languages, Cultures, Media* (Bloomsbury, 2017); *Language, Ideology and Identity in Serial Killer Narratives* (Routledge, 2011); and *Deviance in Contemporary Crime Fiction* (Palgrave, 2007), nominated for the Edgar and Anthony Boucher awards.

Jesper Gulddal is Associate Professor in Literary Studies at the University of Newcastle, Australia. He has published books and articles on anti-Americanism in European literature, mobility and movement control in the modern novel as well as on crime fiction, including essays on Agatha Christie, Ed McBain, Dashiell Hammett and Pierre Bayard's "detective criticism". Recent journal articles have appeared in *New Literary History*, *Comparative Literature*, *Comparative Literature Studies*, *Symploke* and *Textual Practice*. His current work on crime fiction includes the co-edited volumes *Criminal Moves: Modes of Mobility in Crime Fiction* (Liverpool University Press, 2019) and *The Cambridge Companion to World Crime Fiction* (Cambridge University Press, forthcoming 2021), both with Stewart King and Alistair Rolls.

Cynthia S. Hamilton is Professor Emerita in American Literature and Cultural History at Liverpool Hope University and Visiting Professor in English at Edge Hill University. Her research concerns the politics of agency, particularly in relation to race and gender, within popular literatures. She has been Senior Visiting Fellowship at the Rothermere American Institute, Oxford, and held a Peterson Fellowship at the American Antiquarian Society, Worcester, Massachusetts. Hamilton is the author of *Western and Hard-boiled Detective Fiction in America* (1987) and *Sara Paretsky: Detective Fiction as Trauma Literature* (2015) as well as numerous essays on detective fiction.

Michael Harris-Peyton is Adjunct Professor at the University of Delaware. His research focuses on transcultural adaptation in world literature, crime fiction and the postcolonial politics of genre. His dissertation, "Holmes in the Empire", argues for a more rigorous and inclusive model of crime fiction as a global genre. His research has appeared in the collections *Crime Fiction as World Literature* (2017) and *Criminal Moves: Modes of Mobility in Crime Fiction* (2019).

Thomas Heise is Assistant Professor at Pennsylvania State University (Abington). His research focuses on the representations of city life and city culture in post-1945 American literature. He is the author of the monograph *Urban Underworlds: A Geography of Twentieth-Century American Literature and Culture* (2011), the experimental novel *Moth* (2013), the poetry collection *Horror Vacui* (2006) and essays in *African American Review, Modern Fiction Studies, Twentieth-Century Literature, Journal of Urban Cultural Studies* and *American Literary History*. His current research project on contemporary crime fiction maps "the death of the city" in the era of rapid gentrification.

Heather Duerre Humann is an instructor in the Department of Language and Literature at Florida Gulf Coast University. She is the author of four books, including *Gender Bending Detective Fiction: A Critical Analysis of Selected Works* (McFarland, 2017), which made the American Library Association's Over the Rainbow Recommended Book List in 2018. Recent journal articles have appeared in *Clues: A Journal of Detection* and *Interdisciplinary Literary Studies*.

Nicole Kenley is a lecturer in the English Department at Baylor University, Texas. Her research focuses on twenty-first-century detective fiction and global crime as well as contemporary anglophone literature. Her scholarship has appeared in the journals *Mississippi Quarterly, Clues: A Journal of Detection* and the *Canadian Review of Comparative Literature* as well as in the edited collections *Crime Uncovered: Antihero* (Intellect, 2015) and *Teaching Crime Fiction* (Palgrave Macmillan, 2018) and *Animals in Detective Fiction* (Palgrave Macmillan, forthcoming). She is currently at work on a monograph exploring the relationship between detective fiction and globalisation.

Stewart King is Senior Lecturer in Spanish and Catalan Studies and teaches international literatures at Monash University, Australia. He has published extensively on Spanish and Catalan crime narratives and on crime fiction as a form of world literature. He is the author of *Escribir la catalanidad* (Tamesis, 2005), *Murder in the Multinational State: Crime Fiction from Spain* (Routledge, 2019) as well as the seminal article on crime fiction and world literature (*Clues*, 23(2), 2014). His current work on crime fiction includes the co-edited volumes *Criminal Moves: Modes of Mobility in Crime Fiction* (Liverpool University Press, 2019) and *The Cambridge Companion to World Crime Fiction* (Cambridge University Press, forthcoming 2021), both with Jesper Gulddal and Alistair Rolls.

Aino-Kaisa Koistinen works as a postdoctoral researcher at the University of Jyväskylä, Finland. Her research interests revolve around popular culture, media studies, gender studies, posthumanism and violent fiction, and she has published on speculative fiction and crime

Contributors

fiction. She is the co-editor of *Reconfiguring the Human, Nonhuman and Posthuman in Literature and Culture* for Routledge (2019, with Sanna Karkulehto and Essi Varis).

Susanna Lee is Professor of French and Francophone Studies at Georgetown University, where she also directs the program in Comparative Literature. She is the author of *Detectives in the Shadows: A Hard-Boiled History* (Johns Hopkins University Press, 2020), *Hard-Boiled Crime Fiction and the Decline of Moral Authority* (Ohio State University Press, 2016) and A *World Abandoned by God: Narrative and Secularism* (Bucknell University Press, 2006). She has written numerous articles on the nineteenth-century novel, crime fiction, and law and humanities and edited the Norton Critical Editions of Proust's *Swann's Way* and Stendhal's *The Red and the Black*.

Victoria Lei is Associate Professor of Translation and Literary Studies at the University of Macau. Combining traditional research with new tools, such as automatic corpus analysis technology, her research covers literary history, comparative literature, cognition and translation. While pursuing an academic career, she has also been an active conference interpreter and translator. One of her long-term endeavours is translating Chinese classics not yet available to Western readers into English, including *Words of Warning in Times of Prosperity* by the late Qing reformist Zheng Guan Ying.

Matthew Levay is Associate Professor of English at Idaho State University. He is the author of *Violent Minds: Modernism and the Criminal* (Cambridge University Press, 2019), and his articles on the intersections of modernism and crime fiction have been published in *Modernist Cultures* and the *Journal of Modern Literature.* He has also published essays on Chester Gould's crime comic *Dick Tracy* (in the *Journal of Modern Periodical Studies*) and the early history of *Ellery Queen's Mystery Magazine* (in *The Centrality of Crime Fiction in American Literary Culture,* Routledge, edited by Alfred Bendixen and Olivia Carr Edenfield). He is currently conducting research on Patricia Highsmith and generic form, and beginning a book manuscript on modernism and seriality.

Helen Mäntymäki is Senior Lecturer at the University of Jyväskylä, Finland. Her research interests include popular culture, particularly contemporary crime narratives. She has published on gender, violence, affect and constructions of human versus animal in crime fiction, and is currently working on ecological disasters in TV crime series.

Ruth Mayer holds the chair of American Studies at Leibniz University in Hannover, Germany. Her research focuses on transnationalism, seriality, the formation of modernities and mass culture. Her work has appeared in *New Literary History, Modernism / modernity, Screen* and *Velvet Light Trap.* Her most recent book publications are *Serial Fu Manchu: The Chinese Super-Villain and the Spread of Yellow Peril Ideology* (2014) and the co-edited volumes *Kurz & Knapp: Zur Mediengeschichte der kleinen Formen* (2017) and *Modernities and Modernization in North America* (2019).

Neil McCaw is Professor of Victorian Literature and Culture at the University of Winchester, where he teaches on numerous aspects of the nineteenth century. He has published on a wide range of elements of Victorian culture, including historiography, popular journals and crime and detective fiction. In addition to *Adapting Detective Fiction: Crime, Englishness and the TV Detectives,* McCaw has written books on George Eliot, Anglo-Irish literature and Sherlock Holmes.

Contributors

Rebecca Mills is a lecturer in English and Communication at Bournemouth University. She has published articles on elegy and essays on bodies in the Golden Age and spaces in Agatha Christie's novels. Recent projects include co-editing *Agatha Christie Goes to War* (Routledge, 2019) with J.C. Bernthal.

Sam Naidu is Professor of Literary Studies in English, Rhodes University, South Africa. She is the coordinator of the Intersecting Diasporas Research Group. Her main areas of teaching and research are crime fiction, and literature of migration and diaspora, especially of the African, South Asian and Latin American diasporas. She is the author of *A Survey of South African Crime Fiction* (2017) and editor of *Sherlock Holmes in Context* (2017). She is the editor of crime fiction-themed special issues of *Current Writing* (25(2), 2013) and the *Journal of Commonwealth and Postcolonial Studies* (4(1), 2016).

Andrew Nestingen is Professor of Scandinavian Studies at the University of Washington as well as adjunct in cinema studies. His books include *Transnational Cinema in a Global North* (co-edited with Trevor Elkington), *Crime and Fantasy in Scandinavia*, *Scandinavian Crime Fiction* (co-edited with Paula Arvas) and *The Cinema of Aki Kaurismäki*. He has published on crime fiction, Nordic noir, Nordic cinema, the cinema of Aki Kaurismäki and auteur cinema. He served as Review Editor for *Scandinavian Studies* and Associate Editor of *Journal of Scandinavian Cinema*. He is working on a book about Nordic noir.

Louise Nilsson is Senior Lecturer in the Department of English, Stockholm University. She is currently working on the project *Mediating the North in a Transnational Context: Vernacular and Cosmopolitan Places in Nordic Noir* within the research programme Cosmopolitan and Vernacular Dynamics in World Literatures. She holds a PhD in History of Science and Ideas, and in addition to her historical research on early twentieth-century marketing, she focuses on contemporary popular culture and specialises in crime fiction. She is the co-editor of the collection *Crime Fiction as World Literature* (Bloomsbury, 2017) with Theo D'Haen and David Damrosch.

Andrew Pepper is Senior Lecturer in English and American Literature at Queen's University Belfast. He has written extensively about crime fiction over a twenty-year period and is the author of *Unwilling Executioner: Crime Fiction and the State* (Oxford University Press, 2016), *The Contemporary American Crime Novel: Race, Ethnicity, Gender, Class* (Edinburgh University Press, 2000) and co-editor, with David Schmid, of *Globalization and the State in Contemporary Crime Fiction* (Palgrave, 2016). He is also the author of five detective novels set in nineteenth-century Britain and Ireland, all published by Weidenfeld & Nicolson, including *The Last Days of Newgate* (2006), *The Detective Branch* (2010) and *Bloody Winter* (2011).

Barbara Pezzotti is Lecturer in Italian Studies at Monash University, Australia. Her research interests include crime fiction and popular culture, literary geographies and utopian literature. She has published on Italian, Spanish, New Zealand and Scandinavian crime fiction. She is the author of *The Importance of Place in Contemporary Italian Crime Fiction: A Bloody Journey* (FDU Press, 2012), *Politics and Society in Italian Crime Fiction: An Historical Overview* (McFarland, 2014) and *Investigating Italy's Past through Crime Fiction, Films and TV Series: Murder in the Age of Chaos* (Palgrave Macmillan, 2016). She is co-editor (with Jean Anderson and Carolina Miranda) of *The Foreign in International Crime Fiction: Transcultural Representations* (Continuum, 2012), *Serial Crime Fiction: Dying for More* (Palgrave Macmillan, 2015) and *Blood on the Table: Essays on Food in International Crime Fiction* (McFarland, 2018).

Contributors

Maarit Piipponen is a university lecturer in the languages unit at Tampere University, Finland. Her research focuses on constructions of gender and ethnicity as well as mobility and spatiality in crime fiction. She is the co-editor of *Topographies of Popular Culture* (2016, with Markku Salmela) and *Mobility and Transgression in Contemporary Crime Narratives* (forthcoming, with Helen Mäntymäki and Marinella Rodi-Risberg).

Gill Plain is Professor of English Literature and Popular Culture at the University of St Andrews. Her research interests include twentieth-century war writing, crime fiction, British mid-century cinema, gender and feminist theory. Her publications include *Women's Fiction of the Second World War* (1996), *Twentieth-Century Crime Fiction: Gender, Sexuality and the Body* (2001), *Ian Rankin's* Black and Blue: *A Reader's Guide* (2002), *John Mills and British Cinema: Masculinity, Identity and Nation* (2006) and *Literature of the 1940s: War, Postwar and 'Peace'* (2013). She has also edited a number of volumes including *A History of Feminist Literary Criticism* (co-edited with Susan Sellers, 2007), and *British Literature in Transition 1940–1960: Postwar* (2018).

Robert Prickett is Professor of English Education and Associate Dean of the College of Arts and Sciences at Winthrop University in Rock Hill, South Carolina. His research interests include adolescent literature, graphic novels and secondary education. His work has been published in *Clues: A Journal of Detection*, *The SIGNAL Journal* and *The ALAN Review*, as well as various chapters in edited collections. With Casey Cothran, he is currently beginning work focused on graphic novel mysteries.

Marta Puxan-Oliva is a postdoctoral researcher at the Universitat Oberta de Catalunya and Assistant Lecturer at the Universitat de Barcelona. She is a specialist on narrative theory, ecocriticism, world literature, postcolonial studies and racial comparative studies. Her first book *Narrative Reliability, Racial Conflicts and Ideology in the Modern Novel* has just been published by Routledge. She has co-edited the special issues "Rethinking World Literature Studies in Latin American and Spanish Contexts" for the *Journal of World Literature* 2(1) (2017) with Annalisa Mirizio and "Historicizing the Global: An Interdisciplinary Perspective" for the *Journal of Global History* 14(3) (2019) with Neus Rotger and Diana Roig-Sanz. She is currently working on oceans, crime and literature, a topic on which she has published the article "Colonial Oceanic Environments, Law, and Narrative in Herman Melville's *Benito Cereno* and Juan Benet's *Sub rosa*" in *English Studies* 99(4) (2018). She is a member of the research group GlobaLS.

Heta Pyrhönen is Professor of Comparative Literature at the University of Helsinki, Finland. She has published books and articles on detective fiction, Gothic literature, Jane Austen, the fairy-tale tradition in women's writing (*Bluebeard Gothic*, Toronto University Press, 2010), romance fiction and adaptation. Her many publications on detective fiction include *Murder from an Academic Angle: An Introduction to the Study of the Detective Narrative* (Camden House, 1994) and *Mayhem and Murder: Narrative and Moral Problems in the Detective Story* (Toronto University Press, 1999). Recently she co-edited a volume of essays, *Reading Today* (University College London Press, 2018).

Kate M. Quinn is lecturer in Spanish and Latin American Studies at the National University of Ireland, Galway. She has published essays on Southern Cone crime fiction, particularly on Chilean *novela negra* and the legacy of state violence. She is co-editor along with Marieke Krajenbrink of *Investigating Identities: Questions of Identity in Contemporary International Crime*

Fiction (Rodopi, 2009) and is cofounder of a network of researchers who have been running biennial conferences on crime fiction at universities across Ireland since 2005. Her more recent work engages with the boom in crime fiction writing in Ireland.

Alistair Rolls is Associate Professor of French Studies at the University of Newcastle, Australia. His research is primarily focused on twentieth-century literature, in particular, the works of Boris Vian. He also has a keen interest in detective fiction. His recent books in the field include *Paris and the Fetish: Primal Crime Scenes* (Rodopi, 2014) and, with Clara Sitbon and Marie-Laure Vuaille-Barcan, *Origins and Legacies of Marcel Duhamel's Série Noire* (Brill, 2018). He is the co-editor, with Jesper Gulddal and Stewart King, of *Criminal Moves: Modes of Mobility in Crime Fiction* (Liverpool University Press, 2019).

Shampa Roy is Associate Professor of English at Miranda House, Delhi University, India. Her articles on topics ranging from Victorian *memsahibs'* writings to postcolonial pedagogy have appeared in international journals like *Feminist Review, Interventions* and *Studies in Travel Writing*. She has co-edited *Towards Freedom: Critical Essays on Rabindranath Tagore's Home and the World* (Orient Longman, 2007) and *'Bad' Women of Bombay Films* (Palgrave, 2019). She is also the author of *In Zenanas and Beyond: Representations of Indian Women in British Colonial Texts, 1800–1935* (Lambert Publishing, 2011) and *Gender and Criminality in Bangla Crime Narratives: Late Nineteenth and Early Twentieth Centuries* (Palgrave, 2017). Her current work includes a translation of some early Bangla crime writings titled *'True Crime' Writings in Colonial India: Offending Bodies and Darogas in Nineteenth Century Bengal* (Routledge, forthcoming 2020).

Eric Sandberg is Assistant Professor at City University of Hong Kong and a Docent at the University of Oulu. His research interests range from modernism to the contemporary novel, with a particular interest in the borderlands between literary and popular fiction, especially crime writing. He co-edited *Adaptation, Awards Culture, and the Value of Prestige* with Colleen Kennedy-Karpat (Palgrave, 2017), and edited *100 Greatest Literary Detectives* (Rowman & Littlefield, 2018). He is an assistant editor of the Edinburgh University Press journal *Crime Fiction Studies*. He has recently published on Dorothy L. Sayers in the *Journal of Modern Literature*, and on Thomas Pynchon's use of the hardboiled form in *Partial Answers*.

José V. Saval is Reader in the Department of Spanish, Portuguese and Latin American Studies at the University of Edinburgh, where he has been head of Hispanic Studies. His publications are mostly concerned with sociopolitical aspects of contemporary Spanish literature. He has published several monographs on Spanish authors Carlos Barral and Eduardo Mendoza, and a biography of Manuel Vázquez Montalbán. He has also co-edited a volume on the works of Eduardo Mendoza, and another on theatre from the Spanish Golden Age to contemporary plays. He is the main editor of the journal *Cuadernos de estudio Manuel Vázquez Montalbán*.

Karen Seago has recently retired from City, University of London where she taught translation theory and genre theory applied to the translation of popular literary texts. Her research interests are in the translation and reception of genre literature, focusing on how genre conventions pose specific constraints in translation. Publications on crime fiction in translation include co-editing a special issue of the *Journal of Specialised Translation* on "Crime in Translation", articles on translating misdirection, on translatorial self-censorship in the translation of violence and on feminist appropriations of the hardboiled format, as well as crime fiction as world literature with a specific focus on English-Chinese iterations of *Judge Dee*.

Contributors

Emmett Stinson is Lecturer in Writing and Literature at Deakin University, Australia. He is the author of *Satirizing Modernism* (Bloomsbury, 2017) and *Known Unknowns* (Affirm Press, 2010), and a co-author of *Banning Islamic Books in Australia* (Melbourne University Press, 2011). He is currently a chief investigator on the Australia Research Council Grant entitled "New Tastemakers and Australia's Post-Digital Literary Culture".

Jakob Stougaard-Nielsen is Associate Professor in Scandinavian Literature at University College London. He is the author of *Scandinavian Crime Fiction* (Bloomsbury, 2017) and co-editor of *World Literature, World Culture: History, Theory, Analysis* (Aarhus University Press, 2008) and *Translating the Literatures of Small European Nations* (Liverpool University Press, 2019). He has published articles and book chapters on Scandinavian crime fiction, Nordic noir television drama and the welfare state, globalisation, cultural appropriation and disability. In 2010, he founded the London-based Nordic Noir Book Club (https://scancrime.wordpress.com).

Carlos Uxó is Senior Lecturer in Spanish and Latin American Studies at Monash University, Australia. He has published books and articles on representations of Afro-Cuban characters in Cuban literature (*Representaciones del personaje del negro en la narrativa cubana. Una perspectiva desde los Estudios Subalternos*, 2010), Cuban crime fiction (*The Detective Fiction of Leonardo Padura Fuentes*, 2006) and other issues related to contemporary Cuban society. His current work on crime fiction includes a monograph on Cuban crime fiction, *Policial, Neopolicial y pseudopolicial en Cuba* (Peter Lang, forthcoming 2020) and a comparison of Cuban and East German police television series.

Tanja Välisalo is a university teacher and doctoral candidate at the University of Jyväskylä, Finland, and she also works in the Academy of Finland project Centre of Excellence in Game Culture Studies. Her research focuses on fictional characters in transmedial contexts with an emphasis on reception and active audiences.

Nicoletta Vallorani is Professor of English Literature and Cultural Studies at the University of Milan. She has published essays on formula fiction, with particular reference to science fiction and speculative fiction (from H.G. Wells to today). She has authored essays on Joseph Conrad (*Nessun Kurtz. Cuore di tenebra e le parole dell'Occidente*, 2017), urban geographies (*Millennium London. Of Other Spaces and the Metropolis*, 2012) and the intersections between crime fiction and migration studies ("Postcolonising crime fiction. Some reflections on good and evil in global times", 2014). She coordinates the project *Docucity. Documenting the Metropolis*, on documentary filmmaking and urban geographies and is co-director of the online journal *Other Modernities*. Her most recent published essays reflect on crime fiction and the Other.

ACKNOWLEDGEMENTS

The editors are especially indebted to Polly Dodson at Routledge for her enthusiastic support for this project. We also wish to thank two people who have played an important role at either end of production of the *Companion*. At the beginning, when this project was just an idea, Alistair Rolls offered valuable input on approach and structure. At the other end of production, Stephanie Jaehrling carefully proofread the entire manuscript. We are very grateful to both of them.

INTRODUCTION

New directions in crime fiction scholarship

Janice Allan, Jesper Gulddal, Stewart King and Andrew Pepper

It is in the nature of handbooks and companions to have a certain retrospective feel about them, and to lag behind, if only slightly, the state of the art in the field they set out to chart. This is due not only to their ambition to account for developments and tendencies that have proved influential over long periods of time, but also to the fact that new research paradigms take time to achieve critical mass and win broad acceptance by the scholarly community. From the point of view of editors presenting a new companion volume, the inherently retrospective nature of the format makes it challenging to innovate and carve out new research areas. Yet, simply accepting that innovation is not necessarily the order of the day would involve the risk of replicating, perhaps with minor additions, what was already convincingly set out in the last generation of handbooks, thereby begging the question why a new volume is required. This risk is particularly acute in crime fiction studies, a field that is already blessed with numerous handbooks and introductions, many of which, in spite of the acuity of their insights and the depth of their scholarship, are structured in remarkably similar ways, telling a familiar story, drawing on the same examples and covering many of the same themes.

In planning the *Routledge Companion to Crime Fiction*, we wanted to approach the concept of the crime fiction companion in a different way. More specifically, we have sought to produce a volume that couples the retrospective orientation with an emphasis on the present and indeed the future of crime fiction as a field of academic study. Foolhardy as it may seem, this ambition informs a number of key editorial decisions. First, the volume discusses some of the new developments in crime fiction itself, particularly its hybridisation of forms, its engagement with digital technologies and social media, its interventions in the major political issues of our time, its transnationality and, perhaps most strikingly, its global circulation. Second, it indexes and theorises what we consider to be an ongoing dual paradigm shift in recent crime fiction studies: From emphasising the genre and its subcomponents to highlighting the complexity and idiosyncrasies of the individual text, and from studying crime fiction in the context of separate national literary traditions to examining the genre as a transnational and global phenomenon. This latter ambition demands a revision of the standard narrative of crime fiction.

The story of crime fiction, as it has traditionally been told in the academy, has assumed a now-familiar quality. This story, in turn, has tended to give shape to many critical studies of the genre, not to mention university courses. In very broad terms, it begins with Edgar Allan Poe's "The Murders in the Rue Morgue" (1841) and then moves through a selection of English "classics" such as Wilkie Collins's *The Moonstone* (1868), a handful of Arthur Conan Doyle's Sherlock Holmes stories, an exemplary Agatha Christie novel, e.g. *The Murder of Roger Ackroyd* (1926), before arriving in the US where Dashiell Hammett and Raymond Chandler are treated as overlapping and yet diverging bedfellows of the hardboiled school. The ending of this standard narrative is the proliferation of subgenres or types of crime writing in the post-World War II period, such as police novels, thrillers, transgressor and serial killer narratives, metaphysical detective stories, etc. With the emergence of new critical and theoretical approaches in the last decades of the twentieth century, we have also seen a new focus on contemporary and "recovered" examples that rework a prescriptive account of the genre according to "new" imperatives of race, ethnicity, gender, sexuality and other typologies of difference.

Despite such forays into less familiar territory, the "grand narrative" of crime fiction has continued to dominate many of the volumes designed to usher new students and scholars into the field. Like all such narratives about national literary traditions or the emergence and development of generic fields over extended periods, this one is shot through with multiple problems, as many recent accounts of crime fiction, both as a contemporary and historical phenomenon, have duly pointed out. For a start, it privileges and reproduces an Anglo-American perspective whereby the development of crime fiction, both historically and in terms of more recent mutations, is understood almost exclusively as an anglophone affair; US and British national traditions, which are seen as autochthonous and self-contained, are, by and large, preserved. Occasionally French crime fiction and, more recently, "Nordic noir" are given some kind of equivalent status. Generally, however, these accounts marginalise non-anglophone crime fiction and they certainly ignore the extent to which crime fiction has always circulated globally, both in the original language and in translation and, as such, has always been a resolutely transnational genre. The connections, such as they are pursued between examples of US hardboiled crime fiction and British "classical" crime fiction, tend to produce over-simplified accounts of the genre in two main ways. First, writers such as Hammett and Chandler and Doyle and Christie are typically bundled up together, overlooking the ways in which their works differ formally, thematically and politically from each other, and second, the British examples tend to be treated as more formally and politically "conservative" than their "radical" American counterparts, so that the hardboiled school, which is thereby cast as a major rupture or point of departure in any account of the genre's development, is taken to be the most persuasive evidence of the genre's potential for far-reaching social and political critique.

There are other limitations that accrue from such readings of crime fiction. All originary points are to some extent arbitrary, but to see the genre as beginning with Poe overlooks strong evidence tying crime fiction's emergence as a self-designating genre, with its own archetypes, codes and readerships, in the nineteenth century, back to earlier antecedents in the eighteenth and even seventeenth centuries (e.g. criminal biographies, Gothic novels, gallows sermons). Poe is most often cited as the "father" of the genre because he gave us not merely the first "crime scene" with clues and traces that could be read backwards towards the violent act and its circumstances, but also a detective capable of using a deductive method to accomplish this feat. If Poe's status as originating figure has retroactively sanctified "detection" as the pre-eminent trope of crime fiction – so that crime and detective fiction are often taken as synonymous – this critical tendency also obscures alternative genealogies of crime writing that explore affinities with Gothic, sensational and supernatural works, urban fiction, legal, medical and religious writing, political and philosophical tracts, and spy and espionage fiction (Ascari 2007).

Introduction

Poe is an intriguing figure in this regard. While his anointment as the genre's original voice ignores the claims of earlier writers and alternative traditions, Poe's fraught, ambivalent, unruly tales, together with his own incipient transnationalism (as he and his stories move between the US, Britain and France) have been used by recent scholarship to enact and underwrite two of the key claims of this collection: First, that we need a transnational or global framework for analysing crime fiction (as opposed to merely a national one); and second, that it is time, once and for all, to move away from prescriptive generic concepts (e.g. detection) to an emphasis on individual, non-conforming and innovative features that make crime fiction more than just a reworking of pre-existing formulae. Indeed, it is a mistake to regard a global or transnational outlook as something characteristic only of contemporary crime fiction and it is equally problematic to ignore the way in which crime fiction from its beginnings was defined by a willingness to innovate and contest the established orthodoxies of the genre. We should instead seek to trace these practices back not just to Poe but to earlier figures like Vidocq, Godwin and Defoe and to other traditions beyond the Anglo-French axis that tend to dominate even revisionist accounts of the genre's early history. This is the case, for example, in scholarship about the thousand-year history of crime stories in China (Seago and Lei 2014).

The standard account of crime fiction, where the genre is understood or misunderstood as the gift of its chief or most canonised practitioners, has in recent times come under sustained assault and has lost a lot of its critical purchase; hence it now constitutes something of a critical "straw man" – something that is easy to shoot down but that does not necessarily reflect present scholarship. It would be a brave or foolhardy critic who would today claim Poe to be *the* founder of crime fiction, who would neglect crime fiction traditions in the non-anglophone world or who would downplay the ways in which the genre has been shaped and defined by the circulation of texts across national traditions. Likewise, contra efforts to "fix" certain crime novelists according to already prescribed formal and political designations (e.g. Christie as "conservative" vs. Hammett as "radical") there has been much excellent recent scholarship that has paid close attention to the nuances, ambivalences, contradictions and tensions of individual texts. Thankfully, a companion like this one does not exist in a critical vacuum and it makes no special claim to think and say things that have not been thought or said before. Insofar as our companion seeks to account for the tension between genre and textual individuality in crime fiction, while at the same time developing a fuller understanding of the genre's rapid globalisation and its constitutive transnationalism, we are especially indebted to two related (and unrelated) strands of crime fiction criticism.

First, there are those works, predominantly edited collections, that argue for a comparatist, international or postcolonial approach to the study of crime fiction, contemporary or otherwise (Matzke and Mühleisen 2006; Krajenbrink and Quinn 2009; Pearson and Singer 2009; King and Knight 2014; Pepper and Schmid 2016). These studies place their emphasis either on non-anglophone examples and the emergence of crime fiction traditions outside of the "big three" of France, Britain and the US or on the multiethnic character of these "dominant" national traditions or indeed the idea of crime fiction as a "contact zone" (Pratt 1992), whereby new hybridised forms are produced by encounters between US and European examples and local crime fiction from all parts of the globe. Whether a genuinely globalised crime novel can ever emerge vis-à-vis the strictures of institutionalised justice, which tends to operate at a state level, is one line of critical enquiry pursued (Pepper and Schmid 2016).

This approach has been complimented by studies carried out within discrete national traditions arguing for greater awareness of how the flow of people, ideas and objects (including literary texts themselves) across borders and continents disrupt our understanding of national exceptionalism and produce new accounts of the relations between crime, policing, justice and the national/supranational/global (Nestingen and Arvas 2011; Pezzotti 2014). There remains a concern, however, that such works, despite best intentions, end up reproducing a logic of national distinctiveness even as this logic is scrutinised and, in part, questioned. Hence, such approaches have been superseded by a related emphasis on crime fiction as world literature, whereby the return of world literature as a paradigm of literary studies has resulted in new works dedicated to making sense of the global production, circulation and reception of crime fiction, both as a historical and contemporary phenomenon (King 2014; Nilsson et al. 2016; Pepper 2016; Gregoriou 2017). Here the emphasis is placed on the global reach of the genre as texts circulate in their source languages and also in translation, acquiring new forms and meanings as they do so, as well as on the "international connections between these works", in order to develop innovative reading strategies that account for the genre's global reach (King 2014: 10, 14–16).

The second body of critical work to which we are indebted emphasises the endlessly adaptable, endlessly mutating character of individual crime fiction texts. Rather than trying to fix or tie down crime fiction texts according to a set of prescribed typologies (detective fiction, mystery, noir, cosy, hardboiled, suspense, police, forensic, etc.), these studies examine the multiple and complex ways that individual texts appropriate pre-existing generic tropes, features, forms and characteristics and, in doing so, become something distinctive and even unique, so that genre itself is something we need to understand not in fixed, static terms (e.g. as a container) but as mutable, fluid and transgressive (Gulddal et al. 2019). These critical studies may focus on individual authors and seek to offer new ways of understanding them without tying down or fixing the meanings of their novels according to already prescribed formal and/or political imperatives (e.g. Makinen's reading of Christie (2006)), or on a literary period where the emphasis is placed on the complexities and ambivalences of a body of work over a ten- or twenty-year timeframe (e.g. Clarke's claims about late Victorian crime fiction (2014)). They may also offer readings of crime fiction across discrete spaces and times that play up the genre's inherent discontinuities, differences and ambiguities (Plain 2001; Knight 2004; Horsley 2005). In all these cases, a "dialogic" approach emphasises "the ambiguity, or indeed the contradictoriness, of individual texts and hence the different ways of reading them" (Horsley 2005: 2). In other words, genre itself is understood not as a rulebook where individual authors end up replaying the same characteristics and features over and over again, but as a more open-ended foil for literary originality and innovation. Efforts to police the distinction between "literary" and "popular" fiction thereby fall away.

And yet our larger point is that whereas much crime fiction scholarship has responded in relevant, compelling ways to the aforementioned challenges, handbooks, companions and introductions to the genre have, by and large, tended to reproduce a nation-centred approach, and to reinscribe the Anglo-American monopoly, or indeed sought to interpret and present the genre according to a fixed set of precepts. Existing handbooks, then, have either not fully recognised the globality of crime fiction, or they have consigned crime fiction in languages other than English to discrete, ghettoised chapters, making it impossible to address either the transnational roots of crime fiction or the international proliferation of the genre in the past twenty or thirty years. Rather than including chapters that look at particular national or regional crime fiction traditions in isolation (e.g. French, Italian, Japanese, Scandinavian) – an approach that only reinforces the idea that crime fiction is always the product of relationships and arrangements within national traditions – this volume has been designed to explore the international connections between individual works and also to uncover the global and globalising dynamics always-already present in crime fiction (e.g. transnational policing and security practices; stories involving the trafficking of goods, people and money across borders;

Introduction

or forms of generic intertextuality where the affinities or indeed discontinuities cross specific national traditions).

This second shift in crime fiction studies, which challenges the notion that the relationship between the genre and individual crime stories is one of embodiment (i.e. that these texts merely embody pre-existing tropes and characteristics), is also not represented particularly well by crime fiction handbooks or companions which tend to place the emphasis on types of crime fiction. While literary studies in general may have recently pivoted towards quantitative methodologies and "distant" reading practices (Moretti 2013), crime fiction studies is arguably only now discovering the full potential of paying close attention to individual texts and textual specificities (Gulddal et al. 2019). This critical neglect manifested itself in numerous ways. First, the desire to fix crime fiction as one thing (e.g. the story of the crime being superseded and eventually replaced by the story of the investigation – see Todorov 1977) has fed into long-standing claims about the difference between crime and/or popular fiction and "literary fiction", where the latter is seen as characterised by formal innovation and a corresponding sense of political subversion and the former by its adherence to particular rules and hence to literary and political conservatism. Second, this approach has paid too much attention to the ways in which crime narratives are resolved and hence to a logic that emphasises the return to some kind of equilibrium or status quo rather than a mobile, restless, inquisitive ethos that is central to all crime stories, regardless of how they are resolved and whether the resolution is partial, incomplete, ambivalent or critical of existing social and political norms. And third, this approach has ignored the extent to which crime stories engage with complex philosophical and/or political ideas and do so in ways that do not merely thematise existing ideas or claims but which produce new political and philosophical frameworks that throw into doubt orthodox thinking about the relationships between law, justice, crime, policing and morality and which, instead, ask far-reaching questions about whether crime is socially or individually produced or about the ethical issues at stake in the representation of violence.

To demonstrate what is possible if we look at crime stories as individual texts, rather than embodiments of fixed generic norms (and hence as examples of popular as opposed to literary fiction; as end-driven narratives that produce straightforward and "comforting" endings; and as politically and/or philosophically derivative or quietist texts), it may be useful to look briefly at a handful of examples from approximately the same period: Dashiell Hammett's *The Maltese Falcon* (1930); Agatha Christie's *Murder on the Orient Express* (1934); Georges Simenon's *The Bar on the Seine*, first published in 1932 as *Le Guinguette à deux sous*; and by the same author, *The Man Who Watched the Trains Go By*, first published in 1938 as *L'Homme qui regardait passer les trains*. If we treat these novels together we might pay attention to their collective attempts to provide solutions or answers to the mysteries that set the stories in motion, such as, what is the nature or object of the quest in *The Maltese Falcon*?, who murdered Samuel Ratchett in Christie's novel?, who is the killer in *The Bar on the Seine*? or what drives Kees Popinga to escape his old life and commit murder in *The Man Who Watched the Trains Go By*? If we read *Murder on the Orient Express* as an instance of "classical" or Golden Age crime fiction and *The Maltese Falcon* as a "hardboiled" crime novel, or if we distinguish between *The Bar on the Seine* as a straightforward detective story featuring Inspector Maigret and *The Man Who Watched the Trains Go By* as a noir-esque "*roman dur*" (literally, hard novel), we might construct an argument about the politically radical Hammett as opposed to the socially conservative Christie or about the resolution-driven story of the Maigret novel, where answers are provided and justice is served, versus the *roman durs* where no definitive answer as to Popinga's motivations and intentions is given to the reader. Yet if we treat all these novels as individual texts, probing them for their ambiguities and

5

complexities, their nuances and their contradictions, and if at the same time we take them out of their specific national contexts, then a very different picture starts to emerge.

Such an individual and textually attentive approach might place pressure on claims about hardboiled crime fiction as *the* archetypal American genre, not least as the hunt for Hammett's eponymous statuette – which moves from Western Europe to Russia to the Far East and eventually to the west coast of the US – draws attention to the same global networks that the novel and its translations circulate by and through. In doing so, Hammett's novel – ostensibly about the US – is defamiliarised and transformed and its thematisation of global finance requires us to think about the role of debt, currency and power at a supranational level. Christie's *Murder on the Orient Express*, meanwhile, also enacts or thematises transnational mobility as the train's passengers move between the Levant and Europe and, moreover, exhibits some of the same anxieties regarding the relationship between law, power and justice that we see in "hardboiled" fiction (see King 2018). The ending, which might provide clear answers and offer some kind of reassurance to readers (while at the same time raising new questions, cf. Gulddal 2016; Rolls 2018), also exposes the limits of the (supranational) criminal justice system, when lifted out of its state-bound contexts, to provide appropriate or adequate restitution, particularly when complex jurisdictional and ethical questions are taken into account. Likewise, Simenon's Maigret novel, *The Bar on the Seine*, might offer us the kind of answers or explanations that are lacking in his (non-Maigret) novel, *The Man Who Watched the Trains Go By*, so that in the end we do discover who murdered Marcel Feinstein, a Parisian tailor, in a way that we do not fully comprehend Kees Popinga's murderous spree as he flees Groningen for Paris. But in both novels, Simenon conjures a pervasive atmosphere of bafflement and dread in which all certainties run up against a sense that life, for Maigret and Popinga alike, is as arbitrary as it is confusing and disappointing – a move that echoes the lessons of the Flitcraft parable in *The Maltese Falcon* (Pepper 2016: 141–42). Ultimately, these examples demonstrate that it makes less sense than commonly assumed to categorise crime fiction using broad generic concepts such as "classical", "Golden Age" or "hardboiled", especially where these designations are linked to particular aesthetic and political predispositions. Instead we should acknowledge the hybridity and indeed mobility that has always been the genre's dominant *modus operandi*.

This of course brings up the question of whether we are identifying a historical or contemporary phenomenon. Certainly this volume is seeking to steer a course away from the "historical survey" approach that has tended to structure crime fiction handbooks and companions, in which readers are carefully led through clearly demarcated literary periods and (re)introduced to the genre's already canonised "great" writers. Our approach in this volume is perhaps closer to "genealogy" as defined by Foucault rather than straightforward history. Rather than searching for some unsullied moment of origin or arranging the past into orderly segments, the task of the person who writes "effective" history, Foucault tells us, is to trace the emergence of particular patterns and discontinuities as they develop in relation to the mess of overlapping and competing historical forces (1991: 83). The ambition here is not wilful historical iconoclasm but rather a call to reflect upon and engage with the genre's subversive energies, its rule-bending hybridity and its inherent transnationalism as both a historical and contemporary phenomenon. The present companion includes essays that look at crime fiction histories but here, as elsewhere, the emphasis is placed on approaches that challenge orthodox readings or understandings of these histories and engage critically with individual crime narratives rather than on prescribed typologies. At the same time, the overall emphasis of the collection is forward- rather than backward-looking and seeks to connect the genre's traditional preoccupations with the modern, the scientific, the urban and the "real" with an interest in border crossings, migration, human and drugs trafficking, environmental concerns, war, forensics, digital technologies, new security

Introduction

practices and global capitalism. If there is what we might call a "cosmopolitan" ethos behind this kind of pursuit and behind attempts to bring about justice and find commonality and shared affinities between diverse global populations, this volume also emphasises crime fiction's willingness to countenance a set of diametrically-opposed sentiments or positions: a lack of shared understanding, the breakdown of justice systems, global disunity and the threat of the apocalyptic, brought about by environment degradation, social inequality, corporate and individual greed and political fragmentation.

The structure of the *Companion* reflects this restlessness, this desire to challenge and rework orthodox accounts of crime fiction histories and this willingness to embrace the hybrid, multiple, contradictory, heterogeneous nature of individual crime fiction narratives. Rather than offer a comprehensive history of the genre with chapters dedicated to individual periods or subgenres, an approach which – as we have argued – tends to privilege the Anglo-American tradition and reinforce the belief that individual crime fiction texts are, by and large, manifestations of particular generic features, this companion adopts a less programmatic case study approach in which the specific aspects or features (aesthetic, formal, political, etc.) of individual texts are emphasised over some kind of overarching idea of genre or type. In doing so, the companion aims to produce more complex, open-ended discussions of crime fiction's multiplicities, its transnationalism and globality, and the ways in which individual crime fiction narratives produce their own unique accounts of what the genre is or means or does. To promote a more transnational account of crime fiction, we have sourced contributions from around the world and from academic disciplines other than English literature; further, we have encouraged contributors to use examples not just from across the English-speaking world but also from non-anglophone literatures. We have not, however, aimed to achieve some kind of global proportional representation in terms of the nationality of the contributors or the origin of the works discussed as this would unnecessarily distract from the primary aim of presenting the current state of crime fiction criticism.

Although a number of chapters discuss crime fiction on television, film and other media, the volume as a whole focuses on print narratives. We are aware, of course, that there are considerable overlaps and interactions between the various crime fiction media, and that this makes it hard to maintain a neat distinction. Further, we recognise that televised serials have arguably become the most significant manifestation of crime fiction due, in large part, to their global reach and marketplace success, but also thanks to their formal and thematic innovation. However, precisely because of this significance, and because of the sheer volume of crime fiction on the small screen, this is a topic that deserves to be treated comprehensively and not just given one or two tokenistic chapters in a book otherwise dedicated to literature.

The companion is divided into three parts: *Approaches*, *Devices* and *Interfaces*. The first part (*Approaches*) explores the main theoretical currents of crime fiction studies today; this part emphasises the international, global or non-anglophone proliferation of crime fiction, with individual essays dedicated to examining world literature, crime fiction in translation, transnationality, colonialism and decolonialism, but it also engages with the publishing industry and new formats (adaptation and graphic crime novels), together with efforts to think through the now long-standing manoeuvrings away from the centrality of the straight, white male detective and white, male heteronormative accounts of the genre. The second part (*Devices*) explores a range of literary devices which between them are constitutive of the genre understood as diverse, elastic, open-ended and multiplicitous. These essays advance a more theoretical understanding of these constitutive devices which are formal (beginnings and endings; plotting; clues), thematic (place; criminals; victims; detectives), conceptual (affect; alterity) and categorical (metafiction). We recognise that crime fiction as a varied and diverse body of work engages with

7

contemporary reality in complex and often un- or under-acknowledged ways. To this end, the final part (*Interfaces*) seeks to further our understanding of the connections between these texts and pressing debates and issues relating to the modern world. In addition to exploring those "interfaces" which have traditionally been central to our understanding of crime fiction, such as modern science, the police, theories of justice, war, and realism, this part also examines the ways in which crime narratives engage with debates about the environment, migration, trafficking, global capital, the future and the emergence of new digital forms or media.

What emerges from these reflections on the current state of crime fiction criticism is a call for theoretical and methodological innovation; to look to the future, rather than the past. If, as we have argued, traditional handbooks and companions are retrospective in nature, taking their readers through the well-cultivated paths of the past, the ambition for this volume is to venture into the future via routes less travelled. Endpoints, like origins, are always arbitrary and to aim to bring any such volume to the point of "the present" is to always-already have failed. And yet, our hope is that by promoting the approach outlined above – one that focuses on the inherent complexities and contradictions of the individual text without losing sight of the fact that such texts are part and parcel of a transnational and global phenomena – we will point a way to the future of crime studies; encouraging those that follow to travel further and continue to map new ground.

Bibliography

Ascari, M. (2007) *A Counter-History of Crime Fiction: Supernatural, Gothic, sensational*, Basingstoke: Palgrave Macmillan.
Clarke, C. (2014) *Late Victorian Crime Fiction in the Shadows of Sherlock*, Basingstoke: Palgrave Macmillan.
Foucault, M. (1991) "Nietzsche, genealogy, history", in P. Rabinow (ed.), *The Foucault Reader*, New York: Penguin.
Gregoriou, C. (2017) *Crime Fiction Migration: Crossing languages, cultures and media*, New York and London: Bloomsbury.
Gulddal, J. (2016) "'Beautiful shining order': detective authority in Agatha Christie's *Murder on the Orient Express*", *Clues: A Journal of Detection*, 34(2): 11–21.
Gulddal, J., King, S. and Rolls, A. (eds) (2019) *Criminal Moves: Modes of mobility in detective fiction*, Liverpool: Liverpool University Press.
Horsley, L. (2005) *Twentieth-Century Crime Fiction*, Oxford: Oxford University Press.
King, S. (2014) "Crime fiction as world literature", *Clues: A Journal of Detection*, 32(2): 8–19.
———. (2018) "*E pluribus unum*: a transnational reading of Agatha Christie's *Murder on the Orient Express*", *Clues: A Journal of Detection*, 36(1): 9–19.
King, S. and Knight, S. (eds) (2014) "Global crime fiction", *Clues: A Journal of Detection*, 32(2).
Knight, S. (2004) *Crime Fiction 1800–2000: Detection, death, diversity*, Basingstoke: Palgrave Macmillan.
Krajenbrink, M. and Quinn, K. (eds) (2009) *Investigating Identities: Questions of identity in contemporary international crime fiction*, Amsterdam: Rodopi.
Makinen, M. (2006) *Agatha Christie: Investigating femininity*, Basingstoke: Palgrave Macmillan.
Matzke, C. and Mühleisen, S. (eds) (2006) *Postcolonial Perspectives: Crime fiction from a transcultural perspective*, Amsterdam: Rodopi.
Moretti, F. (2013) *Distant Reading*, New York and London: Verso.
Nestingen, A. and Arvas, P. (eds) (2011) *Scandinavian Crime Fiction*, Cardiff: University of Wales Press.
Nilsson, L., Damrosch, D. and D'haen, T. (eds) (2016) *Crime Fiction as World Literature*, New York and London: Bloomsbury Academic.
Pearson, N. and Singer, M. (eds) (2009) *Detective Fiction in a Postcolonial and Transnational World*, Farnham: Ashgate.
Pepper, A. (2016) *Unwilling Executioner: Crime fiction and the state*, Oxford: Oxford University Press.
Pepper, A. and Schmid, D. (eds) (2016) *Globalization and the State in Contemporary Crime Fiction: A world of crime*, Basingstoke: Palgrave Macmillan.

Introduction

Pezzotti, B. (2014) *Politics and Society in Italian Crime Fiction: An historical overview*, Jefferson, NC: McFarland.

Plain, G. (2001) *Twentieth-Century Crime Fiction: Gender, sexuality and the body*, Edinburgh: Edinburgh University Press.

Pratt, M.L. (1992) *Imperial Eyes: Travel writing and transculturation*, London and New York: Routledge.

Rolls, A. (2018) "Ex uno plures: global French in, on and of the Rue Morgue and the Orient Express", *Arcadia*, 53(1): 39–60.

Seago, K and Lei, V. (2014) "'Looking east and looking west': crime genre conventions and tropes", *Comparative Critical Studies*, 11(2–3): 315–35.

Todorov, T. (1977) *The Poetics of Prose*, trans. R. Howard, Oxford: Basil Blackwell.

PART I

Approaches

1
GENRE

Jesper Gulddal and Stewart King

Genre is an ambiguous term in crime fiction studies – one that has undeniable descriptive value and serves to guide both authors and readers, yet also one that is often used too cavalierly in ways that homogenise rather than highlight the multiplicity of the field. Crime fiction authors are often self-consciously writing within (or against) the crime genre, appropriating its conventions and drawing on the work of both classic and contemporary writers in this genre for models and inspiration. Genre is also a crucial factor when publishers assess manuscripts and position individual titles within commercial frameworks such as book series or sections in online or physical bookstores. More generally, genre impacts on how crime titles are designed, marketed, reviewed and finally purchased by readers who may read crime novels exclusively, and whose expectations are guided by their deep familiarity with the tropes of the genre. However, the concept of genre can also be limiting. The term "genre fiction" has a derogatory ring to it, suggesting that the individual books that make up the genre, in this case crime fiction, are defined substantially by their adherence to established devices and narrative patterns. It also implies that these books are intended for entertainment only and have little need of the careful readerly attention that is lavished upon Literature with a capital L. Here, the concept of genre suggests that crime fiction is easy reading, a product of the cultural industry and therefore lacking textual complexity as well as broader critical agendas.

In this chapter we present some of the classic accounts of the crime fiction genre and proceed from there to identify two contemporary shifts in how the genre is conceived. If the older criticism emphasised the stability and prescriptiveness of genre norms, the first shift involves a redescription of crime fiction as a motley and spacious genre defined by hybridity and mobility rather than adherence to rules. The second shift is occurring as a result of the internationalisation of the crime fiction universe, which results in new amalgamations of established (Western) crime fiction tropes and literary traditions outside the traditional focal points of crime fiction in the UK, the US and France. Our case study text, Antti Tuomainen's apocalyptic crime novel *Parantaja* (2010) [*The Healer*, 2013], has been selected to illustrate both these shifts and the new conception of the crime genre that they have produced.

The aim of the chapter is not to *define* the crime genre. As will become immediately apparent, we see crime fiction as a field, characterised internally by a multiplicity of formats, styles and themes, and externally by porous borders to the wider field of literature, especially the realm of (elite) Literature. As such, any attempt at a definition would be provisional and run counter to the mobile understanding of genre that we develop here. Based on this understanding, the concluding section offers a reflection on the crime genre as a fluid agglomeration of texts united by certain resemblances yet allowing for all kinds of uniqueness.

Classic definitions

When used simply to label narratives focusing on crime and investigation, the term "crime fiction" seems uncomplicated to the point of being self-explanatory. However, when we reflect critically on this genre designation, significant problems start to appear, above all because of the vast and diverse range of books, written over a long period, that the concept is meant to encapsulate. When and where did the genre originate? How can it meaningfully be subdivided into distinctive formats and types? Should certain murder mysteries be excluded due to their literary or philosophical aspirations (think of *Hamlet* or *Crime and Punishment*)? At which point does genre-bending or hybridisation lead authors across the border into new generic territory? And is violent crime – pre-eminently murder – the only acceptable topic, or might crime fiction equally focus on financial, environmental or digital transgressions?

Because of these complexities the definition of crime fiction has been a long-standing preoccupation of crime fiction studies and continues to inform critical discussions of the genre. As is to be expected, the question "what is crime fiction?" is asked routinely and explicitly in introductions to the genre (e.g. Rzepka 2010; Symons 1992) and often elicits sophisticated answers that acknowledge the tension between the conventionality and innovation inherent in crime fiction. However, instead of surveying these contemporary attempts at a definition, we want to examine the definitional desire itself – the desire to impose order and stability on the field – by highlighting three classic and paradigmatic ways of understanding the crime genre.

Firstly, some of the early attempts to define crime fiction – and particularly the detective format – promote what may be called a *ludic*, or game-based, understanding of the genre, conceptualising the detective novel as an intellectual rather than aesthetic pursuit akin to crossword puzzles, parlour-room games or sport. American crime writer S.S. Van Dine, in his much-quoted "Twenty Rules for Writing Detective Stories" (1928), explicitly defines detective fiction as a "game" (1928: 189). Rather than engaging in "literary furbelows and style and beautiful descriptions and the projection of mood", detective novels should "state a problem, analyse it, and bring it to a successful conclusion". In doing so, it must adhere to certain rules, for example, that the murder mystery must be solved by means of "logical deductions" (#5), that supernatural explanations must be avoided (#8) and, most importantly, that the reader must have the same access to relevant information as the detective (#1, #2, #15). These rules ensure "fair play", a key value of Golden Age detective fiction. Needless to say, this notion is fraught with difficulties; in fact, as Pierre Bayard and others have shown, the classic detective story often goes to extreme lengths to conceal the truth from the reader (Bayard 2000: 19–30). However, in spite of its inbuilt problems, the ludic conception of crime fiction has value as an early example of a contract theory of genre and as such highlights how genre is crucial as a means of establishing a shared frame of reference for authors and readers (Jameson 1975).

Secondly, the crime genre has been defined as *formula fiction*. Based on a long-standing preconception of crime fiction as a standardised form of literature, this understanding developed in the 1970s and represents an early attempt to take the genre seriously as an object of academic study. The most nuanced account of the formulaic nature of crime fiction can be found in John G. Cawelti's *Adventure, Mystery and Romance* (1976). For Cawelti, the concept of a literary formula spans two meanings. On the one hand, a formula is an archetypical plot structure that is rooted in human psychology and therefore occurs across cultures and historical periods (e.g. stories of revenge, betrayal or forbidden love). On the other hand, the concept refers to a conventional way of representing something or someone that is specific to a particular cultural setting (e.g. the hardnosed private investigator and the femme fatale). On the basis of this distinction, Cawelti defines formula fiction as "embodiments of archetypical story forms in terms of specific cultural materials" (1976: 6). In the context of crime fiction, this definition opens up a line of enquiry focusing on how crime novels use standard narratives of murder and investigation, or of revenge, treachery, jealousy, etc., as a means of exploring the conflicts and tensions of specific social and cultural settings. While this definition potentially enables sophisticated inquiries into the relationship between the crime text and its social and cultural context, the notion of literary formulas often leads to more reductionist forms of analysis that strip away the specificity of the individual crime story so as to foreground its formulaic core. Tzvetan Todorov's "The Typology of Detective Fiction" is a characteristic, albeit unusually astute, example. In this seminal essay, Todorov argues that while the masterpieces of "literary fiction" are characterised by flouting established conventions and creating a genre of their own, those of detective fiction strive to embody those conventions as perfectly as possible: "The whodunit par excellence is not the one which transgresses the rules of the genre, but the one that conforms to them. *No Orchids for Miss Blandish* is an incarnation of its genre, not a transcendence" (1977: 43). Based on these assumptions, and drawing further on structuralist narratology, Todorov proposes that the genre encompasses just three different types: the whodunit, the thriller and the suspense novel.

The third account of the genre regards crime fiction as an *interface* that links specific narrative forms to particular sociocultural questions and concerns. This understanding has rarely been articulated theoretically, yet it is often implied in critical practice and provides the basis for the third part ("Interfaces") of the present book. In this view, crime fiction is not just a form of popular entertainment, characterised by its constant recycling of commercially successful conventions. Rather, it is a narrative vector for exploring a range of wider social, political, cultural or philosophical issues that do not necessarily have anything to do with crime in themselves, yet are significantly implicated and framed by the criminal/investigative plot. The key question here concerns neither text nor context, but what ties them together – how the crime narrative is shaped and informed by the world it represents while also providing a unique means of analysing it. Key topics include the modern city, migration, global capital, the environment and narcotics (see Part III).

Hybridity and mobility

Like all popular genres, and perhaps all literature, crime fiction is based on the dual principles of iteration and variation; on the one hand, crime narratives always draw to some extent on the history and conventions of the genre, even if only in the sense of having a primary focus on crime and investigation; on the other hand, every crime narrative inhabits the genre in an individual way, positioning itself somewhere on a scale that ranges from subtle appropriation to aggressively rewriting the rulebook. In this sense, crime fiction is shaped by a dialectics of "genre performance" and "genre negation" (Gulddal 2016: 55). Older scholarship, particularly the ludic and formula-based understandings discussed in the previous section, tended to emphasise the iterative aspect, possibly overestimating crime fiction's difference from "Literature" by reading it from the point of view of its rule-bound sameness rather than its rule-bending difference. If more recent scholarship has given greater weight to the variability of crime fiction, it reflects a broader shift in our understanding of genre, epitomised by Jacques Derrida's deconstructive questioning of the "law of the genre" as a delimiting and norm-setting principle (1980). Crime fiction tends to be seen today as a field in flux where mutation, contamination and innovation take precedence over the purity of canonical forms.

While this shift was related to the rise of new forms of crime writing, particularly postmodern formats that blurred the boundaries between popular and literary fiction, it is important to stress that historical forms of crime fiction are much less "pure" than is often assumed. In fact, as Martin Kayman (1992) and Maurizio Ascari (2007) have shown in a number of "counterhistorical" studies of the genre, the history of the genre has often been written in light of later developments, that is, by privileging texts that seem to be steps on the way towards the main line of crime fiction; conversely, texts that do not point towards this canon have typically been marginalised. This view challenges the traditional account of crime fiction as a limited vocabulary of subgenres, each precisely defined and associated with canonical authors who are seen as genre founders and as prescriptive models for subsequent writers to follow. Against such monocausal and linear historiography, Ascari's detailed historical analyses highlight how crime fiction as we have come to know it originated in a nineteenth-century field of competing popular genres – adventure novels, Gothic fiction, sensationalist literature, true crime, urban mysteries – traces of which are still present in the supposedly pure acts of genre-foundation in the stories of Edgar Allan Poe and Arthur Conan Doyle.

Yet, even if the origin of crime fiction lies in the happy amalgamation of multiple types of literature, the critical identification of the genre was followed by a certain homogenisation, and it was only in the post-war period that authors, reacting to the prescriptiveness of genre, started in earnest to play with conventions and violate generic borders. Previously an exception, hybridity has become a central norm of crime fiction and has seen the crime novel meld with a range of other genres, for example, historical fiction in Umberto Eco's *The Name of the Rose* (1980, trans. 1983), fantasy in China Miéville's *The City & The City* (2009), science fiction in Philip K. Dick's *Do Androids Dream of Electric Sheep?* (1968), the spy thriller in James Sallis's *Death Will Have Your Eyes* (1997) and climate fiction in Antti Tuomainen's *The Healer*, which we discuss in detail below.

There are several reasons why hybridisation has become such a widespread narrative strategy. One factor is commercial. The marketplace for crime fiction – and genre fiction more broadly – has traditionally been seen as a homogenising force, creating conventional and standardised products. However, as the market for crime novels reaches a point of saturation, authors are increasingly incentivised towards differentiation, and hybrid forms represent an attractive way of standing out in a crowded field. Further, as Heather Humann argues in Chapter 6 of this book, hybridisation is also an effect of a postmodern playfulness in the use and combination of genres that have traditionally been kept separate. This playfulness can be a way to gain standing in the field of literature. While popular genres in themselves are typically perceived to be simple, entertaining and intended for mass consumption, combining them shows a metafictional awareness of genre history and is often perceived as sophisticated and smart; in this sense, hybridisation enables authors with literary ambitions to draw on crime fiction plot models while nevertheless avoiding the stigma of writing genre fiction.

Hybridisation also has a wider functionality. In its purer forms, crime fiction offers a narrative model particularly suited to exploring interpersonal relations and social structures, and by virtue of its formal characteristics alone it tends, with numerous exceptions, towards certain accounts of human nature, society and politics. Hybridisation is a way of complicating this model, thereby creating a bi- or multifocal lens that can be used to explore a range of other issues. Hybrid narratives expand and change the constituent forms, increasing their capacity to represent the complexities of human society. Miéville's *The City & The City* is a case in point. In this novel, the police procedural plot, focusing on the murder of an American student, becomes a vehicle for the exploration of the surreal setting – the overlapping yet rigorously segregated cities of Beszel and Ul Qoma, where the people have learned to "unsee" and "unhear" the other place, even though the border runs through the streets and houses where they live. The result is a crime narrative that throws a sideways glance at the contemporary anxieties that attach to the border as a safeguard of established collective identities, as a means of upholding inequalities and as a medium of transnational mobility and exchange.

Building on the new conception of the genre in crime fiction studies, the authors of the present chapter, with Alistair Rolls, have suggested an approach to crime fiction based on the concept of mobility. Working from the assumption that "crime fiction, far from being static and staid, must be seen as a genre constantly violating its own boundaries" (Gulddal et al. 2019: 1), the authors analyse different forms of nonconformist mobility in crime texts, including what they call the "mobility of genre". This concept amounts to a rejection of the view – represented by Todorov, among others – that the relationship between the individual text and the genre is one of embodiment or adherence to rules and conventions. A mobile account of genre highlights instead the experimental and transgressive aspects of crime fiction and in particular locates the dynamism of the genre in a constant tension between the affirmation and negation of genre norms.

Transnationalising crime fiction

A second factor driving genre evolution is the growing awareness of the global dimensions of crime fiction towards the end of the twentieth and beginning of the twenty-first century. While Julian Symons could once claim that "little sparkles" in foreign crime fiction (1992: 314), this is no longer the case, as evidenced by the decision of the UK Crime Writers' Association to exclude crime fiction in translation from the Gold Dagger prize, after three non-English-language writers were awarded the prestigious prize between 2001 and 2005. This global awareness of non-anglophone traditions was driven primarily by the international success of so-called Nordic noir, particularly as publishers realised the potential attraction of new voices and new crime scenes for a readership more and more interested in crimes set abroad.

While the increased translation, circulation and consumption of crime fiction is to be applauded, the internationalisation of the genre has led to further restrictive or reductive categorisations being imposed on the genre. Indeed, as we will show below, at the very moment in which the genre opens up to its multicultural multiplicity, it becomes reduced to an exclusively Western model. Moreover, despite the internationalisation, individual crime novels are again reduced, this time to the discrete national context in which they are produced. Both of these limitations on the genre emerge paradoxically through the most recent manifestation of World Literature Studies.

Accounting for the global circulation of literature has been a central preoccupation of recent World Literature Studies. In one of its founding texts, "Conjectures on World Literature" (2000), Franco Moretti develops, first cautiously and then fully, a "*law of literary evolution*" that explains the dissemination of the novel throughout the world, and which can be used to account for the international development of the crime genre. Through his distant reading method – the analysis of over twenty studies of the novel around the world – he argues that "when a culture starts moving towards the modern novel, it's *always* a compromise between foreign form and local materials" before clarifying that this compromise consists of three elements: "foreign *plot*"; "local *characters*; and then, local *narrative voice*" (2000: 65; emphases in original). Moretti's conjecture-turned-law is based on a centre-periphery model in which a central "western formal influence (usually French or English)" expands inexorably outwards to peripheral cultures where it is adapted and localised (58). The form, however, largely remains the same.

In the area of crime fiction, *The Cambridge Companion to Crime Fiction* (2003), edited by Martin Priestman, provides a salient example of Moretti's argument even if the authors of this excellent collection do not engage with his ideas. The *Cambridge Companion* contains a central cast of British, American and some French authors, but the periphery is so peripheral as to be almost entirely absent, the exception being the metaphysical crime stories of Argentine Jorge Luis Borges. To be fair, the *Cambridge Companion* was published at a moment when such an approach was still entirely possible. More recent introductions to the genre are more attuned to its global dimensions. Richard Bradford's *Crime Fiction: A Very Short Introduction*, published by Oxford University Press in 2015, is a telling example, as in addition to brief discussions on pre-cursor crime narratives from Classical cultures and the Middle East, Bradford dedicates approximately one-fifth of the entire study to a chapter on international crime fiction, including often underrepresented East Asian and Latin American crime writers other than Borges. While this engagement with the genre's diversity is to be commended, Bradford's study is limited by his definition of crime fiction as stories that exploit the tension "between what is not known and the procedure by which the facts are known" (2015: 2). As such, although he recognises the existence of different crime fiction traditions, like the Chinese "court case" stories which pre-date Poe's "Murders in the Rue Morgue" by at least six centuries, he ultimately dismisses them because the crime and mystery "are incidental and subordinate to other more significant themes and to read them in expectation of Todorov's notion of excitement-by-disclosure would be both perverse and ultimately frustrating" (2015: 3).

Bradford's taxonomical definition draws attention to the way in which the crime genre, despite its international spread, is largely understood as a Western form and that when scholars venture abroad they tend only to recognise as crime fiction those stories from the rest of the world that are already familiar to them – that is, crime stories that are told in a way that Western authors tell them. Such an approach reinforces the centrality of Western models and ignores Asian crime writing traditions in China, India, Malaysia and Indonesia that feature magic and horror, a recent manifestation being Indonesian writer Eka Kurniawan's *Lelaki Harimau* (2004) [*Man Tiger*, 2015], in which the young male protagonist is possessed by a female tiger. Although scholars like Bradford acknowledge alternative crime writing traditions from around the world, the lack of engagement with them because they are perceived to be too different places limits on how far we are willing to go to understand the diverse narrative forms that make up the world's crime fiction. As such, the question that is often raised – what is crime fiction? – should perhaps be reframed as, what is Western crime fiction?

Moretti's focus on the foreign form and the local features combines neatly with a nation-centredness that is typical of literary practice and this, in turn, has led to a further reductive categorisation that is applied to the genre: that of national origin. Outside the British and American norm, which, "like the greenback, acts as an international currency against which all other crime fiction traditions are valued and compared" (King 2019: 196), crime fiction is almost exclusively framed within the national context in which it was produced. That is, the novels are understood as explaining something about the places in which they are set, whether this be Algeria, Guatemala or New Zealand. In such readings, the crime plots can become exoticised and subservient to their ethnographic interest, thus reinforcing their difference and distance from the British and American norm. In the case study below, we explore the ways in which genre hybridisation and transnational mobility open up innovative generic formations and new ways of imagining crime fiction.

Genre

Vanishing borders in Antti Tuomainen's *The Healer*

Finnish author Antti Tuomainen's *Parantaja* (2010) [*The Healer*, 2013] is illustrative of crime fiction's increasing generic hybridity and transnational fluidity. Set in a very contemporary but dystopic Helsinki, *The Healer* combines the crime genre's investigation into a mystery – here the disappearance of the narrator's journalist wife while she was investigating a series of brutal murders enacted by the titular self-styled "Healer" – with climate fiction's exploration of the consequences of environmental catastrophe. In Tuomainen's novel, climate change is no longer a question of debate or, indeed, of scepticism. It is real. A TV screen informs the viewers (and Tuomainen's readers) of its current effects on the world: droughts and floods, pandemics, wars – thirteen in the European Union alone – rising sea levels, uncontrolled fires in the Amazon, and an estimated 650–800 million climate refugees (2014: 5).

The merging of the crime genre with climate fiction, or cli-fi, as it is also known, allows Tuomainen to bring these two genres into dialogue with each other and to push the narrative beyond the generic borders of each. Initially, the climate catastrophe largely functions as a backdrop:

> I got off the bus at the Herttoniemi metro station. [...] There was a break in the rain and the strong, gusting wind couldn't decide which direction to blow. It lunged here and there, grabbing onto everything with its strong hands, including the powerful security lights on the walls of the buildings, which made it look as if the houses themselves were swaying in the evening darkness. I walked briskly past the nursery school that had first been abandoned by children, then scrawled on by random passers-by, and finally set on fire. The church at the other side of the junction had an emergency shelter for the homeless and it looked like it was full – the previously bright vestibule was half dim with people.
>
> *(21)*

Although frightening, for the poet-cum-investigator protagonist Tapani Lehtinen, the dystopian world in which he lives is less important than finding out what had happened to his wife, Johanna. Yet, as Tapani's search proceeds, the climate catastrophe takes on a greater importance and not just because Johanna is missing due to her own investigation into the titular Healer's desire to punish the "super-rich, who [...] masked their own interests under the mantle of economic growth for the common good" over the short term, the result of which was the defeat "of the long-term common good" by a rampant consumerism that "sped up the cycle of destruction" (138–39). The human causes of climate change thus become the crime that Tuomainen wants to draw to his readers' attention through the interaction between the two genres. As such, the first crime – the kidnapping of Johanna – is only important because it reveals the second crime – the environmental disaster. Indeed, as the novel progresses, moving between and merging the two generic categories of crime and climate fiction, the text highlights the severe cost of unchecked climate change for everyone. The novel's dénouement reinforces the futility of the protagonist's quest to rescue Johanna from her kidnapper. The small-scale crime pales into insignificance in light of the bigger crime. In this regard, the blending of crime and climate fiction in *The Healer* further reinforces an important shift in contemporary crime fiction; that is, a move from the interrogation of subjective crimes to larger systemic crimes which individual investigators cannot resolve.

The interaction between the two genres also challenges the discrete national categorisation that has tended to dominate the study of world crime fiction. Indeed, *The Healer* dismisses the nation as a useful framework for analysis and understanding by decentring it altogether.

Although set in Finland, the Finnish context is only important insofar as the country is a temporary refuge for the Finns and other nationalities who have fled due to the ongoing climate catastrophe. As the narrative morphs generically from crime fiction to climate fiction, the increasing irrelevancy of the nation-state in the face of global catastrophe becomes evident. While set in Finland and written in Finnish for a – in the first instance – Finnish readership, the novel eschews the nation as a referent and, instead, develops a planetary perspective. In essence, *The Healer* is about the world.

Conclusion

Given the account of the crime genre that we have developed in this chapter, it is clear that the seemingly simple question "what is crime fiction?" does not have an equally simple answer. The critical attempts to define the genre, and taxonomise it by further defining its various subforms, have largely been abandoned by scholars, not least as a result of the challenges posed by hybrid and transnational crime fiction. Accordingly, it seems that we can only speak of the genre as a loose grouping of texts, tentatively held together, not by any essential or constant feature, but by what Wittgenstein calls "family resemblances" – networks of overlapping connections that unite otherwise distinctive entities in the same way as the concept of a "game" covers everything from board games to tennis to a child throwing a ball against a wall and catching it again (1958: §66). While such resemblances provide some degree of structure to a complex field, it might be a more promising move to resist the definitional desire altogether and explore instead how the crime genre is *used* by various agents in the literary field. The uses of the genre are multifarious and include the marketing strategies of publishers, the creative processes of authors and the reception practices of readers. At the level of textuality, however, this focus on how the crime genre is used foregrounds how individual crime texts never simply embody the genre, but appropriate it, repurposing its tropes and splicing it to other genres in ever-new combinations. In this view, far from being the epitome of literary standardisation, the crime genre is a font of innovation.

Bibliography

Ascari, M. (2007) *A Counter-History of Crime Fiction: Supernatural, Gothic, sensational*, London: Palgrave Macmillan.

Bayard, P. (2000) [1998] *Who Killed Roger Ackroyd? The mystery behind the Agatha Christie mystery*, trans. C. Cosman, New York: The New Press.

Bradford, R. (2015) *Crime Fiction: A very short introduction*, Oxford: Oxford University Press.

Cawelti, J.G. (1976) *Adventure, Mystery, and Romance: Formula stories as art and popular culture*, Chicago, IL: University of Chicago Press.

Derrida, J. (1980) "The law of genre", trans. A. Ronell, *Critical Inquiry*, 7(1): 55–81.

Gulddal, J. (2016) "Clueless: Genre, realism, and narrative form in Ed McBain's early 87th Precinct novels", *Clues* 34(2): 54–62.

Gulddal, J., King, S. and Rolls, A. (2019) "Criminal moves: towards a theory of crime fiction mobility", in J. Gulddal, S. King and A. Rolls (eds), *Criminal Moves: Modes of mobility in crime fiction*, Liverpool: Liverpool University Press, 1–24.

Jameson, F. (1975) "Magical narratives: romance as genre", in *New Literary History*, 7(1): 135–63.

Kayman, M.A. (1992) *From Bow Street to Baker Street: Mystery, detection and narrative*, Houndmills: Palgrave Macmillan.

King, S. (2019) "The private eye of the beholder: reading world crime fiction", in J. Gulddal, S. King and A. Rolls (eds), *Criminal Moves: Modes of mobility in crime fiction*, Liverpool: Liverpool University Press, 195–210.

Moretti, F. (2000) "Conjectures on world literature", *New Left Review*, 1: 54–68.

Genre

Priestman, M. (ed.) (2003) *The Cambridge Companion to Crime Fiction*, Cambridge: Cambridge University Press.

Rzepka, C. (2010) "Introduction: what is crime fiction?", in C. Rzepka and L. Horsley (eds), *A Companion to Crime Fiction*, Chichester: Wiley-Blackwell, 1–9.

Symons, J. (1992) *Bloody Murder: From the detective story to the crime novel*, 3rd rev. edn, New York: The Mysterious Press.

Todorov, T. (1977) "The typology of detective fiction", in *The Poetics of Prose*, trans. R. Howard, Oxford: Basil Blackwell, 42–52.

Tuomainen, A. (2014) [2010] *The Healer*, trans. L. Rogers, London: Vintage.

Van Dine, S.S. (1928). "Twenty rules for writing detective stories", *The American Magazine* (September): 26–30.

Wittgenstein, L. (1958) *Philosophical Investigations*, Oxford: Basil Blackwell.

2
COUNTERHISTORIES AND PREHISTORIES

Maurizio Ascari

Far from being objective entities, literary genres should be regarded as cultural constructs, the development of which can be analysed in a "meta-critical" mode. During the course of modernity, crime fiction underwent a process of specialisation due to societal and epistemological changes that brought about an increasing focus on the investigation. Yet, this process never severed the ties between this highly successful and partly formulaic literary output and the much broader body of crime narratives. This chapter aims not only to remind us of this phenomenon, but also to investigate the concomitant critical and theoretical constructions, starting from the early twentieth century, when detective fiction crystallised into a literary genre that resulted from complex interactions between literary production and reception. It will then move on to the second half of the century, when this theoretical perspective was progressively deconstructed, also in response to the renewed experimental freedom claimed by practitioners of the genre. Having traced the shift from *detective fiction* to *crime fiction*, that is, from the restrictive theoretical and historical paradigms that characterised Golden Age detective fiction to the current emphasis on the creative power of cross-genre pollination, these pages will finally show how this counterhistorical awareness can lead to a renewed interest in the prehistory of the genre.

The canonisation of detective fiction

Following the success of the Sherlock Holmes saga, an increasing number of detective fictions came to be characterised by intertextual connections and variations on a set of conventions. Readers' expectations correspondingly became more defined, in relation to the serial character of detective fiction, its transnational circulation (also thanks to translation) and the development of critical discourses. Terms such as *detective stories/novels* and *mystery stories/novels* started to appear within critical essays (which were often authored by creative writers) in an attempt to vindicate the literary status of narratives that – despite their popularity – were often regarded as inferior and even dangerous. G.K. Chesterton's "A Defence of Detective Stories" (1901) and Arthur B. Reeve's "In Defense of the Detective Story" (1913) are indicative of this prejudice. Under the sign of realism, detective fiction bore the birthmark of its original sin – its proximity with crime, as Chesterton remarks:

many people do not realize that there is such a thing as a good detective story; it is to them like speaking of a good devil. To write a story about a burglary is, in their eyes, a sort of spiritual manner of committing it. To persons of somewhat weak sensibility this is natural enough; it must be confessed that many detective stories are as full of sensational crime as one of Shakespeare's plays.

(1902: 118–19)

With his flair for insightful paradox, Chesterton portrays Shakespeare as a sensationalist, while praising detective novelists for singing "the poetry of modern life" (119), notably of London, and the "romance of detail in civilization" (121), thanks to their use of clues. Detective stories are also described here as reviving the tradition of the epos, casting policemen in the role of knights-errant while depicting criminals as "old cosmic conservatives, happy in the immemorial respectability of apes and wolves" (123).

Reeve's defence of the new genre opens with half-ironical references to the "psychology of the hosts of readers of detective stories", wondering whether "we are all as full of crime as Sing" (1913: 91). He then moves on to analyse the transnational genesis of this literary phenomenon across the United States, France and Great Britain, tracing a Euro-American canon featuring E.A. Poe, Émile Gaboriau, Fortuné du Boisgobey and Arthur Conan Doyle. The article also discusses the European translations of dime novels of the Nick Carter sort, and the "nearly nine million copies of such books" (92) that are sold annually in Russia. As might be expected from the author of serial detective Craig Kennedy, Reeve underlines the positive impact of what he labels the "scientific detective story", since "the whole field of science lies open to be drawn on by the clever detective – from fingerprints, the portrait parlé, the dictagraph and detectaphone [sic], to chemistry and physics in general" (93).

Together with Carolyn Wells's *The Technique of the Mystery Story* (1913), these essays testify to an incipient process of genre-making that climaxed in the so-called Golden Age of detective fiction, in the aftermath of World War I. The shadow of war hovers over Golden Age novels, as shown by Agatha Christie's *The Mysterious Affair at Styles* (1920), in which Hercule Poirot is a refugee from Belgium and Arthur Hastings is on sick leave from the front, and even more by Dorothy Sayers's *Whose Body?* (1923), which expands on detective Peter Wimsey's shellshock symptoms. The Golden Age quest for order may be regarded as a therapeutic response to the violence and epistemological uncertainty associated with World War I, but Golden Age writers and critics emphasised detection to the detriment of crime also in order to "exorcise" the emotional dimension of previous crime writing, inviting a detached (at times ironical) approach, a mode of reading that was akin to reassuringly orderly intellectual pastimes such as crossword puzzles or chess. The ensuing competition between author and readers for the solution of the mystery was regulated by the fair play principle, whereby readers should be offered the same pieces of evidence detectives have under their eyes. This is the age of locked room and country house mysteries, with their variants in the shape of train/boat/plane mysteries. The emphasis rests on a geometry of confined spaces and communities, as well as on authorial ingenuity. This focus on highly contrived, and correspondingly bloodless, murdering techniques was meant to sanitise crime writing, depriving it of its sensational components and turning it into a rational exercise, or so it was believed.

Coherently with this strategy, Golden Age critical essays reveal a prescriptive, rather than descriptive, tendency, which marks both synchronic and diachronic accounts of the genre. In the attempt to gentrify detective fiction, distancing it from a multifarious literary territory that reeked of transgression, Golden Age historians routinely described the genre as originating from Poe's tales of ratiocination. Detective fiction was thus "severed" from neighbouring genres such as sensation fiction and the burgeoning thriller. Not all critics subscribed to this view, as shown by Régis Messac's monumental *Le "Detective Novel" et l'influence de la pensée scientifique* (1929). T.S. Eliot's "Wilkie Collins and Dickens" (1927) can also be mentioned as an attempt to problematise the prevailing view of this genre by contrasting two literary traditions – one featuring *infallible* detectives such as Poe's Dupin, and the other featuring *fallible* detectives like Wilkie Collins' Inspector Cuff, but such critical openness is the exception rather than the rule.

Unconsciously mimicking the epistemological attitude that prevailed at the time, mainstream writers and critics came close to conceptualising the system of genres as a set of adjacent pure forms that could be conveniently pigeonholed, rather than exploring the unceasing cross-pollinations that lead to literary evolution. Ronald Knox and S.S. Van Dine even attempted to foster this purity in contemporary authors, prompting them to write literary works that conformed to sets of rules. The ostensible idea was to ensure that writers played fair, and an oath to this end had to be taken in order to become a member of the London Detection Club, which around 1930 brought together most prominent British detective writers. What was initially intended as a game for literati, however, became dogma, triggering misguided attempts at critical eugenics. I wish to clarify that these considerations are not intended to stigmatise the Golden Age, whose profile is actually much more varied and hybrid than some of its practitioners would have us believe. Thus, while debunking the Golden Age myth of generic purity, we should also reassess our present view of the "Golden Age" of detective fiction in order to eschew any simplistic rendering of what proved to be a period of extraordinary creative and critical vitality.

From detective fiction to crime fiction

While the dominant narrative formulas and critical discourses of the Golden Age pivoted on rational detection, crime fiction had actually never lost contact with the everyday brutality of street violence, as shown by the American hardboiled, which triggered its own theorisation through essays such as Raymond Chandler's "The Simple Art of Murder" (1944). Nor had crime fiction lost contact with its Gothic roots, although this phenomenon arguably acquired full visibility only in the early 1940s, thanks to a number of Hollywood Gothic melodramas at the core of which is the experience of the female victim; Alfred Hitchcock's *Rebecca* (1940), based on Daphne Du Maurier's 1938 novel, comes to mind. Many other films contributed to the flourishing of the psychological thriller, including Hitchcock's *Spellbound* (1945), which encapsulates the popularisation of psychoanalysis in the aftermath of World War II. This season culminated in what is now a classic of American Gothic, Robert Bloch's *Psycho* (1959), which appeared in the same year as Shirley Jackson's masterpiece of psychological horror, *The Haunting of Hill House*.

Despite this climate of experimentation, which invited critics to explore new directions, the prevailing critical paradigm resisted change, as shown by Alma E. Murch's scholarly *The Development of the Detective Novel* (1958), where the genetic links between the detective story, the crime story and the mystery story are acknowledged, but the focus is unambiguously on the clue-puzzle. Almost echoing the above-mentioned anti-sensational prejudice, Murch defines detective fiction in relation to the reader's response as a literary form in which "the reader's sympathy is invariably engaged, if only by inference, on the side of law and order, and the hero is not the criminal, but the detective" (1968: 12). As if to highlight the intellectual matrix of this genre, "Humour and love-making" are correspondingly presented as marking the crime story and conversely as having "no real place" in detective stories (12).

The flimsiness of these definitions becomes apparent if we take time to ponder the Golden Age itself. Ronald Knox's *The Viaduct Murder* (1925) and *The Three Taps* (1927) or Anthony Berkeley's *The Poisoned Chocolate Case* (1929) are characterised by a parodic, ironic, self-deconstructive mode that typifies many other interwar texts, as acknowledged by Bruce Shaw in *Jolly Good Detecting: Humour in English Crime Fiction of the Golden Age* (2014). How is it possible that otherwise excellent scholars failed to see such relevant aspects of the phenomena they were investigating? The answer resides in the subliminal power of the theoretical paradigm that ruled mainstream discourses on detective fiction, impairing the critics' power of observation. It is widely agreed that a good detective should never let any preconceived hypothesis direct their inquiry, but detective fiction was canonised by trimming down the lush tree of crime fiction so that it took on a geometric shape. All the branches that did not fit within this pattern simply had to go, even if this critical representation failed to correspond to the complexity of literary phenomena.

It was crime writer Julian Symons who undertook the first sustained attempt to reverse this tendency. His *Bloody Murder. From the Detective Story to the Crime Novel: A History* (1972) is the first of many studies that in the course of the last fifty years have reassessed the Golden Age, highlighting its "situated" – rather than objective – character and its reductive penchant for delimiting and excluding non-orthodox texts to the detriment of connections and diversity. As Symons writes,

> Historians of the detective story have been insistent that it is a unique literary form, distinct from the crime or mystery story, not to be confused with the police novel, and even more clearly separate from the many varieties of thriller. Those who believe as I do that such classifications are more confusing than helpful, and that the most sensible sort of naming is the general one of crime novel or suspense novel (and short story) have to begin by countering a considerable weight of opinion.
>
> *(1985: 13)*

Following in the footsteps of Symons, Stephen Knight published his *Form and Ideology in Crime Fiction* (1980), in which he not only embraced an expanded notion of this literary genre, but also outlined a new methodological agenda for the investigation of popular literature, in the attempt to probe "the ideological nature and function of crime fiction" (1980: 3). Scholars such as Martin A. Kayman, Andrew Pepper, Gill Plain, Martin Priestman, Charles Rzepka, John Scaggs and Heather Worthington have subsequently contributed – together with others, including myself – to this reassessment of the genre at large under the more comprehensive heading of crime fiction.

What might be labelled postmodernist crime criticism is more text-based than its antecedents, in the conviction that each crime text deserves to be studied with an individual focus, rather than being considered as the materialisation of a formula. The approach is bottom up rather than top down. It values diversity and mobility rather than conformity. A new emphasis on transnational and transcultural connections concurs to render the complexity this mass-market genre has achieved in terms not only of global production and circulation, but also of narrative scope and themes, as investigated by Andrew Pepper and David Schmid's *Globalization and the State in Contemporary Crime Fiction: A World of Crime* (2016). Recent crime writing, moreover, embraces a variety of both old and new media, from cinema and television to digital storytelling, including fanfiction. Criminography is now considered as a network of ideological discourses (often mirroring social conflicts and frictions), in the attempt to uncover the exchanges between crime fictions, journalism, forensic science, pseudoscientific theories and even supernatural worldviews.

Due to an accelerating process of cross-pollination between crime, the Gothic and horror, our present is marked by a range of supernatural thrillers and other related subgenres, as shown by TV series such as *Angel* (1999–2004), *Ghost Whisperer* (2005–2010), *Medium* (2005–2011), *Supernatural* (2005–present) or the first season of *True Detective* (2014), to name but a few. Although transgeneric exchanges have recently reached unprecedented levels within the mass culture industry, this phenomenon is far from new, and Golden Age critics were well aware of the connection between neighbouring genres within the realm of popular fiction. The title of Dorothy Sayers's *Great Short Stories of Detection, Mystery and Horror* (1928) is revealing of this awareness, and in H. Douglas Thomson's *The Mystery Book* (1934) the umbrella term of *mystery* likewise embraces "Stories of Mystery and Adventure" (11), "Stories of Crime and Detection" (13) and "Stories of the Supernatural" (15).

In these Golden Age texts, however, the emphasis is not on generic overlaps, but rather on the difference between adjacent literary territories. Thus, adopting an evolutionary paradigm, Thomson regards detection as the mark of modernity, while describing "the more primitive stories of the supernatural" as "born of superstition, the fear of death, and our childlike terror of the dark" (8). These words resonate with the Golden Age defence of detective fiction as a progressive force within society, in opposition to the genre's shady past and equally shady literary neighbours. A similarly exclusionary attitude interestingly characterises H.P. Lovecraft's *The Supernatural Horror in Literature* (1927), where the adventures of occult detectives Carnacki and John Silence are described as "marred by traces of the popular and conventional detective-story atmosphere" (1973: 97).

While in the early twentieth century generic purity was valued, current criticism challenges what Agnieszka Kotwasińska labels as "generic anxiety" (2014: 86), and conversely aims at reconstructing the network of transgeneric traits that pertain to individual literary works. This new emphasis on hybridity is the result of various factors, starting from the intellectual openness and deconstructive attitude of the postmodernist period, as marked by a nonchalant attitude towards canonicity, a playful indifference to the distinction between "high" and "low" literature. No wonder the concept of mobility is acquiring increasing currency in crime fiction criticism, as shown by *Criminal Moves: Modes of Mobility in Crime Fiction* (2019), which editors Jesper Gulddal, Stewart King and Alistair Rolls have organised around three axes – mobility of meaning, mobility of genre and transnational mobility.

The current conceptualisation of crime fiction reflects the evolution of the genre in the direction of diversity through a network of transnational exchanges between texts, genres and media, together with metatextual experimentations and concerns. To fully understand this phenomenon, one should also mention the important role that gender, ethnic and class identities have come to play, both as writerly concerns and as critical categories, having led to the rediscovery of numerous literary texts by women. Dilys Winn's *Murderess Ink – The Better Half of the Mystery* (1979) and Patricia Craig and Mary Cadogan's *The Lady Investigates. Women Detectives and Spies in Fiction* (1981) testify to the early stages of this canonical revision. More recently, digitalisation has made available a number of journals, magazines and other materials (from broadsides to chapbooks) that in the past could be found only in a small number of libraries, and this has further changed our approach to the study of past popular fiction.

Every prehistory is a counterhistory

This new critical and conceptual openness, together with the accrued availability of previous marginal/ised texts, has given rise to a new interest in the prehistories of modern crime fiction, of which detective fiction is now regarded as a subgenre. Rejecting both the Golden Age focus on rational detection as the defining element of this genre, and the contemporary monogenetic theories that located its inception in a single urtext (the Dupin trilogy), critics have delved into the many traditions that have intertwined across the centuries. As a result, detective fiction is now regarded as a mid-nineteenth-century phenomenon that flourished in relation to the increasing professionalisation of society, notably of disciplinary agents such as policemen, physicians and lawyers.

The roots of this subgenre, however, can be traced back in time to Gothic novels. In "Philosophy of Composition" (1846), Poe himself mentions William Godwin and the unity of design he achieved in his 1794 novel, *Caleb Williams*. A philosopher, Godwin conceived this tight-knit, suspenseful plot through a technique of reverse composition, starting from the end of the story and working his way backwards. Combining an emphasis on rational detection that we can regard as a fruit of the Enlightenment with a resurging interest for the criminal mind, under the aegis of the sublime, this novel was both preceded and followed by other specimens of Gothic narratives that paved the way for the rise of detective fiction proper. The hectic pace of reading Godwin targeted had previously been theorised by novelist Thomas Holcroft in his preface to *Alwin* (1780) and even earlier by Horace Walpole, who describes the narrative of *The Castle of Otranto* (1764) as tending "directly to the catastrophe. Never is the reader's attention relaxed. [...] Terror, the author's principal engine, prevents the story from ever languishing" (1968: 40).

The identification of Gothic fiction as a precursor of nineteenth-century detective and sensation fiction is only a fragment of a huge literary fresco that potentially takes us back in time to Greco-Roman Antiquity and to the Bible, straddling the divide between popular literature and canonical texts. The emphasis can be on both rational and supernatural forms of detection, as shown by medieval and early modern providential fictions, or conversely on crime itself, while other texts simultaneously explore both dimensions, as shown by Sophocles' archetypical tragedy *Oedipus Rex* (c. 429 BC), where the "detective" is famously revealed as the murderer.

Despite being a product of antiquity, Oedipus shares the problem-solving ability of modern detectives, as shown by his unveiling the riddle of the Sphinx, which leads him to become King of Thebes. The key to power here is not physical prowess but insight. Portrayed as highly rational, Oedipus is, however, unable to know himself, acting instead as a pawn in the hands of destiny. Oedipus is a living enigma whose name (*swollen foot*) betrays the secret of his origin. It is not by chance that Delphi – the seat of the famous oracle, who prophesised in a temple bearing the motto *know thyself* – is repeatedly evoked in this tragedy. It is to Delphi that Oedipus sends his brother-in-law Creon to inquire into the origin of the plague that besets Thebes. And it is at a junction between three roads – one of which leads to Delphi – that Oedipus kills King Laius (without knowing that Laius is his father), thus fulfilling the prophecy from which he has been fruitlessly trying to escape. In this story of endogamic crime, knowing oneself ultimately leads to horror. The light of reason, which defeats the Sphinx, withdraws before the abyss of guilt. In response to the revelation of his identity and of his crime, Oedipus chooses the darkness of blindness – a gesture of self-punishment in which we can also read a tragic act of self-compassion, a veiling of reality. The inquiring self is vanquished in this archetypical psychological thriller. The tree of knowledge yields its fruit when the season of evil is over.

This classical text fully acknowledges the complexity of human beings; our inability to attain objective knowledge of ourselves. Despite our rational ability to master external reality, we are still prey to dark forces, potent drives, urges that rise from below. While in the early twentieth century, scientific detection came to symbolise a Positivist view of civilisation as resting on the individual's ability to shed light on reality, what we find at the origins of crime fiction is an acknowledgement of the constitutive darkness of the human.

If we take time to reflect, we can see that darkness is also at the core of Poe's seminal trilogy. In "Murders in the Rue Morgue" (1841) Dupin is actually presented as a Gothic creature of the night who spends the entire day in the darkness of his dwelling, reading, dreaming and conversing with the narrator, while it is only at night that the two roam the streets. This lifestyle befits a character whose analytical ability rests on the creative faculty of the imagination rather than on the combining power of fancy, as the story clarifies in its introductory section. The message is reiterated in Dupin's third adventure, "The Purloined Letter" (1845). With a revealing paradox, on receiving the Prefect, who has come to consult him on a case, the detective comments: "If it is any point requiring reflection, […] we shall examine it to better purpose in the dark" (1984: 494). Darkness and light have entwined in many different ways in the long history of crime fiction, and from our current observatory we are well placed to appreciate this phenomenon in all its complexity, as reflecting the worldviews and ideological concerns of different societies, epochs and authors.

Changing paradigms of detection in *Hamlet*

I conclude these reflections with a brief analysis of *Hamlet* (c. 1600) as an early manifestation of detective fiction. Early modernity was a time of transition, when the medieval paradigms of knowledge made way for a new interest in the testimony of the senses and in the workings of logic, notably in inductive reasoning. A new episteme of empiricism ripened in this period, as evidenced by Francis Bacon's approach to knowledge, which crystallised in works such as *The Advancement and Proficience of Learning Divine and Human* (1605) and *Novum Organum Scientiarum* (1620).

Detective comes from the Latin *de-tegere*, which literally means *un-cover*. While according to the *Oxford English Dictionary* the first occurrences of this word date back to the 1840s, the verb *detect* and the noun *detection* had already come into use between the fifteenth and sixteenth centuries. The increasing relevance of this term is proved by the fact that Robert Cawdrey's *A Table Alphabeticall* (1604), the first monolingual dictionary of English, has an entry for *Detect*, which it defines as "bewray, disclose, accuse" (1966: Fol. D2r.). This verb reappears in *Hamlet* when the hero explains that he intends to stage a play mimicking his father's death. Being invited by Hamlet to observe the king's reaction, Horatio replies:

> […] If a steal aught the whilst this play is playing,
> And scape detecting, I will pay the theft.
> (3.2.81-82)

This passage posits Hamlet as a proto-detective, and Horatio as his assistant, although the tools they employ have little to do with Holmes's forensic science or Dupin's analytical powers. Both Hamlet and Horatio, however, are presented as studying at the University of Wittenberg, a qualification that suits their investigative status, marking an advance on the traditional supernatural paradigm of justice that is embodied by the ghost of Hamlet's father. According to popular belief, God enabled victims to denounce their aggressors from the netherworld. Yet the conception of the afterlife itself dramatically changed in early modernity as a result of the Reformation. This religious and cultural fault line is mirrored in the uncertain status of Hamlet's father's ghost, whose description of his torments evokes a suspiciously Catholic view of Purgatory:

> I am thy father's spirit,
> Doomed for a certain term to walk the night,
> And for the day confined to fast in fires,
> Till the foul crimes done in my days of nature
> Are burnt and purged away.
>
> (1.5.9-13)

Since purgatory had been abolished by the Church of England, as spelled out in its *Thirty-Nine Articles of Religion* (1571), what did Shakespeare mean when he had the ghost of Hamlet's father describe his provenance in Catholic terms? Why did he choose to have Hamlet and his friends study at the University of Wittenberg, where Luther had been a professor of moral theology? While the ambivalences of this play have been effectively tackled by Stephen Greenblatt (2013), what matters to us is the fact that both Horatio and Hamlet suspect the ghost of actually coming from hell with the intention to damn Hamlet by inducing him to suicide (as hinted by Horatio, 1.4.50) or homicide:

> [...] The spirit that I have seen
> May be the devil, and the devil hath power
> T'assume a pleasing shape; yea, and perhaps
> Out of my weakness and my melancholy –
> As he is very potent with such spirits –
> Abuses me to damn me. I'll have grounds
> More relative than this. The play's the thing
> Wherein I'll catch the conscience of the King.
>
> (2.2.575-82)

Far from uncritically accepting the victim's postmortem denunciation of his murder, Hamlet verifies it by means of a psychological test, a play he calls "The Mouse-trap", during a conversation with the king himself.

Obliquely hinting at the conflict between the religion of the "fathers" and post-Reformation dogmas, Shakespeare has Hamlet opt for the intellectual paradigm of university studies in his attempt to ascertain truth, thus turning Hamlet into the emblem of early modernity as an age of secularisation. The dawn of modernity placed increasing emphasis on the rational investigation of phenomena, as shown by Bacon's essay "Of Studies" (1597), where the empiricist thinker presents wisdom as "won by observation" (1883: 255). Although Hamlet still subscribes to a preternatural principle of justice ("Foul deeds will rise, / Though all the earth o'erwhelm them, to men's eyes" [1.2.256-57]), sensory knowledge is central to his investigation. When Hamlet is told by Horatio about the apparitions of the ghost, he approaches this supernatural phenomenon along empirical lines. After Horatio concludes his eyewitness account of this prodigious encounter with words that leave no doubt – "I knew your father; / These hands are not more like" (1.2.211-12) – Hamlet starts questioning him to make sure of the ghost's identity: "His beard was grizzly, no?" (1.2.239). Then he proceeds to ascertain his motive for coming back to Earth:

HAMLET Then saw you not his face?
HORATIO O, yes, my lord, he wore his beaver up.
HAMLET What looked he? Frowningly?
HORATIO A countenance more
In sorrow than in anger.
HAMLET Pale or red?
HORATIO Nay, very pale.

(1.2.226-31)

Endowed with psychological insight, Hamlet exerts his talents to sift the evidence he encounters, inquiring into both Horatio's testimony and the silent message of the ghost.

These reflections on Hamlet as a proto-detective should not distract us from the fact that detection played only a minor role in early modern crime literature, which was marked instead by a prevailing interest in criminal lives and in criminal minds, as shown by Shakespeare's own *Macbeth* (c. 1606). Both *Hamlet* and *Macbeth*, however, call our attention to the momentous transition from an epistemological paradigm of supernatural revelation to one of empiricist observation, which proved central to the evolution of crime fiction. The modern phenomenon of detective fiction stemmed from the central status that rationality, science and professionalism slowly acquired in Western societies, but it is only by contextualising it within the wider realm of crime fiction – both synchronically and diachronically – that we can fully appreciate its cultural relevance. Far from being restricted to the narrow boundaries of a literary formula pivoting on ingenuity, narratives of crime and detection interrogate fundamental aspects of the human experience, opening up to a whole range of philosophical and existential concerns. It is only by recognising their mobile nature, their ability to metamorphose in response to a variety of ideological and other concerns, that we can appreciate their richness and depth, getting to the core of the energies they convey.

Bibliography

Bacon, F. (1883) [1597, 1625] "Of studies", *The Essays*, Intro. Henry Morley, Chicago: Donohue, Henneberry.

Cawdrey, R. (1966) [1604] *A Table Alphabeticall*, ed. Robert A. Peters, Gainesville, Florida: Scholars' Facsimiles & Reprints. https://extra.shu.ac.uk/emls/iemls/work/etexts/caw1604w_removed.htm (accessed 13 November 2019).

Chesterton, G.K. (1902) [1901] "A defence of detective stories", in *The Defendant*, London: R. Brimley Johnson, 118–23.

Gulddal, J., King, S. and Rolls, A. (2019) "Criminal moves: towards a theory of crime fiction mobility", in J. Gulddal, S. King and A. Rolls (eds), *Criminal Moves: Modes of mobility in crime fiction*, Liverpool: Liverpool University Press, 1–24.

Knight, S. (1980) *Form and Ideology in Crime Fiction*, London: Macmillan.

Kotwasińska, A. (2014) "Looking for ghostly crimes: cross-pollination of crime and Gothic fiction in Edith Wharton's 'Mr. Jones'", *Polish Journal for American Studies*, 8: 85–100.

Lovecraft, H.P. (1973) [1945] *Supernatural Horror in Literature*, Intro. E.F. Bleiler, New York: Dover.

Murch, A.E. (1968) [1958] *The Development of the Detective Novel*, London: Peter Owen.

Poe, E.A. (1984) [1845] "The purloined letter", in G. Clarke (ed.), *Tales of Mystery and the Imagination*, London: Dent, 493–511.

Reeve, A.B. (1913) "In defense of the detective story", *The Independent*, 75: 91–94.

Shakespeare, W. (1997) "[c.1600] Hamlet", in S. Greenblatt (ed.), *The Norton Shakespeare: The tragedies*, New York and London: Norton.

Symons, J. (1985) [1972] *Bloody Murder. From the detective story to the crime novel: A history*, New York: Viking.

Thomson, H.D. (ed.) (1934) *The Mystery Book*, London: Odhams Press.

Walpole, H. (1968) [1764] "Preface to the first edition of *The Castle of Otranto*", in M. Praz (ed.), *Three Gothic Novels*, Harmondsworth, Middlesex: Penguin, 39–42.

3
THE CRIME FICTION SERIES

Ruth Mayer

Crime, investigation, interrogation, confrontation, disclosure: A serial pattern informs the very plot logic of crime fiction. Seen in this way, all crime stories are serial narratives – regardless of their mode of publication. As early as 1925, Siegfried Kracauer observed that the (stand-alone) detective novel presents itself as an "endless series" (*unendliche Reihe*) in which the detective does not so much seek out adventures or challenges but is faced with "cases" that "happen to him or are assigned to him" (1979: 58, my translation). Affording more agency to the serial features of the narrative than to its central characters – the detective or the criminal – Kracauer directs our attention from the crime story's plot to its form. The serial logic manifests itself on several levels: the microlevel of the individual narrative, the intermediate level of the story or book series, and the macro level of the genre. In the course of the genre's maturation and profession-alisation in the nineteenth and twentieth centuries, crime fiction came to be inscribed with seriality (Anderson et al. 2015a: 1).

On all levels of serial writing, traditions and conventions play an incisive role. Due to the dynamics of markets and infrastructures, as well as changes in the conceptualisation of authors, narratives, media and audiences over the course of the last two centuries, popular serial story-telling has become subject to faster feedback loops and cycles of remediation. Most of the narrative patterns and plot contrivances that were established in the evolving literatures of crime and detection in the nineteenth century are still present today, functioning as points of departure, ironic references or signals of reassurance. Since the beginning of the twentieth century, a successful crime story calls first for a sequel and second for a media change – today mostly in the guise of a film or TV adaptation that, if successful, will undergo further processes of serialisation through remakes or series production.

In what follows, I will first explore the history and the structural implications of the serial form in crime narration, with a focus on the beginning of the twentieth century. Then I will look more closely at one particular case of serialisation: The publication history and serial aesthetics of Edgar Wallace's first novel, *The Four Just Men* (1905). Finally, I discuss the ways in which the crime series has become the standard form of crime narration in the digitised twenty-first century.

Serial narrative structures

Reflecting on the successful formula of Ian Fleming's James Bond series, Umberto Eco points out the significance of Fleming's strategic transition from a "psychological method [of narration] to a formalistic one", in the course of which the series' protagonist turns from a character into a flat figure, while the series becomes a "narrative machine" (1979: 146; see also Mayer 2014: 1–26). Like Kracauer, Eco highlights the self-propelling force of genre narration and, more narrowly, crime fiction, in which formulas, character constellations and plot conventions gain momentum on their own and become active agents, as it were. Eco was one of the first critics to take popular seriality seriously by emphasising the effectiveness of its oscillation between repetition and variation (or innovation) as a narrative forcefield (1985). He also insisted on the importance of the archives of storytelling, highlighting the creative energy of intertextual borrowings that may be conscious or unconscious, but which keeps literature, and particularly genre literature, going.

The traditions of the French *feuilleton* and the American dime novel proved especially instrumental for the evolution of modern crime narration. Two major serial patterns established themselves in this respect. On the one hand, closed and episodic narratives evolved, which kept drawing upon the same cast of characters and often the same settings, but which enacted their stories without an underlying continuity or overarching chronology. In this serial pattern, characters turn into serial figures that undergo a "virtual beginning" with each new staging, "ignoring where the preceding event left off", as Eco wrote of Superman (1979: 117). This is the structure used by the American dime novels and British detective stories of the nineteenth century. The second pattern manifests in the French *roman-feuilleton* or German *Fortsetzungsroman*, which are genres that tended to pursue one consecutive storyline and chronology across their instalments. These narratives allow their characters to develop, mature and (occasionally) die, and they create storyworlds that can become complex, epic and entangled (Pagello 2015: 21–24). In the twentieth century, crime series often made use of both formats intermittently, allowing for the construction of continuity or coherence, but still presenting the individual instalments as more or less independent pieces.

The two patterns converge exemplarily in the Sherlock Holmes stories, which gesture toward an ongoing larger narrative universe with its own consecutive logic, yet still unfold in individual short stories. These stories are actually always several stories folded "into a tightly compacted frame", as Michael Chabon points out, elaborating that "[n]early all the Holmes stories [...] are stories of people who tell their stories, and every so often the stories these people tell feature people telling stories" (2008: 47). In keeping with other approaches to the field, Chabon diagnoses an intrinsic propensity for narrative self-reflection in the detective plot (see also Gulddal and Rolls 2016). In contrast to other self-reflective literary genres, however, the Sherlock Holmes stories do not indulge in displays of "digression, indirection, or the overtly self-referential" (49), but call to mind, in their conflation of self-reflection and seriality, the contemporary principles of industrial production, acting as "storytelling engines, steam-driven, brass-fitted, but among the most efficient narrative apparatuses the world has ever seen" (47). Chabon identifies this principle of storytelling very closely with what he sees as the genius of Doyle, but it owes at least as much to a larger scene and system of crime narration unfolding, at the time, in a periodical publishing market on both sides of the Atlantic. Doyle's stories are tightly coiled, but at the same time they serve as nodal points in storytelling networks, allowing for innumerable backstories and extensions, imitations, reviews and repercussions, not to mention the fan fictions which still regularly take off from Baker Street many years after Sherlock Holmes's inception.

Moving far beyond the boundaries of its originary texts, the success of Sherlock Holmes hinges on the figure's recognisability and capacity for variation. These qualities characterise many of the most popular characters in twentieth-century crime fiction – and they do not only apply to detectives, but quickly also take over the stylisation of the criminals. At some point around the turn of the century, the fascination with the plots of ratiocination and investigation seems to have flipped to reveal a more disturbing interest in the character of the criminal, as the master criminal became an iconic figure in the urban fiction of modernity. This is how Fu Manchu in England, Zigomar and Fantômas in France, and Dr Mabuse in Germany entered the scene in the 1910s (Mayer 2014).

By the first decades of the twentieth century, the pattern had consolidated itself in transatlantic popular entertainment. By then, recurring detective and criminal figures abounded, most of them signalling back to the success stories of Holmes and his evil counterparts. In 1915, the short story "The Last Adventure of Craig Kennedy" by Frank R. Adams appeared in the magazine *The Smart Set* and engaged ironically with the multilayered seriality of the crime fiction craze. The story signals the hugely popular fiction series of Arthur Reeve and his "scientific" detective Craig Kennedy, who had shortly before transitioned from book to screen, or, to be precise, from his serial manifestation in short stories published in *Cosmopolitan* magazine (eighty-two stories between 1910 and 1918) to his reincarnation in serial film, where Craig Kennedy first made an appearance in the Pearl White vehicle, *The Exploits of Elaine* (1914), and again in subsequent films.

The Smart Set, the "little" magazine steered by its editors H.L. Mencken and George Nathan, with a keen sense for trends, positioned itself deliberately at the borderline between mass entertainment and refined taste. Adams's story uses the popular detective figure against itself by making fun of its omnipresence, the self-perpetuating quality of its success and the larger logic of outbidding inscribed into the genre: "[Sherlock Holmes] only had to make one magazine a month", muses this detective's serial sidekick and chronicler Walter Jameson, while Craig Kennedy has to "fill contracts with six monthlies, two weeklies, and a newspaper syndicate" (Adams 1915: 395). The short story's title announces that it will put an end to the master detective's career and the story culminates in his self-arrest. Detective and perpetrator here turn out to be one and the same person by an absurd confluence of events that lead to the detective's conviction, after which he self-destructs like a malfunctioning machine.

Obviously, the story did not manage (or intend) to end Craig Kennedy's career, which experienced a second boost in the pulp detective magazines of the 1920s and 1930s (although not in H.L. Mencken's own pulp venture, *Black Mask*). But it does manage to capture the workings of serialised detective fiction by showcasing the structural similarity between the main (stock) character and the genre's affinity with the principle of automation: Crime stories "write themselves" in ceaseless recursion, as it were, trying out possible variations and alternatives one after another until they have run their course. The series ends once the variations are exhausted, usually without a grand finale or a final overarching resolution. In their famous "Cultural Industry" essay, Max Horkheimer and Theodor W. Adorno recognise this procedural and reifying logic, although they do not acknowledge its creative potential: "The cultural industry cheats its consumers out of what it endlessly promises. The promissory note of pleasure issued by plot and packaging is indefinitely prolonged" (2002: 111). Indeed, crime series work by way of teases and promises, and their protagonists veer in their function from active agents to props. The pleasure they afford derives at least as much from the joy of watching complex operations unfold smoothly as from a reassuringly revelatory ending.

Serial infrastructures

It has been argued that the formation of industrialised nation-states across the globe was contingent on the invention of "print capitalism" that gained traction in the nineteenth century and relied heavily on the formats of the periodical publishing market with its synchronised production and reception practices (Anderson 1991). Benedict Anderson identified a "logic of the series" (1998: 34) behind this convergence of publishing techniques and politics, and indeed the core practices of nation formation comply with serial patterns – they rely on repetitive rituals and thereby turn isolated individuals into collectives (Mayer 2014: 14–17). The very same mechanisms are at the heart of the popular entertainment media that attained unprecedented significance in the nineteenth century: Dime novels, penny papers, illustrated magazines, sensational newspapers all employ serial formats and they all cater to transregional (at times transnational) audiences (Bold 2012). These media are part and parcel of an early participatory culture in which readers were regularly alerted to the verisimilitude or even veracity of the events depicted. Real or faked true-crime narratives invited their readers to seek correspondences between fiction and reality, to the point of enlisting them to literally solve the crime (Flanders 2014: 140–82; Haugtvedt 2017: 8–12).

In the course of the nineteenth century, a two-tiered anglophone publishing market evolved on both sides of the Atlantic, which increasingly attributed serial publication forms to popular entertainment, while associating literary value with stand-alone "works". Crime narratives came to be identified with the lower rung of the literary scene. This is the arena for the work of Edgar Wallace, whose phenomenal success in the crime genre attests to his fine-tuned sense of the possibilities of the genre and its financial potential. Before launching his career as a writer, Wallace held many odd jobs, working as a war correspondent, newspaper editor, and, most importantly, crime reporter and special correspondent for the tabloid *Daily Mail*. The publication history of his very first novel, *The Four Just Men*, illustrates his flexibility and strategic career planning.

The book first appeared in 1905 in serial instalments in the *Daily Mail*. To promote the publication, Wallace started an extensive media campaign, running advertisements on billboards, buildings, buses and in the press, which announced the ongoing serial publication as well as a forthcoming book edition, and tendered a £500 prize to whoever guessed the correct solution to the complicated plot. The campaign was successful but not successful enough. Wallace had underestimated the profit margin and the cost of the campaign and failed to carefully define the terms of the competition. He was unable to pay all the winners, and the *Daily Mail's* owner, newspaper magnate Alfred Harmsworth, had to lend him the money to safeguard the paper's reputation (Davies 2012: xii–xiii). Yet, while the entire venture was "financially disastrous" (xiii), the novel became a bestseller and the entire episode provided a decisive boost to Wallace's career. He went on to write more than 170 books, in addition to plays, film scripts and hundreds of short stories. "Using a Dictaphone, Wallace could polish off a 70,000-word novel in a weekend, and work on three stories at once, leading to jokes about 'the mid-day Wallace' on sale from railway newsvendors" (Glover 2004: 314). *The Four Just Men* prompted five sequels – three more novels (1908, 1918, 1924) and two story collections (1921, 1928). It was twice adapted to film and served as an inspiration for a popular TV series in the 1960s, long after Wallace's death.

The Four Just Men exhibits the operative logic of serial crime narration with its mix of careful planning and audience management on the one hand, and in its expansive, concrescent and autonomous dynamics on the other. At the beginning of such projects there is often a calculated consideration, which has at least as much to do with business interests as with creative impulses. Popular serial production is thus closely modelled on industrial production – streamlined, synchronised and efficiently attuned to the technical media that allow for the fast processing and circulation of data: The dictaphone, the typewriter, the telegraph, the offset press and many more. The serial momentum then tends to leave individual authors and texts behind, spinning off variations of narrative figures and figurations instead, branching out and pushing onwards, and availing itself of any carrier medium that comes its way (Mayer 2014: 27–58).

But *The Four Just Men* is not only of interest because of its publication history. Its narrative strategies are also indicative of larger trends in crime series narration that would take shape over the course of the twentieth century. This may sound counterintuitive, since neither Wallace's novel nor his oeuvre as a whole really feature what is commonly regarded as *the* most typical element of a crime series: A central recurring detective figure on a par with Inspector Lecoq or Sherlock Holmes, Hercule Poirot or Lord Peter Wimsey (with the exception of the six-volume "Inspector Elk" series, which got lost among the bulk of the author's prolific publications). And while *The Four Just Men*'s central characters veer markedly between seeking justice and perpetrating crime, and derive their fascination from staying off-stage – "four men whom no person had ever consciously seen" (23) – they are no phantom-like supervillains like Fantômas or Fu Manchu, not least because there are four of them. Faceless, flat, exchangeable, they are of interest not because of any outstanding qualities but because of their forceful impact. By today's standards, they are terrorists: They take the law into their own hands, threatening to kill high-ranking government officials and politicians all over the world if they do not do their bidding, and follow up on their threats mercilessly and skilfully. In the first novel of the series, it is the Foreign Secretary of the UK whom they put in their crosshairs.

In their course of action, the four men resemble the very media that serve to publicise their schemes. They are, in a manner of speaking, serial repercussions of the sensational periodical press. Significantly, the novel starts, after a short prologue, with a first chapter which epitomises at the level of the plot what the novel also aspires to achieve formally: Information management. Modern reality is awash in unfiltered and unprocessed data that needs to be sorted and correlated. Wallace's novel responds to this imperative by showcasing how modern mass media work. We are introduced to the four men's devious scheme in the exact same manner in which this scheme is (at first inefficiently) disclosed to a larger public. At the beginning of the first chapter, the reader's attention is drawn to "a tiny paragraph [...] at the foot of an unimportant page in London's most sober journal" (8). The little notice, issued by government authorities, divulges a death threat to the Secretary of State for Foreign Affairs and offers a reward for any information about its instigator(s). This mode of promulgation is pitifully inadequate, as the novel's author, of all people, would know, since he had just made use of the reach of a tabloid paper to solicit reader engagement. In the novel, the obvious fictional equivalent of the *Daily Mail*, "a very bright newspaper" (8) called the *Megaphone*, picks up the obscure notice, recognises it for what it is, and then sets out to turn it into "a great story" (13). The paper's editor-in-chief, "that great man" (9), proves particularly adept at assembling the bits and pieces of evidence about the four men's scheme into a coherent "plot", thus turning random data into a narrative.

While tabloid reporting is usually represented in terms of exaggeration, if not outright falsification, here it is treated as the one medium that can meet the demands of a fast-paced, chaotic and expansive modern reality. It does so by stringing isolated episodes together in a manner that gives scope to the alarming size of the problem and its global dimensions. The investigation reveals that the threatening letter's signatories, the four just men, have been actively "correcting the law" in "almost every country under the sun" (11), interfering with politics by threatening and killing politicians whenever they felt that things went wrong. Until the *Megaphone*'s involvement, "no one crime has been connected with the other" (11). The tabloid meticulously lists the sites, dates and criminal acts of the four perpetrators in consecutive order, and the chapter closes with a glance at the disclosure's effects in equally iterative (and cumulative) form:

> The Editor-in-Chief, seated in his office, read it over again [...]. The reporter – whose name was Smith – read it over [...]. The Foreign Secretary read it in bed [...]. The chief of the French police read it – translated and telegraphed – in *Le Temps*.
>
> *(13)*

Until the sequence is broken up: "In Madrid, at the Café de la Paix, in the Place of the Sun, Manfred, cynical, smiling, and sarcastic, read extracts to the three men [...]" (13). The four men, it turns out, are both the subject matter and the addressees of this news item, and they also seem to be the real driving forces behind its circulation. The smoothly running process of news production and dissemination may not be as neutral and disinterested as the editor believes; it seems to be orchestrated and monitored by sinister forces that pursue their own agendas.

The fact that the four just men commit crimes in order to right the wrongs of world politics is presented as by and large ethically unproblematic in this first volume of the series (later, the four lose their vigilante features and turn into more conventional investigative figures acting on their own account). But at the same time, the four are too unspecific and shadowy to lend themselves to sympathetic identification. They have this in common with the entire cast of the novel (and many of Wallace's characters in general): The characters are functions rather than individuals. The police, thus, are just as shadowy as the criminals – but far less efficient. At one point, the editor, observing the futile efforts by the police to get the better of the four men, remarks critically that he has "read almost everything that has been written by Gaboriau and Conan Doyle, and [believes] in taking notice of little things" (39). The editor misses out on much himself, but at least he is aware of what needs to be done. The "little things" – the hints and clues and tracks – are all over the place, but the crime still happens as announced and is resolved only in retrospect by the police. But then, the police might not be the most important investigative authority in this book: toward the end of the action we learn about "a great number of letters [sent to the police] from all kinds of people containing theories" about what happened, and that the police are "eager to receive suggestions [...] and will welcome any view however bizarre" (97). This is the very logic of participation – of getting the readers involved – that lies at the heart not only of the narrative, but also the book's marketing, Edgar Wallace's entire career and, perhaps, of serial crime fiction more generally.

Obviously, after the heyday of Golden Age detective fiction, the "clue-puzzle" pattern was complemented by other methods of storytelling, in which the readers were not enlisted as detectives (see Chapter 20 in this volume). But still, serial storytelling, and crime story-telling in particular, recast reading as a challenge that needs to be tackled step by step (and which, if mastered, will be rewarded – with a satisfactory resolution, a sense of closure, perhaps even a literal prize, as in Wallace's case – only to fuel the desire for more of the same). The narratives aim to enlist their readers and to keep them engaged, turning them into what could more appropriately be called "fans" (Chabon 2008: 56–57) via the different levels of the crime story's seriality: In the cliffhangers, recap paragraphs and story arcs that organise the serial publication of a text; in the alternation of recognition and surprise fostered by the book series; and in the overarching patterns of affirmation and variation organising the crime genre at large.

Seriality unbound

In the course of the twentieth century, serial crime fiction branched out into a panoply of different forms and formats. There is no subgenre of crime fiction that remained unaffected by seriality (Anderson et al. 2015a: 1), and serial modes of crime storytelling, which had never been limited to print media, made increasingly more use of the broad spectrum of narrative media emerging over the course of the century. In addition, popular serial storytelling spread across the globe, and Edgar Wallace availed himself exemplarily of this global trajectory to expand the reach of his writing and to further his career. Wallace's extraordinary success is tightly linked to the emergence of a global market of popular fiction and the "high translatability" (Jeannerod 2015: n.p.) of his writing, both in a linguistic and a medial sense. The writer died in 1932 in Hollywood, where he had been hired as a scriptwriter.

For most of the twentieth century, serial storytelling in general and crime fiction particularly retained the reputation of being cheap and fast, and increasingly, literary and cinematic formats intersected. This coincided with a cultural and scholarly disdain that abated only in the second half of the century, when postmodern artists and critics came to appreciate the formally compelling qualities of popular narration, and Cultural Studies scholars embraced the popular as an arena of resistant and subversive self-fashioning. In the course of this logic, serial crime narration became one of the most apt expressions of a twenty-first-century sensibility. Thus, the phenomenally successful TV crime drama *The Wire* (HBO, 2002–2008) was celebrated for its "novelistic" quality, calling to mind the masterpieces of nineteenth-century writing, while critics simultaneously emphasised the series' unsentimental engagement with real-life concerns, linking its putative accuracy and authenticity to showrunner David Simon's former employment as a police reporter at the *Baltimore Sun* (Kelleter 2014: 20–21). This both ennobles crime narration as quality storytelling *and* introduces an "ethnographic imaginary" (Williams 2014: 11–36) that suggests an unbiased and scientific take on social realities and experiences. Both claims advanced the series' transmedial impact and contributed to the reinvigoration of the "true crime" genre at large.

As in earlier serial crime fiction, the seriality effect of the new "true" crime genre rests heavily on techniques of audience engagement. Viewers, listeners and readers are invited to be involved in the process of investigation; they collect evidence, weigh testimony, compare perspectives and correlate disjointed bits and pieces of information and misrepresentation. An exemplary case in point for this operative mode is the audio podcast *Serial* (Chicago Public Radio *WBEZ*, 2014–), whose weekly instalments draw on the toolboxes of investigative journalism and crime narration to tackle actual court cases and to invite audiences to reflect on questions of veracity and deception. As Erika Haugtvedt has shown with regard to the podcast's first season, it signals to the sensational storytelling traditions of the Victorian era, when the concepts of "news" and "novelty" were intricately conjoined to generate entertainment with the thrill of actuality.

But the most pertinent feature of the "true" crime narration of our days, which reaches out from its carrier media to the vast landscape of social media channels and online discussion fora, may well be its unresolved and open-ended character. Thus, the overarching title of the audio podcast – *Serial* – could serve as the title of all sorts of contemporary true-crime narratives, in print and other media. Their narratives take over the storytelling techniques of the detective novel and the police procedural and, like their predecessors, they use seriality to bind their audiences in loops of tension and release. But unlike classical crime fiction series, the true-crime series more often than not fails to offer a resolution at the end. Reviewing the storylines of the most successful audio, televisual and print true-crime narratives of 2018, Jen Chaney concludes that "even after investing eight or 13 or more hours in trying to find out" what happened, all the series refuse to provide a clear-cut answer. For Cheney, this is the end result of televisual training in the wake of the complex TV series. I would argue, however, that the crime series was always as much about the joy of conjecturing and the fascination of pursuit than about the confirmation and the catch. Seen in this way, the current true-crime craze may very well be just another boost of serial intensification (or outbidding) – another episode of the serial narration of crime.

Bibliography

Adams, F.R. (1915) "The last adventure of Craig Kennedy", *The Smart Set*, 14(1): 395–401.

Anderson, B. (1991) *Imagined Communities: Reflections on the origin and spread of nationalism*, London: Verso.

———. (1998) *The Spectre of Comparisons: Nationalism, Southeast Asia and the world*, London: Verso.

Anderson, J., Miranda, C. and Pezzotti, B. (eds) (2015a) "Introduction", in Anderson et al., 1–10.

———. (2015b) *Serial Crime Fiction: Dying for more*, New York: Palgrave.

Bold, C. (ed.) (2012) *The Oxford History of Popular Print Culture*, volume six of *US Popular Print Culture, 1860–1920*, New York: Oxford University Press.

Chabon, M. (2008) "Fan fictions: on Sherlock Holmes", *Maps and Legends*, San Francisco: McSweeney's, 35–57.

Chaney, J. (2018) "How the TV landscape teed us up perfectly for true crime", *Vulture*, 2 August, www.vulture.com/2018/08/why-we-watch-true-crime-tv.html (accessed 11 December 2018).

Davies, D.S. (2012) "Introduction", in E. Wallace, *The Complete Four Just Men*, i–xvii.

Eco, U. (1979) *The Role of the Reader: Explorations in the semiotics of texts*, Bloomington: Indiana University Press.

———. (1985) "Innovation and repetition: between modern and postmodern aesthetics", *Daedalus*, 114(4): 161–84.

Flanders, J. (2014) *The Invention of Murder: How the Victorians revelled in death and detection and created modern crime*, London: St. Martin's.

Glover, D. (2004) "'Speed, violence, women, America': popular fictions", in L. Marcus and P. Nicholls (eds), *The Cambridge History of Twentieth-Century Literature*, vol. 1, Cambridge: Cambridge University Press, 304–17.

Gulddal, J. and Rolls, A. (2016) "Crime fiction: the creative/critical nexus", *Text: Journal of Writing and Writing Courses*, 37, www.textjournal.com.au/speciss/issue37/content.htm (accessed 31 October 2019).

Haugtvedt, E. (2017) "The ethics of serialized true crime: fictionality in *Serial* season one", in E. McCracken (ed.), *The* Serial *Podcast and Storytelling in the Digital Age*, New York: Routledge, 7–23.

Horkheimer, M. and Adorno, T.W. (2002) *Dialectic of Enlightenment: Philosophical fragments*, Stanford: Stanford University Press.

Jeannerod, D. (2015) "Edgar Wallace and the global thriller", *International Crime Fiction Research Group*, 15 April, https://internationalcrimefiction.org/2015/04/15/edgar-wallace-and-the-international-field-of-crime-fiction/ (accessed 11 December 2018).

Kelleter, F. (2014) *Serial Agencies:* The Wire *and its readers*, Winchester: Zero Books.

Kracauer, S. (1979) [1925] *Der Detektiv-Roman: Ein philosophisches Traktat*, Frankfurt/Main: Suhrkamp.

Mayer, R. (2014) *Serial Fu Manchu: The Chinese supervillain and the spread of yellow peril ideology*, Philadelphia: Temple University Press.

Pagello, F. (2015) "The myth of the gentleman burglar: models of serialization and temporality in early twentieth-century crime fiction", in Anderson et al., 21–30.

Wallace, E. (2012) *The Four Just Men. The complete four just men*, Ware, Hert.: Wordsworth.

Williams, L. (2014) *On the Wire*, Durham: Duke University Press.

4

CRIME FICTION IN THE MARKETPLACE

Emmett Stinson

This chapter examines the international market for crime fiction within the context of the larger international book trade. It briefly surveys the success of crime fiction in the largest national markets and considers key drivers of crime fiction sales over the last decade. It then examines the way that texts move within and across national markets through a case study of Jane Harper's *The Dry* (2016) – a work that rose to prominence by winning an award for an unpublished manuscript in a secondary English-language market (Australia) and subsequently became an international bestselling work that is being adapted into a major motion picture.

The international book trade

Crime fiction is – in every sense – a popular genre in high demand across international markets. Any analysis of the international market for crime fiction requires an understanding of the broader worldwide market for books. A note of caution also needs to be sounded from the outset: Differences in population, urbanisation and literacy rates can dramatically affect national markets. Access to technology can also produce uneven development: Japan had a small ebook market as early as in the late 1990s, while Indonesia, in 2019, has almost no ebook market at all. International competition from other countries with a shared language can also be a major factor. In smaller English-speaking markets, such as Australia and New Zealand, local titles compete with titles from other anglophone countries like the United States and United Kingdom, whereas Italy, on the other hand, primarily experiences such competition from translated titles.

Different national markets also experience varying demand for books across the broader categories of non-fiction, fiction and children's books; for example, Nielsen BookScan data from 2015 shows that over 45% of the Australian market by volume was children's books, and non-fiction accounted for less than 35% of sales by volume; in China, however, non-fiction sales were nearly 60% of the market by volume, and children's fiction accounted for less than 35% ("Nielsen Book Research" 2015: 8). In this sense, there really is no such thing as an exemplary or normative national market for books, and it would take a monograph to account for local variations in the book trade.

While it is difficult to make generalisations across book markets, most of the value in the international book trade is concentrated in a handful of countries. In 2015, the top six national book markets accounted for 70% of all worldwide book revenue: These six major national markets are the United States (33%), China (17%), Germany (8%), Japan (5%), the United Kingdom (4%) and France (3%) (Wischenbart 2017: 5). The market in the United States alone is larger than all of the markets outside of the big six countries. These large markets have also experienced significant economic headwinds over the last decade; between 2011 and 2018 none of these markets except for China has experienced annual growth greater than inflation (Wischenbart 2018: 4). In Germany alone, for example, the market lost an estimated six million book buyers between 2012 and 2016, or roughly one out of every six readers (Wischenbart 2018: 6). A variety of factors have contributed to this lack of growth, including bookstore closures, discount pricing practices, changes in readership demographics and increased competition from other media, such as online video streaming and gaming.

Translated fiction remains very significant for many major markets. In 2016, for example, eleven of the top twenty-five works of bestselling fiction in Germany were translated, and in France, three of the six top-selling works were translated (Wischenbart 2017: 6). In December 2018, ten of the top twenty-five bestselling works of fiction in China were translated works, including works by Khaled Hosseini, Higashino Keigo, Gabriel García Márquez, Claire McFall and Gabrielle Zevin – a very international list of writers (Anderson 2019). Anglophone markets in general, and the United States in particular, are comparatively inhospitable to translation; while translations comprise 40% of the German trade fiction market, they are usually thought to comprise 3% or less of the US market (Suppressa 2015). The Japanese market is similarly dominated by local works.

Finally, it is worth noting that the global book trade is primarily driven by authors rather than imprints (Squires 2007: 87). As John B. Thompson has noted, the "track record of the author" in selling books is the "first thing" that publishers look at when they consider acquiring a title or the rights to a title (2010: 197). This has become more important with the rise of Nielsen BookScan, which counts point-of-sale data at physical and online book retailers (198). For readers, authors function as "brands" that signal quality in a crowded international market.

The international market for crime fiction

Crime fiction is a subset of the global fiction market, which is itself a subset of the broader global book trade. But despite being a subset of a subset, the international market for crime fiction is significant. Data shows that crime fiction is among the bestselling genres of fiction in major international book markets across languages. In the UK, crime fiction was the third best-selling genre of adult book sales by volume in 2013 (14%) and 2012 (13%) behind only general fiction (18% in 2013 and 16% in 2012) and thrillers (22% in 2013 and 19% in 2012), a genre closely related to crime fiction. Crime ranked well ahead of other commercial genres, such as fantasy (10% in 2013 and 8% in 2012) and romance (8% in 2013 and 7% in 2012), although erotic fiction did outsell it in 2012 (16%), likely due to the breakout success of E.L. James's *Fifty Shades of Grey* (2011), before returning to a much lower volume in 2013 (5%) ("Genre Distribution of Adult Fiction Book Sales Volume in the United Kingdom (UK) in 2012 and 2013" 2014).

Crime fiction holds a similar place in the US market. Crime/mystery fiction was listed as the fourth most popular genre (with 14,884,000 unit sales in 2013 and 14,304,000 in 2014), behind suspense/thrillers (22,161,000 in 2013 and 20,111,000 in 2014), romance (34,585,000 in 2013 and 30,885,000 in 2014), and general fiction (36,314,000 in 2013 and 33,524,000 in 2014) (Milliot 2015). The difference between the US and UK markets is thus the comparative popularity of romance in the United States. Crime sales in the US have fallen slightly across all formats over the last several years (11,225,000 in 2016 and 12,099,000 in 2017), but thrillers (21,901,000 in 2016 and 21,839,000 in 2017) and romance (24,989,000 in 2016 and 21,492,000 in 2017) have recorded similar declines (Milliot 2018). These figures include both print and digital sales.

Continental Europe also has a strong market for crime fiction; in January 2018, the "Crime, Thriller, and Mystery Genre" comprised nearly 10% of all Amazon sales in Italy and Germany and 20% of sales in Spain (Wischenbart 2018: 7). Crime novels comprised 30% of all Amazon Kindle ebook sales in France in 2018 (Wischenbart 2018: 7). The two bestselling paperbacks in Germany in 2018 (Rita Faulk's *Kaiserschmarrndrama* and Jean-Luc Bannalec's *Bretonische Geheimnisse*) were both crime fiction titles. Perhaps the highest-selling crime fiction series in the world – the *Millennium* series, which had already sold 60 million copies worldwide by 2016 (Nilsson 2016: 2) – was produced by Swedish author Stieg Larsson, and there continues to be strong international demand for so-called "Nordic noir"; for example, Swedish author Lina Bengtsdotter's debut crime novel, *Annabelle,* was published on 27 June 2017, and by 5 July 2017, translation rights to the book had already been sold to ten different countries (Anderson 2017).

Crime fiction has a perhaps more tenuous position in the Chinese market, which may stem from the fact that, despite the existence of local forms of detective fiction, crime fiction was essentially banned in China between 1949 and 1976 (Kinkley 2000: 2). As a result, there is a comparative paucity of data on crime fiction within the Chinese market. While there are significant local writers of crime who have been successfully translated around the world, Chinese bestseller lists do not prominently feature local crime titles. However, the top twenty-five works of fiction in December 2018 did include four translated novels by the Japanese mystery and detective fiction author Keigo Higashino (Anderson 2019). Moreover, Liu Cixin's internationally bestselling science-fiction trilogy, *Three-Body Problem*, which held the second, third and fourth spots on the December 2018 bestseller list, features a detective named Shi Qiang and employs crime fiction tropes.

As the above examples indicate, crime fiction is one of the most popular genres in the international market, even in the face of a largely stagnant or declining global book trade. If anything, crime fiction's relative importance has increased over the last decade as the result of a transmedia publishing environment that includes print books, audiobooks, ebooks and a variety of other digital platforms. This media environment is very important for crime fiction, since, as Rüdiger Wischenbart notes, "all general fiction bestsellers, but also crime fiction, romance, fantasy and science fiction are the kinds of books that consumers prefer to download to read on a screen or listen to as audio files" (Wischenbart 2017: 9). Thus, new forms of bookish media, like ebooks and audiobooks, are a significant driver of crime fiction sales in markets that have wide access to this technology. While crime fiction constituted 10% of all paperback sales and 4.7% of hardback sales in the UK in 2015, it comprised 28.4% of ebook sales and 17.7% of audiobook sales, making it the dominant genre in both formats ("Nielsen Book Research" 2016: 40). Crime is thus a genre that thrives in multimedia environments and new reading platforms.

Although the available data is exemplary rather than comprehensive, it helps to establish the general contours of both the international market and major national markets. It does not clarify how the marketplace functions, or how individual works enter the world marketplace and are transmitted across national and linguistic borders. As Beth Driscoll, Lisa Fletcher, Kim Williams and David Carter have argued, the field of genre publishing can be conceived of as a "publishing ecosystem" composed of the networks of roles, institutions and technologies that form the conditions of possibility for the publication of a book (Driscoll et al. 2018: 203). To extend this metaphor, the international crime market presents a series of such ecosystems whose relationships are not linear: A bestselling author in one country is not necessarily guaranteed high sales in another. Instead, these ecosystems are linked – both internally and between each other – through a series of complex mediations among different agents and institutions that Robert Darnton described as the "book communications circuit" (Darnton 1982). This includes not only authors, publishers and readers, but also mediators throughout the entirety of the publishing process, such as literary agents, editors, marketers, booksellers, literary prizes, creative writing programs, online reviewing sites, social media and so forth. This process of transmission can be illustrated through a case study of Jane Harper's *The Dry* (2016), which was first published in Australia and combines the landscape of the remote countryside in the state of Victoria with recognisable tropes from the noir crime novel.

The crime fiction market in action: Jane Harper's *The Dry*

The writing of *The Dry* was deeply embedded in key processes of mediation from the outset. The work originated as part of a twelve-week online novel-writing course during which Harper generated a 40,000-word draft manuscript. This creative writing course was not university-based but offered by the UK literary agent Curtis Brown Creative. Indeed, Curtis Brown heavily features its brand as a literary agency in the marketing materials for these courses: "While we can't guarantee publication or representation, we lavish our expertise on our students. The agents of Curtis Brown and C&W are hungry for new authors and actively looking for clients among our students" (Curtis Brown Creative 2019). Here, its close relationship to the industry is emphasised, as is the possibility that students could become clients; this also implicitly signals a difference from university-based courses, which might emphasise other matters (such as aesthetic concerns). Harper's book was thus conceived and written in a specific milieu within the broader publishing ecosystem.

The second key moment of mediation for *The Dry* occurred in 2015, when it won the Victorian Premier's Unpublished Manuscript Award. This is a prestigious prepublication literary prize with a record of identifying works that have subsequently had national and international success; past winners include Miles Allinson's *Fever of Animals* (which won in 2014 and was published by Allen and Unwin in 2015), Maxine Beneba Clarke's *Foreign Soil* (which won in 2013 and was published by Hachette in 2014) and Graeme Simsion's *The Rosie Project* (which won the award in 2012 before being published by Text in Australia in 2013 and subsequently republished in forty other countries). Winning a prepublication prize effectively consecrates an author's work in advance and greatly increases the likelihood that a publisher will take it on.

As John Thompson notes, debut works like *The Dry* actually have an unexpected advantage in the marketplace:

> Ironically, in a world preoccupied by numbers, the author with no track is in some ways in a strong position, considerably stronger than the author who has published one or two books with modest success and muted acclaim, simply because there are no hard data to constrain the imagination, no disappointing sales figures to dampen hopes and temper expectations. The absence of sales figures sets the imagination free. The first-time author is the true tabula rasa of trade publishing.
>
> *(200)*

Unpublished manuscript awards, then, are doubly valuable because they combine the untapped potential of the first-time author with a public form of consecration. Although Harper had no authorial track record, the benefit of winning this award placed her in a uniquely advantageous position in the industry. This is what Thompson describes as an authorial "platform", which is

Crime fiction in the marketplace

to say the "position from which an author speaks, a combination of their credentials, visibility and promotability, especially through the media" (2010: 203). But Harper also had authorial advantages already beyond this, since she had worked as a reporter at the *Geelong Advertiser* and later at the *Herald Sun*. Having media connections is significant for publishers because the "media are the milieu in which an actual or potential author creates a platform", enabling them "to reach an audience" (Thompson 2010: 203). Harper's frequent appearances on television and in print interviews were certainly aided by the fact that she was already a known figure within the Australian media.

Harper was represented by Curtis Brown in Australia and the influential agent Clare Forster, but also had UK agents. There was a seven-way bidding war over *The Dry*, which included every major publisher in Australia; Harper signed a three-book deal with the Australian division of the multinational publisher Pan Macmillan. This deal was followed by the quick sale of international rights. By the end of 2015 – before the book had even been published – *The Dry* had already been sold to nineteen foreign territories, including translation into French, German, Hebrew, Hungarian, Italian, Japanese, Korean, Norwegian, Polish, Romanian, Russian, Serbian, Slovene, Spanish, Swedish and Turkish ("*The Dry* Goes Global" 2015). This development represents a transfer from the local publishing ecosystem out into others across the globe. While these transmissions are not always direct, there are key mediators who specialise precisely in sales across markets. In the case of *The Dry,* this first wave of international transmission was facilitated by Eva Papastratis in Curtis Brown's translation rights department ("*The Dry* Goes Global"). Having dedicated teams for international rights sales is a key advantage that literary agents can offer clients.

While such deals are often made based on existing connections between agents and various international publishing houses, many international rights deals are also brokered at international book fairs, the most significant of which is the Frankfurt Book Fair. The Frankfurt Book Fair can trace its history back to 1454, but the modern version of the fair is a complex international market for an industrialised book industry: "It is at once a sort of workshop for the creation and realization of book projects, a pool of rights available worldwide, an exchange, an orientation centre in market comparisons, and a weathervane for recognising new trends" (Weidhass 2007: 258). Frankfurt remains the key meeting point for the various worldwide publishing ecosystems. As Simone Murray notes, the fair has a dedicated Literary Agents and Scouts Centre, which the 2008 organisers described as "the most important working centre at the Frankfurt Book Fair" (Murray 2012: 57). *The Dry* was the subject of at least twelve publishing deals in Frankfurt alone.

While most books would be lucky to have the success that *The Dry* had experienced up to this point, it experienced one more particularly significant form of mediation. Just prior to the Frankfurt Book Fair, the film rights to *The Dry* were optioned by Hello Sunshine, the media company founded by US actor Reese Witherspoon. Hello Sunshine describes itself as "a media brand anchored in storytelling, creating and discovering content that celebrates women and puts them at the center of the story" (Hello Sunshine 2019). While the company works across media, it has a particularly close relationship with the publishing industry as a result of Reese's Book Club – a monthly book club series that engages with readers through social media and television appearances. Book clubs associated with major media personalities have been deeply influential for decades in the publishing industry; as Beth Driscoll notes, twenty-first-century book clubs are both overwhelmingly female in their orientation and are "integrated with the commerce of book publishing [as] vehicles for disseminating books" across personal networks and recommendations rather than through formal channels of bookselling (Driscoll 2014: 56).

Book clubs generate added sales by accessing these networks. *The Dry* was included as a recommended title by Witherspoon, who discussed the book on Instagram as "an unpredictable page-turner about a man from a small Australian town who goes home to help investigate a local crime. You won't want to put it down [...]" (Witherspoon 2017). While this may seem like standard book marketing (and it is), it is hard to overemphasise the influence such recommendations can have on sales. As Thompson notes, book club selection matters because it is "a mark of distinction that singles out a small handful of books and classifies them as members of an exclusive club" and this distinction can be "recycled continuously in the marketplace" as a form of branding (275).

Beyond simply recommending a book, however, Hello Sunshine has also begun adapting it into a feature-length film. Adaptation affects book sales in a similar manner to book club selection: "A book that becomes a movie has been selected by someone as worthy of being made into a movie. Even if the movie has been trashed and didn't do well, sales of the book go through the roof" (Thompson 2010: 278). The Frankfurt Book Fair even has a Film and Media Forum "designed specifically for publishers, agents and producers to trade screen and other non-book rights", which emphasises the increasing importance of adaptation for the international market for books (Murray 2012: 57). Film adaptation – or even the announcement of a future film adaptation – encourages further rights sales. But adaptation also can have a huge effect in the originating market: In Harper's case, the adaptation of her book by Witherspoon and Hello Sunshine led to a series of appearances on Australian television, which further promoted her book to local audiences. International success can reinforce local success – though this is not always a guarantee.

It is also worth considering the role that nationality has in terms of selling a book both generally and in the specific instance of *The Dry*. Nationality can manifest in the international market in two ways: Firstly, through the nationality of an author and, secondly, through the depiction of a nation within a given work of fiction. Harper was born in Australia but raised in the UK – a potential advantage that enables her to claim native status in two anglophone markets. But the setting of her book, which occurs in drought-stricken regional Victoria, is unambiguously Australian. Regional Australian settings are in high demand within the local book trade, manifesting most famously in the genre known as "RuRo", or rural romance. The Australianness of *The Dry* might seem to be a potentially negative factor for international sales, however. Although romances about the Australian outback have historically sold into the UK market, there has been a limited international market for such tales. Here, however, Reese Witherspoon's Hello Sunshine has played a large role in making Australian works internationally prominent. This is partially due to the fact that Witherspoon's long-time production partner, Bruna Papandrea, was born in Adelaide, South Australia. Witherspoon's high-profile TV adaptation of the novel *Big Little Lies*, which was based on the book of the same name by Australian novelist Liane Moriarty, has heightened the visibility of Australian works in the international marketplace. As John Thompson notes, publishers often make decisions about the potential future success of books by looking at "comps" or comparable books; while everyone involved "knows that there is an element of speciousness in the citing of comparable books", mediators in the industry play "the game nonetheless" because citing comparable books serves to "put a positive gloss on a new book" and gets other buyers to think of it in those terms (201–2). It is clear that nationality or regionality can be a basis for comparability, and the success of "Nordic noir" testifies to such recent trends. While Australian fiction is not as big a phenomenon as Nordic noir, the Australianness of *The Dry* could nonetheless be leveraged as a selling point in the wake of successes like *Big Little Lies* – and the two works, although in different genres, do engage with similar themes, particularly in relation to the effect of male violence on the lives of women.

Finally, *The Dry*'s journey through the international ecosystems of publishing has been deeply influenced by its status as a work of crime fiction that self-consciously evokes noir tropes. As Claire Squires has argued, genre "is a crucial component in the marketplace" because it serves as "one of the primary means by which authors and readers communicate" through shared conceptions of the tropes and elements that comprise a genre (70). As Squires suggests, a given genre's features are not static, but in fact regulated "by the perception of prevalent structures at a given historical moment"; while perceived structures do have an enormous effect on the markets for given books, these expectations can ultimately be altered by the writer, who can "take part in this process of development and change, by styling his or her writing to fit what they perceive to be popular genres in their era (or, in fact, to write in opposition to fashion)" (70).

The Dry enacts this in a scene where the protagonist, Detective Aaron Faulk, opens a book belonging to a murder victim. The book, of course, is "a battered paperback crime novel":

> A woman, an unknown figure lurking in the shadows, a body count. Standard stuff. Not quite to his taste, but he wouldn't be in the job he was in if he didn't enjoy a good mystery. He lay back against the pillow and started to read.
>
> *(186)*

Faulk finds the book formulaic, describing it as "an obvious storyline, nothing special" (186), but this perception is altered when a slip of paper falls out of the book that contains both the name of a potential suspect and Faulk's phone number. Here, *The Dry* knowingly acknowledges its own links to the key tropes of crime fiction, and the joke only works because its readers presumably *share* this knowledge of the genre. But the novel pushes this identification further by making both its protagonist and victim crime fiction readers who are familiar with these tropes. This, of course, is one of the persistently interesting and unusual features of commercial works of crime fiction: They are commodities that often reflexively comment upon their commodity status.

Conclusion

There is a robust, international market for crime fiction, which, by any measure, is one of the most successful and highest-selling genres of fiction across the globe. Works of crime fiction feature prominently in the bestseller lists of the six largest national markets for books (the United States, China, Germany, Japan, the United Kingdom and France), which comprise 70% of the value of the international book trade. In point of fact, crime fiction's footprint is probably larger than much of the data suggests because literary works and works in other genres often conspicuously borrow tropes from crime fiction, and thus arguably form part of the genre. Translations of crime fiction frequently sell well across virtually all major markets, including the anglophone markets that are traditionally seen as inhospitable to translations. In this sense, crime fiction is not only one of the bestselling genres internationally but also arguably the most globalised.

Crime fiction has remained a pre-eminent international genre, despite a sluggish and often declining book trade over the last decade in most of the largest national markets. Although there is some data to suggest that aggregated crime fiction sales have declined in many major markets, these declines tend to be in line with broader falls. Arguably, the importance of crime fiction is actually increasing. This is the case because crime fiction is particularly suited to a transmedia environment, and much of the growth within the book industry is being driven by new media forms such as ebooks and audiobooks, where crime fiction has a larger market share than in the print market. As the book industry increasingly relies on digital formats, crime fiction is likely to become an even more significant driver of sales.

Despite the appearance of new electronic formats and digital methods of publication, however, the market for crime fiction continues to rely on established networks of mediators across the industry. The success of a novel can be heavily affected by influential institutions and agents in the field. In the case of Jane Harper's *The Dry*, winning a prestigious prepublication literary award as well as representation by a highly regarded literary agent gave her a strong authorial platform that formed the basis for international rights sales. Many of these sales occurred at the Frankfurt Book Fair, which remains the most important event for crime fiction international rights sales, including national/territorial copyright licensing, translation rights and film or television adaptation rights. The success of crime fiction titles can also be amplified by key mediating institutions outside of the publishing supply chain. Two particularly important examples of this are book clubs and film adaptations, which in the case of *The Dry*, encouraged sales both internationally and in the originating country.

The international marketplace for crime fiction is thus a hybrid market that combines the traditional value chain of an older publishing industry with new media. Although traditional gatekeepers – such as publishers and literary agents – are still very important in imbuing works with symbolic capital that later can be converted into economical capital in the marketplace, new mediators have taken on an increasingly important role. In the case of *The Dry*, a newer prepublication prize arguably had the largest early effect on the novel's success. Similarly, the later sale of its rights for adaptation and appearance as a selection in an online book club were also of huge significance. In this sense, the market for crime fiction is determined both by traditional modes of taste-making and reception and promotion across new media.

Bibliography

Anderson, P. (2017) "Rights update: Swedish crime writer's debut book sells to 10 territories", *Publishing Perspectives*, 5 July, https://publishingperspectives.com/2017/07/ights-update-bonnier-lina-bengtsdotter-debut-rights-deals/ (accessed 12 March 2019).

————. (2018) "China's book market: 2018 in review and December's bestsellers", *Publishing Perspectives*, 21 January, https://publishingperspectives.com/2019/01/chinas-book-market-2018-in-review-and-decembers-bestsellers/ (accessed 12 March 2019).

Curtis Brown Creative. (2019) "Three-month novel-writing course with Suzannah Dunn", www.curtisbrowncreative.co.uk/course/three-month-online-novel-writing-course-with-suzannah-dunn/ (accessed 12 March 2019).

Darnton, R. (1982) "What is the history of books?", *Daedalus*, 111(3): 65–83.

Driscoll, B. (2014) *The New Literary Middlebrow: Tastemakers and reading in the twenty-first century*, London: Palgrave Macmillan.

Driscoll, B., Fletcher, L., Wilkins, K. and Carter, D. (2018) "The publishing ecosystems of contemporary Australian genre fiction", *Creative Industries Journal*, 11(2): 203–21.

"Genre distribution of adult fiction book sales volume in the United Kingdom (UK) in 2012 and 2013". (2014) www.statista.com/statistics/329143/adult-fiction-sales-volume-by-genre-uk/ (accessed 9 March 2019).

Harper, J. (2015) *The Dry*, Sydney: Pan Macmillan.

Hello Sunshine, "Our story" (n.d.) https://hello-sunshine.com/our-story (accessed 15 March 2019).

Kinkley, J. (2000) *Chinese Justice: Fiction, law, and literature in modern China*, Stanford: Stanford University Press.

Milliot, J. (2015) "The hottest (and coldest) book categories of 2014", *Publishers Weekly*, www.publishersweekly.com/pw/by-topic/industry-news/bookselling/article/65387-the-hot-and-cold-categories-of-2014.html (accessed 12 March 2019).

————. (2018) "Nonfiction categories continued to grow in 2017", *Publishers Weekly*, 19 January, www.publishersweekly.com/pw/by-topic/industry-news/bookselling/article/75877-nonfiction-categories-continued-to-grow-in-2017.html.

Murray, S. (2012) *The Adaptation Industry: The cultural economy of contemporary literary adaptation*, London: Routledge.

"Nielsen book research: 2015 in review" (2016) https://quantum.londonbookfair.co.uk/RXUK/RXUK_PDMC/documents/9928_Nielsen_Book_Research_In_Review_2015_The_London_Book_Fair_Quantum_Conference_2016_DIGITAL_FINAL.pdf (accessed 10 March 2019).

Nilsson, L. (2016) "Uncovering a cover: marketing Swedish crime fiction in a transnational context", *Journal of Transnational American Studies*, 7(1): 1–16.

Squires, C. (2007) *Marketing Literature: The making of contemporary writing in Britain*, London: Palgrave Macmillan.

Suppressa, L. (2015) "Four key trends impacting foreign rights agents", *Publishing Perspectives*, 6 August, https://publishingperspectives.com/2015/08/4-key-trends-impacting-foreign-rights-agents/ (accessed 19 March 2019).

"*The Dry* Goes Global". (2015) http://janeharper.com.au/News-Engine/ID/4/The-Dry-goes-global (accessed 19 March 2019).

Thompson, J.B. (2010) *Merchants of Culture: The publishing business in the twenty-first century*, Cambridge: Polity.

Weidhaas, P. (2007) *A History of the Frankfurt Book Fair*, trans. C.M. Gossage and W.A. Wright, Toronto: Dundurn Press.

Wischenbart, R. (2017) "Business of books 2017: it's all about the consumers", White Paper for the Frankfurt Book Fair, www.buchmesse.de/files/media/pdf/whitepaper-the-business-of-books-frankfurter-buchmesse.pdf (accessed 1 March 2019).

———. (2018) "Business of books 2018: new tunes for an old trade", White Paper for the Frankfurt Book Fair, www.buchmesse.de/files/media/pdf/FBM_WhitePaper_The_Business_of_Books_2018.pdf (accessed 1 March 2019).

Witherspoon, R. (2017) Instagram, www.instagram.com/p/BPNvmDlgf8H/?hl=en&taken-by=reesewitherspoon (accessed 21 March 2019).

5

ADAPTATIONS

Neil McCaw

Crime fiction is surely the most globalised of all popular genres. Since the nineteenth century, an ever-increasing international readership has been seduced by the familiar comfort of classic detective fictions, with – among a number of others – the "Lecoq" novels of Émile Gaboriau and Arthur Conan Doyle's Sherlock Holmes stories quick to establish their appeal across national and linguistic borders, through translations, retellings and pastiche versions. And it was as such no surprise that this burgeoning appetite for tales of crime and detection consequently fuelled a related growth in regionally and ethnically specific full-blown adaptations of these very same narratives, which over time resulted in a complex intermingling of texts that is now a chief characteristic of numerous crime adaptation franchises.

The international bestselling "Wallander" novels of crime author Henning Mankell, for instance, were adapted into a tranche of Swedish films soon after publication, followed by a series of native-language, feature-length television episodes, and then an English-language serial production for the BBC, starring Shakespearean stalwart Kenneth Branagh in the lead role. Each set of adaptations was also translated into a range of other languages, as was also the case with the original novels, establishing a cacophony of differing versions of the "same" stories, coexisting as part of a network of interlinked, transnational, transmedial texts. In their interrelatedness, such specific networks mirror the wider framework of all of the international crime fiction adaptations, as well as illustrating their essentially migratory nature in the ways they crisscross an increasing plurality of forms, including films, books, stage, television, radio, computer games, social media and apps, as well as transcending an ever more diverse array of national and ethnic identities, to the point of becoming a prominent touchstone of what could be seen to be a truly global popular culture.

Crime adaptation criticism

The multifaceted reality of the manifold body of crime fiction adaptations is mirrored by the varying range of critical approaches that typify the academic study of the subject area, reflecting on the one hand, fluid, deconstructive understandings of "adaptation" itself, as well as a nuanced and sophisticated grasp of the changing nature of the genre of crime and detective fiction itself, over time. Consequently, critical attention has been directed towards a proliferation of texts, both those that evidence a much more explicit, even at times self-conscious relationship

Adaptations

between adaptation and informing source text, as well as others that imply a far less explicit and more of a disguised, subtle, intertextual relationship. Taken as a single body of critical studies, this amounts to a wider acknowledgement – even general consensus – that crime adaptations are multifaceted and shifting forms of text that are defined as much by their relations to other works as they are by any inherent features or characteristics unique to them. Each text occupies its own place within a wider "infinite play of dissemination" (Stam 2000: 58), functioning and interacting in any of a multiplicity of ways across the broad "constellation of tropes – translation, reading, dialogization, cannibalization, transmutation, transfiguration, and signifying" (Stam 2000: 62). This amounts to a palimpsestuous, polychromatic dialogism that facilitates an extraordinary diversity of interrelated meanings and interpretations.

The critical studies of crime fiction adaptation that examine more explicit one-to-one connections between specific original and adapted crime fiction texts as part of a comparative analysis include Archer (2014), which interrogates the processes and outcomes of the novelisation of the Danish police procedural television series *The Killing*, exploring how medium-specific facets of one text are reimagined in another as part of transferring the series from Danish primetime television into popular fiction. Creechan (2016) also offers a comparison of text with text, examining the transposition of the ideological implications of J.M. Rymer's Victorian Gothic bestseller *The String of Pearls* within the process of adapting the novel into two popular stage musicals, and in particular considering how the supposed "lowbrow" nature of the nineteenth-century penny dreadful was appropriated in the name of a musical theatre critique of modern capitalism. Louttit (2016), in turn, examines the reworking of the early detective novel *The Mystery of a Hansom Cab* (1888) for Australian mainstream television, considering how the original text – a "popular classic" – was reimagined as a period adaptation in an effort to appeal simultaneously to a modern "literary" audience as well as to those more receptive to mainstream popular cultural texts. In such comparative critical studies, the focus is thus essentially on the challenges and limitations of adapting one text into another, and how adaptors establish their own sense of the "essence" of each original work which they can then reimagine in their own way.

Such espoused relationships between texts and the wider questions of medium-specificity are sidestepped in crime adaptation criticism where, instead, the focus is on what Linda Hutcheon has called "treating adaptations as adaptations" (2006: 6). The intention in such studies is to explore adaptive texts not for the relationships and connections that supposedly define them, but rather for how they function as cultural texts on their own terms, with the discussion moving away from questions related to the nature of the adaptive process, and towards an attempt to better understand what makes "crime adaptation" a distinct genre in its own right. Field (2009), for example, analyses the mid-twentieth-century series of Sherlock Holmes films starring Basil Rathbone and Nigel Bruce, and considers them as a serial articulation of national and nationalist ideology during World War II, part of the wider ongoing campaign of allied wartime propaganda. This contextual-cultural approach is also apparent in Berger (2016), wherein intertextual dialogue between discrete forms of Nordic noir adaptation is examined through the lens of the politics of intercultural communication and the role of popular and social media. Ultimately, Nordic noir is the subject of a so-called "synchronous" reading that seeks to juxtapose multiple texts and contexts in interrelation.

The implicit acknowledgement that the adaptive process takes place within a network of other texts extends the scope of "adaptation" into other forms of textual interrelation, notably intertextuality and translation, facilitating a broader exploration of how different writers reference and draw from both predecessors and contemporaries. It is an intertextual, intra-writerly focus apparent in Guest (2010), which analyses the various ways in which the Tibetan novelist Jamyang

Norbu appropriates Doyle's Sherlock Holmes, using the original Holmes stories to define the essential features of the Great Detective and then reworking and reshaping these for a native audience – simultaneously striving to ensure that, as a Holmes story, it also appeals to a wider international Holmesian readership. Elsewhere, both Raw (2010) and Stuchebrukhov (2012) unpack, in their own specific ways, facets of the intertextual relationships between particular adaptive texts, with the former exploring the nature of the intra-textual connections between a range of 1970s cinematic reworkings of Raymond Chandler's crime narratives, and the latter interpreting two films by Woody Allen, deploying Mikhail Bakhtin's notions of polyphony and diachrony, as meditations on Fyodor Dostoyevsky's conception of crime and punishment.

These comparative, cultural and intertextual strands of crime adaptation criticism fuse in studies of the nature of the adaptive process as a specific instance of a fundamentally transnational cultural dialogue. Seago (2014), for instance, views crime translation as a form of adaptation across national and ethnic borders, part of the wider flow or mediation of crime narratives across value systems and ideologies, and as such an element of wider international transmedial relations. And the nature of this multidirectional journey is considered in more detail in Gregoriou (2017), which analyses the synonymity of ideas of "migration" and evolving, more open-ended conceptualisations of the process of "adaptation", wherein crime narratives are viewed as essentially itinerant texts that become fundamentally changed not just by transformations in form, but also through their crossing of national borders. A similar interest in the intersection between the intertextual and the intercultural informs Jones (2015), which offers insight as to the nature of the Japanese appropriation of Doyle's character of Sherlock Holmes, through graphic art and Manga comic books. The use and re-use of the figure of Holmes is read not just as an expression of the deeper national fascination with the Great Detective, but also as a barometer of a shifting Japanese self-image, in that Holmes comes to be remodelled to embody those characteristics and values that are either most needed, or most valued, by the modernising nation.

Theories of crime adaptation

The critical history of crime fiction adaptation thus demonstrates a lack of what Kamilla Elliott has called "a presiding poetics", evidencing a degree of diversity that creates the impression of an "*especially* divided field" (2013: 23). In truth, however, the lack of a framing theoretical coherence is more a refraction of the manifold, healthy vitality of this area of scholarship than of any particular absence or lack, for the field has been energised by the ever more multiplicitous and complex understanding of adaptation and the adaptive process, with the malleability and inclusiveness of "adaptation" allowing for a far greater number of possibilities as to how texts can be seen to interrelate. As such, an essentially plural, evolving sense of the adaptive process demands critical approaches that more sensitively accommodate the distinct, discrete ways in which crime narratives can be transposed from one form or medium to another, and which indicate an awareness of the differing natures of texts rooted in "imitation […] transmission […] mutation […] repetition […] variation […] replication […] [and] selection" (Hutcheon 2006: 176–77).

The growing prominence of the concept of the "rhizome" in critical discussions of crime fiction adaptation is symptomatic of this ever-wider scope, particularly in light of its pervasive global presence by the time of the twenty-first century. It provides a poignant metaphor for the root-like, organic but non-linear expansion and extension of adaptations, adroitly capturing the inherent and at times undefinable interrelation of adaptive forms as "nodes" within an open, dynamic "rhizomic" network (Schober 2013: 100). Therein it offers a basis for better coming to terms with the ways in which adaptations engage in an ongoing, interchangeable, seemingly unending intercontinental dialogue, an international circulation of crime adaptations facilitated by the technological, cultural and political infrastructure of globalisation. This network of adaptive texts has at its core a synthesis of global and local energies that combine as part of the process Roland Robertson has called "glocalisation" (2012: 191), whereby adaptations emerge out of the struggle between the innate tendency of globalisation to homogenise, or iron out, the distinct features of particular national cultures and identities, imparting "shared" cultural values and texts around which everyone can congregate, and the regional pushback that comes as a reaction against these globalising, homogenising pressures, as local cultures and identities re-assert their own ethnicity and culture. Crime fiction adaptations bear the imprint of such contest and disjuncture.

Viewing these adaptations as part of a global network of texts and influences thus demands a reconsideration of ideas of adaptation and adaptive practice, extending them far beyond simplistic questions "of resemblance or equivalence" (Deleuze 1994: 1). Parallel critical territories such as palimpsestuousness, intertextuality, translation and transmediality become equally focal matters of concern, with crime adaptation consequently viewed as kaleidoscopic, in terms of both its processes and texts, refuting linear connections between "originary" and "derived" works, or between "models" and "copies" (125). Instead, adaptation becomes a coexistence of interlinked, overlapping elements, motivations and objectives, an extension of Roland Barthes's idea of the text as a "multi-dimensional space in which a variety of writings, none of them original, blend and clash" (1977: 146). Crime fiction adaptations are as such works "drawn from many cultures and entering into mutual relations of dialogue" (148), facets of a much more all-encompassing form of what has become known as "transtextuality". Thus, fully grasping their relative significance and meaning is conditional on an ever-deeper understanding of their place within an implied, mutually dependent web of relations between crime texts of all kinds.

Such a fundamental shift away from attenuated comparisons of adaptations and their supposed source texts thus opens up a range of other interwoven lines of critical enquiry. It redirects the critical focus towards: Exploring the relationships between adapted crime texts and other texts (adapted or otherwise); examining crime adaptations across linguistic, ethnic and cultural borders; interrogating global cultural identities as represented in and evidenced by specific crime texts; discussing the production history of specific crime adaptations (including the how, why, when?); analysing the status of adaptive crime texts as cultural texts in and of themselves; mapping the glocalisation of crime adaptations and their synthesis of global and local identities; and, unpacking the variety of ways in which crime adaptations appropriate and redeploy other genres and forms.

The precise nature of the critical approach deployed depends on the nature of the text under consideration, i.e. deciding which are most likely to tease out the particular features and characteristics of the "adaptation" at hand. In the case of the film *Detective Byomkesh Bakshi!* (2015), the approach needs to draw out its inherent characteristics as an adaptive text, notably: its reworking of the Byomkesh Bakshi crime stories (1932–1970) written by the Bengali writer Sharadindu Bandyopadhyay; its standing as a critically well-regarded though commercially unsuccessful Hindi-language film adaptation; its status as a film of Bengali origin produced by a Hindi production company and directed by the well-known Indian director Dibakar Banerjee; its place within the context of the wider interest in adaptation evidenced by the Hindi film industry; and, its relationships with the wider body of film and television adaptations of the Byomkesh Bakshi short stories, which include the Hindi television series *Byomkesh Bakshi* (1993–1997), the Bengali series *Byomkesh* (2014–2015), as well as Bengali-language films from *Chiriyakhana* (1966) to *Byomkesh Gotro* (2018).

With these features in mind, a reading of the film as a crime adaptation might focus on:

(a) A relative comparison of the Hindi film and the originary Bandyopadhyay fictions, considering the extent to which the film reworks specific Bengali stories; this could compare and contrast particular aspects of the different mediums, such as characterisation, setting, dialogue, genre, tone, soundtrack, cinematography, etc.
(b) An analysis of the film in terms of other film/television/cultural adaptations of the Byomkesh Bakshi stories, viewing its relations to these, potentially focusing on aspects including characterisation, setting, dialogue, genre, tone, soundtrack, cinematography, etc.
(c) An exploration of the ways in which Bengali and Hindi ethnic identities and cultures have shaped the adaptation, with reference to any of the many specific characteristics of the film medium.
(d) A reading of the film in terms of Arthur Conan Doyle's Sherlock Holmes stories and the wider international legend of Sherlock Holmes; this could focus on the features of both film and fictions, or else could explore the diverse aspects of the global Holmes phenomenon as a feature of world culture.
(e) An interpretation of the film in light of its production history, including the questions of when(?), how(?), and why(?) it was conceived, developed, produced and disseminated, and its place within the wider engagement with adaptation as a form/genre within Hindi film culture.
(f) A close reading of the film in and of itself – as an adaptive cinematic text in its own right, divorced from questions related to its adaptive relationships or the nature of the adaptation process; instead it would be interpreted in terms of its inherent characteristics, including plotting, characterisation, setting, dialogue, tone, genre, cinematography, soundtrack, etc. Ultimately, it will be read as an example of its type – the extent to which it illuminates our knowledge of adaptation and the adaptive process.
(g) An exploration of the film as an interaction between global and local identities, the glocalisation of the Byomkesh Bakshi franchise and the wider Bengali, postcolonial culture from which it emerged – and how it thus embodies facets of identifiably "Indian" culture and identity via its depiction of the cosmopolitan city of Calcutta during the 1940s in juxtaposition with a more internationalist, globalising perspective.
(h) An analysis of the film not in relation to the Byomkesh Bakshi stories themselves, but rather with reference to other potentially influential aspects of Bengali and broader Indian literary culture such as earlier examples of Bengali detective fiction, such as the writings of Bhuban Chandra Mukhopadhyay (1842–1916), Panchkori Dey (1873–1945) and Dinendra Kumar Roy (1869–1943).

What follows is an analysis of the film adaptation that focuses primarily on (a), (d) and (g) above, exploring the intertextual relations between the film and the Bengali source stories, attempting to understand the film in terms of the wider international Sherlock Holmes phenomenon, and analysing how the intertextuality of the film straddles national, ethnic and linguistic boundaries. It is a layered approach that allows for the fluidity of contemporary understandings of "adaptation", ensuring a multifarious, interrelated interpretation of the filmic text as a form of Indian crime fiction homage, as well as a reworking of the legend of Sherlock Holmes.

Detective Byomkesh Bakshi!

From the outset the film illustrates a number of intertextual connections with the originating Byomkesh Bakshi short stories, reworking elements of several specific tales, most notably in its central plot premise, which is the domestic arrangement of a group of working men who share a common living area or "mess", a feature derived from the very first Byomkesh short story, "The Inquisitor". This particular story is also the origin of the screen portrayal of a disguised, international drug-smuggling ring exploiting the poverty and desperation of the economically disenfranchised population of Calcutta, which Byomkesh eventually uncovers and has a hand in bringing down. However, most of the other aspects of this story have a less explicit connection with the film, especially as its events take place during the earlier 1940s as opposed to the original 1930s setting, so that the primary backdrop becomes the military conflict and international tensions of World War II. There are some broad similarities to other tales, such as the way the film recycles its depiction of a dysfunctional family unit racked with internecine rivalries and materialistic tensions, which bears a distinct likeness to that portrayed in "Where There's A Will", but despite such narrative echoes, most of the detailed specifics in the film script – especially its narrative structure – have only tangential relations to Bandyopadhyay's fictions. Instead it offers a somewhat distilled, almost pastiche-like version of the world of Byomkesh Bakshi culled from a more general sense of the "essence" of the wider canon of stories and a much more melodramatic tone and style than any of the original narratives, with a greater propensity for graphic violence and grievous criminality than any of the individual stories that were initially published in the leading Bengali literary magazine *Basumati*. Byomkesh Bakshi is placed within a world of international wartime intrigue, with the very future of the city of Calcutta seemingly in jeopardy owing to the threat of an imminent Japanese invasion, the detective crossing swords with a greater array of exaggerated, vividly drawn characters that frequent an extremely violent drug-dealing underworld. It is a version of India characterised by political and military tensions that is a long way from that which features in most of the stories on which the film is loosely based.

That said, the portrayal of Byomkesh Bakshi himself as the self-styled "Truth Seeker" does echo Bandyopadhyay, establishing the detective as someone for whom investigations are less about the systematic application of law enforcement procedures and more an outlet for his own innate human desire to seek the truth, related to his almost obsessive need *to know*. As Byomkesh says, "I am truth seeker – my hobby and my passion is to find out the truth" (Bandyopadhyay, 2003: 22). But what is less clear is the extent to which this aspect of the film characterisation of Byomkesh Bakshi can be directly attributed to the originating fictions, or else vicariously to Doyle's portrayal of Sherlock Holmes, which was clearly a significant influence on the original Bengali stories. In numerous stories (notably "The Man with the Twisted Lip" and "Charles Augustus Milverton"), Holmes is shown to be more interested in deciphering the truth than in strictly enforcing the law, privileging his own sense of natural justice over formal legal statutes, and thus in reiterating this aspect of Byomkesh Bakshi, the film could be seen as channelling Doyle as much as it is more self-consciously adapting Bandyopadhyay.

Such a form of underlying Holmesian influence can also be deciphered in the way the stories characterise Byomkesh's trusty companion, Ajit, wherein – as with Holmes's partner Dr Watson – he becomes the chronicler of the adventures, writing them up for magazine publication and serving as amanuensis and helpmate to the truth seeker. Together the two men display a commitment to investigating the truth similar to that of Doyle's famous pairing, even sharing some of their detective methods, such as utilising newspaper advertisements both to share information and manipulate the criminals (in the story "The Man in a Red Coat"), and depending on particular facets of forensic evidence gathering (such as in "Room Number Two"), including showing an awareness of the investigative significance and scientific basis of fingerprinting. And there are even certain Byomkesh adventures that more closely follow Holmesian plotlines, evident in the similarities between the central quest to discover a collection of hidden gems that have been secreted inside a set of hand-forged statues that is the narrative spine of both the Byomkesh Bakshi adventure "The Hidden Heirloom" as well as of the Holmes story "The Adventure of the Six Napoleons".

In portraying Holmesian features such as the symbiotic homosocial bond between Ajit and Byomkesh the film is indebted as much to the intertextual influence of the Sherlock Holmes stories as it is to those originally featuring Bakshi himself. It is an intertextual influence that becomes yet more apparent as the film version of the detective starts taking on other aspects of Doyle's depiction of the character of the Great Detective, especially his dismissive, aloof, rude tactlessness. In particular, Byomkesh Bakshi's patronising behaviour when he first meets Ajit is very reminiscent of the way the canonical Sherlock Holmes treats those he deems intellectually inferior. Ajit arrives to consult Byomkesh regarding the mysterious disappearance of his own father, having already been warned that those who consult the truth seeker usually end up wanting to "smash his teeth in". And this is then born out when Byomkesh is tactlessly discourteous, telling Ajit that his father has run off with another woman. At which point, the outraged son loses his temper and punches Byomkesh in the face, much to his surprise.

This filmic moment is significant because in the Bengali stories, Byomkesh Bakshi rarely behaves like this. He is a much more reasonable, typical member of the Bengali middle-class – the so-called *bhadralok* – which was becoming increasingly prominent during the 1930s. This class of the so-called "respectable" members of polite society were said to have been deeply influenced by the values and codes of behaviour of the Raj but were at the same time independent-minded in their respectful resistance to the perceived excesses of imperial rule. Likewise, the Byomkesh of the original stories is mannered and compassionate – outspoken in his quest for truth but also self-conscious about his relative good fortune in belonging to what Broomfield calls a "socially privileged and consciously superior group". He is as such an embodiment of an aspirant, socially mobile class known for its "command of education […] pride in its language […] literate culture and its history", always striving to "adapt and augment to extend its social power and political opportunities" within Bengali culture (Broomfield 1968: 5–6). And a crucial element of this is his normalcy, on the basis of which readers have been able to empathise with him. This explains why Bandyopadhyay associated him with quotidian habits such as smoking and tea drinking rather than more ostentatious eccentric, Holmesian pastimes like drug taking or erratic violin playing.

Equally important in shaping the supposed ordinariness of the character's lifestyle is Bandyopadhyay's depiction of his heteronormative sexuality. For whereas the archetypal Holmesian detective is asexual, the originating version of Byomkesh lived out a heterosexual narrative arc, across the canon of stories gaining a wife and family and living a largely conventional life aside from his investigations. He is portrayed as a man of the people rather than one who remains aloof from everyday society. And this is something that also partially translates into the film, such as when Byomkesh becomes enamoured with the woman who will later become his wife, Satyabati. Thus, his ordinariness seems to co-exist with his assumed detective genius, being readily praised for his unusually well-developed deductive skills while also being shown to enjoy the more mundane aspects of his life with Ajit, something poignantly captured by a conversation between the men towards the end of the film. Byomkesh wryly points out that the two of them are, like most citizens of Calcutta, fundamentally orthodox, which is why the criminals were allowed to get away with their crimes for so long. He then asks his friend: "Do middle-class folk like us stand up for their country?", to which Ajit replies – addressing both Byomkesh and also by implication the members of the cinema audience themselves – "No, we go to the movies".

As such, *Detective Byomkesh Bakshi!* embodies an uneasy truce between "global" and "local" identities. For while Byomkesh as a man ultimately conforms to many of the typical features of a respectable native middle-class identity, located within the context of a specific historical representation of Bengali Calcutta, the character also resonates with the influence of the most popular of all international crime franchises, Sherlock Holmes. Whether this is an element of a deliberate marketing strategy, or an homage, or else simply a manifestation of the pervasiveness of the archetypal Holmesian detective, the hero-detective is a fundamental feature of the film's wider transtextuality. This is made most explicit at the conclusion of the film, when a local newspaper publishes a tribute to Byomkesh for thwarting the planned Japanese invasion of India. It praises him as "brave and talented" with "broad chest, keen moustache, eyes like embers", and to emphasise his grand status it suggests an appropriate new nickname that reflects his success. Henceforth, in the eyes of the residents of Calcutta, he will be known as "Our Sherlock Holmes", leaving little doubt as to who he was supposed to be all along.

Conclusion

Reading the film *Detective Byomkesh Bakshi!* as such a heterogenous crime adaptation brings it to life in new ways, providing an increasingly nuanced, sophisticated grasp of the text in and of itself. It also implicitly illustrates the multifacetedness of critical debates regarding adaptive forms. But perhaps most importantly, it demonstrates that any attempt to systematise or categorise such fundamentally complex "adaptive" texts is likely – no matter how sensitive and diligent – to fall short, to prove too delimiting in dealing with multifarious materials such as these. In particular, one of the key ways to underestimate this textual interrelatedness is to fail to come to terms with the array of glocal reworkings of crime and detective narratives, and the way they – in being mediated across cultures and identities – inherently accommodate international and regional sensibilities. Crime adaptation is such a multilayered, rhizomic, global cultural interaction, within an almost limitless range of forms and media and across a plethora of nations, that individual adaptations themselves need always to be read against this vast, international backdrop. Crime adaptations routinely flesh out the television schedules, swamp the cinema timetables, fill out the bookshop shelves, populate the theatres and fuel all number of different, contradictory forms of cross-cultural bricolage, in many if not most of the countries of the world. It is a genre that embodies the dynamic interrelations of world culture, and which provides a window onto the very nature of cultural globalisation itself.

Bibliography

Archer, N. (2014) "A novel experience in crime narrative: watching and reading *The Killing*", *Adaptation*, 7(2): 212–27.

Bandyopadhyay, S. (2003) *Byomkesh Bakshi Stories*, trans. M. Dhar, New Delhi: Rupa.

Banerjee, D. (dir.) (2015) *Detective Byomkesh Bakshi!*, motion picture, produced by Dibakar Banerjee and Aditya Chopra, Yash Raj Films, Mumbai.

Barthes, R. (1977) *Image-Music-Text*, trans. S. Heath, London: Fontana.

Berger, R. (2016) "Everything goes back to the beginning: television adaptation and remaking Nordic noir", *Journal of Adaptation and Film in Performance*, 9(2): 147–61.

Broomfield, J. (1968) *Elite Conflict in a Plural Society: Twentieth century Bengal*, Berkeley: University of California Press.

Creechan, L. (2016) "Attend the tale of Sweeney Todd: adaptation, revival, and keeping the meat grinder turning", *Neo-Victorian Studies*, 9(1): 98–122.

Deleuze, G. (1994) *Difference and Repetition*, trans. P. Paton, New York: Columbia University Press.

Elliott, K. (2013) "Theorizing adaptations/adapting theories", in J. Bruhn, A. Gjelsvik and E.F. Hanssen (eds), *Adaptation Studies: New challenges, new directions*, London: Bloomsbury, 19–45.

Field, A.J. (2009) *England's Secret Weapon: The wartime films of Sherlock Holmes*, London: Middlesex University Press.

Gregoriou, C. (2017) *Crime Fiction Migration: Crossing languages, cultures and media*, London: Bloomsbury.

Guest, K. (2010) "Norbu's *The Mandala of Sherlock Holmes*: neo-Victorian occupations of the past", *Neo-Victorian Studies*, 3(2): 73–95.

Hutcheon, L. (2006) *A Theory of Adaptation*, London: Routledge.

Jones, A.M. (2015) "'Palimpsestuous' attachments: framing a Manga theory of the global neo-Victorian", *Neo-Victorian Studies*, 8(1): 17–47.

Louttit, C. (2016) "*The Mystery of a Hansom Cab*, the classic adaptation and the Australian canon", *Adaptation*, 9(1): 58–67.

Raw, L. (2010) "The skopos of a remake: Michael Winner's *The Big Sleep* (1978)", *Adaptation*, 4(2): 199–209.

Robertson, R. (2012) "Globalisation or glocalisation?", *Journal of International Communication*, 18(2): 191–208.

Schober, R. (2013) "Adaptation as connection – transmediality reconsidered", in J. Bruhn, A. Gjelsvik and E. Frisvold Hanssen (eds), *Adaptation Studies: New challenges, new directions*, London: Bloomsbury, 89–112.

Seago, K. (2014) "Introduction and overview: crime fiction in translation", *Journal of Specialised Translation*, 22: 2–14.

Stam, R. (2000) "Beyond fidelity: the dialogics of adaptation", in J. Naremore (ed.), *Film Adaptation*, London: Athlon, 54–76.

Stuchebrukhov, O. (2012) "'Crimes without any punishment at all': Dostoevsky and Woody Allen in light of Bakhtinian theory", *Literature/Film Quarterly*, 40(2): 142–54.

6

HYBRIDISATION

Heather Duerre Humann

While hybridisation has always been a feature of crime fiction, there has, in recent years, been an outpouring of texts that reveal this tendency. Whether by appropriating qualities of other literary genres, or by reflecting the cultural specificity of a locale beyond the anglophone world, crime fiction texts have demonstrated both the elasticity of the genre and the willingness of writers of crime fiction to bend the genre to suit their narratives. Indeed, a comprehensive examination of the current state of crime fiction requires discussion of the concept of genre hybridity due to the recent spate of narratives wherein two or more forms are present to such a degree that neither dominates. While it is true that genres are always in flux, storylines about crime and its consequences tend, particularly in the twenty-first century, to combine features of different genres to such an extent that they can best be understood as hybrid narratives. Thus, these recent works of crime fiction demonstrate cross-cultural connections while also reflecting the postmodern tendencies toward rejecting boundaries between (so-called) high and low art forms and blurring, when not altogether dissolving, generic distinctions.

Locating and identifying this tendency within crime fiction opens up a space to consider the evolution of the genre as well as to highlight the importance of generic categories. As Ivo Ritzer and Peter W. Schulze argue in *Genre Hybridisation*, genres "shed light on the aesthetic, economic, and social dimensions of the particular conditions under which they were made and which they represent respectively" (2016: 9). In this respect, genres operate as cultural categories, largely due to their association with the cultural practices of the society in which they are produced. Moreover, generic structures "help to observe and analyse complex (inter) medial and (inter) cultural exchanges"; this is due, in part, to the fact that they are "subject to transformation" (Ritzer and Schulze 2016: 9). When writers make use of a genre which has traditionally been an avenue of expression for another culture or group, they attempt to make that form of expression relatable to other cultures and groups of people.

The hybridisation of crime fiction

In the case of crime fiction, the genre has, in fact, evolved significantly and grown to include many different offshoots and subgenres (such as mysteries, hardboiled detective novels, police procedurals, spy novels and thrillers). Not only does the genre encompass a range of styles, but crime writing also transcends national boundaries. It is true that crime fiction has always been an elastic literary form. Moreover, both social and political critique have long been part of the genre. These very qualities, which have remained essential and intrinsic to the genre, have also made crime fiction both malleable and responsive to changing times, thus ultimately contributing to the increasing hybridisation of the genre, which has taken place in tandem with – and as a result of – its increasing globalisation. A trend that has been particularly apparent in recent years, the genre now encompasses a number of notable hybrid texts, many of which serve to blur generic boundaries and call into question our current understanding of genre itself.

To be sure, as Christiana Gregoriou points out in *Crime Fiction Migration: Crossing Languages, Cultures and Media*, the genre is not only perennially popular but also constantly "on the move": "migrating", or crossing languages, media formats and cultures (2017: 2). In the process, texts have been reinterpreted and received across cultures (2017: 3). This migration opens the door for both cross-pollination and exposure to different national and local generic trends. Nonetheless, among these hybridised literary works, a focus on crime and its detection remains present and, in fact, continues to unite the diverse outgrowths and subgenres of crime narratives.

Within these hybridised literary works – as in more traditional crime fiction – the investigation accounts for the bulk of the novel, with the solving of the crime taking place toward the story's end. The rationale behind this formula – and a hallmark of many classical crime narratives – is that society is typically ordered, but the social order has become disordered as a result of a crime. However, in the case of many contemporary texts, these very notions (and the order/disorder nexus) are being called into question. Thus, a trend among the hybridised crime fiction that has grown so popular in recent years is that this formula still exists but is re-worked. Indeed, in the case of hybridised crime fiction, narratives tend to exist at the intersection of (two or more) literary genres. Consequently, in the case of many recent works of crime fiction, it is impossible to discuss the narrative in terms of genre, without also addressing notions such as globalisation, postcolonialism and postmodernism.

As Barry Langford stresses, genres actively produce meaning by calling attention to family resemblances between different texts (2005: 1). One result of this focus on resemblances is that selections belonging to the same genre demonstrate a noticeable degree of intertextuality, which proves satisfying for readers (the consumers of the texts) since they are able to recognise tropes and features across different texts. In the case of crime fiction, some traits are so common that they have helped to define the genre. Nonetheless, authors have revised (and reinvented) the formula by adapting it to suit the times and their own purposes. Indeed, authors have oftentimes done this deliberately – in essence, both relying on the formula and departing from it in order to mould the kinds of stories they want to tell. As Dennis Porter argues:

> No other genre is more conscious of the models from which it borrows and from which it knowingly departs. From Wilkie Collins and Conan Doyle down to Raymond Chandler, Georges Simenon, and Ian Fleming, the most interesting detective fiction is read in large measure for its differences, for its capacity to remain faithful to a tradition at the same time that it reinvents it in unexpected ways.
>
> *(1981: 54–55)*

While it is true that crime fiction has long been a flexible form, there has recently been a major expansion of the genre's boundaries – this expansion has taken place alongside and in response to both globalisation and postmodernism (with its anti-essentialist push and rejection of rigid generic categories), with the result being that crime fiction has become an increasingly hybridised form of storytelling. Although this tendency can be observed in much crime fiction, the texts discussed in detail later in this chapter exemplify the trend.

Hybridisation and the expansion of the genre

Hybrid literary forms – that is, modes of storytelling that cross genres or reimagine a genre – have gained in popularity alongside, and in direct response to, postmodernism, with its overt rejection of fixity, purity and authority in favour of pluralism and indeterminacy. Indeed, as Mike Featherstone argues in *Undoing Culture: Globalization, Postmodernism and Identity*, postmodernism has resulted in "previously sealed-off cultural forms more easily" flowing over what were once "strictly policed boundaries", thus bringing about the production of "unusual combinations and syncretism" (1995: 4).

These tendencies have also helped to shape contemporary crime writing. Particularly in the twenty-first century, authors of crime fiction – anglophone and non-anglophone alike – borrow from and blend techniques used in other literary genres. This trend reveals a greater willingness on the part of authors to innovate as well as suggests their desire to create something new. At the same time, it reflects a more widespread willingness to adapt and be open to new forms. The combined effect is that hybridisation has opened up space for new possibilities within crime fiction, while also allowing the genre to not only transcend its original formulas but also, as a global genre, to move beyond national boundaries. As crime fiction has become more hybridised, it has also become a more suitable vehicle to call into question existing social norms, raise awareness about global issues and critique prevailing sociopolitical structures.

Social transformation demands new (that is mixed and hybridised) generic forms to reflect and interrogate the forces that bring it about. As Audre Lorde has famously argued, "the master's tools will never dismantle the master's house" (1984: 112). What Lorde means by this is that new tools and strategies are needed to disrupt the status quo. Just as social structures are transformed within a changing twenty-first-century world, within fiction, boundaries are also being negotiated; meanwhile, "realities" are questioned as part of these ongoing constructions. It is in this sense that contemporary crime writers – a much more diverse group than in past eras, not least due to the many female and non-white writers who are penning remarkable works of crime fiction – push the boundaries with respect to the genre, frequently transforming stories about crime and its consequences into hybrid or cross-genre works of fiction. From Stieg Larsson, the Swedish author of the internationally bestselling *Millennium* trilogy, to Mur Lafferty, an American writer who creates a murder mystery in space, to Natsuo Kirino, a Japanese noir writer, Kenyan writer Mũkoma wa Ngũgĩ, and Italian author Carlo Lucarelli, contemporary crime writers have constructed hybrid works which push the limits with respect to genre. As a closer examination of these authors' novels will demonstrate, cross-genre writing offers opportunities for opening up debates and encouraging discussion, while also stretching our definition of what it means to write crime fiction.

Testing boundaries: Larsson and Nordic noir

Swedish journalist-turned-crime writer, Stieg Larsson is a prominent example of a crime fiction writer who tests generic limits and boundaries. Indeed, Larsson's *Millennium* trilogy defies easy generic categorisation. Consisting of *The Girl with the Dragon Tattoo* (2005) [2008], *The Girl Who Played with Fire* (2006) [2010b] and *The Girl Who Kicked the Hornet's Nest* (2007) [2010a], the trilogy deals with crime and its consequences while at the same time reflecting the globalisation that has come to characterise life in the twenty-first century. In many respects, his novels rely on the generic archetypes of crime fiction while also conflating features more commonly found in other modes of fiction. Particularly due to his treatment of cybercrime and his representation of sexual taboos, not to mention his willingness to test boundaries with respect to depicting gender in non-normative fashion, Larsson's trilogy comes across as a hybrid text.

Although his novels have been frequently classified as Nordic noir, it is because of the range of topics he addresses, as well as his reliance on generic markers of other subgenres – such as the techno-thriller, spy novel and conspiracy tale – that Larsson's crime fiction transcends this label. His trilogy incorporates different generic formations – and thus relies on qualities that best serve his narrative purposes – in order to make a sustained critique of social and political structures. In short, and as I demonstrate in the closer examination that follows, Larsson borrows from and blends conventions of the genre in his mode of storytelling, thus exemplifying the ongoing hybridisation of the genre as well as his masterful use of technique. Due, in part, to the fact that Larsson's novels provide readers with multiple – and shifting – viewpoints, they allow readers the opportunity to peer into characters' lives and illustrate the kinds of dilemmas they face. This exploration into topics that are both timely and controversial shows Larsson's willingness to call into question the social order while also bringing to light twenty-first-century controversies and concerns.

As analysis of these novels demonstrates, Larsson relies on many of the generic markers of Nordic noir, but he ultimately creates hybrid texts by incorporating features of other popular modes of storytelling. Indeed, critics have been quick to identify the degree to which Larsson both relies upon and veers away from tradition in writing this trilogy. For example, Steven Peacock notes one of "the most striking aspects of the *Millennium* trilogy is each entry's affiliation with different subgenres of crime drama" (2013: 9). Peacock delineates how each of the novels in the series maps in terms of its generic markers:

> *The Girl with the Dragon Tattoo*, in introducing post-punk cyber-hacker Lisbeth Salander and investigative journalist Mikael Blomkvist, soon settles into a variation of Agatha Christie's "locked room" mysteries, with a family's secret murky history playing out on their own private island. The second book, *The Girl Who Played with Fire* expands the mythos of the Millennium universe to detail a government-led conspiracy against Salander, harking back to Cold War political thrillers and antics akin to James Bond's brand of derring-do. The third and final novel, *The Girl Who Kicked the Hornet's Nest* continues in this vein before moving towards a courtroom finale of the kind more often seen in Hollywood legal thrillers.
>
> *(2013: 9)*

In essence, by splicing different generic frames and archetypes, Larsson, throughout his *Millennium* trilogy, breaks new ground. By addressing contemporary (and once taboo) issues such as sex trafficking, sexual violence, child abuse and domestic violence, his novels adeptly raise awareness about current political and social problems. Yet, by positioning these discussions alongside his fictional explorations of organised crime and political corruption (which, in the case of his trilogy, take place within Sweden, a country which has been heralded as a progressive, liberal democracy), he creates hybrid texts which accomplish more than simply raising awareness.

There are, of course, both formal and thematic issues tied to the manner in which Larsson constructs his narrative. With respect to Larsson's use of the noir form, what he adds to this long-standing popular genre is his use of irony to critique and call attention to modern-day problems. Thus, in the case of the *Millennium* trilogy, the implications of moving between these different types of narrative structure work alongside his thematic exploration of contemporary controversies.

Larsson's commitment to exploring these controversial topics has added a political dimension to his crime fiction, a quality that scholars have noted. As Bronwen Thomas argues (2012), Larsson manages to incorporate social campaigning and politics into the crime fiction genre, thus using his fiction to critique multiple manifestations of injustice in contemporary Swedish society. To an extent, this is typical of Nordic noir. Yet, in the case of Larsson's trilogy, especially because of the sustained focus on Salander – who shatters archetypes by the way she is depicted – there is a noticeable degree of hybridisation at work. In his portrayal of Salander, who champions underdogs (by, for example, seeking to vindicate victims of domestic abuse) and fights those who abuse their power, Larsson merges localised social issues with global concerns and contemporary controversies. Larsson also pushes the boundaries because of Salander's sexuality and unconventional lifestyle, demonstrating the degree to which he is willing to call into question the status quo through his construction of a disruptive, but ultimately justice-seeking, outsider. Indeed, because of this character, Larsson is successful in adeptly tackling political issues while also addressing contemporary controversies related to human rights and social justice.

Lafferty's genre-bending exploration of crime in space

While Larsson is remarkable for the way he pushes boundaries, he is far from the only contemporary author to pen crime fiction that demonstrates the contemporary move toward hydridisation within the genre. Especially recently, with the spate of international crime novels being published, crime fiction has become more diverse, with popular titles being written by women and non-white writers alike. A shining example of the diversity of contemporary crime fiction is Mur Lafferty's novel *Six Wakes* (2017). A crime thriller set in space, this novel is remarkable for the way Lafferty blurs and blends different literary genres as part of her storytelling, thereby creating a work of crime fiction that relies on elements common to science fiction as well as confessional literature. The result is a deft combination of different genres and forms in a text where a murder mystery takes centre stage. In this sense, Lafferty's *Six Wakes* represents a type of stylistic eclecticism which, like the other texts discussed in this chapter, underscores the impulse toward postmodernism so common in twenty-first-century storytelling.

While Lafferty's novel is, all told, about the investigation of unsolved murders, *Six Wakes* leans on the genre of science fiction in many respects. Along with its extraterrestrial setting (the novel's action takes place exclusively aboard a starship), Lafferty relies upon a futuristic science fiction scenario, with the events of the book taking place during the twenty-fifth century and centring on a group of cloned beings. Moreover, its premise, that human cloning has advanced to the point that it is possible to download an individual's consciousness into an artificially created body, is undoubtedly the stuff of science fiction.

While Lafferty incorporates science fiction tropes into this narrative, she also relies heavily upon traits common to crime fiction. The degree to which this novel veers toward crime fiction is apparent in the way Lafferty sets up the mystery, which she uses to propel the novel's plot and establish mood.

Reviewers of the novel have noticed the degree to which Lafferty leans on both genres, labelling *Six Wakes* not only a work of science fiction, but also a murder mystery. However, these observations can be taken a step further since *Six Wakes* is specifically a "closed circle" (or "locked room") mystery, with the setting precluding outsiders from having a direct role in the murders. Moreover, Lafferty showcases the versatility of the crime fiction genre by, as Jason Heller argues, constructing a narrative which "shifts from whodunit to howdunit to whydunit with a breathless sense of escalation" (2017). In this sense, Lafferty reveals her familiarity with – and resolve to utilise – formulas common to crime fiction. Yet, by transplanting these formulas to a science fiction setting, Lafferty creates, in the end, a hybridised work.

Further suggesting the degree to which *Six Wakes* is a hybridised novel, Lafferty also borrows from the genre of confessional literature. This becomes clear especially in the way she constructs multiple narrative viewpoints, which emerge via the book's shifting narrative perspectives. Since these various narrative strands provide backstories of the main characters – each of whom has something to hide – and are told from their individual perspectives, the tone comes across as confessional. Confessional literature tends to focus on the process of "un-masking", offering readers glimpses into the interior psychology of characters who unspool their secrets.

When this type of "un-masking" occurs in a work of crime fiction, confession in a literary sense is tied to confession in a legal sense. As Peter Brooks underscores, there is a connection "between legal and literary discourses on the nature and contexts of the confessional act" (1996: 115). In the case of *Six Wakes*, this relationship proves significant. Not only is it crucial plot-wise, since the action of the novel relates to solving crime (the murders that propel the novel's initial mystery), but the use of the confessional voice also serves as a technique which subverts traditional literary genres.

As Mary Beth Harrod explains in *Making Confessions: The Confessional Voice Found among Literary Genres*, "while the lines of literary conventions separate genres, confessional writing tends to blur those lines by bringing the message of the work to the forefront" (2007: i). The dynamic that Harrod describes can be seen in *Six Wakes*, since Lafferty's use of the confessional voice disrupts the traditions of both science fiction and crime fiction. Indeed, in *Six Wakes*, Lafferty blurs and blends different genres to the point that by novel's end, it becomes clear that she has turned traditional storytelling on its head, thus revealing that she can stretch genre to suit her purposes.

Globalisation and hybridisation

While both Lafferty and Larsson are notable for the ways they rely on genre elasticity, there are many other remarkable crime writers from all over the globe who deserve attention for their hybridised works of crime fiction. For instance, Carlo Lucarelli, Mũkoma wa Ngũgĩ and Natsuo Kirino have similarly enriched the field of crime fiction through the publication of their hybridised literary works. Both Lucarelli's *Almost Blue* (1997) and Ngũgĩ's *Nairobi Heat* (2009) are cases of contemporary novels which deal with subjects typically found in crime fiction – one concerns serial killings in Bologna and the other is about a transatlantic murder mystery – but in these novels, "formulas and codes are displaced through red herrings and misdirections, necessitating relocations and reconfigurations" (Nilsson et al. 2017: 6). In the case of Natsuo Kirino's *Out* (1998), a novel which initially seems to conform to patterns common to crime fiction by presenting what seems to be a murder mystery, proves to have additional layers not typically explored in the genre.

In *Almost Blue*, the investigation and goings-on surrounding a string of murders are narrated in a rather unconventional manner since there are multiple perspectives shown: That of the detective, the killer and a third unlikely source, a blind man who becomes key to the investigation when he overhears potentially relevant information on his scanner (Lucarelli 1997: 5–6). Beyond its use of these shifting narrative voices, *Almost Blue* also sets itself apart from typical crime fiction since it adopts a topic popular in crime fiction set in the US (serial killings) but relies, instead, on an Italian setting. Thus, *Almost Blue*, as Tilottama Tharoor argues, uses "structures of American crime fiction playing over the Bologna scene" (2017: 35). In this sense, the novel demonstrates how genre-bending operates as a mechanism for cross-cultural exchange.

Nairobi Heat is another interesting case, since it uses traits common to crime fiction, but bears the obvious influence of both postmodernism and postcolonialism. While on the surface level, *Nairobi Heat* follows the formula of crime fiction – especially of the action thriller and noir variety – the way the narrative straddles two cultures (being set in both Madison, Wisconsin and Nairobi, Kenya), this crime novel ultimately proves to be anything but typical. Instead, *Nairobi Heat* sets itself apart by the way its "American detective thriller format contends with local police methods and local histories and politics", including those of "white settler colonialism" (Tharoor 2017: 34). Again, the implication for the genre is that there is an important degree of cross-cultural exchange taking place, yet, as part of this dialogue, the politics of postcolonialism are both foregrounded and re-introduced via the narrative's focus on the intersection between local and global concerns.

Like *Almost Blue* and *Nairobi Heat*, Natsuo Kirino's *Out* stretches the genre of crime fiction while also demonstrating the genre's global reach. *Out*, which was first published in Japan in 1998 and translated into English in 2003, concerns a brutal murder in the Tokyo suburbs. The novel centres on a female factory worker named Yayoi Yamamota who kills her abusive husband and then, with the help of three of her co-workers, covers up the crime. Because her killing was in response to her husband's abuse, the book reads as part social protest novel, but its gritty realism, combined with its exploration of the violent underbelly of Japanese society, link *Out* to the tradition of the noir thriller. In his article, "Work and Death in the Global City", Christopher Breu situates *Out* as a work of noir, calling Kirino's crime fiction "perhaps the riskiest, darkest, and most stylistically assured noir to appear from Japan" (2016: 41). Yet, in the case of Kirino's fiction, the added elements of social protest push the novel beyond the typical boundaries of crime fiction; in this respect, Kirino's construction of narrative demonstrates that she is a writer who will play with tropes but ultimately veer into new territory in crime fiction by creating a mixture of horror, feminism and class critique. In this respect, Kirino shares much in common with contemporary writers like Carlo Lucarelli, Mūkoma wa Ngūgī, Mur Lafferty and Stieg Larsson, all of whom rely upon techniques from other literary genres in their crime fiction.

Crime fiction at the boundaries

While the selections discussed in this chapter are meant to be representative, they are not exhaustive. Indeed, in recent years, a number of other writers of crime fiction have revised – and sometimes reinvented – the formula. The result is that authors who push boundaries are opening up a space for new possibilities within crime fiction.

Crime fiction has long been recognised as a useful vehicle for social commentary as well as a mode of storytelling with mass appeal. As Jason Pinter relays in "The State of the Crime Novel", crime fiction is responsible for "telling some of the most important stories and peeling back society's flesh to reveal its bare bones" (2010). As important a role as traditional crime fiction has played, because of their penchant for hybridisation, contemporary writers can deliver an even stronger message and reach different readers – a feat easier to accomplish when not writing in a given box. Thus, they can offer new kinds of stories to both new readers and fans of more conventional crime fiction, and in doing so, raise awareness about important issues and use their fiction to question the status quo. Crime writers such as these push the limits with respect to the genre while also showing the increased hybridisation that has come to typify the genre in recent years.

While the plots of many crime novels follow a familiar formula, contemporary writers have shown they can break new ground by making their crime fiction about more than just crime and its consequences. These writers make their readers want to do more than simply "read for the ending", which is what Fredric Jameson once claimed that readers of crime fiction tended to do (1979: 132). Indeed, by their conclusions, the crime fiction discussed herein prove to be more than about the investigation and solving of crime. In writing hybridised works, contemporary authors demonstrate the versatility of the genre while also making a case for its sustained cultural relevance and ensuring continued evolution of the genre.

Bibliography

Breu, C. (2016) "Work and death in the global city: Natsuo Kirino's *Out* as neoliberal noir", in A. Pepper and D. Schmid (eds), *Globalization and the State in Contemporary Crime Fiction: A world of crime*, New York: Palgrave, 39–57.

Brooks, P. (1996) "Storytelling without fear? Confession in law and literature", in P. Brooks and P. Gewirtz (eds), *Law's Stories: Narrative and rhetoric in the law*, New Haven, Connecticut: Yale University Press, 114–34.

Featherstone, M. (1995) *Undoing Culture: Globalization, postmodernism and identity*, London: Sage.

Gregoriou, C. (2017) *Crime Fiction Migration: Crossing languages, cultures, and media*, London; New York: Bloomsbury Academic.

Harrod, M.B. (2007) *Making Confessions: The confessional voice found among literary genres*, Master's thesis, The College at Brockport: State University of New York.

Heller, J. (2017) "*Six Wakes* is a nerve-tingling interstellar murder mystery", *NPR: Books*, 31 January, www. npr.org/2017/01/31/512042753/six-wakes-is-a-nerve-tingling-interstellar-murder-mystery (accessed 16 October 2019).

Jameson, F. (1979) "Reification and utopia in mass culture", *Social Text* (1): 131–48.

Lafferty, M. (2017) *Six Wakes*, New York: Orbit.

Langford, B. (2005) *Film Genre: Hollywood and beyond*, Edinburgh: Edinburgh University Press.

Larsson, S. (2008) *The Girl with the Dragon Tattoo*, trans. R. Keeland, New York: Alfred A. Knopf.

———. (2010a) *The Girl Who Kicked the Hornet's Nest*, trans. R. Keeland, New York: Alfred A. Knopf.

———. (2010b) *The Girl Who Played with Fire*, trans. R. Keeland, New York: Alfred A. Knopf.

Lorde, A. (1984) "The master's tools will never dismantle the master's house", in *Sister Outsider: Essays and speeches*, Berkeley, California: Crossing Press, 110–14.

Lucarelli, C. (1997) *Almost Blue*, trans. O. Stransky, New York: City Lights.

Ngũgĩ, M. wa. (2010) *Nairobi Heat*, New York: Melville House.

Nilsson, L., Damrosch, D. and D'haen, T. (2017) "Introduction", in L. Nilsson, D. Damrosch and T. D'haen (eds), *Crime Fiction as World Literature*, New York: Bloomsbury Academic, 1–9.

Peacock, S. (2013) *Stieg Larsson's Millennium Trilogy: Interdisciplinary approaches to Nordic noir on page and screen*, New York: Springer.

Pinter, J. (2010) "The state of the crime novel", *Huffington Post*, 25 August, www.huffingtonpost.com/jason-pinter/the-state-of-the-crime-no_b_342918.html (accessed 19 October 2019).

Porter, D. (1981) *The Pursuit of Crime: Art and ideology in detective fiction*, New Haven, CT: Yale University Press.

Ritzer, I. and Schulze, P.W. (2016) *Genre Hybridisation: Global cinematic flow*, Marburg: Schüren Verlag.

Tharoor, T. (2017) "Red herrings and read alerts: crime and its excesses in *Almost Blue* and *Nairobi Heat*", in L. Nilsson, D. Damrosch and T. D'haen (eds), *Crime Fiction as World Literature*, New York: Bloomsbury Academic, 33–46.

Thomas, B. (2012) "Kicking the hornet's nest: the rhetoric of social campaigning in Stieg Larsson's *Millennium* Trilogy", *Language and Literature,* 21(3): 299–310.

7
GRAPHIC CRIME NOVELS

Robert Prickett and Casey A. Cothran

Graphic novels have been entangled with stories of crime since their beginnings. In the United States, the genre has been closely linked with stories of heroes and villains, and thus with narratives that deal with the perpetrators, the consequences and the costs of crime. Indeed, the name used by powerhouse American comic book and graphic novel publisher "DC Comics" came from the company's popular series, "Detective Comics", which featured Batman's debut in 1939 (Morrison 2012: 17). Popular early comics featured The Shadow and Dick Tracy and, as Gerard Jones writes, "American fascination with crime had the fervor that comes with profound indifference [...] Dick Tracy was filling the daily pages with lunatic murderers dying horrible deaths [...] and selling more papers all the time" (2004: 94). As such examples suggest, the tradition of crime was ingrained in the medium from its early days as comic strips and pulp magazines, and this trend continued as the form evolved.

Nickie D. Phillips and Staci Strobl, in *Comic Book Crime: Truth, Justice, and the American Way*, observe how superheroes dominate the genre in the twenty-first century (2013: 4–5). In 2018, according to Diamond Comic Distributors, Marvel and DC Comics held 68% of the total market sales of comic books and graphic novels in comic book specialty stores. The medium is often used to explore complex questions about heroism, violence and crime, even when superheroes are not a part of the narrative. Phillips and Strobl describe how "meanings about crime and justice are negotiated and contested in comic books"; they also claim that "these imaginings form part of a broader cultural context in which readers absorb, reproduce, and resist notions of justice" (2).

Of course, a variety of modern mediums meaningfully present crime narratives; characters who seek to reject the codes that order society appear in books, television, film and video games. While each new medium presents readers and viewers with new ways to tell the story of crime, the graphic novel is unique in that it combines two modes of storytelling (image and text) and because it routinely forces the reader to imaginatively engage with both the shown and the not-shown in order to follow the events of the story. In *Crime Fiction*, John Scaggs notes that a key component of all crime fiction is "the process of interpretation itself" (2005: 4). The process of interpretation also exists as a key activity that readers of the graphic novel medium must engage in as they read. Thus, in the graphic crime novel, genre and medium complement one another.

The medium of graphic novels

Graphic novels tell stories by deliberately ordering pieces of art and segments of writing to create a narrative. Robert S. Petersen traces the evolution of the medium from prints in China, to European Medieval and Renaissance popular prints, to caricatures in Britain, to modern art, to French humour magazines; he sees American comics, which are clear forerunners of the twenty-first century graphic novel, as arising from this long and storied tradition (2011: 95). Scholars typically trace the literary origins of the modern graphic novel by observing the progression of comics to comic strips to comic books to graphic novels. The genre developed most significantly over the course of the twentieth century in the United States, although today there is a proliferation of graphic narratives worldwide, both in print and on digital platforms.

The medium has struggled historically with a reputation for providing juvenile, simplistic or lowbrow stories. Nevertheless, recent scholarship has shown that graphic novels provide readers with complicated reading experiences. Brian W. Sturm writes, "Reading graphic novels is a very complex process that combines decoding what is provided in the text and pictures with filling in the gaps in the story left by the author and illustrator" (2013: 58). Graphic novels push readers to interpret simultaneously what is pictured and what is written; additionally, the reader must imagine the parts of the story that do *not* directly appear in the many, variously sized panels that comprise the text. Theorist Scott McCloud postulates that the "gutters" between panels, a convention of the medium, influence reading, arguing that they inspire a cognitive process that he calls "closure". For McCloud, closure requires the reader to think critically:

> The closure of electronic media is continuous, largely involuntary, and virtually imperceptible. But closure in comics is far from continuous and anything but involuntary. Every act committed to paper by the comic artist is aided and abetted by a silent accomplice. An equal partner in crime known as the reader.
>
> *(1993: 68)*

These gaps in narration, placed alongside potentially meaningful fragments of text and evocative illustrations, influence the experience of reading the graphic narrative. The graphic novel format requires readers to simultaneously study visual images, read textual inserts and visualise action that is not shown or described in order to decipher the story.

Because the medium has evolved rapidly within the past fifty years, there is much debate over terms, and specifically over the definition of the term "graphic novel". Petersen argues "graphic narrative" is the appropriate term, writing, "The term 'graphic narrative' allows our focus to rest on two essential ideas: *graphic*, a composed and non-animated visual form, and *narrative*, a crafted story" (2011: xv). Nevertheless, despite scholars' exploration of a variety of nomenclature, "graphic novel" seems to be the popular term used to describe longer narrative works of sequential art today, although national categories, such as "manga", "manhwa", "cergam" or "fumetti" often are recognised.

Medium and message

Graphic crime novels allow for a combination of the familiar and the disruptive, of "imitation and transformation" (Anderson et al. 2015: 1). Indeed, because graphic novels can be challenging as a medium (to read and to interpret), they are an excellent vehicle for *challenging* crime narratives: And here we mean challenging as "complex" and challenging as "problematising". The graphic novel medium provides multiple avenues to inform the reader about potential themes, tropes, morals and messages. Meaning is conveyed within dialogue bubbles, blocks of narrative text, in images, in framing, in stylistic illustration choices and in the use of colour (or lack of colour). The text is a conduit that allows the crime narrative to be reformed in new and thought-provoking ways. The medium's representational modes (art, text and gutters between panels that indicate the absence of art or text) can retell the age-old story of crime and punishment in a new aesthetic.

For example, *The Private Eye*, written by Brian K. Vaughan, illustrated by Marcos Martin and coloured by Muntsa Vicente, pushes the reader to think critically and creatively in order to unravel both an intricate crime narrative and an embedded critical commentary on modern issues of technology, privacy and authority. This series began as a webcomic (available in English, Spanish, Catalan and Portuguese) in March 2013 and was reproduced in print as a compilation graphic novel by Image Comics in December 2015. The text provides readers with the familiar narrative of the private investigator who discovers large-scale corruption while trying to solve a single murder; the setting is 2076, in a world where all internet access and smart technology has been discontinued. Despite the flamboyant futuristic setting of this sci-fi mystery, subtle references to twenty-first century dilemmas are embedded in the art and the text, providing readers with opportunities to reinterpret familiar challenges.

Additionally, this text, by its nature, reworks familiar aspects of the crime narrative. One example: The authors use panels to disrupt the flow of a chase scene, a typical element of the crime narrative formula. In *The Private Eye*, static images must represent actions and movements in time, but the arrangement of these images can challenge the reader. In one significant chase scene, depicted on a one-page full spread, the illustrator uses as a background the maze-like tubes on the edges of town. Overlaid on these tubes are small boxes that graphically represent the three people in the chase, highlighting specific moments of their movement within these tubes: Knocking over a trash can, climbing a ladder, removing a mask, sliding down a tube, all culminating (as the reader's eyes move from the left to the right of the page) in an image on the bottom far right that shows the object of the chase being hit in the head with a helmet. On the next two pages, numerous panels highlight the interrogation. On one page many small panels are used, and on another there is a full-page illustration. In each piece of the narrative progression, the reader is given the option to rush over the material presented, or to linger on specific panels of narration and images. Successful reading of the action requires interpretive ability. The reader must follow the timeline of the chase by looking at a series of images from left to right, rather than being distracted by the whole page of graphics; they must then navigate the dialogue of the moment after the chase, even though dialogue bubbles are not always attached to the character who is speaking, but placed artistically around a close-up of one face (requiring the reader to guess which character would say what line). Thus the chaotic chase scene, so common in crime fiction, is reformed, presented as a puzzle to be solved rather than a pleasurable ride. The chase becomes an intellectual challenge rather than an adrenaline rush.

As noted above, *The Private Eye* provides a strong example of how a formulaic plot element can be refigured in the graphic crime novel; however, many, if not all, graphic novels employ this sort of reconfiguration. In *Graphic Storytelling and Visual Narrative*, Eisner notes that readers have different experiences with different mediums; specifically, he explores text, film, interactive video (games) and comics. Part of the reason one may argue that the graphic novel invites complicated crime narratives arises from the differences between these mediums. Specifically, the nature of the narrative can vary based on the reader's involvement in the speed of the narrative (reading), in the viewer-reader's need to receive the narrative at the creator's pace (film), or in the player-reader's potential to manipulate the narrative action (video games). Eisner notes the importance of the reader's involvement in comics. Although "the quality of the telling hinges on the arrangement of text and image", the reader "is expected to participate. Reading the imagery requires experience and allows acquisition at the viewer's pace" (2008: 69). It may be argued that crime narratives can lose their appeal when they become too predictable or formulaic. Because the graphic crime novel presents familiar plot elements in new, potentially unfamiliar formats, the reader is inspired to make an effort to follow the narrative. Reader participation results from the medium's demands for energy, attention and analysis.

In addition to adding complexity to typical narrative tropes, graphic crime novels can engage with some of the social functions of the modern crime narrative. In her groundbreaking text, *Twentieth-Century Crime Fiction*, Gill Plain (2001) describes how the crime genre has evolved over the course of the century, moving from a form that excluded the Other (the dangerous female, the atypical masculine, the homosexual, the different body) to a form that incorporates and values these characters. Plain also argues that the evolution of the genre has led to a reconsideration of what is not-crime. By including sympathetic characters, or even detective figures, who do not fit society's stereotypes, the author of crime fiction can show how problematic it is for readers to assume something is criminal simply because it is unfamiliar. Looking again at the graphic novel *The Private Eye*, one can note how this text explores cultural interest in potentially disreputable costumes, masks and cosplay. The reader is regularly shocked or titillated by colourful drawings of human bodies wearing fish or bug or monster masks while going about the routines of everyday life. Costumes and cosplay are historically relegated to an event such as Mardi Gras or Comic-Con; images of people in masks on park benches and motorcycles transforms mask-wearing into normal human behaviour.

Building on Plain's observations, Bran Nicol, Patricia Pulham and Eugene McNulty argue that "Crime culture incorporates the fluid definition of crime in the modern period – it responds to changing identifications and perceptions of what constitutes crime and revises, redefines, and questions them in artistic production" (2011: 9). This type of fluid exploration of the nature of criminality marks not just the art but the world of *The Private Eye*. In this graphic crime novel, there is no longer an internet because, in the past, the cloud which stored everyone's "deepest darkest secrets" (Vaughan and Martin 2015: Chapter 1, 22) experienced a massive failure. Thus, "every message you thought was safe, every photo you thought you deleted, every mortifying little search you ever made [...] It was all there for anyone to use against you" (Chapter 1, 23). In consequence, humans have discontinued their use of the internet and have taken extensive steps, including wearing masks daily, to hide their identities. In contrast to the social world of the novel, where identity is a closely kept secret, "Free Assange" posters appear on the walls of rooms in P.I.'s house. This subtle, background reference to the founder of WikiLeaks prompts readers to consider questions about privacy, identity, access and personal freedom. The text of the narrative also promotes the reader to engage with these themes. Characters debate and discuss the merits of a world with and without the internet in a series of speech bubbles. Specifically, P.I. and his grandfather, a tattooed senior citizen who misses Facebook, discuss "teevee", the legality of childhood ADD meds and the merits of staying off the grid. These contrasting visual and verbal messages are heightened by the size and placement of the panels that make up the text. While other crime narratives can certainly accommodate embedded political messages, the structure and formatting of graphic novels, and particularly the focused nature of the individual comic panel, enables these commentaries on crime and not-crime to be presented in ways that inspire readerly examination.

Graphic crime novels

Another important aspect of the crime narrative that can be explored by the graphic novel's combination of words, images and blank spaces is the complexity of the criminal character. *Blacksad* (Canalez and Guarnido 2010) is an international, award-winning, bestselling graphic crime novel series written by Juan Diaz Canalez, illustrated by Juanjo Guarnido and with lettering by Studio Cutie. Originally published in France, the series has been translated into over twenty different languages and has won numerous awards. To date, volumes have been collected and published by Dark Horse Comics (English translation) into *Blacksad* (2010); *Blacksad: A Silent Hell* (2012); and *Blacksad: Amarillo* (2014). This noir series follows John Blacksad, a black cat and private detective, through various mysteries, adventures and distractions. The stories range from murder to kidnapping to revenge to travelogue to conspiracy, all set within an imagined 1950s America and populated with various anthropomorphic animals. In the *Blacksad* comics, the nature of various characters is represented by their animal identity. For example, the violent white supremacist of one story is a polar bear, the shady businessman of another story is a lizard and the professor-scientist is an owl. Jane Hanley notes that these animal images evolve over the course of different comics to reflect behaviour: "Characters' choices become more complex and morally ambiguous. Simultaneously, their graphical depiction is altered such that different aspects of their animal characteristics come to the fore" (2012: 386).

This versatile illustrative technique challenges readers to reimagine the nature and presentation of stock characters in noir crime fiction. Pim Higginson, in his discussion of the noir genre, explores the dual nature of the noir "femme fatale": He describes how she is simultaneously the vulnerable damsel who needs to be rescued and the dishonest monster who attacks the chivalric detective-hero (2015: 59). While this multifaceted character frequently appears in crime fiction, the graphic novel can add additional intricacy and interest to this and other character types. *Blacksad*'s presentation of such familiar types (the femme fatale, as well as the beautiful and doomed actress, the sleazy reporter and the corrupt millionaire) as animals, sometimes with humanoid bodies (two-legged and voluptuous yet covered in fur), provokes a sense of the uncanny in the reader. The characters' mannerisms, gestures and actions can seem very human as they get into fistfights, have sex, drive cars and smoke cigarettes. Nevertheless, characters also can bare their teeth, catch fish in a stream or reference their cold-blooded nature. The use of the anthropomorphic in these texts highlights the absurdity of the human claim of superiority over creation; while animals act like humans, it is really humans who act like animals. Hanley further notes, "the artist seems to refuse readers the simplicity of using characters' species to make reliable moral evaluations" (2012: 390). The femme fatales in various episodes of *Blacksad* can transition between the roles of innocent and villain; in addition, a femme fatale character may be drawn in one episode as a female cat and in another episode as a female bear. As the medium pushes readers to visualise animals as humans and humans as animals, the genre makes possible a multifaceted understanding not only of characters in the narrative but of human nature more generally. Just as twenty-first-century crime fiction has worked to explore the deeper psychology of villains, victims and the people who seek to enact justice, this graphic novel, through its use of interesting character art and development, participates in this movement.

This visual exploration of character is also a major component of manga, a Japanese form of comics, where slapstick moments feature sloppily-drawn figures and serious moments feature the same figures drawn carefully and beautifully. Moving away from the realism of American graphic novels, manga uses multiple art styles – as well as icons or textual symbols – to express mood, tone or the complexity of identity. Adult characters may suddenly be drawn as a childlike "chibi", indicating a state of extreme feeling; in turn, a red symbol resembling a hashtag or star (called an "anger symbol" or "vein pop") may appear above a character's head, indicating anger. Regional or cultural graphic novel styles and iconography, like those found in manga, enrich and complicate the crime narratives that may be found in those regional or cultural graphic crime novel texts.

Identity Crisis #1–7 © 2004, 2005 DC Comics

By their very nature, superhero narratives are crime narratives, as villains must exist in order for superheroes to act. Phillips and Strobl have argued that "the repetition of cultural meanings in comic book narratives often reinforces particular notions of justice, especially the punishment philosophies of retributive justice and incapacitation" (2013: 3). In addition, they claim that "these types of punishments are meted out by crime-fighting heroes and superheroes who are depicted as predominantly white males defending a nostalgic American way of life" (3).

Graphic crime novels

Identity Crisis (2015) was written by Brad Meltzer and pencilled by Rags Morales; it began as a seven-issue comic book limited series, published by DC Comics from June to December 2004. Notably, it brings to light the problematic way that readers automatically assign heroic motives to violent and powerful superheroes. As this graphic crime novel is a mass market American superhero story, its revaluing of the assumptions that are typical in generations of superhero comics is noteworthy. Through the graphic novel's multifaceted storytelling techniques, this text radically repositions superhero characters within crime fiction. The reader must act as a detective, decoding images and text in order to uncover an unexpected narrative about heroes as criminals. This revising of the superhero mythos reflects recent trends in crime fiction where authority figures like policemen, detectives and attorneys are shown as potentially flawed and dangerous individuals who perceive their questionable behaviours as moral and just. Additionally, this revision encourages understanding, if not sympathy, for the plight of the criminal who is captured or arrested by vigilantes acting as agents of good.

Despite featuring numerous DC superheroes, this narrative is, in essence, a locked room mystery. In addition to a baffling murder, it also features postmortem medical examinations, CSI activities and various superheroes who act as detectives. The story begins when Elongated Man, traditionally seen as a minor, supporting character in the DC Superhero Universe, discovers that his wife Sue Dibny has been murdered. The main story arc follows Elongated Man and members of the Justice League as they track down suspect Dr Light. Years prior, he attacked and raped Sue Dibny. Afterwards, he threatened to continue such attacks, revealing his insight that he could harm seemingly invulnerable superheroes by going after their vulnerable family members. In response to his threats (and perhaps in retribution for what he had done to Sue), Zatanna altered his memory by request of the larger group. Over the course of the narrative, it is revealed that this was not the only time that the group had chosen to wipe someone's memory and weaken his/her mind. It is ultimately revealed that the murderer is not a supervillain but the lonely ex-wife of The Atom, Jean Loring, who believes that by threatening superheroes' families, she can inspire The Atom to return to protect and love her. While she gets her wish, for a time, her actions force the superheroes to confront past amoral actions. Historically, the superhero genre gave readers a black-and-white sense of authority, transgression and justice. This modern re-telling angered many long-time readers of DC comics; however, it provides an important reflection on the complexity and ubiquity of crime. Nicol, Pulham and McNulty connect crime narratives to the rise of modernity, noting that "crime culture is the point where no easy separation between the criminal and the normal or non-criminal is possible: politics, society, perhaps even modernity itself is shaped by criminality and is impossible to divorce from it" (2011: 9). *Identity Crisis* presents readers with a modern take on the classic superhero narrative, transforming the familiar story of superhero and villain into the unfamiliar superhero crime narrative.

This text exists as a unique piece of graphic crime fiction as a result of its graphic design, textual style and visual iconography. In terms of graphic design, multiple parallel images cause the reader – perhaps unconsciously – to act as a detective, questioning the generic conventions of the superhero/supervillain narrative. For instance, the placement of side-by-side panels throughout the graphic novel pushes the reader to analyse the parallel behaviours of different characters, as that behaviour is emphasised by repetition. One specific moment is of note: As superheroes speculate on the likely guilt of various criminal elements, they form into their traditional squads in order to force confessions from a variety of supervillains. Here, the illustrations reveal how their violent behaviour looks more like that of vigilantes than of superheroes. This juxtaposition of images showcases the violence within each team.

71

Identity Crisis #1–7 © 2004, 2005 DC Comics

Identity Crisis #1–7 © 2004, 2005 DC Comics

Thus, the graphic design (as well as the plot of the story) raises questions about the nature of both crime and punishment, as a variety of characters are and have been sentenced to disturbing and creative punitive measures, without trials, by superheroes who are not impartial, and who perhaps are not even emotionally stable.

Another way that this text works to reform the crime narrative is through textual style. Spoken dialogue appears in standard white speech bubbles; characters' thoughts are visually and verbally depicted as colour-coded rectangular boxes of text. For example, Green Arrow's narration is white lettering placed within a green text box while Robin's narration is presented as red-inked lettering in a yellow text box. In addition to these character boxes, there is an unidentified narrator who announces settings, time and the relationship status of the characters of the story. Because readers have to distinguish between dialogue, thought boxes and narrative analysis by the omniscient narrator, they are reminded that characters they define as a team are individuals who have different rationales and opinions. The colours add another layer as the internal narrative may or may not match the visual imagery being represented in the panel. Readers must employ critical thinking skills in order to decode each panel. In addition, this series, with its varied perspectives, rewards the avid, serial DC comic book reader with its inclusion of a wide range of superheroes and supervillains. Notably, the use of multiple narrators destabilises the stories told by different actors.

The text also exploits established iconography in order to challenge readers. Particularly effective are Meltzer and Morales's depictions of Superman. In his first appearance, Superman is reduced to Clark Kent: An awkward farm boy, crouched in a small kitchen chair, scolded by his Ma. In another sequence of panels, he appears as Superman; here, the panels gradually fade from white to a close-up panel shot of Superman's iconic "S", his arms crossed in front. The decision to focus squarely on the "S" – and its symbolism – for two panels is striking. While not a main character in this story, Superman (as first superhero) is omnipresent in the superhero genre. The early boyish posture contrasted with the later icon of the "S" problematises the historical character of Superman as noble and all-powerful. Thus, the reader's narrative expectations are challenged by the text's visual reframing of familiar symbols.

Conclusion

Crime fiction depicts "characters [...] seek[ing] to break or subvert the codes that regulate modern society" (Nicol et al. 2011: 1), and the disrupting medium of the graphic novel "offers range and versatility with all the potential imagery of film and painting plus the intimacy of the written word" (McCloud 1993: 212). When the story of crime is presented in the medium of the graphic novel, the resulting graphic crime novel combines images and text to tell the story. Readers must actively engage with the medium's format (of the seen combined with the unseen, not-shown) in order to unlock the action and the resolution of the crime narrative. As readers interact with the story of crime and with the medium, deciphering all aspects of plot and form, multiple interpretations become possible. Crime is a complex and significant topic, and notions of criminality arise from personal, moral and societal norms and beliefs. These norms and beliefs vary from person to person and from culture to culture. As the graphic novel provides space for multiple readings (visually, narratively and imaginatively), it also provides a space for writers, artists and readers to rethink the nature of crime.

Bibliography

Anderson, J., Miranda, C. and Pezzotti, B. (eds) (2015) *Serial Crime Fiction: Dying for more*, London: Palgrave Macmillan.

Canalez, J.D. and Guarnido, J. (2010) *Blacksad*, trans. A. Flores and P. Rivera, Milwaukie, OR: Dark Horse Books.

———. (2012) *Blacksad: A silent hell*, trans. K. LaBarbera, Milwaukie, OR: Dark Horse Books.

———. (2014) *Blacksad: Amarillo*, trans. K. LaBarbera and N. Adams, Milwaukie, OR: Dark Horse Books.

Eisner, W. (2008) *Graphic Storytelling and Visual Narrative: Principles and practices from the legendary cartoonist*, New York: W.W. Norton.

Hanley, J. (2012) "Noir justice: law, crime and morality in Diaz Canales and Guarnido's *Blacksad: Somewhere within the shadows* and *Artic-Nation*", *Law Text Culture*, 16: 379–410.

Higginson, P. (2015) "Armed and dangerous: *Le Poulpe* and the formalization of French noir", in Anderson et al., 52–62.

"Industry statistics: publisher market shares: 2018", www.diamondcomics.com/Home/1/1/3/237?articleID=224185 (accessed April 2019).

Jones, G. (2004) *Men of Tomorrow: Geeks, gangsters, and the birth of the comic book*, New York: Basic Books.

McCloud, S. (1993) *Understanding Comics: The invisible art*, New York: William Morrow.

Meltzer, B. and Morales, R. (2015) *Identity Crisis*, Burbank, CA: DC Comics.

Morrison, G. (2012) *Supergods: What masked vigilantes, miraculous mutants, and a sun god from Smallville can teach us about being human*, New York: Spiegel & Grau.

Nicol, B., Pulham, P. and McNulty, E. (2011) *Crime Culture: Figuring criminality in fiction and film*, London: Continuum International Publishing Group.

Petersen, R. (2011) *Comics, Manga, and Graphic Novels: A history of graphic narratives*, Santa Barbara, CA: Praeger.

Phillips, N. and Strobl, S. (2013) *Comic Book Crime: Truth, justice, and the American way*, New York: New York University Press.

Plain, G. (2001) *Twentieth-Century Crime Fiction: Gender, sexuality, and the body*, Edinburgh: Edinburgh University Press.

Scaggs, J. (2005) *Crime Fiction*, London: Routledge.

Sturm, B.W. (2013) "Creativity in the space between: exploring the process of reading graphic novels", *Knowledge Quest*, 41(3): 58–63.

Vaughan, B.K. and Martin, M. (2015) *The Private Eye*, Berkeley, CA: Image Comics.

8
WORLD LITERATURE

Jakob Stougaard-Nielsen

Crime fiction is arguably the most internationalised genre of popular literature; its basic conventions are recognisable across time, space and media, but also rich in local variations and cultural contexts. This confluence of transnational forms and local specificity makes crime fiction a pre-eminent vehicle for exploring the mobility of literary genres, cultural practices and social values across national borders. Crime fiction, therefore, is a pertinent example of world literature, a literary phenomenon, or a mode of reading, which has received increasing attention in twenty-first-century literary studies.

In this chapter, I shall discuss how a world literature approach may set askew the national horizon that has dominated crime fiction studies. Drawing on seminal critical studies by David Damrosch and Franco Moretti, I shall consider attempts to apply these perspectives to the study of crime fiction, including two notable publications with identical titles: Stewart King's article "Crime fiction as world literature" (2014) and the essay collection *Crime Fiction as World Literature* (2017), edited by Louise Nilsson, David Damrosch and Theo D'haen. Finally, I shall discuss the Swedish writer Henning Mankell's *Den vita lejoninnan* (1993) [*The White Lioness*, 1998] as an example of how a world literature perspective may help us read crime fiction across borders.

Though crime fiction has a long history of cross-cultural exchanges, most studies have been concerned with individual national traditions. Particularly in the US and the UK, scholars have rarely engaged with crime fiction beyond the anglophone world, focusing instead on an exclusive canon of "foundational" works from Edgar Allan Poe and Arthur Conan Doyle's "original" detective stories to Agatha Christie's trademark British whodunit and Dashiell Hammett and Raymond Chandler's American hardboiled crime novels. While the dominant presence of Anglo-American crime fiction studies has tended to "universalise" crime fiction in English, studies of crime fiction from outside the English-speaking world have tended to construct their own national canons following the model of the Anglo-American "centre". Traditionally, such studies have noted how foreign "originals" were first translated, then imitated by local writers until, finally, writers began to add nation-specific content, which then helped shape unique national traditions. A representative example is Kerstin Bergman's recent history of Swedish crime fiction. Bergman notes that the first generation of Swedish crime writers in the early twentieth century often used Anglo-American pen names and took Sherlock Holmes as the model for their detectives. In the 1940s, Stieg Trenter added local colour to the British whodunit in his Stockholm mysteries, before Maj Sjöwall and Per Wahlöö's police novels in the 1960s and 1970s "invented" the socio-critical police procedural, which would take root in Sweden, across Scandinavia and beyond (2014: 14–15).

The foregrounding of national frameworks and literary scholarship's preoccupation with literary evolution may go some way towards explaining the dynamics that have shaped crime fiction as a locally-embedded genre with a global reach. However, such a perspective might also overlook more dialogic, unpredictable and border-crossing dynamics, which have become all the more evident in a contemporary transnational marketplace for crime fiction.

Broadening the canon of crime fiction to include a wider range of languages, locations and cultures is not only an issue of inclusivity. We ignore the wider world of crime fiction at the peril of missing a significant trait of the genre: Its intrinsic transnational origins, modes of circulation and attachments. According to Andrew Pepper, "a focus just on the relationship between English and American archetypes overlooks the extent to which the production and circulation of crime fiction has always been a transnational phenomenon" (2016: 7).

Recently, crime fiction scholarship has ventured out into the wider world, bringing the traditional American and European centres into closer proximity with other locations. In addition to offering discussions of works from central crime fiction traditions, Pepper and Schmid's *Globalization and the State in Contemporary Crime Fiction: A World of Crime* (2016) demonstrates the global reach of the genre by making inroads into less well-known locations such as Mexico, Japan and Sweden. A broader selection of traditions allows this collection to explore how crime fiction presents multiple ways in which the central role of the state mediates between the local and the global, and how crime fiction as a genre presents diverse narrative strategies for engaging with the sociopolitical realities of unequal globalisation.

While much can be gained from attending to the global networks through which crime fiction is produced and circulated, generic attachments, intertextual references, linguistic expression, plot and the cultural content of crime narratives (settings, criminal behaviour, the experiences of detectives, etc.) have always crossed borders even when crime narratives appear most local. Doyle's very "British" detective stories, to use an obvious example, took inspiration from traditions and writers from the United States to New Zealand. His stories have spread throughout the world via periodical presses, translations, international and locally-produced TV and film adaptations. Sherlock Holmes's Victorian London was itself intricately connected to faraway places, including those of the British Empire, where Doyle's stories have since been translated, adapted and rewritten to reflect new local contexts. A world literature perspective would consider such transnational networks intrinsic to our understanding of Holmes's literary world and its vast appeal to readers in multiple locations. The stories' international circulation through translations is not only evidence of how different cultures receive and produce their own versions of the famous detective stories, but also of how such new transnational perspectives allow us to see aspects of the original Holmes stories that have previously been overlooked.

Crime fiction is world literature in an entangled world

In his seminal article "Crime fiction as world literature", Stewart King calls for a "denationalization" of crime fiction studies. I shall return to how King describes what such a perspective might entail, but first it must be noted that while world literature is a term with a long history – often associated with Johann Wolfgang von Goethe in the early nineteenth century – it re-entered critical debates around the turn of the millennium as a response to an already ongoing globalisation of literary scholarship and education as well as of the literary field itself.

As a contemporary critical perspective on "literature from around the world", however, world literature has not been accepted without contention. The debate largely hinges on whether a world literature perspective in practice offers an inclusive cosmopolitan approach to the study of literature, as a way to break down the exclusive canon of Western-European literature. To some, a global view of literature may result in an unfortunate homogenisation of a rich diversity of literatures from around the world. By appropriating distinct foreign-language literatures in selective anthologies and translations into "global English", a world literature perspective may, against its cosmopolitan ideals, simply reproduce Anglo-American cultural hegemonies. In other words, the current debate around world literature reveals that a difference in opinion persists about what denationalisation entails in a deeply unequal and mostly "untranslated" world.

King shares concerns with cosmopolitan writers of the nineteenth century such as Goethe who insisted that a national perspective on literature is too narrow and urged his contemporaries to further the course of a universal world literature. The literary field today certainly is more internationalised than it was at any time before the 1970s, when the publishing business, as Eva Hemmungs Wirtén (2009) explains, became dominated by multinational publishing conglomerates, international book fairs and a growing trade in translation rights. However, inequalities in access and dissemination still persist between global and regional publishing centres and their peripheries. Even the most successfully globalised genre fiction enters transnational circulation in a field where "almost 50 percent of all translations are made from English into various languages, but only 6 percent of all translations are into English" (Wirtén 2009: 400). World literature today, then, presents us with a less optimistic cosmopolitan vision of the future than Goethe envisioned. It is, perhaps, better perceived as an entangled economic, cultural, aesthetic and, therefore, methodological problem for literary scholarship rather than simply an intrinsic literary trait that somehow belongs to a universal canon of influential works.

A world literature approach necessarily considers such multiple entanglements in a transnational perspective. If we follow Damrosch's basic definition of world literature as literary works that circulate beyond their culture of origin, then we should consider *how* these works circulate, and what economic or cultural obstacles they have to overcome (2003: 4). A world literature approach to crime fiction may productively consider the networks of the book trade and wider media market that propel the books to reach audiences beyond the culture of origin (Steiner 2014: 316). What, for instance, enabled Stieg Larsson's *Millennium* trilogy, written in a minor language, to become one of the most globally successful publishing phenomena in the first decades of the twenty-first century?

Several chapters in *Crime Fiction as World Literature* take the book trade as a starting point for exploring how crime narratives circulate outside their culture of origin. Karl Berglund proposes that Larsson's success must be viewed in connection with the importance of book fairs, the rise of literary agents and their ability to sell Larsson's appropriation of a globally familiar genre infused with exotic Swedish locations (2017: 84). On the latter point, Jean Anderson, Carolina Miranda and Barbara Pezzotti (2012) have argued that crime fiction trades in such "exotic environments", which bring the genre "into close proximity to travel writing", revealing a genuine interest in other cultures or, perhaps, a less cosmopolitan "desire for a kind of cultural Disneyland" (3).

The ability of contemporary crime writing to enter into transnational circulation might in some cases have less to do with the thrill of the investigation and more to do with desired local settings and cultural representations. The growing interest in crime fiction from around the world may, therefore, eventually lead away from a cosmopolitan world literature perspective to a

World literature

consideration of crime fiction as nothing more than a pertinent example of "global literature", propelled by market forces that capitalise on the exposure, management and exploitation of exotically different local expressions.

Such reflections on the obstacles and opportunities for the circulation of crime stories are in tune with King's understanding of a world literature perspective, which entails "a shift from studying the production of crime fiction to its consumption. That is, a shift from writers to readers" (13) – with the caveat, I would add, that consumer behaviour in the global marketplace for crime fiction is intricately entangled with the conditions and modes of production that drive the book trade. According to King, a "world-literature approach could profitably study the reception of particular novels in different parts of the world" (16).

It is not only contemporary crime fiction that can fruitfully be viewed from the perspective of its impact on readers and writers around the world. With this perspective we can also study how classic texts have travelled, found readers and new meanings along existing routes of trade and empire. A pertinent example is offered by Damrosch, who explores Holmes's global connections in the exiled Tibetan writer Jamyang Norbu's widely acclaimed "Holmes novel", *The Mandala of Sherlock Holmes* (1999). Damrosch argues for considering Norbu's crime novel an example of Tibetan world literature by emphasising the author's use of Doyle's global model of detective fiction as a frame, his creative use of linguistic and cultural hybridisation, and the novel's indebtedness to local Tibetan history and religion. Norbu's hybrid adaptation or rewriting of Doyle's Holmes produces thereby a new, localised version imbued with an anti-imperialist and humanist purpose, which, Damrosch argues, is already encoded, but rarely seen by Western readers, in the "original" Holmes tales themselves (Damrosch 2017).

A world literature perspective, therefore, finds literary value in translated and transformed texts, traditionally held to be corrupted versions of original national literatures. This is a keystone in Damrosch's understanding of world literature as literature that "gains in translation", which points to the added and changing meanings gained when a work of literature travels beyond its country and language of origin (2003: 281).

Crime fiction is world literature that gains by generic reproducibility

Franco Moretti is arguably the literary scholar who has presented the most obvious, but also controversial, method for the study of crime fiction as world literature. Usually associated with "distant reading" (considering large samples of literary works studied through selections of shared devices, as opposed to more traditional, detailed "close reading" of fewer texts), Moretti's studies of how novels have spread over time and geographical space to form a "literary world system" place genre at the very centre of inquiry (2000: 57). Moretti's mapping of how genre devices travel across national traditions is one way in which we may read crime fiction from a "denationalized" perspective. A "distant reading" method would allow us to consider a much wider sample of crime fictions from around the world, thereby providing us with "insights into the global reach of the genre" (King 2014: 10).

Paradoxically, the most significant aspect of crime fiction, which until relatively recently made it a marginalised form within literary studies, turns out to be its most suggestive asset if viewed from Moretti's world literature perspective – that is, the reproducibility of conventional forms across languages and periods (King 2014: 15). In Moretti's distant view of the diffusion of the modern novel, waves of foreign forms interfere with the rooted tree-like structures of national traditions, a process which adds new dimensions to the global form of the novel itself (2000: 67). When perceiving world literature from a more distant view on the scale of genre, Moretti holds, literary texts are "*always* a compromise between foreign form and local materials" (60). Viewing the history of crime fiction from this perspective could lead us to explore how, for instance, the hardboiled detective novel has evolved from Chandler's mean streets of Los Angeles to Ian Rankin's Edinburgh or Jo Nesbø's Oslo, and how the "foreign form" of the hardboiled genre has interfered with the "local materials" of their different national settings and traditions.

In a similar vein, King has pointed out that crime fiction scholars could practise a world literature approach by analysing "the use of a particular literary device across time and place" (15). King suggests one could productively study the so-called "locked-room mystery", which is what David Schmid has attempted. Schmid's discussion of the diffusion of this spatial genre device begins with the locked room as it represents "the smallest functioning unit of space in the genre" (2012: 10). Schmid then proceeds to scale up the represented spaces from country houses and "mean streets" to end with neoliberal capitalism and global crimes encroaching on local lives in Mexican crime novels. This scaled-up model of how crime fiction genres have evolved, from the very local to the global, begs the question whether the genre is as capable of representing the mostly invisible violence of neoliberal globalisation as it has been able to frame solutions to the puzzle-crimes of the locked-room mystery.

Damrosch is to a lesser degree than Moretti interested in the evolution of formal aspects of literature or in mapping the spread of genres across borders. He holds that world literature essentially is a "mode of reading", what he calls "a detached engagement with a world beyond our own", one that helps us "appreciate the ways in which a literary work reaches out and away from its point of origin" (2003: 297, 300). While Moretti sees world literature as presenting a "formal compromise" between foreign genres and local content, Damrosch insists on the codependence of the domestic and the foreign, the local and the global, as central to a world literature perspective: "works become world literature by being received into the space of a foreign culture, a space defined in many ways by the host culture's national tradition", making a single work of world literature "the locus of a negotiation between two different cultures" (283). This perspective is applied in several of the contributions to *Crime Fiction as World Literature*. Here examples of crime fiction from around the world are considered "glocal": Mexican narconovelas and a transnational detective novel such as Mũkoma wa Ngũgĩ's *Nairobi Heat*, for instance, are taken to exemplify how global forms and transnational crimes both penetrate and are transformed by local lives, traditions and communities: "[a]t once highly stylized and intensely localized", the editors of the volume conclude, "crime fiction is a pre-eminently 'glocal' mode of literary creation and circulation" (4).

A world literature perspective on genre, according to Wai Chee Dimock (2006), may be the tool literary scholars need in order to rethink their analytical object, their field, beyond the traditional divisions of "discrete" national literatures. For Dimock, genres are always "in transit", where likeness is determined by open-ended kinships rather than based on direct lines of ancestry (2006: 86). In this view, she departs from Moretti's more evolutionary centre-to-periphery conjectures on the geographic spread of genres, as she emphasises the reversibility of influences and suggests a more contingent basis on which to explore generic likeness across history and cultures. An example of how to read crime fiction as a glocal genre in transit between different local settings is Pepper's study of how the genre has been used over three centuries in different locations: "to assimilate complex, ambivalent critiques of state power, and society as it is organized under capitalism, into narratives which imaginatively weigh up the competing and overlapping claims of the individual, morality, community, justice, and the law" (2016: 5). The aim of Pepper's world literature approach is to:

draw attention to the multiple influences and constituent parts and indeed elasticity of the form, something that encourages variety and allows writers to inflect their narratives in different ways and in relation to different political ends and different historical contexts.

(5)

While asking us to track how books and genres move across the globe and take residence in diverse locations, a world literature perspective on crime fiction also asks us to compare the multiple ways that crime fiction imagines and theorises entangled locations and worlds; for instance, how the genre is both informed by and takes part in shaping cultural and social perspectives on questions of justice and the law, race, gender and class. To this end, King suggests that a world literature perspective could productively investigate how crime novels provide their readers with "windows" through which diverse societies might be observed (14). We could, for instance, ask how crime novels from different countries and traditions "give local expression to such global phenomena as human trafficking, human rights, upheavals in gender, class, or political relations, and globalization itself" (Nilsson et al. 2017: 5).

Crime fiction can enter world literature by processes very different from the transnational circulation of stories through translation or generic reproducibility by simply, as Damrosch suggests, "bringing the world directly into the text itself" (2018: 107). This occurs most explicitly when writers send their characters abroad or when works are set abroad, whereby narratives will inevitably engage "in a process of cultural translation, representing foreign customs for the writer's home audience" (108). Crime writers have sent their detectives abroad and explored multiple locations throughout the genre's history; by the twenty-first century, crime fiction covers the globe and fictional detectives track border-crossing crimes sometimes across continents.

Henning Mankell's Wallander series as world literature

The Swedish writer Henning Mankell has not only been central to the international success of Scandinavian crime fiction, offering readers "windows" through which to see his native Sweden, but has also contributed to the "worlding" of the genre by sending his Swedish detective abroad. His series featuring the melancholic police inspector Kurt Wallander has been translated into more than forty languages and has been remade for the screen in both Swedish and British adaptations. Beginning with *Mördare utan ansikte* (1991) [*Faceless Killers*, 1997] the series is mostly set in the small Swedish town of Ystad on the Baltic coast, where Wallander is, on the one hand, the police novel's generic representative of the state and, on the other, someone who finds himself out of place and out of time in this role. Far from a cosmopolitan, Wallander is a troubled nostalgic, increasingly anxious about a rot eating away at his ideal, socially harmonious Swedish welfare state: A corrosion variously connected, in his assessment, to an increase in violence, rampant racism, a general lack of solidarity and social conflicts arising from the arrival of foreigners in Sweden. Mankell's Wallander novels are, therefore, an obvious case for consideration within a world literature perspective as they are locally anchored, reproduce an international genre, have been widely translated and even found new life in TV adaptations outside of Sweden – the latter of which is particularly interesting from an intermedial world literature perspective. Set in Sweden using mostly British actors, the BBC production featuring Kenneth Branagh as Wallander employs set design and locations beset with nostalgic longing for an exotic 1950s Golden Age Sweden, reflecting both contemporary British imagologies and Wallander's own nostalgia, while the darker Swedish adaptations foreground his melancholic demeanour. Mankell's Swedish police novel, therefore, exemplifies Damrosch's notion of world literature as "a literary work [that] manifests differently abroad than it does at home" (2003: 6), and is another example of contemporary "glocal" crime fiction.

Slavoj Žižek has suggested that the significance of Mankell's police procedural is that it is a "perfect illustration of the fate of the detective novel in the era of global capitalism" (2003: 24). The Wallander series illustrates how the crime novel's setting has become bounded by "the specific locale, a particular provincial environment" as a "dialectical counterpart" to the globalised world, where, Žižek concludes, "a detective story can take place almost anywhere" (2003: 24). However, what makes Mankell's police procedural a good example of crime fiction as world literature, is not merely its rootedness in a "provincial environment"; it is, perhaps more importantly, the always present and uneasy attachments of himself and his affluent Sweden to global Others and elsewhere, as suggested by the fact that several of the novels' brief prologues are set in the "Global South" (the mostly low-income and often politically marginalised regions of Latin America, Asia and Africa) before the action moves to Ystad.

Rather than suggesting that the senseless violence and the general denigration of morals in the Swedish welfare state are caused by outside forces, Mankell employs Swedish and foreign localities as windows into disparate locations that, as Žižek suggests, "stand for different aspects of the same constellation". There might be echoes of each locality in its opposite, yet "the effect is an insistence on the irreparable split in the global constellation" (2003: 24). To Žižek, Mankell's most important insight is that the two worlds will necessarily remain separated; no translation is possible between the two in an age of globalised capitalism. Therefore, Žižek does not care much for those Wallander novels where Mankell has sent his detective out of Ystad and where the plot is divided more equally between home and abroad.

However, it is precisely in *The White Lioness*, set partly in South Africa, that we may see how this Swedish crime novel can be read as world literature. It is a crime novel that circulates outside of its national tradition, engages with (unequal) international exchange, and presents a spatial structure of cultural interferences. Through its form and narrative, *The White Lioness* offers windows into other worlds that also reflect back on the detective's Swedish home, a home that has already from the first novel, in Wallander's mind, become a foreign country itself. With *The White Lioness*, Wallander becomes, in the words of Michael Tapper, "a small time cop in a drama of world politics" (2014: 171), as he hunts and is being hunted by a former KGB agent. Together with a local black South African, the Russian mercenary is working for a racist, secretive Boer society and has been tasked with assassinating the recently freed Nelson Mandela. By setting geographical nodes off against each other (the fall of the Soviet Union, Sweden's post-welfare state and post-apartheid South Africa) Mankell uses the transnational police procedural to explore changing and competing notions of race, justice and sociopolitical change. Set partly in the globally exposed early years of post-apartheid South Africa, the novel's dramatisation of competing worldviews specific to such other "worlds" inevitably affect even the "small", local world of a brilliant but also notoriously flawed, at times bigoted, Swedish cop.

It is ultimately Wallander's personal flaws and his inability to comprehend the global scale and ideological undercurrents driving the changes he is witnessing from his peripheral perspective that allow him to become "transformatively entangled with Others", as Andrew Nestingen has suggested (2008: 252). Rather than confirming an inevitably split and "untranslatable" world order, at least part of Wallander's global popularity and his influence on South African crime writers such as Deon Meyer, relates to his very human solidarity – a solidarity not devoid of ambiguities but one that "challenges one's own worldview and rational categories" (252). Meyer, whose first crime novel was published in Afrikaans (the language of the apartheid oppressors) in 1994, became part of a surge in crime fiction published in post-apartheid South Africa. Reminiscent of Mankell's ambiguous detective, Meyer has used crime fiction and the thriller to investigate South Africa as a postcolonial contact zone, where the borders between guilt and innocence, perpetrators and victims, are fraught and blurry. For instance, his thriller *Heart of the Hunter* (2003), also written in Afrikaans, whose hero is a black anti-apartheid former KGB assassin, inserts a compromised hero into an unfolding border-crossing narrative about the complex history and ongoing political tribulations and transformations of his country.

When Mankell in the early 1990s uses his crime novel to explore the vulnerable political transition of post-apartheid South Africa, the narrative becomes one of entanglements between a global story about the dark forces that seek to maintain authoritarian and racist regimes around the world and a Swedish story about a country still traumatised by the assassination of the Social Democratic Prime Minister Olof Palme in 1986. Palme being a famously outspoken anti-apartheid advocate, conspiracies have circulated in Sweden about the involvement of vengeful supporters of apartheid in his murder – a still unsolved case that has haunted and tainted the Swedish police and provided material for countless Swedish crime novels.

In *The White Lioness*, Mankell offers a localised Swedish window through which to view unfolding historical events on a different continent – local events that were, of course, thoroughly entangled with Sweden's own recent past and a wider world of geopolitics. Ultimately, a world literature perspective on Mankell's Wallander series and border-crossing crime fiction in general demonstrates the extent to which the transnational crime genre provides a literary form to contain the vast scale of a globalising world as it is saturating and affecting the small scale of localised human experience and even the worlds of "small time" detectives. Necessarily, the worlding of Mankell's crime novel will translate differently into various host countries and may give rise to adaptations, genre mutations and new localised ways in which to imagine the possibility for dialogue, solidarity and cosmopolitan visions across multiple borders.

Bibliography

Anderson, J., Miranda, C. and Pezzotti, B. (eds) (2012) *The Foreign in International Crime Fiction: Transcultural representations*, London: Continuum.

Berglund, K. (2017) "With a global market in mind: agents, authors, and the dissemination of contemporary Swedish crime fiction", in Nilsson et al., 77–90.

Bergman, K. (2014) *Swedish Crime Fiction: The making of Nordic noir*, Milan: Mimesis.

Damrosch, D. (2003) *What is World Literature?* Princeton, NJ: Princeton University Press.

———. (2017) "A sinister chuckle: Sherlock in Tibet", in Nilsson et al., 257–70.

———. (2018) *How to Read World Literature*, 2nd edn, Oxford: Wiley-Blackwell.

Dimock, W.C. (2006) "Genre as world system: epic and novel on four continents", *Narrative*, 14(1): 85–101.

King, S. (2014) "Crime Fiction as world literature", *Clues*, 32(2): 8–19.

Mankell, H. (2012) *The White Lioness*, trans. L. Thompson, London: Vintage.

Moretti, F. (2000) "Conjectures on world literature", *New Left Review*, 1: 54–68.

Nestingen, A. (2008) *Crime and Fantasy in Scandinavia: Fiction, film, and social change*, Seattle: University of Washington Press.

Nilsson, L., Damrosch, D. and D'haen, T. (eds) (2017) *Crime Fiction as World Literature*, New York: Bloomsbury Academic.

Pepper, A. (2016) *Unwilling Executioner: Crime fiction and the state*, Oxford: Oxford University Press.

Pepper, A. and Schmid, D. (2016) "Introduction: Globalization and the state in contemporary crime fiction", in A. Pepper and D. Schmid (eds), *Globalization and the State in Contemporary Crime Fiction: A world of crime*, London: Palgrave Macmillan, 1–20.

Schmid, D. (2012) "From the locked room to the globe: space in crime fiction", in V. Miller and H. Oakley (eds), *Cross-Cultural Connections in Crime Fiction*, Houndmills: Palgrave, 7–23.

Steiner, A. (2014) "World literature and the book market", in T. D'haen, D. Damrosch and D. Kadir (eds), *The Routledge Companion to World Literature*, London: Routledge, 316–24.

Tapper, M. (2014) *Swedish Cops: From Sjöwall and Wahlöö to Stieg Larsson*, Bristol: Intellect.

Wirtén, E.H. (2009) "The global market 1970–2000: producers", in S. Eliot and J. Rose (eds), *A Companion to The History of the Book*, Oxford: Wiley-Blackwell, 395–405.

Žižek, S. (2003) "Parallax", *London Review of Books*, 25(22): 24.

9

TRANSLATION

Karen Seago and Victoria Lei

Translation is central to crime fiction – from its very beginnings, the genre has constituted itself in and through translation with global patterns of circulation and influence. Edgar Allan Poe's stories of ratiocination (1841–1844), written in English by an American, set in Paris with a French amateur investigator, perfectly illustrate the transnational interconnectedness of the genre. Translated into French in 1856 by Charles Baudelaire, the Dupin trilogy shaped Emile Gaboriau's influential detective novels (1866–1876), and these in turn inspired successful and influential detective writers in America, Australia and, most famously, Arthur Conan Doyle in Britain. Much of the critical literature argues that the Anglo-American model is the dominant form which either introduced crime fiction as a genre (Stougaard-Nielsen 2016: 2), or which displaced resident national traditions across Europe and beyond, primarily through translations of Doyle's Sherlock Holmes stories and Agatha Christie's novels. But there is evidence of early forms of the genre in many countries and recent research indicates that such uni-directional transmission from English to other languages and cultures does not in fact capture the circulation and locally-specific iterations of detective fiction. The Dutch market not only imported English detective fiction but also translations from the German and French, as did Turkey, China and, to a lesser degree, Spain and Italy.

Much of the research into crime fiction as an international genre addresses historical developments in genre conventions, how national canons are shaped in specific cultural and socio-lingual contexts and how the movement across these contexts may influence the receiving culture. Bassnett (2017), for example, outlines the interconnectedness of European crime fiction writers whose critical-political focus on working through the traumas of the past she compares to the open-endedness of the American hardboiled thriller. She contrasts this to the formulaic clue puzzles of Agatha Christie or the TV series *Midsomer Murders* with their idealised Englishness and reassuring closure. The unprecedented sales figures of translated crime fiction indicate for Bassnett that critical and escapist crime fiction cater for different readers and their varied needs, which range from reassurance in an uncertain world via an interest in the foreign through armchair tourism to a critical engagement with global criminality. One of the problems in (some) edited collections with an international focus is that even though they recognise the genre's interconnectedness and the transnational flow of texts and conventions, the relationship between national traditions is not explicitly addressed (King 2014: 12). There is a need for crime fiction research to widen its perspective and consider writers, texts and readers in dialogue with each other across borders.

In much of the research, translation is considered only as an enabling mechanism for border crossing without discussing the act of translation itself. The body of work on the reception of translated texts, the influence and effects of translation as well as the genre-specific constraints of crime fiction translation is smaller. In this chapter we discuss these aspects in terms of how the lowbrow status of the genre on the one hand, and of Anglo-American prestige on the other directly impact on editorial policies (what to translate) and translation strategies (how to translate), shaping how individual national traditions and genre conventions develop over time. A case study of the international circulation of Chinese *Judge Dee* stories illustrates the evolution of this tradition in and through translation. Our contention is that although crime fiction is embedded in a specific time and place with its legal, social and cultural norms, translation strategies tend to domesticate this cultural specificity. The second part of the chapter focuses more specifically on the process of translation. What are the effects of domesticating translation choices on the puzzle-solving, armchair tourism or social critique of crime fiction and what are the specific translation challenges which the generic requirements of crime fiction pose?

Translation and the development of national traditions

English translations decisively affected local traditions. In the mid-1930s, 40% of all detective fiction published in Germany was translated from the English (Sturge 2004: 181) and was so prestigious that home-produced detective fiction tended to be published under English-sounding pseudonyms. They were set in Britain or America with Anglo-American characters, suggesting to the reader that they were also imported texts. The combination of English translations and pseudo-translations dominating the publishing environment is surprisingly consistent across Europe in the first half of the twentieth century. France, with its own strong tradition, presents a slightly different picture – we see a playful intertextual engagement, for example, in Maurice Leblanc's *Arsène Lupin Versus Herlock Sholmès* stories (1906–1907) where the French gentleman thief matches his wits against the English prototype (Fornasiero and West-Sooby 2019: 31–32). It was only after World War II that translations and pseudo-translations took up a similarly central position and French-authored texts written in the American style monopolised the market, offering a "redefinition of the French national identity" (Rolls et al. 2016: 139). Established in September 1945 by Marcel Duhamel, Gallimard's *Série Noire* celebrates its seventy-fifth anniversary in 2020 with a list that still focuses primarily on translations. The first three books in the series were translated by Duhamel in what became the series' translation policy of adapting and heavily domesticating, and marketed as American even though the branding *traduit de l'américain* was a "hoax": They were written by British authors posing as Americans (Rolls and Sitbon 2013: 43, 50). French originals were only published as pseudo-translations in the late 1940s and early 1950s and the series *Minuit* (founded in 1941) published nothing but pseudo-translations (Robyns 1990: 24–6). Translations of the hardboiled novel introduced more complex narration, free indirect discourse and longer descriptive passages, shaping the development of French crime tradition into the late 1960s and early 1970s (38). The Anglo-American model similarly inspired and shaped emergent Spanish and Italian traditions.

In the second half of the twentieth century, all European literatures established strong local crime fiction traditions; nevertheless, translation remains an integral feature of the crime fiction market with a share of up to 30% in European countries, and even the notoriously low 3% of translation into English is somewhat higher for crime fiction (Büchler and Trentacosti

2015). Of course, European crime fiction was translated into English, notably by Simenon and Swedish writers Sjöwall and Wahlöö, but it was only in the early twenty-first century that the success of Scandinavian crime novels and TV series led to a boom of translation into English. The "Scandinoir" phenomenon opened the English-speaking market to crime fiction from other European countries, contributing to a reported rise in revenue of 12% in translated crime fiction between 2005 and 2010 (Alter 2010: online) according to the latest figures available. Branding became an important feature in placing European crime for an English reader. Texts from Germany, Italy, Spain and other countries were marketed as "Euronoir", while Scandinavian texts, such as Pia Juul's Danish *The Murder of Halland* (2015), which despite its title was not crime fiction proper in its country of origin, in translation became a crime text under the Scandinoir label. In their border crossing, these books not only transferred the text into a new lingua-cultural environment but experienced marked paratextual changes so that their cover design, typeface and endorsements contributed and conformed to the brand identity of a genre in translation – in this case, Scandinavian or Nordic crime fiction (Broomé 2014: 109).

Translation strategies and editorial policies

Status, whether the prestige of the Anglo-American "import" or the disregard for a lowbrow, pulp genre, is at the core of translation and pseudo-translations in the crime genre. Resistance by critics, writers, academics, the Church and the authorities to the cheap entertainment of genre literature also shaped translational and editorial policies, especially with state intervention regulating translation and publication of foreign texts in Germany and Italy in the 1930s and 1940s and in Spain until the 1970s. Sturge, for example, shows how the majority of texts translated into German were abridged – often to fit with series formats – with an average 20% of material omitted. In extreme cases all elements that did not contribute directly to the plot were cut, and deleted text could go up to just under 50%. Problematic features such as effeminacy or swearing were adjusted, while gender stereotypes were reinforced, removing agency from women but increasing masculine decision-making and self-sufficiency (Sturge 2004: 167, 211).

But it is not only state censorship that enforces strict rules on style and content in the translation of crime fiction. Publishing restrictions and editorial input also play a decisive role in strategic decisions on how a text is positioned in the target market. A good example of this is Duhamel's translation policy for the *Série Noire* which laid down strict guidelines on length, tone and style. This created an invented working-class/gangster argot, privileging humour, action, violence and anxiety (Higginson 2015: 60) and producing a distinctive voice and atmosphere. Only very few texts by famous authors were not subjected to omissions in the process of translation. Overall, the textual and stylistic complexity was reduced and characters, setting, mode and voice were subordinated to plot requirements (Robyns 1990: 37).

Such interventionist approaches are rare these days, but in any translation, decisions have to be made to what degree a text needs to accommodate the target language and culture. Translation strategies are determined by a number of factors: The status of the respective languages involved, the status of the text or author to be translated, and whether the receiving culture is familiar with the genre or author. Translation into English and translation of minor genres tends to adapt to target norms linguistically, culturally and generically. But accommodating the target reader by replacing culturally specific features with general ones removes the text from its context and impacts on layers of meaning that may convey social critique and cultural identity. An example is the small-time crook Nathan in Jay Rayner's *The Oyster House Siege* (2007) who seeks to construct his identity through wearing expensive labels, whose associations with class, old money and respectability as well as a distinct sense of place and entitlement may be lost in translation:

> He was wearing a salmon pink shirt with a double cuff by Lewin's of Jermyn Street and a wide-shouldered navy-blue double-breasted suit from Gieves and Hawkes of Savile Row. His brogues were from Church's and his tie [...] came from Liberty.
>
> *(Rayner 2007: 270)*

Reed (2016) discusses how domesticating or generalising translation choices of culturally specific features smooth out the otherness of the Australian outback and of Aboriginal identity in the French translation of Philip McLaren's *Scream Black Murder* (2002). She shows, for example, how the rendering of "community canteen" as "salles des fêtes village" (village hall) obscures both the function of social management and the rudimentary nature of life in the Australian outback. Community canteens were established to limit illicit drinking by providing a very basic pub-like shack and the French replaces this with genteel associations of afternoon teas and village fetes. Historical space and geographical place are crucial in crime fiction: Physical locations, the textures of social and cultural life, the boundaries of legality and the fabric of laws, norms and conventions are known by the reader of the original text from direct experience. In translation, this background knowledge needs to be conveyed in a way that does not interfere with the reading experience but avoids dislocating or relocating the text.

In transnational circulation, this embodiment of culture in a text creates a "national allegory", especially in a genre that is so embedded in its national context (Rolls et al. 2016: 137). Reed shows how the French translation frames an Australian national representation which neutralises and misrepresents Aboriginal identity. Under Duhamel's editorship, the *Série Noire's* "national allegory" reads the translated American hardboiled as a space of engagement with the harsh realities of occupation and liberation in France, creating a multilayered myth of the USA in and of post-war France (Rolls and Sitbon 2013: 40). King and Whitmore (2016) discuss how the development of Catalan crime fiction contributes to the emergent identity and independence of a minority culture in two ways: An "incorporation and adaptation of an American national allegory" (146) through translation into Catalan (rather than the dominant Spanish) and an exportation of a Catalan independent identity through translation into European languages.

Judge Dee in international circulation

If crime fiction is a privileged means of presenting and re-presenting the nation, then Chinese crime fiction in its exchanges with Western forms of the genre offers a fascinating study of its international circulation and multidirectional influences. The translational afterlife of the ancient Chinese *Gong An* (court-case fiction) format is a case in point. Compiled into print collections between the sixteenth and seventeenth centuries, these often rambling stories with large casts of characters focus on a celebrated judge who solves crimes through insight but also with supernatural help (Seago and Lei 2014: 320). Chinese translations of the first four Sherlock Holmes stories appeared between October 1896 and May 1897 in the *Current Affairs Newspaper* (*Shi Wu Bao*), which was the most important newspaper for the late Qing reformists; and another twenty-five stories followed by 1906. The Holmes translations contributed decisively to China's engagement with modernity in terms of social equality, rational scientific argument and democratic freedom (Seago and Lei 2014: 321). The initial impact of Doyle's stories was more in terms of content than of generic innovation: These early translations were adapted quite heavily to the conventions of *Gong An* with its lack of suspense and linear narrative structure.

Translation

For example, early Holmes translations tended to reveal the solution to the mystery in the title: Doyle's 1891 story "A case of identity" was translated with the title "A case about a step-father defrauding his stepdaughter" (1897). The narrative was re-structured to conform to the linear model of *Gong An*, and Watson's first-person narrative account becomes a more distanced, omniscient third-person narrator providing additional explanatory background information.

This early phase of adaption to the Chinese model also saw a passionate debate over literary conventions leading to a gradual shift towards adopting the Western paradigm and creating a modern tradition of Chinese detective fiction. Depicting a modern, rational, just and law-governed society, the *Zhen Tan* replaced the older *Gong An* tradition. Due to a number of political and cultural developments, including several periods when the traditional stories were explicitly banned, *Gong An* were no longer available in China by the mid-twentieth century, although anecdotal evidence suggests that books were kept and passed on in private possession. It was the interest of Western scholars and authors in "authentic Chinese crime fiction" that unearthed copies of two examples, the *Dee Gong An* (anon: c. 1890[1]), translated by the sinologist Robert van Gulik as *Celebrated Cases of Judge Dee* (1949), and the *Long Tu Gong An* (anon: c. 1600), translated by Leon Comber as *The Strange Cases of Magistrate Pao: Chinese Tales of Crime and Detection* (1964). Both translations were extracts – the first thirty chapters of the *Dee Gong An* and only six stories out of over a hundred in the *Long Tu Gong An* – and their selection and translation strategies construct a particular view – a national allegory – of China's brutal past and exotic orientalism comprising supernatural interventions, torture and sexually voracious women, especially in the case of Comber's translation (Seago and Lei 2014). In contrast, van Gulik's interest was a more scholarly, literary and cultural one, concerned to introduce the *Gong An* as a genre to Western readers. To conform to some extent to Western expectations, van Gulik smoothed out some of the "excesses" of the Chinese versions by reducing the large number of characters, the rambling story lines, irrelevant details, the focus on torture and punishment and reliance on the supernatural. But he attempted to keep as many of the Chinese tropes as possible, creating an image of an ancient culture with wise but exotic deployment of justice. His English translation was very successful (it is still available in print) and was the basis for relay translations into other languages, among them French and German. Between 1953 and 1966, van Gulik also wrote his own *Judge Dee* series, motivated by the wish to keep alive a genre that was no longer current in China. These authored stories were then translated into Chinese by Chen and Hu in the 1980s and 1990s, but van Gulik also self-translated at least one of them in 1953. Chen and Hu's quite faithful rendering formed the basis for intersemiotic translations into fourteen episodes of a TV series, *Dee Case Legend*, in 1986, followed by a further fifty episodes in 1996, which are still available on the internet. The success of the *Dee Case Legend* meant that in 2004, China Central TV commissioned the *Detective Dee* series, which by 2018 had reached 226 episodes and is still ongoing. This series was based on Chinese-authored scripts by Qian Yanqiu, which were compiled into a four-volume novel and published by China Social Sciences Publishing House between 2006 and 2011. Between 2014 and 2015, two different TV spin-off series, *Young Sherlock* and *The Famous Detective Dee*, were produced by three different mainland TV studios with a total of fifty-two episodes, and in 2010 and 2013, Hark Tsui directed two internationally successful, award-winning films: *Detective Dee and the Mystery of the Phantom Flame* and *Young Detective Dee: Rise of the Sea Dragon*.

This complex circulation of *Judge Dee* from Chinese into English and English into Chinese translation, as well as in the form of pseudo-translations within English and intersemiotic translations within Chinese, offers fascinating insights into flows of adaptation and development between central and peripheral literatures. It shows that the reintroduction of an English-adapted Chinese genre on the whole does not result in a restitution of Chinese tropes.

Changes do occur in the Chinese TV spin-offs and film adaptations, but the representation of gender is the only feature which returns to the more traditional conceptualisations of *Gong An*. Torture, the supernatural and bloated narratives generate considerable audience discussion in blogs and posts, which clearly reject these features. In many original stories, the supernatural plays a constitutive role in identifying the criminal in the Chinese text. In all translations and adaptations, this feature is either omitted, replaced with rational explanations or discredited through plot developments that suggest supernatural intervention, which is subsequently unveiled as a villainous deception. Focus on the two ancient Chinese tropes of torture and supernatural intervention reveals a certain anxiety over the image of China as a modern, rational and just state and this becomes explicit in the film *Detective Dee and the Mystery of the Phantom Flame* (2010) when Judge Dee says: "never use torture to gain a confession because that is what makes our regime unpopular". Narrative excess in terms of plot development and large casts were both reduced, and this economy was maintained even in the TV series, a format which permits less end-focused storytelling and a much larger cast of characters. But audience reception clearly indicated a lack of interest in reintroducing the narrative digressions of traditional Chinese *Gong An*, with viewers commenting favourably on the lack of redundancies and the tight narrative. Viewer feedback and blogs explicitly addressed to what extent the translations and TV series were "faithful" to van Gulik's pseudo-translations; the status of van Gulik's stories as the authoritative model is further reinforced by negative audience reception to the Chinese-authored TV scripts, which were condemned for their flabby narrative structure and plot-irrelevant digressions. Thus, the anglophone model of crime fiction has largely replaced Chinese *Gong An* tropes, to the point that Chinese fans appear to view the van Gulik pseudo-translations (and their Chinese translations) as the original *Judge Dee*, erasing the traditional Chinese *Gong An* version. However, digitisation and widespread internet access have made many supposedly lost *Gong An* collections available and they are increasingly popular, with *Gong An* and Western-inflected van Gulik stories existing side-by-side. This raises the question whether perhaps Chinese reception does not perceive van Gulik's versions of *Judge Dee* as an adapted form of *Gong An*, but sees it as a separate, distinct strand of traditional Chinese detective fiction. This is a question for further research.

Translation effects and genre-specific challenges

Research into the effects of translation on the text addresses how variable sociocultural expectations shape the rendering of culturally specific features, the handling of tropes, style and non-representational language, as well as particularities of place, history and social context. The translation of issues such as slang and swearing, representations of non-normative sexuality or gender performance under conditions of censorship has garnered particular interest, with consistent findings indicating that these aspects are frequently omitted or standardised (Linder 2011; Epstein 2011). However, gender norms continue to exert considerable influence in shaping translation decisions around women's use of slang, swearing and non-standard language in "inappropriate" contexts. Translations of American crime writer Sarah Paretsky's feminist PI, Swedish female characters in novels by Maj Sjöwall and Per Wahlöö and Stieg Larsson's Lisbeth Salander show that the use of non-standard language by these female characters tends to be standardised, or at least toned down, but is maintained or increased if used by sexually "deviant" characters (Epstein 2011, Seago 2018). Dialect poses particular problems, especially when it supports characterisation as in Andrea Camilleri's Inspector Montalbano, who uses a mixture of standard Italian, Sicilian and a made-up Sicilian-inflected version of Italian, depending on who he talks to. This gives insights into degrees of familiarity, respect or contempt, which is

Translation

lost in the toned-down and to some extent standardised rendering. The loss of *sicilianità* in particular means that the strongly emphasised cultural context is reduced to clichés about food, the Mafia, etc. (Kapsaskis and Artegiani 2016), replacing regional diversity with a national stereotype. Translated crime fiction arguably conforms to a greater extent to genre requirements than originally written crime fiction, foregrounding plot and losing literary, aesthetic and cultural complexity. Anderson, for example, has shown how translations of Léo Malet lose the stylistic dimension and ludic play which characterise his work (Anderson 2014), while Sturge's analysis shows that extraneous detail including doubt, self-parody and humour is removed or slimmed down (Sturge 2004: 235).

So far only two edited volumes (Cadera and Pavić Pintarić 2014 and Seago et al. 2014) focus on the specific demands of translating crime fiction and to what extent genre conventions may impose constraints on translational choices and decisions. Cadera and Pavić Pintarić bring together detailed analyses of source and target texts which address the creation of suspense through voice, perspective and narrative structures across a range of literary and audiovisual formats. Seago et al. also address the generic demands the translator has to negotiate, analysing, amongst others, rhetorical structures, place and stereotyped discourse. Crime fiction is, of course, highly culturally specific; legal frameworks determine what counts as a crime and these definitions differ across cultures, even in relation to apparently universal criminal acts such as murder or internationally understood criminal organisations such as the mafia. Terminology in crime fiction comes from a wide range of fields, including politics, jurisprudence and law enforcement, as well as associated areas of expertise in medicine, forensics, pathology, psychology, IT technology and any field that impacts on the investigation or is relevant to the plot. Getting the discourse of experts right plays an important role in creating a plausible and believable textual world, but part of this verisimilitude is also the ability to negotiate the code-switching between specialist communication, general language and in-group slang used by the police, medics, legal experts, IT boffins and also, of course, criminals.

Terminology can be researched, but much crime fiction translation requires in-depth and nuanced cultural and social knowledge in both the source and target culture for the translator to be able to pick up on the suggestions, clues and misdirections which create a text whose coherence needs to be constructed and reconstructed. The different subgenres of crime fiction will have a different focus on puzzle-solving, social critique, action or suspense, all of which pose a variety of different translatorial challenges. But they all rely on a narrative structure which involves the solution to the why, who, what and how of the crime. And it is not only the detective in the text who is investigating the motives, means and suspects, identifying potentially relevant information, assessing evidence and building a case towards some form of (re-) solution. It is also the reader who participates in tracking fragmented narrative strands, shifting (character) perspectives as well as a temporally and spatially disrupted story, which often involves intentionally manipulated, partial or misleading information. Such plot requirements demand heightened attention to detail and absolute accuracy in rendering seemingly irrelevant features, even overriding what would be an idiomatic solution. For example, in Val McDermid's *The Wire in the Blood* (1997), a potential murder suspect attacks a police officer, pulling her hair with one hand, which, in the English original, is identified as "his free hand". Rather than translating literally (which would be grammatically acceptable), the German translator has chosen an idiomatically more elegant rendering "mit der linken Hand" (with the left hand). However, one of the suspects has a metal prosthesis and would not have been able to perform this action with his left hand, which means that the German text effectively reduces the uncertainty of the English original by excluding this one suspect.

Similarly, a character's transgression of (minor) social or moral norms may flag them as a potential suspect. Regionally or socially marked register variation, specific geographical settings or culturally evocative attributes in clothing, housing, reading habits, etc. may perform plot-relevant functions and need to be rendered, however minor they may be. The translator needs to convey unconventional behaviour to a reader not attuned to the boundaries of what is "normal" without too much explanatory intervention which would introduce unintentional foregrounding or lead to the loss of narrative momentum. The translator walks a tightrope of demands for absolute accuracy, attention to minute detail and plot-relevant repetition, while rendering ambivalence, ambiguity and multiple meanings in a way which explicates culturally specific connotations but maintains sufficient uncertainty for the reader to remain involved.

Arguably, the central challenge for the crime fiction translator is to maintain reader involvement, specifically by keeping intact the cognitive challenge of disentangling plot strands and recognising clues, the affective responses of suspense or fear, or the interest derived from experiencing the foreign as a form of armchair tourism. However, genre constraints should not override the literary, social and cultural complexity of many crime texts. As noted above, language play, irony, linguistic variation and metaphor are essential features. These are too often ignored in translation, resulting in flat, formulaic texts which highlight generic conventions at the expense of social critique, stylistic complexity or exploration of character and environment. But editorial guidelines and publishing formats contribute to a privileging of the generic features at the expense of engaging with the complexities of the foreign literary text.

Note

1 English references give the eighteenth century, most likely because van Gulik's title identifies *Judge Dee* as an "authentic eighteenth-century detective novel". Contemporary Chinese scholarly works place it in the late Qing Dynasty (1871–1908) and the earliest edition found is from 1890.

Bibliography

Alter, A. (2010) "Fiction's global crime wave", *The Wall Street Journal*, 1 July, www.wsj.com/articles/SB100 01424052748703426004575338763878488670 (accessed 23 July 2019).

Anderson, J. (2014) "Hardboiled or overcooked? Translating the crime fiction of Léo Malet", *JoSTrans*, 22: 28–43.

Bassnett, S. (2017) "Detective fiction in translation: shifting patterns of reception", in L. Nilsson, D. Damrosch and T. D'haen (eds), *Crime Fiction as World Literature*, London: Bloomsbury, 143–55.

Broomé, A. (2014) "Swedish literature on the British market 1998–2013: a systemic approach", unpublished doctoral thesis, University College London.

Büchler, A. and Trentacosti, G. (2015) *Publishing Translated Literature in the United Kingdom and Ireland 1990–2012: Statistical report*, Aberystwyth: Literature Across Frontiers, Mercator Institute for Media, Languages and Culture, www.lit-across-frontiers.org/wp-content/uploads/2013/03/Translation-Statistics-Study_Update_May2015.pdf (accessed 14 November 2019).

Cadera, S. and Pavić Pintarić, A. (eds) (2014) *The Voices of Suspense and their Translation in Thrillers*, Amsterdam: Rodopi.

Epstein, B. (2011) "Girl with the dragon translation: translating thrillers and thrilling translations", *FIT XIX Congress Proceedings*, San Francisco, August 1–4.

Fornasiero, J. and West-Sooby, J. (2019) "Behind the locked door: Leblanc, Leroux and the anxieties of the Belle Époque", in J. Gulddal, S. King and A. Rolls (eds), *Criminal Moves: Modes of mobility in crime fiction*, Liverpool: Liverpool University Press, 27–44.

Higginson, P. (2015) "Armed and dangerous: *Le Poulpe* and the formalization of French noir", in J. Anderson, C. Miranda and B. Pezzotti (eds), *Serial Crime Fiction: Dying for more*, London: Palgrave Macmillan, 52–62.

Kapsaskis, D. and Artegiani, I. (2016) "Transformations of Montalbano through languages and media: adapting and subtitling dialect in *The Terracotta Dog*", in A. Esser, I. Smith and M. Bernal-Merino (eds), *Media Across Borders*, London: Routledge, 85–98.

King, S. (2014) "Crime Fiction as World Literature", *Clues*, 32(2): 8–19.

King, S. and Whitmore, A. (2016) "National allegories born(e) in translation: the Catalan case", *The Translator*, 22(2): 144–56.

Linder, D. (2011) *The American Detective Novel in Translation: The translations of Raymond Chandler's novels into Spanish*, Salamanca: Ediciones Universidad de Salamanca.

Rayner, J. (2007) *The Oyster House Siege*, London: Atlantic.

Reed, S. (2016) "Howdunnit? The French translation of Australian cultural identity in Philip McLaren's crime novel *Scream Black Murder/tueur d'Aboriginènes*", *The Translator*, 22(2): 157–75.

Robyns, C. (1990) "The normative models of twentieth century *belles infidèles*: detective novels in French translation", *Target*, 2(1): 23–42.

Rolls, A. and Sitbon, C. (2013) "'Traduit de l'americain' from Poe to the Série Noire: Baudelaire's greatest hoax?", *Modern & Contemporary France*, 21(1): 37–53.

Rolls, A., West-Sooby, J. and Vuaille-Barcan, M.-L. (2016) "Translating national allegories: the case of crime fiction", *The Translator*, 22(2): 135–43.

Seago, K. (2018) "'Philip Marlowe in drag?' – the construct of the hard-boiled detective in feminist appropriation and translation", *Ars Aeterna*, 9(2): 39–53.

Seago, K. and Lei, V. (2014) "'Looking east and looking west': crime genre conventions and tropes", *Comparative Critical Studies*, 11(2–3): 315–35.

Seago, K., Evans, J. and Rodríguez de Céspedes, B. (eds) (2014) "Crime in Translation", *Journal of Specialised Translation*, 22.

Stougaard-Nielsen, J. (2016) "Nordic noir in the UK: the allure of accessible difference", *Journal of Aesthetics and Culture*, 8: 1–11.

Sturge, K. (2004) *"The Alien Within": Translation into German during the Nazi regime*, Munich: iudicium.

10

TRANSNATIONALITY

Barbara Pezzotti

A transnational approach is one of the most recent developments in crime fiction scholarship. This new strategy challenges the traditional anglophone perspective on the genre and advocates a more inclusive reading of crime fiction. By highlighting the extent to which this kind of literature has always circulated globally, both in the original language and in translation, the most recent scholarship argues that a transnational perspective is fundamental for an analysis of the past and the future of crime fiction.

"Transnationality" is still an elusive term that has been construed in many diverse ways in different disciplines such as geography, social sciences, cultural studies and literary studies. The initial aim of this chapter is to give an overview of the debate over "transnationality", especially in contraposition to other terms, such as "cosmopolitanism", and "global", with which "transnational" is often confused. In particular, following Smith (2001), Sassen (2006) and Trousdale (2010), this chapter will offer a definition that highlights the fluidity and transformative nature of transnationalism in contrast with the unconscious elitism that is often implicit in notions of cosmopolitanism. Secondly, the chapter explores in greater depth why "transnationality" is a category that particularly fits crime fiction. By using the works of Seago (2014), Pepper and Schmid (2016) and Gregoriou (2017) it argues that transnationalism has been an inseparable feature of the genre since its origins. The chapter will then proceed to illustrate the most recent trends in scholarship, including a focus on the transnational detective whose analysis is often interlinked with a postcolonial perspective on crime fiction; the representation of transnational crime and its problematic dynamics with the institution of the nation-state; the transnational reader of a genre that often functions as a cultural mediator (in the best examples) or a tourist guide for the armchair traveller; and the transnational brand and its most successful creature, the Nordic noir. Finally, I will conclude by arguing that in crime fiction scholarship a theorisation of the actual transnational (geographical) space of investigation is still lacking.

Crime fiction as transnational literature

In the 1990s the influence of globalisation on the field of geography spurred a renewed interest in definitions of place and space, and the articulation of various theories of place, characterised by their emphasis on connectivity, mobility and exchange. Jameson's study has famously emphasised the dissolution of borders and disruption of horizons, which may generate a sense of postmodern anxiety at the loss of reference points (Jameson 1991). By contrast, other scholars, such as Massey, have argued that the local does not dissolve. Place is instead transformed into a "meeting place" that is the location of the intersections of particular bundles of activity spaces, of connections and interrelations, of influences and movements (1995: 59). Likewise, Pratt has coined the term "contact zones" to identify "social spaces where disparate cultures meet, clash, and grapple with each other" (1992: 4).

The concept of place as a "meeting place" or a "contact zone" is an invitation to discard the traditional views of "national" in favour of a transnational or globalised view of the world, and the term "transnational" has been increasingly scrutinised. For example, Trousdale defines transnationalism as a state or condition under which national borders and identities, while no longer acting as a mode of differentiation, are still present and significant (2010: 3). The discourse on transnationalism intertwines with an analysis based on cosmopolitanism. Recent approaches to cosmopolitanism highlight the presence of the local and the global. Beck argues that there has been a shift from a national to a "cosmopolitan" outlook, which is characterised by a "conceptual reconfiguration of our modes of perception" (2006: 2). This reconfiguration results in an epistemological shift in which the traditional national paradigm is replaced with a perspective of "inclusive differentiation" (5). In this new cosmopolitan logic, binary opposites such as local and global, national and international, and internal and external are interconnected and express the overlapping coexistence of possible worlds. This new definition attempts to overcome criticism against the abstract and rootless idea of cosmopolitanism as the "perfect civil union of mankind" provided in Kant's "Idea for a Universal History with a Cosmopolitan Purpose" (1784). However, by implying a free movement in space (a luxury still denied to a significant part of the world population), the new cosmopolitanism retains an unconscious elitism that transnationalism avoids. Equally interestingly, the concept of the "nation" eventually fades in the dialectic between local and global. By contrast "transnationality", in Smith's words, "insists on the continuing significance of borders, state policies, and national identities even as these are often transgressed by transnational communication circuits and social practices" (2001: 3). In other words, unlike cosmopolitanism, transnationalism crosses borders and acknowledges them, fuses separate places and recognises their separation. As Trousdale puts it "[t]ransnationalism, despite its potential for inclusivity, is also a means of preserving national difference" (12). This is particularly relevant when we analyse crime and its fictional representations as global crime and crime organisations are increasingly pursued by national institutions.

In the past twenty years, after more than a century of scholarship dominated by a focus on national literatures, the study of transnational literature has enlarged understanding of the literary process, and the concept of national literature has partially lost its power. The study of literature has increasingly begun to map its mobility across national and cultural borders. If the expression "transnational literature" often refers to literatures written in a second language; or to literatures with a cross-cultural theme, Seyhan opens up to a more comprehensive view of transnational literature as "a genre of writing that operates outside the national canon, addressing issues facing deterritorialized cultures, and speaks for paranational communities and alliances" (2001: 10).

Among the literary genres, crime fiction appears to be intrinsically transnational. First of all, as Pepper and Schmid argue "the production, circulation, and translation of crime fiction, from the genre's roots in the criminal stories circulating in London and Paris from the early eighteenth century, has always been an inherently transnational phenomenon" (2016: 1). Translation and circulation characterise much fiction, but it is particularly relevant for crime fiction which has long been one of the most popular genres in terms of sales, translations and adaptations.

It can also be argued that, by its importation and adaptation of a "foreign" format, crime fiction in languages other than English has, by default, always been "transnational". The ongoing success of the genre that Gregoriou perceptively defines as "crime fiction migration" (2017: 3) is supported by "consistent popularity and attractiveness irrespective of time, place as well as people" (3). Seago explains that the broad appeal of this genre lies in the ability of crime fiction to offer "insight into the cultures that produce it" (2014: 2). Furthermore, since the definition of what constitutes a crime is constantly changing, cross-border movements, translations, interpretations and cross-fertilisations of detective stories have the potential to "offer access to intercultural, intracultural anxieties, cultural and social shifts and the merging construction of a popular literary form" (2).

Despite transnationalism being an inherent characteristic of crime fiction, scholarship has only recently analysed the genre through a transnational lens. So far, researchers have mainly concentrated on analysing anglophone crime fiction, though a few scholars have developed national and regional perspectives beyond the anglophone world. This approach has been a welcome attempt to fill a persistent void in academia: Since crime fiction scholarship has traditionally concentrated on American and British output, the publication in the last decade of studies in English focusing on the German, Italian, Spanish or Japanese traditions among others, has had the merit of opening the discourse regarding the development of the genre to what was mistakenly perceived as the periphery of crime fiction. Equally importantly, edited scholarly collections of international crime fiction have highlighted the contribution of non-anglophone novels to important issues, such as migration, border control and gender violence. The subsequent and logical step has been a transnational take on the genre. So far, a limited number of monographs and collections of essays have specifically tackled transnationality in crime fiction, such as Matzke and Mühleisen (2006), Pearson and Singer (2009), and Pepper and Schmid (2016). Among these publications, four trends emerge: The analysis of the so-called "transnational" detective, mainly in postcolonial crime fiction; the analysis of the representation of transnational crimes in an increasingly globalised world; consideration of the transnational experience of the reader exposed to crime fiction; and a development of the transnational brand, with a focus in particular on the so-called "Nordic noir", one of the most successful marketing stories of the last decade.

The detective, the crime, the reader and the brand

The transnational turn in the study of the genre initially concentrated on the most important figure of the genre: The detective. Detective figures, such as Raymond Chandler's Philip Marlowe, are liminal figures, able to deal with different social classes, in spite of being (mostly) white, male and middle-class. More recent crime fiction has increasingly featured men or women belonging to different social, cultural and ethnic backgrounds. The detective's external negotiation with various strata of society throughout the investigation has been internalised and the detective increasingly needs to negotiate who he or she is and what they stand for before facing scrutiny by society. Recent critical works focus on the character of the sleuth in mainly postcolonial or transcultural terms (Matzke and Mühleisen 2006), or identify a recent evolution in the so-called hybrid detective "whose role acknowledges cultural multiplicity" (Anderson et al. 2012: 2).[1] However, "transnationality" is specifically at the core of *Detective Fiction in a Postcolonial and Transnational World* (Pearson and Singer 2009). In their edited collection, Pearson and Singer argue that while crime fiction at its origins was linked to imperialism and constructions of race and national identities, the genre has progressively evolved into a potent tool for narrating the complexities of modernities, citizenship and justice in a postcolonial

Transnationality

world. Pearson and Singer also argue that in this sense transnational studies share with recent postcolonial theories a commitment to overcome a national framework and centre-periphery models in favour of "worldviews, that effectively comprehend not just liminal states, but liminal forms of statehood, and that articulate or legitimize multiple trajectories of belonging and identity" (2009: 9). While observing that transnational encounters also take place in classic detective fiction, these authors identify the American hardboiled novel as the first subgenre where transnationalism developed in full. Pearson and Singer argue that despite racial and ethnic stereotyping in this subgenre, "detectives inhabit denationalized, multiethnic modern cities" that impose a new multiethnic way of life to which the hardboiled detective has adapted (5). Pearson and Singer note that the hardboiled subgenre is the template for the postcolonial, transnational or racially marginalised detective for a range of contemporary authors, from Chester Himes to Vikram Chandra. Drawing on the hardboiled tradition, these authors expand "the detective's role to nationalities and cultural minorities that have been marginalized or exoticized in previous crime fiction" (5).

This is an interesting perspective, even though it tends to replicate the traditional chronological history of crime fiction which sees a linear development of crime fiction as conformity to a pre-existing formula, in this case the so-called "whodunit" and the hardboiled story. It can also be argued, as the editors of this collection do in their introduction, that Edgar Allan Poe's stories are essentially transnational for their being written by an American author and set in France with a French detective as protagonist. Interestingly, however, Pearson and Singer make the case for a crime fiction at the intersection of postcolonial and transnational studies that expresses not so much a broadly conceived borderless globalisation of culture, but rather specific concerns about

> the vexed relationship between detection and statehood, which alternatively creates and vitiates legal and ethical frameworks, and between detection and national, cultural, ethnic, or racial identity, factors which demand that investigators cross borders both external and internal, figurative and literal.
>
> *(10–11)*

Studying this through the lens of transnationalism means recognising that the nation-state – as a fact or an aspiration – remains a salient category for this unique ability to secure universal rights and provide individuals the freedom to think and move freely between their local and global citizenship (9).

Just as crime is increasingly seen as a transnational phenomenon, policing is also becoming a set of networked activities connecting national police forces and supranational intelligence or security agencies across the globe. This is reflected in an increasing number of crime novels and, especially, TV series that feature transnational and international investigative teams. Together with the transnational detective recent scholarship has also tackled the issue of transnational crime and border crossing. Pepper and Schmid argue that, despite the genre's long-standing transnational characteristics, "it is only in the last twenty years or so that crime fiction has really mushroomed beyond the familiar scenes of its foundational texts […] to become a truly global literary genre" (1). As a global genre, Pepper and Schmid continue, crime fiction needs to be analysed for its ability to reflect in a critical way "on the process of globalization in general, or on the growing transnationalization of crime and policing networks in the contemporary era" (2). Pepper and Schmid highlight how, in a globalised world, the state still plays a role in mediating between the local and global (4). Indeed, according to Sassen, the nation-state remains "the prevalent organizational source of authority" even though its political power is increasingly detached from "its exclusive territory" and embedded in a "multiple bordering system" (2006: 419–20). Interestingly, border control remains a tangible and controversial manifestation of state authority. Likewise, as Chandler puts it "there can be no international law without equal sovereignty, no system of [universal] rights without state-subjects capable of being its bearers" (2003: 34). In crime fiction the discourse is complicated by the state's centrality to the historical development of crime fiction and by its significance to the genre. If nothing else, issues of power and corruption – traditionally at the centre of much crime fiction – are now problematised by the complex relationship between "national", "international" and "transnational". A transnational analysis of crime fiction allows scholarship to tackle the genre in its increasingly globalised form without forgetting the "national" as a foundational category and at the same time, as Pepper and Schmid hope, to scrutinise the ability of crime fiction to critique global capitalism and contemporary geopolitics (8). In so doing, as Beyer also argues, crime fiction – due to its wide readership – may have a significant impact on the public awareness of contemporary transnational evils, such as child and sex trafficking (2018: 90).

Apart from key elements in the narrative, such as the detective and the crime, transnationality can also be a key term for the relationship between crime fiction and the reader. As King argues, the act of reading is "the convergence of two locals – that of the reader and that of the text" (2019: 206). In other words, the strong position of crime fiction in the global market points to a potential disconnection between a reader and the national tradition in which a crime novel was produced. King proposes a reader-centred approach to crime fiction that "draws attention to the porosity of [...] borders and points to the coexistence of the nation and the world beyond and within it" (207). The result is a transnational experience that positions a work of fiction somewhere between travel guide and act of cultural mediation. Indeed, not only crime fiction can be seen as a transcultural contact zone into which individual authors bring their ideas about alterity (Anderson et al. 2012: 1), but also as a space where readers embark on journeys that, in the best examples, allow them "to scrutinize different cultures and societies and, in so doing, to better define themselves" (1–2).

Finally, intertwining place and marketing, Nilsson examines the complexity of a domestic crime fiction becoming what she called "a globally shared literature" (2016: 540). This is a new field of study since the role of the commercial aspect of crime fiction, especially in the international market, has seldom been investigated. In particular, Nilsson argues that "[c]rime fiction functions as entertainment and a social critique, tied to a specific vernacular and a local place that, once circulating in a transnational context, becomes a cosmopolitan imaginary" (541). Through an analysis of book covers and other marketing tools, Nilsson shows how branding and marketing have been able to create an imaginary of the north that has contributed to the success of the "Nordic noir" in the worldwide scene (542). It can be added that Nordic noir is a particularly relevant case because it intertwines the transnationality of the setting with a transnational branding in a transnational market. In other words, visual marketing strategies have astutely put together different national cultures and identities – as expressed in Danish, Norwegian and Swedish crime fiction – into one transnational reality or, to an imaginary world of snowy and bleak landscapes as well as a Viking spirit, and advertised it as a unified brand. The acceptance of this transnational brand into the transnational market of crime fiction has generated a powerful shared imaginary of the north, arguably the most successful case study in contemporary crime fiction.

Transnationality in Andrea Camilleri's *The Snack Thief*

Il ladro di merendine (1996) [*The Snack Thief*, 2003] both embodies and reflects some of the above-mentioned transnational themes in crime fiction. *The Snack Thief* is one of the first novels in a

Transnationality

long-running series written by Andrea Camilleri (1925–2019), arguably the most famous Italian crime writer in the world. The Inspector Montalbano series has been translated into thirty-two languages, was adapted for Italian television and successfully broadcast in the UK, US and Australia. In *The Snack Thief* the investigation revolves around two cases: In the first an elderly man is stabbed to death in an elevator in the small fictional Sicilian town of Vigàta (where all Montalbano's investigations take place) and his maid, the Tunisian Karima, disappears, and in the second a Tunisian crewman on an Italian fishing trawler is machine-gunned by a Tunisian patrol boat off Sicily's coast. The inspector's life is endangered when he finds out that these cases are related. Ultimately, his investigation unveils government corruption and international intrigue.

The novel presents several transnational elements. First of all, the crime investigated turns out to be international terrorism and the inquiry involves the Italian and Tunisian governments and their respective police forces and secret services. Secondly, the transnational structure in which the detective's identification with a national (and regional) space and the simultaneous transcendence of their borders is mediated through the act of investigating. In particular, the enquiry allows Inspector Montalbano, a proud Sicilian, to interact with Tunisian characters and to appreciate for the first time the deep transnational and transcultural roots of his homeland. The tone is set in the novel when, while describing a suburb of the fictional Montelusa (the city of Agrigento), the narrator pictures Arab immigrants not as foreigners, but as people who simply come back home after hundreds of years (2017: 107); the reference here is to the Arabic domination of Sicily between 831 and 1091 on the one hand, and the recent wave of migration from Northern Africa to Italy, on the other. This topic is dear to Camilleri who, in a previous novel, *Il cane di terracotta* (1996) [*The Terracotta Dog*, Camilleri 2004], had introduced the idea of a common history between Sicily and Tunisia. In this novel Montalbano meets Master Rahman, a teacher from Tunisia. The teacher's knowledge of the community of the seaside village of Mazara del Vallo is vital for the investigation, as Rahman explains to Montalbano the reasons for the pacific coexistence of Mazarese and Arabs:

> We're family. Al-Imam al-Mazari, the founder of the Maghrebin juridical school, was born in Mazara, as was the philologist Ibn al-Birr, who was expelled from the city in 1068 because he liked wine too much. But the basic fact is that the Mazarese are seafaring people. And the man of the sea has a great deal of common sense; he understands what it means to have one's feet on the ground. And speaking of the sea – did you know that the motor trawlers around here have mixed crews, half Sicilians half Tunisians?
>
> *(268)*

As we can see from this passage, the sea – which holds the potential to act as a borderline – resists this role: Its fluid borders are symbolised by the mixed crew in the Sicilian fishing boats. In *The Snack Thief*, the encounters between the detective and various witnesses reinforce the idea of "fluid borders" between Italian and Tunisian culture and history. This happens when Montalbano interviews Aisha, the Tunisian landlady of Karima. The language barrier between the two is overcome by a common interest in food. Montalbano, who proudly only eats Sicilian dishes, enjoys some Tunisian homemade delicacies: "the kebab had a tart, herbal flavor that made it a little more sprightly" (2017: 80). During the investigation, Montalbano also meets and befriends François, Karima's child. United by a tragic destiny (Montalbano also lost his mother when he was a child) one night, on the beach "[they] started talking, the inspector in Sicilian and the boy in Arabic, and they understood each other perfectly" (177). Indeed, in this novel, the sea, the beach and – metaphorically – the language barrier are boundaries that, using Bhabha's words, become transnational places "from which *something begins*" (1994: 7). It is not by chance that at the end of the investigation the inspector decides to adopt François. Ultimately, the investigator crosses borders "both external and internal, figurative and literal" (Pearson and Singer 2009: 11). Whereas the current political moment in Italy and the rest of Europe is marked by a countermove towards stasis, borders and exclusion, this novel shows how cultural, historical and linguistic "contact zones" are multiple, attesting to continuous mobility back and forth across the Mediterranean. Camilleri exposes the anti-immigration rhetoric as a political construction that aims at diverting the public opinion's attention from the inability of right-wing governments to solve Italy's economic issues. Thus, *The Snack Thief* becomes a political and social manifesto against the new xenophobic political climate. Camilleri's political stance in this regard is relentless. Reference to Mediterranean history and culture are present throughout the series and are at the centre of the narrative in *Il giro di boa* (2003) [*Rounding the Mark*, 2006] and *L'altro capo del filo* (2016) [*The Other End of the Line*, 2019] where the Sicilian author tackles the topical issue of the illegal migrant emergency on the Italian coasts.

The Snack Thief is also notable because, through a fictional case of international terrorism, Camilleri operates a critique of the war on terrorism. Prophetic in its treatment of this hot topic, in a pre-2001 climate, the Sicilian author highlights the immorality and cynicism of governments in fighting this war. In the novel, the cooperation between the Italian and Tunisian agencies aiming to eliminate a dangerous terrorist leads to the death of several innocent people, François's mother, Karima, and Aisha among others. With no possibility for the detective to bring Karima's and Aisha's murderers to justice, Camilleri's novel focuses on "the vexed relationship between detection and statehood" (10) that Pearson and Singer highlight. A confrontation between Montalbano and a colonel of the Italian secret service illustrates this troubled relationship:

> "As I'd suspected," said Lohengrin Pera, "you've figured it all out. Now I ask you to pause and think. You, like me, are a loyal, devoted servant of our state. And so –"
>
> "Stick it up your ass," Montalbano said softly.
>
> "I don't understand."
>
> "Let me repeat: you can take our state and stick it up your ass. You and I have diametrically opposed concepts of what it means to be a servant of the state. For all intents and purposes, we serve two different states. So I beg you please not to liken your work to mine."
>
> *(2017 : 254)*

Through the recurrence of transnational "contact zones", this novel provides a powerful counter-narrative to the current xenophobic discourse. Through the refusal of the detective to identify himself with a state that crushes innocent lives in the name of a war on terrorism, *The Snack Thief* also provides the criticism of "contemporary geopolitics" called for by Pepper and Schmid (2016: 8). Finally, it provides fascinating material for an investigation of the transnational geographical place, a topic still little explored in crime fiction scholarship.

Transnationality is a new approach in crime fiction that defies the traditional anglocentric take on the genre and opens to a more inclusive reading of crime fiction. So far this strategy has intersected with postcolonialism, global studies, marketing and branding studies. Recent studies show how the transnational is an essential tool to investigate issues such as social inclusion, ethnicity and racial identity, global crime and policing, readers' experience and branding. However, there is scope for further development. For instance, this concept could also be fruitfully applied in relation to the field of literary geographies. As place is an important element in crime fiction, an analysis of transnational geographic places would complicate the discourse on the impact of place and space in the crime narrative. As in the case with Camilleri, it would add to an analysis of the political use of place in literature. More generally, it would also enhance the discourse on the impact of fictional representations in shaping attitudes towards specific environments. This new angle would open the opportunity for a re-reading of crime fiction classics transnationally. Finally, it would also facilitate an analysis of the process through which domestic crime fiction may become a globally shared literature.

Note

1 Crime fiction in terms of postcolonialism is analysed in Chapter 13 of this collection, therefore I will not discuss this issue at length in my chapter.

Bibliography

Anderson, J., Miranda C. and Pezzotti, B. (eds) (2012) *The Foreign in International Crime Fiction: Transcultural representations*, London: Continuum.

Beck, U. (2006) *The Cosmopolitan Vision*, London: Polity.

Beyer, C. (2018) "'In the suitcase was a boy': representing transnational child trafficking in contemporary crime fiction", in C. Gregoriou (ed.), *Representations of Transnational Human Trafficking: Present-day news media, true crime, and fiction*, Palgrave Pivot, 89–115.

Bhabha, H.K. (1994) *The Location of Culture*, New York: Routledge.

Camilleri, A. (2004) *The Terracotta Dog*, London and Oxford: Picador.

———. (2017) *The Snack Thief*, London and New York: Picador.

Chandler, D. (2003) "International justice", in D. Archibugi (ed.), *Debating Cosmopolitics*, London: Verso, 27–39.

Gregoriou, C. (2017) *Crime Fiction Migration: Crossing languages, cultures and media*, London and New York: Bloomsbury Academic.

Jameson, F. (1991) *Postmodernism, or the Cultural Logic of Late Capitalism*, London: Verso.

King, S. (2019) "The private eye of the beholder: reading world crime fiction", in J. Gulddal, S. King and A. Rolls (eds), *Criminal Moves: Modes of mobility in crime fiction*, Liverpool: Liverpool University Press, 195–210.

MacLeod, A. (2014) "The contemporary fictional police detective as critical security analyst: insecurity and immigration in the novels of Henning Mankell and Andrea Camilleri", *Security Dialogue*, 45: 515–29.

Massey, D. (1995) "The conceptualization of a place", in D. Massey and P. Jess (eds), *A Place in the World? Places, cultures and globalization*, Oxford: Oxford University Press.

Matzke, C. and Mühleisen, S. (eds) (2006) *Post-colonial Postmortems: Crime fiction from a transcultural perspective*, Amsterdam: Rodopi.

Nilsson, L. (2016) "Mediating the north in crime fiction", *Journal of World Literature*, 1: 538–54.

Pearson, N. and Singer, M. (eds) (2009) *Detective Fiction in a Postcolonial and Transnational World*, Farnham and Burlington: Ashgate.

Pepper, A. and Schmid, D. (eds) (2016) *Globalization and the State in Contemporary Crime Fiction*, London and New York: Palgrave Macmillan.

Pezzotti, B. (2012) "Who is the foreigner? The representation of migrants in contemporary Italian noir fiction", in J. Anderson et al., 176–87.

Pratt, M.L. (1992) *Imperial Eyes: Travel writing and transculturation*, New York: Routledge.

Sassen, S. (2006) *Territory, Authority, Rights: From medieval to global assemblages*, New York: Princeton University Press.

Seago, K. (2014) "Introduction and overview: crime (fiction) in translation", *Journal of Specialised Translation*, 22: 2–14.

Seyhan, A. (2001) *Writing Outside the Nation*, Princeton: Princeton University Press.

Smith, M.P. (2001) *Transnational Urbanism: Locating globalization*, Oxford: Blackwell.

Trousdale, R. (2010) *Nabokov, Rushdie and the Transnational Imagination*, New York: Palgrave Macmillan.

11
GENDER AND SEXUALITY

Gill Plain

Thinking about gender in relation to crime fiction is not simply a matter of representation; it is also the case that the genre itself – its formal structures and stylistic features – has long been considered gendered. This is particularly evident in the mid-twentieth century when, thanks in no small measure to the rhetorical excess of Raymond Chandler's influential essay "The Simple Art of Murder" (1944), the dialogic tough talk and urban grit of the so-called "hardboiled" school came to be regarded as a "masculine" mode, against which the clue-puzzle world of amateur intellects and well-regulated crime was rendered irredeemably "feminine". The instability of such a binary is evident – but it acts as a potent reminder that detective fiction has, throughout its history, valorised modes of knowledge conventionally associated with masculinity: Rationality, logic, the primacy of empiricism and the refusal of emotion. Against this can be set the counterhistory explored by critics such as Maurizio Ascari, a lineage rooted in the Gothic, the supernatural and the sensational that mobilised discourses of pseudo-science and the occult to explore the irrational and forbidden, and to negotiate – amongst other things – the "widespread fear of decline" that accompanied the Victorian "faith in progress" (2007: 146). The transgressive desires and social taboos confronted by the sensational resist rational explanation and demand an investigation process open to the culturally feminine categories of the inexplicable, the chaotic and the corporeal. This chapter will consider some of the critical debates emerging from the perception of gendered modes of detection, and the changing constructions of masculinity and femininity at play in the genre. It will also explore the centrality of desire to plot and character and consider the emergence of the detective as a transgressive figure.

Gendering the genre / gender in the genre

Hammett wrote at first (and almost to the end) for people with a sharp, aggressive attitude to life. They were not afraid of the seamy side of things; they lived there. Violence did not disturb them; it was right down their street. Hammett gave murder back to the kind of people that commit it for reasons, not just to provide a corpse; and with the means at hand, not with handwrought duelling pistols, curare, and tropical fish.

(Chandler 1964: 195)

Gender and sexuality

To paraphrase: Hammett wrote for men, he wrote about men, and he did so in a manner that was not just recognisably but assertively masculine. In this quotation "people" stands for the universal white male subject of patriarchy. People are emphatically gendered male and exhibit the stereotypical features of traditional masculinity: Aggression, courage, resilience. They even, in their capacity to murder for a reason, reveal a perverse relationship to the anti-emotionalism of the Holmesian tradition. These may be tough guys, not intellectuals, but they still have the self-control and restraint that sets them apart from "the flustered old ladies – of both sexes (or no sex) and almost all ages – who like their murders scented with magnolia blossoms and do not care to be reminded that murder is an act of infinite cruelty" (Chandler 1964: 196). Chandler's dismissal of the Golden Age tradition, however, is not simply a case of a salesman asserting the superiority of his product. Rather, his vehemence emerges from profound cultural anxieties that shaped the interwar period in Britain and America.

Both the popularity of the clue-puzzle form and the emergence of a "hardboiled" idiom have been linked to the impact of World War I. While the archetypal noir sensibility reeks of disillusionment, the clue-puzzle formula functions as a panacea for a wounded culture needing rehabilitation from war's violent excess. It is, in Alison Light's redolent phrase, "a literature of convalescence" (1991: 69). This is not simply a matter of escapism. The relative bloodless-ness of the stories, their self-contained formal complexity and their refusal of emotion, speaks to a post-traumatic culture distrustful of exactly those traditional masculine virtues that had once been seen as central to self and nation (1991: 9). Equally significant is the transformation of the detective. A rejection of conventional masculine authority is evident in characters as diverse as Agatha Christie's Hercule Poirot, a vain Belgian refugee with an egg-shaped head, dyed hair and a pair of immense moustaches; Margery Allingham's vacuous man-about-town Albert Campion and Gladys Mitchell's Mrs Bradley – "a shrivelled, clever, sarcastic sort of dame [who] would have been smelt out as a witch in a less tolerant age" (Mitchell 2014: 6). When male authority does appear, it is frequently ridiculed and undermined, as is the fate of the aptly named Inspector Boring in Mitchell's *Speedy Death* (1929). As Light concludes, "both male and female writers in the period found a kind of modernity in making fun of heroes" (1991: 70).

The transformation of the detective's body was accompanied by changes in his, and her, methodology. Writing of Christie's first novel, Stephen Knight observes that she

> alters Doyle's pattern towards a passive problem-solving that rejects romantic male heroism as a protecting force. Hercule Poirot is a fussy, unheroic figure. His physical vanity is foolish but his brain works well: what is of value in him is not tied to mas-culine stereotypes.
>
> *(1980: 108)*

Poirot's passive problem-solving can be set alongside the later emergence of Miss Marple as a figure who detects less through the scientific scrutiny of empirical evidence than through an understanding of social networks – a form of anthropological study combined with psycho-logical profiling that enables her to read both corpse and community as part of recognisable patterns of human nature. Miss Marple can detect criminal activity because she has, in some form or another, seen it all before. Her age, and her position on the margins of society, are transformed into sources of knowledge and power, albeit the latter needing to be channelled through an obliging line of police assistants.

Miss Marple is an unofficial psychologist, Mrs Bradley, by contrast, is a professional psy-choanalyst, and her approach to crime represents another challenge to conventional modes of masculine detective agency. Mrs Bradley is a dedicated Freudian: "We are all murderers, my friend [...]. Some in deed and some in thought. That's the only difference" (Mitchell 2014: 106). Mrs Bradley's paraphrase of Freud's "Thoughts for the Times on War and Death" (1915) aligns her detective with a modernist cynicism that rejects conventional pieties, and Mitchell is radical in bestowing the authority of this new and increasingly influential hermeneutic mode upon an elderly woman who resembles a pterodactyl.

The hardboiled tradition can equally be seen to challenge conventions of masculine rationality, but with a very different aim. As with the clue-puzzle formula, it is a reactionary formation that responds to the upheavals of modernity. Indeed, Lee Horsley suggests that the "noir thriller is one of the most durable popular expressions of the kind of modernist pessimism epitomised in *The Waste Land*" (2001: 1). Like the clue-puzzle it is distrustful of rhetoric and high ideals, but it manifests this distrust in a hermeneutic of suspicion that extends to institutional authority and structures of power. This fundamentally urban mode of crime fiction generates a radically different relationship of form to gender. Masculinity here is not something to make fun of, it is something to admire and defend.

The emphasis placed on the restoration and reassertion of masculinity by the tropes of hardboiled narrative means that no other form of crime fiction so potently insists upon the "otherness" of women. Underpinning the gender taxonomy of private-eye novels and noir thrillers is a more or less virulent subscription to the binary representation of women as virgin (victim, valuable, innocent, passive, to be protected) or whore (criminal, amoral, irrational, desiring, active, to be punished). The accompanying stereotypes of masculinity are almost as limiting, but these may be complicated and subverted, as for example, in the sensual homoeroticism that characterises much of Chandler's fiction (Plain 2001: 62–63; Abbott 2002: 81–89). Equally unexpected is a novel such as Hammett's *The Glass Key* (1931), where the self-annihilating masochism of the protagonist "shatters [...] the fiction of a psychically invulnerable and impermeable masculinity" (Forter 2000: 17). *The Glass Key* is also remarkable for its "surprisingly positive" representation of women (44), but this is the exception, not the rule and, at the level of formula, women's roles are limited to victim, helpmeet or the desirable, and therefore potentially deadly, *femme fatale*. This figure weaponises femininity, either through a straightforward assault on the detective's libido, or through the deceptive performance of feminine vulnerability. Hammett's Brigid O'Shaugnessy in *The Maltese Falcon* (1930) relies on her performance of stereotypical feminine weakness to escape male scrutiny, just as she deploys her body to challenge the privilege of male power. Her agency is evident in the successful emasculation of the lustful Miles Archer; the flaw in her sexual power is exposed by the homosexual Joel Cairo, who is, as Sam Spade wryly observes, "out of [her] reach" (1992: 87).

Although the interwar period provides a particularly rich example of the complex imbrication of gender and genre, this relationship has been integral to crime narrative across its history, determining the possibilities of both detection and transgression. The Victorian assumption that women – as the "weaker" sex – were in need of greater social and moral policing, for example, rendered their criminality doubly deviant. As Heather Worthington observes, the female villain was "not only acting in defiance of the (patriarchal) law but also rejecting her 'proper' feminine role" (2011: 42). Transgressive women thus figure as sensation, spectacle and warning, while also often reiterating the pervasive cultural association of femininity and madness (43). Yet, the assumption of women's fundamental otherness can also be seen, ironically, to enable early manifestations of the female detective and to shape their methodology. It takes a woman to catch a woman – as is evident from Baroness Orczy's *Lady Molly of Scotland Yard* (1910). When the finest police minds prove unable to solve a case requiring both feminine tact and intuition, they turn to Lady Molly who waits to be summoned whenever the inexplicable world of

Gender and sexuality

women needs interpretation. In "The Fordwych Castle Mystery", it is only Lady Molly's keen eye that can distinguish between the law-abiding transgressions of the emotionally aloof, golf-playing "new woman" and the murderous deviance of the actual criminal, who has deployed an exquisite performance of conventional femininity to turn public opinion against her suspiciously masculine sister.

Lady Molly was far from being the first female investigator: As Sally Munt observes, women writers and female detectives had been engaged in a "process of intrepid infiltration" of the genre since at least the 1860s (1994: 5). However, women detectives remained exceptional, provisional, or in need of justification, until the rise of second-wave feminism and the identification of crime fiction, and hardboiled narrative in particular, as a form that might be adopted for political ends. Yet, while popular fiction is ideally suited to the interrogation of the contemporary, its capacity actually to effect change has been much debated. Munt (1994) offers a nuanced account of the feminisms shaping crime narrative in the 1970s and 1980s, from the "liberal" feminism of writers such as Sara Paretsky and Sue Grafton, through socialist feminism, to psychoanalysis and postmodernism. The book also examines lesbian "inverstigators" and the emergence of black feminist writers such as Barbara Neely and Rosa Guy. A novel such as Neely's *Blanche on the Lam* (1992), argues Munt, presents a persuasive critique of culture and form, offering a "view from the underside" that deconstructs the detective's romantic individualism and asserts the value of community as a model of resistance (116). Blanche's position on the margins enables her to see differently and makes her an acutely sensitive cultural reader. The skills she needs to survive are equally those that make her an effective detective (117).

While acknowledging such successes, and the satisfaction of seeing patriarchy indicted, Munt nonetheless posits a structural tension at the heart of feminist appropriations of the genre. Whether liberal or lesbian, the decision to adopt a genre dependent to some measure on the upholding of the established social order ensures that the "radical charge" of feminist crime narratives will always be "constrained within an overall conformity" (31). Not all commentators agree. Priscilla Walton and Manina Jones argue, by contrast, that the crime genre *enables* political critique: "The feminist appropriation of the hard-boiled mode can redefine textual and cultural boundaries precisely because it comes into intimate contact with them [...] it is a *practical* application of *political* tenets expressed through a *popular* form" (1999: 87).

Integral to the debates surrounding feminist crime fiction, then, is the question of how do women detect? In the case of professional detectives, such as Paretsky's V.I. Warshawski, they follow the confrontational, tough-talking methodology of the hardboiled detective, albeit with reservations, dark humour and a considerable degree of self-consciousness. They also share this figure's ambivalent relationship to authority, often putting friendship and social justice above strict adherence to the law. Accidental detectives, from Barbara Wilson's printer Pam Nilsen (*Murder in the Collective*, 1984) to Denise Mina's abuse survivor Maureen O'Donnell (*Garnethill*, 1998), draw on countercultural networks and non-traditional forms of knowledge, but have disturbingly little agency. Both are uncertain investigators, in marginal positions, and both, across the narrative arc of their fictions, cross the boundary dividing detective from victim. They share the archetypal detective's outsider perspective, but without any of "his" power. Female police detectives face different challenges, their detective agency circumscribed by the law they are obliged to enforce. Yet the presence of women within the squad fundamentally changes, and exposes to scrutiny, homosocial and patriarchal structures previously unquestioned by the form.

Finally, the legacy of Miss Marple persists in detectives such as Alexander McCall Smith's Precious Ramotswe. *The Number One Ladies Detective Agency* (1998), and its many sequels, reveals the resilience of a detective methodology based upon the reading of "human nature" and women's supposed "emotional intelligence". It also suggests a nostalgic desire for a world, and a detective fiction, grounded in the illusory security of a stable homogenous society. These examples form a diverse field, but what unites them, and also enables the male detective's evolution, is the investigator's socially embedded status. Detectives now have backgrounds and baggage; actions taken in one novel have repercussions still felt in the next, and the process of investigation is complicated by the detective's responsibility not only to truth or justice, or any other abstract concept, but also to interpersonal relationships, communities and beliefs. The detective's gradual transition from hermeneutic cipher to intersectional actor, often developed across series fictions and long-form television drama, is a significant formal transition that can be traced to the post-World War II appropriation of the genre as a means of investigating identity. Detectives now are mothers, fathers, daughters, lovers – implicated in the social fabric of their investigations and frequently motivated by the personal. The case study that follows anticipates this transition.

Dorothy L. Sayers, *Strong Poison* (1930)

Published only two years after the introduction of universal suffrage, Dorothy L. Sayers's *Strong Poison* is an early example of a crime writer using the malleability of the genre to tackle cultural taboos. The novel features Sayers's serial detective Lord Peter Wimsey, whose introduction in *Whose Body* (1923), situated him as part of the fashion for feminised detective figures. Looking as if his "long, amiable face [...] had generated spontaneously from his top hat, as white maggots breed from Gorgonzola" (9), he lists detection amongst his hobbies and cultivates a foolish persona to disguise his status as a shell-shocked war veteran. This more serious dimension of Wimsey's personality grows in importance across the series, and *Strong Poison* can be seen as a turning point brought about by the introduction of Harriet Vane, murder suspect, crime novelist, Oxford graduate and – eventually – wife.

Harriet is introduced in a *tour de force* opening sequence much commented on by feminist critics (Heilbrun 1990; Hoffman 2016). On trial for the murder of her erstwhile lover, she risks being condemned to death for failing to pander to the male ego. As the judge summarises the evidence, we learn that Vane had lived outside marriage in apparent bohemian happiness with Philip Boyes, an avant-garde writer. This continued until Boyes unexpectedly proposed. As Harriet later explains to Wimsey,

> I quite thought he was honest when he said he didn't believe in marriage – and then it turned out that it was a test, to see whether my devotion was abject enough. Well, it wasn't. I didn't like having matrimony offered as a bad conduct prize.
>
> *(41–42)*

To Wimsey, in the process of evolving into a proto-feminist detective, this makes perfect sense. To the police investigation, the prosecution, the judge and most of the jury, Harriet's refusal is incomprehensible. The judge carries most weight in articulating the view of a patriarchal status quo that, irrespective of post-war social change, persists in infantilising women, assumes their inferiority and is unable to see them as subjects independent of male authority. Indeed, the judge implies, in her financial independence, her lack of familial ties and her transgression of conventional social proprieties, Harriet must be "a person of unstable moral character" (8). He furthermore comes close to asserting that it is a small step from sexual impropriety to murder. Women's assumed distance from patriarchal law – their inability to reason and withstand the pressures of emotion – is evident in these assumptions and yet, paradoxically, Harriet stands

Gender and sexuality

equally accused of "unwomanly conduct" (Heilbrun 1990: 258). Multiply transgressive, she has stepped outside the boundaries of acceptable middle-class morality, and insisted on her status as an independent agent in the public sphere (Hoffman 2016: 65–66; Reddy 1988: 22). This is all the more troubling because Harriet's work not only maintains her, it also supports Boyes. Her most egregious transgression in the end, then, is that cited by Boyes's friend, Ryland Vaughan:

> Harriet Vane's got the bug all these damned women have got – fancy they can do things. They hate a man and they hate his work. You'd think it would have been enough for her to help and look after a genius like Phil, wouldn't you? […] Genius must be served, not argued with.
>
> *(76–77)*

Vaughan conflates gender and literary value. Harriet's mind is inferior because she is a woman; her writing is inferior because she is a crime novelist. Her "middlebrow" literary productions cannot be compared with the hard-edged masculinity of highbrow modernist art (Light 1991: 7). Sayers's novel, however, dismisses such distinctions and figures Harriet as "a woman who has, metaphorically, killed and abandoned her lover when she outgrew him" (Heilbrun 1990: 258).

Beyond the character of Harriet, and the examination of double standards that she enables, *Strong Poison* has been read as a proto-feminist crime novel on account of the radical changes it initiates in the detective's methodology. As Horsley has observed, the secrets that must be uncovered, "lie in recesses that [Wimsey] cannot himself penetrate" (2005: 51), resulting in an undermining of conventional detective agency. As the frustrated Wimsey stands in his library, surrounded by the wisdom of the ages, he is forced to acknowledge his impotence. Traditional forms of knowledge will not solve the case, nor will the heroic male agent (Rowland 2001: 30). Rather, the investigation will progress through the creative thinking and performative skills of women and the working classes (Horsley 2005: 51). At the heart of this process is Miss Climpson's clandestine detective agency, the "Cattery". This discreet bureau, populated by women "of the class unkindly known as 'superfluous'" (46), provides employment for the invisible women of heteronormativity. Spinsters, young and old, run schemes to expose fraud and criminal activities. For Miss Climpson herself, employment and freedom of movement represent a welcome escape from separate spheres ideology, but it is, ironically, her ability to infiltrate specifically female communities that enables her detection.

Arguably, then, *Strong Poison* offers an early manifestation of the detection by network and affiliation characteristic of later feminist re-appropriations of the genre. The rule of law is questioned – if not actually destabilised – and justice served through an alliance of outsiders: Bill Rumm, the evangelical former safe-breaker; the undercover secretarial operative, Miss Murchison; the artist Marjorie Phelps and Harriet's loyal lesbian friends, Sylvia and Eiluned. Miss Murchison, in particular, triumphs as a detective through her performance of femininity: She scares away her employer by becoming overly familiar; she pretends "feminine" carelessness and lack of professionalism to gain time to investigate; and, because others assume she will not understand the world of finance, she is able to access valuable information. Miss Murchison's "career" highlights the opportunities that are closed to women. Harriet, as an Oxford-educated woman, has seemingly managed to escape such conventional constraints, but rather than celebrating this "freedom", *Strong Poison* works to demonstrate how vulnerable this makes her. Through the example of Harriet's public humiliation, women's emancipation is revealed as provisional and precarious, easily overwritten by the ongoing force of patriarchal gender normativity.

For all the radical potential implicit in plot, character and methodology, critics have also noted the limitations of Sayers's feminist vision. Megan Hoffman suggests that while the spinsters' detection saves Harriet, their activities also "perform the function of manoeuvring the heteronormative romance plot into place" (2016: 67). Wimsey falls in love with Harriet and begins to emerge from the comfortable homosocial dyad he had occupied with his loyal manservant Bunter. A figure who had himself been somewhat queer and part of the period's habit of "making fun of heroes" becomes over the course of the series increasingly serious and manly. Beneath the foolish "epicene" exterior (145) a wiry strength is revealed and, by *Gaudy Night* (1935), a diplomat, negotiator and Oxford scholar has emerged. Yet this cultural authority is unstable and Wimsey's shell shock, which returns to haunt the final novel, *Busman's Honeymoon* (1937), speaks to the impossible pressures of the patriarchal ideal. Sayers's sequence of novels maps a rapidly changing sociopolitical context, in which post-war frivolity and post-traumatic denial mutates into pre-war anxiety and a return to the security of gender normativity. The tidy ending of Harriet and Peter's marriage provides some resolution, but it cannot overwrite what the earlier novels have revealed about the instability of gender roles in interwar Britain.

Detecting desire

The gender dissonance evident in Wimsey's homosocial dependence on Bunter, and in Philip Marlowe's homoerotic fascination with "big" men, offer early indications of the genre's capacity to offer a space for the exploration of non-normative sexualities. Megan Abbott's *This Street was Mine* (2002) offers a nuanced exploration of the complex desires underpinning the hardboiled detective's quest, while J.C. Bernthal's *Queering Agatha Christie* (2016) similarly works to expose the transgressive possibilities at play within seemingly conventional Golden Age fictions. More explicit representation of desire and its implications for the process of investigation, however, would have to wait for the post-war, and largely post-Stonewall, emergence of lesbian and gay detective narratives.

Judith Markowitz dates the inception of queer detection to Lou Rand's 1961 pulp novel *Gay Detective* (2004: 3), but by far the most influential early figure was Joseph Hansen's Dave Brandstetter, whose debut, *Fadeout* appeared in 1970. Brandstetter, an insurance death claims investigator and war veteran, is an urbane, cultured, quietly authoritative figure, ideally configured to counter representations of homosexuality as deviant and pathological. The trajectory of the twelve-novel series follows Brandstetter from grief for a lover who has died of cancer, through a failed relationship, to a new long-term partnership with a much younger black journalist. A recurring cast of queer friends populates the texts, each of whom at some level exposes the bleak dysfunctionality of heteronormative American society. The final novel's title, *A Country of Old Men* (1993), is also its theme. The exhausted detective grieves for friends lost to old age and AIDS and struggles with his own failing body. Ending in the darkness of a heart attack, the book forms an epitaph for a particular mode of homo-paternalism and marks a generational endpoint.

Lesbian detection arrived later (Markowitz dates its origins to Eve Zaremba's Helen Keremos in 1978), but rapidly outstripped its male counterpart in scale and popularity (Walton and Jones 1999: 41–43). The lesbian's status as a spectral figure on the margins of society – neither legal nor illegal, stereotyped and yet invisible – fitted her ideally for the role of detective outsider, and writers revelled in the creation of female characters who simultaneously mobilised and parodied concepts of detective agency. From Mary Wings's Emma Victor to Val McDermid's Lindsay Gordon and Barbara Wilson's Cassandra Reilly, lesbian detectives

Gender and sexuality

pleasurably appropriated everything from the hardboiled detective's idiom to the *femme fatale*'s body in a series of adventures in which textual play coexisted with serious political intent. These were investigations that worked to question rather than consolidate the established social order and conventional categories of identity, resisting closure and radically reimagining the detective's role.

Less playfully, but equally politically, lesbian detectives also infiltrated the police procedural – a process exemplified by the Kate Delafield novels of Katherine V. Forrest. Delafield begins the series as a grief-stricken and closeted figure, and the series maps her necessary transition from alienated outsider-within to part of both a lesbian and a law enforcement community. In *Murder by Tradition* (1991), which maps the brutal murder of a young gay man, the prospect of justice seems bleak: Although the meticulous Delafield identifies the murderer, it seems likely that he will escape by means of a "gay panic" defence. This novel, then, turns from a straightforward whodunit to a much more detailed procedural examination of how a law biased towards repressive heteronormativity might be outwitted. Victory for Delafield and a community of reformers is eventually achieved through the assertion of gay visibility. The murder victim was out and proud: The killer must have seen this and acted with intent to commit a hate crime.

Forrest's battle to rehabilitate the justice system from within is continued by the legal detective fictions of Michael Nava. The extreme legal probity of Nava's gay LA lawyer, Henry Rios, works to challenge a repressive right-wing orthodoxy but, as *The Burning Plain* (1997) demonstrates, finding legal remedy against the massed forces of corporate money, heteronormative privilege, religious bigotry and homophobia is far from straightforward. Before the case can be solved, many of Rios's cherished law-abiding principals have been abandoned. In the courtroom, Rios is the calm professional heir of Brandstetter and Delafield; in private, he is angry – and Nava taps into archetypal hardboiled structures as Rios confronts homophobes in a series of tough-talking stand-offs, many of which also function as impassioned advocacy for equality in an age of insidious institutional prejudice. In the years since 2000, gender non-conforming detectives have increasingly moved to the mainstream – perhaps most obviously in the figure of Lisbeth Salander, the bisexual computer hacker at the centre of Stieg Larssen's *Millennium* trilogy (2005–2007). Salander's sexual preferences are the least of her worries, and while this might be regarded as a positive sign of social change, it sits alongside a plot that emphasises the foundational and ongoing misogyny of global late capitalism.

Conclusion

The relationship between gender and genre is thus both formally and politically significant. Gendered conceptions of power and knowledge shape detective agency; they also determine the reading of bodies, both living and dead. Who detects, how they detect and what they detect matter, and the vitality of crime fiction as a genre can – at least in part – be attributed to its capacity to interrogate the structural inequalities, cultural anxieties and psychic pressures of modernity. Yet, while the landscape of detection has undergone radical transformations in relation to gender and sexuality, the same cannot be said of desire – which remains a disruptive narrative force destabilising detective agency. While investigators have been liberated to desire whomsoever they choose, the formula still largely insists upon the impossibility of more than transitory fulfilment. As the genre's catalogue of divorced, lonely, grief-stricken, alienated and addicted detectives reveals, it remains the case that the work of detection is fundamentally incompatible with the pleasures of desire.

Bibliography

Abbott, M.E. (2002) *The Street Was Mine: White masculinity in hardboiled fiction and film noir*, New York: Palgrave.

Ascari, M. (2007) *A Counter-History of Crime Fiction: Supernatural, gothic, sensational*, London: Palgrave.

Bernthal, J.C. (2016) *Queering Agatha Christie: Revisiting the golden age of detective fiction*, London: Palgrave.

Betz, P.M. (2006) *Lesbian Detective Fiction: Woman as author, subject and reader*, Jefferson, NC: McFarland.

Chandler, R. (1964) [1944] "The simple art of murder", in *Pearls are a Nuisance*, Harmondsworth: Penguin.

Forter, G. (2000) *Murdering Masculinities: Fantasies of gender and violence in the American crime novel*, New York: New York University Press.

Hammett, D. (1992) [1929] *The Maltese Falcon*, London: Serpent's Tail.

Heilbrun, C.G. (1990) *Hamlet's Mother and Other Women*, London: The Women's Press.

Hoffman, M. (2016) *Gender and Representation in British Golden Age Crime Fiction: Women writing women*, London: Palgrave.

Horsley, L. (2001) *The Noir Thriller*, Basingstoke: Palgrave.

———. (2005) *Twentieth-Century Crime Fiction*, Oxford: Oxford University Press.

Knight, S. (1980) *Form and Ideology in Detective Fiction*, Basingstoke: Macmillan.

Light, A. (1991) *Forever England: Femininity, literature and conservatism between the wars*, London: Routledge.

Markowitz, J.A. (2004) *The Gay Detective Novel*, Jefferson, NC: McFarland.

Mitchell, G. (2014) [1929] *Speedy Death*, London: Vintage.

Munt, S.R. (1994) *Murder by the Book? Feminism and the crime novel*, London: Routledge.

Plain, G. (1996) *Women's Fiction of the Second World War: Gender, power and resistance*, Edinburgh: Edinburgh University Press.

———. (2001) *Twentieth-Century Crime Fiction: Gender, sexuality and the body*, Edinburgh: Edinburgh University Press.

Reddy, M. (1988) *Sisters in Crime: Feminism and the crime novel*, New York: Continuum.

Rowland, S. (2001) *From Agatha Christie to Ruth Rendell: British women writers in detective and crime fiction*, Basingstoke: Palgrave.

Sayers, D.L. (1968) [1930] *Strong Poison*, London: Hodder and Stoughton.

———. (1989) [1923] *Whose Body?*, London: Hodder and Stoughton.

Walton, P. and Jones, M. (1999) *Detective Agency: Women rewriting the hardboiled tradition*, Berkeley: University of California Press.

Worthington, H. (2011) *Key Concepts in Crime Fiction*, London: Palgrave.

12

RACE AND ETHNICITY

Sam Naidu

This chapter examines contemporary crime fiction's creation of innovative textual strategies such as shifts from individual crime to entangled webs of sociopolitical crimes, and from a local or national focus to a transnational one, in the quest for social justice. Crime fiction reflects, at times, the racism of its specific milieu, as well as evolving, reformist views and debates about race and ethnicity. Presenting often a morass of social relations with varying levels of resolution, contemporary crime fiction can be, depending on the author and reader, comfortingly conservative, disquietingly retrograde, radically progressive, or acutely critical.

Historically, and depending on location, crime fiction has taken up various positions in relation to race and ethnicity, either maintaining the status quo or providing a popular platform for ideological and ethical questioning of race and ethnicity. First, however, the terms "race" and "ethnicity" are highly contentious and their usage in this chapter requires definition. Based in social constructivism, Cornell and Hartmann describe race as

> a human group defined by itself or others as distinct by virtue of perceived common physical characteristics that are held to be inherent [...]. Determining which characteristics constitute the race [...] is a choice human beings make. Neither markers nor categories are predetermined by any biological factors.
>
> *(1998: 24)*

Cornell and Hartmann's inclusion of "choice" in their definition suggests human will, which may be internal or external to the group in question. On the other hand, they define ethnicity as a sense of common ancestry based on cultural attachments, past linguistic heritage, religious affiliations, claimed kinship, or some physical traits (19). Race and ethnicity, then, are terms which describe socially constructed groups based on distinctive physical and cultural characteristics, but additionally, "a relational dimension that indexes a group's location within a social hierarchy" needs to be acknowledged (Ford and Harawa 2010: 251). With these social constructivist, contiguous definitions in mind, this chapter examines how crime fiction has concerned itself with race and ethnicity, bringing to the fore intertwined, often troubled, relations between groups as well as transgressions or misdeeds specific to certain groups and contexts.

Dominant images

British and American crime fiction of the nineteenth century concerned itself generally with upholding hegemonic notions of law and justice through rational, epistemological quests, rooted as they were in cultures which were increasingly concerned with crime, punishment, discipline and the threat posed by the racial "other". These concerns were mediated in the literature through a prescriptive and pervasive discourse of race based on a white-black binary. White metropolitan authors such as Arthur Conan Doyle served to legitimate imperialist and colonialist ideologies by constructing Anglo-Saxon whiteness as dominant or superior to all "others", especially foreign races and ethnicities. Not always rendered as inferior but rather evoking an exotic intrigue, Anderson et al. note that "foreign characters and foreign settings have [had] a privileged space in crime fiction since its origins" (2012: 1), due to their association with mystery, adventure and the "other", specifically the colonial "other". Scholars such as Caroline Reitz (2004) and Tobias Döring (2006) have interrogated "the inextricable link between crime fiction and the imperial enterprise" (Döring 2006: 4), demonstrating that imperial authority, order and discipline were affirmed through the fictional investigation of crime and the reconstruction of social stability. Döring, for example, denounces the often xenophobic, racist and stereotypical portrayals of foreigners, in particular of migrants from the colonies, found in the Holmes stories (74).

Attesting, however, to the complexity of attitudes regarding race found in early crime fiction, authors such as Doyle also attempted to interrogate and understand racial and ethnic differences. In "The Adventure of the Yellow Face" (1893), for example, at the heart of the mystery is an interracial marriage and a child of mixed race. Thwarted by this strange difference,[1] Holmes fails to detect, and the hero of this story is therefore the tolerant and compassionate Grant Munro who does not repudiate his wife for having been previously married to an African American and who lovingly accepts the child as his own.

Context-driven, textual encoding of race and ethnicity through dominant imagery persisted in the British cosy whodunits of the early twentieth century. Novels by Agatha Christie, Dorothy L. Sayers or Margery Allingham rarely feature black or foreign characters (with the notable exception of Hercule Poirot himself, of course) and the dominance of whiteness was reinforced through their homogenous, monocultural casts and their determined preservation of the status quo. Ethnic "others", such as the Belgian Poirot, or Americans, Jews and Middle Eastern characters do feature as exceptions to the norm, often with undesirable or suspicious traits. Studying ethnicity in Christie's oeuvre, Jane Arnold notes that a great deal can be gleaned about "the place of Jews in English society", concluding that "they are not an easy part of the society she describes, neither are they entirely alien" (1987: 275–76). While Arnold observes the reinscription of certain stereotypes, she concedes that "No particular Jewish characteristic is completely negative" (276), such that, while dominant images and ideologies are discernible, these texts also reflect that crime fiction's engagement with racial and ethnic categories and relations was by no means always essentialist or binary.

The dominance of whiteness was also inscribed in the US hardboiled novel. According to Maureen Reddy, the criteria of whiteness, heterosexuality and masculinity encoded in texts by authors such as Dashiell Hammett and Raymond Chandler confer on the detective his heroic status (2003: 10), consolidating that dominance. At this point also, crime fiction's involvement in the delineation of racial and ethnic categories, or as Andrew Pepper puts it, its implication in the "hegemonic ambitions of those who have benefitted from the unequal distribution of power" (2000: 7), and its concurrent resistance to those categorisations and questioning of the ideology underpinning them, became more bold and far-reaching.

Race and ethnicity

Examples of that resistance and questioning of dominant racial and ethnic ideologies are found in the works of African American author, Chester Himes. Himes's Harlem series describes a wide range of poor, black characters who are transplanted from the rural South to urban Harlem. Himes's vivid and mordant descriptions of Harlem draw attention to the desperate, impoverished and often abject lives of black people in the US at the time. In the final, incomplete novel in the series, *Plan B* (1993), Himes creates a detective figure, Thomsson Black. Black, signalling a new form of overt engagement with race and ethnicity, is an ingenious character who articulates a strong political manifesto about the need for black people to reclaim their dignity by starting "at the bottom, at the chitterling of the hog" (Himes 1993: 166). Initially defined by his race and poverty, Black overturns this interpolation to lead an insurrection against racism.

In creating Black, Himes exhibits a keen awareness of the need to counter racial stereotypes found in mainstream crime fiction. Operating within the main parameters of the genre, Himes nevertheless troubles and inverts some of the genre's conventions, such as casting a white male as the lead detective, and female or other races and ethnicities as peripheral, often villainous characters.[2] Challenging persistently racist images in crime fiction and in US culture is, according to Norlisha Crawford (2017), Himes's primary project. Crawford's account of Himes's subversion of mainstream crime fiction highlights his disruptive use of characterisation, his repudiation of hegemonic racial categories and his intersectional treatment of history, setting, class and culture. This subversion is a legacy that Himes passed down to contemporary black authors such as Walter Mosley, who created Easy Rawlins deliberately and consciously to address the scarcity of "black male heroes" in American literature. Commenting in an interview on the emphatic representation of race in his work, he claims that "hardly anybody in America has written about black male heroes [...] There are black male protagonists and black male supporting characters, but nobody else writes about black male heroes" (Neuman 2011: n.p.). This paucity of black male heroes persists in mainstream crime fiction, but in recent African noir novels such as Mũkoma wa Ngũgĩ's *Black Star Nairobi* (2013) and Leye Adenle's *When Trouble Sleeps* (2018), black male heroes, and moreover, black female heroines are being inscribed, consequently modifying notions of heroism in diverse social contexts and configurations.

Transnational and postcolonial renderings

At the end of the twentieth century, scholars and critics took note of the emergence of a range of authors, detective figures and voices in crime fiction. While some took this growing diversity to signify a dismantling of racism and a newfound harmony, others warned against facile celebrations of multiculturalism (Pepper 2000) or disingenuous disregard for structural and systemic racism (Reddy 2003). A distinct recent advance in crime fiction scholarship has been the development of a transnational approach which compares and contrasts crime fiction from across the globe (Krajenbrink and Quinn 2009).

Concomitantly, having moved beyond metropolitan settings and concerns, literary endeavour and academic attention shifted significantly to constitute various new subgenres of crime fiction, one of which is postcolonial crime fiction. Matzke and Mühleisen's *Postcolonial Postmortems: Crime Fiction from a Transcultural Perspective* (2006), for instance, convincingly shows how postcolonial crime fiction, has extended and reshaped the genre to address notions of community, beliefs, race, gender and sociopolitical and historical formations in order to contest them. The new postcolonial are characterised by hybridity, especially the postcolonial detectives who blend "western police methods and indigenous cultural knowledge" (Christian 2001: 13), thus rendering them more effective in their respective settings.

Postcolonial crime fiction such as Tony Hillerman's series set in Native American reservations of the American Southwest draws on and subverts the heritage of classic crime fiction in order to expose how "western" discourses of rationality, with their particular racial bias, while limited in any context, are particularly inadequate when it comes to solving crimes in the postcolonial context, where racial and ethnic difference, and its attendant power dynamics, carry such historical weight. Indeed, the very definition of "crime" is questioned and reimagined to include the violations and abuses of colonialism, slavery, genocide, and in the South African context, also apartheid. For Hillerman, recuperating Navajo history and culture is a prevailing concern, but also emphasised through the characterisation of his two detectives, Leaphorn and Chee, is the notion of hybridity. Leaphorn, the earlier Hillerman creation, studied anthropology at the University of Arizona and rejects certain aspects of Navajo culture in favour of logical reasoning. Leaphorn syncretises his academic learning, his intimate knowledge of Navajo social customs, and his respectful responsiveness to the environment and topography of the reservation in order to detect. Similar to Leaphorn, Chee works for the Navajo Nation Police and studied anthropology at university, but in contrast, Chee, a trained shaman, is a romantic dreamer who prefers to use emotion and intuition to detect. Hillerman's engagement with race and ethnicity deliberately blurs boundaries between discrete categories and definitions. Leaphorn and Chee are thus entangled in Native American and white American social systems. Both detectives have to blend different knowledges to detect individual crimes on the reservation, and their liminal positioning points to wider, systemic crimes.

As seen in Hillerman's texts, one of the main ontological interrogations prevalent in postcolonial crime fiction has to do with race and ethnicity: How are social racial taxonomies constructed historically in the post-colony? How do these racial hierarchies impact on the current society and politics? How are the crimes of today linked to the violent and oppressive racist regimes which gave rise to such systems of oppression? How can a society so riven by racial difference ever be reconciled? In South Africa, where a particularly pernicious and tenacious racist regime took root and flourished after the colonial era, these questions are very prominent in its crime fiction.

Entanglement and muddledness – South African post-apartheid crime fiction

Crime fiction in South Africa today is just as concerned with social disorder and political instability as it is with individual, sensational crimes around which thriller plots are constructed, as authors such as Deon Meyer, Margie Orford, Angela Makholwa and Andrew Brown present narratives with entangled histories and subjectivities, highlighting difference and sameness amongst crimes, and divisions and contiguities amongst racial and ethnic groups. Postcolonial, post-apartheid South Africa, far from being the "rainbow" nation that was envisaged in the early 1990s, is an economically unstable and politically fractured flailing democracy with racially marked power differentials, human rights abuses and iniquitous social stratifications. Given this status quo, crime fiction in South Africa functions as "a form of social hermeneutics [...] within an ethically muddled topography" (de Kock 2015: 48). But this hermeneutics, I argue, is uniquely limited. This muddledness, especially when it comes to racial categories and race relations, rather than being "solved" in the literature, is its distinguishing feature, as authors, characters and readers grapple with it and remain, to a large extent, baffled and bewildered. The result is that the form of South African crime fiction is distinctive in that detection is limited to the level of abduction and, while racism is very much a concern, race and ethnicity as concepts have become destabilised and are often rendered as distorted or vague.

Significantly, South African fictional detectives explore, in an ontological sense, the entanglements between individuals and groups within an "ethically muddled topography". Characters burdened by the racist typologies of apartheid share the condition of "entanglement":

> Entanglement is a condition of being twisted together or entwined, involved with; it speaks of an intimacy gained, even if it was resisted, or ignored or uninvited. It is a term which may gesture towards a relationship or set of social relationships that is complicated, ensnaring, in a tangle, but which also implies a human foldedness. It works with difference and sameness but also with their limits, their predicaments, their moments of complication.
>
> *(Nuttall 2009: 1)*

Rather than rehearse the simplistic binaries of colonial or apartheid discourse (which could potentially reinforce them and thus be politically retrograde), South African crime fiction attempts to depict the condition of entanglement or hybridity, just as Hillerman was at pains to portray his Native American detectives as liminal subjects, operating in racial or ethnic spaces that are in-between and derived of many influences and affiliations. South African crime fiction concerns itself with the imbrication of individuals and groups, the peculiar intimacy wrought from past trauma and the current crises to which such propinquity gives rise.

Despite generally featuring a white male as the detective figure and adhering to the traditional hardboiled tradition in many respects, Deon Meyer's novels exhibit this ineluctable folded-togetherness of the different racial and ethnic groups in South Africa. Over the years Meyer's texts have expressed differing and even contradictory views about race and ethnicity. Taken together, his novels could be described as muddled about the topic of race and yet every plotline in the chronological present of a Meyer novel has an explication in South Africa's colonial or apartheid past. In effect, Meyer offers, for every crime committed in contemporary South Africa, a backstory of intricate entanglement, including the story of how racial and ethnic typologies were created.

Building on this notion that race and race relations are entangled in both social and chronological dimensions, Meyer also depicts South Africa's complex colonial and apartheid history by describing the growing prevalence of transnational criminal networks which criss-cross the globe. In a parallel move, he has downgraded his detectives' narrative of white injury which coloured his earlier novels and curtailed the contrived presentation of black characters through awkward racial and ethnic epithets. In their place, Meyer has endeavoured to compose a portrait of entanglement that, muddled as it may appear, is effective in capturing the disorderly tangle of race and ethnic categories and relations in post-apartheid South Africa. When applied to Meyer, the term accentuates the muddledness with which he repeatedly attempts to express the disillusionment and disorder of contemporary South Africa. *Cobra* (2014) therefore conscientiously and entertainingly captures South Africa's evolving and entangled systems of authority and power, cultural transformations and growing global networks, all of which are shown to have their roots in South Africa's racist past.

Re-visiting race and ethnicity: Entanglement and transnationalism in *Cobra* (2014)

By no means a coherent or consistent comment on race and ethnicity in post-apartheid South Africa, *Cobra* offers a problematisation of race and ethnicity through a deliberate emphasis on entanglement, and, relatedly, the extrapolation from various national, historical criminal elements to transnational or global ones. Writing in Afrikaans, Meyer's earlier novels aggregate to a recuperation project aimed at rehabilitating white men of Afrikaner ethnicity, through the figure of the detective-hero, all of whom have integrity, serve the nation-in-transition, and are ostensibly not racist despite having trained within the apartheid system. In *Cobra*, Benny Griessel, who has become a serialised protagonist, is haunted by the horrors of current crimes more so than the racist brutalities of the past regime. He is an intrepid, courageous detective who blurs racial lines through his class background. Impoverished and with little education, he exhibits an unswerving adherence to his own concept of a transcendent justice, having rejected apartheid's skewed justice and post-apartheid's muddled justice.

In so doing, he is shown to throw off the taint of his racial category and ethnicity, albeit while exposing himself as an idealistic fool. In previous novels, however, Griessel embodied a white injury narrative through references to his being passed over for promotion or to his frustration with his incompetent, black superiors. In *Cobra*, however, there is undoubtedly a shift and he is consolidated as a hero of the victims of crime, regardless of race or ethnicity. At worst, Griessel's white injury narrative and heroism appeal to a white readership, and Meyer is thus able to achieve white bonding and assuage white guilt. At best, however, Griessel is a racialised white detective, an interdependent member of a multi-racial detective team, who is anti-racist, especially in his conceptualisation of justice, and, further, his investigations force him to interrogate systems and structures which engender material, racial inequalities. Consequently, Meyer's Griessel is a convincing postcolonial detective who is "in process [...] learning, adjusting, changing, compromising, rejecting, resisting" (Christian 2001: 13), a muddled detective operating in a muddled setting.

Griessel's stature as a rehabilitated Afrikaner white man post-1994 is reinforced by the black subsidiary characters, in particular his colleagues Vaughn Cupido and Mbali Kaleni, who like and respect him. Originally, in previous novels they appeared as token black characters. Here, although substantially evolved, they still function to provide "authenticating commentary by a person of color" (Reddy 2003: 119), commentary which is required to exonerate the white detective and provide "an experience of absolution and affirmation for white readers who do not believe themselves to be racist" (120–21).

Cobra is a hardboiled, police procedural thriller pivoting on the intersection of political intrigue with transnational financial networks. These networks are in league with terrorist organisations and governments, with British Intelligence Services, South Africa's State Security Agency and with a petty pickpocket called Tyrone Kleinbooi, who is black or, to be more specific he is "Coloured" – this is the racial designation used by the apartheid government and which is still in common usage to describe a diverse group that is descended from Dutch colonisers, indigenous San and Khoi-San people, and various other racial, cultural and ethnic antecedents, including slaves from Asia. Through an emphasis on Tyrone's race and ethnicity as "Coloured" (in one sense indeterminate and hybrid, but from another perspective very specific and fixed in terms of social and cultural positioning), South Africa's apartheid past and post-apartheid present are brought under the spotlight.

A complex web of global and local criminal threads are thus woven together and at the centre is the local petty criminal, Tyrone. With this intricate plotting,[3] Meyer examines how entangled individual characters' lives and criminal systems are, and how race determines one's position in the web. Ultimately, the paltry criminal who is initially portrayed as a victim of his sociopolitical circumstances emerges as one of the heroes of the novel. Like Himes's Black, Tyrone has very few resources with which to fight "against overwhelming odds" (Himes 1993: 166), and yet he succeeds, subverting long-established categories of race and power.

Griessel's black sidekicks, Cupido, a "Coloured" captain in the Hawks team, and Kaleni, who is Zulu, the only female member of the team, provide further exploration of entangled

Race and ethnicity

race relations. Cupido, who is straight-talking and sharply dressed, explicitly and provocatively comments on racial and class inequalities. Rather than Griessel, Meyer deploys this character with his demotic speech (the original Afrikaans and his Cape slang are retained in the English translation) to make acute comments about South Africa's colonial past, racism, class and transnational crime. Remarking on the kidnapping of the wealthy white British mathematician from the luxurious wine-farm, he asks of the sympathetic Griessel:

> And what is this here? German owner of a Boer farm with a French name where a Brit is kidnapped. Fucking United Nations of Crime, that's where we're heading. And why? 'Cause they bring their troubles here. Like those French at Sutherland, and the Dewani thing, and who gets the rap? South-*fokken*-Africa.
>
> *(19)*

Here Cupido voices not only a type of xenophobia resulting from South Africa being maligned in international media, but also a postcolonial critique about how South Africa has historically been exploited by, mainly European, foreigners. Noteworthy is how Cupido's character has been developed over a number of novels into a less-caricatured, more nuanced portrait with racial and ethnic features conveyed through speech, dress and anti-racist sentiments. This character is, however, complicated by being at times xenophobic or racist himself, thus touching on a complex chain or entangled pattern whereby the victim of racism, deeply steeped in a cognitive framework, becomes a perpetrator. Cupido ends the above-quoted rant with a telling racially-loaded line: "But they screen the little *volkies* in slave uniforms and let them clean up after their whitey backsides until ten o' clock at night" (19). Here Cupido is referring to the exploitation of "Coloured" workers ("*volkies*") on luxurious wine estates and guest farms in and around Cape Town, alluding also to the region's colonial and slave era and the fact that racial power dynamics have remained disturbingly similar for three-and-a-half centuries.

In contrast to Cupido's quips and irreverence, Captain Kaleni is Griessel's formal, dignified, black, female boss. She is shown to have a strong emotional response to her work and to be ethically the strongest member of the team. When placed under pressure by corrupt police administrators to drop the case, Kaleni responds by making a surprising comparison between the democratic black-majority government and the apartheid white-minority government (172–73). With this act of defiance Kaleni simultaneously shames her superiors, presents a potted history of the anti-apartheid struggle, points to South Africa's entangled histories and political systems, and, counterintuitively it would seem, deracinates South Africa's most corrosive crime – corruption. Meyer is adroit in devising that Kaleni, a black woman, indicts the apartheid and post-apartheid regimes for the same crime. Just like Griessel, Kaleni is purposely shown to be committed to a cause, in this case, democracy, rather than to a racial group. Thus, the two detectives are aligned, one serving justice and the other democracy, with both espousing a discourse of non-racialism. Together, the trio of Griessel, Cupido and Kaleni, entangled as they are through shared histories, forced intimacies and a common (over-burdened) profession, form a multi-racial, multiethnic detective team. Such teams are found also in the novels of Margie Orford or Andrew Brown, where great care is given to these portraits of polygonal entanglements. This development in form, the move away from a lone detective to a group or team of interdependent, united members, is common in South African crime novels in which synthesis of difference or hybridity is required to detect, and, thematically, the intention is to signal a burgeoning multiculturalism.

In *Cobra* Meyer attempts to redefine the hardboiled tradition by presenting a motley trio of detectives and an underdog, black hero pitted against the most potent transnational criminal forces. In so doing, he creates a somewhat muddled, in terms of political commitment, characterisation and thematic thrust, but highly entertaining South African postcolonial, post-apartheid crime thriller with formulaic and conservative images of race and ethnicity, as well as progressive, transformative ones.

Conclusion

Many critics may view Meyer's crack at representing race and race relations in contemporary South Africa as disingenuous or naïve. While this choice of protagonist does not on the surface transform orthodox depictions of racial difference, a closer examination of Griessel reveals a white character grappling with guilt, trauma, frustration and the desire to effect a sort of universal, non-racial justice. Not entirely devoid of the Eurocentric and Americentric elements of the genre which undergirded its structural relationship with whiteness, *Cobra* nevertheless presents a white detective who is undergoing a slow and painful metamorphosis, a work in progress. This muddledness is not exclusive to white detectives. Andrew Brown's Eberard Februarie in *Coldsleep Lullaby* (2005) and Diale Tlholwe's Thabang Maje in *Ancient Rites* (2008) are black detectives experiencing a similar muddledness as they navigate a bewildering terrain of complicated entanglements, cultural hybridity and increasingly blurry racial and ethnic categories.

One of the paradoxes of this crime fiction is that, while systemic and structural racism are rendered hyper-visible in contemporary crime fiction, such texts are intent on dismantling those categories on which such systems and structures were built. Most saliently, in terms of engagement with race and ethnicity, contemporary crime fiction facilitates a view of intricate current relations between nations as being linked to a past, colonial era. This feature of contemporary crime fiction extends the interrogation of race and ethnicity beyond the confines of national settings, to explore how global networks of oppressive and exploitative systems and structures "once thought of as separate" now intersect in "unexpected ways" (Nuttall 2009: 11). Reflecting the contradictory trends of increasing "tribalism" and transnationalism of the world today, contemporary crime fiction creates multiple, entangled locations and time frames in which to view issues of race and ethnicity.

Notes

1 This strange difference for Holmes is an unknowable (in terms of ratiocination) social configuration of a family comprised of a white mother who had been married to a black man, a white father and a mixed-race child who is the product of the previous marriage.
2 See Maureen Reddy's thesis that this hypermasculine, heterosexual, white, male central consciousness of the hardboiled tradition is defined against the "others" of the narrative (2003: 9).
3 For a more detailed account of *Cobra* see Naidu (2016).

Bibliography

Anderson, J., Miranda, C. and Pezzotti, B. (eds) (2012) *The Foreign in International Crime Fiction: Transcultural representations*, New York: Continuum.
Arnold, J. (1987) "Detecting social history: Jews in the works of Agatha Christie", *Jewish Social Studies*, 49(3–4): 275–82.
Brown, A. (2005) *Coldsleep Lullaby*, Cape Town: Zebra Press.
Christian, E. (2001) "Introducing the post-colonial detective", in E. Christian (ed.), *The Post-colonial Detective*, New York: Palgrave Macmillan, 1–16.
Cornell, S. and Hartmann, D. (1998) *Ethnicity and Race: Making identities in a changing world*, Thousand Oaks, CA: Pine Forge Press.

Crawford, N.F. (2017) "The South as literary space in African-American hard-boiled detective fiction: challenging images that persist and matter in U.S. culture", in J. Claude and A. Mills (eds), *"Polar Noir": Reading African-American detective fiction*, François-Rabelais University Presses, https://books.openedition.org/pufr/5804 (accessed 20 May 2019).

de Kock, L. (2015) "From the subject of evil to the evil subject. Cultural Difference in post-apartheid South African crime fiction", *Safundi: The Journal of South African and American Studies*, 16(1): 28–50.

Döring, T. (2006) "Sherlock Holmes – he dead: disenchanting the English detective in Kazuo Ishiguro's *When We Were Orphans*", in Matzke and Mühleisen, 59–86.

Doyle, A.C. (1893) "The adventure of the yellow face", in *The Memoirs of Sherlock Holmes*, London: George Newnes, 17–28.

Ford, C.L. and Harawa, N.T. (2010) "A new conceptualization of ethnicity for social epidemiologic and health equity research", *Social Science and Medicine*, 71(2): 251–58.

Hillerman, T. (1986) *Skinwalkers*, New York: Harper.

Himes, C. (1993) *Plan B*, Jackson: University Press of Mississippi.

Krajenbrink, M. and Quinn, K.M. (eds) (2009) *Investigating Identities: Questions of identity in contemporary international crime fiction*, Amsterdam and New York: Rodopi.

Matzke, C. and Mühleisen, S. (eds) (2006) *Postcolonial Postmortems: Crime fiction from a transcultural perspective*, Amsterdam: Rodopi.

Meyer, D. (2014) *Cobra*, London: Hodder & Stoughton.

Naidu, S. (2014) "Writing the violated body: representations of violence against women in Margie Orford's crime thriller novels", *Scrutiny 2*, 19(1): 69–79.

———. (2016) "Crime travel: a survey of representations of transnational crime in South African crime fiction", *Journal of Commonwealth and Postcolonial Studies*, 4(1): 3–22.

Naidu, S. and Le Roux, B. (2017) *A Survey of South African Crime Fiction*, Pietermaritzburg: UKZN Press.

Neuman, J. (2011) "The curious case of Walter Mosley", *Moment Magazine*, September-October, www.momentmag.com/the-curious-case-of-walter-mosley/4/ (accessed 20 May 2019).

Nuttall, S. (2009) *Entanglement: Literary and cultural reflections on post-apartheid*, Johannesburg: Wits University Press.

Pearson, N. and Singer, M. (eds) (2009) *Detective Fiction in a Postcolonial and Transnational World*, Aldershot: Ashgate.

Pepper, A. (2000) *The Contemporary American Crime Novel: Race, ethnicity, gender, class*, Chicago & London: Fitzroy Dearborn Publishers.

Reddy, M. (2003) *Traces, Codes, and Clues: Reading race in crime fiction*, New Brunswick, New Jersey and London: Rutgers University Press.

Reitz, C. (2004) *Detecting the Nation: Fictions of detection and the imperial venture*, Columbus: Ohio State University Press.

Templeton, W. (1999) "*Xojo* and Homicide: The postcolonial murder mysteries of Tony Hillerman", in A.J. Gosselin (ed.), *Multicultural Detective Fiction: Murder from the other side*, New York: Garland, 37–59.

Tlholwe, D. (2008) *Ancient Rites*, Cape Town: Kwela Books.

13

COLONIALITY AND DECOLONIALITY

Shampa Roy

Crime fiction is an excitingly protean form and has generated a veritable heteroglossia of genres across cultures. When adapted and indigenised in different cultures – especially those to which it travelled as a result of colonisation – crime narratives have seen several shifts and changes and have been the site of conservative colonial and racial politics as well as of radical decoloniality and varied expressions of dissent. This chapter maps the terrain of decoloniality in crime writings within some colonised and postcolonial cultures and ends by examining the ideologically resistant mutations of Eurocentric models of crime fiction within colonial Bengal in India.

Crime novel and the empire

Postcolonial criticism over the last few decades has alerted us to the ways in which much of nineteenth-century Western literature – both literary and popular – is embedded in imperialist contexts and racist knowledge systems. Words like the "East"/the Orient, that are used in such writings, allow condescending generalisations about vast swathes of geographical spaces and become unexamined signifiers of savagery, unrestrained sexuality and criminal propensities that help legitimise imperial control. Both canonical fictions as well as popular texts like crime fictions written during the apogee of imperialist politics drew upon and consolidated racial and imperial attitudes and ideologies. The iconic Victorian *Bildungsroman* about a spirited governess – *Jane Eyre* – that deploys the mad, bad and dangerous figure of a Jamaican heiress, Bertha Mason, to gesture at the horrors attendant upon an interracial marriage was written in the same decade as the first generic formulation of crime fiction – "The Murders in the Rue Morgue" (1841) – which doubles as a racial allegory by attributing a pair of gruesome murders to a Bornean orangutan. While several nineteenth-century fictions implicitly endorse such attitudes and assumptions, there are rare instances – like Wilkie Collins's *The Moonstone* (1868) – that problematise them to a certain extent. Lauded by T.S. Eliot as "the first and greatest of English detective novels" (2015: 167), *The Moonstone* is undeniably saturated with disparaging racial and colonial stereotypes. It describes India as one of "the outlandish (places) of the earth", "full of thieves and murderers" (88), and Indians/Orientals as "tigerish", "snaky", "rogueish". At the centre of the plot is an Indian diamond that poses a terrifyingly alien threat to orderly English domesticity, secured by the "blessings of the British constitution" (35): "Here was our quiet

Coloniality and decoloniality

English house suddenly invaded by a devilish Indian Diamond – bringing after it a conspiracy of living rogues" (35). Racial contempt for the mysterious and menacing group of Indians intersects with anxieties about violation of the imperial centre by the diabolical periphery. Paranoia about such infiltration is also articulated through the biracial Ezra Jennings, "born and partly brought up in one of our colonies" (467).

And yet, easy cultural binaries are also undermined in the novel. The diamond had been stolen from an Indian temple by an unscrupulous Englishman and the final murder of another thieving Englishman by the mysterious group of Indians helps restore it to its place of origin. The invoking of a particularly violent moment in the history of British colonial expansion in India – the defeat of Tipu Sultan in 1799 and the vicious storming of his capital Seringapattam – as the context for the theft of the diamond, draws attention to the imperial project as characterised by unconscionable acts of invasion and plunder. And despite Sergeant Cuff's misgivings about hybrid roses, Ezra Jennings plays a crucial role in the solving of the mystery of the stolen gem, and is represented sympathetically as imaginative, astute and courageous.

The ideological ambivalence that marks Collins's novel, however, all but disappears once the great white, upper-class English male detective Sherlock Holmes makes his debut and dazzles the audiences with his formidable ratiocinative powers. Created by a writer who sought to make detection an "exact science", the fiercely rational detective and his purportedly unbiased observations and deductions only strengthened racial prejudices by refusing to see/expose them as ideological constructions. Ostensibly based on forensic acumen and dispassionate truth-seeking, Holmes's investigative process drew upon and embellished contemporary ethnographic and anthropological findings to demonise racial "others" and played upon his readers' fears of alien contagions that might have travelled from the colonies. In *The Sign of Four* (1890), for instance, Holmes's conjecture about the murderer's ethnicity, based on his authoritative know-ledge of ethnographic data, prepares his readers for a savage "other". What is then revealed of the Andaman Islander Tonga – "as venomous as a young snake" (1986: 1531) – only confirms the typological discourse invoked with precision by the erudite detective. This discursive con-struction helps elide the history of Britain's vicious colonisation of the islands in 1858 that wrecked the lives of the indigenous Andamanese population and justifies "that strange visitor's" brutal end "in the dark ooze at the bottom of the Thames" (1986: 1158). Furthermore, while describing the Indian rebels of the 1857 Mutiny/First War of Independence, the novel refuses to distinguish between them and putative criminals like Tonga. The Mutineers' questioning of the legitimacy of the Empire is dismissed through derisive references to them as "two hundred thousand black devils let loose" (1986: 1291).

And even when there are no Oriental malefactors in the Holmes stories, spaces like South America, Africa and India are synecdochically represented through strangely horrific indi-genous poisons (or even a poisonous snake), all of which are used in murders within England. Jefferson Hope (*A Study in Scarlet*) uses South American arrow poisons; Bartholomew Sholto is killed by a thorn dipped in "some powerful vegetable alkaloid" (1986: 563); the Tregennis family succumbs to the fumes of an African root ("The Adventure of the Devil's Foot", 1910, 1986: 428); the "speckled band" is a deadly snake brought from India by Dr Grimsby Roylott, "a clever and ruthless man who had an Eastern training" ("The Adventure of the Speckled Band", 1892, 1986: 368) to kill his stepdaughter.

Thus, by a neat sleight of hand, imperial violence wrought on the colonies by the English is completely erased, whereas savagery and motiveless malignancy that threaten to invade English peace are represented as inextricable features of the East/Orient. And needless to say, the English detective's stature is spectacularly enhanced when he demonstrates his ability to read and destroy every trace of "identifiable foreignness" that causes metropolitan anxiety (Thomas 1994: 659).

Racist assumptions and stereotypes were rife in Anglo-American crime novels well into the twentieth century. The immensely popular Fu Manchu series, which was first published from 1913, for instance, was centred around a Chinese "devil doctor", "the yellow peril incarnate in one man" (Seshagiri 1913, 2006: 162) and his nefarious schemes of global domination. Although English xenophobia is mocked to a certain extent in Christie's fictions, the narratives are insistently focused on a small group of western, white, middle-class characters, even when set in British colonies like Egypt or the Caribbean. Furthermore, disparaging remarks made casually by characters in her novels about Arabs as "dirty dark-yellow" (1936, 1962: 73), or about black workers in the Caribbean as lazy ("for blacks don't work themselves to death at all, so far as I can see. Was looking at a fellow shinning up a coconut tree to get his breakfast, then he goes to sleep for the rest of the day" [1964: 150]) suggest complicity in contemporary racist ideologies that underpinned colonial politics.

Plotting decoloniality

Despite its early history of entwinement with colonial and racial ideologies, crime fiction has undergone continuing changes and seen radical deconstruction of the ratiocinative process when adapted into an immensely diverse array of cultural and linguistic contexts all over the world. Moving across national and linguistic boundaries, it has experienced a great deal of exciting "genre-bending" (Matzke and Mühleisen 2006: 5).

Early manifestations of the genre in some of the cultures, like India, that had experienced colonisation were influenced by or even simple mimicries of the immensely popular Anglo-American models. But subsequently they came into their own and began "speaking to the varying needs of local communities of readers" (Knepper 2007: 1436) and "interrogating the imperial histories and racial ideologies that helped spur their (own) generic development" (Pearson and Singer 2009: 8). As a result, such crime fictions

> stretch over a wide range of registers, themes and styles, from pulp fiction to highly literary novels with elements of crime, from cosy mysteries with a sense of closure to fragmented narratives focusing on racial tensions, gender conflicts or the morals of violence.
>
> *(Matzke and Mühleisen 2006: 3)*

Even when borrowed conventions are not entirely discarded, ideas of criminality and policing begin to acquire layered significations when explored by diverse writers responding to the social and political exigencies of their specific colonial and postcolonial contexts. The investigation of crimes in such novels is invariably tied to examining the crimes of colonial regimes and what has followed in their wake from the perspectives of previously colonised subjects. The detective protagonists help open up wider possibilities by giving a voice to those who are disenfranchised within colonial contexts and marginalised or demonised by Eurocentric fictions. Many such remappings of the Eurocentric model refuse to conform to the representational constraints associated with classic solution-oriented mysteries. They are not plotted around the detecting authority's self-assured assumption that justice will be done and an infallible social order restored once the audacious criminal is unearthed and punished. Instead they suggest that the epistemological certainties of conventional detective fictions are limited by their refusal to locate individual culpability in larger socioeconomic causes of crimes or to examine the contradictions and iniquities of the social order. Questions of criminality and justice are revealed as being far too complexly embedded in social and economic realities and

Coloniality and decoloniality

in inequalities of class (in the case of India, also caste), gender and race to be resolved by a single detective's spectacular feats of logic or the discovery of individual villainy. Brutally unjust systems of colonial governance have either created or exacerbated inequalities and despite political decolonisation, many postcolonial cultures continue to be beleaguered by the legacies of systemic oppression and injustices. What constitutes a crime and a criminal can be revealed as being fractious sites of struggle for power by contending social agents. The assumption that a Holmesian kind of detective can plug the gaps in an otherwise unquestioned social order, becomes naïve and incongruous given that the social order itself is exposed as riddled with continuing histories of injustices and inequities. Solace-inducing denouements are therefore often sacrificed in such fictions for the sake of a deeper and more problematised viewing of crime through an engagement with material realities.

In South Africa, for instance, where a huge diverse population of black African people were colonised by various European countries for over 300 years and subsequently governed by a white minority government which imposed apartheid for most of the twentieth century, the entire history of its written literature, with its roots in colonialism and apartheid, from a certain vantage point, might be seen to be the history of criminality or the response to it (Warnes 2012: 982). While crime fiction became enormously popular in post-apartheid South Africa, writers like Wessel Ebersohn, who wrote even during apartheid South Africa, extended and reshaped the genre for social analysis so that, "the investigation of a single case widens out into an analysis of the 'condition of the nation itself'" (Davis 2006: 186).

Post-apartheid crime fiction writers in South Africa produce their fiction within a context where despite official liberation, the long shadow cast by the depredations of its colonial and apartheid history continues to be felt in the imbalances of power and wealth, economic uncertainties and the widespread prevalence of corruption and violent crimes. As such, crime fiction has become one of the most apposite forms for engaging with contemporary contexts and many writers use the genre for a searing analysis and critique of the rot in inherited institutions like the police, judiciary and state bureaucracy. Crime writer Roger Smith's assertion, "I believe a crime writer working in a country like South Africa has an obligation to present an honest picture of the realities. Crime fiction is more than entertainment" (Fletcher 2013: 91) refers to the particular relevance of this genre in a crime-ridden society and also its need to go beyond the traditional attractions of formula-driven whodunits. Ebersohn, while talking about the untenability of a definite and comforting closure in his novel *Closed Circle* (1990) based on the unsolved killings of left-wing activists during apartheid, says,

> the problem with *Closed Circle* was that I am aware that there have been many of these sort of killings in South Africa and in almost no cases have the killers been brought to justice. So I simply couldn't have the fictitious characters brought to justice.
>
> *(Green 1994: 13)*

The idea of a just order being restored after the solving of the central mystery continues to be demystified by post-apartheid writings that describe dystopic contexts where politicians and police are as dangerous as criminals, organised crime is a powerful presence and the senseless deaths and violation of women and children an everyday reality.

The gruesomely violated female bodies in Margie Orford's novels like *Daddy's Girl* (2009) and *Like Clockwork* (2006), for instance, are reminiscent of and yet starkly different from the female corpses in Poe's early crime fictions, for Orford's novels bring to light stories of appalling and widespread misogyny that bewilder and haunt readers long after the mystery has been formally "resolved". While the ethical dimensions of such graphic descriptions of violated female bodies have been debated by critics, they are not just a set of clues for the detective to decipher but become tragic symbols of "a war against women" and the gross systemic failures of post-apartheid society.

The detective protagonists in the works of writers like Orford, Deon Meyer or Michiel Heyns, are often scarred by traumatic memories and bewildered by present-day horrors. The criminality they confront is shaped by a society where the violence of the present is a living legacy of the different kinds of violence (state-sponsored and oppositional) during the colonial and apartheid regimes, so that their engagement with it is different from that of the coldly ratiocinative sleuth or even the cynically detached hardboiled detective. The vicious crimes they encounter are accompanied with morally complex challenges and conundrums, and the lines between offender and victim, justice and revenge seem contingent and ambivalent. As Mpayipheli, a character in Meyer's *Devil's Peak* (2007), who has operated as an assassin outside unjust laws during the apartheid era and is now forced to seek vigilante justice in the post-apartheid system, muses:

> How do you describe to a child the strange, lost world you lived in – explained about Apartheid and oppression and revolution and unrest? [...] He sat down with his back to a rock and he tried. At the end he said you must only take up a weapon against injustice; you must only point it at people as a very last resort. When all other forms of defence and persuasion were exhausted.
>
> *(2007: 80)*

In Australia, even though crime fiction written over several decades explored the lawlessness of colonial society in the outback and the imported British hierarchy imposed upon the continent's urban centres, these were all written from white settler perspectives and Aboriginals' voices and their horrific history of displacement and killing remained occluded until recently. In the late 1920s, a mixed-race protagonist, Detective Inspector Bonaparte (Bony), created by Arthur Upfield, became popular with Australian audiences. Although Bony is important for being the first Aboriginal investigator, his construction endorsed certain patronising stereotypes about Aboriginals, and Bony himself is represented as being untouched by racial discrimination and as espousing racist prejudices against interracial unions. It was with the advent of Indigenous writers of crime fiction, like Philip McLaren, that Aboriginal perspectives in crime fiction were placed at the centre and racial and colonialist stereotypes typical to white settler fictions were challenged.

McLaren's first novel *Sweet Water-Stolen Land* (1993) is woven around the nineteenth-century Myall Creek massacre in New South Wales where ten white Europeans and one black African killed thirty unarmed Indigenous Australians and it became the first (and last) time that the colonial administration intervened to ensure that the Aboriginal people got justice. McLaren plots his novel around this historical case and examines the colonisers' imposition of *Terra Nullius,* their rampant killings of Aboriginals, arbitrary grabbing of their lands and twisting of religious and ethnographic discourses to legitimise the violence.

His novel, *Scream Black Murder* (1995), inspired by the unresolved case of the 1989 murder of an Aboriginal, David Gundy, by policemen who went unpunished, has two Indigenous detectives, Fuller and Leslie. The detectives pursue a killer who attacks Indigenous women and whose crimes have gone undetected until now, largely because of the lax attitude of the authorities towards their murder. Unlike Bony, who seems to have never suffered the effects of racial discrimination or been discomfited by it, McLaren's investigators suffer as a result of the former assimilation policy. Detective Leslie, for instance, asserts that he has joined the police force because "he was furious that deaths of Aboriginal people were not investigated properly", "well-documented mistreatment and abuses by authorities were allowed to pass" and "the loss of black lives was largely unexplained" (2001: 14). And Detective Fuller frequently broods on her forcible separation from her mother as a child and on being forced to work as a domestic for a white family – two experiences that are based on actual historical experiences of the Aborigines, referred to as the Stolen Generations and Stolen Wages, respectively.

Crime fictions of the kind written by Meyer, Orford and McLaren make statements about their country's political past and through investigations of present-day crimes, critique and intervene in contexts that continue to be crippled by the power hierarchies and dominant ideologies that characterised colonial systems of governance.

Colonial Bengal and the rise of *Goyenda* (detective) fiction

In colonial India, it was in Bengal, the administrative centre of the British colonial government and the focal point of colonial power for over a century, that crime fictions written in an Indian language – Bangla – emerged for the first time. In Calcutta, the capital of Bengal, a dedicated detective department was set up in 1868 as part of Calcutta Police, and from the end of the nineteenth century, the genre of crime fiction began to be explored by several Bangla writers.[1] Initially, writers and publishers of such fictions felt they could only appease their readership – the English-educated, middle-class Bengali *bhadralok*, many of whom were fervent anglophiles and readers of Vidocq, Poe and Doyle – with writings that were "*chhayabalamban*" (De 1905: 1), a word that hints at a slippage between an exact reflection and adaptation of the Eurocentric models. However, as the genre began to flourish in Bangla from the 1890s, it became evident that there were enough readers who welcomed crime fictions which could overcome the regurgitatory impulse and were not "incompetent translations of English or French crime writings", but written in ways that were "entirely the writers' own" (from the weekly journal *Bangabashi* (June 1906), qtd. in Ghosh 2011: 7). Thus was born the indigenised *goyenda*, who was marked by the historical moment of his articulation.

Goyenda fiction emerged during an epistemic break, when for the first time colonised Bengalis asserted their desire for a decolonised nation and identity through the idea of *swadeshi*.[2] Racist and oppressive government policies created an atmosphere of simmering anti-colonial resentment from the last decade of the nineteenth century, and it finally exploded in what came to be known as *swadeshi* protests in Bengal that led up to and continued to simmer in the wake of the colonial government's arbitrary decision to partition the region in 1905. A revivification of the Bengali Hindu subjectivity, perceived as having weakened over the past few centuries, was felt to be needed by large sections of the *bhadralok*. Though fraught with regressive implications in terms of gender, caste and religion, this ideal helped express the colonised subjects' growing resentment against years of racial slights and injustices and the need to challenge the colonial regime.

Produced within this volatile context, early *goyenda* fiction, despite being a legatee of colonial education and western models of writing, helped consolidate anti-colonial and nationalistic masculine identities. Located at the intersection of the Bengali *bhadralok*'s fascination with European goods, the English language and literature as markers of *adhunikata* (modernity) and their intensifying disenchantment with the colonial regime, this fiction represents the colonised subjects' negotiation of a modernity that was fractured and fraught with contradictions. The *bhadralok*, though unable to forfeit their admiration for European languages and literatures, saw the importance of writings that would strengthen Bangla, widen the horizons of its literature and help in the assertion of a strong linguistic identity capable of resisting the colonial privileging of English.

The imagining of the early *goyenda* hero resists the derisive and racist stereotypes of the dull and servile Bengali *babu* – "fitted by nature and by habit for the foreign yoke" – popularised by colonial writers like Macaulay and Kipling (Macaulay 1845, 1910: 39).[3] Even when the *goyenda* is employed by the colonial government as a police detective, he is represented as being completely untrammelled by colonial authority, capable of acting with admirable inventiveness and freedom and venerated by his British superiors. Since the humiliation of drudgery-filled *chaakri/keranigiri* (employment in clerical jobs) was also tied by contemporary social commentators in Bengal to the middle-class Bengalis' over-dependence on a colonial education that discouraged independent thinking, it is not surprising that *goyendas* are constructed as being distanced from the egregious consequences of such education. Eschewing academic pursuits, the *goyenda* relies on his agility and resourcefulness to outwit diabolical antagonists. In one of the earliest Bangla *goyenda* fictions, for instance, *goyenda* Haridas is condescendingly described by the narrator, his old childhood friend, as an inveterate failure within the school system. However, when the narrator meets his old friend during a criminal investigation, he is awe-struck by Haridas's *goyenda* resourcefulness in identifying and apprehending the culprits (Sarkar 1895).

Promoda

Written and published in the same year that Bengal's first arbitrary partitioning was announced by Lord Curzon amidst massive *Swadeshi* outcry, Kshetramohan Ghosh's novel *Promoda* has as its hero a young *goyenda*, Jadunath, who embodies the ideal of physically heroic and dynamic Bengali masculinity that had come to be seen as intrinsic to Bengal's militant anti-colonial protest.[4] Perhaps it is no coincidence that Jadunath is about the same age as many of the iconic adolescent revolutionaries of the time who were idolised for their single-minded commitment to the *Swadeshi* cause. Readers are meant to marvel at the indomitable courage and commitment of the young *goyenda* as he chances upon a case of criminal conspiracy against Promoda, a wealthy heiress, and becomes obsessed with solving the mystery. Jadu does not have Holmes's scientific knowledge and forensic acumen, but his *odhyobshyay* (tenacity) and *protyutponnomoti* (ready-wittedness) are foregrounded as qualities that have been instrumental in his rise as a successful detective.

Impulsive and unafraid of taking risks, Jadu, an inveterate rule-breaker, disrupts the ideal of the *bhalo/shanto chhele* (the archetypal "good/virtuous boy" admired for his compliance and quiet devotion to academic pursuits) which had traditionally encapsulated the Bengali subjects' unquestioning acquiescence in the colonial system and their belief that their industriousness would be duly rewarded by entry into lucrative professions. The erosion of the Bengalis' faith in an assumed equation between *lekhhaa poraa* (studying) and *boro hoyaa* (social advancement) – the idea of hard-earned cultural capital leading to personal and professional growth – is expressed through the emergence of a young subversive hero like Jadu who shuns both colonial classrooms and safe professional choices: "Jadunath was not more than 15 years old [...] He never was terribly interested in learning to read and write [...] [Being a detective] had sharpened his wits while sitting in classrooms had made the others rusty" (1905: 8).[5]

Jadunath's adventures in the novel begin on a stormy night when he espies two men taking a sleeping young woman (Promoda) into an asylum run by a sinister English woman called Helena. Criminality and chicanery in the novel are inseparably intertwined with the colonisers. A criminal conspiracy has been hatched against Promoda by her Eurasian half-sister Lily, Lily's brutish English fiancé Tomary, his friend John and two Bengali *babus*, a doctor and a lawyer. Their plan was to imprison Promoda in an asylum for the rest of her life and to have a fake funeral to prove her death so that Lily could become the sole heir to their father's wealth. Lily's

Coloniality and decoloniality

ruthlessness and avarice are tied to her Eurasian identity (readers are informed early on that she is the product of an ill-advised union between a Bengali *bhadralok* and an Englishwoman) and Helena's harsh arrogance is "the result of the white blood that flowed in her veins" (Ghosh 1905: 21). The two wily *babus* are perfect examples of complicity in the prevalent power structures produced by colonial education.

Consequently, the investigation becomes a battle of wills between the disenfranchised, colonised hero and his powerful colonial adversaries. Viewing Jadu through the prism of entrenched racial attitudes – as an illiterate native lout who can be easily brushed aside or brow-beaten – Tomary and his cronies fail to perceive him as a threat, and it is this complacency that leads to their final comeuppance. In fact, Jadu is shown using the derogatory stereotype of the obsequious and cowardly Bengali as a guise to dupe his arrogant adversaries.

Another voice from the margins that becomes crucial in the crime-solving is that of a poor carriage driver, a man rendered all but invisible by his class, caste and race. Despite his modest assertion that, "We are mere carriage drivers, poor men who have to toil everyday to earn a livelihood. All we are interested in is getting our fare. We really don't need to bother our heads over things that happen around us", his witness statement indicates remarkably acute observation and memory (1905: 65). By finding and using such witnesses who are bullied and dismissed by the police, the *goyenda* privileges subaltern voices and gestures at alternative modes of crime-detection that are far more effective than boorish forms of colonial policing that one contemporary social commentator describes as "worse than the criminal excesses of dacoits" (Chattopadhyay 1892: 35).

In the final encounter, after unmasking the conspirators, young Jadu's audacious declaration to the bewildered Englishmen, "*Sahib* what are you staring at? I'm impossible to put down. Even if you bury me inside the ground, I will spring right back", acquires a political edge (1905: 113); it warns of a resistant force that will not be intimidated or defeated until it has ful-filled its aspirations of justice.

Like Jadu, the crime fiction of the colonised or previously colonised writers is often a resistant force. It moves away from "classic" detective fiction and its formal conventions in order to engage critically with the compelling sociopolitical issues that shape the crimes of its specific context, and to lay bare its inextricable links with power hierarchies and injustices related to the colonial period. Whether it is through a radical reimagining of the investigator, settings that reflect irretrievably damaged social and political order or open-ended closures, crime fictions that have emerged in colonial and postcolonial contexts often question the hege-monic discourses that underpin the Eurocentric explorations of this genre.

Notes

1 Crime fiction in Bangla continued to be written in the postcolonial period, but for this essay I have restricted the focus to writings that were published in the colonial period.
2 *Swadeshi* translates literally as "of one's own nation". It began largely as an agitation against the partition from 1903 and subsequently enlarged into a more broad-based anti-colonial movement.
3 Kipling's *Hurree* Babu in *Kim* (1901) strengthened the discursive construction of Bengali masculinity as effete and cowardly.
4 This crime novel in Bangla, like others published in the first decade of the twentieth century, was popular with contemporary readers, but has subsequently neither been translated nor received any crit-ical attention. The translations from Bangla in this essay are mine.
5 The proverbial *bhalo chhele/subodh balak* (good/virtuous boy) was made popular by school primers in which two boys, the well-mannered Gopal and the reckless Rakhal, were constructed as Manichean opposites.

Bibliography

Chattopadhyay, R. (1892) *Pulish o Lokrakhha*, Calcutta: Nobin Chandra Pal Publishers.

Christie, A. (1962) [1936] *Murder in Mesopotamia*, London: Fontana.

———. (1964) *The Caribbean Mystery*, London: Harper Collins, Kindle edition.

Collins, W. (1868) *The Moonstone*, Kindle edition.

Davis, G. (2006) "Political loyalties and the intricacies of the criminal mind: the detective fiction of Wessel Ebersohn", in C. Matzke et al., 181–99.

De, P. (1905) *Govindram*, Calcutta: Bengal Medical Library.

Doyle, A.C. (1986) *Sherlock Holmes: The complete novels and stories*, New York: Bantam.

Eliot, T.S. (2015) [1927] "Wilkie Collins and Dickens", in F. Dickey, J. Formichelli and R. Schuchard (eds), *The Complete Prose of T.S. Eliot: The critical edition, 1927–1929*, vol. 3, Baltimore: John Hopkins University Press, 164–74.

Fletcher, E. (2013) "South African crime fiction and the narration of the post-apartheid", Master's thesis, University of the Western Cape, https://core.ac.uk/download/pdf/58915337.pdf (accessed April 2019).

Ghosh, B. (2011) (ed.) *Pachkari De Rachnabali*, vol. 1, Kolkata: Karuna Prakashani.

Ghosh, K. (1905) *Promoda*, Kolkata: Seal Press.

Green, M. (1994) "The detective as historian: A case for Wessel Ebersohn", *Current Writing Text and Reception in South Africa*, 6(2): 93–112.

Knepper, W. (2007) "Remapping the crime novel in the francophone Caribbean: the case of Patrick Chamoiseau's 'Solibo Magnifique'", *PMLA*, 122(5): 1431–46.

Macaulay, T. (1910) [1845] *Essay on Lord Clive*, London: George Harrap.

Matzke, C. and Mühleisen, S. (eds) (2006) *Postcolonial Postmortems: Crime fiction from a transcultural perspective*, Amsterdam: Rodopi.

McLaren, P. (2001) *Scream Black Murder*, 2nd edn, Broome, Australia: Magabala Books.

Meyer, D. (2007) *Devil's Peak*, trans. K.L. Seegers, London: Hodder and Stoughton.

Pearson, N. and Singer, M. (eds) (2009) *Detective Fiction in a Postcolonial and Transnational World*, Farnham: Ashgate.

Sarkar, S. (1895) *Shabash Churi!!*, Kolkata: Mohan Press.

Seshagiri, U. (2006) "Modernity's (yellow) perils: Dr. Fu-Manchu and English race paranoia", *Cultural Critique*, 62: 162–94.

Thomas, R. (1994) "The fingerprint of the foreigner: colonizing the criminal body in 1890s detective fiction and anthropology", *ELH*, 61: 655–83.

Warnes, C. (2012) "Writing crime in the new South Africa: negotiating threat in the novels of Deon Meyer and Margie Orford", *Journal of Southern African Studies*, 38(4): 981–91.

14

PSYCHOANALYSIS

Heta Pyrhönen

Detective fiction and psychoanalysis share many points of convergence. Both date from approximately the same time period: "an era that saw increasing doubt about logic and reason as ways to govern the world and that questioned humanity's ability to redeem itself through progress and knowledge" (Yang 2010: 596). Sigmund Freud liked detective fiction, especially Doyle's Sherlock Holmes and Poe's stories (Yang 2010: 597). Doyle provides a strong point of connection given that he, like Freud, was a physician by training. Both fashioned their texts as "cases", narrating the vicissitudes of a patient's life or of a perplexing crime. Doyle relied on the method of thinking taught to him by the medical professor Joseph A. Bell (Eco and Sebeok 1983). Logicians call this method abduction. Abduction accounts for a pre-existing fact (a symptom that ails the patient or a clue of the crime) that appears inexplicable: Both psychoanalyst and detective reason backwards, postulating from an existing fact a rule that explains it. The abductive operation may rely on unconscious perceptions of the world (Sebeok and Umiker-Sebeok 1983: 18–19).

Carlo Ginzburg explains that Freud and Holmes adhere to an epistemological model that was emerging in the late nineteenth century. It held that details and marginalia provided the key to an individual's "innermost core", because his or her individuality is linked with elements beyond conscious control (1983: 87). The psychoanalyst and the detective share a similarly cautious approach to the details, participants and narrated accounts of a psychological or criminal case. In his extensive study of Freud, Paul Ricoeur speaks of a "hermeneutics of suspicion" (1970: 26, 32) that calls for a "[reading] against the grain and between the lines" with the aim of drawing out "what a text fails – or wilfully refuses to see" (Felski 2015: 1).

This emphasis on suspicion as a guiding principle of reading is inscribed in the genre, because by inviting readers to solve the crime, it encourages them, not only to think like a detective, but also to think like a criminal. If readers are able to think like a criminal, then they may be able to imagine committing crimes under certain circumstances. The genre asks that readers pry and peep into matters related to crime under the guise of detection. This attitude endows the investigation with a voyeuristic quality, rendering this activity guilt-free and making reading pleasurable (see also Porter 1981: 240–41).

Psychoanalytical discussions tend to conclude that the genre stubbornly avoids the "truth" at which it is continually hinting: Detective fiction prevents readers from fully applying the critical method of suspicion to themselves as readers. It does not make them aware that their (unconscious) desires are at work while reading fiction about crimes. Hence, when the time comes to reveal the criminal's identity, readers may smugly disengage themselves from the desires underlying the crime (Žižek 1991: 59).

Scholars have examined various thematic and structural analogies between detective fiction and various psychoanalytic approaches. In this chapter, I concentrate on the most influential ways in which psychoanalysis has been brought to bear on the genre. I build my discussion on Doyle's short story "A Case of Identity" (1891) in order to illustrate how Holmes's reading strategy both converges with and departs from the psychoanalyst's. Their shared reading strategy provides a fruitful entry point for a discussion of how psychoanalysis has contributed to detective fiction criticism. I read this story in light of the French poststructuralist psychoanalyst Jacques Lacan's analysis of Edgar Allan Poe's "The Purloined Letter" (1844). I also consider a more recent psychoanalytic approach to detective fiction: Pierre Bayard's "detective criticism". Doyle's story, by focusing on the question of identity, overlaps with the analysands' probing of their identities in psychoanalysis.

Details in detection

"A Case of Identity" opens with Holmes letting his imagination fly. He says to Dr Watson:

> If we could fly out of that window hand in hand, hover over this great city, gently remove the roofs, and peep in at the queer things which are going on, the strange coincidences, the plannings, the cross-purposes, the wonderful chain of events, working through generations, and leading to the most *outré* results, it would make all fiction with its conventionalities and foreseen conclusions most stale and unprofitable.
>
> *(1989: 50)*

This flight of the imagination suggests that the present case addresses strange incidents with excessive outcomes. It may also be read as a poetic description of the psychoanalytic process during which the analysands, with the analyst's help, acquire a new insight into their psyches and the surprising associations these psyches house.

This connection with psychoanalytical thinking is strengthened when Holmes observes the client, Miss Mary Sutherland, before meeting her in person. He sees her nervously moving back and forth on the pavement. He treats her nervous movements as *symptoms* of her mental suffering. On this basis, he formulates an abduction according to which "oscillation upon the pavement always means an *affaire du coeur*" (51). His conjecture is proven correct, for the client narrates a case that deals with the mysterious disappearance of Hosmer Angel, a London cashier, to whom Mary was engaged. Her mother and stepfather did not want her to participate in social gatherings, but, nevertheless, she had met Hosmer at a ball. Hosmer had wooed her by inviting her for walks and sending letters. Setting out for church on the wedding day in separate carriages, Hosmer disappeared before the vehicles arrived. The groom had insisted that she swear on the Bible to stay true to him no matter what might happen. The jilted bride begs Holmes to find out what happened to Hosmer.

Hosmer's letters provide key clues. Acting the role of armchair detective, Holmes solves the case simply by listening and writing a note to verify his conjectures. He begins with the fact that the letters are typewritten from start to finish, including the signature. Typically, one writes love letters by hand and, in particular, signs them by hand. Moreover, the letters are not only void of emotion but also of any sense of personality. Slavoj Žižek explains that fictional detectives are capable of "looking awry", that is, of spotting an odd detail in the design of the crime. The solution lies in such odd minutiae, for Holmes notices that the typewritten e's are slurred and the r's tailless; additionally, there are fourteen other specificities about the keys (60). In placing himself in a position from where such details appear meaningful (Žižek 1991: 11–12, 114, 125–26), Holmes deciphers their purport. He concludes that Mary's stepfather, Mr Windibank, has adopted the role of Hosmer Angel. The fact that Hosmer appears only when Mr Windibank is travelling suggests that two men are in fact the same person. Furthermore, this conjecture explains Hosmer's appearance and personal characteristics: He has disguised all features – his distinctive eyes, voice, facial characteristics and handwriting – that would have enabled the shortsighted Mary to recognise him.

In planning the crime, the criminal manipulates the intersubjective realm of meaning: The letters disclose Hosmer's amorous intentions. Holmes takes this deceitfulness as a starting point. In this respect his approach resembles that of a psychoanalyst who treats all details of the analysand's demeanour and speech as potentially meaningful. By positioning himself within the symbolic domain of language, reason and logic, the detective identifies that which remains unconscious (the criminal's desire) in his deception. The typewriter's worn keys, spotted only by Holmes, have "really quite as much individuality as a man's handwriting" (60). Mr Windibank has unwittingly given himself away in the impersonality of the typewritten text. Moreover, Holmes considers what Mr Windibank achieves by actions that poorly fit the framework of intimacy. He treats these details as symptoms of the culprit's suppressed desire. Thus, when Mr Windibank justifies himself by claiming he only played a joke on Mary (62), Holmes spells out the mercenary nature of the stepfather's deception that made Mary invest in him emotionally. The desire underlying this crime is thereby briefly verbalised. However, in order to probe the topic of unconscious desire, we need to look closer at how Hosmer Angel's letters circulate in the story.

Letters in circulation

Jacques Lacan used Poe's "The Purloined Letter" to illustrate the basic tenets of his psychoanalytic theory. Poe's story revolves around letters stolen from a woman of high rank. Even though Hosmer's letters are not stolen, Lacan's analysis throws light on the story, for both repeat a similar design. As this design is repeated twice in Poe's story, it crystallises the story's narrative pattern. This structure becomes apparent in the way the letter organises the characters in triads whose shape emerges from three kinds of glance with which they see the letter: The first glance is blind; the second sees the blindness of the first, but does not perceive that it, too, is being seen; whereas the third sees what the first two glances leave exposed. As this third glance sees the whole configuration, it marks the place of analysis and analyst.

In Poe's story, a woman, perhaps the Queen of France, has received a compromising letter that she must conceal from her husband, the King, who enters the room. She hides the letter by leaving it among other papers in full view on her table. Her tactic succeeds, for the King does not spot it. The letter, however, is stolen from the Queen in the husband's presence by Minister D–. The King is blind to what is taking place, while the Minister sees his blindness; the Queen, however, observes both her husband's blindness and the Minister's cunning: He can steal the letter, knowing that she cannot intervene, because by so doing she would alert her husband's attention to the illicit letter. For Lacan, this situation serves as the story's first scene.

Doyle's story is set in middle-class surroundings. The illustrious persons are replaced by a typist and a merchant stepfather, yet the camouflaged tension is similar. Mr Windibank forbids Mary all social outings, because a woman "should be happy in her own family circle" (54). As

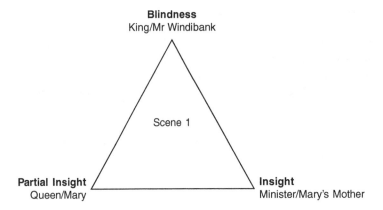

Fig. 1 Character positions – Scene 1

in Poe's story, she has to hide her desire from a man in an authoritative position. The dissatisfied Mary "wants her own circle" (45). In this first scene Mary believes that Mr Windibank occupies the King's position of blindness, while Mary holds the position of Poe's Queen, that of partial knowledge, partial ignorance, for she trusts that Mr Windibank is ignorant of her correspondence with Hosmer. Given that Mary believes her mother to be on her side, she is fully ignorant of the fact that the mother is Mr Windibank's accomplice. Therefore, at this stage, the mother holds the position of power. If she wanted to, she could disclose her husband's treachery and deflect blame from herself. The interpersonal relationships may be presented in triangular figures (Fig. 1). Here I rely on Shoshana Felman's analysis of Lacan's essay (1988: 145).

Lacan observes that the first scene is repeated in the story, and that this repetition puts the stolen letter in circulation, changing the characters' positions relative to each other. In the second scene of Poe's story, the Prefect of Police, whom the Queen has hired to retrieve the stolen letter, moves into the position of blindness, for although he has enlisted Dupin's help, he is not informed of the detective's investigation. What sets Dupin apart from Minister D– is his realisation that the letter exerts influence on its holder by making him repeat the former recipient's actions. Indeed, Minister D– has hidden the letter by using the Queen's strategy: He has placed it in a card rack in full view. While visiting the minister's apartment in disguise, Dupin notices that the adversary has resealed the letter and closed it with his own seal – who would send a letter to himself? This gaffe is the equivalent of a Freudian slip, a parapraxis or an unconscious error that betrays unconscious wishes or intentions. By using the same strategy of hiding as the Queen, the minister self-assuredly proclaims his superiority. Simultaneously, however, he loses his dominant position, gliding into the place the Queen occupied before, for he is unaware of Dupin's investigative intervention. Stealing the letter back, Dupin occupies the position of analysis.

In Doyle's story, Mary loses her place of partial knowledge, for she has no control over Holmes's investigation. Like Minister D–, Mary's mother loses the upper hand, sliding into the position of partial knowledge, partial ignorance: She knows the truth, but has neither knowledge of nor control over Holmes's actions. At this stage, Holmes has the advantage, for he has solved the case and has decided what action to take on his client's behalf. He reasons that the stepfather Mr Windibank is Hosmer Angel. In order to prove his conjecture, he sends a letter to Mr Windibank, requesting a meeting. When Mr Windibank replies by typing a note to Holmes, his message equals the minister's seal. He unwittingly puts key evidence in

Psychoanalysis

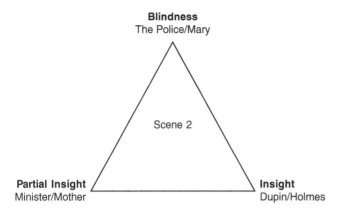

Fig. 2 Character positions – Scene 2

Holmes's hands, enabling the detective to demonstrate that Hosmer's letters were typed on the same machine as the stepfather's note. Lacan observes that the possession of the letter feminises the holder: Minister D– adopts the Queen's strategy of concealment and imitates her handwriting, while Mr Windibank types his letters, thus stepping into Mary's professional sphere. As a typist, Mary could have spotted the same features in the typewritten script as Holmes does (Fig. 2).

For Lacan, Poe's story dramatises the split between the conscious self that is constructed in the symbolic order (the realm of language and culture), and the unconscious that is also structured like a language, but one that has its own "grammar", evident in dreams and various kinds of slips. In its ceaseless movement, the stolen letter is comparable to a psychic symptom, a repetitious and displaced symbolic substitution for something the unconscious has repressed. Thus, Poe's story stages the mechanisms of the repetition compulsion. As the characters of the two stories illustrate, their actions are not only steered by their conscious intentions, but also by their unconciouses. Hence, both stories dramatise structural repetition: The letter as a symbol of the unconscious governs their actions by making them take up certain positions vis-à-vis others without being aware of it. In a similar fashion, unconscious desire, though repressed, survives in displaced, symbolic form, shaping subjects' lives and actions without their being aware of its meaning or of the repetitive patterns it structures. Dupin succeeds because he is able to stay within the realm of the symbolic, outside the circuit of desire: Like a psychoanalyst, he translates into conscious form that which remains unconscious in the repetitive structure. Poe's story concludes with the return of the letter to the Queen, suggesting that Dupin helps her to get rid of the dangerous "symptom" of her desire that threatened her status at court.

Mary is the recipient of letters of affection from Hosmer. Doyle modifies the theft of the letter. The letters are from the start "stolen", for with them, Mr Windibank steals the feelings Mary would in a usual situation direct at a man outside the family circle. Doyle's story departs from Poe's in a crucial respect: Dupin has the letter returned to the Queen, whereas Holmes refuses to tell Mary the truth. He insists that Mary would not believe him: "You may remember the old Persian saying, 'There is danger for him who taketh the tiger cub, and dangers also for whoso snatches a delusion from a woman'" (64). Holmes decides not to divulge the deception whose target is the woman on whose behalf he has acted. This decision raises the question of Holmes's motives. Unravelling them helps us to assess his part in the case. Such deliberation is the concern of what Pierre Bayard calls detective criticism.

Holmes's misdirected reading

Pierre Bayard, a French professor of literature and a psychoanalyst, has questioned the status of the fictional detective as a model reader after whose methods we ought to fashion our reading. In a series of playful books, starting with the bestselling *Who Killed Roger Ackroyd? The Mystery Behind the Agatha Christie Mystery* (2000), Bayard not only claims that the solutions to these famous genre classics are wrong, but also that their insufficiency directly stems from the inadequate reading practices of the detectives. Bayard takes on the role of master sleuth, solving these cases "correctly". His alternative solutions are based on textual evidence and draw on clues that the fictional detective disregards.

Bayard argues that his reading method succeeds where the strategies of Sherlock Holmes and Hercule Poirot fail, because he applies "detective criticism", an interventionist reading strategy aiming at discovering the true culprits of fictional crimes (2008: 59). Bayard claims that many alleged solutions to fictional crimes are wrong. These errors derive from the detective's disregard of his or her individual psychology and unconsciousness. By applying detective criticism, claims Bayard, readers can arrive at true solutions to any fictional crime. Given his goal of cutting through the fictional detective's delusional reading, his approach is both deconstructive and steered by the hermeneutics of suspicion.

Bayard conceives of the text as a gapped entity (2008: 64–66). The reader fills in the gaps by inferences, thus producing an intermediate world through reading as the completion of these gaps. Given that readers' subjectivities affect their reading, the intermediate world is partly conscious, partly unconscious. Shoshana Felman observes that "there is no language in which interpretation can itself escape the effects of the unconscious, the interpreter is no more immune than the poet of unconscious delusions and errors" (1988: 152). From this feature stems the delusional nature of the detective's reading. Bayard explains this affinity by referring to the subjectivity of the theoriser. Theoretical constructions rely on the theoriser's subjective efforts to produce meaning (Bayard 2000: 90–91). Holmes's pseudoscientific method eliminates the element of individual psychology in the mysteries he is trying to solve. He never explicitly considers how his own subjectivity, proclivities and biases affect his choices and reasoning.

"The Case of Identity" opens with a frame narrative of Holmes and Watson admiring a golden snuffbox, "a gift in the case of Irene Adler papers" (51). Holmes refers to a previous case, "A Scandal in Bohemia" (1891), which involved the alluring adventuress Irene Adler. This short story adapts "The Purloined Letter" in multiple ways (Sweeney 1990). "To Sherlock Holmes", Watson begins his account of that case, "she is always *the* woman […] In his eyes she eclipses and predominates the whole of her sex" (9). Applying Bayardian detective criticism shows that Holmes's refusal to tell Mary of Mr Windibank's treachery is rooted in the Adler case.

Unravelling "The Case of Identity" is child's play for Holmes. He probes Hosmer Angel's disappearance in terms of physical absence – one moment a man is present and the next, whenever the stepfather is at home, he is not. There is no legal crime. Nevertheless, the case involves an instance of a *double life* that leaves questions open: What relationship exists between Mr Windibank's two sides? Is he primarily a stepfather or a suitor sexually interested in his stepdaughter? His wife is his senior by fifteen years, while Mary is the same age as him. Moreover, his wife, Mary's mother, is an active accomplice in the deception. Holmes never considers these issues. Given Bayard's psychoanalytical approach, he links detective criticism to the myth of Oedipus, claiming that the "question of the guilt of Oedipus is posed anew for each reader" (2008: 69). In this case, the ending leaves readers puzzling over the oedipal dynamic in the Windibank household: Is Mr Windibank sexually attracted to his stepdaughter or is Mary interested in him? Mary's mother has been keener on the relationship and fonder of Hosmer than Mary. In fact, it is at the mother's prompting that Mary acquiesces to court with Hosmer. Does the collusion of Mary's mother in the deception signal worry or jealousy? Be that as it may, Mary's wish for her "own [family] circle" (54), suggests that she desires a man from outside the family. Readers surmise that knowledge of the deception would help Mary to disengage herself from this callously self-serving family. The question of Holmes's motives for remaining silent thus persists.

The clues to Bayard's corrective readings rely on intertexts, and it is surprising that he does not explicitly discuss this fact. Similarly, in gauging Holmes's motives I rely on "A Scandal in Bohemia". The ease with which Holmes solves the Hosmer Angel case by sitting in his arm-chair is due to the fact that this case shares features with the previous one. These features make it familiar, facilitating the formation of conjectures. The previous case also involved a man in disguise, a compromising document, a woman cruelly wronged and a carriage ride to church. Therefore, Holmes can easily reason that two men are, in fact, the same person.

Holmes's decision not to tell Mary Sutherland the truth starkly departs from the method of a psychoanalyst who helps the analysand to deal with the facts of the case. Holmes justifies his choice by claiming that Mary will not believe him, and she cannot tolerate losing her delusion: She would become as dangerous and rageful as a tigress from whom her cub is snatched. Following Irene's coach to the church, the disguised Holmes is made an official witness to her marriage to the lawyer Norton. In the light of this story, it is Holmes who actually is the angered party. Thus, Irene is out of the detective's reach for good. The comparison of Mary to a tigress is particularly revealing, for by not confiding the truth to Mary, Holmes makes sure that she will most likely never become a mother with child. The detective knows that she is not allowed to attend social gatherings. He knows she has sworn on the Bible that "she would be true to him" (55) and hears her say "I shall be true to Hosmer. He shall find me ready when he comes back" (57). By remaining silent, Holmes plays directly into the hands of Mr Windibank and Mary's mother. Holmes becomes their accomplice, for he locks Mary in the family circle.

This state of affairs suggests that Holmes confuses his own situation with Mary's – it is he who is forever pledged to Irene Adler. In fact, he can conjecture that "oscillation upon the pavement always means an *affaire du coeur*", because he and Watson have paced "to and fro in front of [Irene's] house" (22). For Holmes, Irene remains "*the* woman" (28). Where Mary has pledged herself to Hosmer, by withholding the truth, Holmes turns Hosmer into *the* man in Mary's life. Given the similarity of these names, one may wonder whether Holmes's decision includes a projection of his wish that he be *the* man in Irene's life. Consequently, Mr Windibank is not the only "cold-blooded scoundrel" (63) in the story. As a reading strategy, detective criticism does more than simply refashion the endings of detective stories by uncovering "true" criminals. It makes us aware of alternative ways of formulating the problems the detectives are solving: In this case, it poses questions about the character and aspirations of the *petit bourgeois* man as the head of his family – and about the detective who protects this man's privilege.

Transference in reading

It is crucial to notice that the last scene in Poe's story involves a third repetition of the triangular pattern that has already been repeated twice. When Dupin steals the letter from the minister, he leaves behind a substitute letter that declares his hatred of the adversary due to an unspecified wrong the minister has caused Dupin in the past. Thereby, Dupin becomes fully participant in the intersubjective triad. Similarly, by not trusting Mary with the truth, Holmes participates in and reinforces the deception of which she is the victim. As Jacques Derrida points out, at the conclusion it is Lacan as a reader who sees this third unconscious repetition and occupies the position of the symbolic. Thus, Lacan's analysis envisages a position outside the triangle from whose vantage point the interactional patterns of the triangle emerge. Derrida observes that Lacan forgets to consider the role that writing and narration play (1988: 198). Like Poe's story, Doyle's narrative highlights writing in the form of the letters as well as Watson's allusions to himself as the chronicler of Holmes's cases. Derrida emphasises that both writer and reader are participants in the drama the narrative stages.

Derrida's criticism highlights yet another sense in which the letter circulates in "The Purloined Letter". Poe's story is self-inclusive, as its title is eponymous with the story's central object. Similarly, in Doyle's narrative the reader is made privy to Hosmer's letters over Holmes's shoulder. In both stories the reader is envisioned as the letter's ultimate recipient. Consequently, through the letter's circulation the author invites the reader to enter the story as an active participant in creating the narrative's design and meaning. Such a mutual dialogue characterises psychoanalytic *transference*, which consists of the dialogic relationship between the analyst and the analysand as they construct and interpret the analysand's life narrative. Together they attempt to understand the force of desire (comparable to the circulation of the purloined letter) that speaks in and through this narrative (Brooks 1994: 47). In reading, the transferential relationship takes place between text and reader: We treat the text as the place of meaning and as the vehicle for the knowledge that reading imparts. Peter Brooks states that in this transferential reading relationship, readers have two roles. First, they fill in narrative gaps, in light of their understanding of the dynamics of desire in the text. Second, they are steered by their subjectivity and psychic histories. Thus, they become fully involved in what they read. Brooks suggests that readers constantly shift positions from one place to the other in reading. It is this constantly shifting movement that makes the transference relationship between author and reader an inherent part of the structure and meaning of the narrative text (Brooks 1994: 50, 72). I have traced that movement of desire in this chapter. The psychoanalytic reading strategy follows how desire runs through the text, whether it be figured in a letter, a body or some other trope. Of interest is the manner in which its movement shapes the characters' interaction – and spills over to structure our reading.

To make these complex ideas more tangible, I conclude by briefly looking at Colin Dexter's short story "A Case of Mis-identity" (1993), an explicit adaptation of Doyle's story. Dexter has retained Doyle's basic narrative problem but includes Holmes's ingenious brother Mycroft alongside Watson in the scene where the client tells her story. Dexter's active engagement as the recipient of Doyle's story is illustrated by the fact that in reconstructing it, he has Holmes, Mycroft and Watson take turns in presenting their solutions. Thus, this adaptation illustrates how each of these three men receives and contextualises the client's story in accordance with his interpretation of how desire shapes the client's and her family's interaction. Holmes's solution repeats the one he offers in Doyle's story, but Mycroft pinpoints many logical fallacies in his brother's account. Mycroft's solution identifies the client and her mother as the deceivers; they have connived together in order to get rid of the stepfather. Mycroft's solution turns the least likely suspect, the client, into the culprit. In the end, Watson proves both brothers wrong. He has just treated the client's fiancé. Hosmer Angel was on his way to church, stopped to withdraw cash for the honeymoon from his bank, and was then robbed and maimed. There is no deception, but a man with honourable intentions who came to harm.

In placing himself as the recipient of Doyle's story, and in interpreting and then reconstructing it as his own story, Dexter illustrates the workings of transference in reading stories about crime. The dynamic of his reinterpretation is comical and crowned by a twist as regards the hermeneutics of suspicion that Holmes and Mycroft put into play. Watson, who is proved correct, has

Psychoanalysis

stayed, as it were, on the surface of things and has luckily hit on the truth. Most readers are not writers like Dexter, yet each of us engages in idiosyncratic ways with "the psychic investments of rhetoric, the dramas played out in tropes" while we read (Brooks 1994: 44).

Bibliography

Bayard, P. (2000) *Who Killed Roger Ackroyd? The mystery behind the Agatha Christie mystery*, trans. C. Cosman, New York: New Press.

———. (2008) *Sherlock Holmes Was Wrong: Reopening the case of "The Hound of the Baskervilles"*, trans. C. Mandel, London: Bloomsbury.

Brooks, P. (1994) *Psychoanalysis and Storytelling*, Oxford: Blackwell.

Derrida, J. (1988) "The purveyor of truth", trans. A. Bass, in Muller, 173–212.

Dexter, C. (1993) "A case of mis-identity", in *Morse's Greatest Mystery and Other Stories*, New York: Ivy Books. E-book.

Doyle, A.C. (1989) *Sherlock Holmes: The complete illustrated short stories*, London: Chancellor.

Eco, U. and Sebeok, T. (eds) (1983) *The Sign of Three: Dupin, Holmes, Pierce*, Bloomington: Indiana University Press.

Felman, S. (1988) "On reading poetry: reflections on the limits and possibilities of psychoanalytic approaches", in Muller and Richardson, 133–56.

Felski, R. (2015) *The Limits of Critique*, Chicago: University of Chicago Press.

Ginzburg, C. (1983) "Clues: Morelli, Freud, and Sherlock Holmes", in Eco and Sebeok, 81–118.

Irwin, J. (1994) *The Mystery to a Solution: Poe, Borges, and the analytic detective story*, Baltimore: Johns Hopkins University Press.

Lacan, J. (1988) "Seminar on 'The Purloined Letter'", trans. J. Mehlman, in Muller and Richardson, 28–54.

Muller, J. and Richardson, W. (eds) (1988) *The Purloined Poe: Lacan, Derrida and psychoanalytic reading*, Baltimore: Johns Hopkins University Press.

Pederson-Krag, C. (1983) "Detective stories and the primal scene", in G. Most and W. Stowe (eds), *The Poetics of Murder: Detective fiction and literary theory*, New York: Harcourt.

Porter, P. (1981) *The Pursuit of Crime: Art and ideology in detective fiction*, New Haven, CT: Yale University Press.

Ricoeur, P. (1970) *Freud and Philosophy: An essay on interpretation*, New Haven, CT: Yale University Press.

Rycroft, C. (1968) "The analysis of a detective story", in *Imagination and Reality: Psycho-analytical essays 1951–1961*, London: Hogart, 114–28.

Sebeok, T. and Umiker-Sebeok, J. (1983) "You know my method: A juxtaposition of Charles S. Pierce and Sherlock Holmes", in Eco and Sebeok, 11–54.

Sweeney, S.E. (1990) "Purloined letters: Poe, Doyle, Nabokov", *Russian Triquarterly*, 24: 213–37.

Yang, A. (2010) Psychoanalysis and detective fiction: a tale of Freud and criminal storytelling", *Perspectives in Biology and Medicine*, 53(4): 596–604.

Žižek, S. (1991) *Looking Awry: An introduction to Jacques Lacan through popular culture*, Cambridge, Mass.: MIT.

PART II

Devices

15

MURDERS

Michael Harris-Peyton

Murder occupies a special place in discussions of crime fiction. It is not unusual, among anglophone readers, to refer to the entire body of crime fiction as "murder mysteries"; likewise, it is not uncommon for scholarship and reference materials about the genre to rely on that metonymy. For instance, any casual newcomer to the genre who resorts to searching for "murder mysteries" on Wikipedia will be automatically redirected to the entry on "crime fiction" as a whole. Reading scholarship on crime fiction, too, reveals an historical preponderance of murder-related titles, like Haycraft's *Murder for Pleasure* (1941) and Symons's *Bloody Murder* (1972), to name just two. Contemporary scholarship on crime fiction has more diversely themed titles, but still has a tendency towards murder: Flanders's *The Invention of Murder* (2011), for instance, and King's *Murder in the Multinational State* (2019). Participatory media themed around crime – board games, video games and the like – generally prioritise content about this violent, mysterious version of death. Century-old proclamations on the formula of detective fiction, like Van Dine's "Twenty Rules" (1928), assume that murder is at the core of the content.

Importantly, a lot of crime fiction is not about murder at all. Despite its special visibility as a constituent part of crime fiction, murder routinely steps aside in favour of petty thefts, disappearances, frauds, bank robberies and kidnappings, along with more contemporary forms of criminality, like cybercrime and eco-crime. Still, murder has an iconic status in the genre. In order to investigate this unusual position, this chapter poses two related questions:

1. Why is murder enshrined as the preferred crime of crime fiction?
2. How is murder, as an important trope or device, useful to crime fiction?

Answers to the second question are much more common in scholarship than answers to the first. The status of murder as the preferred crime is generally regarded as incidental (especially in early scholarship) or so obvious as to not require a particularly deep answer. Meanwhile, crime fiction criticism privileges questions of how the presentation and metaphorical use of murder change over time, rather than why the genre employs murder as a device at all. Such criticism also tends to rely on the stereotypical history of the genre critiqued in this collection's introduction. For instance, a common narrative asserts that murder in early crime fiction moves from being sensational (in, for example, Poe or Doyle), to being a sanitised puzzle element (in

"Golden Age" texts), to being described in extensive detail (in contemporary crime fiction); in essence, this narrative forms a trajectory between "conservative" and stereotypically Victorian crime writing to an American-dominated genre dependent on graphic depictions of bodily violence.

Such histories and subgenre categories are more descriptive than explanatory: The specific deployments of murder as a genre device and the shape of crime fiction or "murder mysteries" change over time, but the genre does not always change collectively – it is frequently going in several directions at once. Nonetheless, critical responses to murder in crime fiction generally fall into two overlapping camps: Murder as the instigating element for a mystery story and its central puzzle, and murder as a symptom of larger, often social or political, criminality. For instance, both of these interpretations occur within a single paragraph of Raymond Chandler's seminal article "The Simple Art of Murder" (1944) – murder, as an event, carries "sociological implication", but the mystery novel has "a depressing way of minding its own business", or avoiding any sociological discussion (223). While Chandler's characterisation is simplistic, it illustrates a key point of this chapter: Murder has been consistently understood as indicative or symbolic across several generations of scholarship, even when such a role undercuts other long-held beliefs about the genre, such as the Golden Age dependence on murder as sanitised, isolated acts of deviancy or the inherent conservatism of the genre as a whole.

Scholarship and the occasional murder

While it would be easy to propose a grand, stereotypical narrative where crime fiction comes to rely more and more on murder as the core criminal event, on an individual basis, texts in the crime fiction genre resist that generalisation. A safer generalisation might be that crime fiction deploys murder as one particularly sensational device for directing the attention of an investigator or reader to a larger instigating circumstance. Furthermore, this motive for using murder is not a peculiarity of one specific historical variety of crime fiction, but a consistent trope across the genre's myriad, transnational and transhistorical forms. This chapter argues that the answer to our second question – why is murder useful in the genre? – is that murder is an historically useful signpost for broader social deviancy or criminality. In fact, scholarship on crime fiction, especially in the last three decades, has taken this position for granted. This is especially true in late twentieth-century critical work, where re-reading crime fiction texts through an ideological, sociological or psychological lens was the norm. It remains true in much of the scholarly work of the early 2000s, which generally focused on recovering lost histories, influences and texts in the genre – extending it beyond the efforts of white, heterosexual male writers – and on critically examining the impact of crime fiction on popular notions of diversity, democracy, justice, colonialism and bodily violence. Murder can generally be understood as a sensational, attention-grabbing symptom of some larger issue. Murder, in other words, is an *occasion*, a special, unusual event that invites attention to its causes and effects, thus inspiring the formation and (for detectives) the recovery of a *narrative*.

This dual-narrative structure – the narrative of investigation occasioned by the murder, and the recovered narrative that explains the murder – is commonly understood as a definitional feature of detective-driven crime fiction. Identified and described by Tzvetan Todorov in terms of the "fabula" (the story as presented in the narrative) and the "sujet" (the chronological order of events), the murder in crime fiction (or whatever criminal event) serves to position those two aspects of narrative "side by side", in contrast to other fiction which merges the two (1977: 46). This observation gets taken up by theorists like Franco Moretti, who uses this structure to interrogate how clues work (1983: 130–56), and John Cawelti, from whom we get the clearest formal characterisation of crime fiction as a genre desiring to bring order to a disordered system (1976: 13–14). In all cases, the murder is a narrative-initiating event, and mandates the recovery or application of larger meaning to that fatal event.

Work on recovering the history, generic roots and multiple origins of crime fiction similarly depend on murder as a definitional (and sometimes, an originating) feature. Maurizio Ascari argues, in *A Counter-History of Crime Fiction*, that the genre has its roots, at least in English, in the Gothic or sensational fiction and true-crime reportage of the eighteenth and nineteenth centuries as well as in the interaction between scientific positivism and fantasy (2007: xi). Heather Worthington, preceding Ascari, traces the influence of nineteenth-century true-crime reportage on detective-driven crime fiction first theorised by Stephen Knight (Worthington 2005; Knight 1980). In both cases, the presence of death (and particularly, of violent or unexpected death and the out-of-place presence of a corpse, i.e. sensational murders) is a common subject matter, and constitutes an aspect of those products' transgressive or sensational appeal. Ascari's analysis limits itself to the genre in a transatlantic or Euro-American context, and Worthington's is likewise limited to a British context; yet crime fiction is famously global not just in its contemporary popularity but in its inception and production.

Other scholarly work has proposed alternative histories and counter-histories for the genre that transcend a purely European or North American context. For example, Mukherjee's *Crime and Empire* covers some of the same ground as Ascari and Worthington, asserting that British sensation fiction and non-fiction crime writing marks the features of crime discourse on a global scale. Mukherjee's key observation is that this genre is dependent on colonial strategies of police investigation that Britain devised for its colonised territory and later applied to Britain itself (2003). Regardless, murder occupies a central role in all these historical narratives, as the trope that shapes and later identifies a genre.

Early crime fiction criticism, often undertaken by authors of crime fiction or enthusiastic editors, typically aimed to provide a history and general formula for the genre which emphasised the role of murder as a device for gaining readerly attention. Haycraft's 1941 book *Murder for Pleasure*, for example, takes the centrality of murder to the genre so much for granted that it is not explicitly examined as a device or writerly choice except in one key instance. In a chapter dedicated to "The Rules of the Game", Haycraft cautions aspiring writers that attempting to write a crime novel about a "lesser crime" is unwise, noting "murder has come to be the accepted theme of the detective novel, for reasons too numerous and obvious to require attention" (1941: 234). His later description of the do's and don'ts of murder (in an aptly named subsection of the chapter, "Devices") describes how murder should work for an entertaining narrative but leaves murder's structural role as instigating incident and call for meaning unsaid (248–55).

Murder, in Haycraft and his contemporaries' definitions of crime fiction, is simply assumed to be the crime, while leaving room for variants of crime fiction to focus on crimes like theft, kidnapping or espionage if the author is brave enough. For instance, in S.S. Van Dine's "Twenty Rules for Writing Detective Stories", the seventh rule stipulates that "[t]here simply must be a corpse in a detective novel, and the deader the corpse the better. No lesser crime than murder will suffice. Three hundred pages is far too much pother for a crime other than murder". Van Dine's answer for why, specifically, it has to be murder and why there has to be a corpse boils down to sensation and catharsis: It stimulates the readers' "sense of vengeance and horror" so that they will engage in the puzzle or game of the story with the desire to bring the perpetrator to fictional justice (1928: n.p.). This characterisation, like Haycraft's, cites murder's potential for sensation and attention-grabbing without confronting *why* – Van Dine atomises or individualises murder as a plot device, but implicitly operates on the assumption that murder's sensational draw is linked to larger ethical or sociological cachet.

By the mid to late twentieth century, however, enough critical material on crime fiction had accumulated to draw attention to the motives for the persistence of murder as a central feature of the genre. Murder's role, as an indicator of some deeper problem, gets denormalised in this scholarship. In other words, the fictional prevalence of murder ceases to be an unremarkable aspect of the genre, and scholars begin to look for why murder is such a common device and how it is connected to the other crimes featured in crime fiction. Marxist and Freudian approaches to crime fiction, especially during the mid-twentieth century, analysed murder as a byproduct of those approaches' preferred underlying causes: Capitalist property politics and subconscious psychology, respectively. East German scholar Ernst Kaemmel, in an example of the Marxist approach, argued in a 1962 essay that murder in crime fiction is the expression of insecurity in the capitalist order – murders are always about property and bourgeois values, but the revolutionary knowledge that capitalist systems of justice fail is contained by the glorified individual detective (1983: 55–61). Semiotic and psychoanalytic perspectives on crime fiction were taken up by Lacan in his influential "Seminar on 'The Purloined Letter'" (1983). Julian Symons, in his 1972 book *Bloody Murder*, offers two explanations for why we read crime fiction that are predicated on the psychological and sociological value of murder – murder is shocking and transgressive, and the detective story solves the murder, reinforcing a belief in a moral, ordered world (1972: 20–24). Later, Stephen Knight's account of the development of the genre, predicated on true-crime genres like the *Newgate Calendar* and early police novels, extends Symon's assertion, figuring the genre in ethical or juridical terms, as the restoration of social order threatened by the irreversible act of murder and the punishment of the transgressor (1980: 266–68).

Murder is thus a stand-in for a larger psychological, social or economic issue and a transgressive event that draws readerly attention to those issues. Murder is a device and an occasion. This common way of examining murder, however, meshes poorly with some other early pronouncements on crime fiction. The belief that murder is a purely discursive device (a puzzle to be solved with no wider meaning), as in the earliest crime fiction scholarship, facilely ignores why murder is attractive to readership. Contemporary scholarship on crime fiction has challenged that argument, changing how the genre is structured, historicised and read in the process. As a result of these challenges, murder has persisted as the assumed crime in crime fiction but is widely understood as a means for the genre to engage in commentary – even if that commentary is simplistic. Newer scholarship has replaced or updated our lenses for looking at perpetrators, victims, investigators and their contexts, but has generally sustained this notion that murder is a powerful device the genre uses to organise the narrative and direct reader attention to the text's potential for commentary. Murder is a storytelling device and an ideological signal-flare – "the story is worthy of your attention" and "there is greater meaning here".

Murder in crime fiction as a world literature

The prevalence and versatility of murder highlights the importance of recent efforts to read crime fiction as a world literature. The atomisation of murder in early criticism – the tendency to view it purely as a singular puzzle element, without larger implications, even when citing its emotive or sensational potential – is made possible, in part, by viewing crime fiction as a monocultural enterprise. This narrow approach to murder as a device reinforces facile notions that anglophone crime fiction is conservative, formulaic or apolitical and that other traditions, as "translations" of the genre, inherit this nature. Reading the genre as a world literature emphasises the plurality of traditions in the genre and reveals that murder's success as a central trope is not incidental. Murder's potential for political or social commentary, far from being a recent development or an exceptional feature of one regional or linguistic tradition of the genre, is a common, transcultural feature. To borrow language from postcolonial and environmental critic Rob Nixon's *Slow Violence and the Environmentalism of the Poor*, murder is "fast violence" that makes forms of "slow violence" like social inequality, sexism, corruption and colonialism visible in a transcultural genre (2013). Viewing crime fiction through compartmentalised national or linguistic traditions, like viewing murder as a device devoid of politics, forecloses questions of why murder is such a successful device in an already successful transnational genre.

The case for crime fiction as a world literature, rather than a Eurocentric or variously regional series of genres, is clearly laid out in Stewart King's 2014 essay "Crime Fiction as World Literature". Noting that a great deal of scholarly work has recovered overlooked histories and bodies of crime fiction, King argues that splitting these developments up as regional histories or recoveries maintains the illusion that the genre is an anglophone cultural domain. By viewing the genre as a single, global (or at least, internationally networked) phenomenon, it becomes possible to acknowledge the genre's complex influences, courses of development and deployments of form and politics (2014: 9–11). The capacity of crime fiction to explore political or social issues in a variety of local and global contexts within this world literature framework has been explored in the edited collection, *Crime Fiction as World Literature* (Nilsson et al. 2017), and elsewhere. Other works, like Andrew Pepper's *Unwilling Executioner* (2016), focus on the often unexpected places that commentary emerges in the genre (2016: 14).

Reading the genre as a global literature denormalises the prevalence of murder: In the global genre of crime fiction, as in anglophone fiction, murder, as a device, is never just murder – it is a mechanism for enabling both narration (and by extension, authoring) and commentary. In global crime fiction broadly, murder's value as an attention-garnering narrative event is based on its social or emotive impact, its greater social and ideological implications. The case study that follows is meant to suggest that this deployment of murder for political commentary is the rule, rather than the exception: Even the most "conservative" Golden Age-style crime fiction texts are capable of social critique via the device of murder. Even the most allegedly "derivative" or generic crime fiction, the most stereotypical murder mystery, is politically charged because the act of deploying genre tropes and the practice of describing crime as an exceptional or narrative-worthy event, are political acts.

Murder as a clue to a greater crime – Cheng Xiaoqing's "The Shoe"

Cheng Xiaoqing's mystery story "The Shoe" is a good example of a conventional (or, we might say, genre-conscious) Golden Age-style mystery that deploys the device of murder in a way that subverts the conventional individualisation of murder. Writing during the brief Republican period after the end of the Qing dynasty in China in 1912, but before the communist revolution of 1949, Cheng Xiaoqing primarily worked as a translator of Western fiction (Wong 2007a: 209). Motivated by a desire to "awaken readers to the advantages of careful observation and rigorous reasoning", Cheng began to write his own detective stories featuring the sleuth Huo Sang and his companion and narrator, Bao Lang (Wong 2007b: vii–x). Operating in an intercultural space, and very aware of the generic trappings of British, American and French detective fiction as well as Chinese crime writing and local audience demands, Cheng's mysteries offer an interesting opportunity to explore the function of murder within the genre, since the stories are produced with both a deliberate pedagogical aim and a strong, structural awareness of what crime fiction is expected to do.

As a typical Huo Sang mystery, "The Shoe" plays upon the generic expectation that the murder, in a "murder mystery", is central and that, as this chapter has asserted, murder both points to a larger commentary and works to occasion the narrative. The murder of a young woman occasions the story, and the sensational presence of the victim's body and an unusual, foreign object in the crime scene (the titular lone shoe) is ascribed disproportionate importance by everyone investigating the crime *except* the rational Huo Sang. In the end, the titular shoe, like the body of the murder victim, is revealed as incidental to the actual crime (financial malfeasance) while also causing Huo Sang's presence on the case and, coincidentally, causing the murder – the shoe and the murder are, ironically, red herrings in the mystery narrative established by their presence. Instead, the text's use of murder opens up an avenue for the detective character, and the author, to launch a critique of unregulated financial practices and the impact of those practices on interpersonal relationships.

The story is structured by the expectations of crime fiction as a genre: Individual sections of the story are titled by their function in the mystery "puzzle" – "The Crime Scene", "A Point of Contention", and the like, making the text's function as a demonstration of rational or scientific problem-solving methods clear (e.g. Cheng 1923: 1, 8, 16). "The Shoe" begins with Huo Sang and Bao Lang being contracted by the police to investigate the murder of Ding Fangzhu, the wife of Hangzhou bank manager Gao Youzhi. At the scene of the crime, the lack of witnesses and material evidence stumps police detective Ni Jinshou and his "narrow-minded", bureaucratic superior, Lieutenant Fan (1–4).

The police make a series of common-sense deductions which are gradually revealed as faulty. Huo Sang walks Ni Jinshou through the process of investigation, challenging his assumption that a locked chest means that nothing was taken (a thief could very easily re-lock the chest afterwards), and scolds Ni Jinshou and Lieutenant Fan for missing mundane but indicative clues, like the presence of burned correspondence (4–13, 17). They quickly determine that the men's shoe – stylish and youthful – is not the correct fit for the victim's absentee husband, a middle-aged bank manager. Suspicion falls instead on a young man witnessed cat-calling the victim when she sat on her balcony, whose personal style would match the style of the lone shoe (14). Lieutenant Fan, a judgemental and irrational character, prematurely asserts that the motive was "cuckoldry" and that the murderer is the suspicious young man (17), though Huo Sang dissents that this interpretation is based more on sensational storytelling tropes than good puzzle-solving techniques, mounting a thinly veiled critique of other popular mystery fiction (16–19).

Huo Sang's unsensational logic is validated – Ding Fangzhu's locked jewellery box is revealed to have been emptied of valuable jewels and then re-locked (28). The shoe's owner is identified, and he explains that, in a fit of drunken infatuation, he tossed one of his shoes from the street into Ding Fangzhu's chambers, but never entered there himself (34). Huo Sang then methodically pursues the contents of the destroyed letter at the local post office (40). As Huo Sang explains to Bao Lang, the shoe and the victim's corpse are incidental to the core crime, which centres on the missing jewellery and the destroyed letters. The murder, ultimately, is the result of tragic miscommunication: The victim's husband had made several bad investments for his bank, and seeing no way to make the money back, planned to flee the country with his wife. He sends her a letter setting up a clandestine meeting while all the household staff are out. Upon his arrival, he sees the shoe (and spots the young, infatuated man) and concludes that Ding Fangzhu is cheating on him and has revealed his secret plans to her lover. Panicked, he murders her and steals her jewels to finance his escape. He then ensures the destruction of his letter and sets up the scene with the shoe and his wife's body to suggest an illicit affair in order to cover his tracks.

The husband, thanks to Huo Sang's ability to see through these red herrings, is caught while trying to flee the country (43–44).

The story ends with Huo Sang noting the effect financial speculation (and, by extension, any ungrounded speculations) had on the lives of the husband and wife and entrusting Ni Jinshou with the appropriate legal and juridical actions (44). The true crime is revealed: This murder, the jewel theft and casual police sexism are all products of the Republic's involvement in the unregulated predations of international neocolonial capitalism. The capture and punishment of the husband, as a symptom and victim of these political and economic injustices, is never dramatised in the text, reinforcing the story's use of murder as an occasion for mounting this social critique. Likewise, the murder victim, thoroughly dehumanised both before and after death by the stigma of infidelity, stands as an indictment of Republican China's gender politics (44).

Fictional murder, true crimes and terminal legibility

Even in crime fiction as self-consciously formulaic as "The Shoe" – which quite literally labels its narrative parts – murder is not simply a puzzle to be solved. While it is true, as Pepper notes in the introduction to *Unwilling Executioner*, that not all crime fiction is necessarily engaging in political commentary, or at least not always willingly (2016: 2–5), murder as a device and as an exceptional social event inherently has the potential for commentary. The shift in crime fiction scholarship over time, at first preferring to assume murder's necessity to the story, then theorising about its implications on a textual scale, then examining the device as a transcultural practice, means that we might now be able to theorise answers to this chapter's two guiding questions.

First, murder's special prominence in crime fiction is a result of the genre's roots in various forms of sensational, fictional and nonfictional storytelling globally. The stakes of this central position are that crime fiction, like crime reportage, is always already prepared to engage in social or political commentary even if it proposes to take no stance beyond "this murder is worthy of reader attention". That argument for attention is a form of commentary: murder is an exceptional state, a failure or exposure of the machinations of power, and it must be narrated, investigated or contained (e.g. Pepper 2016: 1–3).

Second, the function of murder, as a generic device, has generally been understood as a popular (but not exclusive) choice for calling a narrative into existence, and as an event which must be addressed and given meaning. This understanding of murder as occasion for narrative marks crime fiction scholarship – it is a foundational or basic premise of the study of crime fiction. For example, if one imagines a crime fiction text which contains a murder, or indeed, any other crime that is *not* investigated, one of the driving questions of that text, given its generic position, would be "why is nobody investigating that murder?". Murder, in this sense, is semiotically unavoidable – as a narrative event in the genre of crime fiction, it must be confronted. Unlike other forms of crime, however, murder constitutes a terminal state – the crime is already complete – and so investigation is framed as informational recovery, rather than as prevention, interdiction or property recovery.

A succinct way to understand the device of murder in crime fiction is that it makes commentary *terminally legible*, i.e. it conclusively ends a series of events which must be made to produce readable meaning. As the impetus for narrative, murder makes that larger meaning unavoidably readable to the story's real-world audience and the fictional investigator or investigators – thus, terminally legible. To solve the murder requires the exposure or recovery of this larger meaning as well as the specific events of the murder itself. Even to avoid solving the murder is, itself, a form of addressing the murder – a political or ideological statement. To avoid describing, solving or narrating murder (or any other crime) in crime fiction is a strange proposition indeed, especially if one continues to insist that such a text is, somehow, crime fiction. Thus, crime in crime fiction is always involved in the process of political or social critique. Regardless of the reason for its deployment, murder in crime fiction is never simply the appearance of a context-less, apolitical corpse.

Bibliography

Ascari, M. (2007) *A Counter-History of Crime Fiction: Supernatural, Gothic, sensational*, New York: Palgrave Macmillan.

Cawelti, J.G. (1976) *Adventure, Mystery and Romance*, Chicago: Chicago University Press.

Chandler, R. (1947) [1944] "The simple art of murder", in H. Haycraft (ed.), *The Art of the Mystery Story: A collection of critical essays*, New York: Grosset and Dunlap, 222–37.

Cheng, X. (2007) [1923] "The shoe", in *Sherlock in Shanghai: Stories of crime and detection by Cheng Xiaoqing*, ed. and trans. T.C. Wong, Honolulu: University of Hawai'i Press.

"Crime fiction", Wikipedia, https://en.wikipedia.org/wiki/Crime_fiction (accessed May 2019).

Flanders, J. (2011) *The Invention of Murder: How the Victorians revelled in death and detection and created modern crime*, London: Harper Collins.

Haycraft, H. (1941) *Murder for Pleasure: The life and times of the detective story*, London: D. Appleton-Century.

Kaemmel, E. (1962) "Literature under the table: the detective novel and its social mission", in Most and Stowe, 55–61.

King, S. (2014) "Crime fiction as world literature", *Clues: A Journal of Detection*, 32(2): 8–19.

———. (2019) *Murder in the Multinational State: Crime fiction from Spain*, New York: Routledge.

Knight, S. (1980) "… 'Some men come up …' – the detective appears", in Most and Stowe, 266–98.

Lacan, J. (1983) [1973] "Seminar on 'The Purloined Letter'", in Most and Stowe, 21–54.

Moretti, F. (1983) "Clues", *Signs Taken for Wonders: Essays in the sociology of literary forms,* trans. S. Fischer, D. Forgacs and D. Miller, London: Verso.

Most, G.W. and Stowe, W.W. (eds) (1983) *The Poetics of Murder: Detective fiction and literary theory*, New York: Harcourt Brace Jovanovich.

Mukherjee, U.P. (2003) *Crime and Empire: The colony in nineteenth-century fictions of crime*, Oxford: Oxford University Press.

Nilsson, L., Damrosch, D. and D'haen, T. (2017) *Crime Fiction as World Literature*, New York: Bloomsbury Academic.

Nixon, R. (2013) *Slow Violence and the Environmentalism of the Poor*, Cambridge, MA: Harvard University Press.

Pepper, A. (2016) *Unwilling Executioner: Crime fiction and the state*, Oxford: Oxford University Press.

Symons, J. (1972) *Bloody Murder: From the detective story to the crime novel: A history*, London: Faber and Faber.

Todorov, T. (1977) *The Poetics of Prose*, trans. R. Howard, Ithaca, NY: Cornell University Press.

Van Dine, S.S. (1928) "Twenty rules for writing detective stories", reproduced at The Thrilling Detective, www.thrillingdetective.com/trivia/triv288.html (accessed May 2019).

Wong, T.C. (2007a) "About Cheng Xiaoqing", in Cheng, 207–10.

———. (2007b) "Preface", in Cheng, vii–xi.

Worthington, H. (2005) *The Rise of the Detective in Early Nineteenth-Century Popular Fiction*, New York: Palgrave Macmillan.

16
VICTIMS

Rebecca Mills

Victims spend the crime fiction text being resurrected and effaced by the detective. In narratives of violent crime, victims' bodies are investigated for clues, as are their lives and personalities. This reconstruction of victims is often designed to evoke sympathy or identification from readers, but on occasion reinforces the sense that victims deserve their fates. In many texts, particularly murder stories, these processes dehumanise and de-individualise the victim, as the corpse becomes evidence (or is sidelined during the investigation), and the personality is reduced to a type. The criminal's psychology and method, and the behaviour and motivations of suspects, witnesses, even the detective, often take over the narrative. This privileging of the living undermines the detective's function as an advocate for the dead, as the narrative focus shifts to unearthing and resolving the detective's own trauma, or an abstract invocation of law, order and justice. The detective may restore order, as in the classic formulation, but he or she cannot bring the dead back to life. The restoration of order and the implementing of justice, then, can mean the effacement of the dead.

This chapter examines the positioning and readings of the murder victim and the responsibility of the detective in crime fiction and scholarship. Victims inhabit a fluid position in the criticism of crime fiction, shifting from the centre of the reading to the margins, according to the theoretical framework applied. Narratological critics such as Heta Pyrhönen view the victim as a piece of the puzzle, a necessary point of contact between detective and crime (1999: 131–32). In poststructuralist, queer, feminist and socially conscious criticism, the victim *is* the puzzle. The bodies of murder and assault victims are dissected into their primary signifiers of race, gender and age, and placed within the wider societal and cultural implications that each signifier carries. Gill Plain remains an influential critic in this mode; Glen S. Close, for instance, builds on her analysis of the social and gender signification of the corpse (2018). Plain and Close, among others, invoke Julia Kristeva's *Powers of Horror: An Essay on Abjection* (1982) when investigating the corpse: "The corpse, seen without God and outside of science, is the utmost of abjection. It is death infecting life. Abject [...] disturbs identity, system, order" (1982: 4). As Plain observes, Kristeva's "theorisation of the abject is almost painfully appropriate to the dialectic of fascination and repulsion that motivates the production and consumption of criminal fictions" (2014: 9–10). While Kristeva's formulation is useful in this context, it can lead to an emphasis on the corpse as an object rather than the victim as a subject.

Recent commentary is often concerned with crime narratives on both page and screen that sideline women characters while presenting graphic accounts of violence against them. Both viewing the victim as a catalyst for a puzzle and mapping the victim as a scene of society's crimes elides the victim's own subjectivity but inscribes their symbolic significance in different ways. This chapter concludes by discussing Dorothy B. Hughes's noir novel, *In A Lonely Place* (1947). This novel foregrounds young women's victimhood rather than corpses, suggesting that the vulnerability of women can be addressed without graphic violence and abject horror.

Puzzle and purity

Not all crime narratives centre on murder or violence. John Scaggs notes an "escalation from the stories of Poe, and later the stories of Doyle, neither of whom concerned themselves exclusively with the crime of murder" to the emphasis on murder in English Golden Age mysteries (2005: 43). In the Sherlock Holmes canon, mysteries are often related to inheritance, blackmail and other financial threats, rather than murder. Scaggs remarks that in Wilkie Collins's *The Moonstone* (1868), the "first detective novel written in English" (23), it is "the centrality of the mystery or puzzle of the moonstone, and its final solution, that qualifies the novel as a crime story in its purest sense" (24). Scaggs's survey of the genre naturally offers a chronology rather than in-depth analysis, but his summary of *The Moonstone* erases the original colonial theft and murder involved in acquiring the diamond, as well as the collateral victims of the mystery (the suicide of the servant girl Rosanna Spearman, and the murdered jewel thief). The appreciation of "puzzle" and "purity" inflects criticism of the Golden Age, as early commentators place the purely conventional and structural aspects of the mystery at the centre of their readings, while marginalising the presence and significance of the victim. In "The Simple Art of Murder" (1944) Raymond Chandler suggested that fellow hardboiled author Dashiell Hammett "gave murder back to the kind of people that commit it for reasons, not just to provide a corpse" (1974: 234), implying the former to be a more realistic representation of crime than the formula of the Golden Age.

Privileging the puzzle over the political is a mode of analysis with implications for both reading and writing the victim. S.S. Van Dine's "Twenty Rules for Writing Detective Stories" (1928) has one rule about victims: "There simply must be a corpse in a detective novel, and the deader the corpse the better. [American readers] wish to bring the perpetrator to justice" (1974: 190). This instruction makes the corpse the object of murder rather than a subject. Ronald Knox's "Ten Commandments" (1929) for mysteries do not mention corpses or victims at all (1974: 194); Knox focuses on the relationship between detective and murderer, and detective and reader. This pairing of the detective and reader at the expense of the victim continues in literary criticism. Roger Caillois observes in "The Detective Novel as Game" that:

> [a] detective in a novel uses his ingenuity to answer the same traditional questions that an actual investigator puts to himself: Who? When? Where? How? Why? These questions do not invoke equal interest, however: one of them – how? – usually constitutes the central problem.
>
> *(1983: 3)*

Caillois's question "who" refers to the criminal, not the victim. Similarly, Pyrhönen suggests in her examination of the ludic structure of the detective novel that:

> In the author's game with the reader, the detective functions as a central textual component with whose help the narrator instructs, manipulates, or cajoles the reader into forming this or that ethical view of life. We may interpret this ground rule broadly as involving the reader's task of evaluating morally a detective's investigative performance.
>
> *(1999: 165)*

In such a reading, the victim is a counter in the game, a way of measuring ethical currency. Pyrhönen observes that "Christie often underlines a substantial moral difference between the criminal and the victim. [...] [B]ut in some instances there is no moral quality whatever setting the victim apart from the criminal (e.g. *Appointment with Death*)" (308), suggesting that even Christie, often perceived as formulaic, could and did play with the rules of victimhood.

The victim, then, is often considered subordinate to the plot. Carl Malmgren examines "murder fiction" as a "quest narrative" involving the roles of "the Sender, the Subject, the Object, the Helper, the Opponent, and the Receiver" (2010: 153). His "functional reading" of Christie's *The Mysterious Affair at Styles* (1920) reveals that, "For the purposes of this analysis the victim is negligible. The real story starts when the body appears, for that is when the unknown quantity is inserted into the narrative and the quest for knowledge begins" (153). The distinction between victim and body in Malmgren's reading is crucial; the corpse is necessary to the story, but the victim's individuality and subjectivity are not. This distinction informs the persistent notion of the "curiously sanitised and bloodless corpses" of the era (Scaggs 2005: 43). And yet, particularly in Christie's later fiction, detective work is predicated on knowing who the victim *was*, beyond merely reading the corpse. In *Evil Under the Sun* (1941), for instance, Poirot comments:

> You do not comprehend, Captain Marshall. There is no such thing as a plain fact of murder. Murder springs, nine times out of ten, out of the character and circumstances of the murdered person. *Because* the victim was the kind of person he or she was, *therefore* was he or she murdered! Until we can understand fully and completely *exactly what kind of a person Arlena Marshall was*, we shall not be able to see clearly exactly *the kind of person who murdered her*. From that springs the necessity of our questions.
>
> *(2008: 111–12; emphasis in original)*

Malmgren remarks further that "Because victims are marginalized and those affected by the crime frequently stereotyped, the detective in mystery fiction occupies the center stage" (156). Poirot's determination to centralise Arlena challenges this notion of the victim in the margins. Indeed, part of the resolution of the mystery is that while her body is interchangeable with that of another woman, Arlena's personality as expressed through her clothing makes her unique. From a structuralist perspective, however, focus on the victim's personality as well as the corpse reassigns the victim the role of Helper in the detective's quest.

Christie and other English Golden Age writers were keenly aware of generic conventions of role and structure. The Detection Club, including Christie and Dorothy L. Sayers, swore to stick to puzzles that the reader could solve, as well as to avoid clichéd characters and plots. However, as Lee Horsley, among others, has pointed out, "One of the most obvious ways in which writers could vary the formula was to disrupt such apparently predictable elements as the reliable narrator and the reliably 'fixed' triangle of characters – detective, victim, criminal" (2005: 41). Horsley notes that "Both [Sayers and Christie] play with the victim/murderer relationship, Christie in *Peril at End House* (1932) and Sayers in *Strong Poison* (1930)" (42). The mention of "playing" here suggests Callois's and Pyrhönen's delineation of the ludic nature of the detective novel, but in these examples, the author is playing against rather than with the reader. In Christie's *Endless Night* (1967) an innocent and rich young woman is presented via the narration of her predatory and amoral husband, who intends to kill her, inherit her money and marry someone else. This reversal, however, supports a narrative structural trick, not experimentation with immersing the reader in a sense of inevitable victimhood.

Horsley contextualises these structural games by quoting Susan Rowland's argument that "by manipulating formal expectations in this way writers like Christie and Sayers critiqued the idea of a stable, knowable self in modern society" (qtd. in Horsley 2005: 42). These manipulations suggest continuity between the performance of roles in the Golden Age, noir and contemporary iterations of crime fiction. In contemporary crime fiction, the instability and inscrutability of the self is taken for granted, and doubled or even tripled character roles are expected rather than transgressive. This is partly due to the influence of the noir mode in both fiction and film. As Horsley writes,

> The victim might, for example, become the aggressor; the hunter might turn into the hunted or vice versa; the investigator might double as either the victim or the perpetrator. Whereas the traditional mystery story, with its stable triangle of detective, victim and murderer, is reasonably certain to have the detective as the protagonist, noir is a deliberate violation of this convention.
>
> *(2009: 10)*

Similar to *Peril at End House*, Gillian Flynn's domestic noir *Gone Girl* (2012) presents an unstable young woman as a victim – until reader expectations are overturned, in a commentary on female roles and male desires in contemporary society. In Stieg Larsson's *The Girl with the Dragon Tattoo* (2005), it is society that has created a complex victim. Lisbeth Salander is both victim of state-enabled rape and abuse, and vigilante. She is a hacker who operates outside the law, but flirts with conformity and stability when helping journalist Mikael Blomkvist solve cases of murder and corruption in Sweden. And yet, the roles of victim/hero/helper do not easily overlap in this novel – the revelation of the other women who have been victimised and murdered by a man driven by Biblical fanaticism suggests that church and state are powerful villains. For structuralist analysis, the victim is part of the problem to be solved rather than an entity with its own inscribed meanings and agency; patriarchy is perhaps too vast a problem to be solved.

Identifying the body

A sense of stark distinction between the "realistic" American hardboiled crime tradition and the mannered English Golden Age of detection has in recent years been eroded, and an understanding of relationship and continuity between the different genres of detective fiction has emerged. The "bloodless corpse" (Scaggs 2005: 43) and the "slashed body" (Messent 2012: 44) of contemporary authors such as Thomas Harris, Kathy Reichs and Patricia Cornwell no longer seem as distant from each other as they did when Chandler argued that Sayers's "kind of detective story was an arid formula which could not even satisfy its own implications" (qtd. in Haycraft 1974: 232). After all, Larsson cites Sayers in *The Girl with the Dragon Tattoo*:

> "I understand that something happened to Harriet here on the island," Blomkvist said, "and the list of suspects consists of the finite number of people trapped here. A sort of locked-room mystery in island format?"

Vanger smiled ironically. "Mikael, you don't know how right you are. Even I have read my Dorothy Sayers."

(93)

And one of Sayers's corpses spurts blood, in a scene as gruesome and abject as any in contemporary crime:

> It was a corpse. […] Indeed, if the head did not come off in Harriet's hands, it was only because the spine was intact, for the larynx and all the great vessels of the neck had been severed "to the hause-bone", and a frightful stream, bright red and glistening, was running over the surface of the rock and dripping into a little hollow below.
>   Harriet put the head down again and felt suddenly sick.
>
> *(2016: 6)*

In the late twentieth century, critical attention turned to re-evaluating the Golden Age texts beyond genre and structure and, by extension, to re-situating the role of the victim and the body. Feminist and queer theory readings recover the victim's identity as a metonym for wider social and sexual concerns and debates (Bernthal 2016). Precise historicity informs the investigation of how the Golden Age authors responded to post-World War I anxieties and social change, rather than insulating themselves from them. The "air-brushed depictions of death in Golden Age fiction" (Scaggs 2005: 44) have thus been contextualised and challenged from multiple perspectives.

Plain explicitly attempts to recover the body and its meanings from this notion of airbrushing, while challenging the perception of an insular Golden Age. Not only does Plain argue that "The resolution of the mystery in Christie frequently depends, as it does in Chandler, on an accurate reading of the female body" (2014: 31), but she queries whether "Christie's corpses [are] as bloodless as their reputation suggests?" (31). Plain argues that Christie's *Murder on the Links* (1923) and *Murder in Mesopotamia* (1936) offer a knowable corpse, or a corpse that can be mapped and understood, to replace the unmournable and uncountable victims of World War I: "The sacred requires a sacrifice, and postwar society needed a body in order to grieve. Detective fiction provided this 'grievable' body" (42). Christie's corpses, then, are deeply significant:

> Christie does not need to litter her pages with the manifold corpses of Chandlerian "realism", for those few bodies that she does deploy are freighted with the abject terrors of historical reality. Palliative medicine it may be, but in its deployment of the corpse, detective fiction transforms the inarticulable griefs of mortality into an all-in package tour through the process of bereavement.
>
> *(42)*

This association of the detective novel with rituals of mourning is significant because in Christie's books, victims are rarely explicitly mourned. Inquests are usually given more space than funerals, and grief and loss are repressed or non-existent. Nobody is truly sorry that Arlena is dead in *Evil Under the Sun*, for instance. The detective's duty to the dead, however, and duty to recover the dead and read the signifiers inscribed upon the victim in the interests of justice, perhaps makes a satisfactory substitution, while emphasising the impossibility of adequately mourning the dead.

Rebecca Mills

Beyond the Golden Age and the page

Christiana Gregoriou works along similar lines to Plain in presenting the body as a site of recovery. Discussing the forensic crime genre of Reichs and Cornwell, she suggests that "the dissecting of bodies is seen as an alternative metaphor for looking at crime" (2007: 146) – a re-situating of the victim rather than the criminal at the centre of the narrative. This occurs, she suggests, because:

> It is a genre that is focused on the scientific as opposed to the police procedural aspect of crime investigation, and concentrates on the victim rather than the perpetrator. It is more concerned with establishing the identity of victims and their physical and emotional state at the time of death as opposed to the identity and state of mind of the killer.
>
> *(150)*

The forensic project, then, is linked to discourses of the detective as an agent on behalf of the dead. The scientific invasion of the body may lead to answers, but it can be dehumanising for both corpse and detective. In *Bones* (Fox, 2005–2017), the television adaptation of Reichs's series, forensic anthropologist Temperance Brennan favours empiricism over empathy, which is presented as a flaw in character and social skills.

Current commentary connects the frequently recurring victimisation of women (and other marginalised and othered identities) to contemporary social contexts. Its scope includes depictions of violence against women in television and film. Alice Bolin's essays articulate a personal response to the troubling cultural phenomenon of what she terms the "Dead Girl Show". Examples include *Twin Peaks* (ABC, 1990–1991, Showtime 2017), *Pretty Little Liars* (ABC, 2010–2017) and *True Detective* (HBO, 2014-present). Bolin highlights the misogyny of these series, observing alarming parallels between real-world violence and toxic masculinity and the patterns of threat on these shows. She suggests:

> The Dead Girl Show's notable themes are its two odd, contradictory messages for women. The first is that girls are wild, vulnerable creatures who need to be protected from their own sexualities. [...] The other message the Dead Girl Show has for women is simpler: trust no dad. Father figures and male authorities hold a sinister interest in controlling girl bodies, and therefore harming them.
>
> *(2018: 16)*

These anxieties resonate with Larsson's trilogy and the novels of contemporary women crime writers such as Tana French, Megan Abbott and Gillian Flynn, but they are not a strictly contemporary concern. Nineteenth-century Gothic and sensation fictions are preoccupied with the vulnerability of the virgin and the threat of the sexually active woman; this spotlight on women's bodies and behaviour continues in the victimisation of both virgins and sexually active women in twentieth- and twenty-first-century fictions of crime and horror.

In Hughes's noir novel *In a Lonely Place* (1947), both vulnerable and experienced women are under threat from a strangler, suggesting that no woman is safe. The novel is focalised through Dix Steele, the monosyllabic and hypermasculine name evoking Hammett's Sam Spade and Mickey Spillane's Mike Hammer. Christopher Breu observes that Steele "becomes a darker, more overtly misogynist version of Raymond Chandler's Philip Marlowe" (2009: 204). However, unlike these morally ambiguous but ultimately reassuring private investigators, Dix

Victims

Steele is a serial killer, whose victims are young women "in the wrong place at the wrong time". Steele hunts in the "lonely places" around Los Angeles, such as foggy bus stops, back alleyways and deserted beaches:

> He didn't get up again, instead he slumped down there on the slope of a dune, and he buried his head in his arms.
> [...]
> And the red knots tightened in his brain.
> [...]
> The dog was nuzzling him when the girl came out of the fog. Dix looked up at her and he said, "Hello." She wasn't afraid. She said carelessly, "Hello."
> He smiled. She didn't know that behind that smile lay his hatred of Laurel, hatred of Brub and Sylvia, of Mel Terriss, of old Fergus Steele, of everyone in the living world, of everyone but Brucie. And Brucie was dead.
>
> *(2015: 535)*

The "girl" in the fog is a stranger to Dix, but the litany of names her presence summons are people he is intimately connected to. Dix threatens both women he knows (Laurel, Sylvia and Brucie) and anonymous women, reinforcing Hughes's point that no woman is safe in a misogynistic world. Brub is Dix's best friend and brother-in-arms during the war, and Sylvia is Brub's wife. Brub is a policeman and Dix serves as his unofficial partner, investigating the rapes and murders that he himself has committed. The novel negotiates a similar policing of female sexuality that Bolin observes in later texts and encourages the undermining of trust in male authority via this doubling of criminal and investigator, and the inability of Brub, a policeman, to realise his closest friend is a killer. The woman Dix murders in the dunes is a sacrificial victim who serves as a substitute for all his other objects of hatred. Bolin links the idea of the "perfect victim" to sacrifice:

> Dead Girls help us work out our complicated feelings about the privileged status of white women in our culture. The paradox of the perfect victim, effacing the deaths of leagues of non-white or poor or ugly or disabled or immigrant or drug-addicted or gay or trans victims, encapsulates the combination of worshipful covetousness and violent rage that drives the Dead Girl Show. The white girl becomes the highest sacrifice, the virgin martyr, particularly to that most unholy idol of narrative.
>
> *(23)*

The "red knots" in Dix's brain evoke this "violent rage", while his attitude towards his actress girlfriend Laurel veers between worship and contempt. Throughout the novel, he struggles to see women as individuals: "[Laurel] was like all women, curious about your private life" (443), feeling anger towards them all. Brucie, mentioned above, was Dix's girlfriend in the armed forces, his "only love" (497) whom he strangled when she wanted to return to her husband. It is still the "white girl" (Bolin 2018: 23) in the wrong place that often gets the most news coverage; as media scholar Sarah Stillman notes, "Sensationalised news coverage of young white women and girls in peril is so common in the USA that commentators have coined a name for it: 'The missing white girl syndrome'" (2007: 492).

Bolin's intensive investigation of the "dead girl" echoes Close's discussion of the "necropornographic sensibilities" (17) of American and Spanish crime fiction. Drawing on

Kristeva's theory and building on Plain's work on the signification of the corpse, Close poses similar questions:

> I wondered why cadavers, those most inert of literary characters, seemed to me to be ultimately the most dynamic element of crime novels. Why are novel readers and television viewers the world over compelled to consume, time and again, narratives in which cadavers elicit minute examination and give rise to elaborate investigations and explanations of the circumstances of death? And why are dead female bodies treated so distinctively and incessantly as sex objects?
>
> *(4)*

This misogynistic fetishising of the tortured female corpse is a recurring trope. Godsland comments of Spanish crime fiction that:

> The pages of many male-authored detective fictions are littered with women's lifeless bodies that have been sexually misused by male protagonists. [...] Many male writers of crime fiction across the globe allegedly formulate these fantasies of control as a response to women's move into the public arena.
>
> *(2007: 89)*

In response, she suggests, "Spanish women who write female victims are also voicing their own concerns and those of their countrywomen about the extent of male violence against women in Spain" (90).

To some extent this atmosphere of masculine threat resonates with *In a Lonely Place*. Dix is a war veteran returning to a changed America; he wishes to resume his comradeship with Brub but he has been replaced by Sylvia: "Things weren't the same. There was a girl there, a girl who had a right to be there" (13). Breu argues that instead of a response to a "postwar crisis of masculinity" (2009: 200) caused by the presence of women in the industrial workforce, the noir novel demonstrates a *lack* of crisis: "Thus it is not a crisis of masculinity so much as an aggressive reassertion of male privilege that lends postwar noir its specific gendered charge" (201).

Cormac Ó Cuilleanáin, in his study of Dublin-set crime fiction, observes the civic duty of the detective to the citizens of his community:

> Implicit in the detective's quest is a commitment to post-mortem democratic values, [...] that the quest of the detective, shuttling between the worlds of the living and the dead, projects something of the equality of death back onto the living. This could be one reason why social justice is a legitimate concern of the crime writer.
>
> *(2013: 59)*

Brub's function in Hughes's novel is to restore justice and speak for the victims, but, as he comments, "Los Angeles is too big" (34) for him to do his civic duty. The city of the silver screen and glamorous modernity has too many lonely places. The reader can never access his commemorative or potentially restorative role without Steele's mocking, gleeful presence:

> "Her name was Mildred Atkinson. She was still waiting when the girls' bus came along. She waved goodbye to them. No one saw her after that."
> Sylvia had stopped eating. "It's horrible," she said.

"Yes, it's horrible," Brub agreed. "There's no reason for the pattern. If we could just get at what's behind it."

Dix put on a thoughtful frown. "Have you no leads at all?"

(421)

The victims in this novel disappear into the columns of newspaper reports, as Hughes does not graphically describe their rape or murder, but neither does she allow reading their characters or bodies either. This is why noir is disorienting; there is no reassuring pathologist or Poirot figure. If this novel is a game, it is stacked against the (female) reader. Dix reads a newspaper report about his victim: "'Mildred was a good girl,' the parents sobbed. She'd never let a man pick her up, her girl friends chorused, but they wondered how much they hadn't known about Mildred" (428). Laurel, ironically, comments to Dix "Someday maybe those dopes will learn not to pick up strange men" (444). There is no one who can "read" the victim; even those closest to her (possibly) never fully knew her, and even young women who were "good girls" in life can lose their reputations in death.

Detectives, victims and society

In his essay on the conventions of the detective novel, W.H. Auden observed,

Murder is unique in that it abolishes the party it injures, so that society has to take the place of the victim and on his behalf demand restitution or grant forgiveness; it is the one crime in which society has a direct interest.

(1948: 407)

In Christie's and Sayers's novels, the detective speaks for society on behalf of the victim, against the murderer, and responds to society's demand for resolution, by eliminating or containing the murderer. In later noir novels this duty remains but its fulfilment is by no means certain. The authority and insight of the detective are undermined, the villain is often triumphant rather than defeated, and the victim is destroyed by society rather than functioning as a symbol of its breakdown.

Bibliography

Auden, W.H. (1948) "The guilty vicarage: notes on the detective story, by an addict", *Harper's Magazine*, https://harpers.org/archive/1948/05/the-guilty-vicarage/ (accessed 11 March 2019).

Bernthal, J.C. (2016) *Queering Agatha Christie: Revisiting the golden age of detective fiction*, Basingstoke: Palgrave Macmillan.

Bolin, A. (2018) *Dead Girls: Essays on surviving an American obsession*, New York: HarperCollins.

Breu, C. (2009) "Radical noir: negativity, misogyny, and the critique of privatization in Dorothy Hughes's *In a Lonely Place*", *MFS Modern Fiction Studies*, 55(2): 199–215.

Caillois, R. (1983) "The detective novel as game", in G.W. Most and W.W. Stowe (eds), *The Poetics of Murder: Detective fiction and literary theory*, New York: Harcourt Brace Jovanovich, 1–12.

Chandler, R. (1974) [1950] "The simple art of murder", in Haycraft, 222–37.

Christie, A. (2008) [1941] *Evil Under the Sun*, London: HarperCollins.

Close, G.S. (2018) *Female Corpses in Crime Fiction: A transatlantic perspective*, Palgrave Macmillan.

Cuilleanáin, C.Ó. (2013) "Crimes and contradictions. The fictional city of Dublin", in L. Andrew and C. Phelps (eds.), *Crime Fiction in the City: Capital crimes*, Cardiff: University of Wales Press, 47–64.

Flynn, G. (2012) *Gone Girl*, London: Orion Group.

Godsland, S. (2007) *Killing Carmens: Women's crime fiction from Spain*, Cardiff: University of Wales Press.

Gregoriou, C. (2007) *Deviance in Contemporary Crime Fiction*, New York: Palgrave Macmillan.

Haycraft, H. (ed.) (1974) *The Art of the Mystery Story: A collection of critical essays*, New York: Carroll and Graf.

Horsley, L. (2005) *Twentieth-Century Crime Fiction*, Oxford: Oxford University Press.

———. (2009) *The Noir Thriller: Contrary states*, Basingstoke: Palgrave.

Hughes, D.B. (2015) [1947] *In a Lonely Place*, in S. Weinman (ed.), *Women Crime Writers: Four suspense novels*, The Library of America.

Knox, R.A. (1974) [1928] "Detective story decalogue", in Haycraft, 194–97.

Kristeva, J. (1982) *Powers of Horror: An essay on abjection*, New York: Columbia University Press.

Larsson, S. (2009) [2005] *The Girl with the Dragon Tattoo*, London: Penguin Random House.

Malmgren, C. (2010) "The pursuit of crime: characters in crime fiction", in C.J. Rzepka and L. Horsley (eds), *A Companion to Crime Fiction*, New York: Wiley-Blackwell, 152–63.

Messent, P. (2012) *The Crime Fiction Handbook*, New York: Wiley-Blackwell.

Plain, G. (2014) *Twentieth Century Crime Fiction: Gender, sexuality and the body*, London: Taylor & Francis Group.

Pyrhönen, H. (1999) *Mayhem and Murder: Narrative and moral problems in the detective story*, Toronto: University of Toronto Press.

Sayers, D.L. (2016) [1932] *Have His Carcase*, London: Hodder & Stoughton, Kindle edition.

Scaggs, J. (2005) *Crime Fiction*, Oxford: Routledge.

Stillman, S. (2007) "'The missing white girl syndrome': disappeared women and media activism", *Gender and Development*, 15(3): 491–502.

Van Dine, S.S. (1974) [1929] "Twenty rules for writing detective stories", in Haycraft, 189–93.

17
DETECTIVES

David Geherin

Mysteries and the effort to solve them are integral parts of the human experience, and crime fiction gives narrative form to the desire to try to figure out something that demands an explanation. Sophocles's King Oedipus, who can arguably be called the first detective in literature, took it upon himself to solve the mystery of what was causing the plague that had fallen upon Thebes. He learns from the Oracle at Delphi that the plague will end only when the murderer of the previous king has been found. Tragically, solving the mystery has mixed results: The resolution to the mystery means the plague ends, but in a plot twist as clever as any in an Agatha Christie novel, it turns out that Oedipus himself is the murderer he was searching for when he discovers that the old man he once killed in a confrontation was the previous king. Worse still, he learns that the king was his father, and his wife, the queen, whom he subsequently married, is his mother. As later detectives will learn, solving the mystery does not always solve all the problems.

Over the distinguished history of crime fiction since the appearance of Edgar Allan Poe's "Murders in the Rue Morgue" in 1841, the responsibility for solving mysteries has fallen upon three main types of detective: The amateur; the private eye; and the policeman. All are, to one degree or another, tasked with finding answers to knotty problems. A close look at the differences among the three illustrates important developments in detection and helps us see how the functional aspects of the detective work undertaken in turn tell us something about the complex ideologies and typologies at play in the works themselves and in crime fiction generally.

The amateur detective

Poe's C. Auguste Dupin was an intellectual genius who solved baffling crimes by employing his superior analytical skills. But it was Poe's successor, Arthur Conan Doyle, who in the towering figure of Sherlock Holmes created the most famous detective of all time, and the model for a generation of sleuths to follow. No one put the science of deduction to better use than Holmes.

"The Blue Carbuncle" (1892) is a typical example. The story begins with a display of Holmes's amazing deductive ability, in this case what a simple hat tells him about its owner – that he is a middle-aged intellectual who has fallen on hard times, that within the last three years he has taken to drink, and that his wife has ceased to love him. Holmes then goes on to solve the theft of a priceless jewel, though in the end it becomes clear that it is not justice that motivates him, but personal satisfaction. As he explains to Dr Watson, "Chance has put in our way a most singular and whimsical problem, and its solution is its own reward" (Doyle 1994: 151). And then in the spirit of the Christmas season, he chooses to let the guilty party go free. Justice, he insists, is not his responsibility nor is it his job to make up for the deficiencies of the police, and while this sets up an adversarial and indeed hierarchical relationship between the waged policeman and the amateur sleuth (who must always in the end triumph), it also raises the prospect that the state and criminal justice system are unable, on their own, to bring crime, in all of its guises, under control.

Doyle inspired the creation of Agatha Christie's Hercule Poirot, who made his debut in *The Mysterious Affair at Styles* in 1920. A short, dandyish man with an egg-shaped head, Poirot is retired from the Belgian police force and is now living in England as a refugee from the war. Like Holmes, he only accepts challenging cases – "For Hercule Poirot nowadays only the cream of crime" (Christie 1983: 3) – which in his opinion the police lack the imagination or intellectual ability to solve. Also like Holmes, he relies on a superior intelligence, which he refers to as his "little gray cells", combined with a careful arranging of clues that enable him to connect the links in the chain that reveals the truth. The larger point is that detectives like Holmes and Poirot are driven as detectives to solve crimes for personal and not social values, i.e. they are driven by hermeneutic compulsion rather than a desire for justice, even if their detective work delivers justice and therefore has significant social or ideological value (see Porter 1981).

Although Holmes spawned a long line of genius detectives like Dorothy Sayers's Lord Peter Wimsey and John Dickson Carr's Gideon Fell, not all of the classical detectives were intellectual giants who craved the spotlight. Some were more modest crime solvers. In *The Murder at the Vicarage* (1930), for example, Christie introduced Miss Jane Marple, an elderly spinster who lives in the bucolic English village of St. Mary Mead. Unlike Dupin, Holmes or Poirot, she relies on her keen observation and a deep understanding of human evil based on a lifetime study of the people living around her to solve the mystery.

Christie's novels ushered in an era of mystery fiction known as the Golden Age, which spanned the years between the two world wars. The genre featured amateur detectives of all types who were motivated by the thrill of the game, the challenge of solving a knotty problem, and often the personal satisfaction of demonstrating their superiority over the police. And whether these sleuths employed ratiocination or knowledge of the criminal mind derived from a life spent observing human behaviour in a tiny village, the novels they appeared in followed a similar formula: A murder is committed and a clever detective solves the crime.

In these books, crime is more of a logical problem than a social or moral issue and the emphasis is always on the mystery of whodunit; plots were carefully constructed to create elaborate puzzles for the detective to unravel (and for the reader to engage in a usually fruitless battle of wits to beat the detective to the solution). The world the classic detective inhabited was rational and comprehensible, governed by the laws of logic and sufficiently uncomplicated so that a person with a special gift could always be counted on to figure out the solution to a crime. These detective stories also served the purpose of supplying comforting, reassuring endings as a diversion for readers as the world began to experience troubling times following World War I. They operated on the naïve assumption that all mysteries could be explained by the right kind of detective whose solution they hoped would then restore a sense of order to a temporarily disturbed world.

One common complaint about such novels is their lack of reality and emphasis on plot over character development. The puzzle formula needed little more than a "functional stylization" in the sense that the novels required "characters only in sufficient numbers, and sufficiently fleshed out, to give its puzzle an anthropomorphic semblance and to preserve the reader from boredom for as long as the veil of its 'mystery' is drawn" (Grossvogel 1979: 41). Traditionally, critics have read the "clue-puzzle", following this interpretation, as a socially conservative form, whereby readers could happily "escape" into a world in which "all the mysteries will be explained, all the problems solved, and peace and order will return to that mythical village which despite its above-average homicide rate, never really loses its tranquility or its innocence" (James 2009: 75). However, more recently scholars have examined British detection and detectives in the interwar years as more (socially and politically) conflicted and, indeed, ambivalent (Light 1991, Bernthal 2017), and have subsequently sought to explore instructive connections between this type of crime writing and US hardboiled crime fiction, which has been more often characterised as socially expansive and politically complex (King 2018).

The private detective

At about the same time the Golden Age was reshaping the genre for a new era and new readers, there occurred another revolution in crime writing, in the US this time, that would also change the nature of the detective figure. As noted above, the classical whodunit is predicated upon a benevolent and knowable universe that the sleuth is confident can be forced to surrender a solution to any mystery if one diligently applies the laws of logic. But the horrors of World War I and its aftermath cast a dark shadow over that assumption and led many to conclude that the world was neither as benevolent nor as rationally ordered as previously believed. In the US, this sense of disillusionment was intensified by the institution of Prohibition in 1920, which led to the widespread perception that many cities were being taken over by gangsters who ran the bootlegging industry. "The Great Good Place", the term W.H. Auden used to describe the world of the classical mystery, was rapidly turning into "The Great Wrong Place" (1948: 151). The time was ripe for the creation of a new type of detective.

Dashiell Hammett was the perfect writer to lead the revolution. Before turning to writing, Hammett had worked for several years for the Pinkerton Detective Agency, at the time the largest private law enforcement agency in the US. Put off by what he considered the unreality of stories about the amateur intellectual sleuths that were so popular at the time, he was determined to bring a more convincing sense of realism to the figure of the detective. In 1923, he began publishing a series of stories in *Black Mask* magazine based upon his own experiences about an unnamed detective employed by the Continental Detective Agency known only as the Continental Op. A few years later, he created tough-talking private eye Sam Spade in *The Maltese Falcon* (1930).

The classical detective and the private eye or hardboiled detective differ in both motivation and methods. Amateur detectives are driven by the thrill of the chase, the intellectual challenge or a healthy sense of being better at solving crimes than the police. Though the private detective is a professional in the business of solving crimes, he is not motivated entirely by money. He is drawn to cases the police cannot or will not solve, not by a desire to demonstrate how much smarter he is than they are but by a personal code that demands that justice be served and a wrong righted.

Their respective methods of detection are also radically different. The private eye's success comes not from logical deduction but from methodical trial and error. "Aggressive action, not analytic thought, is his forte", notes J.K. Van Dover. "The hard-boiled detective doesn't think; he does" (2005: 99). His cases often require him to get his hands dirty and sometimes his nose punched while he scrambles around employing his wits and street smarts to find the clues that enable him to identify the guilty party. He cannot simply settle down in a comfortable armchair and smoke his pipe while patiently putting the pieces of the puzzle together. Dashiell Hammett once likened the challenge the private eye faced to being "a blind man in a dark room hunting for the black hat that wasn't there" (1989: 78).

Raymond Chandler praised Hammett for taking murder "out of the Venetian vase" and dropping it "into the alley" and credited him with giving murder "back to the kind of people that commit it for reasons, not just to provide a corpse; and with the means at hand, not with hand-wrought dueling pistols, curare, and tropical fish" (1995: 989). In the character of Philip Marlowe, he created the prototype of the American detective hero that would dominate the genre for the next several decades. Chandler brought two important innovations to the figure of the detective. On the opening page of *The Big Sleep*, Marlowe spots a stained-glass panel in the hallway of a potential client's home depicting a knight in armour rescuing a naked woman tied to a tree.

> The knight had pushed the vizor of his helmet back to be sociable, and he was fiddling with the knots on the ropes that tied the lady to the tree and not getting anywhere. I stood there and thought that if I lived in the house, I would sooner or later have to climb up there and help him.
>
> *(Chandler 1992: 3)*

Thus was born the figure of the private detective as Arthurian knight, rescuing damsels in distress and working on behalf of the helpless and the needy. "I'm a romantic", Marlowe confesses. "I hear voices crying in the night and I go see what's the matter. You don't make a dime that way. You got sense, you shut your windows and turn up more sound on the TV set" (Chandler 1995: 651). To detectives in the Marlowe mode who bravely venture onto the mean streets of the big city, a case becomes a mission, and the goal is not simply solving a mystery but searching for the truth and helping the innocent. They know, however, that they can do nothing to restore innocence to a fallen world. They also know that success is not guaranteed: Failure is a real possibility.

Chandler's other major innovation was making the detective the narrator of the story. The formula built around the brilliant intellectual detective had its limitations. For one thing, the reader could not be given access to his thought processes; to do so would have spoiled the triumph of the detective as they reveal the identity of the murderer. To keep the master's deductions from us, Doyle, Christie and the others usually employed another character as narrator, a Watson or Hastings, who serve as recorders of their brilliant friend's successes but are never privy to the actual process of detection that led to the solution to the crime. Having the detective tell his own story allowed the reader to see how his mind works as he sometimes fumbles his way to the solution. In turn, this brings a vulnerability to Marlowe's character that sits sometimes uneasily alongside his jaundiced humour and indeed the distinctive style of his – and Chandler's – narration, which should not be mistaken for realism. What we are given in these stories is not realism, despite Chandler's claims about Hammett and Venetian vases, but a highly stylised first-person commentary on the peculiarities and idiosyncrasies of Los Angeles life. This would become one of the most notable features of the private-eye genre as writers began to use the detective-hero not just as a crime solver but also as a sharp-eyed social commentator.

Detection and diversity

For the next several decades, the private-eye genre remained almost exclusively male as the torch passed from Marlowe to dozens of knightly private eyes like Ross Macdonald's Lew Archer and

Robert B. Parker's Spenser. Then in a five-year period beginning in the late 1970s, Marcia Muller, Sara Paretsky and Sue Grafton each introduced a female version of the hardboiled detective. These were certainly not the first female detectives in crime fiction – the figure of the female detective is traceable as far back as the 1860s and 1870s – but Muller's Sharon McCone, Paretsky's V.I. Warshawski and Grafton's Kinsey Millhone, were all modelled on Philip Marlowe rather than on female amateur detectives like Miss Marple. Less violent and tough-talking than their male predecessors, these smart, feisty women embodied the rapidly changing role of women in society and enacted or practised different modes of detection; in Paretsky's case, eschewing the explicit and by the 1970s hackneyed individualism of the earlier gumshoes for a more collective, communitarian ethos where Warshawski comes to rely on a wider network of like-minded friends and affiliates to solve crimes (see Schmid 2012).

Though these and other female writers of private-eye fiction often engaged in overtly feminist critiques of society, they also addressed other social, political and even environmental concerns. Warshawski, for example, is a fierce defender of the poor and powerless and her investigations raise larger social issues relating to law and justice in society. This earned her recognition for consistently confronting "the organizational crime – corporate, union, professional or otherwise – that hides behind the glittering facade of the contemporary urban agglomerations" (Bertens and D'haen 2001: 32), and for bringing a degree of sociopolitical activism to the genre, which has been picked up and developed by more recent crime writers (e.g. Alicia Gaspar de Alba).

The predominantly all-white fraternity of private eyes underwent another significant transformation thanks to the emergence of African American writers such as Walter Mosley, who introduced Easy Rawlins in *Devil in a Blue Dress* in 1990. Observing the world through the eyes of a female or a minority detective expanded the perspective of the private-eye novel to include issues related to gender and race. Mosley's novels, for example, are set in LA in the late 1940s and beyond and illuminate the post-war African American experience in the city.

Because the private eye is an urban version of the prototypical Western hero represented by legendary nineteenth-century frontier heroes such as Davy Crockett and Daniel Boone as well as literary heroes like James Fenimore Cooper's Natty Bumppo, it has largely remained a quintessentially American hero. Nevertheless, it has indeed found a home in a number of foreign locations. Inspired by the question of what Raymond Chandler might have written if he had moved from England to Berlin instead of to Los Angeles, Scottish writer Philip Kerr created Bernie Gunther in 1990, a private eye modelled on Philip Marlowe, who operates in 1930s Berlin during the rise of Hitler's Third Reich and who, despite his opposition to the Nazis, ends up working for several of Hitler's notorious henchmen. Paco Ignacio Taibo II's Héctor Belascoarán Shayne, a Mexico City based private eye, was featured in a series of novels that infused the hardboiled detective genre with a Kafkaesque surrealism well suited to an exposé of evils perpetrated by the Mexican state. In the latter case, Shayne's status as "private" means he can distance himself from the violence and corruption of the state, a move that Kerr's Gunther practises too, though as a former cop, he cannot help but become entangled in the mechanisms of state power. As Pepper (2016) has shown, detectives, public and private, have always had an awkward, ambivalent relationship to the workings of criminal justice, a tension that becomes more pronounced in the guise of our final figure, the police detective.

The police detective

The police have appeared in crime novels from the beginning, but in many instances their image was anything but positive. Classical detectives like Dupin, Holmes and Poirot often had a competitive relationship with the police and took great delight in routinely demonstrating their superiority over them. The police in hardboiled detective novels were frequently depicted as antagonistic forces who sought to prevent the private eye from intruding on their turf. But the image of the cop underwent a major change thanks to Belgian author Georges Simenon.

French novelist Èmile Gaboriau is often credited with creating the first police detective in the person of Monsieur Lecoq in 1866, but it was Simenon who brought the figure into prominence. In a series that began in 1931 and spanned four decades, his Chief Inspector Jules Maigret of the Paris Police Judiciaire Crime Squad became one of the most important figures in the genre. Unlike many of the classical detectives, Maigret is a seasoned professional who relies on the assistance of several fellow officers in his investigations. A student of human nature, he also feels the need to understand the criminals he pursues, which is instrumental in helping to shift "the centre of gravity of crime fiction from the *who* and *how* to the *why*" (Weisz 1983: 180).

Equally important as an influence on the establishment of the modern police procedural is Ed McBain, who believed that the only valid persons capable of dealing with crime were policemen, who are officially charged with enforcing the laws set by the government. In 1956 he launched a series that featured a squad of detectives assigned to the 87th Precinct in the fictional city of Isola, a stand-in for New York City. While Detective Steve Carella often took centre stage, McBain emphasises the collective nature of policing by surrounding him with a team of fellow cops who work together to solve whatever crime is committed on their watch. He also prefaced each novel with the assurance that while the city and the people are fictitious, the police routine is based on established investigatory techniques. His books highlight the kind of procedural realism that established the model that successive writers in the genre would follow.

McBain's novels were introduced to Swedish readers in translations done by the husband-and-wife team of Maj Sjöwall and Per Wahlöö. But the two of them accomplished much more than this when in 1967 they began publishing a series of ten police procedurals that centred around Martin Beck and his fellow officers on the Stockholm police department. Like McBain, they describe in detail each investigation, but they transformed the genre by exploiting its potential as a vehicle for social and political commentary. The search for a bank robber in *The Locked Room* who shot a bystander during a robbery eventually turns into a critique of the failure of Sweden's so-called Welfare State in addressing the desperate needs of the poor and the powerless. The authors also cast a critical eye on the official police organisation itself, which Beck feared was increasingly turning into a paramilitary force: "What could a man do as he witnessed the gradual decay of his own organization?" another policeman asks himself as he "heard the rats of fascism pattering about behind the wainscoting" (Sjöwall and Wahlöö 1973: 57).

The generic shift from the private-eye tale to the police procedural was largely prompted by the recognition that "the marginal position and limited perspective of the PI hero or heroine makes for an ineffectual, and even irrelevant, figure as far as the representation of criminal activity and its containment goes" (Messent 1997: 2). In the real world, it is the police who solve most crimes by working as a team using the latest investigative technology – from fingerprints and DNA samples to mobile records and surveillance videos – that is simply unavailable to amateur detectives and private eyes. Using a collective group of detectives also allows for the telling of multiple stories, as the police ordinarily work several cases simultaneously, and since it is their duty to investigate whatever crime occurs in their jurisdiction, they must deal with a much greater variety of crimes.

Detectives in crime fiction are not limited solely to the three main types described above. Amateur detectives come in an infinite variety of identities, and professional investigators in related fields – lawyers, journalists, forensic scientists – often assume the role of the detective who solves the crime. The function of the detective also continues to evolve as the world of crime fiction has expanded from Miss Marple's sleepy village and the confined parameters of the locked room to the global village and the infinite space of the digital world. As crimes have become increasingly international in scope and their perpetrators more difficult to police, some have questioned whether the crime novel is capable of adequately representing "the transnational, even global, totality that defines this kind of crime" (Schmid 2012: 21). One example of a new kind of detective who does possess some of the specialised skills needed to combat the latest crime-solving challenges, which are global or at least transnational rather than simply local, can be found in Stieg Larsson's *The Girl with the Dragon Tattoo* (2005).

The Girl with the Dragon Tattoo

No one would ever think Sherlock Holmes when looking at Lisbeth Salander, a pale, anorexic-looking twenty-four-year-old woman with a pierced nose and eyebrows, a wasp tattoo on her neck, and a dragon tattoo on her left shoulder. She looks like "she had just emerged from a week-long orgy with a gang of hard rockers" (Larsson 2008: 32). As a child she was declared emotionally disturbed and is still subject to court-ordered social and psychiatric guardianship. All of this has left her angry, sullen and fiercely antisocial ("Seven minutes of another person's company was enough to give her a headache" [312]).

But this school dropout possesses a brilliance even Holmes would admire. With both a keen mind and a photographic memory, Salander is, by her own estimation, the best computer hacker in Sweden. Her hobby is digging into the lives of people and exposing their secrets. Her talent in this regard has landed her a job at Armansky Security, where she was given the assignment of preparing a background report on financial journalist Mikael Blomkvist, who had just been found guilty of libelling and defaming prominent Swedish financier Hans-Eric Wennerström.

Despite a reputation for integrity and investigative prowess prior to this incident, Blomkvist, who is convinced he was set up and deliberately fed false information, is nonetheless forced to leave his job at *Millennium*, a magazine he helped found. But then he gets an unexpected offer of a most unusual new job. Eighty-two-year-old Henrik Vanger, patriarch of a powerful manufacturing empire, offers to hire him to do two things: 1) write a history of his large, dysfunctional family; and 2) solve a thirty-six-year-old mystery. On the day when a tanker accident closed all access to and from Hedeby Island where he lived, his beloved sixteen-year-old niece Harriet mysteriously disappeared. Her body has never been found and Vanger is convinced she must have been murdered by one of the few dozen people trapped on the island. What makes the case so baffling is that he is tormented each year on his birthday by receiving a pressed flower in the mail, a habit Harriet began when she was eight. If Blomkvist agrees to accept his job offer, Vanger promises to give him proof of Wennerström's crimes.

Blomkvist and Salander do not actually meet until halfway through the novel when he tracks her down after discovering she had hacked into his computer to gain personal information in order to write her report on him. After spending six months looking into Harriet's disappearance, he has uncovered some promising leads but has reached the point where he needs help. A person with Salander's advanced computer skills might be useful in his investigation.

While Blomkvist assumes the role of the conventional detective whose methodical snooping is able to turn up important evidence about Harriet's disappearance as well as the identity of a serial killer who might have murdered her, Salander plays a more essential role than that of a mere sidekick: She rescues Blomkvist from the clutches of the serial killer who is about to kill him; she later arranges for an illegal phone tap that provides the information that solves the mystery of Harriet's disappearance; and then she spends twelve-hour days in front of her computer tracking down Wennerström's 3,000 separate accounts and bond holdings all over the world and downloading all the evidence Blomkvist needs to prove Wennerström's criminality.

Salander determines that Wennerström's cyber empire is secretly involved with the Russian mafia and Colombian drug cartels in global crimes involving illegal arms dealing, money laundering, attempts to purchase enriched uranium on the black market in Ukraine, even the child sex trade in Mexico. Salander does more than merely expose his crimes. Using her computer wizardry, she systematically transfers the millions in each of Wennerström's many accounts into her own. She is not then surprised when Wennerström is subsequently gunned down by some Colombians; only she knows why he is unable to pay the debt he owes them.

As crime fiction becomes increasingly more international in scope, we will likely see the emergence of even more detectives like Salander who possess the kind of specialised digital/ IT skills capable of combatting the threat posed by the new kinds of transnational crimes proliferating around the globe. As a vigilante figure concerned primarily with exacting a more individualised form of justice, there is perhaps also something familiar and even reassuring about her actions and even her violence. But just as Salander's IT expertise speaks to or about important changes in the nature of crime and detection, the issue of whether a single detective figure, capable of uncovering networks of criminality spanning continents and pursuing justice outside or beyond the nation-state, will continue to dominate the crime novel remains to be seen.

Bibliography

Auden, W.H. (1948) "The guilty vicarage", in *The Dyer's Hand and Other Essays*, New York: Random House, 147–58.

Bernthal, J.C. (2017) *Queering Agatha Christie: Revisiting the golden age of detective fiction*, Basingstoke: Palgrave Macmillan.

Bertens, H. and D'haen, T. (2001) *Contemporary American Crime Fiction*, New York: Palgrave Macmillan.

Chandler, R. (1992) *Raymond Chandler: Stories and early novels*, New York: The Library of America.

———. (1995) *Raymond Chandler: Later novels and other writings*, New York: The Library of America.

Christie, A. (1983) *The A.B.C. Murders*, New York: Bantam.

Doyle, A.C. (1994) *Sherlock Holmes: The major stories with contemporary critical essays*, ed. J.A. Hodgson, New York: Bedford St. Martin's.

Grossvogel, D. (1979) *Mystery and its Fictions: From Oedipus to Agatha Christie*, Baltimore: Johns Hopkins University Press.

Hammett, D. (1989) *The Dain Curse*, New York: Vintage.

James, P.D. (2009) *Talking About Detective Fiction*, New York: Alfred A. Knopf.

King, S. (2018) "*E pluribus unum*: A transnational reading of Agatha Christie's *Murder on the Orient Express*", *Clues*, 36(1): 9–19.

Larsson, S. (2008) *The Girl with the Dragon Tattoo*, trans. R. Keeland, New York: Alfred A. Knopf.

Light, A. (1991) *Forever England: Femininity, literature and conservatism between the wars*, London: Routledge.

Messent, P. (1997) "Introduction", in P. Messent (ed.), *Criminal Proceedings: The contemporary American crime novel*, London: Pluto Press, 1–21.

Pepper, A. (2016) *Unwilling Executioner: Crime fiction and the state*, Oxford: Oxford University Press.

Porter, D. (1981) *The Pursuit of Crime: Art and ideology in detective fiction*, New Haven: Yale University Press.

Schmid, D. (1995) "Imagining safe urban space: the contribution of detective fiction to radical geography", *Antipode*, 27(3): 242–69.

Detectives

———. (2012) "From the locked room to the globe: space in crime fiction", in V. Miller and H. Oakley (eds), *Cross-Cultural Connections in Crime Fictions*, New York: Palgrave Macmillan, 7–23.

Sjöwall, M. and Wahlöö, P. (1973) *The Locked Room*, trans. Paul Britten Austin, New York: Pantheon.

Van Dover, J.K. (2005) *We Must Have Certainty: Four essays on the detective story*, Selinsgrove, PA: Susquehanna University Press.

Weisz, P. (1983) "Simenon and 'Le Commissaire'", in Bernard Benstock (ed.), *Art in Crime Writing: Essays on detective fiction*, New York: St. Martin's Press, 174–88.

18

CRIMINALS

Christiana Gregoriou

This chapter addresses the portrayal of crime fiction's most vital character type: The criminal. This character is most often defined solely on the basis of their criminality and social deviance, the latter being "a quality of people's response to an act and not a characteristic of the act itself" (Price 1978: 147). Portraying such characters one-dimensionally and reactively is problematic, but so are the socially-produced constructions of criminality itself. In line with Nils Christie's (1986) criminological theory, the ideal offender is expected to be large, evil and completely unknown to their victim. In accordance with such expectations, criminals are also assumed to be physically powerful, unrepentant and entirely to blame for their actions, assumptions which also need to be challenged. Crime fiction is known to both corroborate and question stereotypical expectations of this kind which, in turn, encourages readers to do the same.

The chapter opens with a discussion of the genre's construction of the criminal before proceeding to identify key criminal archetypes as well as the correlations the genre tends to make between criminal and non-criminal aspects of both behaviour and status. The discussion will then turn to crime fiction writers whose work allows access to the criminal mind, before defining what I refer to as "criminal mind style". Lastly, Val McDermid's *Mermaids Singing* (1995) will be subjected to a criminal mind-style analysis to draw out some of the features previously outlined and showcase the form that such stylistic analysis can take. Though examples drawn on in this chapter mostly suggest that crime fiction accounts of criminal behaviour can be reductive and problematic, the figure of criminality is itself a complex one, the actual criminal phenomenon complicated and ambiguous and the line between criminal and non-criminal behaviour very often blurred and hard to discern.

Constructing criminals

In contrast to criminals, the fictional detective figure is typically a positively connoted one, even if inevitably somewhat conflicted. Much like criminals, detectives are portrayed as highly intelligent yet troubled and obsessive individuals, sacrificing themselves to their work, their suffering producing knowledge, insight and results. Fictional detectives are also characters who relate to, identify with, or engage in transference with, criminals, mirroring them so as to predict their next move. Most importantly, fictional detectives find themselves needing to break the law to catch criminals. And yet, because of the cultural and legal labelling of these two character types (see Gregoriou 2007: 91–94), crime fiction readers tend to be far more tolerant of detectives' rule-breaking than that of the criminals they pursue. Reader judgement of characters' abnormal behaviour clearly depends on context, an issue that the genre of crime fiction works to expose.

Where ideal criminals are strong, evil and blameworthy, ideal victims are weak, respectable and blameless (see Christie 1986). As I have discussed elsewhere (Gregoriou 2011), the most undeserving of victims are also defined by their youth, female gender, innocence, vulnerability and even beauty, whereas the most deserving of crime victims are characterised, if not defined, by their supposed social deviance. Where victims are themselves criminalised or otherwise stigmatised through their own deviant actions – or actions defined by others as deviant (where, for example, their sexual behaviour supposedly puts them at risk of harm) – they find themselves stripped of their victim status. Not only are such victims treated as *deserving* of whatever crime they have been subjected to, but they might even be thought of as *responsible* (see Schmid 2005: 226–29). Just as detectives can resemble criminals, discourses of victim responsibilisation can criminalise victims. By portraying victims as responsible for the acts committed against them, the responsibility of the perpetrator is mitigated.

The genre's preferred, and most significant, criminal archetypes are the "monster", the "vampire" and the "spoilt child" (Gregoriou 2007). The first two types are reminiscent of the age-old nature/nurture debate. The monster refers to those fictional criminals who supposedly act criminally because this is the sort of behaviour to which they were predisposed from birth (i.e. nature). In texts of this kind, criminals are portrayed as "the embodiment of a cold, calculating evil" (Peach 2006: 156), the characters' monstrous psyche being at times reflected even in their physicality (a correlation I return to shortly). This criminal archetype is drawn upon in novels that favour metaphors which refer to criminals as having always been inhuman/monstrous. In contrast, the vampire archetype refers to those fictional criminals supposedly made into such, their criminality being the consequence of previous trauma (i.e. nurture). In such contexts, killers are seen as "a product of a dysfunctional childhood" (Peach 2006: xv; see also Seltzer 1998: 256) and therefore not accountable for their criminal actions. I refer to such fictional criminals as vampiric given that, as per folklore, vampires are not born as such, but turned into Gothic creatures through, for instance, blood transfer. Lastly, I have employed the term "spoilt child" to refer to fictional criminals who act criminally, not because of nature or nurture, but simply because they like it, and because they can. They enjoy criminal behaviour, cannot help but indulge in it and refuse to take responsibility for it.

These variant fictional archetypes open up a range of questions which not only address our need to understand criminals and explain their behaviour, but also to examine the extent to which criminality is socially produced. Thus, the genre forces us to examine our own role or contribution to crime through, for instance, various gender-, race- and sexuality-related ideologies we have come to internalise. Despite such tendencies, crime fiction has found itself evolving in response to a changing world, adapting to social standards of female, racial, gay and transgender equality. In so doing, modern crime fiction has come to challenge the masculinity, whiteness, straightness and cisgenderness of the genre by featuring non-male/white/straight/cisgender criminals, and hence challenging traditional expectations as to who criminals can actually be.

Even though crime fiction has evolved to embrace more progressive politics of identification, the fictional portrayal of killers is persistently characterised by various contradictions. According to the myth around serial killers, for instance, such criminals may be seen as setting themselves apart as "abnormal" (physically unappealing "others" and loners) while also having the ability to look "normal", and hence remain unseen when hiding amongst and acting like us. Similarly, in *Natural Born Celebrities*, Schmid (2005: 6–8) argues that the serial killer celebrity figure inspires contradictory feelings of repulsion and attraction, condemnation and admiration, contrasts which offer "evidence of the collapse of the difference between fame and notoriety" (2005: 6–8). Peach proposes a related contradiction:

> [T]he language in which criminality is written about, whether scientifically or imaginatively, occupies a kind of "double time" in that even in the most scientific accounts, it is caught between objectivism and fascination, and between distance and involvement. For the most part, this is because criminologists and authors know that their readers are themselves poised between objectivism and fascination in their relationship to crime.
>
> *(2006: 4)*

In other words, the fact that readers cannot help but be ambivalent about criminals as a character type may, perhaps, explain their attraction.

The discourse through which fictional criminals are portrayed is also problematic. Though such narratives often examine the extent to which criminals are the result of bad families (a question of nurture), the misogynistic ideologies which often underlie such portrayals result in mother-blaming more than father-blaming, as mothers are often seen as creators of not only the body but also the character of their children (a question of nature). Such "bad mother"-related discourse (see also Boyle 2005: 10) makes the mothers of criminals culpable for the actions of their offspring.

The correlation between supposedly bad mothering and the child's ultimate criminal behaviour is not the only problematic connection made by fictional crime narratives. Another is the correlation between sex and criminal violence. In line with conservative and indeed negative views of sex, such narratives tend to suggest that sexual needs or issues may well relate to, if not cause, criminal violence, with even consensual sex being seen as a form of such violence. In such contexts, the problematic suggestion is that, for all criminals, sex, violence and crime are all inextricably linked. Similarly, by deeming sexually innocent victims as less deserving of criminal actions than their sexualised counterparts, sex comes to be problematically viewed as a form of social deviance which supposedly enables, and encourages, criminal behaviour.

A third correlation the genre tends to make between criminal and non-criminal aspects of behaviour is that of reading/watching fictional violence (in books/films/TV), writing about fictional violence (say, in a creative writing class) or even engaging in *fictional* violence (in a video game, for example) and *actually* being criminally violent. Despite there being some evidence that actual criminals may pattern themselves on fictional ones, and that fictional criminal construction is often inspired by official accounts, which in turn often draw on fictional accounts (see Seltzer 1998 and Jenkins 1994), one ought not assume that an interest in fictional crime could cause criminal behaviour.

A fourth correlation that bears relevance to this discussion is that between foreignness/racial identity and criminality. The discourse around criminality is often patterned around our need to belong, which ultimately generates divisions between groups. Contrasting pairings between "non-criminal/potential victim us" and "criminal them" are not uncommon but need to be contested. A community's (perceived) outsiders are often treated as the ultimate scapegoats as their non-local/not-like-us status is interpreted as relevant to any of their (criminal) behaviours. Much as misogynistic agendas inform representations of mothers being to blame for their offspring's actions, so do xenophobic/racist agendas inform discussions of a foreigner's supposedly deviant or criminal behaviour. Such discourse suggests that foreign or racial minority status may well predetermine criminal behaviour. Outsiders therefore supposedly need to be feared as potential criminals, acting against innocent natives who can only be seen as their potential victims.

The fifth and final correlation that needs questioning is that between physical or psychological disability, difference or illness and criminal status. Chandonne, a "monstrous" criminal who appears in Patricia Cornwell's *Black Notice* (2000), can be used to illustrate this association. What makes Chandonne's monstrous classification possible is not only his psychopathic behaviour, but also his physical makeup, in that he emits a strange body odour because of a rare metabolic disorder. This sort of criminal portrayal is linked to the previously described myth of criminals as physically "abnormal". Suggesting (most often causal) links between a supposedly abnormal physicality and criminal behaviour must be challenged, particularly because of assumptions regarding the extent to which certain physicalities are themselves deemed unappealing compared to others. The same holds true for correlations between mental illness and criminality. This is in line with media discourse around criminals, which also uses one's supposed mental illness as an "explanatory resource", naturalising the "mundane notion that only madness could account for [certain criminal] actions" (McCarthy and Rapley 2001: 161). In Jim Thompson's *The Killer Inside Me* (1952), for instance, the killer refers to his criminal tendency as a "sickness" (6, 8, 22, 68, *passim*), a "disease" or a "condition" (201). Problematically, the suggestion that mental illness is related to criminal behaviour could imply that all individuals with mental health issues are prone to criminal violence, an association that stigmatises mental illness and those experiencing it. Having said that, those suffering from psychopathic disorders often prove good exemplars of criminal archetypes, particularly as psychopathy is the area where mental disorder and violent, or indeed, criminal behaviour actually interact. Texts, such as Thompson's, that are focalised through one psychopathic criminal, not only allow access to the criminal's worldview but, in addition, tend to be concerned with investigating the precise nature of psychopathic criminal minds.

Accessing criminal mind(style)s

Kate Watson (2012: 203) lists a range of authors whose work is narrated and focalised through the unreliable voice of a murderer, including Charles Brockden Brown, James Hogg, Edgar Allan Poe, Wilkie Collins, Agatha Christie and Val McDermid, the last of whom will be the focus of a stylistic analysis below. To this list, I would add James Patterson and Jeff Lindsay, whose works I have previously subjected to a stylistic analysis (see, correspondingly, Gregoriou 2007 and 2011), with an eye to unlocking the criminal portrayal and investigating the means through which these novelists portray not only psychopathic killers, but also the various ideologies underlying their representation. Before offering an overview of these analyses, I outline the key theoretical concepts that underpin a stylistic approach to such texts.

Roger Fowler first coined the term "mind style" to refer to language used to portray a particular mental self. For Fowler, mind styles are projected via systematic linguistic and textual patterns which cumulatively, and consistently, cut the presented world into patterns in such a way as to "give rise to an impression of a world-view" (1977: 76). Since I take mind style to refer to the way in which a particular reality is perceived and conceptualised in cognitive terms, I, in turn, have coined the phrase "criminal mind style" to refer to language that reflects a criminal's worldview, and relates to the mental abilities and tendencies of an individual criminal, traits that may be completely personal and idiosyncratic, or ones that may be shared, for example, by people with similar cognitive habits (see Gregoriou 2007: 71). Since criminality is often mystified, linguistic analysis of criminal mind styles offers readers access to the criminal worldview and thereby potentially demystifies the criminality in question.

Linguistic engagement with texts of this kind can entail analysis of the texts' grammar and lexis, but also their use of metaphor, an area I will concentrate on below. In accordance with the cognitive view of metaphor (see Lakoff and Johnson 1980), one would traditionally indicate how the target domain (i.e. the item described) is referred to via the metaphor's source domain (i.e. what it is described through). A focus on those source cognitive domains corresponding to the target domain of criminals can reveal not only the poetic structure of the criminal mind, but also various underlying ideologies surrounding criminals and criminality.

In James Patterson's *Along Came a Spider* (1993) and *Cat and Mouse* (1997), for example, killers are firstly metaphorically conceptualised as spiders ("He had spun his web perfectly" [1997: 5]) or other predatory animals ("Here comes Mr Fox", [1993: 5]). Such metaphors dehumanise these killers but also naturalise their actions, the assumption being that the killers somehow kill to survive (their victims being "food"), much like animals kill to feed themselves. Similarly, Dexter's acts of murder are framed along the lines of hunting in Jeff Lindsay's *Darkly Dreaming Dexter* (2004): "And so I hunted" (81), or "Harry had helped me control my Dark Passenger, feeding him stray pets" (157). Such reductive accounts of criminality are not uncommon in crime fiction but neither, in fact, are nuanced ones. Nevertheless, simplistic accounts of this kind are significant in portraying criminality as yet another human act driven by supposed necessitation. Besides, such metaphors are in line with Richard Tithecott's discussion of the acts of serial killers being "figured as continuous with the craving of food, as one of the more recent and extreme examples of man fulfilling his ever-changing needs" (1997: 63).

Lindsay's Dexter is portrayed as belonging to an inhuman species ("Perhaps because I'll never be one, humans are interesting to me" [63]) and as monstrous ("I am a very neat monster" [11]), metaphors which, in "othering" Dexter, prove helpful in explaining his otherwise inexplicable behaviour, but also perhaps highlight what is monstrous within ourselves. Similarly dehumanising is Patterson's conceptualisation of criminals as machines that carry out their vicious intentions automatically and without agency: "Gary was like a programmed machine from the moment he spotted the police" (1993: 180). Referring to killers as machines assumes a lack of accountability on one hand and, contradictorily perhaps, a clear purpose or function on the other. Lastly, portraying "[t]he figure of the killer as [an] unfeeling, programmed machine" allows "the writer of the program [to remain] a mystery" and explains the mechanical repetitiveness found, for instance, in the serial killing act (Tithecott 1997: 98).

Criminal behaviour is also linked to play-acting, often referred to as a film or play: "This was his movie" (Patterson 1993: 52); "The scene of the crime-to-be, the scene of the masterpiece theatre" (Patterson 1997: 20). Killers are portrayed as actors partly because there is a level of literal performance to what they do (how they lure their victims in, how they hide their intentions from others), but also because the performative element itself implies an audience. A related metaphor is that of killing being likened, by Dexter, to art ("this artist – excuse me, I mean 'killer' of course" (Lindsay 2004: 96)). Referring to murder as any type of art suggests that killers are engaging in action which is meant to impress, inform and entertain (non-criminal) readers. Problematically, this implies that we admire their criminal actions rather than abhor them. A related conceptual metaphor is that of crime as a game or criminals as players ("It's time for more fun, more games" [Patterson 1993: 171]; "*Make no mistake about it. I will win*" [Patterson 1997: 55]; "[W]as [the killer] saying, 'Hi! Wanna play?'" [Lindsay 2004: 123]). Such metaphors suggest not only a competition, rules and a desire to show superior skills, but also that all participants in the game (including detectives and victims) are willingly and pleasurably engaged in playing.

Criminals

The next section critically engages with the criminal portrayal in McDermid's *Mermaids Singing*, the novel which first introduced the author's recurring protagonists, Detective Inspector Carol Jordan and clinical psychologist and profiler Tony Hill. I first illustrate some of the previously identified theoretical themes before engaging in brief criminal mind-style analysis of extracts, focusing not only on the novel's psychopathic killer Angelica, who is portrayed as mentally ill (through, for example, references to her doctors prescribing her tranquilizers), but also on Hill's psychological profiling of Angelica, as he engages in transference with her throughout; as Hill admits to himself, "if I'm going to be the best at what I do, I have to think like a villain" (224).

Val McDermid's *Mermaids Singing*

Much like the Patterson novels referred to above, McDermid's novel is only partly focalised through a psychopathic criminal. Angelica is a male-to-female transgender serial killer who reconstructs medieval torture devices with which to attack and kill the men who refuse her advances. As Barbara Pezzotti notes, the genre tends to use the transvestite as "an easy *escamotage* to guarantee a surprise turn of events and an unpredictable ending to the mystery" (2018: 10). Here, further to transgenderism being put forward as a trait that, problematically, helps explains Angelica's criminal behaviour, it also allows her to be positioned as the ultimate and dangerous outsider, both physically and psychologically. And yet in opting for a transgender killer in a series of "non-gender-specific narrative" extracts (i.e. extracts that do not reveal the focaliser's gender), McDermid generates expectations of the killer being a cisgender male, only for Angelica's transgenderism and her choice of male victims to ultimately "challenge the traditional grand narrative of crime fiction that defines the male as killer and the female as victim" (Watson 2012: 195). Unlike Patterson's novels, where the parts focusing on the criminal are in the third person, passages focusing on Angelica are written in the first person, an effective device with which to disguise Angelica's female gender. The Angelica-focalised sections are also in italics, the font choice graphologically foregrounding the perpetrator sections as deviant and "other" to the main narrative (Seago 2018: 923) where Hill's psychological profiling of the killer appears in a non-inflected font throughout.

Save being female, Angelica closely resembles the ideal offender described above; she was, after all, born male, large and strong. She is also evil, unknown to her victims, unrepentant and entirely to blame for her pre-planned actions. She is described as homophobic as she appears to reject both her own, and others', homosexuality. When reflecting on her male past, she notes:

> *I'd never had much interest in girls. And although I found men attractive, I knew I wasn't a poof. They disgust me, with their pretence at normal relationships when everybody knows that it's only men and women that can fit together properly.*
>
> *(McDermid 2003: 368)*

While crime narrative discourse tends to "demon[ise] homosexuality by arguing that it is intimately connected (indeed, almost identical) with violence" (Schmid 2005: 209), it is Angelica's homophobia that is demonised here and proves to be the root of her violent behaviour. Though the victims' bodies being dumped in areas known primarily for their use by the gay community initially leads the investigative team to presume they are gay, Angelica's victims are later revealed to be straight, which interestingly comes to invite more sympathy for them. What the text ultimately suggests, and invites the readers to problematise, is the assumption that gay male victims might be construed as more deserving of their fate, as they are deemed less respectable and more blameworthy than straight victims, all by virtue of their sexuality. As Hill finds noted in a newspaper editorial, "authorities value the lives of gay men less than those of other members of the community" (98). As will be seen, this is an assumption that McDermid implicitly invites readers to ponder over and ultimately reject.

In accordance with the serial killer myth, Angelica is portrayed as partially integrated into society through her job in computer science, but also as physically unappealing (Hill describes her as "distinctively ugly" [350]) and a lonely figure who thus finds herself obsessing over her reconstruction of torture devices. She has an interest in playing dark video games (50) which, along with her own computer expertise, leads her to video her acts of torture and murder, subsequently employing specialised software with which to voyeuristically create further manipulated and animated fictionalised scenarios involving both sexual intercourse with, and violence directed at, her victims. Note how the narrative here suggests a link between Angelica's violent fantasies, fiction-making and actual violence, all supposedly contributing to each other, perhaps even causatively so. Such links problematically suggest that aspects of one's behaviour (such as enjoying being alone, having interests and playing video games) are not unrelated to one's tendency for violence, when in fact they might well be so.

Angelica depicts features that are characteristic of all criminal archetypes previously described. She fits the spoilt child archetype, according to which she does what she likes (i.e. acts violently as a result of her lack of emotional and sexual fulfilment) and without any concern for others. As Hill concludes while psychologically profiling a (then) presumed male killer: "[h]e has the egocentric view of the spoiled child, and has no insight into the impact of his behaviour on others" (248). Angelica is also portrayed as a monster of sorts, in the archetype's physical sense at least (an angry neighbour describes her as an "ugly cow" who "look[ed] like a brick shit-house in drag" [379]), the text implying that it is her unsightly appearance that initially led her victims to reject her, and hence to her murderous response. Lastly, she may also be classified as a "vampire", as the narrative suggests that Angelica's dysfunctional and abusive family background contributed to her violent actions as an adult; she "*spent more time locked in the cupboard than most people's coats do*" (367). Unsurprisingly, the narrative here demonstrates more mother-blaming than it does father-blaming. Neglected and ultimately abandoned by her father, Angelica was raised by an abusive and alcoholic prostitute mother, which is relevant to Angelica later not only being abusive herself, but also her prostituting herself to sailors, in order to fund her sex-change surgery (see Watson 2012: 205).

As for the text's criminal mind style, readers mostly encounter extended metaphors to do with criminal behaviour being related to "*work*" (143, 268, 309), which Angelica loves and takes pride in. Hill, for instance, refers to her as a "career killer" (92), while Angelica herself characterises the killings as "*achievements*" and "*accomplishments*" (310, 345). Referring to criminal activity along such lines suggests that killing is a set task undertaken in a formal and legitimate capacity, not to mention one that others value. A case in point is Angelica's description of each victim as an "*assistant*" or "*partner*" in the killing "*experience*" (52, 325, 187); in other words, as willing participants in their own torture and murder.

Not unrelated to the work metaphor is that of killing as a craft or an art for which Angelica has a "*natural bent*" and "*extraordinary talent*" (212). One of the torture devices is referred to as a "*toy*" (3) and victim remains as "*handiwork*" (309, 346). Further examples include Hill's code-naming of her as a "Handy Andy" (76) whose work he was dangerously close to admiring (35), and Angelica's references to a torture museum having served as "*a muse*" (4) and to her killing devices as "*masterpiece[s]*" she "created" (188, 85). Elsewhere, one encounters metaphorical representations of Angelica's violence as a specific art form: "*drama*"/"*performance*" (1), encompassing of "*choreographed move[s]*", and her planning violent events much like "*a theatre director plans the first production of a new play*" (24). Referring to killing as art is reminiscent of the previously outlined analyses of novels by Patterson and Lindsay and suggests that killing may be a mere creative expression of oneself, but also that killers as artists are not only creatively generative but also worthy of admiration. Ultimately, then, metaphorical characterisations of criminality arguably reflect, but also shape, our understanding of criminal behaviour and the various ideologies related to it.

Conclusion

In this chapter, I have argued that rule-breaking and deviance is not limited to criminals alone; in addition to such behaviour being typical of detective figures, victims can also be portrayed as responsible for their own deaths due to their own supposed social deviance. And while the genre's preferred criminal archetypes force us to examine the extent to which criminality is socially produced, they also lay bare several contradictions, myths and problematic correlations which writers often draw upon in their attempts to explain criminal motivation. Fictional narratives are prone to mother-blaming, and also tend to link sexual needs and/or an interest in fictional crime to real criminal tendencies. Further, the genre tends to correlate "otherness" to criminality, relying on an indexical relationship between deviance and racial, national, physical or psychological difference.

McDermid's *Mermaids Singing* features a criminal that, in many ways, aligns to the genre's preferred archetypes, but Angelica's transgenderism and homophobia also play with conventional approaches to crime, gender and sexuality. McDermid challenges the genre's typical gender role-related reader expectations and perhaps proposes a demonisation, not of homosexuality, but of homophobia instead. Though characterisations in other crime novels may well be more complex and ambiguous, in the case of the metaphors highlighted in the examples above, criminality is revealed not to be a universal concept, but one always in flux, always in need of contextualisation as social expectations and ideologies continue to evolve. Close analysis of the genre's portrayal of criminals opens up key questions relating to such ideologies, questions to which we might next begin to respond.

Bibliography

Boyle, L. (2005) *Media and Violence: Gendering the debate*, London: Sage.
Christie, N. (1986) "The ideal victim", in E.A. Fattah (ed.), *From Crime Policy to Victim Policy*, London: Palgrave Macmillan, 17–30.
Coates, L. and Wade, A. (2004) "Telling it like it isn't: obscuring perpetrator responsibility for violent crime", *Discourse and Society*, 5: 499–526.
Fowler, R. (1977) *Linguistics and the Novel*, London: Methuen.
Gregoriou, C. (2007) *Deviance in Contemporary Crime Fiction*, Basingstoke: Palgrave.
———. (2011) *Language, Ideology and Identity in Serial Killer Narratives*, London: Routledge.
———. (2017) *Crime Fiction Migration: Crossing languages, cultures, media*, London: Bloomsbury.
Jenkins, P. (1994) *Using Murder: The social construction of serial homicide*, New York: de Gruyter.
Lakoff, G. and Johnson, M. (1980) *Metaphors We Live By*, Chicago: University of Chicago Press.
Lindsay, J. (2004) *Darkly Dreaming Dexter*, London: Orion.
McCarthy, D. and Rapley, M. (2001) "Far from the madding crowd: psychiatric diagnosis as the management of moral accountability", in A. McHoul and M. Rapley (eds), *How to Analyse Talk in Institutional Settings: A casebook of methods*, London: Continuum, 159–67.
McDermid, V. (2003) [1995] *The Mermaids Singing*, London: HarperCollins.
Patterson, J. (1993) *Along Came a Spider*, London: HarperCollins.
———. (1997) *Cat and Mouse*, London: Headline.
Peach, L. (2006) *Masquerade, Crime and Fiction: Criminal deceptions*, Basingstoke: Palgrave.

Pezzotti, B. (2018) "Transvestism and transgender in the crime fiction of Andrea G. Pinketts", *Clues*, 36(2): 9–18.

Price, R.H. (1978) *Abnormal Behaviour: Perspectives in conflict*, 2nd edn, New York: Holt, Rinehart and Winston.

Schmid, D. (2005) *Natural Born Celebrities*, Chicago: University of Chicago Press.

Seago, K. (2018) "Translating violence in crime fiction", *Perspectives: Studies in Translation and Practice*, 26(6): 916–29.

Seltzer, M. (1998) *Serial Killers: Death and life in America's wound culture*, New York: Routledge.

Tithecott, R. (1997) *Of Men and Monsters: Jeffrey Dahmer and the construction of the serial killer*, Wisconsin: University of Wisconsin Press.

Watson, K. (2012) "Engendering violence: textual and sexual torture in Val McDermid's *The Mermaids Singing*", in C. Gregoriou (ed.), *Constructing Crime: Discourse and cultural representations of crime and deviance*, Basingstoke: Palgrave Macmillan, 194–208.

19

BEGINNINGS AND ENDINGS

Alistair Rolls

At the beginning of her study of luck and ethics in Greek tragedy and philosophy, Martha C. Nussbaum explains that one might expect a rigorous and objective analysis to be founded on the principles of "traditional philosophical discourse" and an expedient selection of "*examples*" (2001: 14, emphasis in original). This is, however, precisely what Nussbaum wishes to avoid. She is determined instead to "read the tragedies whole and to discuss them in all their poetic complexity" (2001: 14). Through this choice, Nussbaum is critiquing the very beginnings of a critical tradition of reading fictional texts by "philosophical" authors as vehicles for philosophy, for getting various important points (which is to say, points deemed interesting according to academic conventions) across to various target audiences. The fictional vehicles of the philosophy, which necessarily contain more packaging than philosophical package, are dismissed as precisely this – excess matter useful for enabling the lay reader to take away at least something of the message, presumably some trace or homeopathic dosage, but which the scholar can simply excise in order to get directly to the key philosophical truths within. For Nussbaum, the problem with this model of reading and explaining philosophy is that it reduces complex thought to a series of snapshots, which, reframed, can then be distorted.

My aim here is to develop a reading strategy focused on maintaining all the packaging that literary criticism, in the field of crime fiction in our case, has deemed extraneous; indeed, it is my contention that what is articulated in Nussbaum's project is applicable to all academic critique of literary texts. And I use the term "literary texts" advisedly here, for this is precisely what I consider crime fiction, and especially the more enduring classics that constitute its corpus, to represent.[1] Seán Burke describes literature's place in Nussbaum's work as a "specialised arena in which moral issues and dilemmas are represented as invitations or indeed imperatives to philosophical reflection" (2010: 38–39). It strikes me that there is a similar ethical imperative on readers to accept the invitations made in crime novels to reflect on the fictional nature of what they are reading. Thus, I shall consider here whether certain crime fiction texts, by the very nature of their beginnings and endings, and the relationship between the two, do not in fact call upon readers to reassess and to question the solutions that are revealed and, ostensibly at least, sanctioned as truth.

Endings *versus* the whole text

The distinction that Nussbaum draws between a philosophical argument and the messy inde-terminacy of tragic drama can be mapped fruitfully onto crime fiction. Jesper Gulddal, for example, predicates his argument against the detectival authority of Hercule Poirot on just such a dichotomy. Specifically, Gulddal (2016) compares the detective's aspiration to "beau-tiful shining order", which, when applied with all the power of Poirot's ratiocinative logic, to the murder committed on the Orient Express, produces the now famous solution to the great multiplicity of events, including clues used and not used by Poirot, that make up the whole text of *Murder on the Orient Express* (1934). The result, for Gulddal, is a reassessment of Poirot's authority and the authoritative solution of the novel that stands in contradistinction to the interpretation that has otherwise gone unchallenged by scholarship. Gulddal's argument is that academic critique of this work, and other works of the genre (and indeed, we might add, of the construction of such a genre, which then stands itself in contradistinction to the literary[2]), has tended to remain so conspicuously subservient to the authority of the detective, which is typically also considered to be commensurate with that of the author (none other than Agatha Christie herself in this case), because the work itself engages in its own self-interpretation. This internal resolution of both crime and meaning is ultimately the very basis of the genre's clas-sification as "crime fiction". The privileged site for the closure of the case and its attendant exhaustion of textual meaning is, for Gulddal, the ending:

> The classic detective novel is structurally tilted toward the ending as the moment where the mystery finds its solution, and social order is re-established. The ending is meant to offer narrative closure by tying up loose ends and demonstrating that all individual events are part of a coherent picture. However, this finality has an authori-tarian aspect: the ending is the point where the authoritative stance of the protagonist is vindicated and his solution consecrated as the final word in the matter, to the exclu-sion of all other interpretive possibilities.
>
> *(2016: 12)*

If Gulddal's critical praxis here can be likened to Nussbaum's, it is because, like her, he calls on us to read the novel not through the lens placed on it at the ending, but in its entirety, and thus the *whole text*. In this, Gulddal's work builds on the pioneering studies of Gill Plain (2001) and Merja Makinen (2006). While Plain's subject is the body in crime fiction, including the body of the text, with ample referencing of the works of Agatha Christie, Makinen focuses exclu-sively on Christie. It is perhaps only fitting that the development of a whole-text approach to crime fiction should draw so heavily on Christie's works, for she has become the very embodi-ment of the rules and techniques that are now synonymous with the genre, especially in its "cosy", whodunit form. And yet, as Gulddal argues, it is in Christie's works that we find some of the most compelling arguments for reading the whole text; indeed, it can be argued that no one has done more to debunk the authority of Poirot's revelations than Christie herself. Certainly, when Pierre Bayard (2000) challenges the solution offered by Poirot in *The Murder of Roger Ackroyd*, he goes to some lengths to negotiate the path between the readerly activity (which poststructuralists like Roland Barthes in fact call a *writerly* endeavour on the reader's part) demanded by the *messiness* of literary text and another, parallel kind of readerly attentive-ness, which involves in this case reading, and reassessing, the whole gamut of clues provided by the text rather than simply accepting Poirot's (equally subjective) analysis of selected examples. In other words, Bayard's brand of detective criticism draws on the textual plurality (which lies behind Nussbaum's engagement with both the messiness and the power, beauty even, of Greek tragic plays) of poststructuralism while being careful to insist that the keys to producing an alternative solution are clearly present in the text and available to all readers (and all equally provided by the author). As a critic, Bayard places himself inside the text, reading the same facts as the detective; and when he presents his own solution to the murder of Roger Ackroyd, he deems his interpretative act to be nothing short of a pardon for Dr James Sheppard, a correction of a miscarriage of justice. In this light, Bayardian detective criticism is the closest crime fiction scholarship has come to acting on an ethical imperative to reinterpret crime fiction's great revelations and, in so doing, to engage with the entirety of their respective texts.[3]

Despite the prevalent assumption that readers enjoy crime fiction because they like to pit their wits against the detective (and thus, by logical extension, the author), and therefore that they read the whole text in search of the truth, their submission to the detective's final revelation (whether the reveal dashes their attempts by disproving their chosen solution, or whether it endorses it by indicating the same guilty party) demonstrates that their reading process has, in the final analysis, been conditioned by the ending in a much more reflexively staged way than can typically be seen to be operating in any other form of literature. For scholars of crime fiction's status as popular fiction, reading a crime novel in fact embodies the pleasure that Barthes et al. associated with *readerly text*, which is to say, a story whose meaning readers passively digest. In such a scenario, the pleasure of having the guilty punished and the status quo restored arguably trumps the thrill of chasing the culprit alongside, or ahead of, the detective. Either way, the desire to find out who the guilty party is promotes a practice of fast reading, which is opposed to the savouring of lines and words associated with those texts that, for Ken Gelder (2004: 35–39), can properly be termed literary. This approach, which the reader may be considered to desire, and which the genre's practitioners and scholars have tended to promote, is labelled "end-orientation" by those who seek to break down the taxonomical boundaries between crime fiction and literature.

The paradox of end-orientation, especially as it pertains to the whodunit, lies in the fact that the whole novel appears designed to reveal how a locked room can nonetheless be shown to have been subject to ingress and/or egress (and ultimately, of course, never to have been locked at all). Under the weight of the final revelation, however, it becomes locked once again, and this time more irresistibly. Far from seeking to break free from this conundrum, the response of criticism has been by and large to describe the mechanics of these systems of enclosure; indeed, while the texts have remained closed, the descriptions of this enclosure have proliferated into at times dizzying permutations of (re)classification. Thus, crime novels that aspire ostensibly to a higher degree of literariness are variously described as examples of analytic, metaphysical and postmodern crime fiction (Irwin 1994; Merivale and Sweeney 1999). The result of such taxonomising is further to enclose the more neutrally couched centre. How can the works of Agatha Christie be considered literature when they are so much less literary than those of recognisably "literary crime fiction"? Interestingly then, we fail to read the whole text of crime fiction because we have been told that it is crime fiction. As has been noted elsewhere, this is not how crime fiction began (Gulddal et al. 2019); rather, it is a critical equivalent of the detective's great revelation and comes, like death, at the end, ensuring that we forget all the rich (and, let's say it, literary) possibilities that crime novels lay before us.

Beginnings *versus* the whole text

The response to the locked room of end-oriented reading that I have outlined so far is the focus on the whole text. I wish to add to this debate here by balancing out critical response to end-orientation with an examination of that section of the crime novel that is the most easily forgotten. Famously, for J. Hillis Miller, the beginning of a novel has been referred to as something magical: "For me the opening sentences of literary works have special force. They are the 'Open Sesames' unlocking the door to that particular work's fictive realm. All it takes is a few words, and I become a believer, a seer" (2002: 24). Given the power that these privileged lines have to transport us, it seems almost unthinkable that a genre has been founded on their obfuscation. In fact, these "Open Sesames" are there and function within the economy of the crime novel precisely as Miller suggests, unlocking the door to that particular work's fictive realm in spite of, and in parallel to, the ineluctable progress of the investigation narrative towards the closure of the case (and the opening of the locked room).

Crime fiction, with its special focus on sleight of hand and red herrings, which force us not to see the truth (so as to heighten our reading pleasure by delaying, but only delaying, the revelation of the truth), has caused us *not* to see. In particular, we readers have become conditioned not to see crime novels' beginnings (which is to say, we read them, but our attention is already distracted by what is to come). Who will remember at the end of the complex investigative twists of *The Body in the Library* (1942), for example, that the novel began, not with the discovery of a body in the library at Gossington Hall, but with Dolly Bantry having a dream about the vicar's wife parading around the church in a bikini? To forget to see this scene (or rather, to see it only to forget it by the end) is not simply a pity; it is to deny an important element of crime fiction's literariness. As Miller notes, "[t]he irruptive, transgressive violence of [these] beginnings is often proleptic or synecdochic, part for the whole, of the work that follows" (2002: 27). Indeed, in the case of *The Body in the Library*, the beginning functions metonymically, standing for the novel, not in its absence, but in contiguity, in parallel to the investigation text (Rolls 2015). The text of Dolly's dream of lesbian desire is a whole novel, both told and not told, present and absent, which is screened by what will pass as the diegesis proper, whose focus is on the body in the library, the only body that we readers remember seeing by the time we have read Miss Marple's final solution. In this case, the body of the text, or the novel that follows the opening paragraphs, serves effectively to screen the body glimpsed in those moments where Dolly and reader are still opening their eyes to the new day and new novel, respectively. In such a scenario, the novel's investigation is arguably not *real* at all but something of a book-length red herring; it stands to cover up another text that is both real and virtual (because out of sight).[4]

That crime fiction's beginnings open up a transgressive space where the crime novel can be itself (a crime narrative) and its Other (a literary text) *at the same time* without any abstracted theoretical moves on the part of the critic can be demonstrated with reference to a case study. In this case, I shall look at the paradoxical "Open Sesame" of Christie's *Hallowe'en Party* (1969). *Hallowe'en Party* is an Hercule Poirot novel in which Joyce, a girl of thirteen, is murdered at a Hallowe'en party because she claims to have witnessed a murder in the past. The murderer turns out to be the organiser of the party, Mrs Rowena Drake, who acts to keep secret the crimes that she and her lover, the gardener Michael Garfield, have committed. The investigation contains any number of interesting elements, including infanticide, witchcraft and the role of storytelling. For the purposes of this case study, however, I shall limit myself to a close reading of the beginning of the novel, which highlights quite another set of critical and generic possibilities.

Agatha Christie's *Hallowe'en Party* (1988)

The opening scene of *Hallowe'en Party* constitutes nothing less than a provocation: It thrusts into the reader's view "a scene of chaotic activity" against a backdrop of pervasive obliviousness (11). The extreme busy-ness of the scene, of the very business of a Hallowe'en party, is immediately contrasted with the gaze of Christie's author *en abyme*, Ariadne Oliver, who is the very opposite of business and who, as such, becomes the embodiment of the *other business* of *Hallowe'en Party*, which is to say, what the novel can be said to be besides the narrative of its investigation text. Amid the hustle and bustle, Oliver "held up a large yellow pumpkin, looking at it critically". This critical gaze immediately takes on a reflexive edge, as she hesitates over the core constituents of the titular party: "It was to be a Hallowe'en party for invited guests of an age group between ten and seventeen years old". The party will involve a great many examples of produce that cause her, following her experiences of Hallowe'en in the United States, to hesitate still further, in this case as to "the difference between a pumpkin and a vegetable marrow" (11). This hesitation is both intertextual, insofar as it references the prominent role of vegetable marrows in *The Murder of Roger Ackroyd* and Dr James Sheppard's repeated instances of hesitation on thresholds, and generic: Here a crime writer is staged thinking about her trade while blocking the intense, creative energy of the titular Hallowe'en party narrative. As Oliver interrupts the flow of the party preparations with an outpouring of apparently incoherent verbiage, causing other "busy women" (11) to fall over her, the very first scene concludes with a further reference to the failure, when acting in haste, to pay attention to what is happening before one's eyes: "[but] they were not listening to her. They were all too busy with what they were doing" (12). Reflexively, the scene opposes the writer of crime fiction and her readers, who, busy, task-focused and end-oriented as they are, have been present, but have not paid attention, to the hesitation at this point of the text; instead, like the "busy women", Christie's readers are keen for the party to begin and to be a success, and not to listen to an old woman wonder what a story about (around, on the edges of) a Hallowe'en party might look like.

Clearly, we may question who is cluttering whose scene here: The women and Oliver get in one another's way. If order is to be extracted from this chaos, from Nussbaum's tragic messiness, then something will have to give. And yet, one may also wonder whether the chaos needs to be undone, whether this is not, after all, legitimate party business. In his study of loiterly literature, Ross Chambers (1999: 7) reminds us of the origins of triviality, which lie in the Latin term *trivialis*, a word denoting "a three-way crossing" and the business that occurred there. For, at its origin, *trivialis* conjured up images of business transactions (and all that accompanied them, including base and seedy activities). The ethical imperative on the reader here is to hold on to this scene in the face of the chaos to come and to tease apart the insignificant from the significant at this moment of intense triviality.

For Chambers, loiterly literature

> has this characteristic of the trivial: it blurs categories, and in particular it blurs those of innocent pleasure taking and harmless relaxation and not-so-innocent "intent" – a certain recalcitrance to the laws that maintain "good order". In so doing, it carries an implied social criticism.
>
> *(1999: 8–9)*

The criticism here is not merely social (in the sense of the decline of traditional English mores in the late 1960s), but also, and especially, generic, the categories being blurred including the literary, in the neutral, unmarked sense, and texts classified according to genre, in this case crime fiction. In light of this, Chambers's continued description of "loiterature" reminds us of the binary pairing of (the scatterbrained) Oliver and (the logical) Poirot:

> It casts serious doubt on the values good citizens hold dear – values like discipline, method, organization, rationality, productivity, and, above all, work – but it does so in

the guise of innocent and, more particularly, insignificant or frivolous entertainment: a
mere passing of the time in idle observations or witty remarks.

(1999: 9)

Clearly, Joyce's apparently insignificant comment about having seen a murder is taken quite
seriously by Poirot. It is important to remember, however, that at this point of the beginning (as
it were, at the nonetheless substantial, and busy, beginning of the beginning), Joyce's comment
(which is at the origins of the murder and its resolution) *has not yet been made.*

What we are present to at this stage of the novel is an eddy caused by a flow of irrepressible
activity hitting a counter-current of creative thought. The result is the creation of a second,
loiterly text at the point of origin of the end-oriented crime narrative. Crime fiction's crime
narrative is predicated on end-orientation – that much is clear; its beginning, on the other hand,
counters this pull with loiterly resistance and a genuine openness to alterity. Crime fiction, in
other words, at its origin surpasses the constraints and very definitions of its own genre. In order
for the crime narrative to win out over its loiterly Other, secondary readings must be closed
down, since, in Chambers's words, "the trivial, as that which is overlooked, can stand for that
which, in any generic situation, has to be repressed for the genre's authority to exert itself"
(1999: 40).

In light of this, it is perhaps understandable that Rowena Drake, who is the murderer
in what I am reading as the embedded crime narrative, should give another name to the
text: "I'm not calling this a Hallowe'en party, although of course it is one really. I'm calling
it the Eleven Plus party" (1998: 12). Alternatives, including alternative names, abound as the
novel questions precisely what it *really is.* These extend to a proliferation of virtual witches,
the most obvious of which is the local cat-lady, Mrs Goodbody, but Rowena Drake must
also strike the reader as a name purpose-built for a Hallowe'en party, and indeed Poirot's
questioning of her takes on the edge of a witch hunt on more than one occasion (see especially 43–47). The most obviously witch-like performance at the beginning of the novel,
however, is that of Ariadne Oliver herself, most notably when the soon-to-be-murder-
victim, Joyce, drops the apples that are destined for the game that will constitute her own
crime scene, and of which Oliver is notoriously fond: "[the apples] stopped, as though
arrested by a witch's wand, at Mrs. Oliver's feet" (13).

Not only is the crime scene proleptically signed here, but its author is also quite reflexively
designated as such, for Joyce immediately engages Oliver on the topic of the latter's crime
novels. When, for example, she suggests that "[w]e ought to have made you do something
connected with murders. Have a murder at the party to-night and make people solve it", Oliver
replies: "Well, I did once, and it didn't turn out much of a success" (13). The reference here is
to Christie's *Dead Man's Folly* (1956), in which Oliver's murder hunt at a garden party becomes
a Poirot investigation when an innocent, and again rather unintelligent, young girl, Marlene
Tucker, is murdered. Oliver's creative mind begins to tick over at this point (as she eats her apples
and Rowena Drake prepares the game of apple-bobbing). The conversation turns, apparently
insignificantly, to the relative value of galvanised buckets *versus* plastic pails, and the leitmotiv of
nostalgia for times past and the problems with the youth of today. More importantly, I should
suggest, it also introduces the murder weapon. Thus, when we read the following lines, we
perhaps ought to notice that the party, or game, is being shared by Ariadne Oliver: "[Oliver]
surveyed the room full of people critically. She was thinking in her authoress's mind: 'Now, if
I was going to make a book about all these people, how should I do it?'" (14). Rowena Drake
has already renamed her event the Eleven Plus party; as such, she has abandoned control of the
titular party to others: To a creative Other, and also to other textual possibilities.

It is my contention here that the beginning of *Hallowe'en Party* gives way to the body of the crime novel proper, not at the point when Joyce claims to have seen a murder, but just before, when she claims to have read one of Oliver's crime novels. In particular, what seals her fate is her criticism of Oliver's chosen method of murder: "'I read one of your books,' said Ann to Mrs. Oliver. '*The Dying Goldfish*. It was quite good,' she said kindly [...] 'I didn't like that one,' said Joyce. 'There wasn't enough blood in it. I like murders to have lots of blood'" (15). Interestingly (or trivially), these words mimic almost exactly the critical comments made about Oliver's murder game by the soon-to-be-victim of *Dead Man's Folly*: "I'm not going to have any blood on me. [...] No. Just strangled with a cord, that's all. I'd of liked to be stabbed – and have lashings of red paint" (Christie 2014: 65). While Marlene Tucker dies according to Oliver's *mise-en-scène*, albeit in the economy of the crime novel rather than in the murder game, Joyce's bloodless murder will in fact repay the insult given to *The Dying Goldfish*, for that is precisely what Joyce will become, drowning in her own bowl of water. When the ostensibly fatal lines come therefore ("'I saw a murder once,' said Joyce" [15]), the die is already cast. In the alternative text of the beginning, she dies not because she has seen another's murder, but because she has read her own death before (analeptically, in Christie's *Dead Man's Folly*) and, at the same time, because she has foreseen it (proleptically, through the title of Oliver's virtual novel). And when Poirot is summoned to solve the murder of the crime narrative, he offers himself to Oliver as another, sympathetic and, crucially, more open-minded critical reader. What he will provide can be read in two ways: First, as the solution of *Hallowe'en Party* qua crime novel; and second, as that of Oliver's Hallowe'en party murder game. When asked, before he begins his investigation, whether the solution will be simple, he replies "it could be and it could not be" (1988: 26).

Conclusion

For crime fiction to be considered literary, its endings, which tell the reader precisely what it means and how it functions according to the conventions of the genre, must always be read in conjunction with its beginnings, which always contain, and often open up and act on, the possibility for other meanings and escape from these same conventions. Beginning-oriented readings enable the pursuit of alternative murderers (what Pierre Bayard considers nothing short of justice) and the unmooring of the text from the strictures of the detective's final revelation. In this way, crime novels can finally come a little closer to offering what they have always appeared to promise readers: A chance to compete with the detective and to co-construct the investigation on an equal footing. Importantly, whole-text reading should not be considered an alternative to beginning-orientation, as it is to end-orientation; rather, it benefits from the plurality that must emerge from new beginnings. Such plurality, such richness and, indeed, such internal contradictions have long been considered the domain of the literary. If crime fiction requires a narrative that revolves around a criminal act, it is not the case that this is all that crime fiction has to offer. Crime novels, when read individually *and* as a whole (when you have read one Agatha Christie, you have not read them all ...), can be considered so much more than the sum of their criminal parts. As I hope to have demonstrated here, Agatha Christie's novels are not classics of the genre because they contain such ingenious plots; instead, it is because their ingenuity contains room for doubt and opens up plural (although not necessarily secondary) plots within one primary narrative. To return to Nussbaum's imperative to read actively, Christie's novels, and good crime novels more broadly, do not cast aside their packaging, however much attention is paid to the logical deductions that they contain. If Christie can be said to have written great literature, therefore, it is because her novels refuse exhaustion and privilege the messiness that reasoning only ever partially resolves.

Notes

1 I use the words "enduring classics" advisedly, too: They appeal here to Stephen Knight's *Secrets of Crime Fiction Classics* (2015).
2 As we shall see, the opposition of genre fiction to the canon of literature is promoted by critics of crime fiction like Ken Gelder (2004).
3 One might argue that it is all too simple to substitute one murderer for another in any of Christie's novels, given that she famously remained open as to the question of whodunit while writing her stories. In this sense, her approach to their writing mirrors the reading experience that crime novels present: They are wide open, and reflexively so, until the very end, at which point they are hermetically sealed. It is nonetheless true that it took Bayard's pioneering detective criticism to break this critical seal.
4 The model of text-within-a-text that I am arguing for here is typical of Agatha Christie's beginning-orientation. This does not mean that it is limited to Christie or, indeed, to the classics of the Golden Age. The works of contemporary French author Fred Vargas also provide examples of such ambiguous beginnings (see Rolls 2014).

Bibliography

Bayard, P. (2000) *Who Killed Roger Ackroyd? The mystery behind the Agatha Christie mystery*, trans. C. Cosman, New York: New Press.

Burke, S. (2010) *The Ethics of Writing: Authorship and legacy in Plato and Nietzsche*, Edinburgh: Edinburgh University Press.

Chambers, R. (1999) *Loiterature*, Lincoln and London: University of Nebraska Press.

Christie, A. (1988) *Hallowe'en Party*, in *Agatha Christie Crime Collection: Hallowe'en Party, Passenger to Frankfurt, The Thirteen Problems*, Sydney: Lansdowne Press, 7–174.

———. (2014) *Dead Man's Folly*, London: Harper.

Gelder, K. (2004) *Popular Literature. The logics and practices of a literary field*, London and New York: Routledge.

Gulddal, J. (2016) "'Beautiful shining order': detective authority in Agatha Christie's *Murder on the Orient Express*", *Clues: A Journal of Detection*, 34(1): 11–21.

Gulddal, J., King, S. and Rolls, A. (eds) (2019) *Criminal Moves: Modes of mobility in detective fiction*, Liverpool: Liverpool University Press.

Irwin, J.T. (1994) *The Mystery to a Solution: Poe, Borges and the analytic detective story*, Baltimore and London: Johns Hopkins University Press.

Knight, S. (2015) *Secrets of Crime Fiction Classics: Detecting the delights of 21 enduring stories*, Jefferson, NC: McFarland.

Makinen, M. (2006) *Agatha Christie. Investigating femininity*, Houndmills: Palgrave.

Merivale, P. and Sweeney, S.E. (eds) (1999) *Detecting Texts: The metaphysical detective story from Poe to postmodernism*, Philadelphia: University of Pennsylvania Press.

Miller, J.H. (2002) *On Literature*, New York and London: Routledge.

Nussbaum, M. (2001) *The Fragility of Goodness: Luck and ethics in Greek tragedy and philosophy*, Cambridge: Cambridge University Press.

Plain, G. (2001) *Twentieth-Century Crime Fiction: Gender, sexuality and the body*, Edinburgh: Edinburgh University Press.

Rolls, A. (2014) *Paris and the Fetish: Primal crime scenes*, Amsterdam: Rodopi.

———. (2015) "An ankle queerly turned, or the fetishized bodies in Agatha Christie's *The Body in the Library*", *Textual Practice*, 29(5): 825–44.

20

PLOTTING

Martin Edwards

Plot, according to E.M. Forster, is "a narrative of events, the emphasis falling on causality" (1958: 82). Forster argued that the plot of a novel demands intelligence and memory on the part of readers, and that "mystery is essential to a plot" but warned that "[s]ometimes a plot triumphs too completely. The characters have to suspend their natures at every turn, or else are so swept away by the course of Fate that our sense of their reality is weakened" (1958: 89).

Forster's remarks draw attention to a more general concern about crime fiction vis-à-vis other specifically literary forms; i.e. that the specific requirements of the crime fiction plot – e.g. the committing of a crime and the need for an investigation – might weaken some general notion of "quality" and that this was a particular risk in the field of crime fiction. Thus, Anthony Trollope said of Wilkie Collins's writing: "The construction is most minute and most wonderful. But I can never lose the taste of the construction" (in Page 1974: 223). Another of Collins's friends, Charles Dickens, complained about *The Moonstone* (1868): "The construction is wearisome beyond endurance, and there is a vein of obstinate conceit in it that makes enemies of readers" (qtd. in Page 1974: 169).

Reservations of this kind have persisted. Leading crime novelists of the second half of the twentieth century, for instance, often downplayed the importance of plot. Raymond Chandler drew a distinction between "the people who can plot but can't write [and] the people who can write and, all too often can't plot" (1973: 56). As Julian Symons pointed out: "plotting was never something [Chandler] really enjoyed [...]. Chandler thought that 'plotting may be a bore even if you are good at it'" (1992: 230). Symons too confessed to "a lack of interest in constructing a tight and watertight plot" (qtd. in Walsdorf and Allen 1996: xxxii), and he was dismissive of "the Humdrum school of detective novelists [who] had some skill in constructing puzzles, nothing more" (1992: 104). Arguably, the views of Chandler and Symons simply reflected the fashion of the times and a reaction against the strong emphasis on ingenuity of plotting during the "Golden Age of detective fiction" between the two world wars. Yet in recent years, many cleverly plotted but long-forgotten Golden Age whodunits by neglected authors have been reprinted, while an increasing number of newly written novels of crime and detection with highly elaborate plots have enjoyed widespread commercial and critical success.

Peter Brooks defines plot as "the design and intention of narrative, what shapes a story and gives it a certain direction or intent of meaning" (1992: xii). This broad formulation does not imply that a well-made plot is inconsistent with literature of distinction. But with regards to crime fiction, there are a number of plot formations that are worth paying attention to, notably Todorov's description of the duality of the typical whodunit plot which "contains not one but two stories: the story of the crime and the story of the investigation" (1977: 44). This in turn presupposes some kind of distinction between the reader's desire to know what really happened (e.g. who the murderer is and what motivated them to kill) and the pleasure derived from the postponement or referral of this revelation. Regardless, there is no logical reason why skill at plotting such stories should be incompatible with skill at characterisation or any other desirable literary attribute.

Dickens himself praised "the extraordinary care" of Collins's work on *The Moonstone*, pointing out that it comprised a "series of 'Narratives'" (qtd. in Page 1974: 169), with the events related from the viewpoints of different characters. This technique of construction, with the crime novel taking the form of a "casebook", is of crucial significance, because it enables Collins to conceal the truth about the theft of the eponymous jewel from the reader, even though he supplies clues to the truth. The novel exemplifies the intimate relationship between a crime story's structure and its plot, and demonstrates that a well-designed plot may, and often does, possess its own aesthetic beauty.

The influence of *Trent's Last Case*

The catalyst for the plot-driven Golden Age detective novel was a book intended as a satiric response to the omniscience of Sherlock Holmes and his rivals. Edmund Clerihew Bentley's original aim was "to write a detective story in which the detective was recognisable as a human being" (1940: 252). While working on an idea for a novel, he came up with "the most pleasing notion of all [...] the notion of making the hero's hard-won and obviously correct solution of the mystery turn out to be completely wrong" (1940: 254). Bentley regarded *Trent's Last Case* (1913) as "not so much a detective story as an exposure of detective stories" (1940: 254).

The prime reason for the book's popularity, however, was not the element of satire, or even the quality of Bentley's prose, but the originality of the construction of the murder mystery plot, with the detective's false solution followed by a twist revealing an unexpected "least likely person" culprit. This approach to plotting fired the creative imaginations of members of the new generation of crime writers that emerged after World War I. Increasingly, the detective story came to be treated as an intellectual exercise, a game between author and reader requiring an understanding of the relationship between plot and rules: Could the readers solve the puzzle before the great detective revealed all? The novel was better suited to this type of story than the short story form because the extra length made it easier to complicate the plot with red herrings and hidden clues – something that pleasurably deferred the final revelation where the detective would unmask the murderer. Some authors included a formal "challenge to the reader" (e.g. Ellery Queen) at that point in the text when all the information necessary to solve the puzzle had been presented.

To write an effective story of this kind, skill at plotting was essential, and in an early survey of the genre, Dorothy L. Sayers said:

> connoisseurs [...] call for a story which puts them on an equal footing with the detective himself, as regards all clues and discoveries.
>
> Seeing that the demand for equal opportunities is coupled to-day with an insistence on strict technical accuracy in the smallest details of the story, it is obvious that

the job of writing detective-stories is by no means growing easier [...]. How can we at the same time show the reader everything and yet legitimately obfuscate him as to its meaning?

(1928: 33)

Here, Sayers highlights the way in which Bentley overcame such difficulties in *Trent's Last Case* by means of shifts of viewpoint, and argues that the evolution towards "fair play" in plotting was "a recoil from the Holmes influence and a turning back to *The Moonstone*" (1928: 36).

Agatha Christie's plotting techniques

From the outset of her career as a crime novelist, Agatha Christie displayed a gift for plotting. At a point when Christie had only published a handful of books, Sayers suggested that her principal means of misdirecting the reader was to "cling to the Watson formula" (1928: 33). Just as Holmes's investigations were almost invariably recorded by his admiring and supportive friend Dr Watson, so Hercule Poirot's early cases were recounted by Captain Arthur Hastings. This device, and in particular Hastings's obtuseness, enabled the author to distance the reader from the detective's process of reasoning. Sayers cites *The Murder of Roger Ackroyd* (1926), in which a narrator who takes the same role as Watson and Hastings proves to be the culprit, as

an exceptional handling of the Watson theme [...]. All the necessary data are given. The reader ought to be able to guess the criminal, if he is sharp enough [...]. It is, after all, the reader's job to keep his wits about him, and, like the perfect detective, to suspect *everybody*.

(1928: 34)

Subsequent to Christie's death in 1976, consideration of her body of work has led to increasingly sophisticated analyses of her armoury of plotting techniques. Mary Jane Latsis and Martha Henissart, who co-wrote detective novels as Emma Lathen, argue that:

Agatha Christie's brilliance lies in her rare appreciation of the Laocoon complexities inherent in any standard situation. She herself rarely condescends to misdirect; she lets the cliché do it for her. When a sexually carnivorous young woman appears on the Christie scene, the reader, recognising the stock figure of the home wrecker, needs no further inducement to trip down the garden path of self-deception [...]. Then the solution, the keystone of which is simply the durability of the original marriage or attachment, comes as a startling *bouleversement* for him.

(Lathen 1977: 86)

A more focused study of Christie's strategies of deception by another detective novelist, Robert Barnard, suggested that Christie's reclusive nature informed her approach to plotting: "the way she hides her personality, tastes and attitudes and invites the reader to assume things about her opinions as a way of tricking him [is] one of the most elusive and difficult to guard against" (1980: 69). She kept varying the *Roger Ackroyd* concept, in which a character is excluded from suspicion because the reader is placed in a position of sympathy with him from the beginning. Another favourite trick, borrowed from stage magicians, is to distract the reader from important information by drawing their attention to something else that is irrelevant – for instance, by introducing an attempted murder that is no more than a smoke screen, or by emphasising the importance of a particular murder or supposed murder rather than the one that is crucial to the story.

Barnard cited *After the Funeral* (1953) as a beguiling example of the "smoke screen" method of plotting. While attending Richard Abernethie's funeral, Cora Lansquenet tactlessly remarks, "But he was murdered, wasn't he?". When she is killed, the natural assumption is that the motive is an attempt to cover up Abernethie's murder, yet as Barnard says, Abernethie "is one of the few people in any of Christie's novels to die from natural causes, and the important death is in fact that of Cora Lansquenet" (1980: 76).

Pierre Bayard reformulated the analysis, identifying three fundamental methods by which Christie's plots deceive the reader. First, there is the technique of disguise, so that the truth, or at least one of its basic components, is concealed from the reader. Second, there is the technique of distraction, as in *After the Funeral* and *Three-Act Tragedy* (1934), in which the first murder is motiveless, a mere rehearsal for the crime that the culprit intends to commit; the plot device is artistically appropriate given that the killer is an actor. Third, there is exhibition, as in her first novel, *The Mysterious Affair at Styles* (1920), in which the culprit sets out ostentatiously to incriminate himself, while relying on a quirk of the then law to escape punishment for his crime.

In his study of *The Murder of Roger Ackroyd*, Bayard argued that Christie utilised two narrative techniques to make her plot work. The first is the use of double-edged discourse: "statements that offer two possible but completely contrary, or at least distinctly different, readings" (2000: 34). The second is the lie by omission, which renders her narrator unreliable. The most crucial example in the text of both techniques is the following passage:

> Now Ackroyd is essentially pig-headed [...] All my arguments were in vain.
> The letter had been brought in at twenty minutes to nine. It was just on ten minutes to nine when I left him, the letter still unread.
>
> *(Christie 1997: 40–41)*

During the ten-minute gap, which is mentioned, but without explanation as to what happens in that time (i.e. using narrative lacunae as a key technique), the narrator murders Ackroyd.

The textual ambiguity of *The Murder of Roger Ackroyd* is even more prevalent in another novel narrated in the first person, *Endless Night* (1967). Christie is bold enough to repeat the *Roger Ackroyd* trick, and as Bayard says, since the narrator is a much more obvious suspect than his counterpart in the earlier book, double-edged discourse "becomes even more important [...] as preparation for the murder takes place over nearly a year. Therefore a multitude of events can be recounted in a way that completely skews the reader's perspective and conceals their true sense." The purpose of the double-edged discourse is "to disguise the gaps left by the lie by omission, especially at moments when it is impossible to make whole swathes of reality disappear completely without attracting the reader's attention" (Bayard 2000: 49).

The A.B.C Murders

Christie's *The A.B.C Murders* (1936) exemplifies the art and craft of plotting. The plot is ingenious and original yet owes something to an earlier work − as do almost all the leading texts in the genre. It has in its turn proved highly influential. The story concerns a series of murders apparently committed by a maniac who is killing people in an alphabetical sequence. Before each crime, the murderer sends a taunting letter to Hercule Poirot, warning him of the date and location of his next killing. The messages are signed "ABC" and a copy of the ABC

Plotting

Alphabetical Railway Guide, commonly known as an "ABC", opened at the page of the town where the murder occurred, is left with each corpse. It emerges that someone has been selling silk stockings in the neighbourhood at the time of each of the crimes.

The first victim is Alice Ascher, murdered at Andover, and the second Betty Barnard, strangled at Bexhill. The third victim is Sir Carmichael Clarke, killed at Churston. The sequence falters with the fourth murder, in Doncaster: George Earlsfield is stabbed to death in a cinema, although a man called Roger Downes was sitting nearby, and it seems possible that he was the intended victim.

For the most part, the story is again narrated by Captain Hastings, but here Christie varies the viewpoint, a method she had adopted in a non-series novel, *The Man in the Brown Suit* (1924), where, anticipating the *Roger Ackroyd* device, the second-string narrator proved to be the villain. Of the thirty-five chapters in *The A.B.C Murders*, eight are written in the third person. Most of these adopt the viewpoint of a character with the initials ABC. He is a troubled hosiery salesman called Alexander Bonaparte Cust who happens to be in the vicinity at the time of each murder. Evidence tending to incriminate him mounts up, although at a late stage, it emerges that he has a possible alibi for the Bexhill crime. It appears that the central puzzle differs from those in earlier Poirot novels. The story does not appear to concern whodunit, but rather the pursuit of Cust and the question of how he will be brought to justice, together with – if madness is not the simple explanation – the reason for his committing the crimes and for his fixation on the alphabet.

Christie uses a "smoke screen" or "distraction" (both Bayard's terms) together with the shifts to a third-person perspective to conceal from the reader the story of the crime. That story is based on a principle articulated by G.K. Chesterton in an exchange between his priest-detective Father Brown and the criminal Flambeau:

> "Where does a wise man hide a pebble?"
> And the tall man answered in a low voice: "On the beach."
> The small man nodded, and after a short silence said: "Where does a wise man hide a leaf?"
> And the other answered: "In the forest."
>
> *(1992: 161)*

Christie's masterstroke was to apply this concept to a series of murders, by having a culprit decide to hide a particular crime that he wished to commit among a sequence of apparently random killings. Franklin Clarke's proposed victim was his wealthy brother, Sir Carmichael Clarke, who lived in Churston. Franklin feared being deprived of his inheritance in the event that his brother's ailing wife died and he remarried but was faced with the difficulty that in the event of his brother's death, he would be an obvious suspect. A chance meeting with Cust gave him the idea of the alphabetical plan seeming to connect otherwise disparate crimes, and a convenient scapegoat for the murders.

Christie refined this scenario by giving Franklin Clarke a role to play in the investigation. He proposes to form a "special legion" of friends and relatives of the murder victims to assist Poirot in his attempts to solve the case. This version of the "least likely person" solution to a mystery is a variant of the *Roger Ackroyd* ploy of making the Watson figure, the detective's helper, the culprit. Forming the special legion helps Franklin Clarke to throw suspicion on Cust in the story of the investigation, while enabling Christie to "play fair" with her readers and create an artistically pleasing resolution to the story of the crime, by ensuring that the reader is adequately prepared for the final twist.

Few traditional whodunits have earned as much acclaim or have enjoyed such enduring popularity and influence. It is instructive, therefore, to examine the way in which Christie developed the plot. In studying Christie's private journals, in which she jotted down ideas for stories, John Curran has identified three notebooks which contain fifteen pages of material relevant to *The A.B.C Murders*; they even pinpoint the date on which she started writing the novel as 6 November 1934.

The first reference to the story is: "Series of murders – P gets letter from apparent maniac [...] [the killer] murdered [...] third victim for reasons of his own – 1st and 2nd camouflage [...] idea to fasten guilt on [scapegoat]" (Curran 2016: 229). At this point, Christie was contemplating that the fourth apparent victim, the survivor of an attempted murder, would be the culprit. This was a variation of an idea she used several times during her career, most effectively in *Peril at End House* (1932).

In another notebook, the use of alphabetical surnames for the victims is introduced, but Christie envisages Poirot sending a telegram to himself about the "E" murder. A third set of notes outlines two possible explanations for the crimes; one is close to the motive in the book, whereas the other has strong echoes of *Peril at End House*, perhaps explaining why she rejected it. Taken together, the notes illustrate that Christie's approach to plotting was that advocated by the American crime novelist Fredric Brown in a handbook for aspiring mystery writers: "A writer plots by accretion [...]. It can start with anything – a character, a theme, a setting, a single word. By accretion it builds or is built into a plot" (Brown 1982: 35).

Curran observes that there is no indication in Christie's notebooks as to the source of the idea of the alphabetic sequence of the crimes. It is possible, however, to speculate that Christie drew inspiration from her friend Anthony Berkeley Cox. Cox wrote detective novels as Anthony Berkeley and in 1930 he established the Detection Club, a social network for detective novelists of which Sayers and Christie became founder members and, later, presidents. A telling clue comes from Cust's occupation as a silk-stocking salesman. Anthony Berkeley's *The Silk Stocking Murders* (1928) was an early example of the serial killer whodunit, and Berkeley's initials were ABC.

Ambiguous evidence and multiple solutions

The enduring influence of Bentley's scepticism about the supposed brilliance of fictional detectives, and his deployment of a false solution to a murder puzzle is evident in Anthony Berkeley's work. These elements became central to Berkeley's method of plotting his detective novels, which relies upon the ambiguity of evidence, i.e. the principle that most items of information presented in a detective story are susceptible to more than one interpretation.

Few fictional detectives are as fallible as Berkeley's Roger Sheringham, who repeatedly conjures up ingenious solutions to mysterious deaths only to discover that he was mistaken. Berkeley's most celebrated whodunit began life as a short story, "The Avenging Chance", in which Sheringham solved the mystery of murder by poisoned chocolates. Berkeley elaborated the scenario in *The Poisoned Chocolates Case* (1929), in which Sheringham presides over the Crimes Circle, a literary forerunner of the Detection Club. Each of the six members of the Club comes up with a different solution to the puzzle, sometimes as a result of acquiring fresh information. Sheringham's explanation of the mystery (the same as in the short story), the fourth presented in the novel, is duly debunked by one of his colleagues.

The false solution remains a key technique for authors seeking to create a plot twist, and also lies at the heart of *Who Killed Roger Ackroyd?* (2000), in which Bayard puts forward an alternative to Christie's solution, proposing that the culprit was not the narrator, but his sister. This in turn opens up a set of far-reaching implications regarding the author as the sole guarantor of a story's meaning (see Bayard).

Accretion

Other than Christie's notebooks and "how-to" guides for aspiring writers, there is a dearth of published material exploring in detail the process by which crime fiction authors build their plots. However, Sayers's biographer Barbara Reynolds examined the genesis of *The Documents in the Case* (1930), on which Sayers collaborated with Robert Eustace, a doctor who worked with other detective writers, primarily contributing technical expertise and plot concepts. The authors' correspondence shows how they used the accretion method to build a story which was essentially a "howdunit" rather than a whodunit.

Barton's suggested starting point was a method of murder, the addition of poisonous muscarine to a dish of otherwise innocuous mushrooms. Conscious of Sayers's literary ambitions for the detective genre, he wrote: "We can introduce some very deep and interesting questions into the mushroom story – the subtle difference between what is produced by life and that artificially produced by man" (Reynolds 1993: 214). With the *modus operandi* of the criminal established, Sayers turned her attention to story structure and characterisation, saying: "We shall have to work it powerfully on the emotional side [...]. And we shall have to somehow work the scientific-theological interest solidly into the plot" (Reynolds 1993: 219).

In considering the love affair that is the catalyst for murder, Sayers concluded:

> I don't want to make the villain too villainous, nor yet must the victim be a villain. I think I shall [...] make the victim a harmless sort of bore [...] and have him married to a sort of Edith Thompson woman who eggs on the villain to get rid of the husband. That will allow plenty of human nature.
>
> *(Reynolds 1993: 219)*

Edith Thompson was hanged for the murder of her husband in 1922. The case is widely regarded as a miscarriage of justice because the crime was carried out by her lover, and there was a lack of clear evidence that she encouraged him to commit it. The case has inspired many crime stories, but Sayers was unsympathetic towards Thompson, and this coloured her characterisation of Margaret Harrison, the victim's wife. She took the decision not to use Wimsey as her detective, conscious that she was undertaking a project distinct from the conventional Golden Age detective novel. Her technique for telling the story was borrowed from *The Moonstone*: "I'm rather keen to try the experiment of writing the book in a series of first-person narratives, à la Wilkie Collins. It will be a new line to try" (Reynolds 1993: 222).

When the manuscript was complete, she felt disappointed with the outcome of her labours, telling Eustace that she had "produced a mingled atmosphere of dullness and gloom which will, I fear, be fatal to the book [...]. I wish I could have done better with the brilliant plot" (Reynolds 1993: 221). Yet the ingenuity of the central idea coupled with Sayers's updating of Collins's method ensures that despite its flaws, *The Documents in the Case* exemplifies detective fiction plotting at its most ambitious and innovative.

Post-Golden Age plotting

As early as 1928, Sayers said: "The mystery-monger's principal difficulty is that of varying his surprises [...]. There certainly does seem a possibility that the detective-story will some time come to an end, simply because the public will have learnt all the tricks" (1928: 43). Understandable as such forebodings were, as the genre has evolved, so authors have found fresh ways to fashion their plots, adapting techniques used in the past to types of crime story very different from those in which they were first adopted.

As a consequence of the length of her career and her focus on plotting, the methods used by Christie have proved especially influential. Indeed, we might take a moment to consider why Golden Age plotting has continued to influence contemporary crime fiction, even more so than other types or modes of crime fiction (e.g. hardboiled); and whether this suggests that contemporary tastes somehow favour the intricate plotting techniques derived from Golden Age practitioners like Christie over and above, for example, the hardboiled novel's preference for action, politics and place. That said, we should perhaps be careful about drawing clear-cut distinctions between Golden Age mysteries and urban-based crime stories. The central concept of *The A.B.C Murders*, the distracting of attention from one particular murder by committing other murders which appear to form part of the same sequence, recurs in novels as diverse as the first 87th Precinct police procedural book by Ed McBain, *Cop Hater* (1956) and *The Visitor* (2000), a taut American thriller by British-born Lee Child. It is also to be found in stories which follow the pattern of the traditional whodunit, such as Bruce Hamilton's cruise ship mystery *Too Much of Water* (1958), which makes explicit reference to Christie's novel.

Unreliable narrators have proliferated in recent years, as authors of psychological suspense novels have found them useful in the search for means of creating plot twists. The unreliability of the person recounting the story may, as in *The Murder of Roger Ackroyd*, be due to his or her guilt or to a range of other causes, such as alcoholism, amnesia, experience of psychological trauma, dementia and assorted neurological conditions; each opens up a range of plotting possibilities. Paula Hawkins's international bestseller *The Girl on the Train* (2015) combines three viewpoints with unreliable narration; the eponymous girl on the train is an alcoholic who suffers blackouts and finds herself disbelieved when she reports a missing person to the police.

Tricky structural and plotting techniques are fraught with risk, as in Hawkins's *Into the Water* (2017), which tells the story from no fewer than eleven points of view. As the crime novelist Val McDermid said in a review:

> To differentiate 11 separate voices within a single story is a fiendishly difficult thing. And these characters are so similar in tone and register – even when some are in first person and others in third – that they are almost impossible to tell apart, which ends up being both monotonous and confusing.
>
> *(2017)*

In the twenty-first century, as in the era of Wilkie Collins, successful plotting requires the author to disguise the taste of construction, to sweeten the brew with a compelling setting and atmosphere as well as strong characterisation. A number of recent crime novels with complex plots in the Golden Age manner have become international bestsellers; examples include Anthony Horowitz's *The Magpie Murders* (2016) and *The Word is Murder* (2017) and Stuart Turton's *The Seven Deaths of Evelyn Hardcastle* (2018).

Sophie Hannah, another bestselling exponent of contemporary psychological suspense, as well as the author of novels featuring Hercule Poirot (authorised by the Christie estate), has given the answer to the concerns raised by Forster, Trollope and others:

Plotting

there's [...] a misconception in some people's minds that if you care and talk about and prioritise planning – plotting – that somehow this must mean you don't care about character depth and psychological insight. Plot and character are not rivals – they're co-conspirators.

(2017)

Bibliography

Barnard, R. (1980) *A Talent to Deceive*, New York: Dodd Mead.

Bayard, P. (2000) *Who Killed Roger Ackroyd?*, trans. C. Cosman, New York: The New Press.

Bentley, E.C. (1913) *Trent's Last Case*, London: Nelson.

———. (1940) *Those Days*, London: Constable.

Berkeley, A. (2004) *The Avenging Chance and other Mysteries from Roger Sheringham's Casebook*, Norfolk, VA: Crippen & Landru.

Brooks, P. (1992) *Reading for the Plot: Design and intention in narrative*, Cambridge: Harvard University Press.

Brown, F. (1982) "Where do you get your plot?", in L. Treat (ed.), *Mystery Writer's Handbook*, Cincinnati: Writer's Digest, 35–41.

Chandler, R. (1973) *Raymond Chandler Speaking*, D. Gardiner and K. Sorley Walker (eds), London: Penguin.

Chesterton, G.K. (1992) [1911] "The sign of the broken sword", in *The Complete Father Brown Stories*, Ware, Hert.: Wordsworth.

Christie, A. (1936) *The A.B.C Murders*, London: Collins.

———. (1997) [1926] *The Murder of Roger Ackroyd*, London: Collins.

———. (2012) "Detective writers in England", in *Ask a Policeman*, London: Harper Collins, xiii–xx.

Curran, J. (2016) *Agatha Christie's Complete Secret Notebooks: Stories and secrets of murder in the making*, London: Harper Collins.

Forster, E.M. (1958) [1927] *Aspects of the Novel*, London: Edward Arnold.

Hannah, S. (2017) "Why and how I plan my novels", https://sophiehannah.com/why-and-how-i-plan-my-novels/ (accessed 25 October 2019).

Lathen, E. (1977) "Cornwallis's revenge", in H.R.F. Keating (ed.), *Agatha Christie: First lady of crime*, London: Weidenfeld and Nicholson.

McDermid, V. (2017) *"Into the Water review"*, *The Guardian*, 26 April.

Page, N. (ed.) (1974) *Wilkie Collins: The critical heritage*, London: Routledge.

Reynolds, B. (1993) *Dorothy L. Sayers: Her life and soul*, London: Hodder.

Sayers, D.L. (1928) "Introduction", in *Great Short Stories of Detection, Mystery and Horror*, London: Gollancz.

Sayers, D.L. and Eustace, R. (1930) *The Documents in the Case*, London: Gollancz.

Symons, J. (1992) *Bloody Murder*, London: Faber.

Todorov, T. (1977) *The Poetics of Prose*, Oxford: Blackwell.

Walsdorf, J. and Allen, B. (1996) *Julian Symons: A bibliography*, Delaware: Oak Knoll Press.

21

CLUES

Jesper Gulddal

The clue is by general consent a constituent feature of crime fiction; it is the means by which the detective solves the mystery, the device that keeps the plot together, the interface that draws in the reader. However, as in other cases of overfamiliarity, we often fail to scrutinise this feature and instead put our faith in intuitive or commonplace understandings. This is true also of crime fiction scholarship, which tends to take the presence and narrative significance of clues for granted, but has rarely, with a handful of notable exceptions, made the clue an object of analysis in its own right. More problematically, the standard use of the term conflates two distinct meanings, one referring broadly to all the different types of information that a detective might use to further the investigation, the other denoting a specific type of information closely tied to specific investigative practices. In the latter, more technical sense, which is the one used in the present context, the clue is a textual enigma and needs to be solved by the detective by means of interpretation.

The initial aim of this chapter is to analyse the clue in terms of its textual functions and the theoretical discussions it has occasioned. As a second stage, the chapter attempts to make sense of the clue as a specific representation of the world and the rules and regularities that define it. Drawing on the work of German philosopher Hans Blumenberg, I argue that the clue in its classic form is a manifestation of a longing for the modern social world to be *readable*, for it to have a stable underlying grammar that enables the diligent, rationally inquisitive mind – the mind of a detective – to take it in and understand it in much the same way as one would read a book. Tying the clue to a metaphysical worldview in this way suggests that it comes with a historical end-date, not so much as a literary device (crime novels still abound with clues), but as an advanced way of thinking about crime and detection. In recognition of this, I conclude by highlighting some of the ways in which crime fiction for much of its modern history has been engaged in attempts either to debunk or displace the clue as the lead device of the crime novel.

Aspects of the clue

The word "clue" is a dead metaphor. In its original, literal meaning, a clue is a ball of yarn and refers specifically to the woollen thread that, according to Greek myth, Ariadne gave to Theseus to help him find his way out of the Minotaur's labyrinth. In a metaphorical application of this myth, early modern writers used the term to describe something that provides guidance through existential challenges, later extending this use to anything that might lead to the solution of a mystery or shed light on unexplained phenomena (OED). It is from here that the modern use of the term in crime fiction comes; while clues as literary devices appear sporadically in earlier crime fiction, the word itself seems to have been introduced to the genre – with the spelling "clew" – by Edgar Allan Poe in the "The Murders in the Rue Morgue" (1841). A clue in this sense is a thread that the detective can follow and thereby find the exit from a maze-like murder mystery. Or to demetaphorise this statement: a clue is a piece of information whose correct interpretation, along with that of other clues, together with which it forms a pattern, enables the detective to identify the murderer.

Clues are often material objects: A goose quill, a piece of cambric, a misplaced chair, a wedding ring, a letter, a missing sum of money, to list some of the clues in Agatha Christie's *The Murder of Roger Ackroyd* (1926). Rita Felski notes that detective fiction "turns the random scraps and detritus of daily life into hieroglyphs that glint with mysterious meaning" (2015: 92). However, clues have an indeterminate phenomenology and manifest themselves, not only in the form of objects, but also as utterances, gestures, facial expressions, glances and actions of any kind, not to mention as psychological clues pertaining to the mental dispositions and motivations of the criminal. Every fragment of information in a detective story is potentially tied to the crime and hence a potential clue. One effect of this pervasive meaningfulness is a paranoid reading style that compels readers to look for clues and hidden meaning in every textual detail. Another is the familiar interplay of clues and "red herrings", two textual elements that are in fact indistinguishable until the detective separates them by selecting those pieces of information on which the solution will be based, thereby writing off all other information as either irrelevant or deliberately misleading; as Pierre Bayard comments, a clue "is less a sign already present than a sign *that is constituted after the fact in the movement of interpretation*" (2000: 69).

As an object of knowledge, the clue has significant epistemological implications. An influential semiotic account of it, advocated by some of the classic figures of literary theory, conceives of the clue on the model of signs, codes, marks and encrypted information. The clue is seen as analogous to a linguistic sign insofar as it combines a physical form (signifier) and a meaning (signified) that needs to be uncovered (e.g. Malmgren 2001: 13–25; Moretti 1988: 145–46). Yet, the clue is more than a sign: Not only does it lack the conventional tie between signifier and signified, but it also transcends, as a deeply contextual phenomenon, the self-contained nature of the sign according to Saussurian linguistics. From within the semiotic tradition, Umberto Eco has acknowledged this point by suggesting that the interpretation of clues must be understood as an instance of what Charles Sanders Peirce calls abductive reasoning. As Eco argues, the clue cannot simply be decoded or, as Sherlock Holmes would have it, deduced, but allows the detective to posit, in the manner of an educated guess, a hypothesis that explains it (1983). From the point of view of historical studies, Carlo Ginzburg has likewise argued that the clue belongs to a "conjectural paradigm" that emerges in the late nineteenth century as a counterweight to the dominant methods of the natural sciences. Bringing together practices as diverse as the use of clues in crime fiction, inconspicuous details in art history and symptoms in psychoanalysis, this paradigm consists of interpretative practices where, as in the case of the detective interpreting clues, "infinitesimal traces permit the comprehension of a deeper, otherwise unattainable reality" (1989: 101).

Returning to Felski's characterisation of the clue as a "hieroglyph", the clue can also be characterised more generally as a textual riddle. It relates to the overall mystery as a part to a whole, on the one hand because it rearticulates and multiplies the questions that this mystery poses, and on the other hand because the overall solution depends on the correct reading of each individual clue. Interpreting the clue is therefore a contextual operation that links the isolated detail to suspects, biographies, psychological profiles, alibis, time schedules and, above all, other clues. Only when it has been integrated in the detective's solution has it been fully understood. The clue in this sense is a *hermeneutic object* calling for rigorous interpretation.

This call is addressed in the first instance to the detective, who responds with hermeneutic brilliance, sometimes coupled with specialist or forensic knowledge. In the course of its history, however, the clue has developed an interactive dimension, extending the interpretive challenge to the reader. Franco Moretti (2000, cf. 2004) has traced the evolution of the clue in 1890s British detective fiction as part of an attempt to develop a Darwinian literary history where authors are seen to vie for commercial success by means of incremental experiments with genres and devices. His model posits that the evolutionary path of the clue takes place across four stages, or "bifurcations", adding further attributes at each stage. Through a process of trial and error, writers discover (1) that the presence of clues in the detective story is a device with significant reader appeal and that such clues work better if (2) they are necessary to the investigation as opposed to merely ornamental and (3) if they are visible to the reader as they are discovered rather than simply revealed at the end by the detective.

The interactive or decodable clue follows as the fourth and final step. Moretti attributes its invention to Arthur Conan Doyle, but argues that this type of clue was an accidental discovery and only occurs in a small part of the Sherlock Holmes corpus. Doyle was in fact searching for something different: Not a means of engaging the reader, let alone a means of establishing parity between the reader and the detective, but rather a way of highlighting Holmes's incomparable genius. Yet, in Moretti's evolutionary account of literary history, reader reception trumps authorial intention, the Darwinian principle of natural selection finding its equivalent here in a principle of reader selection. Accordingly, readers discover that they enjoy detective stories using clues (and particularly interactive clues), recommend these stories to others and thereby generate an "information cascade" (2000: 210) that propels stories of this type to fame while causing other types to be forgotten. Some well-placed scepticism is in order here; it seems more plausible, as Christopher Prendergast contends, that Doyle's success was based on a fascination with Sherlock Holmes (2005: 51), an aspect much more likely to be debated among readers than the use of clues.[1] Nevertheless, Moretti's evolutionary model and distinction between the presence, necessity, visibility and decodeability of clues offer important theoretical resources and remind us that the clue as a device manifests itself in a number of historically distinct forms.

In spite of Doyle's experiments, it is not until the interwar period, in the so-called "Golden Age" of detective fiction, that the interactive clue reaches its mature form and becomes the central device of the genre. The detective story as a result acquires a new, ludic dimension. Captured in genre designations such as the "whodunit" and the "clue-puzzle" as well as in frequent comparisons of detective fiction to crosswords, this understanding implies that the storyline is a game devised by the author as a challenge to the reader, and that the reader is given an active, investigative role, competing to reach the correct interpretation of the clues before the detective. "Fair play" thereby becomes a core value of the genre. The attempts in the 1920s to codify the detective genre stress that no clue must be withheld from the reader. Prefacing his "Twenty Rules of the Detective Story" by explicitly asserting that the detective story is a "game" or a "sporting event", and that the author must therefore "play fair with the reader", Van Dine gives pride of place to the rule that "[t]he reader must have equal opportunity with the detective for solving the mystery. All clues must be plainly stated and described" (1928). Roland Knox's "Ten Commandments", which were endorsed by the famous Detection Club of British mystery writers, similarly states that "[t]he detective is bound to declare any clues which he may discover" (1929). However, while the clue-puzzle's intellectual activation of the reader helps explain its enduring popularity, the ideal of "fair play" is often observed only in a very formal or technical manner. As Bayard has shown (2000: 13–30), the clue-puzzle stages an intricate game of show-casing and concealing information, of hiding the truth in plain view. The clues are there for the reader to find, yet they are tangled up with such complex strategies of disguise and distraction, and mixed with so many false leads, that, in the words of Raymond Chandler, "[o]nly a half-wit could guess it" (1995: 984). The idea of the interactive clue thereby turns upon itself: Readers are asked to conduct their own investigations, but they are not meant to succeed.

Finally, the logic of the clue involves an ontology in the sense of an understanding of how the world is ordered and how its elements – people, actions, objects – interconnect to form a coherent whole. While it does not address crime fiction directly, Hans Blumenberg's work on the "readability of the world" offers important tools with which to describe this ontology. Drawing on his long-standing interest in what he dubs "metaphorology", that is, the study of how metaphors structure human experience and thinking, Blumenberg in *Die Lesbarkeit der Welt* ["The Readability of the World"] pursues the metaphor of the world as a book from the Bible to the mapping of the human genome; his key contention is that this metaphor represents a constant human desire to capture the totality of experience and uncover its inherent mean-ingfulness (1981). As an ontological metaphor, the clue claims to fulfil a similar function, namely, to make the modern social world legible and understandable.

The trope of readability is common in classic detective fiction from Poe to Christie and is articulated programmatically, and with direct reference to the metaphorical paradigm of the "book of nature", in Doyle's first Sherlock Holmes novel, *A Study in Scarlet* (1877). In an early chapter entitled "The Science of Deduction", Watson offers a first insight into the incomparable abilities of his newfound housemate. The prompt is an article he comes across in a magazine:

> Its somewhat ambitious title was "The Book of Life," and it attempted to show how much an observant man might learn by an accurate and systematic examination of all that came in his way [...]. "From a drop of water," said the writer, "a logician could infer the possibility of an Atlantic or a Niagara without having seen or heard of one or the other. So all life is a great chain, the nature of which is known whenever we are shown a single link of it. [...] By a man's finger-nails, by his coat-sleeve, by his boots, by his trouser-knees, by the callosities of his forefinger and thumb, by his expression, by his shirt-cuffs – by each of these things a man's calling is plainly revealed."
>
> *(Doyle 2009: 23)*

The narrator initially dismisses these extravagant claims as "ineffable twaddle" (23), yet he soon enough develops an appreciation for Sherlock Holmes's philosophy, for Holmes is, of course, the author of the piece. The central part of this philosophy is the idea of the "great chain", that is, the complete interconnectedness of all elements of the world and the associated idea that any individual link in this chain enables the "logician" to form a precise image of the whole. Although the scope of Holmes's theory is extreme, claiming validity in both the natural and the social worlds, it clearly articulates the ontology implied by the clue: In itself a minute and seem-ingly insignificant detail, the clue allows the skilled reader to deduce the whole of the crime.

Yet, the link between the clue and the ideal of a readable world does not just manifest itself in the form of explicit ideological claims like the ones expressed by Holmes; it is also embedded in the narrative structure of the detective story itself. Firstly, the clue is tied to a principle of cohesion. It guarantees the deep integration of the fictional universe by positing the existence of a stable link between motivations and actions, between actions and material, physical or psy-chological traces, and between these traces and the subsequent investigation and uncovering of the truth; as such, it forms the core of a stable sequence, allowing criminal acts to be detected based on the traces they leave behind. Secondly, the clue embodies a principle of finality. All narratives are to some degree end-oriented, but the ending of the detective story, in the form of the protagonist's solution, presents itself as particularly final and authoritative.[2] Its authority is based on the claim that all clues have been fully elucidated and arranged to form a pattern, which is brought to light in the detective's reconstruction of the story of the crime. What this structure excludes is the polar opposite of the clue, namely contingency. The chance occurrence, the stray object, or the meaningless expression have no structural place in detective stories based on the logic of clues. From the point of view of narrative structure, this logic creates a weave of connections that link all elements of the story – in other words, it imposes a syntax on the social world, particularly the world of crime, thereby replacing its opaqueness with a fiction of readability.

The case of the readable hat

Ellery Queen's *The Roman Hat Mystery* (1929) both embodies and meta-textually reflects on the classic concept of the clue. Pseudonymously authored by Frederic Dannay and Manfred Bennington Lee, this novel marks the launch of the immensely successful, multi-format Queen franchise featuring Inspector Richard Queen and his bookish son Ellery. Epitomising the American version of the clue-puzzle, the Queen novels explicitly flag their commitment to the principle of "fair play" by including a "Challenge to the Reader" – a short interlude towards the end where the narrator directly addresses the reader, indicating, in the wording of the debut novel, "that the alert student of mystery tales, now being in possession of all the pertinent facts, should at this stage of the story have reached definite conclusions" as to the who and how of the murder (324).

The Roman Hat Mystery contains several clues, but only the top hat referred to in the title is truly important; as Richard Queen notes, he "never knew of a case in which a single factor so dominated every aspect of the investigation" (364). When the shady lawyer Monty Field is poisoned during a performance at the Roman Theatre, the investigators quickly establish that his top hat has disappeared, and that it seems not to have left the premises. This makes the theatre staff prime suspects, and the Queens are eventually able to reveal that the murderer is in fact one of the actors, Mr Barry, who removed the victim's hat and left his own stage hat in the dressing room.

An important feature of the missing hat as a clue is the fact that it functions both as a core element of the plot and as a commentary on the clue itself as a narrative device. Firstly, the detectives explicitly regard this clue as a hermeneutic problem. Richard Queen notes that "we were so busy pressing the immediate inquiry at New York's Roman Theatre on Monday night we couldn't grasp the full significance of its absence" and further contends that if "we had analyzed the meaning of the hat's disappearance then and there – we might have clinched the case that very night" (356). The missing hat is the mystery in a nutshell, and the correct interpretation therefore leads to a complete solution. Secondly, the hat also contains the solution in a literal sense. The investigation brings to light that Monty Field was a blackmailer who was murdered by one of his victims. When searching Field's rooms, Ellery Queen finds a secret compartment containing several hats which enable the detectives to deduce the blackmailer's *modus operandi*: Field used them as a convenient way of storing and transporting the incriminating documents with which he extorted money from his victims, and the name of each victim is inscribed with "indelible ink" (310) on the leather inner band of each hat. While the hat with the killer's name is never found, the detectives do discover a top hat marked "MISC." (311), which contains copies of original documents proving that Mr Barry "has a strain of negroid blood in his veins" (376). At the height of the Jim Crow era, keeping this "black taint" a secret is a sufficient motive for murder, and the detective duo therefore quickly move to arrest the actor.

The hat and its contents thus serve as a metacommentary on the clue as a metaphor for the readability of the world. Just as a clue is not simply a sign, but a condensed and encoded yet ultimately interpretable representation of the mystery as a whole, the hat, when unpacked and emptied, contains information that fully elucidates the death of Monty Field. The hat can *literally* be read: It is filled with writing that names the murderer while at the same time supplying the motive and biographical background of the murder. This being the case, it is necessary to violate the principle of "fair play". If the clue were "plainly stated and described", it would ruin the mystery. Accordingly, at the time when the narrator poses his "challenge to the reader" and assures us that we are "in possession of all the pertinent facts" (324), readers know of the telltale hat labelled "MISC.", yet only the detectives know its contents.

Sceptical readers might want to question certain aspects of the hat as a clue. Most importantly perhaps, it is premised on the assumption that no male person would have arrived at the theatre without the appropriate combination of hat and dress. Even if this assumption is supported by contemporary sartorial norms (which it is, but not to the point of excluding the possibility of exceptions), it clearly overestimates the capacity of the ushers to perform their duties while also keeping track of the patrons' headwear. Yet, the slight absurdity of the set-up simply underscores the wider, ontological function of the clue, which is to render the social world orderly and readable. The top hat as a clue not only serves as the central part of a narrative that makes sense of the mystery, it also eliminates all contingent and therefore meaningless and unreadable occurrences – such as, for example, that a person should arrive bareheaded without being noticed by the ushers.

Beyond the clue

The clue in classic detective fiction epitomises the mystery aspect of the plot while at the same time underwriting the genre's claim that the world is an orderly place that can be read and understood in much the same way as a book. This claim of readability is limited both geographically and chronologically; it is tied to a Western epistemological horizon and arguably emerges as a compensatory response to the complexity of modern society, promising order, causality, linearity and predictability where everyday experience sees only chaos and contingency. However, in the twentieth century, especially after World War I, the clue's attempt to contain this social complexity is increasingly linked to a loss of realism. As a result, the logic of the clue is subjected to extensive self-reflexive critique as the crime genre reinvents itself on the basis of new epistemologies better aligned with the modern world. This critique takes three main forms.

The first form manifests itself in the works of Dashiell Hammett and, more generally, in the American "hardboiled" format that emerged in the late 1920s. Hammett's *The Maltese Falcon* (1929–1930), for example, repeatedly mocks and undermines the notion of the clue and its epistemological implications. Not only does the private investigator, Sam Spade, come across several clue-like objects that turn out to be meaningless; he is also exposed as a poor reader of actual clues. When learning that Brigid O'Shaughnessy, his client, lover and antagonist, stopped on her way to the Ferry Building to buy a newspaper, Spade correctly guesses that the newspaper is important. However, even though he knows where O'Shaughnessy is going, and further knows that she and her business associates recently arrived by ship from Hong Kong, he is unable to guess, leafing through the newspaper, that the relevant information can be found in the shipping news section. It is not until the following day, when Spade encounters the same newspaper in a wastepaper basket and notices that this page has been torn out, that he finally draws the right conclusion and heads to the harbour. By then it is too late: Spade's failure to work out even a relatively uncomplicated clue means that he is unable to prevent the murder of Captain Jacobi. The point is a scepticism with regard to the detective's ability to read the world. If Doyle used clues as a way of highlighting Holmes's brilliance, Hammett introduces an array of empty, unnoticed or misunderstood clues to show that Spade's strength as a detective lies in his ability to navigate the unmeaning chaos of modern urban life rather than in his intellectual prowess.

The metaphysical or postmodern crime novel also seeks to escape the logic of the clue. It is sometimes claimed that this format is not a genuine part of the crime genre, but simply draws on its devices and conventions for its own philosophical purposes. However, its godfather, Argentinian author Jorge Luis Borges, was in fact an unashamed crime fiction aficionado. The short story "Death and the Compass" (1942) is an intricate parody of the clue-puzzle and its implied epistemology. The protagonist, Erik Lönnrot, is a cerebral detective who considers himself a modern version of Poe's Auguste Dupin. His firm belief in the readability of the world is seemingly confirmed by the clues of the case, mainly a series of letters that appear to spell the secret name of God, and he responds by making the interpretation of obscure Kabbalistic books his main avenue of investigation. Yet, the clues are in fact a trap laid for him by a criminal mastermind, Red Scharlach, who knows his bookish inclinations. In an inversion of the detective genre's traditional disparagement of the police, Inspector Treviranus's common-sense understanding turns out to be correct while Lönnrot's tortured interpretations are invariably wrong, and it is ultimately his stubborn adherence to the logic of the clue that leads to his death at the hands of his enemy.

Finally, the police procedural, dominant in crime fiction since the 1950s, tends to abandon the hermeneutics of clues in favour of actual investigative practices used by metropolitan homicide units. Ed McBain's early 87th Precinct novels, for example, pour scorn on the clue-puzzle assumption that murders can be solved by a mind brilliant enough to read the signs that the murderer has left behind. In the fictional city of Isola, crimes are solved instead by teams of police officers, supported by forensic scientists, who rely on established procedure and persistence rather than interpretative intelligence. Instead of reading clues, the police officers investigate by following "leads" that might ultimately enable them to catch the killer. The success of this sequential process is never guaranteed, and often the solution is entirely disconnected from any actual police procedures, materialising instead by chance or as a result of police instincts. These innovations amount to a new ontology of crime fiction. Abandoning the reassuring correlation between motivations, actions and signs that underpins the clue as a device, McBain's early work instead evokes a world of contingency in which the mindlessness of modern urban crime can only by countered by diligent and professionalised police work (Gulddal 2016b).

As a result of these and other attacks, the vertical structure of the *clue*, which contrasts surface manifestations and deep meanings and therefore requires interpretation, has to a large extent been replaced by other epistemologies: the horizontal structure of the *lead* (which has no deep meaning but might turn up additional information), the stable correlations of the *symptom* (which links causes and effects with reference to an established code) and, as a branch of the latter, *forensic evidence* (which allows specialists to decode the crime scene using scientific methods). Individual clues continue to play a role in contemporary crime fiction, sometimes prominently so, yet they are mainly soft and ontologically modest clues, decoupled from the fantasy of a readable world.

Notes

1 For an incisive critique of Moretti, see Ascari 2014.
2 The textual realities are, of course, more complex, and the detective's solution is not always able to contain the interpretative possibilities indicated by the main narrative. See Bayard 2000, Gulddal 2016a and Chapter 19 of the present volume (Alistair Rolls, "Beginnings and Endings").

Bibliography

Ascari, M. (2014) "The dangers of distant reading. Reassessing Moretti's approach to literary genres", *Genre*, 47(1): 1–19.

Bayard, P. (2000) *Who Killed Roger Ackroyd?*, trans. C. Cosman, New York: The New Press.

Blumenberg, H. (1981) *Die Lesbarkeit der Welt*, Frankfurt/Main: Suhrkamp.

Chandler, R. (1995) [1944] "The simple art of murder", *Later Novels and Other Writings*, New York: The Library of America, 977–92.

Doyle, A.C. (2009) [1887] *A Study in Scarlet. The Penguin Complete Sherlock Holmes*, London: Penguin, 13–86.

Eco, U. (1983) "Horns, hooves, insteps. Some hypotheses on three types of abduction", in U. Eco and T.A. Sebeok (eds), *The Sign of Three. Dupin, Holmes, Peirce*, Bloomington & Indianapolis: Indiana University Press, 198–220.

Felski, R. (2015) *The Limits of Critique*, Chicago & London: The University of Chicago Press.

Ginzburg, C. (1989) [1979] *Clues, Myths, and the Historical Method*, trans. J. and A.C. Tedeschi, Baltimore: Johns Hopkins University Press.

Gulddal, J. (2016a) "'Beautiful shining order'. Detective authority in Agatha Christie's *Murder on the Orient Express*", *Clues*, 34(1): 11–21.

———. (2016b) "Clueless. Genre, realism, and narrative form in Ed McBain's early 87th Precinct novels", *Clues*, 34(2): 54–62.

Knox, R. (1929) "Ten commandments for detective stories", in H. Harrington and R. Knox (eds), *Best Detective Stories of the Year (1928)*, London: Faber & Faber, 4.

Malmgren, C.D. (2001) *Anatomy of Murder. Mystery, Detective, and Crime Fiction*, Bowling Green: Bowling Green State University Popular Press.

Moretti, F. (1988) "Clues", *Signs Taken for Wonders. Essays in the sociology of literary forms*, London & New York: Verso, 130–56.

———. (2000) "The slaughterhouse of literature", *Modern Language Quarterly*, 61(1): 207–27.

———. (2004) "Graphs, maps, trees. Abstract models for literary history – 3", *New Left Review*, 28: 43–63.

Oxford English Dictionary (OED) (2018) Oxford: Oxford University Press, "clue, *n*", www.oed.com/view/Entry/34830 (accessed 3 December 2018).

Prendergast, C. (2005) "Evolution and literary theory. A response to Franco Moretti", *New Left Review*, 34: 40–62.

Queen, E. (2015) [1929] *The Roman Hat Mystery*, New York: Open Road.

Van Dine, S.S. (1928) "Twenty rules for writing detective stories", *The American Magazine* (September).

22
REALISM

Paul Cobley

Although they seldom define the term, books and articles about crime fiction are often liberally peppered with the word "realism". This is because, as Nicol (2010: 508) states, "Crime fiction has always been dedicated, in different ways, to producing a kind of realism". Generally, such casual use of the term "realism" with reference to crime fiction signals the relationship by which narratives of crime are firmly rooted in the mission to portray an important feature of social formations and its relation to other features of social formations. Furthermore, they are committed to carrying this out in a manner that does not have recourse to the fantastic – as, say, fantasy might – and does not primarily present its objects in allegorical terms – as, say, a theological epic like *The Divine Comedy* or *Paradise Lost* might. Crime fiction's depiction of social formations relies, instead, on reference to broadly familiar institutions, objects, events and relationships. Moreover, it does so in a way that is calculated not to draw attention to itself in respect of excessive poetic licence, straining of the reader's credulity, tropes or expression used principally for metric or rhythmic effect, or any other measures that might be found to be beyond the genre's boundaries or the requirements of the narrative.

Yet, the relation of realism and crime fiction cannot be contained by this short definition alone. Note that Nicol, in his statement, refers to "a kind of realism" rather than just "realism" singular. Writers on crime fiction regularly note the ways in which subgenres of the crime narrative represent an "advance" or "departure" in realism from other genres: The professional private detective as more realistic than the enthusiastic ratiocinator, the motivations of the hardened criminal as more realistic as opposed to the "amateur cracksman", the depiction of geopolitics in the spy thriller as more realistic than the concern with consistent psychology and dialogue in narratives of single murders, and so forth. This acknowledges that "realism" is multifarious, subject to change even within the genre of crime fiction, and not susceptible of one, unitary definition. It is why the question of what constitutes "realism" remains vexed, even in the present, nearly two centuries after the term evolved into general usage.

If "realism" can be condensed into one general problem of representation, within that problem there are nevertheless a number of overdetermined relations for crime fiction. A simple saying and a simple example illustrate the issue. The saying holds that "the rendering of an object can never be the object itself". In the example which might accompany this saying, if I utter the word "knife" that word *cannot be* the knife in question or any knife. Indeed, it is not meant to be in such a relation of substitution, simply because it is a word and not the thing. Instead, the word and the knife it denotes are in a relationship of signifying or representation. Inherent in the relationship is the understanding that the word *stands in* for that which it denotes; the denoted object, therefore, does not even have to be present at the moment of utterance for the relationship to obtain.

What one must bear in mind with this example is that it only features a somewhat abstract act of representation, where one discrete sign is taken to refer to one object. This is seldom the norm in human experience. Moreover, narrative fiction obviously features an array of signs. It derives from a tradition, prevalent in the West and beyond, where narratives are recounted partly in prose – which represents institutions, objects, events and relationships in the manner of the word "knife" standing in for the object *knife* – and partly in imitative mimesis whereby the speech of characters (irrespective of whether they existed) is reproduced verbatim, often within speech marks (Cobley 2014).

Object and psychological realism

So far what has been considered is only the "realism" entailed by fiction's general reference to features of the world. Given that narrative fiction harbours a strong tradition of assiduously presenting the speech of characters, it is not unsurprising that it has also had a history of interest in, and depiction of, characters' psychology. Not only is realistic depiction a matter of general reference, then; it is also sometimes concerned with representation of features of the world through the prism of characters' psychologies. Such "psychological realism", which is common in crime fiction and narrative in general, will present the world, at specific times or throughout a narrative, in relation to a character's perspective. In addition, of course – and, especially in crime fiction which is not devoted to narrating individual psychology alone, but in relation to such aspects of the genre as resolving criminal conspiracies – "psychological realism" will be related to the plot and story events in a narrative. An early sound film example of crime fiction, Alfred Hitchcock's *Blackmail* (1929), is illustrative in this case. The protagonist, Alice (Anny Ondra) grabs a bread knife and stabs to death a man as he is sexually assaulting her. She flees the scene of the murder but is worried that she has left behind evidence of her deed. The next morning, Alice hears her parents (Sara Allgood, Charles Paton) speaking with a neighbour (Phyllis Konstam) who is evidently keen on gossip. They discuss the murder, which has become headline news, and Alice, in a state of high anxiety, zones in and out of the conversation, hearing only one word clearly, the shrill utterance of the word "knife", as it is highlighted on the sound-track. Here, *knife* becomes not just a neutral object in the narrative but an object with specific resonances that serve not just the plot (in which she is blackmailed by someone who saw her exit the flat where she was assaulted) but also, in its prominence on the soundtrack, exemplifies psychological realism.

The implementation of psychological realism and what might be called "object realism", as in the preceding discussion in which institutions, objects, events and relationships are presented in more or less detail as familiar, has been central to crime fiction. The genre's concern with criminal and counter-criminal activities answers a demand that it narrate objects, facts and activities accurately, with fidelity to what is generally known about those things and with attention to the detail of more specialised activities. Thus, crime fiction partakes of general "object realism", but also utilises "forensic realism" (Jermyn 2013) in which professional knowledge usually unavailable to the public becomes part of the narrative. Often, such forensic realism asserts the veracity in its depiction by denigrating other narratives with putatively lesser claims to realism. The following example, from Nick Stone's *King of Swords* (2007), exemplifies this device of realism:

> 'That's the movie version', Gemma said, with a weary sigh. She was glad she'd never gone into teaching. She didn't believe in fighting losing battles. How could you compete with Hollywood myths? 'After death, the skin around the hair and fingernails loses water and it shrinks. And when it shrinks, it retracts, making the hair and nails look longer, and therefore giving the impression that they've grown. But they haven't, really. It's an illusion. Like the movies. OK?'.
>
> *(Stone 2007: 25–26)*

As this example shows, specialist knowledge serves "forensic realism" on the one hand, but also promulgates a more general "object realism". Indeed, this has been the key defining principle in the realism of at least three subgenres of crime fiction that have been devoted to professional minutiae in criminal proceedings: The police procedural, the legal thriller and the many narratives, particularly following the Scarpetta novels of Patricia Cornwell, that are devoted to the investigations carried out by pathologists (notwithstanding the fact that those charged with carrying out postmortem examinations in real life do not conduct investigations into crimes).

The impetus to record detail in realism has also been well observed outside the genre. Jakobson notes the "*depiction of contiguity or the narrative act of focusing on inessential details*" in realism (1987: 25, emphasis in original); Barthes (1989) also suggests that realism often consists of "the reality effect", a narration of the inessential details in, say, the furnishing of a room that appears in the narrative. In such a narration, the presentation of the detail for its own sake theoretically guarantees the realism in the depiction. The strong orientation toward plot in crime fiction, however, means that while such details will not be absent from the genre's prose, they are more likely to be bound to the resolution of the mystery in the narrative and hence tend to be essential. As Gulddal indicates in Chapter 20 of this volume, readers of crime fiction are compelled "to look for clues and hidden meaning in every textual detail".

Equally, the requirements of the mystery entail that "object realism" alone is insufficient to produce compelling narratives focused on crime and the agencies of law. Again, the strong orientation of the genre to plot is important. Plot, since Aristotle, has been understood as the agency of causality in narratives (Cobley 2014) and its workings are closely related to the motive force of characters. Consequently, the protagonists in crime fiction are immensely important because they are either: The causes of the mystery or conspiracy that is central to the genre's narratives; the extraordinary individual(s) who will resolve the mystery; or those who are affected by the mystery but lack the resources to resolve it. For any crime fiction to be at all credible – as opposed to a purely formulaic working-through of the genre's elements – the characters in the narrative, driven by their involvement in the mystery, need to be constituted by some measure of psychological realism.

Psychological realism in crime fiction usually requires a delicate balance of the functional qualities required for characters to perform their roles in the genre and the kind of motivation that is customary to indicate psychological consistency in narrative fiction. Credibility will be strained and realism undermined if heroes, villains and bystanders are mere ciphers, embodying good or evil as if these were pure, allegorical or fantastic qualities. Correspondingly, crime fiction faces the dilemma of presenting the commonplace nature of crime, a quotidian phenomenon in contemporary social formations, in a manner which is dramatic. The chief problem arising here is that, as has been recognised by crime fiction critics as long ago as Haycraft (1941: 228–29), "most real life crime is duller, less ingenious, less dramatic, lacking in what Poe called 'the pungent contradiction of the general idea', as compared with fictional felony". As such, "object realism" is tempered by the demands of drama or narrative drive in crime fiction, while "psychological realism" must negotiate the need to ensure that characters embody "structural" functions (hero, villain, onlooker, etc.).

These dilemmas have been resolved by crime fiction in a number of ways. One move by which the genre has attempted to resolve some of the contradictions in figuring realism is by making murder integral to its narratives. If, as Palmer (1978) argues, crime fiction is defined by the fears of conspiracy prevalent at the time of the genre's inception in the nineteenth century – namely, the fear of theft and the fear of working people's combining for joint action – the inflection of those fears in murder, an unwonted irruption in social life, makes sense. The occurrence of murder as a result of a conspiracy is unusual enough to warrant its resolution by an extraordinary individual, in contrast to theft and the combination of working people which would most likely be combatted by bureaucratic means. In this case, two situations are trumped. The first is the "object realism" in which murder in real life is much less frequent and much more banal than it is in fiction. The second is the "psychological realism" where everyone or no one is exceptional in greater or lesser degree. The requirement to resolve an event as unprecedented in real life as a murder resulting from a conspiracy, yokes realism to the demands of the genre in which conspiracy-inspired murder can proliferate on a precedented scale.

Hardboiled realism?

Another way in which crime fiction maintains its genre credentials while accommodating realism is by focusing on the work of the professional. Irwin notes how the novels of Dashiell Hammett perform this act by shifting emphasis in the process of criminal investigations from ratiocination (exact, rational reasoning) to the challenges of human relationships thrown up by crime. Irwin refers to the so-called "Golden Age" of crime fiction, or the "school of Mayhem Parva", exemplified by the works of Agatha Christie, Freeman Wills Crofts, Dorothy L. Sayers and others which featured isolated murders solved by reasoning over clues by seasoned detectives. As the "object realism" of Golden Age crime fiction's focus on the detail of clues stagnated and seemed to become artificial, at the expense of "psychological realism" in particular, a new approach to accommodating realism in the genre was needed. Irwin writes:

> [I]n striving for greater realism, Hammett turned away from analytic-deductive plots in favor of character-driven narratives resembling novels of manners, but since Hammett's detective stories began as popular fiction appearing in what were essentially men's magazines, he had to find another plot element that would be as interesting and appealing to his male audience as the puzzle aspect of analytic detective fiction. And this element was the conflict between the professional and the personal, between work and relationships, in the detective's life.
>
> *(2006: 184)*

As Irwin suggests, then, the focus on the professional in Hammett's work retained the general object realism and forensic realism that was bound up with the exigencies of investigation but transferred emphasis to psychological realism in depicting occupational relations.

In fact, in the history of crime fiction, the reorganisation in standards of realism discussed here is somewhat emblematic. For some of the contemporary purveyors of crime fiction, the motivation to produce particular kinds of narratives was no doubt inspired, in large part, by a desire to enhance realism in the genre. However, the arguments about realism at this stage of development of crime fiction can be seen as part of a more general movement of stagnation and regeneration or decline and renewal in respect of the parameters of realism. At a moment when the "Mayhem Parva school" and the new, "hardboiled" writing of Hammett and others were both still contemporary rather than historical phenomena, Raymond Chandler, a proponent of the latter kind of crime fiction, took issue with the cosy artificiality of the former school. In a famous passage from his essay, "The Simple Art of Murder" (1944), Chandler wrote:

> Hammett gave murder back to the kind of people that commit it for reasons, not just to provide a corpse; and with the means at hand, not with hand-wrought duelling pistols, curare, and tropical fish. He put these people down on paper as they are, and he made them talk and think in the language they customarily used for these purposes.
>
> *(1995: 989)*

Clearly, this is a herald of the route to greater realism in crime fiction. It lauds Hammett's renewal of psychological realism, noting the importance of the motivation of those who murder. It marries that with object realism – "the means at hand", common objects that will nod to the banality of murder. It also promotes the possibility of mimesis, the ideal of representing people's speech with utmost accuracy.

To some extent, Chandler's lauding of Hammett is a justification of his own approach to realism. A key component of this approach is a specialised implementation of "language", not just in the imitation of the patterns of people's speech but also in narrative prose. As is well known, hardboiled style consists of short sentences, usually without adjectives and adverbs. It features the use of terms from speech rather than the more "flowery" terms used in some literature – for example, "said" is more likely to appear in hardboiled crime fiction than "asserted", "queried" or "expostulated". Nouns are usually concrete and recognisable while, complementing object realism, verbs are stripped to a minimum with a heavy reliance on the verb "to be". Sentences are mainly simple declarative ones and subordinate clauses are generally eschewed. These sentences tend to describe events in the sequence in which they occurred, directly and unmixed with comment. The resultant low-key representation is unemotional and can give the impression of "objectivity" or greater realism. Coupled with the numerous unhappy endings, problematic denouements and lack of resolution in Chandler's narratives, hardboiled crime fiction – in audiovisual as well as print versions – has unsurprisingly become associated with a closer imitation of life (the latter of which, unlike most narratives, also features a predominance of unresolved events and situations).

To a great extent, the hardboiled tendency in crime fiction has become dominant as a means of attempting to ensure heightened realism. Despite the prose initially playing so prominent a part in the identity of hardboiled writing, its influence has spread not just to printed crime fiction but also to audiovisual productions such as *film noir*, where narratives often feature a laconic, first-person voice-over, close imitation of criminal argot and, invariably, night-for-night shooting of scenes for the sake of authenticity. Yet, while the hardboiled was closely associated with *film noir* and later versions of the private-eye film, its influence has been discerned in a number of other areas of crime fiction where a low-key narration has putatively reinforced the realism of the narrative. The spy thriller from the Cold War onwards has employed a hardboiled style (see Harper 1969), often to demonstrate how emotion has been crushed in the lives of the protagonists. Similarly, a broadly hardboiled approach has been evident in a form of crime fiction popular in the last decade and a half: So-called Scandi or Nordic noir. The Danish television crime series *The Killing* (*Forbrydelsen*, 2007), for example, was lauded in the UK as a piece of exceptional realism, deriving from its "sombre aspect, funereal pace, and demands for absolute concentration" by which "it breaks every rule in the TV crime fiction handbook" (Graham 2011: 20). The extended focus of *The Killing* on the impact that the eponymous murder of Nanna has on her parents prompted critics to hail it as a major innovation in realism: "In frequently heartbreaking detail, we have been made aware of the bleak and everlasting effects of the fallout of a premature, violent death upon those who are left behind" (Graham 2011: 20–21). Of course, the realism being applauded is palpably a variant of the hardboiled tendency in crime fiction.

It is here, in examples such as this, that the fault lines of definitions of realism in crime fiction are manifest. Hardboiled fiction is no less a rendering of an object than Golden Age crime fiction. As such, it is every bit as artificial as Golden Age narratives. Indeed, Chandler's criticism of the Mayhem Parva school may also be the setting up of a straw man, since crime fiction from that school is sometimes argued to be by no means as uniform or cosily artificial as the criticism of it might make it seem (see, for example, Light 1991).

What should be apparent from this discussion so far is that, even in the face of the great influence that the hardboiled has enjoyed, there are different kinds of realism which are exercised in crime fiction: Realism in respect of character motivation, realism in respect of dialogue, realism in respect of milieu, realism in respect of technical details, and so on. In turn, these have been contested by different proponents or schools of crime fiction. Furthermore, what is taken to be realism in the genre has been contested by readers or viewers, including critics, sometimes in concurrence with proponents and sometimes with contrasting views to them. These contests, too, have taken place at specific moments in the development of crime fiction and at specific moments in respect of the contemporary period in general. That is to say, what is taken to constitute realism cannot be divorced from the events in, and opinions about, the contemporary world in which crime fiction is consumed. In an attempt to emphasise these points, I will consider *Bodyguard*, a major hit in the television schedules in the UK in autumn 2018 and then worldwide.

Bodyguard: Realism in the court of public opinion

Bodyguard is the narrative of a police officer and ex-Afghanistan veteran with post-traumatic stress disorder, David Budd (Richard Madden), who finds himself elevated to the position of personal bodyguard to the UK Government's Home Secretary, Julia Montague (Keeley Hawes). She, in turn, may be the target of a terror plot in retaliation for her belligerent policies. Budd is at the centre of the action, not just because he is the politician's bodyguard, a relationship complicated further as he and Montague engage in a sexual liaison. In addition, Budd, seriously disaffected by his combat experiences, is a comrade of a scarred ex-veteran of the Afghan campaign, Andy Apsted (Tom Brooke), who is seemingly more disaffected still. The series proceeds through a number of action set pieces and cliffhangers, and the series finale along with the opening, are particularly notable in this respect. The very first scene of the drama lasts 20-plus minutes and features Madden, on a Glasgow-London train, discovering that the journey is endangered by a suicide bomber in the toilet of one of the carriages. Through a tense process of negotiation, he gently stands down the Muslim woman from her position, indicating that he can understand that she has been coerced into carrying out the terror act by jihadi men and, ultimately, with the arriving security forces, procures safety for the woman, himself and the train's passengers.

Amidst the hype and the intense mainstream involvement in this example of crime fiction, what is notable is the extent to which so much of the discussion of *Bodyguard* at the time of its first broadcast was concerned with "realism". Newspapers obsessed over whether former home secretary, Amber Rudd, found the series realistic (Deen 2018); and whether the technologies, terminology and political procedure employed were accurate, according to specialists (largely yes – for example, Clifton 2018; largely no – for example, Turk 2018; Mozafari 2018). In one sense, this fixation on forensic realism and general object realism in a crime fiction is perhaps only remarkable for its scale, attendant on the popularity of the series and the demand for journalists to fill space. Certainly, the way in which *Bodyguard* writer, Jed Mercurio, regularly cited in interviews the meticulous research and expert advice – across the police, the security services and politics – underpinning the series (O'Sullivan 2018) is also fairly routine in below-the-line publicity for crime series and it illustrates the general demand of realism for the genre. What the intense and widespread involvement in *Bodyguard* provides is a picture of how central to crime fiction conceptions of realism are. Any plot inconsistencies – why the connection of veterans Budd and Apsted were not investigated by the police (O'Sullivan 2018), why "a traumatised Afghanistan veteran with a troubled home life was given the most high-profile security job in the country" (Cumming 2018) – were amplified into a matter of national debate.

While the questions of forensic realism picked at the detail in *Bodyguard*, it was clear that another debate over realism was developing. Because the series was seen to have "ticked all the state-of-the-nation boxes" (Cumming 2018), it immediately became embroiled in questions regarding whether its depictions matched social realities or whether they were more a matter of wishful sociopolitical thinking. News sources widely reported social media responses to the preponderance of female characters in roles of authority: Julia Montague, a markswoman, an explosives expert, the Head of the Metropolitan Police's Counterterrorism Command, a Chief Superintendent of detectives, a detective sergeant and a PR advisor to the Home Secretary. It was widely reported that viewers saw such female representation as "political correctness" or "unrealistic" (Noah 2018; Pook 2018). Yet, the matter was, unsurprisingly, far from clear-cut. Mercurio strenuously refuted the claims (Noah 2018), while the *Daily Mail* reported support for the "bold change" in representation (Coen and White 2018). Meanwhile, others pointed to the veracity of the roles, given that three women were currently heading up London's emergency services: Cressida Dick, Head of the Metropolitan Police; Dany Cotton, London Fire Commissioner; and Heather Lawrence, Chair of London Ambulance Service (Pook 2018). Some considered *Bodyguard* as, in the words of Trevor Phillips, former chairman of the Equality and Human Rights Commission, "possibly the most misogynist piece of TV I've seen in years" (*The Scotsman* 2018); others hailed it as "2018's most feminist TV show" (Pook 2018). Yet others accused it of Islamophobia and misogyny combined for its portrayal of the suicide bomber, Nadia, at the beginning and end of the series (Mediaversity 2018).

The case of *Bodyguard* reveals a number of aspects of the relationship of crime fiction and realism. It suggests that object realism is a perennial demand of crime fiction, particularly when large numbers of viewers, channelled by social media and press coverage, are invested in a crime narrative that depicts familiar objects, extraordinary situations and politically sensitive subjects. It demonstrates that there are different kinds of realism – particularly in respect of general object realism and forensic realism, where there is the demand for fidelity to technology, professions, historical events and occupational relations, among others. The case of *Bodyguard* also exemplifies the manner in which realism entails crime fiction conforming to certain standards of representation of social groups at specific moments in the contemporary period in which it appears. Even when it does so conform, its purported realism in one dimension might be subject to challenge from its depictions in another dimension, as well as being subject to contestation in the arena of public opinion. It is notable, especially, that the question of psychological realism in respect of *Bodyguard* tended to arise in those discussions drawing attention to the roles of characters rather than those devoted to the role of occupation in object realism. Even so, if psychological realism is difficult to establish because of the intractability of fully understanding human motivations, it also seems that object realism is also hard to establish definitively.

Conclusion: Realism or verisimilitude

One important conclusion to draw from this discussion is that realism is by no means an established entity that some texts or some genres possess. Indeed, this is not a new realisation: It was expressed as early as 1921 by Jakobson (1987: 25, italics in original) in his list of definitions of realism as "*The conservative tendency to remain within the limits of a given artistic tradition, conceived as faithfulness to reality*" and then "*Realism comprehends the sum total of the features characteristic of one specific artistic current of the nineteenth century*". Yet it is not enough to prevent the continued demotic use of the term, especially in relation to crime fiction. Clearly, what is taken to be "realistic" is constantly changing in response to public opinion or *doxa*. So, while "realism" endures as a term, it is often difficult to elude the fact that it implies some phenomenon that is stable. Given that crime fiction is so profuse, dominating television schedules and print publishing, not only is the demand for realism in the genre wider than it is for other genres, it is arguably more subject to the vagaries of popular changing tastes and predilections than such genres as literary fiction.

One modest proposal for those who wish to engage in scholarly analysis of crime fiction is that the kinds of questions considered above could be addressed within the rubric of "verisimilitude" rather than "realism". The former suggests not a "gold standard" of veracity, but a mutable relationship, with fiction responding to standards of fidelity that are constantly changing in a complex relationship with *doxa* or public opinion (Todorov 1977). This might enable a greater understanding of both the rapid rate of innovation in crime fiction and the aforementioned intimacy to popular taste.

Bibliography

Barthes, R. (1989) "The reality effect", in *The Rustle of Language*, trans. R. Howard, Berkeley: University of California Press, 141–48.

Chandler, R. (1995) [1944] "The simple art of murder", in *Later Novels and Other Writings*, New York: Library of America, 977–92.

Clifton, K. (2018) "BBC *Bodyguard*: Government source lifts the lid on how accurate the TV drama really is", *Evening Standard*, 4 September, www.standard.co.uk/news/uk/government-source-lifts-lid-on-bbcs-smash-hit-drama-bodyguard-a3927331.html (accessed 22 August 2019).

Cobley, P. (2014) *Narrative*, 2nd edn, London: Routledge.

Coen, S. and White, F. (2018) "Women rule the roost in BBC's new drama *Bodyguard* as 7 million tune in to watch first episode", *Daily Mail*, 27 August, www.dailymail.co.uk/news/article-6103817/Women-rule-roost-BBCs-new-drama-Bodyguard-7million-tune-watch-episode.html (accessed 22 August 2019).

Cooke, R. (2018) "*Bodyguard* is convoluted and preposterous – but it's impossible not to get caught up in", *New Statesman*, 29 August, www.newstatesman.com/2018/08/bodyguard-bbc-review-drama (accessed 22 August 2019).

Cumming, E. (2018) "*Bodyguard* finale: why I'm not convinced by the 'best' show of 2018", *The Guardian*, 17 September, www.theguardian.com/tv-and-radio/2018/sep/17/bodyguard-finale-why-im-not-convinced-by-the-best-show-of-2018 (accessed 22 August 2019).

Deen, S. (2018) "Former home secretary Amber Rudd plays coy when asked if *Bodyguard* is realistic", *Metro*, 16 November, https://metro.co.uk/2018/11/06/former-home-secretary-amber-rudd-plays-coy-when-asked-if-bodyguard-is-realistic-8108988/ (accessed 22 August 2019).

Graham, A. (2011) "Lessons of *The Killing*", *Radio Times*, 26 March-1 April, 20–21.

Harper, R. (1969) *The World of the Thriller*, Baltimore and London: Johns Hopkins University Press.

Haycraft, H. (1941) *Murder for Pleasure*, New York and London: Appleton-Century.

Irwin, J.T. (2006) *Unless the Threat of Death Is Behind Them: Hard-boiled fiction and film noir*, Baltimore and London: Johns Hopkins University Press.

Jakobson, R. (1987) [1921] "On realism in art", in K. Pomorska and S. Rudy (eds), *Language in Literature*, Cambridge, MA and London: Belknap Press, 19–27.

Jermyn, D. (2013) "Labs and slabs: television crime drama and the quest for forensic realism", *Studies in History and Philosophy of Biological and Biomedical Sciences*, 44: 103–09.

Light, A. (1991) *Forever England: Literature, femininity and conservatism between the wars*, London: Routledge.

Mediaversity (2018) "*Bodyguard* adds to a long and damaging media trend of depicting brown people as terrorists", 7 December 2018 www.mediaversityreviews.com/tv-reviews/2018/12/5/bodyguard (accessed 22 August 2019).

Mozafari, L. (2018) "BBC's *Bodyguard* has a lot of inaccuracies real-life bodyguards have issues with: 'There's a lot of things we could pick apart'", *Digital Spy*, 28 August, www.digitalspy.com/tv/a864948/bbc-bodyguard-episode-1-2-inaccuracies-real-life-bodyguards-issues/ (accessed 22 August 2019).

Nicol, B. (2010) "Patricia Highsmith (1921–1995)", in C.J. Rzepka and L. Horsley (eds), *A Companion to Crime Fiction*, New York: Wiley-Blackwell, 503–09.

Noah, S. (2018) "*Bodyguard*'s Jed Mercurio hits back at 'politically correct' gripes", *Metro*, 29 August, www.metro.news/bodyguards-jed-mercurio-hits-back-at-politically-correct-gripes/1201979/ (accessed 22 August 2019).

O'Sullivan, K. (2018) "*Bodyguard* creator Jed Mercurio slams critics who question show's accuracy as he debunks massive plot hole", *Daily Mirror*, 20 September, www.mirror.co.uk/tv/tv-news/bodyguard-creator-jed-mercurio-slams-13283069 (accessed 22 August 2019).

Palmer, J. (1978) *Thrillers: Genesis and structure of a popular genre*, London: Edward Arnold.

Pook, L. (2018) "*Bodyguard* is 2018's most feminist TV show – here's why", *Stylist*, 2 September, www.stylist.co.uk/opinion/bodyguard-feminism-tv-keeley-hawes-richard-madden-bbc/224814 (accessed 22 August 2019).

The Scotsman (2018) "*Bodyguard* 'most misogynistic' TV show in years", 22 October, www.scotsman.com/news/uk-news/bodyguard-most-misogynistic-tv-show-in-years-1-4817953 (accessed 22 August 2019).

Stone, N. (2007) *King of Swords*, Harmondsworth: Michael Joseph.

Todorov, T. (1977) *The Poetics of Prose*, Ithaca: Cornell University Press.

Turk, V. (2018) "How realistic is *Bodyguard*? A real personal protection officer tells all", *Wired*, 22 September, www.wired.co.uk/article/bodyguard-finale-realism (accessed 22 August 2019).

23
PLACE

Stewart King

Sometimes referred to as backdrop, setting, location, atmosphere or, more commonly when done well, another character, place is arguably the most important feature in crime fiction. While it is not the defining feature – that, of course, is the presence of a crime – place gives the crime meaning. For in crime fiction, nothing makes sense without place. "Place calls forth the crime", argues Joan Ramon Resina (1997:156).[1] That is, crimes are place-specific in the sense that they are rooted in the particular physical, cultural, political, economic, environmental, social and, of course, legal circumstances of the place where the crime is committed. Place not only calls forth the crime; it also determines the sort of detective who investigates the crime, the criminal who commits it and the victim who suffers from it. The significance of place is not just true of crime fiction; it "is impossible [...] to think of a world without place", argues geographer Tim Cresswell (2013: 1). Despite its importance, Cresswell maintains that how we understand place has been hindered by common-sense or obvious meanings: "Place is a word that seems to speak for itself" (1). The self-evident understanding of place is also common to many crime fiction studies in which, as David Schmid notes, with few notable exceptions (Geherin 2008; Pezzotti 2012), place is taken for granted (2012: 7–8). This chapter seeks to develop a more considered understanding of the role of place both in individual crime fiction narratives and in the experience of reading crime fiction. To comprehend the role of place in crime fiction, the chapter draws on the works of geographers, some of whom have applied their understanding of place to crime fiction, before reflecting on the different functions of place in crime fiction and in crime fiction scholarship. Rather than treating place as a fixed, knowable entity, the chapter will explore the notion of unstable places through an analysis of Catalan crime writer, Teresa Solana's *Un crim imperfecte* (2006) [*A Not So Perfect Crime*, 2008].

Reading geographically

Place is a fuzzy and contestable concept. In part, this ambiguity is due to the different and sometimes contradictory understandings of the concept developed by geographers and philosophers (Cresswell 2013: 15–51). To understand place, geographers contrast it with space, a term with which it is often used interchangeably in popular discourse, but which has different meanings for geographers. "'Space' is a more abstract concept than 'place'"; it is "undifferentiated": "What begins as undifferentiated space becomes place as we get to know it better and endow it with value" (Tuan 1977: 6). Spaces surround places, such that places are spaces imbued with meaning. As Laura Lippard puts it, place

> is latitudinal and longitudinal within the map of a person's life. It is temporal and spatial, personal and political. A layered location replete with human histories and memories. It is about connections, what surrounds it, what formed it, what happened there, what will happen there.
>
> *(1997: 7)*

Lippard here points to something more ephemeral and less tangible than the concrete forms that we usually associate with place. As such, "place is not just a thing in the world but [...] a way of seeing, knowing and understanding the world" (Cresswell 2013: 11).

Place as "seeing, knowing and understanding the world" emerges through three aspects of place identified by political geographer John Agnew, for whom place consists of locale, location and sense of place (1987: 5–6). Agnew's definition of locale aligns with Lippard's, discussed in the previous paragraph. It consists of the social interactions that occur within specific physical environments; that is, the material places where individuals live out their lives and their relationships with others. In the context of crime fiction, locale is the place where the victims and villains, suspects and bystanders, witnesses and detectives live, interact and, of course, die. Place as location responds to the question "where?". It points to a limited geographic place defined by its difference from other places, such as the crime scene in a locked room, the vicar's library, the family home in the suburbs or the mean streets of the inner city. More broadly, location can be expanded to include the entire city itself, a particular region or, as I will discuss later, the nation in the sense of individual crime novels being examples of Australian or Albanian crime fiction. Agnew defines sense of place as "the subjective orientation that can be engendered by living in a place" (5–6). It is this last understanding of place that is most invoked in discussions of place in crime fiction by scholars like Gary Hausladen, for whom sense of place is "essential to creating an authentic locale for the plot of the novel, an authenticity that is absolutely necessary to preserve credibility" (2000: 3).

Place in crime fiction, however, is much more important than Hausladen's more limited sense of place. In crime fiction, place is that which gives the crime and the investigation meaning, especially those tangible and intangible elements that provide some understanding of the society and the culture that, while not explaining the crime, make it possible. To understand place, then, is to make sense of the world. In this sense, the focus given to the creation of a convincing sense of place in individual novels, while important, potentially distracts us from the way in which specific spaces take on meaning to become places. The author of the Father Brown novels, G.K. Chesterton, hinted at the important role of place in the construction of meaning in his 1901 essay, "A Defence of Detective Stories", in which he noted that "there is no stone in the street and no brick in the wall that is not actually a deliberate symbol – a message from some man, as much as it were a telegram or a post-card" (159). If place is space made meaningful, then the task of meaning-making is assigned to the investigator. P.D. James points to this in her reflections on the crime genre, *Talking about Detective Fiction* (2009), in which she argues that "setting, which being integral to the whole novel, should be perceived through the mind of one of the characters, not merely described by the authorial voice, so that place and character interact" (2009: 111). While James does not assign this function specifically to the detective, in crime fiction this figure usually adopts the role of meaning maker. For the reader who seeks an explanation behind the crime, the detective mediates the physical, social and cultural world represented in the text; he or she guides readers, helping them to understand the world in which they live (McCracken 1998: 63). In other words, while "crime fiction texts constantly assure the reader of their mimetic function through continued reference to actual places, dates, people and organizations", the construction of specific places in crime fiction allows "the reader to experience normally inaccessible or forbidden activities" (Porter 1981: 40). That is, fictional crime stories contain an implicit promise to provide readers with knowledge about the particular place represented in the novel itself, to reveal what is hidden from view. It is this revelatory function of the crime novel that has led critics to describe the contemporary genre as an edgy form of tourist literature (Anderson et al. 2012: 1).

In this sense, place is space made legible by the detective. For much crime fiction, the most important place is the crime scene itself. Seemingly mute, crime scenes are places where clues communicate, where the detective makes meaning from the seemingly incomprehensible, where questions find answers. The detective's – and by extension, the crime novel's – meaning-making, however, often ventures beyond the interpretation of clues at any given crime scene. Just as place can incorporate a wide variety of phenomena – "At one extreme a favorite armchair is a place, at the other extreme the whole earth" (Tuan 1977: 149) – so too does crime fiction. Indeed, the crime novel makes any number of places meaningful, including, as David Schmid identifies, locked rooms, manor houses, regions, cities and the entire globe more broadly. In each of these different scales, the representations of place "possess certain features and challenges unique to that type, as well as similarities with other types" (Schmid 2012: 9).

Given the importance of meaning to place and given that meaning is always personal, place is never neutral. Radical geographers like Phillip Howell (1998) point to the political nature of place, in that access to specific places is often policed, leading to exclusions and inclusions, to the creation of groups who don't belong – those who are out of place – and those that belong. Place, then, is experienced differently: It has different meanings for different people, particularly for "characters of different race, ethnicity, and gender, or different social status, wealth, and power" (Hausladen 2000: 184), and to this list I would add characters who identify with the LGBTQI+ community. By way of example, the multiplicity of meanings attributed to place can be illustrated by comparing the ways in which Los Angeles is experienced differently by the protagonists of Raymond Chandler's and Walter Mosley's novels, the white Philip Marlowe and the black Ezekiel "Easy" Rawlins. Whereas Marlowe traverses the city without difficulty, encountering and interacting with people of all social classes and races, Rawlins's movement is hindered by his class and race or, more to the point, by the class and racial prejudices of others, particularly the police. The different experiences the two detectives have of place is performed in the opening scene of Mosley's *Devil in a Blue Dress* (1990), in which he reprises a scene from Chandler's *Farewell, My Lovely* (1940). A white man – Marlowe – enters a black bar, but rather than telling it from Marlowe's perspective, where the blacks are othered, albeit in a non-threatening way, Mosley others the white man, DeWitt Albright, who enters the bar, by narrating the story from Rawlins's perspective. Although Albright continues to occupy a position of power because of the authority invested in his whiteness in 1948 Los Angeles, by othering whiteness, Mosley displaces its centrality to the experience of place, as was typical of much crime fiction of the time.

Crime fiction by women writers also tends to narrate a very different relationship between their female characters and the places they inhabit. In contrast to many male detectives who, like Chandler's Marlowe, move seemingly with ease through the urban mean streets of much crime fiction, the relationship between the city and women is far more complex. In *Estudi en lila* (1985) [*Study in Lilac*, 1987], for example, the Majorcan crime writer Maria-Antònia Oliver draws attention to the dangers the city represents for women. Set in Barcelona, the novel follows an investigation by private-eye Lònia Guiu into the identities and whereabouts of three men who allegedly cheated an antiques dealer, Elena Gaudí. Lònia's investigation reveals that Gaudí had been raped by the three men in the city's symbolic and administrative centre. While the novel highlights that gendered experiences of place are markedly different, it does not just limit itself to representing the risks women experience when they enter public spaces. The novel also represents an attempt to reclaim and wrest back control of urban spaces by women. Lònia, for example, notices the lilac-coloured graffiti appearing on buildings around the city that announce "against rape, castration" (Oliver 1991: 191), a form of justice that Gaudí enacts after Lònia provides her with the identities of the three rapists Lònia had initially believed to be antiques thieves.

The different experience of place – and, hence, the meaning attributed to it – that we see in the Chandler, Mosley and Oliver examples is just one of the ways in which locations are endowed with a multiplicity of meaning by the people who live and operate in a specific place. It is unfortunately beyond the scope of this chapter to provide examples of every sort of meaningful place in crime fiction or the ways in which places take on different meanings for characters of different race, ethnicity, gender, sexuality, class and social status. I do, however, want to focus on one place that becomes central both to reading individual crime narratives and, more broadly, to crime fiction scholarship: The nation.

Place as national allegory

In a 2009 essay titled "Nationality International: Detective Fiction in the Late Twentieth Century", Eva Erdmann claims that contemporary crime fiction has exhausted its narrative possibilities and, as a result, the genre's "main focus is not on the crime itself, but on the setting, the place where the detective and the victims live and to which they are bound by ties of attachment" (2009: 12). Contemporary crime novels, argues Erdmann, "take on the task of describing local cultures and [...] the work of cultural representation", including "the imagological representation of national stereotypes and critical reflection of and upon different milieus and socio-political ideologies, as well as the portrayal of the historical conflicts of individual societies and states" (25). Drawing on a German term that encapsulates the "types of buildings, traditional costumes, customs and values, local dialects" that make up a home locality, Erdmann describes contemporary crime fiction as the new *Heimatroman*, or homeland novel (16). In this place-based reading, individual works of crime fiction take on a national allegorising function irrespective of whether a specific novel articulates national concerns in any substantial way beyond being set in, and depicting, a place – most often, a town or a city – within a specific country.

This national bounding is more often than not attributed to crime fiction produced beyond the British and American tradition, particularly when it comes to postcolonial and other emerging national crime fiction traditions as they become world literature through translation and transnational circulation and reception (cf. Rolls et al. 2016). This division has important implications for how specific texts are read and interpreted. In this process of national allegorising, places – here, nations – create an identity for the texts themselves beyond the nationality of the author or the language in which the text is written. Indeed, in a controversial statement, Erdmann argues that a national crime novel does not have to be written by a national author or in the language of the place where the novel is set; rather, nationality is ascribed to it on the basis of its ability to convey an appropriate national "atmosphere" (2012: 197). As we will see in the following discussion of Teresa Solana's *A Not So Perfect Crime*, the imperative to frame discussion of crime novels exclusively within a national framework can be deeply problematic.

Place

Unstable places in Teresa Solana's *A Not So Perfect Crime* (2008)

Crime novels are not born allegorical, they become so. We can see this in the paratexts to Teresa Solana's *A Not So Perfect Crime*, the covers of which in both the original Catalan and English translation make the connection between the novel and the city of Barcelona through two iconic architectural works that form part of the city's international branding. The Catalan cover includes an image of the mosaic tiles from Antoni Gaudí's Parc Güell, a popular tourist destination which received over ten million visitors a year until the Barcelona Town Council began charging admission. The cover of the English translation by Peter Bush also provides an iconic image of Barcelona: Gaudí's Casa Batlló with its equally mosaiced walls. This connection between crime and place is further reinforced on the front and back covers of the English version through the publisher's description of "Murder and mayhem in Barcelona" and a quote that describes the book as a "hymn to the city of Barcelona". The blurb and quotations on the back cover, moreover, transform this crime novel set in Barcelona into a national allegory, even if there is no agreement on which nation is being allegorised. The publisher's blurb, for example, describes the book as a "satire of Catalan politics", while the quote from the review of the novel on the German literary blog, Krimi-Couch, interprets it as a "scathing satire of Spanish society". Regardless of which nation is represented in the novel, these paratexts serve as a promise to fulfil the readers' desire for knowledge regarding a particular place, in this context, Barcelona – their desire to see things, to find out things hidden behind the city's iconic *modernista* façades.

Yet, Solana's novel resists fulfilling this desire. *A Not So Perfect Crime* is the first of four parodic detective novels which feature twin brother detectives Eduard and Pep Martínez Estivill, although Pep has adopted very pretentious, faux aristocratic names, Borja Masdéu-Canals Sáez de Astorga, to gain the trust of their wealthy clients from Barcelona's northern suburbs. Whereas previous crime fiction from Barcelona, like Manuel Vázquez Montalbán's iconic Carvalho series (discussed by José V. Saval in Chapter 36), featured more typically hardboiled detectives who criss-crossed the city and encountered a wide variety of characters from different social and economic groups which, combined, created a panoramic view of the city and, allegorically, contemporary Spain, Solana uses place differently. While Eduard and Pep/Borja do travel around the city, place is less panoramic and more intimate. Indeed, place is reduced largely to the brothers' office.

Although Solana distances herself from the typical hardboiled representation of place by adopting the isolated crime and well-heeled characters of the classic detective novels of Christie and Sayers, this use of the classic detective formula is not a retreat from reality. Instead, it offers a means of criticising the characteristic concerns and obsessions of postmodern societies obsessed with image. If in the traditional mystery the investigation serves to uncover a hidden reality, this task is complicated in Solana's novel where, from the very beginning, the distinction between surface and substance, fantasy and reality is blurred. This lack of clarity begins with the very detectives themselves who engage in an elaborate ruse in order to win the trust of their clients. A central part of this deceit is their office which, as Eduard describes it, consists of a large, single room in which they have had built into the walls two false doors, replete with brass nameplates that announce their respective titles "director" and "deputy director", despite the twins being the only two employees. The "actual" room they occupy is ostensibly the office of their nonexistent secretary, whose presence is hinted at through a Mac computer that no longer works, an expensive scarf that is carefully draped over the back of a chair, a bottle of Chanel nail polish and, before clients arrive, a subtle spray of a classic French perfume. To explain having to meet their clients in the secretary's office, the brothers invent a story about ongoing renovations that never finish (2008: 14–16). Based on this description, it would be easy to see the twins as little more than upmarket scammers, but their actions differ very little from many of the other characters in the novel – from conservative politicians and artists to Eduard's wife, Montse, the part-owner of a wellness centre and closet smoker – who equally engage in role-play, representation and simulacrum in order to mask their inconsistencies and infidelities.

Geographers warn us "not to conflate the material with the solid, tangible, concrete", so that we understand that place is more than solid structures (Cresswell 2013: 10). Indeed, in Solana's novel, "sense of place" is all there is, as place turns out to be mere mirage, a simulacrum of reality. If the aim of "sense of place", as argued by Hausladen and others, is to provide authenticity, to create a credible representation of the place represented in the novel, then Solana's novel offers us a place that is authentically inauthentic. This has implications for how we read crime fiction because if crime fiction constitutes a new *Heimatroman*, as argued by Erdmann, in which the aim of the investigation is to uncover an ultimate "truth" about a place, then what are we to make of a work in which both reality and homeland represented in the novel are mere artifice? If we read foreign crime fiction to discover something about place, what does it mean when the very meaning that shapes place is so easily manipulated? Solana's novel reveals the inherent instability and the constructed nature of representations of national places and identities. Rather than offering mere alterity associated with the novel's perceived Barcelona-ness, Catalan-ness or Spanish-ness, *A Not So Perfect Crime* undermines the national allegorising imperative attributed to much crime fiction. In so doing, Solana's criticism is targeted not at a specific Barcelonan, Catalan or Spanish condition, but rather at a broader, global, postmodern culture in which surface triumphs over substance and image is more important than reality.

Places of reading

Critics have tended to examine the function of place within specific novels or series of novels, focusing on how places are constructed, whether they contain convincing representations and the ways in which they can inform the very crimes that form the basis of the stories. For Gary Hausladen, the focus on specific places is a way of resisting the homogenising push of globalisation: "in an increasingly integrated world, places are different and unique and that 'sense of place' is about these differences, the inherently unique character of different locations in the world" (2000: 23). This insistence on the "unique character of different locations" reinforces the individuality of specific places and, in so doing, emphasises their otherness. Here, however, I want to draw attention to their connectedness in order to reframe Hausladen's focus on the particularity of place in opposition to globalisation and, instead, re-read place within a global context.

Underlying the approach of scholars like Hausladen, Erdmann and Schmid is an assumption that place is intradiegetic; that is, the place represented within the novel. For example, in his brilliant essay, Schmid analyses the ways in which different crime narratives from Poe to the Mexican authors (and revolutionary), Paco Ignacio Taibo II and the Zapatista National Liberation Army's Subcomandante Marcos, explore social power within the specific frame of place in which the action occurs. As such, Schmid's analysis moves from locked rooms to manor houses to cities in which the detectives operate and, bypassing nations altogether, to the entire planet through the critique of globalised neoliberalism that is articulated in Taibo II and Marcos's novel set in Mexico. While the place represented within a crime narrative is, of course, important, I suggest that place is in fact also experienced extradiegetically, that is outside the text, and that, without ignoring the places within crime novels themselves, when we read place extradiegetically, potential new meanings and new understandings of place emerge. In "The Landscapes of Sherlock Holmes", the geographer Yi-Fu Tuan argues that "People are creators of texts – that is, patterns and systems of meaning – of varying degrees of intensity, transparency, and explicitness" (1985: 60). Following Tuan, I am here interested in the individual reader's experience of the different places represented in different texts from the specific place – a particular town, city, region or nation – where crime novels are read. These extradiegetic places, I argue, are just as important for making meaning, for imbuing place with meaning, as the place represented within the novel itself. Indeed, the place represented in a novel takes on new meanings when read from afar: What is a familiar "detective self" for national readers becomes, for example, a "detective other" for readers of different nationalities.

Whereas traditional scholarship on place in crime fiction assigns the role of meaning-making to the – often local – investigator, it is important to remember that places are connected to other places; that while readers are enticed to enter into the specific place represented in any given crime novel – what Lippard calls the "lure of the local" (1997) – and, in doing so, potentially gaining a deeper understanding of the specific place, readers experience place relationally. That is, our experience of each new crime scene is measured by our experience of other places, including the place in which the reader lives, thus making the experience of reading place a comparative and, when reading novels from outside the country we live, a transnational act. As I have argued elsewhere (King 2019), acknowledging the role that readers play in attributing meaning to places through the very act of reading texts from around the world can lead to the development of a global consciousness that transcends the specific place represented within individual novels.

One such example of this is the growing body of environmental crime fiction, in which place can be read as both localised and cosmopolitan. This localisation occurs intradiegetically through the way in which the crime novel addresses a particular nation's failure to avoid environmental destruction by framing it within a criminal framework, as occurs in Carl Hiaasen's Florida-based crime novels (1994). Cosmopolitan readings, however, can be both intra- and extradiegetic. Finnish author Antti Tuomainen's *Parantaja* (2010) [*The Healer*, 2013] is an example of the former, as the novel uses a concrete place – a dystopic Helsinki set in the not-too-distant future – to reflect on a global catastrophe. In the novel, Helsinki itself is only relevant in that it is the place where we see the planetary consequences of climate change played out. An extradiegetic cosmopolitan reading, however, emerges from reading multiple climate crime fictions set in any number of different places. In such a reading practice, readers recognise that while the consequences of climate change are experienced in specific places, such as Florida in Hiaasen's novels or Helsinki in *The Healer*, individual crime novels can become less about specific places and more about larger, global issues. In a cosmopolitan reading, place becomes the planet, as the reader connects these distinct places – via the reading experience – to the rest of the world.

Scholars and readers alike have often reflected on the popularity of the crime genre, in particular, on why large sections of the world's population are interested in reading about violent depictions of life. The explanations for this fascination range from a desire to escape from the monotony of our lives to, as Heta Pyrhönen argues in Chapter 14, a voyeuristic fantasy to experience what it is to be a criminal. Place is often ignored as a possible reason for our interest in crime fiction and, when readers' interest in place is discussed, it is largely limited to the genre's role as tourist literature. However, geographer and Sherlock Holmes aficionado Yi-Fu Tuan perhaps provides a place-centred explanation for the genre's popularity when he asserts that "[a] fundamental human fear is disorientation, social and geographical" (1985: 58). If the crime novel emerged in response to "the obliteration of the individual's traces in the big-city crowd", as argued by Walter Benjamin (1973: 43), then the investigative process addresses that fear of social and geographical disorientation by making different places meaningful for readers, thus helping us to make sense of the world and our place in it.

Note

1 Unless otherwise specified, all translations are my own.

Bibliography

Agnew, J.A. (1987) *Place and Politics: The geographical mediation of state and society*, Boston: Allen & Unwin.

Anderson, J., Miranda, C. and Pezzotti, B. (eds) (2012) *The Foreign in International Crime Fiction: Transcultural representations*, London: Continuum.

Benjamin, W. (1973) *Charles Baudelaire: A lyric poet in the era of high capitalism*, trans. H. Zohn, London: NLB.

Chandler, R. (1995) [1940] *Farewell, My Lovely*, in R. Chandler (ed.), *Stories and Early Novels*, New York: Library of America, 765–984.

Chesterton, G.K. (1901) *The Defendant*, London: J.M. Dent.

Cresswell, T. *Place: A short introduction*, John Wiley, 2013.

Erdmann, E. (2009) "Nationality international: detective fiction in the late twentieth century", in M. Krajenbrink and K.M. Quinn (eds), *Investigating Identities: Questions of identity in contemporary international crime fiction*, Amsterdam: Rodopi, 11–26.

Geherin, D. (2008) *Scene of the Crime: The importance of place in crime and mystery fiction*, Jefferson, NC: McFarland.

Hausladen, G. (2000) *Places for Dead Bodies*, Austin: University of Texas Press.

Hiaasen, C. (1994) *The Carl Hiaasen Omnibus: Tourist Season; Double Whammy; Skin Tight*, London: Picador.

Howell, P. (1998) "Crime and the city solution: Crime fiction, urban knowledge, and radical geography", *Antipode*, 30(4): 357–78.

James, P.D. (2009) *Talking about Detective Fiction*, London: Faber & Faber.

King, S. (2019) "The private eye of the beholder: reading world crime fiction", in J. Gulddal, S. King and A. Rolls (eds.), *Criminal Moves: Modes of mobility in crime fiction*, Liverpool: Liverpool University Press, 195–210.

Lippard, L.R. (1997) *The Lure of the Local: Senses of place in a multicentered society*, New York: The New Press.

McCracken, S. (1998) *Pulp: Reading popular fiction*, Manchester: Manchester University Press.

Mosley, W. (1992) [1990] *Devil in a Blue Dress*, London: Pan.

Oliver, M.-A. (1991) [1985] *Estudi en lila*, Barcelona: La Magrana.

Pezzotti, B. (2012) *The Importance of Place in Contemporary Italian Crime Fiction: A bloody journey*, Madison: Fairleigh Dickinson University Press.

Porter, D. (1981) *The Pursuit of Crime: Art and ideology in detective fiction*, New Haven, CT: Yale University Press.

Resina, J.R. (1997) *El cadáver en la cocina. La novela criminal en la cultura del desencanto*, Barcelona: Anthropos.

Rolls, A., Vuaille-Barcan, M.-L. and West-Sooby, J. (eds) (2016) "Translating national allegories: the case of crime fiction", Special issue of *The Translator*, 22(2): 135–43.

Schmid, D. (2012) "From the locked room to the globe: space in crime fiction", in V. Miller and H. Oakley (eds), *Cross-Cultural Connections in Crime Fiction*, Houndmills: Palgrave Macmillan, 7–23.

Solana, T. (2008) *A Not So Perfect Crime*, trans. P. Bush, London: Bitter Lemon.

Tuan, Y.-F. (1977) *Place and Space: The perspective of experience*, Minneapolis: University of Minnesota Press.

———. (1985) "The landscapes of Sherlock Holmes", *Journal of Geography*, 84(2): 56–60.

Tuomainen, A. (2013) *The Healer*, trans. L. Rogers, London: Vintage.

24

TIME AND SPACE

Thomas Heise

Detective fiction is a literature animated by dead bodies. From the locked rooms and train cars of Golden Age mysteries to the back alleys and mean streets of hardboiled fiction, dead bodies litter the genre. If the corpse is seemingly a necessity to this literature, we nevertheless are confronted with the question of what the corpse means. For the detective, the initial questions are invariably the hows and whys of a particular murder, yet these quickly deepen, I want to suggest, into more fundamental and categorical questions pertaining to the very nature of time and space in the genre. This is true because the corpse signifies for the detective a past that has to be recovered and reconstructed and a spatial disruption that has to be contextualised and explained. The corpse's shocking presence breaks the seamless flow of time and throws into relief the world around it. Making sense of and correcting these disruptions is a narrative process. Put starkly, the detective narrative is predicated on death: It is founded upon it (a spatial metaphor) and grammatically launched into being because of it (a temporal one). The dead almost always surface at the beginning of these novels, Gill Plain observes, "as a 'tabula rasa' upon which the script of detection will be written" (2001: 31). By functioning as "instigators of narrative causality", deaths in detective fiction fuel the need for narration in the first instance (Plain 2001: 31).

What I suggest here is not unique to detective fiction, and yet it is in detective fiction that this narrative process is formally dramatised in the most existential ways imaginable. In *Reading for the Plot*, Peter Brooks declares that "[i]t is my simple conviction, then, that narrative has something to do with time-boundedness, and that plot is the internal logic of the discourse of mortality" (1984: 22). Brooks's conviction derives from the "simple", but unavoidable textual and ontological fact that all narratives and all lives must come to an end. The retrospective narration of a life begins, he implies, with an awareness of the end that has awaited it from the start. "For plot starts [...] from that moment at which story, or 'life'" is triggered by this knowledge into "a state of narratability, into a tension, a kind of irritation" to discover, as he phrases it, "what has already happened" (103, 25). While Brooks's study is of canonical literature, the detective genre nevertheless serves in his analysis as a kind of master plot, "the narrative of narratives" that lays bare the structures and interpretive work by which plotting reconstructs the past and in doing so "offers the pleasurable possibilities (or illusion) of 'meaning' wrest from 'life'" (108). Kneeling to inspect the corpse, the detective wonders "who was this person?", "where did he (or she) come from?" and "why was he murdered?". For Brooks, the detective is an allegory for the reader and the literary sleuth searching for clues, "reconstruct[ing] intentions and connections", following a digression in hopes that it leads somewhere, and doubling back to earlier scenes to interrogate them once more (5). Brooks's point is that in any narrative, detective or otherwise, the end is in the beginning, because from the start, death is waiting for the narrative to finally reach it so that the sentence might be closed, the meaning of the book of life revealed when it comes to a full stop.

If the work of the detective is to sew the strands of time together again and unveil the intricacy of its knots in the "big reveal" we so often find in the genre's deathbed scenes, gunpoint confessions or post-investigation summaries, the purpose is to try to restore wholeness and order before time and space were thrown out of whack. "The detective", Dennis Porter observes in *The Pursuit of Crime* (1981), "encounters effects without apparent causes, events in a jumbled chronological order, significant clues hidden among the insignificant. And his role is to reestablish sequence and causality" (1981: 30). We see as much in the final pages of Raymond Chandler's *The Big Sleep* (1939) where Philip Marlowe confronts Vivian Sternwood about her murderous plot:

> [I]f I seem to talk in circles, it just seems that way. It all ties together – everything. Geiger and his cute little blackmail tricks, Brody and his pictures, Eddie Mars and his roulette tables, Canino and the girl Rusty Regan didn't run away with. It all ties together.
>
> *(1992: 223)*

Concluding moments like this one, where the detective "ties together" loose strands of the text with a binding thread of interpretation, are a staple of the genre.

To reach its conclusion, the genre is committed "to an act of recovery, moving forward in order to move back", as Porter contends (1981: 29), or moving "in circles", as Chandler states (1992: 223). All of this, of course, takes time, time rendered in narrative form. The ambulatory plots of gumshoe fiction are admittedly convoluted and confusing. After Marlowe walks Vivian through her guilt, she mutters "in a dead, exhausted voice, 'God, how you tire me!'", a sentiment many readers share (1992: 224). What does it mean that detective fiction moves in this repetitive and roundabout fashion? Why all of these red herrings, detours, double-crossings, mistaken identities, false confessions and investigative dead-ends that make up the middle of these texts? Brooks argues that their purpose is to stretch out time so as to engender the pleasures of suspense, "the play of desire in time that makes us turn pages", even while forestalling the inevitable conclusion (1984: xiii). Porter concurs, remarking, "the appeal of the detective story on the level of the anecdote is not in the end but in the process, in what it does to us as we read it rather than in the nature of the secret it withholds for the denouement" (1981: 110).

There is, however, an edificatory function to this process. From the reader's perspective, the detective narrative is not just a pleasure; it is also a kind of work. Nevertheless, there is pleasure to be found in its work, pleasure in the process of "figuring it out", pleasure in the knowledge accumulated along the way as the clues and leads of the investigation, which is always a narrative-in-the-making, are formed into a working hypothesis, an interpretation, a theory. Here time and space come together or, we might say, are mutually constituting, emerging simultaneously in the big bang that both precedes the detective narrative and brings its mysterious universe into being. The temporal process of plotting is irreducibly spatial, a fact underscored by the geographical resonances of the word "plot" itself. This begs the question, what is the space of the detective novel? To answer this question, it helps to step back and focus on the category of space more generally. Henri Lefebvre theorises that space has long proven to be a resistant subject of analysis because of two misleading suppositions: "the illusion of transparency" and "the realistic illusion" (1991: 27, 29). The former conceptualises space "as luminous", "as giving action free rein", as little more than the ether we pass through, while the latter understands it as "natural", as a container of objects, as little more than a category to be empirically described and measured (Lefebvre 1991: 27, 29). Lefebvre works to demystify these illusions by arguing that space needs to be decoded in order to uncover the "*truth of space*" (1991: 9, emphasis in original). Similarly, geographer Edward Soja enjoins us to "see beyond" the "immediate surface appearances" of space to discern how those appearances are constituted (1989: 122). For Lefebvre the "*truth of space*" begins with the recognition that space is a social product, a "materialization of 'social being'" (1991: 102). It is fungible, formed and reformed by social relations that are in turn shaped and reshaped by space itself. Manuel Castells captures this dialectical nature when arguing, "Space is not a 'reflection of society,' it *is* society. [...] [and is] produced, as all other objects are, by human action" (1983: 4). It follows from this, Soja argues, that

> We must be insistently aware of how space can be made to hide consequences from us, how relations of power and discipline are inscribed into the apparently innocent spatiality of social life, how human geographies become filled with politics and ideology.
> *(1989: 6)*

The detective *reads* space and the reader of detective fiction *reads* this reading. Attempting to "see beyond" the "immediate surface appearances" of the setting, the detective searches for signs, clues and motivations (Lefebvre 1991: 122). What the iterations of the genre – Golden Age mysteries, hardboiled novels and police procedurals – all share is a "hermeneutics of suspicion", which is to say an adamant refusal to take anything at face value and a commitment to exposing "the lies and illusions of consciousness" (Ricoeur 1970: 356). The time-consuming circumambulations of the detective novel's plot should be understood as a spatial operation to gather evidence. Evidence of what?, we might ask. For the detective the obvious answer is the evidence of the triggering crime, the fatal mystery that launches the plot. But I want to suggest that the evidence amounts to something larger, an interrogation of the social itself – its structures, ideologies and human and spatial relations – of which crime is only a symptom.

Mapping detective fiction

It makes sense that a genre of social and spatial investigations would also be a genre in love with maps and map-making. The pulp mysteries published by Dell in the 1940s and 1950s, for instance, showcase on their back covers scene-of-the-crime maps of isolated estates, apartment buildings, hotels, individual bedrooms and city streets (O'Brien 1981: 51–3). Accompanied by Dell's trademark of a keyhole icon through which peers an eye, these maps offer the fantasy of both a disembodied, totalising surveillance of buildings, landscapes and entire cities, and a voyeuristic one-point perspective that peeks into singularly lurid events unfolding behind closed doors. The idea of control through surveillance is operative here, but so too is the idea that the genre finds pleasure – one is tempted to say guilty pleasure – in the act of watching and then disciplining social and legal transgressions. Maps are, of course, not neutral instruments. At least since the early modern period, their historical function has been to render abstract and rationalist representations of space for imperialist expansion, the creation of territorial boundaries and the implementation of social, political and economic order (Jarvis 1998: 52). In the context of detective fiction, their function is inseparable from the policing of space as a means of asserting the rule of law in an exercise of state power. The practice of including maps as visual supplements to narratives of detection has faded but has not entirely vanished.

In Gabriel Cohen's police procedural *Red Hook* (2001), for instance, the narrative is prefaced with a map of the titular industrial waterfront neighbourhood of Brooklyn, its name bolded over others in the borough, seemingly to imply that it is an unexplored territory, a place yet to be brought under control. While Cohen's map suggests this, it also provides the reassurance that one can at least see this rough-and-tumble neighbourhood as safely rendered as flat and two-dimensional before one enters its harder to navigate textual thicket of corruption, blackmail and murder. The crime books in Akashic series of anthologies – from *Amsterdam Noir* (2019) to *Zagreb Noir* (2015) – also include maps with the notable design feature of chalk outlines of dead bodies pinned beneath the names of various neighbourhoods corresponding to plot points in the stories. With all other symbols for landforms, historical sites and infrastructure removed from the data frame, Akashic's maps reduce geographical space to a single thing: A container for death that grimly transforms it into an urban graveyard. The irony is that despite the abstract rendering of space, every chalk outline signifies and yet conceals a story about the struggle over the meaning of lived spaces in the city. "[T]here can be no geographical knowledge without historical narrative", Jarvis contends, a truth that detective fiction bears out (1998: 7).

While the distinctions between genteel mysteries and hardboiled fiction are overdrawn, their different conceptualisations of space are noteworthy. In *Murder for Pleasure* (1941), Howard Haycraft proscribed "the rules of the game" for the puzzle-oriented mysteries of Arthur Conan Doyle, Dorothy Sayers and Agatha Christie. Paramount was the requirement that the author set aside any "social and political prejudices" and concentrate instead on the "absolute logicality" of the crime and its solution (254, 258). "Each important plot incident, every structural step of the story, must be", he insisted, "the perfect and logical consequence and result of this central conflict of crime and pursuit" (258). For Haycraft, the genre was purely formal and geometrical. Solving crimes was a process of deduction that entailed a mental mapping of a delimited or sealed-off space, the proverbial locked room. The purpose of crime was, in effect, to create a space for thinking. In his own "Twenty Rules", S.S. Van Dine stressed that "the culprit must be a decidedly worth-while person – one that wouldn't normally come under suspicion" (1992: 191). In other words, the suspect shouldn't be a butler, maid or gardener. Members of the working class, Van Dine implied, were inherently untrustworthy. To make one of them the culprit would spoil the mystery. In such novels, a narrow slice of geography corresponds to a narrow slice of the social fabric. The moral fantasy of these texts is that human actions have a rational explanation, which the detective merely has to uncover, and that guilt is never social or political. Yet, such a fantasy requires a great deal of bad faith. Though "the culprit must be a decidedly worth-while person", one cannot help concluding, perhaps to Van Dine's dismay, that the rich are a murderous lot indeed.

Haycraft's and Van Dine's dictums rule out politics by insisting that space itself is, in essence, innocent. Hardboiled detective fiction, in contrast, underscores the fundamentally political nature of space by unveiling how it both constitutes and expresses relations of power, and how it is always heterogenous and fluid, containing plural networks by which information, capital, material objects, as well as social meanings, are exchanged, appropriated and fought over. Noting this distinction, Fredric Jameson argues hardboiled novels "are first and foremost descriptions of searches", adding "The immediate result of this formal change is that the detective no longer inhabits the atmosphere of pure thought" (2016: 24). Rather than a stationary eye peering through a keyhole, hardboiled novels deploy a roving eye – usually embodied in a first-person narrational perspective – looking into myriad public and private social spaces. Beyond the locked room, the P.I. is "[p]ropelled outwards into the space of his world and obliged to move from one kind of social reality to another" (Jameson 2016: 24). When the Continental Op in

Dashiell Hammett's genre-setting *Red Harvest* (1929) arrives in Personville, he immediately heads "out to look at the city", a polluted town seized by gangs comprised of the strikebreakers that the ruthless Elihu Willsson hired to bust the union at his mines (1992: 3). As the Op snakes his way through the city's "pool rooms, cigar stores, speakeasies, soft drink joints, and [...] street corners", he infiltrates the criminal underworld to set its factions against each other (1992: 70). By the end of Hammett's narrative, every space in Personville is revealed to house some form of nefarious activity.

An inspection of nearly any detective novel will yield examples of where the social life of crime is narratively mapped. In *The Big Sleep*, Chandler's detective charts Los Angeles with a degree of detail that at first may appear superfluous. Readers watch Marlowe drive "across Vine and all the way to Western", then on to "Brittany Place" where it meets "Randall Place" (1992: 53, 54). They learn that Carmen Sternwood's address is "3765 Alta Brea Crescent, West Hollywood" and are informed that Geiger's operation is "on the north side of the boulevard near Las Palmas" (33, 22). Perhaps the most extreme example of this narrative feature is found in Paul Auster's postmodern detective novel *City of Glass* (1985). A two-page walk by the accidental detective Quinn is a block-by-block tour of Manhattan: "taking a westward turn [...] he reached Seventh Avenue [...]. At Sheridan Square he turned east again, ambling down Waverly Place, crossing Sixth Avenue, and continuing on to Washington Square [...]. At 32nd Street he turned right" and so on (1990: 127, 128). Topographical referents – names of cities, neighbourhoods, parks, streets, addresses given with cartographic precision – produce an imagined geography, a reality effect creating the impression of a real story. Yet, such apparent empiricism should be greeted sceptically, given the complex signifying processes of language and the allegorical nature of literature. More than this, the detective genre itself promises not just to describe space, but, as we will see, to peer beneath its surface representations to offer an interpretation of space that lays bare its deeper mysteries.

Plotting a vaster crime

Mapping in the detective genre is a methodological procedure for decoding the underlying "truth" of space. To understand this, it is helpful to turn to Jameson's concept of the cognitive map, a pedagogical function that literature can provide through a totalising image of the affect and structure of our phenomenally complex social reality. Such cognitive maps, Jameson posits, "seek to endow the individual subject with some new heightened sense of its place in the global system" (1991: 54). The circumambulations of the detective plot – literalised in the walking and driving scenes in these novels – can be understood as an effort to accumulate data so as to construct geographical and historical knowledge of the social relations and processes animating surface realities. In the genre, this procedure begins with an investigation into a localised crime, then expands to unveil and indict an entire social system. Marlowe's pursuits along the winding canyon roads of California, for example, take him from the decadence of Sternwood's mansion to the oil fields of LA, from the particle-board house concealing Geiger's pornography racket to the squalor of the Fulwider Building, and finally past Pasadena to the gangster Eddie Mars's hideout on the urban perimeter. These "remote and inaccessible" social spaces in the sprawling city are "all tie[d] together" by a narrative of systemic corruption whose immediate point of origin is the capitalist exploitation of a place (1992: 40, 223). The siphoning of wealth out of the soil, which fuels the chauffeured-lifestyle of the Sternwoods as well as the automobile driven by the middle-class detective, materialises a corrosiveness that stains everyone it touches, including Marlowe himself who in the end, after sheltering his client, realises he too is "part of the nastiness" (230). *The Big Sleep* ends up being a novel not only about murder, but also about complicity.

Circling back to Auster's narration, we must note that its flat, affectless style appears on the surface to scrub clean the bustling and diverse social spaces of Manhattan. It turns out mapping is a prerequisite for the discovery of a social reality that Quinn, isolated in solitude and depression, has failed to notice. At the beginning of *City of Glass*, we are told that during his daily strolls he is perennially "[l]ost [...] within himself" and "it no longer mattered where he was" because "all places became equal" (1990: 4). For Quinn, New York, all evidence to the contrary, is not a place, but a utopia of one, a "nowhere he had built around himself" (4). His social myopia to the world around him structures his individually focalised perspective that enables him to carry the private sphere out into the public. In effect, he transforms the heterogenous social spaces of the city into the pure mental space of the locked-room mysteries. Yet Quinn's hermeticism eventually cracks. On one long walk through Manhattan, he feels an "urge to record certain facts" and when he writes them down, suddenly the urban poor, as a symbol and lived reality of the injustice that is ubiquitous, yet invisible, in New York City, surfaces. In the blink of an eye the novel is populated with "the down-and-outs, the shopping bag ladies, the drifters and drunks" (129). "[T]hey seem to be everywhere the moment you look for them", Quinn says, adding, "Some will starve to death, others will die of exposure, still others will be beaten or burned or tortured" (130). When reaching this moment, readers likely feel they have been duped by Auster, that he has lured them into a plot about the protection of Peter Stillman Jr from his murderous father, only to be given a story about the larger social crime of homelessness in New York. But this act of bait-and-switch is the novel's very point. Quinn's denial of the injustices around him is not only what makes possible the privatisation of his consciousness but is also what makes possible the public neglect and hyper-privatisation of the social sphere that turns the streets of 1980s New York in Auster's novel into the home of the poor. In other words, "all places" are not "equal" (4).

Henry Chang's Chinatown

Two of the most significant and interrelated developments in detective fiction over the past two decades are its growing diversity and global orientation. Increasingly, the genre has been taken up by authors writing from intersecting positions of ethnic, racial, gender and sexual difference who have interrogated the form itself to expose its history of prejudicial representations and redeployed its possibilities in the service of a social critique of global systems of power. Concurrently, the genre has proliferated internationally, as Andrew Pepper and David Schmid show, moving beyond its foundational centres in the US, the UK and France to include work written in Mexico, Brazil, South Korea, South Africa, Australia and other nations and regions (2016: 1–2). While its newly expanded geographical sweep establishes crime fiction as "a truly global literature", Pepper and Schmid argue it is more so the genre's effort to think critically about "the processes of globalization" and the "growing transnationalization of crime and policing networks" that holds the most promise of extending the genre's "formal and thematic boundaries" (2016: 1, 2, 8).

The "Detective Jack Yu" series by the Chinese-American writer Henry Chang exemplifies these two trends. Beginning with *Chinatown Beat* (2006), Chang has mapped Manhattan's Chinatown across expanding spatial scales from the neighbourhood to the city to the nation and ultimately to the globe. One of the most pernicious images of Chinese communities is their supposed insularity, a stereotype that has been used to justify a history of exclusionary practices founded upon the idea that Chinese immigrants and their descendants are inassimilable to the larger skein of American life. Chang exposes such mystifications as partially rooted in social distance. From the outside Chinatown may signify as an undifferentiated Chinese mass that is cognitively unmappable. For the white NYPD officers in Chang's novel, who tellingly live in the suburbs, "Chinatown was like a foreign port [...], full of experiences confounding to the average Caucasian mind" (2006: 8). This totalising Sinophobic description is soon dispelled by Jack's insider view which reveals to readers a neighbourhood of multiple dialects and languages, multiple Chinese ethnicities, and multiple rival tongs with differing class alliances and regional origins whose neighbourhood turf wars are fundamentally battles over the construction of ethnic identity in and through place. "We own the streets", one crime boss states, exclaiming "Chinatown is our life" (2006: 169). Thus, the demystification work that Chang's novels perform is a spatial and temporal operation, which takes shape in plots in which internal feuding between tongs emerges out of efforts to hold on to and expand territory. These feuds are, in turn, tied to human trafficking, the global drug trade and transnational flows of money and credit, all of which are filtered through the perspective of Jack, whose vexed emotions about his own past in a rapidly changing Chinatown imbricates the novels with layers of history and memory. Chang's Chinatown is an increasingly globalised space, its borders porous.

Early in a chapter titled "The City", Jack patrols Manhattan in its entirety, sketching a land-scape of ethnic poverty and crime that serves as the setting for the next several books. Starting at "the corner of Mott and Bayard" in Chinatown, "[h]e rolled through the extended com-munities of Fukienese, Malaysians, Chiu Chaos, settlements stretching east to Essex and north to Delancey, into areas longtime Hassidic, Puerto Rican", driving on to the northern neigh-bourhood of "Morningside Heights and the enclave of Dominicans", "a drug-dealing hub that connected New York, Connecticut, New Jersey", before stopping to stare at "the city spread out before him" (2006: 14–16). Here Chinatown is no isolated preserve, but part of a "patch-work quilt of different communities of people coexisting, sometimes with great difficulty", each thread signifying for Chang a different pattern of immigration (16). And New York City itself is situated as a node in a regional economy, where inner-city communities service a suburban demand for illicit drugs. After mapping Manhattan in this manner, Chang's novel returns to Chinatown to investigate its "Chinese puzzle" (209). The puzzle is solved, or at least clarified, by understanding Chinatown through the lenses of urban and global political economy.

No crime novel's map of the wider social totality is ever complete, or, ever completely free from biases built into the genre itself. Yet the way this literature narratively stitches together what at first appears as a fragmented reality provides evidence of deeper connections. Take for instance when Mona in *Chinatown Beat* stands on the balcony of her apartment building with its rooftop billboard advertising "Luxury Condominiums" for sale and surveys Chinatown's "ghetto detritus" (2006: 19). In this moment, the text asks us to contemplate capitalist spatial contradictions and witness in condensed shape the polarised but contiguous geographies of the contemporary city. Later in *Year of the Dog* (2008), Chang takes readers to "the tallest building in the area", a "sixteen-story mirrored glass office" tower that is anchored by a "Citibank branch and a tourist-trade gift shop" and is home to the "On Yee Merchants Consortium" on the third floor (2008: 70). Concretised in one architectural image is Chinatown's position and role within the global economy. An older closed economy governed by ethnic traditionalism shares space with the marketing and commodification of Chinese culture as cheap consumer goods to outsiders, which shares space with a multinational financial entity through which foreign and local capital passes into and out of the neighbourhood. Even the mysterious triads that fight over turf in the neighbourhood are eventually demystified. Their "Fu Manchu bullshit", Chang reveals in *Year of the Dog*, is a cover for black-market global corporations dealing in illicit commodities – not only drugs, but "video camcorders, digital cameras, Walkmen and laptop computers" through a "network of merchants" "in Europe, and in Central and South America. More recently [...] North America" (2008: 74, 123). "And every time business was transacted", he notes in *Chinatown Beat*, "there were the lawyers, the brokers, the city officials, the bank regulators" (2006: 30).

In Chang's novels, the spaces of Chinatown are saturated with the residue of time. As Jack's investigations lead him on a windy path through Chinatown's secrets, they take him back to the past. His Chinatown is a place of dead bodies, but also metaphorical ghosts. The latter assumes the form of haunting memories of a childhood friend's death by local gangsters and the form of words from Jack's freshly buried father: "*Remember where you came from*" (2006: 83, emphasis in original). While wishing to escape his old neighbourhood, he is continually pulled "back to unfinished business" (2010: 1). For Jack, the conflict over space manifests his internal divisions between competing demands for assimilation and cultural purity and his desire for a future free from his father's shadow. In one telling scene, Jack, watching freighters loaded with goods moving through New York's harbour, describes his life as comprised of "mostly portable, transient, disposable items", a "life in flux" (2006: 60).

In the final analysis, such spatial and temporal conflicts are structural, as much as personal. While detective fiction may not provide a solution to these structural "crimes", what the genre shows is that the struggle over time and space is a struggle over the very meaning of life and death.

Bibliography

Auster, P. (1990) *City of Glass*, New York: Penguin.
Brooks, P. (1984) *Reading for the Plot: Design and intention in narrative*, Cambridge: Harvard University Press.
Castells, M. (1983) *The City and the Grass Roots*, Berkeley: University of California Press.
Chandler, R. (1992) *The Big Sleep*, New York: Vintage Crime.
Chang, H. (2006) *Chinatown Beat*, New York: Soho Press.
———. (2008) *Year of the Dog*, New York: Soho Press.
———. (2010) *Red Jade*, New York: Soho Press.
Hammett, D. (1992) *Red Harvest*, New York: Vintage Crime.
Haycraft, H. (1941) *Murder for Pleasure: The life and times of the detective story*, New York: D. Appleton-Century.
Jameson, F. (1991) *Postmodernism, or the Cultural Logic of Late Capitalism*, Durham: Duke University Press.
———. (2016) *Raymond Chandler: The detections of totality*, London: Verso.
Jarvis, B. (1998) *Postmodern Cartographies: The geographical imagination in contemporary American culture*, New York: St. Martin's Press.
Lefebvre, H. (1991) *The Production of Space*, trans. D. Nicholson-Smith, Oxford: Blackwell.
O'Brien, G. (1981) *Hardboiled America*, New York: Van Nostrand Reinhold Company.
Pepper, A. and Schmid, D. (2016) "Introduction", in A. Pepper and D. Schmid (eds), *Globalization and the State in Contemporary Crime Fiction*, London: Palgrave, 1–19.
Plain, G. (2001) *Twentieth-Century Crime Fiction: Gender, sexuality and the body*, Edinburgh: Edinburgh University Press.
Porter, D. (1981) *The Pursuit of Crime: Art and ideology in detective fiction*, New Haven: Yale University Press.
Ricoeur, P. (1970) *Freud and Philosophy: An essay on interpretation*, trans. D. Savage, New Haven: Yale University Press.
Soja, E. (1989) *Postmodern Geographies: The reassertion of space in critical social theory*, London: Verso.
Van Dine, S.S. (1992) "Twenty rules for writing detective stories", in H. Haycraft (ed.), *The Art of the Mystery Story: A collection of critical essays*, New York: Carroll & Graf, 189–93.

25

SELF-REFERENTIALITY AND METAFICTION

J.C. Bernthal

Sherlock Holmes is not an admirer of detective fiction, dismissing, in his 1887 debut, Edgar Allen Poe's Dupin as "a very inferior fellow" and Émile Gaboriau's Lecoq as "a miserable bungler" (Doyle 2001: 22, 23). As readers learn in *The Clocks* (1963), Hercule Poirot has written a monograph about fictional detectives, expressing his utter disdain for the works of Arthur Conan Doyle. In Henning Mankell's *Kennedy's Brain* (2005), Kurt Wallander deduces that a government official could not possibly understand police work because they enjoy Agatha Christie's novels. As long as crime fiction has been a literary genre, its practitioners have sought to establish their place in its canon via characters claiming that their literary predecessors bear no relation to the reality of detection. As such, they establish their own version of reality where they are superior, and therefore exist in a self-consciously artificial relationship with the world beyond the book.

There is a long-running tendency within crime writing to acknowledge, either obliquely or directly, its own fictional status, and metatextual play is common in both bestselling and "literary" or experimental examples of the genre. This could well stem from the genre's origins in journalism – *The Newgate Calendar* (1795–1866) blended accounts of real and imagined crimes without distinguishing between them, and Poe famously refused to clarify whether his early short stories were works of fiction or memoir.

Crime fiction is, after all, a form of writing in which fundamental questions are raised; where concepts of guilt and innocence are explored, and where certainties – solutions – are provided, interrogated, or at least anticipated. The frequency with which crime fiction refers to either the genre or its own fictional status – thus simultaneously concocting a fictional world and presenting it *as* fiction – inevitably raises issues around what is "real", what is "fictional", and what this means for the broader narratives that structure life and/or literature, as well as those themes – guilt and innocence, right and wrong – that are crime fiction's domain. The aim of this chapter is to outline critical theories and debates surrounding self-referentiality and metafiction in crime fiction, and to speculate briefly on the future of the field as scholars pay increasing attention to diversity within the crime novel.

And/or?

Self-referentiality – when a creative work refers to itself or highlights the process behind its creation – is a literary device going back to mythological texts. The persistence of this practice reminds us that self-reference is a fundamental part of what makes us human; the ability to think in terms of the "I", with all the connotations of self and relationship that that letter has, is a cornerstone of language and distinguishes us, as social creatures, from other animals. Self-reference and self-understanding are also tools for processing and applying new knowledge – something that can both broaden and limit horizons.

Metafiction – a closely related but not identical term – was coined by William H. Gass in 1970. Positing metafiction as the literary equivalent to a metatheorem in mathematics, Gass distinguished it from "drearily predictable" self-referentiality (novels about writers, for example), highlighting works "in which the forms of fiction serve as the material upon which further forms can be imposed" as examples (2018: 655). Metafiction, then, does not simply acknowledge its own artificiality but constantly reminds the reader of its status, and highlights the mechanics of creative writing by mixing, overwriting or combining in unexpected ways elements of competing literary traditions. Coining the term, Gass contributed to a very contemporary artistic and critical movement of the second half of the twentieth century, which also saw the rise of postmodernism. This was a time of widespread interest in self-reflexivity, with artistic and theoretical forms reflecting hostility to the idea that any narrative – religious, political or literary – could command true authority.

Naturally, some critics and theorists applied these ideas to crime fiction, with its (traditional or perceived) central conceit of uncovering and explaining the truth around a disruptive event. Tzvetan Todorov, reading crime fiction from a structuralist perspective, maintained that each such narrative contains two stories: The story of the crime and that of the investigation (1977: 50). The postmodernist Linda Hutcheon developed this to claim that in reading a mystery novel, the reader is automatically engaged in an act of interpretative scholarship, arguing that the genre's "appeal to metafictionists" is inevitable (1980: 73). Mystery fiction is, after all, a genre that, even when it does not advertise its own unreality, is predicated on a gamble between the author and the reader as to the solvability or otherwise of a puzzle. When such a text is additionally self-referential, Hutcheon argues, the act of reading becomes itself creative (151).

A Golden Age monopoly?

Arguably, the most noticeably self-referential branch of crime fiction is so-called Golden Age detective fiction, which can be roughly characterised as puzzle-based mystery fiction produced in the 1920s and 1930s, mostly in Britain. Such texts are rarely without some reference to Sherlock Holmes or detective fiction more generally. In the works of Agatha Christie, Dorothy L. Sayers and others, phrases along the lines of, "If this were a detective story [...]" frequently pre-empt the next plot twist, and the central character will be compared, favourably or otherwise, with established fictional sleuths. With the Golden Age enjoying increased critical attention in recent years, self-referentiality has been the topic of much discussion.

A string of influential critics of the twentieth-century crime novel have noted and upheld a distinction between self-referentiality in "crime fiction" and metafiction in "literary fiction". Lee Horsley draws a line between Golden Age authors' "light-hearted reminders that they are producing a work of fiction", taking the frequency of such references within the genre as proof that these books were written to be read quickly, by people who had read enough detective fiction already to understand the formulae and appreciate each book more as a part of the phenomenon than as an entirely unique text (2005: 13), and a more ambitious narrative

Self-referentiality and metafiction

"that seeks to destabilize our sense of the outside world" (12). However, Horsley also argues that the self-referential nature of some crime fiction lends it power, as the frequent references to fiction invite readers to consider puzzle-based narratives as invitations to "acts of *rereading*" (13, emphasis in original). Not only are clues continually "reread" in light of new knowledge or interpretative frameworks, but reminders of the books' fictional status also encourage readers to judge what they are reading in the context of other novels and stories they have read – and also to consider those other texts anew.

Nonetheless, as scholarship on crime fiction has grown and diversified, elements of critical vocabulary previously denied to genre fiction have been brought to bear. Joanna Stolarek, for example, has argued that the concept of metafiction in genre fiction allows Todorov's famous distinction between the mystery and the thriller to be superseded – when the author's presence is artificially foregrounded, it is narrative itself that is under investigation (2009: 36–37). Cameron McCabe, a pseudonym for German sexologist Ernst Bornemann writing in English, concluded his murder mystery, *The Face on the Cutting-Room Floor* (1937), with a lengthy series of criticisms of his own narrative style, raising questions in the guise of literary criticism as to whether McCabe was the name of the detective, the victim, the criminal or the narrator, and revealing only that it was a pseudonym. The novel was described by one contemporary writer/critic as "the detective story to end all detective stories", and has since been considered as an early example of postmodern metafiction, rooted in genre (Coe 2016: viii-ix).

When readers turning to a famously escapist genre – especially in the uncertain interwar years – encountered frequent references to the fictional status of what they were reading, they might well have been forced to acknowledge the act of escapism itself and its relationship to real life. This is evident when detective novelists with celebrity status created alter egos to appear in the text. Dorothy L. Sayers had Harriet Vane, a crime writer who frequently told her partner – and therefore the readers – that she would prefer to be writing important, socially engaged fiction, thereby drawing attention to the genre's perceived shortcomings. Agatha Christie had an exuberant self-portrait, Ariadne Oliver, who bamboozled through cases complaining that the real murders she was investigating were too messy and not as neatly organised as those in her books, before messily arriving at the correct solution every time. In Sweden, Maria Lang invented Almi Graan, an anagram of Maria Lang, which was itself a pseudonym, as an unglamorous antithesis to her own detective heroes, injecting notes of realism at the most dramatic and exuberant moments. In Golden Age crime fiction, then, there was a vogue for authors acknowledging their own presence in the investigations of fictional crime. On the one hand, this extends the playful artifice, reminding readers that they are participating in a work of fiction and lessening the emotional impact of death on the page. As Ariadne Oliver puts it in Christie's *Dead Man's Folly* (1957), in her world, "Men get killed and nobody minds – I mean nobody except wives and sweethearts and children and things like that" (Christie 2014: 97), relegating the most powerful emotional impact of murder to an afterthought that gains comic value by its negligence. On the other hand, drawing attention to the process of crime writing with such blasé comments invites the reader to consider what is not being said and shown as much as what is.

John Dickson Carr's *The Three Coffins* (1935) contains possibly the most broadly cited chapter in Golden Age crime fiction outside the pages of Christie. Carr's métier was the locked room mystery, and Chapter 17 of the novel is titled "The Locked-Room Lecture". In it, detective Gideon Fell interrupts the narrative, preparatory to explaining the solution to the mystery, with what is essentially an essay on the fictional variations of the locked-room scenario

(2002: 151–64). Responding to an objection along the lines that discussions about fiction have no place in real murder investigations, Fell explains:

> we're in a detective story, and we don't fool the reader by pretending we're not. Let's not invent elaborate excuses to drag in a discussion of detective stories. Let's candidly glory in the noblest pursuits possible to characters in a book.
>
> *(152)*

He goes on to justify what is going to be a highly elaborate solution to the novel's central puzzle by explaining that in fiction, as opposed to in life, the laws of probability work differently so that small and overlooked things are fundamentally more important, and "'improbable' grows meaningless as a jeer" (153). Carr – through Fell – also name-checks his many predecessors, from Poe and Doyle through Jacques Futrelle, Anna Katherine Green and even Carr's own early work – before naming the "types" of solution available to the writer of locked room mysteries (157–59). In so doing, he primes and prepares the reader for the inventiveness of what will follow, and conditions the context in which it will be read.

Malcah Effron calls this moment "detective fiction scholars' benchmark for self-referentiality", noting that it pre-empts crime fiction scholarship itself, acknowledging as it does the artificial, patterned nature of detective novels (2010: 1). It is a more extreme version of the asides that Carr and his peers frequently make in Golden Age fiction, sometimes with a distinct lack of subtlety ("After all", says one character in Edmund Crispin's *The Moving Toyshop*, "Gollancz is publishing this book" [2015: 97]). While Horsley cites the Carr passage as evidence of crime fiction's playful artifice, not only divorced from reality but wearing its irrelevance on its sleeve, and several scholars such as Susan Elizabeth Sweeney and Carl Malmgren have agreed, Effron points out that such asides "create an *impression* rather than an *awareness* of metatextuality", never developing into full moments of metatextual destabilisation, and thus leaving the interpretation to the reader (2010: 4, emphasis in original). Effron also argues that detective fiction blurs the lines between self-referentiality and metafiction, as "self-referentiality's rhetorical function in detective fiction [creates metafictional moments,] suggesting the metafictive tendency of self-referentiality" (42). Metafiction, as Effron understands it in relation to crime fiction, uses self-referentiality as a tool to make its processes accessible, inviting the reader to act as a literary critic with creative input into what the text *means* (55).

Upholding a distinction between "cozy" British mysteries and "hardboiled" American thrillers, Susan Rowland has coined the concept of "cozy metafiction", which "reinforces and blurs the lines between life and death". Rowland argues that cozy metafiction is a way of presenting the corpse as something rooted in a world beyond the narrative but still "solvable", while "ensur[ing] that the drama is simultaneously accepted as *fiction*" (emphasis in original), so that "[d]eath is 'solved' and 're-solved' by the solution that banishes its ability to poison an essentially recuperable world" (2016: 158). Here, Rowland is using "metafiction" in much the same way as Horsley uses "intertextual play and gamesmanship" (2005: 16) to maintain that Golden Age crime fiction represents an engineered retreat from real life (Rowland 2016: 172). However, others have pointed out that when detective novels highlight the artificial nature of their puzzles and – crucially – the solutions, they undermine the certainties and reassurances such tidy resolutions appear to present in the real world (see Effron 2010). The key point of difference in interpretation, then, is whether metafictional elements of crime writing diffuse or draw attention to the reality of violence. The following case study provides examples of a text read in both ways, and as a revelry in escapism that facilitates social commentary.

The metanarrative in the library

Halfway through Agatha Christie's *The Body in the Library* (1942), the investigators are interrupted by an annoying child, who reads too much detective fiction. He proudly boasts that he is an autograph hunter, and that he has "got autographs from Dorothy Sayers, Agatha Christie and Dickson Carr" (1972: 63). Here, Christie positions herself amongst her peers (both incompletely named), as if their work forms some kind of great continuum that is so unconnected to professional detective work that its champion is a child who sees death as a game, and whose knowledge of the genre actively hampers a "real" criminal investigation. It is a strategically placed moment of self-referentiality: It comes at the centre of the book, breaking up some dialogue-heavy interviews with suspects and acting in much the way that, traditionally, a second murder would to avoid narrative-dragging and bring in more colour. It is quite a significant self-referential moment, but it is not isolated, since the whole novel ostensibly pillories the conventions of Golden Age detective fiction, advertising its own unreality.

The title, *The Body in the Library*, was itself a cliché when Christie published the novel in 1942: In 1929 Sayers had a character, believing themselves a natural victim, declare, "Me for the corpse in the library" (2012: 6), and Christie herself had Ariadne Oliver identified as "the one who wrote *The Body in the Library*" in 1936 (Christie 1982: 17). In her introduction to the Penguin edition of the novel, Christie wrote that she was pillorying "clichés belonging to certain types of fiction" (1972: 5). The body in the library is deliberately "incongruous" with the surroundings: It is "a blonde", with bleached hair and a tacky sequined dress – in other words, a corpse belonging to a pulp fiction book cover thrust into the setting of an upper-middle-class mystery novel. The story opens with a middle-aged woman who has fallen asleep reading a detective novel being jolted awake by the maid announcing that she has discovered a body in the library. At first, Mrs Bantry's husband believes that the novel has seeped into his wife's dreams or unconscious and even after the scene has been viewed and the police have been summoned, no one can quite shed the idea that they are experiencing the kind of thing that "only happens in books" (13). The body itself "doesn't look *real*" and "just isn't *true*" (17, emphasis in original). Significantly, Mrs Bantry invites her friend Miss Marple to "come and watch" the police perform at the crime scene (16). Together, the two women set out to unravel the mystery, not because of the horror of crime but because Marple is "good at murders" and the whole thing "is rather thrilling" (14).

At the outset, then, the story's negotiation of its own unreality is established. This continues with the arrival of an extremely proactive policeman, Inspector Slack, whose ironic name invokes but inverts Charles Dickens's habit of naming his characters according to their virtues or vices. When one character points out that "in books" Scotland Yard is full of stupid men, he is chastised not as a man who reads but as a character in a contemporary novel: "Making fun of the police is very old fashioned" (106). This is not just a self-referential joke, pointing out the novel's status as fiction in a changing marketplace; it is also significant because the reader has just been introduced to the extremely satirical figure of Inspector Slack.

While the book revels in its own fictionality, the corpse itself straddles various levels of reality. The victim's name is Ruby Keene: She was an eighteen-year-old dancer with bleached blonde hair, whose real name was Rosy Legge (so, already her identity is not wholly authentic), and has been identified by her sister. Miss Marple eventually establishes that the body in the library was not that of Ruby Keene but of a missing schoolgirl who was lured by the murderers into believing she would become a movie star, and given hair dye and makeup to look like Ruby before being murdered in order to confuse the time of Ruby's death. Like McCabe's *The Face on the Cutting-Room Floor*, *The Body in the Library* uses the world of filmmaking to bring artifice into thematic as well as textual play. However, here the filmmakers are not real: It is the victim's investment in the rags-to-riches stories of Clara Bow and Vivien Leigh that have led her to trust two bogus studio representatives and allowed them to give her a makeover. They end up killing her. Marple works this out where the police have failed by noticing that the deceased bit her fingernails, the habit of a schoolgirl and not of a professional dancer. The body, then, has at least three identities, and, if we count the schoolgirl's belief that she was entering her own new show business identity, four.

Ruby Keene, however, has an additional fifth identity. There was a real Ruby Keen, a twenty-three-year-old woman strangled and then stripped – as opposed to being strangled and then dressed – in 1937. The case made the news, partly because of how it was solved (Honeycombe 1996: 343–47). The corpse, then, exists as an onion of fictional layers, one (triply false) name being that of a real murder victim. The presence of the schoolgirl, dressed up as Rosy Legge in the role of Ruby Keene, in the shadow of the late Ruby Keen, is more than a nod to unreality. It is a complex confusion of identities, fictions and truths. It is emblematic of the novel's metafictional flourish, celebrating the power of artifice by laying that process bare.

Some observers, most notably the crime writer P.D. James, have held up *The Body in the Library* as an example of detective fiction failing to be socially relevant. James argues that the book stretches suspension of disbelief beyond breaking point: Any pathologist, she points out, would know straightaway that the victim's hair had been dyed, and forensic technology was not so undeveloped in 1942 that the body would have been identified simply on the say-so of her sister. However, James concedes, "we are in Christie Land. We're not dealing with reality. We're dealing with a different form of reality" (qtd. in Thompson 2008: 385). It is possible to read this idea of "Christie Land" as the point of the novel, especially given the stark difference between forensic investigations of the dressed-up fictional Ruby Keene and the undressed real Ruby Keen. Indeed, the real Ruby Keen investigation was remarkable for its then unprecedented dependence on forensic science, as a man was convicted on the strength of a unique fibre found on the victim's person (Honeycombe 1996: 346). From the outset, *The Body in the Library* does not simply inhabit "a different form of reality"; it draws attention to the dissonance between life and fiction from the title page through every self-referential utterance until the end, when Marple argues that the rather complicated murder plot was "no more intricate than the steps of a dance" (1972: 190). That is to say, the crime has been planned and executed artistically, both by the fictional murderers and, as a literary act, by the author herself. To what end depends on one's interpretative framework.

A reading that identifies "cozy metatext" in the novel would posit Ruby Keen(e) as a real-world sacrifice, brought into the stylised pages of fiction only to be given a solution that reality denied her. In the midst of broader national tragedy (the novel was published in the middle of World War II), such deliberate escapism meets a consumer demand to turn real death into unreal death, and to undo the power of evil. A reading of *The Body in the Library* as socially engaged metafiction would similarly uphold a sense of advertised unreality. However, in this understanding it is the self-referential moments in the text – the clichés, the name-checks, and not the corpse alone – that opens the door to metatext. The escapism is not really escapist, then, but another cliché attached to crime fiction and being held up to mockery in the form of the crime-reading child.

The child, naively treating a murder as a fictional mystery and obstructing the police investigation, stands in, explicitly, for the reader. He serves as a reminder that fictional murder is not real murder and should not be approached in the same way, but also – since his methods do unearth evidence that the police have missed – allows the author and reader to celebrate a broadness of perspective that art can bring to real-world problems. The parody employed here can be both enjoyable and, since its unreality is highlighted, conscientious: Underneath all the fun, there is real death, and a real world in which Agatha Christie is not a God but an author writing to a commercial standard and being asked for her autograph.

A shift in application

Having examined the traditional uses of self-referentiality and metafiction in puzzle-based crime fiction, it is prudent now to consider broader and more contemporary applications, and finally to look at how these perspectives might inform one another as the genre continues to develop and diversify. Just as there is no critical consensus on the role of self-referentiality and/ or metafiction in traditional crime fiction, so too is the application of these devices within the genre multivalent. Concurrent with the end of the Golden Age, the largely American hardboiled genre explicitly dealt with the unreality of the classical form it was written against. More recently, Anthony Horowitz, who writes mysteries, claims to have found "something completely new to do within the genre" by putting himself as a character into the narrator-sidekick role and self-consciously building his plots around existing tropes of Golden Age fiction. Horowitz states that, in this way, he has "broken down the wall between us, making you [the reader] aware of me as the writer" with the aim of emphasising the mystery novel's fun, game-playing aspect (Horowitz 2018). On the other hand, postmodern crime writers such as Umberto Eco and Gilbert Adair have been using the same trick for decades to explore the limits of language in constructing solutions within or without fiction, revealing all narratives as artificial and contextually processed.

Eco's *The Name of the Rose* (1980), both a novel and a work of postmodern criticism, is filled with linguistic and structural references to mystery narratives and the creative acts of writing, narrating and reading. The instrument of death in the novel turns out to be a literary manuscript, and ultimately language fails the narrator, who is unable to explain or resolve the matter fully. Gordon McAlpine, in *Holmes Entangled* (2017), uses the form of the detective novel to explore quantum theory. McAlpine's novel is a useful contrast to John Dickson Carr's *The Mad Hatter Mystery* (1933), because both concern a search for a missing manuscript by an acknowledged parent of detective fiction, Edgar Allen Poe. In Carr's novel, the manuscript is almost window dressing, serving to bolster the dominant themes of fact, fiction and ethics (a central character is, like Poe, taking some sensational liberties in his reports of crimes). On the other hand, McAlpine's detectives are Sherlock Holmes and his creator Arthur Conan Doyle, with bookend narration from the quintessentially postmodern novelist Jorge Luis Borges, one of several historical figures who ends up murdered, and Poe's detective narratives are not stories but case studies (it is worth recalling that many of Poe's early readers took his fiction for journalism). The lines between fact and fiction are deliberately, generically and self-consciously blurred, allowing the reader to question the authenticity of any narrative. Ultimately, the literary destabilisation enables McAlpine to explore the scientific possibility that there are multiple universes and that the one he presents, in which Holmes and Doyle are both real people, is just one of many "true" realities.

Elsewhere, metatext can aid a political critique of Western or capitalist structures. Josef Škvorecký's Czech short stories, such as those collected in *Sins for Father Knox* (1973), are all structured around the tropes of British crime fiction and self-consciously set out to break the "rules" of Golden Age crime with or without direct textual allusions, with the effect of pillorying and thereby undermining Western European authority. Michael Ondaatje's postcolonial novel *Anil's Ghost* (2000) is frequently discussed with reference to detective fiction. In particular, Ondaatje's use of multiple "detective" voices, all of whom fail to reach a coherent understanding of truth, has been taken to represent the conflict between seeking justice in any one of a conflicting number of social senses and the need for "justice on an individual scale" which contributes to righting "the social system as a whole" (Davis 2016: 17). Each of Ondaatje's five detectives is deeply invested in a unique approach to ethical politics – which creates an investigative politics self-consciously bound up in conflicting literary traditions. However, the crimes under investigation, though introduced with a skeleton, are broader, less clear-cut, and less formally understood or investigated than artificial murder. The novel concerns war, placelessness and violations of human rights. Using tropes of detective fiction in a self-conscious manner, the postcolonial novel can question overarching metanarratives beyond those of good and evil, in specific socio-geographic contexts. It is this intertextual gesture to multiplicity, and to uneasy solutions, which is gaining increased traction in studies of postcolonial detective fiction (see Munos and Ledent 2019).

British crime fiction in particular is enjoying a Golden Age renaissance in the first quarter of the twenty-first century, one form of which is the presence of Golden Age tropes, characters or even novelists in contemporary crime fiction (most well-known detectives feature in continuation novels; Agatha Christie, Josephine Tey and Dorothy L. Sayers are all investigators in multiple series; and bestsellers like Stuart Turton's *The Seven Deaths of Evelyn Hardcastle* (2018) wear their Golden Age credentials on their sleeves). Sometimes, the Golden Age allusions are purely gestural, almost a requirement of a nostalgic genre. However, the global impact of Scandinavian crime fiction has been representative of a shift in subject focus, from individual crimes and stories to broader national or international crimes and narratives. With metanarratives directly and overtly under scrutiny, there is strong potential for literary self-referentiality to assist the process. As social and political aspects of crime fiction diversify, and a critique of metanarratives overtakes the playfulness of metafiction, it is possible that new areas of referentiality will pervade even the most mainstream crime writing in the coming years.

Bibliography

Carr, J.D. (2002) *The Hollow Man*, London: Orion.
Christie, A. (1972) *The Body in the Library*, London: Fontana.
———. (1982) *Cards on the Table*, Glasgow: Fontana.
———. (2014) *Dead Man's Folly*, London: Harper.
Coe, J. (2016) "Introduction", in C. McCabe, *The Face on the Cutting-Room Floor*, London: Picador, v–xii.
Crispin, E. (2015) *The Moving Toyshop*, London: Collins Crime Club.
Davis, E.S. (2016) "Investigating truth, history, and human rights in Michael Ondaatje's *Anil's Ghost*", in N. Pearson and M. Singer (eds), *Detective Fiction in a Postcolonial and Transnational World*, Abingdon: Routledge, 15–30.
Doyle, A.C. (2001) *A Study in Scarlet*, London: Penguin.
Effron, M. (2010) "'If only this were a detective novel': self-referentiality as metafictionality in detective fiction", PhD thesis, Newcastle University.
Gass, W.H. (2018) "Philosophy and the form of fiction", *The William H. Gass Reader*, New York: Alfred A. Knopf, 641–56.
Honeycombe, G. (1996) *The Crimes of the Black Museum*, London: Book Club Associates.
Horowitz, A. (2018) "The detective story as meta-fiction", *Crime Reads*, 5 June, https://crimereads.com/the-detective-story-as-meta-fiction/ (accessed September 2018).
Horsley, L. (2005) *Twentieth-Century Crime Fiction*, Oxford: Oxford University Press.
Hutcheon, L. (1980) *Narcissistic Narrative: The metafiction paradox*, Waterloo: Wilfrid Laurier University Press.
Munos, D. and Ledent, B. (eds) (2019) *Minor Genres in Postcolonial Literature*, New York: Routledge.
Rowland, S. (2016) "Cooking the books: metafictional myth and ecocritical magic in 'cozy' mysteries from Agatha Christie to contemporary cooking sleuths", in C. Cothran and M. Cannon (eds), *New Perspectives on Detective Fiction: Mystery magnified*, New York: Routledge, 157–72.

Self-referentiality and metafiction

Sayers, D.L. (2012) *Strong Poison*, London: Bourbon Street.

Stolarek, J. (2009) "A crime story or metafictional game? – A definition and redefinition of the status of the detective novel in Martin Amis's *London Fields* and Tvetan Todorov's, Typology of Detective Fiction'", *Anglica Wratislaviensia*, 47: 27–39.

Thompson, L. (2008) *Agatha Christie: An English mystery*, London: Headline.

Todorov, T. (1977) "The typology of detective fiction", *The Poetics of Prose*, trans. R. Howard, Oxford: Basil Blackwell, 42–49.

26

PARATEXTUALITY

Louise Nilsson

The way we view the world is in many ways formed by impressions from film, literature and other media. According to Arjun Appadurai, twenty-first century media have fashioned a "global imaginary" that blurs the lines between the fictional and the real. Art, news and entertainment cultures all converge in a contemporary mediascape where unseen places and unknown actions unfold for viewers around the globe as a part of everyday life through films, posters, books, images or news reports, in print or on screen. These media expressions create the impression of "knowing" a certain place, culture or event (Appadurai 2011: 28–31).

Offering artistic representations of the world, crime fiction is an increasingly significant part of Appadurai's global mediascape. Although the genre often depicts the local and presents a social critique of its own national context, it is, at its heart, global. Gravitating between the local and the cosmopolitan, crime writers across the globe read and influence each other's literary explorations of life, death, crime and punishment, in relation to different values, moral systems and notions of justice (King 2014; Nilsson et al. 2017). Given the genre's popularity and transnational circulation in the form of novels and films, crime fiction is a major contributor to the mediascape that engenders this global imaginary.

How we perceive and understand a book, however, does not begin with the opening line, but with the framework provided by *paratexts*. According to French literary critic Gérard Genette, paratexts are textual elements that frame the actual contents, thereby enabling "a text to become a book and to be offered as such to its readers and, more generally, to the public" (2009: 1). The most palpable example is the book's jacket design and its constitutive elements: Cover image, title, author's name and back-cover blurb. These paratexts guide how consumers perceive the book and serve to guide reader expectations. For example, a book's title has a dual purpose: To represent the narrative and attract buyers. The title in turn resonates with the book-cover design, which positions the narrative within the system of genres on the book market.

This chapter explores how crime fiction narratives – based on paratextual source material – present themselves on the transnational book market. My aim is to examine how paratextual strategies seek to govern our perception of narrative content, and how they shape our understanding prior to reading or viewing a work of crime fiction. I argue that paratextual source material enables us to analyse the interplay between a crime novel's content and its commercial presentation.[1]

Paratextuality

A book's paratexts span from the jacket design to a wide array of external texts such as press releases, reviews, articles about film adaptations, interviews, blog and discussion forum posts and information provided by online booksellers such as Amazon. This chapter focuses primarily on jacket design and book reviews and pays special attention to two forms of paratextuality that are central to the marketing of crime fiction, namely what I call *paratextual validation* and *paratextual authenticity*. Paratextual validation is about positioning the novel within the crime fiction genre as a whole, vouching for its quality and uniqueness as well as for its belonging to a genre with a long heritage. Paratextual authenticity is a matter of lending the narrative an aura of authenticity – a sense that it "could be true". These strategies are both subject to commercial imperatives yet co-exist with crime fiction's aspiration to offer realistic representations of society with a social critical edge.

I begin by presenting a brief introduction to paratextuality as a way of reading crime fiction and proceed from there to discuss the two concepts of paratextual validation and authenticity. On the basis of these theoretical reflections I then analyse a sample selection of paratexts before offering a few concluding thoughts on the role of paratextuality in crime fiction.

Paratexts as methodological approach

The pre-eminent theorist of paratextuality is French narratologist Gérard Genette whose seminal *Paratexts: Thresholds of Interpretation* (1987) analyses the complex relationship between the production of literature and its institutional and cultural contexts. Genette describes the paratext as a "threshold" or a "vestibule" where readers are invited to step in or turn back. The paratextual is "an undefined zone", enjoying a liminal existence both inside and outside the text. It thereby provides a transitional zone involving a pragmatic and strategic "transaction", as it exists to provide the public with "a better reception of the text and a more pertinent reading" (Genette 2009: 1–22).

According to Genette, paratexts can be broken down further into *peritexts* and *epitexts* (2009: 5). Peritexts are found on specific books/ebooks and may consist of text and images; examples include the title, the front cover, the author's name and short biography and the back-cover blurb, sometimes accompanied by quotes from book reviews. Epitexts, on the other hand, are "distanced elements" that appear outside the book: Reviews, interviews or materials accompanying a film adaptation such as DVD releases or promotional photographs and posters; they also include public or private correspondence and diaries (Genette 2009: 5). The distinction between peritexts and epitexts is not clear-cut, however, as epitexts such as book reviews or promotional photographs for film adaptations can be used peritextually as a back-cover review quote or (in the case of a movie tie-in) a front cover image.

Since Genette published *Paratexts* in 1987, a significant shift has occurred from analogue to digital technology, and the international book market has gone through major changes as a result. Genette himself was aware that reading patterns and devices might change and insisted that the text he discussed was "the form (nowadays, at least) of a book" (2009: 1). With the rise of digital technology, physical books co-exist with ebooks and devices such as e-readers, mobile phones and tablet computers, and these latter formats tend to expand the book's epitextual circulation. For example, a book downloaded to a Kindle still has a front cover and paratexts such as a bioblurb and acknowledgements, but websites such as Amazon and Google Books also serve as hosts for online communities of readers who are given the opportunities to discuss the book and review and grade it; these epitextual strategies are a form of marketing derived from the readers themselves and their participation. Further, more generally, the cultural centrality of the book has declined in relation to screen media. This has resulted in the emergence of new marketing strategies that exploit the contemporary impact of film and television, as for example when an adaptation of a novel enables its remarketing with a front cover featuring actors and settings from the adaptation.

The nature of the paratext is therefore changeable and subject to technological and cultural developments. This makes the paratextual corpus almost limitless in size. Any study of paratexts would do well to focus, not on doing justice to this unwieldy whole, but rather on the main functions and aims of paratexts. Drawing mainly on jacket design and magazine articles and reviews as examples of peritexts and epitexts, this chapter argues that crime fiction tends to employ two key paratextual strategies, introduced above as paratextual validation and paratextual authenticity.

Paratextual validation results from statements about the value of the novel, both as an instance of crime fiction and, more broadly, as a literary text. I understand this concept as referring to specific paratexts, such as review quotes, front-cover design, and so forth, that serve to situate individual crime texts within the genre of crime fiction as well as to persuade and convince potential readers about their value and quality. Paratextual validation can take the form of a favourable comparison of a new writer's first novel to the works of an established crime author. Other validation strategies include a dramatic, lurid cover design aiming to catch the potential buyer's attention, often combined with statements about the author's credentials or the crime story's quality.

Paratextual authenticity concerns the individual crime novel's relationship to the real world and serves to highlight how the narrative is intimately aligned with the reality it depicts. Here, the paratextual framing forms part of the genre's aspiration to be authentic in its critical exploration of social phenomena. Authenticity is a versatile concept in the context of crime fiction and the authentic feel of the text is evidently often a result of textual rather than paratextual strategies – in a police novel, for example, the faithful rendition of investigative procedures and social contexts helps establish the narrative as authentic, and this sense of authenticity can, as Jesper Gulddal has argued (2016: 55), be further emphasised by wilfully challenging or negating the established conventions of the genre. However, authenticity is also produced paratextually, in the materials surrounding the text, and serves here as a marketing tool designed to attract buyers and readers. The archetypical example of this is the opening voice-over of the 1950s American television series *Dragnet*, which assured viewers that "the story you are about to see is true. The names have been changed to protect the innocent". Another example is the biographical note, which often turns the author's education, profession, life experience or ability to do research into strategies for framing the fictional narrative as a voice of truth and authenticity. Even if the story is not based on true events, paratexts can be sufficient to evoke a sense of authenticity.

Paratextual validation

An important aspect of paratextual validation is the framing of a novel within a certain aesthetic that enables the reader to identify the work as a *crime* novel. The cover design is particularly important in terms of positioning the crime novel on the book market and within the system of literary genres. The front cover's purpose is to catch the attention of potential buyers, place the book within the genre and highlight that the plot is suitably suspenseful. The main paratextual components are the front-cover image, the title and the author's name. The cover image *visually* positions the crime novel on the market and offers a preview of the narrative's tenor, which is often specified further in the back-cover blurb. Often the image draws on an imaginary of iconic tropes such as knives, blood, guns, crime scene tape, chalk outlines or close-ups of body parts belonging to a murder victim. Often these tropes are represented in colours such as black and red, providing an additional dramatic lure. Another iconic imaginary consists of mood-setting tropes such as black birds, most commonly ravens, eerie, abandoned environments, threatening silhouettes and roads that lead towards a city or through a natural landscape. These iconic images give narratives a familiar framing in popular culture and connect to an aesthetic that is embedded in cultural history, in fairy tales or folklore about monsters in dark forests (Nilsson 2017).

Another common strategy is to merge these tropes with an image that evokes the *place* where the plot is set, whether it is in a city or the countryside. The set of tropes used for this strategy consists of images displaying cityscapes, notable landmarks, forests, deserts, snowy landscapes or beaches, all of which help to place the narrative in terms of country and continent as well as create a link to established cultural perceptions of the setting. This has been a common paratextual strategy for "Nordic noir". A cover image showing a snowy, blood-splattered field against the backdrop of black birds circling a forest serves to inform readers that the book is a crime fiction novel taking place in rural Scandinavia, thereby positioning the novel on the global book market in terms of national origins and genre (Nilsson 2018).

In addition, the validating peritexts on the jacket reveal a complex mediascape and serve as an empirical means of examining how crime fiction circulates transnationally and how individual crime titles are adapted to new cultural contexts. Stieg Larsson's *The Girl with the Dragon Tattoo* exemplifies the paratextual relationship between the novel's title and its circulation outside its native context. The novel launched on the Swedish market in 2005 was titled *Män som hatar kvinnor* ("Men Who Hate Women") in line with the author's wishes and against the pleas of the publisher, Norstedts Förlag. Larsson's refusal to change the title was motivated by a desire to call attention to violence against women in society and culture. This ran counter to the translations, publication and marketing of the novel in new cultural contexts and book markets where this intention was often ignored (Nilsson 2016: 4–8).[2]

Now a bestseller, Larsson's book has become a paratextual validation tool for marketing other crime novels on the global book market. Promoting a new translated novel as written by "the next Stieg Larsson" is, in effect, a paratextual promise that it will offer a suspenseful, exciting reading experience. For example, Japanese crime novelist Keigo Higashino's *Salvation of a Saint* (2012), the second instalment of his Detective Galileo series, features the face of a young Japanese woman and, above the author's name and the title, a quote from an article in the *Times*, "Meet Keigo Higashino, the Japanese Stieg Larsson" (2011). This reference to Larsson – an epitext turned into a peritext appearing on the cover of the English translation – positions Higashino's novel, not simply as crime fiction, but as crime fiction of a certain international quality. This example shows how comparisons to internationally successful authors can be used as a validation tool. Once a work becomes iconic, often after achieving bestseller status, like Larsson's trilogy, it can serve as a reference point to position other works within the genre.

In addition, the *Times* article also states that Higashino's success derives from his depiction of an unseen Tokyo of seedy neighbourhoods, back alleys, homelessness and poverty. Here the reference to Larsson merges with the description of Higashino's own nation-specific uniqueness. Following Appadurai, this exemplifies how a crime narrative may influence the reader's perception of the real world we inhabit, as the novels are framed as authentic depictions of the world. This sample case thereby also highlights the delicate overlap between the paratextual strategies of validation and authenticity. Further, the use of the bestselling Swedish novelist as a reference point for the paratextual framing of Higashino for the anglophone market shows how the "glocalness" of the crime genre can serve as a common denominator when different national contexts are put in play through paratexts and not only help shape how readers perceive the novel, but give an air of authenticity to its depiction of the setting.

A translated novel may also be presented to a domestic market through the paratexts of a specific series. This validation strategy relies on the reputation and familiarity of the series within the domestic context. Often such series – which typically include both domestic and foreign titles – have an aesthetic that helps consumers identify its novels and positions the foreign novelist within the system of genres. Book series focusing on a specific genre, like crime fiction, serve as reassuring brands that provide a marker of quality for books published within the series. An example of this is the French publishing house Actes Sud's launch of Higashino in the series *Actes Noirs*. Here, *The Devotion of Suspect X* (2011) was given a book design consisting of the series' iconic black and red colour palette, featuring eerie imagery that borrows from the aesthetics of fairy tales, surrealism and horror fiction.

Other paratextual validation strategies include references to awards, prizes, placement on bestseller lists or nominations. Being a finalist or nominee, for example, allows the book to enter a distinct part of the literary system that facilitates media exposure. Awards highlight how external literary systems and infrastructures may influence a book's peritextual display. At the same time, publishing houses can nominate novels for these awards and so influence the selection of finalists and nominees. These awards and nominations can be seen as epitextual activities that consolidate specific taste preferences and work as systems of inclusion and exclusion, governed by the committee members and the participating publishing houses. Here, the choices of a select group of professionals become powerful paratextual marketing tools, aiming to convince potential buyers and readers of the novel's worth (Matthews and Moody 2007).

Paratextual validation also occurs via peritexts *within* the book covers, placed before the narrative's beginning or after its end. Introductions, often written by someone other than the novelist, frequently serve as a peritext in new editions or translations. Two examples are the 2004 paperback re-release of Michael Connelly's *The Poet* (1996) for the American market and the translated first-edition paperback release of Joseph Wambaugh's *Hollywood Station* (2006) for the Swedish market in 2010, both of which have introductions/prefaces by writers well-known in the countries where the novels were republished. *The Poet* is introduced by renowned American horror novelist Stephen King while *Hollywood Station* includes a preface by Leif G.W. Persson, a Swedish celebrity criminologist and crime writer whose novels have been translated into English and other languages.

The introductions to *The Poet* and *Hollywood Station* are similar in style and content, despite being written for two different cultural and national readerships, and these similarities are significant, given the different intended markets. While the new edition of *The Poet* is targeted at expanding sales within the domestic market, the translation of *Hollywood Station* features as a new work of foreign literature for the Swedish market. Both introductions praise the authors and their writing as well as calling attention to their earlier works. They also offer personal memories about the authors, information about reading preferences as well as general biographical notes. Finally, Wambaugh and Connelly are compared to other similar, well-established crime writers, which helps to situate them within the genre and its traditions.

Another aspect to consider in regard to both the authors of the novels and the two introductory essays is the subtle overlap between fiction and reality. The avid reader of Connelly knows that he used to work in crime journalism before becoming a full-time novelist, and Persson is also a well-known professor of criminology in his own native context. Such professional links to either law and law enforcement or journalism and the news media are common among crime writers, and they are easily turned into paratextual strategies for highlighting a crime novel's authenticity.

Authenticity by paratext

The notions of authenticity and believability are cornerstones of the crime genre. An example of the way in which paratextual framing helps to position a story as authentic can be found in Caleb Carr's historical crime novel *The Alienist* (1994), which tells the story of the hunt for a serial killer in late nineteenth-century New York. The 1995 American paperback edition published by Bantam Books includes a number of peritexts: Cover image, title, author's name, copyright page with information about previous editions, review quotes, biographical note, a list of the author's other novels, acknowledgements, etc. All these peritexts contribute to shaping readers' preconceptions about the story before they have even read the first sentence. The cover photo, for example, positions *The Alienist* as historical crime fiction, showing the dark silhouette of a cape-covered man from behind, crossing a city street with horses and carriages in the background, suggestive of the late nineteenth or early-twentieth century. The title and the author's name above are printed in gold, harmonising with the sepia-toned black and white photograph.

The cover and photograph are carefully designed to ensure that readers accept the text's authenticity. Belonging to the period and place where the plot is set, it acts as historical documentation, and its accuracy is underlined by the copyright page note that the photograph is from the collections of the Library of Congress. The sense of authenticity is further enhanced by the review quotes that appear not only on the front and back covers, but also inside the book itself. In place of a blurb, the back cover has six positive review quotes in red lettering against a black background. *The New York Times* states that "you can smell the fear in the air"; the *Flint Journal* assures us that it "will please fans of *Ragtime* and *The Silence of the Lambs*"; *USA Today* praises it as "gripping [and] atmospheric"; and the *Detroit News* says that "Caleb Carr's rich period thriller takes us back to the moment in history when the modern idea of the serial killer became available to us". Additional quotes inside echo this praise. The *Buffalo News* describes *The Alienist* as "a remarkable combination of historical novel and psychological thriller" and the *Richmond Times-Dispatch* says it depicts the "Gilded Age metropolis", taking the reader "climbing up tenement stairs, scrambling across rooftops, and witnessing midnight autopsies".

The chosen quotes have a variety of functions. They assure the reader that the book is historically accurate, vouch for the quality of the author's craft, compare the novel to other successful works and link the modern phenomenon of serial killers to the historical time period. By mixing references to quality with references to accuracy and atmosphere, the review quotes bridge the gap between paratextual processes of validation and authentication. For publishers, new editions have the advantage of allowing for epitextual quotes to enhance the jacket's peritext. Paratextual quotations like those cited above create – as epitexts in terms of their origin and peritexts on the book – a shared intertextual universe via references to other crime authors and novels, which vouch for the quality and authenticity of the work.

Before the reader even begins reading *The Alienist*, the paratexts have helped establish the fictional narrative's perceived authenticity. Sometimes claims to authenticity co-exist and intersect with paratextual validation, for example, in the form of accompanying biographical notes. In the present case, the text tells the reader that the novelist was born in New York's Lower East Side, has a degree in history, writes about politics and military affairs and works in television, film and theatre. In offering basic information about the author, these points highlight to the reader that Carr has a deep, native connection to New York, an academic background qualifying him for historical research and a professional background in journalism, media and art, thereby reinforcing the story's perceived authenticity.

The acknowledgements support this peritext. Located at the very end of the book and covering more than two pages, they inform readers of the research that Carr undertook for the novel, which involved a range of archives, museums and libraries in New York as well as the Harvard Archives in Cambridge, Massachusetts. In addition, the author provides a list of scholars whose work he consulted, including serial killer specialists such as Colin Wilson and Robert K. Ressler. Together, the acknowledgements and the biographical note serve to reinforce the story's authenticity – either before, during or after the reader reads the book itself.

The paratexts are sometimes further supported by interviews where the author emphasises the importance of research and the aspiration that the book should be considered true in all elements except in regard to the fictional plot. Interviews, in turn, create connections to the wider crime fiction universe, given that writers often discuss influences and inspiration drawn from other novelists or real-life cases. In an interview with *Strand Magazine* (Anon. 2018) Carr for example highlights his interest in psychological profiling and refers to Thomas Harris's Hannibal Lecter novels as an inspiration for his own writing.

Book reviews also contribute towards establishing a narrative's authenticity. In the case of *The Alienist*, Anthony Quinn's review in the *Independent* offers an illustrative example. Quinn emphasises how Carr's book provides insight into the everyday life of the period, representing "old New York" in detail "[f]rom the fetid reek of 'stale beer dives' to the baronial splendour of bankers' mansions, from dirt-poor tenements to the fanciest French restaurants". Carr's narrative offers a "place to learn, inter alia, about Bowery slang, local card games, and [...] Red Indian burial traditions", all of which play a role in the novel's plot (Quinn 1994).

Supportive epitexts such as these can attach themselves to film adaptations, and these in turn can contribute to reinforcing a text's authenticity. In the case of *The Alienist*, the novel was turned into a TV series that premiered on TNT in 2018. Following the adaptation, the paratextual framing of Carr's novels highlights both the television series and the novels as a crime fiction series. *The Alienist* went from a single book to having a sequel, *The Angel of Darkness* (1997), followed by *Surrender, New York* (2016), which is set in the present and features Dr Trajan Jones, a leading expert on the work of the series' historical protagonist, Dr Laszlo Kreizler. The TV adaptation has resulted in new editions of the novels in ebook and printed editions which display images of the actors and historical surgical tools. Adaptations can also produce new epitexts through interviews with writers, directors and actors, which in turn provide new peritextual material for new editions. Thus, an exchange takes place between the film and novels where both benefit as one product directs attention to the other.

In summary, the paratextual frames of validation and authenticity not only position the crime novel on the book market and highlight its genre identity, but also help guide would-be readers and shape their perceptions of the narrative. This paratextual framing, which consists of the peritextual content of the jacket design and the epitexts of the broader mediascape, opens up a space that allows literature to present itself as an authentic voice depicting a reality through its fictional stories. In addition, the genre as a whole is a part of the multifaceted global mediascape that governs and informs our views on the world as well as our local settings. Paratexts serve as gateways to the presentation of crime fiction as it circulates in shifting cultural contexts in the global book market. Paratextual framing cannot be separated from the narrative content or its intertextual relation to the genre. The paratext is not solely a marketing strategy that governs our reading experience (and therefore cannot be separated from the narrative content); it is also, following Appadurai, a framing device that enables crime novels to contribute to the global imaginary's multifaceted representation of the world.

Notes

1 For further discussion of Genette and paratextuality in the context of crime fiction, see Rolls and Vuaille-Barcan 2011, Effron 2010 and Maher 2016.
2 Other European translations (into French, Spanish and other languages) opted for a literal translation of the original title. For details, see Nilsson 2016.

Bibliography

Anon. (2018) "Interview with Caleb Carr (excerpts)", https://strandmag.com/the-magazine/interviews/interview-with-caleb-carr/ (accessed 4 September 2019).

Appadurai, A. (2011) "Disjuncture and difference", in L. Connell, and N. Marsh (eds), *Literature and Globalization: A Reader*, London: Routledge.

Carr, C. (1995) [1994] *The Alienist*, New York: Bantam Books.

Connelly, M. (2009) [1996] *The Poet*, Warner Books: New York.

Effron, M. (2010) "On the borders of the page, on the borders of genre: artificial paratexts in Golden Age detective fiction", *Narrative*, 18(2): 199–219.

Genette, G. (2009) [1987] *Paratexts: Thresholds of interpretation*, Cambridge: Cambridge University Press.

Gulddal, J. (2016) "Clueless genre realism and narrative form in Ed McBain's early 87th Precinct novels", *Clues: Journal of Detection*, 34(2): 54–62.

King, S. (2014) "Crime fiction as world literature", *Clues: Journal of Detection*, 32(2): 8–19.

Maher, B. (2016) "'La dolce vita' meets 'the nature of evil': the paratextual positioning of Italian crime fiction in English translation", *The Translator*, 22(2): 176–89.

Matthews, N. and Moody, N. (2007) *Judging a Book by its Cover. Fans, publishers, designers, and the marketing of fiction*, Aldershot: Ashgate.

Nilsson, L. (2016) "Uncovering a cover: marketing Swedish crime fiction in a transnational context", *Journal of Transnational American Studies*, 7(1): 1–16.

———. (2017), "Covering crime fiction: merging the local into the cosmopolitan mediascape", in Nilsson et al., 109–30.

———. (2018), "A cosmopolitan north in Nordic noir: turning Swedish crime fiction into world literature", in S. Helgesson, A. Mörte Alling, Y. Lindqvist and H. Wulff, (eds), *World Literatures: Exploring the cosmopolitan-vernacular exchange*, Stockholm: Stockholm University Press, 340–354.

Nilsson, L., Damrosch, D. and D'haen, T. (eds) (2017) *Crime Fiction as World Literature*, New York: Bloomsbury.

Quinn, A. (1994) "The eyes don't have it" (review of Caleb Carr, *The Alienist*), *The Independent*, 6 August 1994.

Rolls, A. and Vuaille-Barcan M.-L. (2011) *Masking Strategies: Unwrapping the French paratext*, Bern: Peter Lang AG.

Varga, S. and Guignon, C. (2017) "Authenticity", in E.N. Zalta (ed.), *The Stanford Encyclopedia of Philosophy*, https://plato.stanford.edu/archives/fall2017/entries/authenticity/ (accessed 14 November 2019).

Wambaugh J. (2010) [2006] *Hollywood Station*, Stockholm: Ordupplaget.

27
AFFECT

Christopher Breu

Like most forms of popular fiction, crime fiction is known to produce affective responses in its readers. One of the defining features of most genre fiction is that it produces effects in the body, whether it is the excitement of adventure, the fear produced by horror, the arousal of pornography, or the sense of longing and fulfilment produced by romance. Indeed, popular fiction is often denigrated precisely because it produces such "vulgar" bodily affects, in contrast to the complex and distanced contemplation instilled by capital "L" literature. The production of such forms of embodied affect may be lamentable for the guardians of high art, but for scholars interested in questions of affect, popular fiction can be seen as a privileged medium. Popular fiction does not just instil affects in the reader, it also narrativises them. Affects attach not only to characters and spaces but to the very workings of narrative itself. As psychoanalytic critics have demonstrated, central to the drive of crime fiction is the desire to know. In conventional crime fiction, this desire to know often manifests itself as a will to mastery. Thus, the classical detective narrative is premised on the movement from fear, suspense and disorientation to mastery, clarity and order. While the hardboiled detective story may forego much of the conventional resolution associated with the classical narrative, it too is predicated on a sense of mastery, even if this mastery is proven to be more about the toughness or endurance of the protagonist rather than any restoration of justice. Similarly, crime fiction that narrates the exploits of the master criminal, from the *Memoirs of Vidocq* (1828) forward, is predicated on the daring and mastery of the criminal.

Whereas the other subgenres of crime fiction are finally about mastering affects (as well as mastery *as an affect*), noir, as a reworking of these other genres, is about the opposite. Noir is predicated on the inability of the protagonist to master the affects dramatised by the narrative. Instead the affects typically master the protagonist (who is unmastered by them) and define the coordinates of the fictional world. Noir thus has a privileged position in understanding affect in relationship to crime fiction. It demonstrates the power of affect to both shape individual actions and the larger landscape in which such actions take place. Noir takes shape as a specific affective mood or atmosphere. Central to noir is the staging of negative affects. Negativity clings to the very bones of the noir crime story. Noir works via the staging of negative affects such as guilt, sadness, (often murderous) rage, cynicism, loss, resentment, fear, anxiety, destructive desire, often including an erotic attachment to death.

Initially, this definition of noir may seem counterintuitive. Noir is often associated in popular culture with a certain kind of nostalgic image of mid-twentieth-century life, featuring tough

Affect

guys, femme fatales, shadows, crime and a dangerous yet alluring urban demimonde. It is also usually associated with film, with such actors as Humphrey Bogart, Lauren Bacall, Veronica Lake, Robert Mitchum, Barbara Stanwyck, Edward G. Robinson and others. Indeed, it has only been in the past thirty years or so that the category of the noir novel has gained critical currency in the work of Christopher Metress, James Naremore, William Marling, myself and others (Breu 2009; Marling 1994; Metress 1994; Naremore 1998). Yet, many film noirs were adaptations from crime novels that shared many of their thematic concerns and narrative structures. Moreover, the novels often were resolutely darker and more disturbing than many of their filmic counterparts, since the latter had to negotiate the Hayes code. Thus, the term noir seems to fit the novels even more fully than the films, even if the naming was belated and the films were named first, if also retrospectively, as Marc Vernet has noted (1993). If we focus just on the noir crime novel (leaving to one side the detective novel), we can construct a timeline that begins with the writings of James M. Cain, Horace McCoy and Cornell Woolrich in the 1930s, gathers steam in the work of such mid-century writers as Patricia Highsmith, Dorothy Hughes, Jim Thompson, David Goodis, Chester Himes, Boris Vian and other writers for the French *Série noire*, and continues into the present with writers such as Megan Abbott, Dennis Lehane, and Gillian Flynn in the US, Natsuo Kirino and Shuichi Yoshida in Japan, Paco Ignacio Taibo II and Eugenio Auguirre in Mexico, to mention only a few contemporary writers and national contexts.

As Christopher Metress has argued, this tradition of crime writing emerged in intimate opposition to the tradition of hardboiled detective fiction (Metress 1994: 55–60). Whereas hardboiled detective fiction privileged the hardboiled male, who was defined by action, working-class toughness, violence and the ability to get the job done, right or wrong, noir focused on criminals, drifters, hustlers, the star-crossed and the down-and-out (Breu 2005: 1–22). Raymond Chandler's detective, Philip Marlowe, for all of his violence and his ostensible toughness, is still descended from chivalric romances (as his name indicates). He is still a kind of hero, if a thoroughly flawed one. Similarly, while the plots in the hardboiled detective story are notoriously inconclusive and ambivalent, there is still typically a patina of a happy or at least acceptable ending. In the context of the noir crime novel, the central characters are typically anti-heroes – think, for example, of Highsmith's Tom Ripley or Shuichi Yoshida's Yuichi in *Villain* (2010), both of whom are murderers on the run – and the endings are typically bleak, often involving the death or imprisonment of a central character (see Jim Thompson's *The Killer Inside Me* (1952) or the fate of Kazue in Natsuo Kirino's *Grotesque* (2003) to cite just two examples).

Noir's elusiveness

While I have just provided a relatively straightforward definition of noir fiction, noir remains an elusive category. Some critics include detective fiction along with crime fiction in the category while others do not; some read noir films and novels together while others argue for their necessary difference. As such, this elusiveness echoes the logic of noir itself. What seems like a problem with fixing a positive definition of noir is precisely what reveals the inherently negative and ambient quality of noir. The problem with the various attempts to define and precisely fix the coordinates of noir is that noir itself is not a positive or fully stable object. Noir, at its most radical, is about the negation of stable categories, affirmative narratives and positive claims. Rather than a specific genre, such as the crime or detective story, noir functions as a deformation or volatilisation of other genres. It works by bringing out the negative affects at work in other genres, revealing a kind of conceptual and textual darkness that is otherwise only an implicit or minor feature of the text. It is, thus, an ambient quality of texts – their ambient negativity. As Slavoj Žižek (2001) argues, film noir is not so much defined by its canted frames, so much as its canted view on life. It reveals the world of nightmares that lurks within the corners, crevices and alleyways of the everyday world. To borrow the title from one of the most celebrated of noir novels and film noirs (about which more below), noir reveals the "nightmare alleys" within the seeming stable grid of city streets. If, as D.A. Miller (1989) has argued, the typical detective narrative works to render city space rational and controllable, noir renders it dream-like and strange. It is in this nightmare world, the everyday world just looked at slightly differently, that noir does this work. It is striking in this regard that in William Lindsay Gresham's *Nightmare Alley* (1946), there is no one nightmare alley. It is not a place, so much as a condition, or to put it more precisely, it is a dream place that is simultaneously a condition. When one leaves the ordered and rational streets of the everyday where the typical protagonist of the crime or detective story lives, one can enter a nightmare alley in which all the personal and social demons of the noir protagonist emerge.

Noir can thus be likened to a kind of dreamwork in the psychoanalytic sense. As in Freud's account of the dream, the dreamwork functions through condensation and displacement, transforming the latent dream thoughts and manifest everyday experiences into scenarios that work to both dramatise and mask specific repressed wishes or traumas (Freud 1955, 4: 227–310). This double movement to both unveil and cover-over produces the characteristic ambivalence of the noir novel in which desire fundamentally moves both toward and away from the unacceptable wish or disavowed truth at the heart of the narrative. The dream presents the acceptable face of something unacceptable. Noir works the same way. It binds its volatile contents to seemingly prosaic narrative forms. Take as one example of the volatilisation of other forms, the moment in Megan Abbott's *You Will Know Me* (2016), when Katie Knox comes to realise that her daughter Devon, who is an Olympic hopeful in gymnastics, has killed the young adult man – legally he is her rapist – with whom she has been sleeping. Katie has this realisation much later than most of the other characters in the novel, many of whom have worked to cover up the crime and protect Devon's Olympic hopes. Katie's world goes from one defined by suburban safety and private family life to a neoliberal landscape of competition, amorality and violence. Yet it is merely the same world looked at differently. She sees this truth for a moment and then turns away from it again at the end of the novel. This is not a crime narrative with a master criminal or a protagonist who makes a clean getaway. Instead, it is a crime narrative about all too ordinary and typical crimes. Crimes not of mastery and daring but of weakness and amorality. It is a nightmare that blooms from the cracks of the everyday. Thus, the crime story is deformed by noir; it becomes primarily about affect rather than action.

Theorising noir affect

Noir thus does a kind of psychoanalytic work around repressed or disavowed materials, not just on the level of the individual protagonist but on a larger cultural level. On the social level, noir can be defined in relationship to the critical category of affect. Affect, as a category, has become increasingly central to contemporary work in critical theory. While the concept has its origin in the philosophical work of Baruch Spinoza, and there is a theoretical trajectory that runs from Spinoza thorough Deleuze, to Lawrence Grossberg, Brian Massumi, Teresa Brennan and others, it also is present at the founding of psychoanalysis and there is an alternative thread that runs through various psychoanalytic thinkers to the writings of the psychologist Sylvan Tomkins and into the work, in literary and cultural studies, of Eve Kosofsky Sedgwick, Lauren Berlant and Sianne Ngai.

Affect

Put simply, affect can be defined as that which affects a body in a given cultural, communicative or intersubjective context. It is both biological and ideational, interpersonal and subjective. Affects can be likened to emotions, and the lineage that runs through psychoanalysis often names affects. For example, Sylvan Tomkins (1995) argues that there are eight basic affects: 1. Interest-Excitement; 2. Enjoyment-Joy; 3. Surprise-Startle; 4. Distress-Anguish; 5. Shame-Humiliation; 7. Contempt-Disgust; 8. Fear-Terror. While these are emotional states for Tomkins, they are also embodied states that have much to do with the state of biological and neurochemical excitation attaching to them. They are thus both somatic and psychic. As such, they give the lie to Cartesian understandings of the mind/body split and complicate Enlightenment concepts of disembodied rationalism. Noir, with its emphasis on the way in which emotions and embodied states complicate any notion of detached rationality, is a privileged form when it comes to this understanding of affect. Reason in such a formation is not separate from feeling or emotion; the two are bound together, as they are in the noir crime novel. Affect in the psychoanalytic genealogy often takes the quality of a symptom – a drive to repeat a state or condition until its logic is worked through. This working-through can be the undoing offered by death as much as the emergence of a different way of being in the world.

In contrast to the psychoanalytic dimensions of affect, the Spinozan and Deleuzian genealogy of the concept emphasises incipience and ambience. In this account, affect is more rigorously disentangled from emotion. Affect is a nonconscious state that precedes any conscious apprehension, perception or feeling. This state is embodied but it can also be collective and atmospheric – the quality of a given space, social formation or time. As Teresa Brennan notes, it is the feeling that's already there when you walk into a crowded room (2004). It is also often articulated in relationship to the virtual or the incipient. Affect, in this sense, can be likened to Raymond Williams's account of "structures of feeling" in *Marxism and Literature*, where it suggests a feeling in the air before a major political or social change takes place (Williams 1978: 128–35). The Spinozan genealogy of affect, then, tends to emphasise becoming and incipience more than fixity and being.

Noir affect borrows from each of these approaches even as it takes them in a more resolutely negative direction. In borrowing the naming of states (without affect being reducible to those states), as well as the emphasis on negativity and repetition, noir affect draws most heavily on the psychoanalytic genealogy of affect. Yet it is also invested in the ambient and collective dimensions of affect emphasised by the Spinozan genealogy. Thus, noir often can be about states of transformation, yet this transformation can be toward death and dissolution as much as possibility and renewal. Indeed, noir affect is most preoccupied with the force and attraction of death itself, and thus can be theorised in relationship to the psychoanalytic dimension of the death drive. To put it simply, noir affect can be defined as various forms of negative affects that are dramatised and explored by those texts that we call noir. These affects include (but are not reducible to) rage, sadness, anxiety, guilt, cynicism, shame, resentment and destructive desire, often including an erotic attachment to death. Indeed, if one can provide any singular definition to the texts we call noir, it is not generic features, formal characteristics or narrative repetitions, but the uncomfortable tarrying with one or more of these affects themselves. Noir enacts a kind of dreamwork in relationship to the repressed wishes and traumas to which we find ourselves returning. It insists, in its repetitions and darkness, that we engage with that which we both desire and abhor.

In engaging negativity, death and dissolution, noir affect also insists that we tarry with the losers of the world. It thus can be read as an antidote to forms of rhetoric that demand happiness, wellness, achievement, success, as well as forms of crime fiction that narrate success (think of Elmore Leonard's *Get Shorty*, for example). Noir affect thus has economic resonances as well. If affect labour (labour in which a person's affect is central to their job), as theorised by Patricia Ticineto Clough, has become increasingly central to neoliberalism and the production of what Michel Foucault terms "human capital", then noir affect serves as a negation to this demand to manage our affect well (Clough 2007: 1–37; Foucault 2010: 227). As such, it can be theorised in productive tension with Lauren Berlant's celebrated concept of "cruel optimism" (2011: 1). Berlant defines cruel optimism as a neoliberal affective state in which people are invested in attachments that hinder their own flourishing. Noir affect is perhaps its flipside. It is what emerges when one stops holding on to such false promises and travels down to the affective heart of capitalism itself, with its ruthless sorting of winners and losers, the worthy from the unworthy, the solvent from the insolvent, the vital from the dying (think of the narration of the dying Walter Huff in the film version of *Double Indemnity* (1943) as just one example).

In its negativity, noir often works against the affirmative rhetoric of capitalism. Noir affect forms in opposition to the boosterish rhetoric of Fordism and early twentieth-century advertising as well as the good life promised by neoliberal self-actualisation. A scene near the end of Natsuo Kirino's *Grotesque* (2003) captures this critique at its most disturbing. The penultimate chapter of the novel is made up of the journal of a prostitute, Kazue, who has been found murdered by a serial killer on a garbage-strewn rooftop. Kazue's journal narrates her decline from private school student, to awkward office worker who is fired during a downturn, to high-priced escort, to the lowest rungs of sex work. Throughout the diary, she continues to use self-actualisation rhetoric even as she sinks lower and lower. This is cruel optimism in a noir frame.

Another feature of noir affect is that it is predicated on an aesthetic of proximity rather than distance. In contrast to notions of distance and detached aesthetic complication associated with high culture, the aesthetic of noir is entirely about the discomfort of the too proximate, of the closeness of the disturbing object or repressed truth. While affect was not a central term in Lacan's revision of psychoanalysis, he does devote one seminar to an affect, *Seminar X: Anxiety*. Anxiety, for Lacan, is produced by an uncomfortable proximity to an object or truth that would destroy the subject's symbolic fictions of the world if it was directly encountered (2016). As Kelly Oliver and Benigno Trigo argue, anxiety is one of the central affects of noir (2003: 1–33). Instead, the symbolic fictions defining the noir world regularly break down in relationship to the proximity of that which has been repressed. Noir affects are what are generated from this proximity. Take, for example, Cornell Woolrich's *I Married a Dead Man* (1948). The opening scene of the novel begins with the main character wondering whether she or her husband killed a blackmailer. Since, as we learn much later, she has repressed the truth that she did the deed, neither husband nor wife can trust each other because each thinks the other did it. This uncomfortable truth, that she killed the blackmailer, warps their marriage and her psyche. This is a proximate truth that can neither be fully disavowed nor fully accepted.

Noir time and space

Because of the distortions produced by such uncomfortable truths, wishes and traumas, noir texts do not merely represent the place or time in which they are produced. Instead, their representations are always distorted, displaced or condensed to a greater or lesser extent by the dreamwork of noir. Thus, spaces tend to be what Mark Augé describes as "non-places" (2009: 63). Typically, they are anonymous, shopworn or serialised spaces. They are places which are inhabited by the down-and-out, the transient, the anonymous. They tend to be all-too-ordinary spaces looked at differently, through the lens of nightmare. The nondescript or shabby street is transformed into a nightmare alley via noir affect (take, for example, the way in which the seemingly picturesque streets of Santa Monica become a hunting ground for Dix Steel, a serial rapist and murderer, in Dorothy Hughes's *In a Lonely Place* (1947)).

The temporality of noir is similarly distorted. Time in noir tends to take on phantasmatic dimensions. Calendrical or clock time becomes distorted, compressed or distended depending on the workings of noir affect. In her celebrated essay, "Lounge Time" (1998), Vivian Sobchack discusses the public time of noir in various spaces of adult modernity, such as the bar, the lounge, the nightclub, the gas station, the diner, the bus station, etc. Yet all these spaces tend to also be a bit down-and-out, worn down, abandoned by the forward movement of modernity. Noir time is a time of repetitions and returns. Often, the fatal choice has already been made (think, for example, of the narration by a dead man floating in a pool in Billy Wilder's *Sunset Boulevard* (1950) or the suicide of the protagonist's wife, which has already taken place when the novel begins, in David Goodis's *Down There* (1956)). Time, in the noir narrative, tends to be structured around the psychoanalytic notion of *Nachträglichkeit*, which is translated into English as differed action or retroactive meaning (Freud 1955, 19: 29–47). The temporality of *Nachträglichkeit* indicates that the significance of trauma is only reproduced through its repetition. So, while past events already haunt the noir protagonist, the meaning of such events are only ever fully significant through repetition. In François Truffaut's adaptation of *Down There*, *Shoot the Piano Player* (1960), the tragedy of the wife's suicide only takes on full significance with the girlfriend's murder at the hands of mobsters at the end of the film. As this suggests, the psychoanalytic concept of repetition compulsion also defines noir time. The characters in a noir often feel compelled to repeat the very traumas, wishes and truths that they spend much of the narrative trying to ward off.

Given that we have defined noir in terms of affect, rather than as a genre, form or historical sequence, the definition of noir proffered here can be associated with different national traditions, periods and mediums. As James Naremore and Jennifer Fay and Justus Nieland have noted, noir is a transnational, if not global, phenomenon (Naremore 1998: 9–39; Fay and Nieland 2009: 1–122). It is not a cycle of films or a specific set of novels, but the artistic engagement with forms of affect and their narrativisation. This artistic engagement may have started in the early twentieth century, but it continues in the present. For this reason, noir is a remarkably promiscuous (in the best sense) practice, having historical and contemporary manifestations in a range of different countries, from the US, Mexico, France, Italy and Britain to Scandinavia and Japan (to just name the most prominent traditions). Similarly, there are not only noir novels and films, but noir television shows, anime, manga, video games and more. Whatever the medium, however, noir pushes its audience to confront uncomfortable truths about themselves and the world they live in.

Nightmare Alley as noir affect

John Lindsay Gresham's *Nightmare Alley* (1946) is a noir that reworks and deforms the genres of the crime novel and the naturalist novel. It also reworks the tropes of investigative journalism, revealing the secrets behind carnival acts, spiritualism and, finally, in its most ironic moment, psychotherapy (which it reveals, meta-textually to the degree that noir itself is psychoanalytic, to be the ultimate and most lucrative con). The novel starts as a naturalist account of carnival life but transforms into a crime novel in recounting the grifts practised by the main character, Stanton Carlisle. We follow Stan as he goes from carnival magician, to mentalist, to spiritualist, to running a psychoanalytically-informed con on a business magnate, to falling all the way back down the ladder and beyond.

At every step of the ascent he manipulates and uses people, from killing the husband of someone he desires with alcohol, through using various women to gain access to forms of knowledge and status he cannot access on his own, to finally being used himself by a woman more powerful and ruthless than him. These violent antagonisms are captured by the sadism visible in Stan's eyes, which are "as hard as a frozen pond" (149). This hardness figures capitalist cynicism and sadistic violence at its purest. The narrative seems to simultaneously embrace and critique these affects. This ambivalence is typical of the noir narrative – it both embraces capitalism at its most unbridled and represents the way in which the very same logic leaves a swath of destruction and violence in its path. Yet, the critique of capitalism and its embodiment in the grifter or crook is not particularly moralistic. The noir text merely records the way in which those who live by such an ethos also come to their undoing by the same. At the end of the narrative, Stan becomes a geek, his deepest fear stemming from his early experience of carnival life. The geek is a carnival performer who bites the heads off animals for the promise of alcohol. The geek is basically an abject drunk who will do anything to feed his fix. Stan, for all his hardness, is haunted by the image of the geek and the addiction and fear it represents.

The geek is a figure that haunts Stan from the beginning of the narrative. As the carnival director Hoately tells him: "Listen kid. Do I have to draw you a damn blueprint? You pick a guy and he ain't a geek – he's a drunk. A bottle-a-day booze fool" (7). What is most striking about this account is the way in which it suggests the arbitrariness of who becomes the geek. Certainly he's a drunk, but he just happens to be picked out (we meet many drunks in the novel who aren't fingered for the same due to their worldly stature or just luck) through a cynical logic of capitalist sorting. What makes Stan, as well as all of us, available to such manipulation and abjection is the fear that stalks him, despite his attempts at mastery and ruthlessness. This fear is captured in the logic of the "nightmare alley" itself, which appears to Stan in a recurring nightmare:

> It was the dark alley, all over again. With a light at the end of it. Ever since he was a kid, Stan had the dream. He was running down a dark alley, the buildings vacant and black and menacing on either side. Far down at the end of it a light burned, but there was something behind him, close behind him, getting closer until he woke up trembling and never reached the light.
>
> *(67)*

The alley is the fear of death; even more, it is the fear of weakness and terror that allows death to overtake one. It is the fear of not being hard enough or tough enough to endure the waking life of everyday competition. Yet, at the same time, it is secretly a wish. It is a desire to give into weakness, passivity and iniquity. It is the desire to not have to fight so hard to win – to give into losing. It is the desire to finally give up on the cruel optimism of hope of the light before one and just succumb to the nightmare. If nothing else, one can live out one's days as a geek, sure of the limits of one's suffering. Even negative repetitions become a kind of comfort. Such are the paradoxes of noir affect.

Conclusion

Noir, then, does something radical with the typical affects produced by crime fiction. In place of mastery and moral certainty that characterises the classical detective narrative, it is organised around failure and moral ambiguity. Similarly, in place of the hardness of the hardboiled protagonist, the noir protagonist is finally vulnerable and death-haunted. Noir thus subverts the will to know that is central to the form. It suggests that we cannot fully know or master the haunted landscape in which we move. Indeed, it suggests that we cannot even know our own mind. Instead, we must navigate the darkness as best we can.

Bibliography

Augé, M. (2009) *Non-Places: Introduction to an anthropology of supermodernity*, trans. J. Howe, London: Verso.

Berlant, L. (2011) *Cruel Optimism*, Durham: Duke University Press.

Brennan, T. (2004) *The Transmission of Affect*, Ithaca: Cornell University Press.

Breu, C. (2005) *Hard-Boiled Masculinities*, Minneapolis: University of Minnesota Press.

———. (2009) "Radical noir: negativity, misogyny, and the critique of privatization in Dorothy Hughes's *In a Lonely Place*", *Modern Fiction Studies*, 55(2): 199–215.

Clough, P.T. (2007) "Introduction", in P. Ticineto Clough and J. Halley (eds), *The Affective Turn*, Durham: Duke University Press, 1–33.

Deleuze, G. (1992) *Expressionism in Philosophy: Spinoza*, trans. M. Joughin, New York: Zone.

Fay, J. and Nieland, J. (2009) *Film Noir: Hard-boiled modernity and the cultures of globalization*, New York: Routledge.

Foucault, M. (2010). *The Birth of Biopolitics: Lectures at the Collège de France, 1978–1979*, trans. G. Burchell, New York: Picador.

Freud, S. (1955) *The Standard Edition of the Complete Psychological Works of Sigmund Freud*, trans. and ed. J. Strachey, London: Hogarth Press.

Gresham, W.L. (1946) *Nightmare Alley*, New York: New York Review of Books Classics.

Grossberg, L. (1992) *We've Gotta Get Out of This Place: Popular conservatism and postmodern culture*, New York: Routledge.

Lacan, J. (2016) *Anxiety: The seminar of Jacques Lacan, Book X*, trans. A.R. Price, Cambridge: Polity Press.

Marling, W. (1994) *The American Roman Noir: Hammett, Chandler, Cain*, Athens: University of Georgia Press.

Massumi, B. (2002) *Parables for the Virtual: Movement, affect, sensation*, Durham: Duke University Press.

Metress, C. (1994) "Living degree zero: masculinity and the threat of desire in the roman noir", in P.F. Murphy (ed.), *Fictions of Masculinity: Crossing cultures, crossing sexualities*, New York: New York University Press, 155–84.

Miller, D.A. (1989) *The Novel and the Police*, Berkeley: University of California Press.

Naremore, J. (1998) *More than Night: Film noir in its contexts*, Berkeley: University of California Press.

Ngai, S. (2005) *Ugly Feelings*, Cambridge, MA: Harvard University Press.

Oliver, K. and Trigo, B. (2003) *Noir Anxiety*, Minneapolis: University of Minnesota Press, 1–26.

Sedgwick, E.K. (2003) *Touching, Feeling: Affect, performativity, pedagogy*, Durham: Duke University Press.

Sobchack, V. (1998) "Lounge Time: Postwar crises and the chronotope of film noir", in N. Browne (ed.), *Refiguring American Film Genres*, Berkeley: University of California Press, 129–70.

Spinoza, B. de (1996) *Ethics*, New York: Penguin.

Tomkins, S. (1995) *Shame and its Sisters: A Silvan Tomkins reader*, ed. E. Kosofsky Sedgwick and A. Frank, Durham: Duke University Press.

Vernet, M. (1993) "Film noir on the edge of doom", in J. Copjec (ed.), *Shades of Noir*, London: Verso, 1–32.

Williams, R. (1978) *Marxism and Literature*, Oxford: Oxford University Press.

Žižek, S. (2001) *Enjoy your Symptom!: Jacques Lacan in Hollywood and out*, New York: Routledge.

28

ALTERITY AND THE OTHER

Jean Anderson

On 15 March 2019, New Zealand Prime Minister Jacinda Ardern responded to the massacre of fifty Muslim worshippers in Christchurch by addressing the killer directly with a declaration that summed up what many felt across the country: "we utterly reject and condemn you" (Small 2019). Ardern's words speak of a strong desire to establish distance between ourselves and criminal violence. Similarly, though, the motivation of the gunman, himself an Australian immigrant, can also be represented as "utterly rejecting" the incomer Other.[1]

Not everyone agreed completely with the Prime Minister's statement. Her declaration that "They are us", referring to the Muslim community, while just as lapidary, was seen by some as reflecting an ambivalence that highlights the fluidity of the constructs of self and Other. In using this expression, Ardern both rallied the nation and underlined the importance given to perceptions of difference. Otherness is (and can only be) viewed from a particular standpoint. That this standpoint is, in itself, as shifting and fluid as constructions of identity – they are us, you are not us, but we are not them – is rarely acknowledged by those who wield the idea of difference as a weapon.

Such "us / not us" statements are founded (on both sides) on an assumption that there is a community of the righteous and an excluded group or groups of those who are different. This urge to disown any connection with outliers, the rejection of those we prefer to see as "not us", can be related to long-established social psychology theories of "ingroups" and "outgroups" (Sherif 1958). In rejecting those we see as Other, we intensify a comforting separation and claim moral superiority. At the same time, Others represent a challenge to our values, and to our sense of security. Fundamentally, the issue is that if the Other is not Other, then we ourselves are Other, an intolerable but perhaps unavoidable conundrum.

Why, then, the widespread attraction to reading about behaviours we (apparently) reject for ourselves? An increasing interest in real-life stories of violence and murder and the steady appeal of crime fiction can be linked to the concept of "safe danger": Reading about, or watching, violent criminal activities allows us to encounter the Other but with "a very low risk of any serious harm" (Martínková and Parry 2017: 88). Peter Messent proposes that "the reader's desire for transgressive excitement [is] balanced by her or his need for security and safety" (2013: 5). Gill Plain describes crime fiction, and particularly detective fiction, as being "about confronting and taming the monstrous. It is a literature of containment, a narrative that 'makes safe'" (2001: 3). The need to "make safe" is accompanied, as Kristeva points out in

Powers of Horror, by ambivalence: "Apprehensive, desire turns aside; sickened, it rejects. [...] But simultaneously, just the same, that impetus, that spasm, that leap is drawn toward an elsewhere as tempting as it is condemned" (1982: 1). We are both attracted and repelled by this Other, just as we might teeter on the edge of a cliff, drawn by vividly imagined danger.

Crime fiction allows us to explore imaginatively what it is to be the criminal Other: Creations like Jeff Lindsay's Dexter (or, arguably, Agatha Christie's Dr Sheppard) place us alongside the murderer. Crime fiction also provides a space in which we can rehearse detecting that same Other, whereas in real life we are restricted to basing our judgements on externalities: At least part of the fascination of serial killers lies in the non-coincidence of appearance and character, such as the quiet ordinariness of Peter Sutcliffe and Fred and Rosemary West, the attractiveness of Ted Bundy or the clown disguises of John Wayne Gacy.

I argue here that we learn this abject attraction-repulsion at an early age. There is an attraction to exposing ourselves to risk and contemplating danger on a visceral level, such as being thrown repeatedly into the air by a parent. More to the point, we transpose this "thrill of the spill" into our reading and viewing preferences. We also learn from early exposure to particular types of narrative: Fairy tales abound in conflicts between good (represented by protagonists with whom we are encouraged to identify) and evil (a dangerous Other, the source of narrative excitement even if destined to be conquered). Without the villain, there is no story. Where crime fiction is concerned, this fairy-tale aspect has been remarked on in passing by Graham Greene, for whom crime stories are "modern fairy tales" (1969: 215). For Bruce Shaw, "many, if not all the stylistic strategies noted for the fairy tale are used to good effect by the best [...] crime writers" (2013: 19). It is no accident, then, that crime narratives contain some of the basic constructs and arguably, purposes, of these so-called children's stories. In essence, we learn through them to read the world, to expect and to predict particular behaviours and outcomes. The quest pattern highlighted by Propp for the fairy tale and applied with variation to crime fiction by Todorov (1977), and the sense of a return to justice are concepts that apply to both fairy tales and classic detective fiction, although there is a growing tendency for contemporary crime narratives to complicate the oppositional good (self) vs. evil (Other) paradigm. In so doing, these narratives recognise the central, driving force of the villain and the attraction-repulsion inspired in readers by the Other.

This chapter will focus on the function of Otherness in crime fiction through various figures: The criminal Other, the victim Other, detective Others and the use of othered places, with a particular focus on the ways in which James Lee Burke's Robicheaux novels both perpetuate and undermine paradigms of Otherness.

If looks could kill: Judging the Other by appearance

In many examples from the Western fairy tale tradition, especially if we exclude Andersen's (scandi-noir?) and the Grimm brothers' dark-toned stories, virtue is rewarded. Particularly in the Disney versions that have replaced their earlier sources, goodness is recognised and triumphs, setting up and repeating a model in which the world operates according to principles of justice. This element is also key to some crime fiction: Russian crime writer Daria Dontsova acknowledges that she writes "fairy tales for adults" in order to reassure her readership that "things will sort themselves out" (Masropova 2008: 113).

Many readers first encounter the monstrous Other via fairy tales in which otherness is portrayed through descriptions of physical appearance and visual categorisations. Wicked witches, trolls and ogres, for example, are ugly, while princes and princesses are beautiful. In many fairy tales, a character's true nature is concealed by appearance and, as in crime fiction, the stories often contain explicit reversals, unmaskings of the hidden Other. Snow White's stepmother is beautiful but villainous; the frog can become a prince; the Beast has an inner goodness; Little Red Riding Hood discovers the danger behind the wolf's disguise.

Physical descriptions of characters also play an important role in crime fiction. Either the evil Others pass undetected (disguised) among us, or their inner nature is reflected in their appearance, written in such a way as to provide readable clues to the truth. Writing crime fiction is largely a matter of concealing that "truth" while allowing some surface indications to guide the reader alongside the detective. The reader is nonetheless never sure before the reveal (if there is one) what the truth might be. In classic crime fiction, it is the role of the detective to reveal the truth by stripping back the concealment afforded by misleading externalities.

Some aspects of appearance do lend themselves to interpretation, leading to an ambivalent response. For Kristeva, otherness is signalled initially through outward signs of difference. In *Strangers to Ourselves*, foreigners or strangers are first and foremost distinguishable by their appearance: "this grasping the foreigner's features, one that captivates us, beckons and rejects at the same time" (1991: 3). Unusual physical traits may be underlined by strangeness in speech or cultural habits: Faced with attacks and/or rejection, the foreigner withdraws into "aloofness" (9), where "hatred provides the foreigner with consistency" (13). Initial indicators of difference are thus crystallised into an increasingly dense and xenophobic layering of impenetrable otherness, repelling the observer and causing the observed to retreat further into opacity. The ethnic Other can rarely "pass" in the same way as unrecognised villains, but not looking different is no guarantee of shared values.

European-based crime fiction, in print and visual forms, provides a testing ground for confronting Otherness at a time when migratory pressures are increasing opportunities for the assimilation or rejection of incomers locked into racial stereotypes. There are numerous instances of incomer (immigrant) criminality playing a major role in crime fiction, from the film *Taken* (2008), in which East Europeans run prostitution rings, and Arab white slavers, whose exact national origins remain unspecified, bid for virgins, to season three of the French series *Engrenages* [*Spiral*, 2010], which features Albanian organised crime. Such examples reiterate the hostility toward Otherness that widens the gap between "us" and "them" and can be seen as instigating new stereotypes of the criminal Other, promoting "aloofness" and distance.

If crime fiction generally can be seen as a space in which this distance might be explored and a degree of empathy with the Other brought to light, this is no easy task. Not all foreigners are seen in a negative light: They may invite sympathy as victims of persecution and stereotyping. Andrea Camilleri's *Il ladro di merendine* (1996) [*The Snack Thief*, 2003] presents a sympathetic view of North African immigrants, with Inspector Salva Montalbano describing them as "family" (Pezzotti 2012: 180–82). Despite this positive attitude, the predominant tendency of other characters is to group "foreigners" into an amorphous threat, rather than to see them as individuals. A further example illustrates the way Otherness as a singular label can be highly resistant to more balanced treatment. Angelina Maccarone, writer for the long-running German television series *Tatort*, defended her script for episode 684 (2007) as an attempt to present an ethnic group as "far from homogeneous", with a storyline that featured a young Alevi Turkish woman sexually abused by her father. This attempt to break the incomer label "Turks" into smaller groupings with individual stories merely split them into further categories of Otherness, creating a scandal among Alevi Turks who saw themselves as doubly othered (Sutherland 2012).

The detective as Other

Identifying and "catching" the criminal reinforces the distinction between the virtuous (and potentially vulnerable) me/us and the perpetrator(s), but it may require the forces of order to

Alterity and the other

cross the normal/abnormal divide. Even that most famous of detectives, Sherlock Holmes, can hardly be said to be socially conformist: His use of disguises in pursuit of the criminal further emphasises his ability to "pass" undetected while detecting. The structural model of the outsider perspective has also been an important element in detective stories where the "gentleman adventurer" epitomises the importance of justice even when attained by unconventional means ("setting a thief to catch a thief"). In Carroll John Daly's *The False Burton Combs* (1922), the detective becomes an outlier by stepping outside social norms (such as class and, later, gender behaviours) in order to defend the society to which these are fundamental. Seen as an early hardboiled investigator, Daly's deceptive detective shares traits with earlier French figures such as Ponson du Terail's Rocambole (1857), Leblanc's Arsène Lupin (1905) or the English writer Hornung's A.J. Raffles (1898). While the hardboiled detective evolves over time, he (or later, she) is by and large a loner working the edges of society, both observer and to a lesser degree, participant.

In such cases, readers may be asked to identify with and simultaneously distance themselves from the detective. While Sax Rohmer's Fu Manchu (1913) and his scheming daughter can be seen as reinforcing the evil Other stereotype, figures such as Charlie Chan (1919) and Hercule Poirot (1920) indicate that outsiderness may be a useful quality for observing the behaviours of others. Thus the insider-outsider paradigm is inverted: The outsider in these examples demonstrates a heightened level of insider perception, while maintaining a degree of distance. This distance owes something to an element of caricature and comic exaggeration of the outsider aspects of the character: Poirot's prissiness and Chan's inscrutability, for example, also evoke some ambivalence in the reader.

It should be noted, too, that using an outsider detective protagonist allows the writer to question local values and norms of behaviour. Investigative teams, like Dominique Sylvain's detecting duo of retired French policewoman Lola Jost and American burlesque dancer Ingrid Diesel, or mixed-origin detectives such as Jakob Arjouni's German-Turkish sleuth Kemal Kayankaya, can be used to achieve this distancing effect and to question the validity of cultural differences by framing them as "Other", as both attractive and unacceptable at the same time.

Laughing it off: Humour as Othering device

In *Powers of Horror* (1982) Kristeva argues that humour is a means of resisting or at least responding to that phenomenon of attraction-repulsion she describes as abjection:

> The one by whom abjection exists is thus a *deject* who places (himself), *separates* (himself), and therefore *strays* instead of getting his bearings, desiring, belonging, or refusing. Situationist in a sense, and not without laughter, since laughing is a way of placing or displacing abjection.
>
> *(1982: 8, emphasis in original)*

The laughter Kristeva refers to is described as "apocalyptic" and deflects or displaces only in a destructive manner (204). In this section, I argue that humour can also be an important narrative choice in facilitating the reader's identification with problematised detective or criminal characters, and that verbal and situational humour, the shared joke, as it were, play a major role not only in creating this affective link but also in distancing violence. The "us-ness" of laughter domesticates violence and turns an imminent threat into a source of relieved amusement. Whether the source of comedy be a slapstick situation in Janet Evanovich's Stephanie Plum or gritty, ironising wordplay in Chandler's Marlowe or Hammett's Spade, it provides a distraction from the sinister reality that people are kidnapped, injured, killed every day. In that sense, humour in crime fiction acts to negate anxieties about vulnerability and is arguably a replacement strategy for the fairy-tale "restoration of order" that may no longer seem possible to the contemporary reader.

More bluntly put, the crimes of comedic "Others" take on a less stressful form, which allows the creation of a (fictional) "kinship" with the reader (Chodat 2006), and thus a sense of community (us) that also soothes the sense of vulnerability by excluding perpetrators of violent crime (them). The crime comedy, or "crimedy", can provide a lighthearted approach to acts of desperate violence that can also allow space for social criticism, as in the case of the (mainly female) practitioners of the Polish and Russian subgenre known as *ironicheskii detectiv*, detective fiction "infused with [...] comedic remarks and situations" (Masropova 2008: 113). Many of these writings are parodic in nature, such as Evanovich's Stephanie Plum series, Marion Chesney's Agatha Raisin or French television series *Candice Renoir*, *Élodie Bradford* and *Capitaine Marleau*, all of which feature unorthodox female investigators.

Historically, the French scene also offers examples of crime fiction where verbal comedy arguably overrides the horror of what is being described, and thus "others" it into an edgy form of entertainment. It is quite different, too, from the gentler kind of humour that characterises many of the "cosy" mysteries, although these may have a deeper layering than is often recognised. Bruce Shaw suggests that "[w]hile the strain of humorist writing has a strong cozy effect, it is subversive as well, introducing serious issues masked behind diverting laughter" (2013: 6); in other words, "safe danger".

The killer as Other and same: James Lee Burke's Dave Robicheaux

The most comforting scenario in crime fiction is undoubtedly one in which the killer is identified as Other and order is restored (Scaggs 2005: 201). The detective's role in such situations is one of hero and the reader can identify his or her restorative role: The (evil) Other is contained or eliminated. In recent years we have seen a proliferation of oddball detectives whose characterisation increasingly stresses variation from the Manichean construct of good versus evil. Lindsay's Dexter series (2004-), for example, thoroughly muddles the reader's perceptions of right and wrong, bringing the killer Other into a relatively sympathetic focus.[2]

Faced with the Other, we have two choices: We can emphasise difference and reduce our Other to an amalgam of the qualities we do not share; or we can attempt to see him or her in their totality, recognising shared elements and learning from differences (Savouret 2010: 17). This challenge to recognise, control and reject the Other is a constant preoccupation of James Lee Burke's protagonist Dave Robicheaux, in his investigative activities and his own internal struggles. A former policeman now working for the sheriff's department, and a recovering alcoholic, Robicheaux is a strong central character in a complex narrative environment filled with Otherness. This analysis of the hero and his world will focus on the 2018 novel, *Robicheaux*, with some reference to earlier works.

The Robicheaux series is set in New Iberia Parish, on Bayou Teche and near the coast in South Central Louisiana, with frequent investigative trips to nearby Lafayette, Baton Rouge and New Orleans, the city in which the protagonist began his career in law enforcement following service in Vietnam. For Robicheaux, the first-person narrator of the novels, the area is historically and in contemporary terms a space of otherness, as he explains in *The New Iberia Blues* (2019): "Acadiana, like New Orleans, is filled with eccentrics primarily because it has never

Alterity and the other

been fully assimilated into the United States. It's a fine place to be an artist, a writer, an iconoclast, a bohemian, or a drunk" (175). Home to the Cajuns (Acadians), French settlers who were chased out of Canada by the British during the *Grand Dérangement* of 1755–1769, it has become a locus of difference, as Robicheaux, himself a Cajun, explains: "Maybe for that reason, we have a greater tolerance for others who are different or who have been collectively rejected" (175). At the same time, wrongdoers – or those accused of wrongdoing – are not always so generously received. In *Cadillac Jukebox* (1996) Burke's protagonist dismisses the possibility of someone's wrongful conviction for murder in a few words: "He had never denied it, had he? Besides, he had never been one of us" (3). The "us" here is ambiguous: Since Robicheaux is the narrative focaliser in each of the novels, the pronoun applies to both those of Cajun origin, seen as the earliest and therefore the authentic settlers in the region, and to those who stay for the most part on the right side of the law.

Almost everyone in Louisiana is Other. Despite the priority accorded to them by virtue of Robicheaux's own origins and centrality to the narrative, Cajuns are by no means the sole occupants of Louisiana, where a high level of *métissage* exists. For example, blacks are often described as having blue eyes, inherited from their French ancestors (2010b: 88; 2018: 181); "redbones" are typically of Indian, French and African descent (1999: 40). Burke also makes frequent mention of "peckerwoods", or Southern white trash; this term generally applies to poor rural whites, many of whom belong to the Klan or, if in prison, to the Aryan Brotherhood.

At the same time as there is much mixing, there is also, as the presence of the last two groups would indicate, a strong emphasis on social and racial divisions. Tensions between poor whites and blacks are influenced by deeply embedded memories of the defeat of the South: "Each morning they [poor whites] got up with their loss, their knowledge of who they were, and went to war with the world", observes Robicheaux in *Black Cherry Blues* (2010b: 88). It is noteworthy that while the protagonist espouses generally liberal views, descriptions of almost every character emphasise appearance, and particularly skin colour. In highlighting diversity, Burke seemingly cannot avoid stressing difference, perhaps because in print as opposed to visual media, telling instead of showing is required. This divisiveness is reinforced by the fact that various locales are referred to in terms of their socially segregated clientele: One Harpo Delahoussey runs "a ramshackle nightclub for redbones" (1999: 40); mixing can occur, in "an end-of-the-line mixed race joint" in *Robicheaux* (2018: 296), but the fact it occasions comment suggests that all locations enforce a particular inclusivity/exclusivity code.

Added to this mix are the various exploiters of Louisiana's resources, outsiders who have essentially destroyed the beauty and fertility of the region:

> the oil and chemical companies who drained and polluted the wetlands; the developers who could turn sugarcane acreage and pecan orchards into miles of tract homes and shopping malls that had all the aesthetic qualities of a sewer works; and the Mafia, who operated out of New Orleans and brought us prostitution, slot machines, control of at least two big labor unions, and finally narcotics [...] they took everything that was best from the Cajun world in which I had grown up, treated it cynically and with contempt and left us with oil sludge in the oyster beds, Levittown, and the abiding knowledge that we had done virtually nothing to stop them.
>
> *(2010b: 42)*

While the Cajuns and other locals are therefore victims, they are also complicit in the villainy that has been perpetrated: "we had done virtually nothing to stop them". The borderlines between good (us, the locals) and evil (them, the incomers) are blurred, particularly since "peckerwoods" and Mafia, or Cajuns and developers do sometimes work together.

Given this blurring of boundaries, how can we tell "us" from "them"? Throughout the series, criminals often have an appearance that sets them apart and marks them as Other. Burke's Robicheaux is particularly unforgiving of corrupt politicians: Bobby Earl, a former Klan Grand Master with ambitions to be governor responds to Robicheaux's persistent inquiries:

> a strange transformation took place in his face. The skin grew taught against the bone, and there was a flat, green-yellow venomous glaze in his eyes, the kind you see only in people who have successfully worked for years to hide the propensity for cruelty that lives inside them.
>
> *(2010b: 97)*

Child abuser Verise Benson in *A Stained White Radiance* has suffered terrible burns, so that his face resembles red putty (2010a: 34); contract killer Eddy Raintree from the same novel has "a head like a pumpkin" (85); Chester "Smiley" Wimple, a hitman for hire and a recurring character, looks like the Pilsbury doughboy, or "an egg with features painted on it", a "toy man with lips as red as a clown's" and a smile that looks like "an open wound" (2018: 283, 378, 342). As a consequence, he has often been mocked, bullied, excluded. Clearly a villain, he is also a victim. Despite his evil otherness, Smiley chooses to execute those who have abused children while sparing targets who have shown him kindness; he is himself a survivor of abuse endured in an orphanage and as a street urchin growing up in Mexico. Positioned within his alterity, he can still find and join an "us". As Robicheaux comments in *The New Iberia Blues*, if he had grown up the way Smiley did, he probably wouldn't be very different (2019: 395).

Leroy Panek's comment that "most writers simply label their villains as psychopaths and leave it at that" (2010: 169) notwithstanding, Burke takes a more exploratory stance at times. Villains can be complex creatures, despite their unconscionable acts. Readers are invited, via Robicheaux's readable descriptions, to see the demarcation lines between good and the evil Other as not always fixed. While some villains are simply villainous, particularly mafia associates, others are treated in a more mitigated way.

There is a deeply significant reason for this occasional sympathy: Given the lack of any clear-cut division, the criminals are not usually entirely Other. Nor are the upholders of the law entirely admirable – far from it. One of the most salient features of Burke's fictional world is the number of crooked policemen: The level of corruption throughout Louisiana is high. While Robicheaux himself is honest, his former partner and frequent offsider, Cletus Purcel, is a well-intentioned drunk who – as a licensed private investigator – frequently has recourse to violence to achieve his ends. While he brutalises only those who "deserve" it, in other words maintaining a degree of self-control and judgement, the same cannot be said of Robicheaux. Acutely self-aware, Robicheaux sees the commonalities between the "good guys" and the "bad": "we share much of the same culture as the lowlifes, and we are more alike than different" (2018: 3). A recovering alcoholic who occasionally falls off the wagon, he spends part of *Robicheaux* half-convinced that he has committed a murder he cannot recall: "The last person I can trust or believe is me" (171).

Just like the so-called psychopath killers, Robicheaux has "a disorder in [his] head", triggered by observing the cruelty of others towards those weaker than themselves (357). However, his murderous attack on a suspect is no act of justice and vengeance calmly meted out; instead, it is abject and uncontrolled violence:

Alterity and the other

I should have pulled the plug. But I knew I wasn't going to. The simian that had lived in me since I was a child was back in town. A cloud that was red and black and without shape seemed to explode inside my head and destroy my vision, although I was able to see my deeds from somewhere outside my body.

(2018: 278)

Here the protagonist's description of his state of mind closely parallels Kristevan abjection in its simultaneous attraction and repulsion. The same ambivalence that characterises many of Burke's descriptions of villains applies to the detecting heroes, society's supposed bastion against the perpetrators of crimes.

In the end, Burke's Robicheaux novels are less about classic detective-catches-criminal certainties and more concerned with the complex and fluctuating boundaries between good and evil, self and other viewed from the outside but also from the inside (good and evil *within* self and other), that not-so-safe danger that is evoked by "the unsettling abject 'other' of Julia Kristeva's theory [...] with its distinctly uncertain boundaries" (Scaggs 2005: 103). There is no reassuring "they all lived happily ever after" here, no "utter condemnation and rejection" but instead an unsettling attraction-repulsion.

There are, in the end, no comforting separations between "us" and "them". The other is within us: "I do not encounter myself outside, I find the other within me" (Deleuze 1986: 105; my translation). Perhaps in the end our fascination with crime, in fiction as in life, is a recognition that we are all Other, and an attempt to understand that Other within ourselves. Crime fiction offers us a harmless and often entertaining close-up insight into the complexities of an impulse to violence that defies and overflows any neat, Manichean division between self and Other.

Notes

1 This chapter will focus mainly on ethnic and social Others. For a discussion of gender as Otherness, see Chapter 11.
2 Humour does not always have a significant place in such role-inversion works; it is largely absent, for example, in UK television's *Luther* (2010-), *Marcella* (2016-) and *Bancroft* (2017-).

Bibliography

Burke, J.L. (1996) *Cadillac Jukebox*, New York: Simon and Schuster.
———. (1999) [1998] *Sunset Limited*, London: Orion.
———. (2010a) [1992] *A Stained White Radiance*, New York: Simon and Schuster.
———. (2010b) [1989] *Black Cherry Blues*, New York, London: Pocket Books.
———. (2018) *Robicheaux*, New York: Simon and Schuster.
———. (2019) *The New Iberia Blues*, London: Orion.
Chodat, R. (2006) "Jokes, fiction and Lorrie Moore", *Twentieth-Century Fiction*, 52(1): 42–60.
Deleuze, G. (1986) *Foucault*, Paris: Minuit.
Greene, G. (1969) "Journey into success", in *Collected Essays*, London: Bodley Head, 215–19.
Kristeva, J. (1982) *Powers of Horror. An essay on abjection*, trans. L.S. Roudiez, New York: Columbia University Press.
———. (1991) *Strangers to Ourselves*, trans. L.S. Roudiez, New York: Columbia University Press.
Martínková, I. and Parry, J. (2017) "Safe danger – on the experience of challenge, adventure and risk in education", *Sport, Ethics and Philosophy*, 11(1): 75–91.
Masropova, O. (2008) "Crime, BYT, and fairy tales: Daria Dontsova and post-Soviet ironical detective fiction", *The Slavic and East European Journal*, 52(1): 113–28.
Messent, P. (2013) *The Crime Fiction Handbook*, Chichester: Wiley-Blackwell.

Panek, L.L. (2010) "Post-war American police fiction", in M. Priestman (ed.), *The Cambridge Companion to Crime Fiction*, Cambridge: Cambridge University Press, 155–71.

Pezzotti, B. (2012) "Who is the foreigner? The representation of the migrant in contemporary Italian crime fiction", in J. Anderson, C. Miranda and B. Pezzotti (eds), *The Foreign in International Crime Fiction: Transcultural representations*, London: Continuum, 176–87.

Plain, G. (2001) *Twentieth-Century Crime Fiction: Gender, sexuality and the body*, Edinburgh: Edinburgh University Press.

Savouret, P.-L. (2010) "L'Autre, c'est moi: la figure littéraire de l'étranger dans les romans policiers de Lorenzo Silva", in P.-L. Savouret (ed.), *Polars. En quête de ... l'Autre*, Chambéry: Presses de l'Université de Savoie, 17–30.

Scaggs, J. (2005) *Crime Fiction*, London: Routledge.

Shaw, B. (2013) *Jolly Good Detecting: Humor in English crime fiction of the Golden Age*, Jefferson, NC: McFarland.

Sherif, M. (1958) "Superordinate goals in the reduction of intergroup conflict", *American Journal of Sociology*, 63(4): 349–56.

Small, Z. (2019) "Prime Minister Jacinda Ardern fiercely condemns Christchurch 'terrorist attack'", *Newshub*, 15 March, www.newshub.co.nz/home/politics/2019/03/prime-minister-jacinda-ardern-fiercely-condemns-christchurch-terrorist-attack.html (accessed 20 February 2019).

Sutherland, M. (2012) "Images of Turks in recent German crime fiction: a comparative case study in xenophobia", in J. Anderson, C. Miranda and B. Pezzotti (eds), *The Foreign in International Crime Fiction: Transcultural representations*, London: Continuum, 188–99.

Todorov, T. (1977) "The typology of detective fiction", *Poetics of Prose*, trans. R. Howard, Oxford: Blackwell, 42–52.

29

DIGITAL TECHNOLOGY

Nicole Kenley

In the conversation surrounding crime fiction's changing identity, digital technology is frequently thought of as a marker of the new in the genre. That is, digital technology stands out as a harbinger of the new types of crime, new criminal methodologies and new crime-solving techniques that mark contemporary crime fiction as somehow distinct from its more analogue forebears. While it is certainly true that the inclusion of digital aspects such as computers, smartphones or GPS (to list but a few popular technologies) marks novels as belonging to the late twentieth or early twenty-first centuries, this tendency to equate digital technologies with newness belies the genre's reliance on technology since its beginnings. As Ronald R. Thomas points out (1999), detective fiction (and crime fiction more generally) has incorporated forensic technologies since its rise in popularity in the nineteenth century. As a result, the reader may well expect that technology plays a role in much crime fiction, contemporary or otherwise. The formulation that technology simply equals novelty is problematic because it obscures the true role of digital technologies, which is not as a marker of newness but rather as a signifier of the choices such innovations force upon society. Brenden Riley notes that

> [w]e make trade-offs when we adopt new technologies. They usually solve one set of problems while bringing with them a new set for society to grapple with. Ideally, the new set will be less burdensome than the old set, but often such problems are so far off as to be unpredictable or inconceivable for the inventors of the new technology.
>
> *(2017: 95)*

Crime fiction imagines those "unpredictable or inconceivable" potential consequences through the ways in which criminals exploit and detectives police digital technologies.

As the examples in this chapter demonstrate, since digital technology in crime fiction may be used either by criminals or those attempting to thwart them, the use of technology by those two groups is reciprocally shaping. A criminal's use of a new digital technology forces a detective to adopt a new methodology in order to prevail, and vice versa. This reciprocally-shaping component demonstrates that, while readers (and detectives) might wish for a straightforward containment of crime via the application of digital technologies, in fact, these technologies reveal the extent to which criminals often exploit new technological opportunities with greater facility than either police or private detectives. As a result, both criminals and detectives innovate, push boundaries and force consideration of broader social issues. These issues may be ripped from current headlines or, as is more often the case, reflect possible, yet currently unrealised, scenarios for exploiting technologies. Frequently, the texts pose large cultural questions about the risks and rewards of (over)utilising digital technologies. Ultimately, as usual, the genre provides a lens through which to view cultural anxieties more broadly. Digital crime, depicting as it does a smaller subset of global crime, represents a strategy through which the genre of detective fiction tries to control a new type of criminality. The conviction that new technologies can contain global crime is revealed by detective fiction to be only partially realisable, troubling a broader expectation about the genre's general function.

In making this argument, the chapter begins with a general overview of the uses of digital technology in crime fiction, from personal computers and hacking, through to the rise of smartphones and social media. Next, in service of the argument that criminals and detectives reciprocally shape the usage of new technologies, the chapter provides an exploration of the relationship between forensic novels and digital technologies. While the overarching view of forensic novels is that they deal with physical rather than digital evidence, many prominent forensic authors include an array of digital technologies in their works, from miniaturised surveillance drones to data mining. This section details how forensic crime novels continually present emerging digital technologies in response to new uses of technology for criminal perpetration and containment. The chapter concludes by looking at Jeffery Deaver's 2016 novel *The Steel Kiss* as a means of examining the tension between digital technology and one of crime fiction's traditional functions, threat containment, to further underscore the relationship between digital technologies, criminals, detectives and risks versus rewards.

Hackers, social media and speculative fiction

As digital technology advances, crime fiction as a genre continues to investigate the ways in which the new options such technology affords offer both security and threats. On the one hand, digital technology provides invaluable tools to detectives in the form of searchable databases and nearly instant access to the kinds of information that would formerly have taken days, weeks or months to obtain. On the other hand, digital technologies can be hacked and weaponised to create unforeseen crimes that detectives struggle to police and contain. The tension between the benefits and risks to detection, between expediency and vulnerability, governs most detective fiction concerned with digital technology. The figure that perhaps best exemplifies this tension is the hacker.

Though novels dealing with hackers date to at least 1984 with William Gibson's cyberpunk novel *Neuromancer*, hackers in detective fiction did not explode in popularity until Stieg Larsson's posthumously published *The Girl with the Dragon Tattoo* appeared in 2005 (2008 in English translation). The sheer volume of scholarship on Larsson's novel and the entire *Millennium Trilogy* (including edited collections from Åström et al. (2013) and Peacock (2013), as well as monographs and articles) speaks to the impact the works have had on the genre. Based on the novel's success worldwide, some suggest that its scope goes beyond detective fiction to influence fiction more broadly: A recent publication survey indicates that in 2016, at least partially thanks to the popularity of *The Girl with the Dragon Tattoo*, "nearly 1 percent of fiction titles featur[e] the word 'girl' in the title" (Mandel 2016). In explaining the Millennium trilogy's popularity, Sarah Casey Benyahia writes that "Salander [...] is a product of society's fears of, and attraction to, cyberspace" (2013: 59). The same claim might be made of detective novels featuring digital technology more generally. In *Dragon Tattoo* and the scores of other detective novels with some sort of digital aspect, from GPS trackers to RFID chips to smartphones to surveillance drones, the technology tends to be introduced at some length by an expert, be it the detective, the criminal or a third skilled party. These introductions function both to tantalise and terrify, highlighting the benefits and dangers created by the technology and forcing the reader to consider which outweighs the other. In *Dragon Tattoo*, the hacker Lisbeth Salander's process underscores the benefits and risks of digital technology:

> If the individual was listed in a computer file, which everyone inevitably was, then the subject quickly landed in her spider's web. If the individual owned a computer with an Internet connection, an email address, and maybe even a personal website, which nearly everyone did who came under her special type of research, she could sooner or later find out their innermost secrets.
>
> *(Larsson 2005 [2008]: 358)*

Of note in this explanation are the types of digital technology described: A computer with an internet connection, email and potentially a blog. These technologies, even in 2005, were so widespread as to make the "nearly everyone did" claim of the text ring true with most readers. They do not seem novel or luxurious – they seem like necessities. Yet these same necessities create vulnerabilities so that "innermost secrets" become accessible to a skilled hacker like Salander. Noteworthy as well is the idea that "everyone inevitably" ends up at least listed in a digital file, forcing readers to realise that the choice has been made for them: In the world of *Dragon Tattoo,* they have already traded security for convenience. This realisation becomes all the more frightening in light of the hacker's unlimited geographical range; as I argue elsewhere, Salander's ability to cross digital borders marks her abilities, and the criminal activities she sometimes combats and sometimes commits, as global crime (Kenley 2014). Thus, few if any borders exist to protect readers from digital attacks, highlighting one consequence of digital technology.

Of course, the consequences of those attacks depend on the skills wielded by the detective. As Sophie Statzel Bjork-James writes, the "seduction of Larsson's novels is that the heroes always use their tech better" (2012: 100). The Millennium trilogy does indeed function this way, raising threats only to show that Salander and her Hacker Republic can contain them through superior skill. The novels also highlight the relative weakness of Säpo, the Swedish police force, when compared with Salander and her crew; as representatives of the state, Säpo must respect legal and jurisdictional boundaries that Salander (and the criminals she pursues) easily bypass. Salander is the "hero" effectively employing technology, and the well-meaning police, though still useful in executing physical tasks like arrests, make a compelling argument for the hacker as an essential twenty-first-century detective by throwing Salander's abilities into stark relief.

While owning a computer or having email makes readers vulnerable, the novels work to reassure them that they remain somewhat safe because the detectives have superior technological skills. Some hacker series, such as Rosie Claverton's Amy Lane series, rely as well on the hacker's consummate skill but introduce further questions about the hacker's allegiances. Still other detective novels featuring digital technology, contrariwise, work to convince readers that the benefits of new technology are outweighed by the costs.

Another trend in crime fiction and digital technology is the rise of social media in the commission and solving of crimes. Many of these novels build on the foundation laid by *Dragon Tattoo* in terms of hacking and then add a social media component. Helen Fitzgerald's *Viral* (2016) explores the consequences of sensitive personal content being hacked and promoted via social media channels. Matthew Blakstad's 2016 *Sockpuppet* centres on a hack of the British government's fictional Digital Citizen program that is solved in part by an online community of both human users and bots. Stav Sherez's 2017 novel *The Intrusions* features his recurring characters Detective Inspector Jack Carrigan and Detective Sergeant Geneva Miller pitted against a hacker using technology similar to that of *Dragon Tattoo,* but also utilising social media to up the ante. *The Intrusions* builds on the same foundation as *Dragon Tattoo,* suggesting that any internet presence makes readers vulnerable to hackers. According to Carrigan and Miller, the killer chooses his victims based on their Twitter activity, then begins an active, two-pronged campaign of psychological warfare. In the first phase, the victims are cyberbullied, with one victim receiving "436 abusive tweets from 67 accounts in the space of two hours" (Sherez 2017: 135). In the second phase, the victim's computers are taken over via Remote Access Technologies, or ratting. The victims are then recorded without their consent; finally, the recordings are trafficked online. In the words of the novel's hackers, "You'll never be alone again. If you use a phone or computer or TV, I'll be there with you" (257). Clearly, in this iteration, the risks of digital technology outweigh the rewards.

In the world of *The Intrusions*, these attacks escalate to murder via old-fashioned drugging, kidnapping and imprisonment in an example of an author working through worst-case scenarios. However, even if this final phase of the attack seems unlikely, Sherez works to make sure his readers recognise that the balance of power has shifted from detective to criminal. Once discovered, the killer tells Miller of his impending capture:

> It doesn't matter. Even if you catch me, there's hundreds of thousands just like me all over the world, cruising the web, looking for prey, and it's only going to get a whole lot worse. You think the things I've done are bad, just wait and see what the next generation is capable of. You'll have nowhere to hide. You'll never feel safe again.
>
> *(329)*

The final statement, while directly addressed to Miller, seems capable of resonating with a wider referent for "you" than merely the detective. Miller, and the reader, are asked to recognise that, for Sherez in this novel and perhaps in detective fiction more broadly, the battle for safety in the war of digital technology has been lost. In a sense, this ending scene reveals the tension inherent in detective fiction's broader drive to provide security via solutions. Though the individual crimes have been solved and answers have been provided, these revelations are not enough for detective fiction to provide the reader with comfort in a digital era.

In the service of exploring the limits of digital technologies, detective fiction sometimes pushes its own boundaries by hybridising with other genres. Such hybridisation allows detective fiction to employ the strengths of other, less strictly realist genres that excel at speculation. Science fiction and crime fiction merge in some series, with the physical and the digital meshing to create cyborg hybrids, as in John Burdett's *The Bangkok Asset* (2015) or Richard Morgan's *Altered Carbon* (2002). As before, the introduction of additional technology allows for a wider range of criminal activity as well as containment options. By introducing the post-human into detective fiction, authors like Burdett and Morgan suggest that detective fiction, too, may need to evolve into a new, post-global iteration if it is to continue to mediate digital spaces. More common are novels that inhabit the mode of speculative fiction, like Dave Hutchinson's Fractured Europe series or Matthew Blakstad's *Lucky Ghost* (2018). Hutchinson's series pairs a Balkanised Europe not unlike that of the present day alongside advanced digital courier suits that enable seamless border crossings. Blakstad creates a fictional-yet-plausible digital currency based on real-world emotions, writing a world distinct from but parallel to the current one. Whether the future spun by these novels is potentially years or decades away, these novels highlight the simultaneously exhilarating and terrifying possibilities digital technology presents.

Digital technology

The exciting yet intimidating potential of digital technology may explain why some contemporary authors of detective fiction choose to avoid engaging it altogether. Sue Grafton's highly successful Alphabet series featuring her hardboiled detective Kinsey Millhone serves as a counterpoint to the constant press of ever-newer technology. The novels begin with *"A" is for Alibi* in 1982 but, though she wrote the series until her death in December 2017, Grafton chose to continue setting her novels in the 1980s, moving forward in monthly increments rather than keeping pace with a real-world chronology. As a result, Grafton's final novel, *"Y" is for Yesterday*, published in 2017, is set in 1989 and uses, as do all the other novels in the series, 1980s technology (one of Kinsey's investigative trademarks is inscribing clues on index cards). Readers experience Kinsey wearing out the proverbial shoe leather hunting for information on trips to city record offices and newspaper bureaus while the readers themselves have access to that sort of data from their smartphones. As Ethelle Bean points out, Grafton's novels indicate that technological newness and nostalgia are relative. In 2002's *"Q" is for Quarry*, set in 1987, Kinsey attempts to solve a cold case from 1969, "often contrasting 1960s-era technology with what was state-of-the-art in 1987" (Bean 2005: 30) and, implicitly, with the technology available in 2002. In addition to indicating a certain reluctance to engage with digital technology on the part of some contemporary authors, Grafton's books highlight a marketable nostalgia for detection before digital technology became widespread. This wistfulness, from readers as well as authors, for a somewhat simpler era in detective fiction only makes sense given the high volume of crime novels that position digital technology as a destructive force.

While detective fiction uses digital technology in a myriad of ways, this central question of whether it mitigates or exacerbates crime remains an open one in the literature and criticism. Contemporary detective fiction exposes the unrealistic fantasy that a new kind of technology can control a new kind of crime and replaces it with the ambivalence and complication that comes with a genre attempting to manage and understand a new frontier. Ultimately, the only thing that seems certain is that, as a police technical expert explains in Sherez's *The Intrusions,* "what technology gives with one hand it takes away with the other" (67). The genre continues to project the possibilities, both positive and negative, attendant on innovation.

The digital forensic

At first blush, the forensic subgenre of crime fiction seems potentially at odds with the digital given its insistence on physical trace evidence. Forensic detectives take both crime scenes and bodies as their purview, and many establish their investigative foci as integral components of their series. Three of the best-known American forensic authors, Kathy Reichs, Jeffery Deaver and Patricia Cornwell, for example, each stake a claim to a slightly different forensic domain of expertise in their series' first instalments. Patricia Cornwell's chief medical examiner Kay Scarpetta studies the interaction between body and crime scene in her 1990 novel *Postmortem.* Following suit a few years later, Reichs's forensic anthropologist Temperance Brennan establishes her niche as an investigator of bones and bodies too decomposed for a traditional autopsy in *Déjà Dead* (1997), while Deaver's forensic criminalist Lincoln Rhyme lays out a grid to cover every square inch of a crime scene in *The Bone Collector* (1997). A body of scholarship has been produced detailing Cornwell's use of bodies as evidence (Head 2011; Mizejewski 2001), Deaver's perspective on crime and mobility (Jakubowicz and Meekosha 2004), Reichs's particular focus on bones as evidence (Povidiša 2008) and forensics in popular culture more widely (Harrington 2007; Littlefield 2011; Palmer 2001). More criticism exists examining forensic detective fiction and its particular technologies than criticism focusing on crime fiction and digital technology generally. Over the nearly thirty-year history of the forensic subgenre, however, the field has shifted to accommodate new digital technologies in tandem with crime fiction more broadly, to the point that some forensic authors (such as Deaver, as shown in the next section) have swung the balance of their novels toward strictly digital technologies rather than crime scene investigation. Further, the focus on forensic detective fiction's interaction with physical clues has obscured the relationship that the subgenre facilitates between the physical and the digital, a role which contributes to the growth of digital technology in detective fiction by facilitating the transformation of physical traces into digital data. Whether the forensic focuses on blood spatter or cybercrime, it has always investigated the relationship between the physical and the digital.

As digital technologies have become nearly *de rigueur* for contemporary detective novels, forensic novels have followed suit, a logical progression considering their existing amenability to the tools that help their detective render bodies and crime scenes legible. The novels of Cornwell, Reichs and Deaver come to feature all manner of digital devices, from GPS transponders (Reichs's *Break No Bones*) to server farms containing vast databases ripe for data mining (Deaver's *The Broken Window*) to surveillance flybots and "Computers, robotics, synthetic biology, nanotechnology, the more off the wall, the better" (Cornwell 2010: 76). Cornwell also includes a main character with a strong digital technology background in her detective's niece and ward, Lucy. Introduced as a preteen with a natural aptitude for computers in the first Scarpetta novel, Lucy quickly grows into a digital technology *Wunderkind*, creating her own internet search engine and selling it to become a dotcom millionaire. Cornwell's inclusion of a character designed to focus on the digital aspects of criminal investigation, and that character's growing prominence as the series progresses, speaks to forensic crime fiction's increasing incorporation of digital technology as the subgenre itself grows and changes.

Beyond high-tech gadgets, the forensic crime novel's stock in trade is technology that renders the physical into the digital. These novels feature laboratories equipped with CT and MRI machines, gas chromatograph/mass spectrometers, scanning electron microscopes and many other devices that take traces left by crimes and digitise them. As with the digital technologies described above, forensic detective fiction, too, uses these technologies to fulfil detective fiction's generic drive to reassure readers that criminals can be apprehended, though as I argue elsewhere, the extent to which authors like Deaver, Cornwell and Reichs endorse this ideology can be situated on a continuum of containment (Kenley 2019). The idea that the digital forensic can render the physical into the more portable and comprehensible digital is not a new one. Thomas notes, again, that detective fiction in general and forensic detective fiction in particular has always worked to make these traces legible: "Each of these detective devices – fingerprint technology, forensic profiling, crime photography – is itself a nineteenth-century invention designed to convert the body into a text to be read" (1999: 4). In contemporary forensic detective fiction, of course, the technologies are frequently digital and concerned with translating the physical into the digital as well, as in the case of DNA sequencing, a common forensic detective novel trope, but the fundamental concept of working to make bodies decipherable remains the same. Further, by digitising these physical elements, they become hackable.

Examples of the hacking of digital forensic technologies abound, but an early one comes from Mizejewski's reading of Cornwell's *The Body Farm* (1994). In the novel, a sophisticated biometric lock system, designed to turn fingerprints into access codes, is hacked by a criminal who exploits the possibility of a breakdown between the physical and the digital (Mizejewski 2001: 16). As the forensic transforms trace evidence into data, it makes that data more comprehensible but also easier to manipulate. Ultimately, the more digital elements the genre introduces, the more it, too, teases out the possibilities for exploitation of new technology, troubling the border between searchability and vulnerability.

Digital technology

The Steel Kiss and the price of security

The Steel Kiss's driving thesis is that the trade-off offered by a new form of digital technology, in this case between convenience and security, comes at too high a cost. Deaver, an American author initially known for his gripping descriptions of forensic crime scene investigations, has in the past decade shifted from primarily writing about physical to digital crime. Deaver still incorporates elements of physical forensic analysis, but his increasing use of digital technologies points to the ways in which even a subgenre originally centred on the physical continues to bend toward the digital. *The Broken Window* (2008), for example, centres on data mining, and the detectives must analyse not only the data but also its metadata to solve the case. Further, Deaver frequently writes about digital crimes based on technologies that are only starting to come into vogue. *The Steel Kiss*, published in early 2016, considers smart appliances, devices equipped with their own internet connections. Such smart appliances only became readily available for purchase a few years prior, circa 2013. Deaver, then, works to create criminals who weaponise cutting-edge technology, spurred by a demand to produce the innovative plots that captivate readers searching for novelty (Wagner 2006: 20–23).

The Steel Kiss operates around the concept that, because smart appliances have internet connections, they can be hacked and thereby weaponised. The novel, like so many others discussed in this chapter, operates around the classic detective fiction formula of introducing a threat, escalating it, and then potentially offering reassurance through containment of that threat. Much contemporary detective fiction, not just but especially that concerning digital technology, hinges on this final question of reassurance and whether or not the genre can realistically provide it in the wake of globalisation. Deaver differs from Sherez in that he does offer some (slim) hope at the novel's end, but even so, he implies that this chance for security will be passed over in favour of a chance for profit. In *The Steel Kiss*, the threat is initially introduced as a freak accident, a malfunction of a commonplace convenience in the form of a mall escalator. An access panel swings open unexpectedly, causing a man to be trapped in the grinding gears of the machine. As Deaver's detectives Lincoln Rhyme and Amelia Sachs continue to investigate, they learn that the escalator has a smart controller installed, which allowed it to be hacked and taken over. As the investigation proceeds, Rhyme and Sachs come to learn that the escalator is just one of many, many devices embedded with a

> smart controller. [...] A lot of products have them built in. Conveyance systems –
> escalators, elevators – and cars, trains, industrial machinery, medical equipment, construction equipment. Hundreds of consumer appliances: stoves, heating systems, lighting in your house, security, door locks. You can send and receive data to and from machinery with your phone or tablet or computer, wherever you are. And control the products remotely.
>
> *(Deaver 2016: 191)*

At this point in the text, the list of devices doubles as a list of potential weapons, hackable devices that can be used to terrorise, maim or kill. Deaver leans on the threats these devices pose to create a culture of fear. A blogger in the novel writes a post about the dangers the smart devices, or the Internet of Things, pose. The post, titled "INDULGENCE = DEATH? THE DANGER OF THE INTERNET OF THINGS", includes two subheadings: "IS YOUR DATA SAFE?" and "IS YOUR LIFE SAFE?" (195, capitals in original). The first section outlines the ways in which smart appliances provide access to personal data, a threat whose profile has risen since the novel's 2016 publication. However, this threat is largely a commercial one – personal data can be collected and sold to marketers to produce more personalised advertisements. The second threat, however, is one of physical danger. The blogger indicts consumers for trading ease for security, writing, "Ask yourself, is convenience worth the price of you and your children's lives?" (198). Thus, the novel works explicitly to inspire fear in its readers, suggesting that, given the long list of common smart devices that people interact with daily, the deal has already been struck. Safety has been traded for expediency.

As the novel progresses, Deaver demonstrates the ways that digital crime can lead to physical harm. The ubiquity of smart controllers opens up threats from commonplace appliances, tools and conveyances that "could be deadly: cars, trains, elevators, defib[rillators], heart monitors, pacemakers, microwaves, ovens, power tools, furnaces, cranes" (228). Deaver follows through on those threats, not only killing the original victim trapped in the escalator gears but killing, injuring or terrifying characters throughout the text with a hacked stove, microwave (in an explicitly weaponised simile, a coffee mug heated so that it "exploded like a hand grenade", [341]), baby monitor, power saw, automobile and water heater. In essence, the smart controllers have taken non-digital devices and, by putting them online, have turned them into digital weapons with physical consequences. As Rhyme notes in the text, he "had no idea a ubiquitous device could be so dangerous" (341). The novel works to create a fear of the digital as an infiltrating force that turns the mundane into the deadly and which cannot, seemingly, be rebuffed.

To contain the threat of these deadly smart appliances, Deaver offers a mix of reassurance and ongoing fear, in effect hedging his bets. If the stances of detective fiction engaged with digital technology exist as a range, with a belief that technology can ultimately contain crime at one limit, and an insistence that digital technologies can complicate but not control crime at the other, *The Steel Kiss* occupies the middle of that range. That is, while he takes care to detail the extensive threats posed by digital technology, Deaver insists as a fundamental underpinning of the text that, since even digital crimes leave trace evidence, thanks to "criminalistics – forensic science – there is not a single crime that cannot be solved. The only question is one of resource, ingenuity, and effort" (23). The novel's conclusion bears out this bold claim, with the killer brought to justice via a mix of forensic analysis and reciprocal hacking. Yet despite his statement about "a single crime", Deaver highlights the fact that identifying this particular perpetrator does not alleviate the overarching threat. Rhyme's investigation reveals that smart appliances could be made, if not impermeable, at least much more secure with greater interest from their manufacturers and consumers. A police detective explains that, in their haste to get products to market, "smart controller companies use existing software for their embedded products – and I mean old, ancient software. Dinosaur-ware. Early Windows and Apple operating systems and some open source code [that] is more vulnerable to security exploits" (229–30). The manufacturers' reliance on outdated technologies leaves consumers vulnerable, but according to the CEO of one such manufacturer, the consumers continue to prefer convenience over security. Security patches take smart devices offline temporarily, and once customers "get used to a convenience it's impossible to take it away from them. [...] Everyone who has a smart product expects it to keep performing. If it doesn't they'll go elsewhere" (242). In essence, Deaver indicts both manufacturers and consumers of digital technology for valuing profit and ease over a greater measure of safety, answering what is in essence the central question of digital technology in crime fiction writ small. Until one or both of these constraints changes, which in Deaver's portrayal they are unlikely to do, digital technologies pose threats not even the tech-savviest detective can contain.

Conclusion

Overall, crime fiction continues to use digital technologies to explore the possible consequences of an increasingly digital society. These texts raise questions based on the complications precipitated by the introduction of new technologies. Rather than accepting innovations as inherently good or uncritically indulging in the fantasy that technology provides pat solutions to digital crimes, detective fiction demonstrates the ways in which digital technologies can be used to contain or foster criminal behaviour. Whether the crimes or containment mechanisms come from hackers, social media or some as-yet-unforeseen digital frontier, detective fiction continues to engage the messy contingencies and consequences attendant on trying to control digital crime. Finally, detective fiction uses digital technology to ask broader questions about accessibility, security, convenience, progress and vulnerability that will only grow in relevance along with the increase in digital technology.

Bibliography

Åström, B., Gregersdotter, K. and Horeck, T. (eds) (2013) *Rape in Stieg Larsson's Millennium Trilogy and Beyond: Contemporary Scandinavian and Anglophone crime fiction*, New York: Palgrave Macmillan.

Bean, E. (2005) "Technology and detective fiction", *Clues: A Journal of Detection*, 24(1): 27–34.

Benyahia, S. (2013) "Salander in cyberspace", in Peacock, 58–78.

Bjork-James, S. (2012) "Hacker republic: cyberspace and the feminist appropriation of technology", in King and Smith, 98–107.

Cornwell, P. (1994) *The Body Farm*, New York: Berkley Publishing Group.

———. (2010) *Port Mortuary*, New York: G.P. Putnam's Sons.

Deaver, J. (2016) *The Steel Kiss*, New York: Grand Central.

Harrington, E. (2007) "Nation, identity and the fascination with forensic science in Sherlock Holmes and *CSI*", *International Journal of Cultural Studies*, 10(3): 365–82.

Head, B. (2011) "A normal pathology? Patricia Cornwell's third-person novels", in M. Effron (ed.), *The Millennial Detective: Essays on trends in crime fiction, film and television, 1990–2010*, Jefferson, NC: McFarland, 36–49.

Jakubowicz, A. and Meekosha, H. (2004) "Detecting disability: moving beyond metaphor in the crime fiction of Jeffery Deaver", *Disability Studies Quarterly*, 24(2): 30 paragraphs.

Kenley, N. (2014) "Hackers without borders: global detectives in Stieg Larsson's Millennium trilogy", *Clues: A Journal of Detection*, 32(2): 30–40.

———. (2019) "Global crime, forensic detective fiction, and the continuum of containment", *Canadian Review of Comparative Literature*, 46(1): 96–114.

King, D. and Smith, C. (eds) (2012) *Men who Hate Women and the Women who Kick their Asses*, Nashville, TN: Vanderbilt University Press.

Larsson, S. (2008) *The Girl with the Dragon Tattoo*, New York: Random House.

Littlefield, M. (2011) "Historicizing the CSI effect(s): the real and the representational in American scientific detective fiction and print news media, 1902–1935", *Crime, Media, Culture*, 7(2): 133–48.

Mandel, E. (2016) "The gone girl with the dragon tattoo on the train", FiveThirtyEight, 27 October, https://fivethirtyeight.com/features/the-gone-girl-with-the-dragon-tattoo-on-the-train/ (accessed 25 January 2019).

Mizejewski, L. (2001) "Illusive evidence: Patricia Cornwell and the body double", *South Central Review*, 18(3–4): 6–20.

Palmer, J. (2001) "Tracing bodies: gender, genre, and forensic detective fiction", *South Central Review*, 18(3–4): 54–71.

Peacock, S. (ed.) (2013) *Stieg Larsson's Millennium Trilogy: Interdisciplinary approaches to Nordic noir on page and screen*, New York: Palgrave Macmillan.

Povidiša, I. (2008) "Bones to read: an interpretation of forensic crime fiction", *Reconstruction: Studies in Contemporary Culture*, 8(3): 24 paragraphs.

Riley, B. (2017) *The Digital Age Detective: Mysteries in a changing landscape of literacy*, Jefferson, NC: McFarland.

Sherez, S. (2017) *The Intrusions*, London: Faber & Faber.

Thomas, R.R. (1999) *Detective Fiction and the Rise of Forensic Science*, Cambridge: Cambridge University Press.

Wagner, H. (2006) "'Readers are Gods': Jeffery Deaver's religion of writing", *Mystery Scene*, 95: 20–23.

PART III

Interfaces

30

CRIME FICTION AND CRIMINOLOGY

Matthew Levay

Criminology and crime fiction are linked in a number of ways, some obvious, some less so. In the broadest sense, both are interested in what counts as a crime and who counts as a criminal as well as the conditions that produce these designations, and both investigate the problem of how to prevent acts of crime through institutional, individual or other means. Both, too, are uniquely concerned with the question of whether the causes of crime should be attributed to groups or individuals, laws or psychologies, and how to diagnose the complexities of criminality in ways that address the specificities of particular acts while also acknowledging their legal and social bases. Perhaps no connection, however, is as significant as the fact that both criminology and crime fiction are remarkably diverse categories commonly misunderstood as rigidly structured according to fundamental precepts. Just as, according to John Scaggs, the genre of crime fiction, "in its sheer diversity, defies any simple classification", the field of criminology is comprised of methodologies taken from sociology, psychology, anthropology and statistics, among other disciplines, and therefore resists any single, limiting framework (2005: 1). Criminology and crime fiction are both messy concepts, and in their messiness are vital to our understanding of how crime manifests and how society perceives that manifestation.

Because criminology, as a field of interdisciplinary knowledge, encompasses a wide array of practices for distinguishing how and why crime appears as it does and offering plausible solutions for its deterrence, it is no wonder that such a field would be an object of fascination for crime writers. Indeed, crime fiction is filled with examples of criminological thought, in which characters voice sometimes prevailing, sometimes emerging notions of criminality that map onto the very same concerns that occupied criminologists of the period. These moments arrive in disparate guises – for instance, through medical or psychiatric practitioners whose scientific approaches challenge stereotypes of the criminal as a moral abomination, or through criminal characters who explain how life circumstances paved the route to criminal activity – but all of them illustrate the genre's investment in approaching criminality from multiple angles, within specific social and historical milieus.

Crime fiction's engagement with criminological thought is never static, as developments in the discipline of criminology continue to yield fresh insights, and thereby influence a continually evolving genre in unexpected ways. It is worth exploring, then, how and why authors draw upon criminological practices in their work, whether they give voice to nascent, popular or antiquated approaches. It is clear that crime fiction engages with both past and contemporary developments in criminology, whether explicitly or implicitly, as part of a broader interest in police procedure; the sciences of detection; biological, sociological and psychological models of criminality; and the shifting public and academic perceptions of crime as a legal category. The primary aims of this chapter are, first, to establish criminology as an interdisciplinary assemblage of fields and practices that attempts to understand the nature of criminality through diverse, often shifting means, and second, to explore how these practices dovetail with crime fiction's long-standing efforts to explore criminality's manifestation in modern society. Throughout, I emphasise the historicist perspective that crime fiction is not a straightforward reflection of criminological thought, but rather constitutes a unique form of popular criminology indebted to key developments in the discipline while at the same time exposing them to critique.

Classical criminology, positivist criminology, sociological criminology

Tracing a complete history of criminology would be impossible in such a short chapter, not least because that history remains subject to debate. As Nicole Hahn Rafter explains, "the term *criminology* did not enter common usage until the late nineteenth century, and criminology as an academic discipline did not take shape until even later" (2008: 11). The field's belated codification is partially due to the variety of its practitioners; Peter Becker argues that, because the early criminal sciences included the work of "physicians, magistrates, police experts, and penologists as well as prison chaplains, phrenologists, and philanthropists", criminology's origins can appear to revolve around an idiosyncratic set of ideas (2018: 35). Any overview of those ideas risks becoming overwhelmed by what Paul Rock characterises as the "propensity of old theories to linger on, co-existing and merging with newer ideas in a variety of combinations" (2017: 22).

Yet one can still trace the major criminological approaches to which crime writers responded, and which they made substantive components of their work. Most historical accounts of criminology attribute the field's birth to eighteenth-century thinkers like Jeremy Bentham and Cesare Beccaria, commonly associated with the classical school of criminology, which sought to balance the rights of free individuals with their debts to the collective. To achieve that balance, classical criminologists asserted that punishment was necessary to prevent future crimes, but also maintained that, as Clive Emsley puts it, any punishment "should be perceived as the logical outcome of committing a crime", "administered in proportion to the seriousness of the crime" and "administered equally, whatever an offender's social rank" (2007: 32). Thus, classical criminologists sought legal remedies to social ills in a way that attempted objectivity, discarding assumptions about moral fitness or economic standing typically applied to criminals. Theirs was a reformist approach aimed at transforming an inconsistently regulated penal system into a more utilitarian venture.

Against the classical criminologists, one can situate those nineteenth-century positivist thinkers who applied scientific and pseudoscientific methods to the identity of the criminal. Easily the most famous exponent of this approach was Cesare Lombroso, the figurehead of the "Italian School" of criminology and the new field of criminal anthropology, who argued that criminals were born rather than shaped, and thus could not be expected to act in a manner inconsistent with their makeup. Positing the notion of the atavistic, or born criminal, Lombroso declared that "the most horrendous and inhuman crimes have a biological, atavistic origin in those animalistic instincts that, although smoothed over by education, the family, and fear of punishment, resurface instantly under given circumstances" (2006: 91). The job of criminal anthropology was to protect the public by identifying those physical aberrations that Lombroso and others believed would reveal the atavistic nature within. Based on photographs of convicted criminals, skull measurements of deceased prison inmates and personal interactions with various offenders, Lombroso devised typologies of criminality that equated physiognomy with specific criminal acts, thereby providing a basis for asserting that criminals could be identified by anyone with sufficient skill in reading the testimony of appearance. The tenets of criminal anthropology were not always accepted, even in the scientific communities of late nineteenth-century Europe; David G. Horn characterises Lombroso's most infamous work, *L'uomo delinquente* – revised multiple times between its publication in 1876 and its final, four-volume iteration in 1896–1897 – as "a heterogeneous text, full of contradictions, inconsistencies, and errors" and "at once organized by an ambition to build a totalizing science of criminal man" (2003: 5). Despite such objections, Lombroso's work garnered a wide audience, and made a lasting impression on the popular literature of the day.

Positivist approaches to criminality, based in a faith in empirical methods even as they could easily be deployed to validate various prejudices, met significant challenges from those who favoured sociological explanations of crime. For instance, Émile Durkheim's concept of anomie – the insufficient regulation of individual desires – or his emphasis on social control theory, which describes how individuals follow the rules of a given society based on the relative strength of communal ties within that society, suggest causal explanations of crime grounded in environmental and social factors. Likewise, the Chicago School steered the critical conversation surrounding criminality toward the influence of environment by adopting an ethnographic approach, tracking Chicago neighbourhood crime rates in order to understand their variation across communities. Coming to prominence in the 1920s and 1930s, members of the Chicago School pioneered the concept of social disorganisation theory, arguably the most durable counterpoint to positivist criminology in its claim that crime, far from being tied to individual characteristics, is actually rooted in the specificities of place. In the broadest terms, social disorganisation theory refers to how a group's central values – typically, to live in a safe environment – are not always upheld, as some communities are unable to maintain strong bonds among residents, leading to lax forms of social control. By mapping the disparities in crime rates between different urban regions, researchers of the Chicago School applied the concept of social disorganisation theory to show that neighbourhoods with high levels of crime were not simply populated by immoral individuals, or by those who, in Lombroso's terms, were born to lives of crime, but instead experienced significant difficulties in maintaining social order. As Robert E. Park and Ernest W. Burgess explained in their landmark study *The City* (1925), the

> sources of our actions are, no doubt, in the organic impulses of the individual man; but actual conduct is determined more or less by public opinion, by custom and by a code which exists outside of us in the family, in the neighborhood, and in the community.
>
> *(104–05)*

Consequently, twentieth-century sociological approaches to criminology offered crime writers of the period a new way of examining an always popular topic: Urban crime.

Similarly, the late 1960s saw the rise of labelling theory as an explanatory model for criminality. This model holds that the manner in which an individual is labelled – for the purposes of criminology, as a criminal or more specific kind of offender – creates the conditions for that individual's future behaviours. Individuals internalise labels that members of the broader group apply to them, and as those labels gain acceptance within and beyond their community, individuals come to inhabit roles not of their own making but constrained by social expectations. In an additional chapter published in a revised version of *Outsiders* (1963), which helped popularise labelling theory, Howard S. Becker contends that

> labelling places the actor in circumstances which make it harder for him to continue the normal routines of everyday life and thus provoke him to "abnormal" actions (as when a prison record makes it harder to earn a living at a conventional occupation and so disposes its possessor to move into an illegal one).
>
> *(1991: 179)*

With the existence of labels comes the expectation that one will behave according to them, a presumption of criminality translating into the real thing once conditions for lawful existence evaporate.

Criminology in crime fiction: Nineteenth century to the present

Given the scale of criminology's changes since the nineteenth century, combined with massive developments in crime fiction during the same period – not to mention the fact that crime fiction is a global phenomenon encompassing multiple languages and national traditions – a history that maps criminological thinking onto the entirety of the crime genre is an impossible project. Instead, this section charts how crime fictions from the nineteenth to the twenty-first century have engaged with significant issues, practices and developments in modern criminology, taking them as frameworks for representing criminality and its detection in novel ways. Indeed, crime fiction has always been marked by its investment in criminological thinking; from nineteenth-century detective fictions and their representations of classical criminological approaches, to the spectre of criminal anthropology in late nineteenth-century crime fiction, to the confluence of generic convention and criminological perspectives in Golden Age mystery fiction, to the urban ethnographies of the hardboiled detective story, to 1980s serial killer fiction and the burgeoning study of psychopathy (itself echoing earlier positivist approaches), and finally to contemporary crime fiction that uses labelling theory and social disorganisation theory to locate the causes of crime within urban and rural networks of poverty and social marginalisation, the history of crime fiction is a history of criminological thinking.

Probably the most notable aspect of criminology's influence on crime fiction arises in the latter's representation of the detective, figured in the nineteenth century as a heroic avatar of logic, empiricism and public safety. According to Ronald R. Thomas,

> [t]he systematic medicalization of crime in criminological discourse during [the nineteenth century] corresponded to the literary detective's development into a kind of master diagnostician, an expert capable of reading the symptoms of criminal pathology in the individual body and the social body as well.
>
> *(2003: 3)*

As several critics have noted, the fictional detective could assuage public fears of crime as an insurmountable occurrence by illustrating the validity of empirical approaches to the subject. In this way, Victorian detective fiction distinguished between criminals and other people, often by asserting that criminality could be successfully "diagnosed", to use Thomas's metaphor, within unfit individuals intent on fracturing a social order to which they cannot belong; such a distinction informs Laura Otis's characterisation of Sherlock Holmes as a "fantasy of a national immune system" who "devote[s] all of his formidable mental powers to identifying and neutralizing living threats to society", often those that moved from the colonies toward the empire's metaphorical heart (1999: 91).

Doyle's early works depict Holmes as a scientifically-minded, albeit eccentric specialist. In *A Study in Scarlet* (1887), one character describes Holmes as "a little queer in his ideas – an enthusiast in some branches of science", indicating a slightly disreputable amateur whose studies nonetheless bear the imprimatur of the empirical sciences (18). When John Watson compiles a list of his friend's accumulated knowledge, the result is a hodgepodge of disciplines that erects a foundation for Holmes's skills in criminal pursuit; whereas Watson admonishes Holmes's ignorance in literature, philosophy and politics, among other subjects, he admits Holmes's prowess in chemistry, anatomy, botany with a specialisation in poisons and sensational literature, the last category moving him to remark that Holmes "appears to know every detail of every horror perpetrated in the century" (35). Here, Watson figures Holmes as an interdisciplinary trailblazer forging his own profession, whose simultaneous detachment from and connection to the sciences provides a vantage point suited to the detection of what otherwise escapes the police's sights.

Holmes is a criminological figure within popular crime fiction, but by this token he is also a representative of the field's internal conflicts and hazy public image, rather than a straightforward exemplar of its reputability. Holmes explains his peculiar studies via the metaphor of a "little empty attic [...] stock[ed] [...] with such furniture as you chose", which he equates with the human brain (32). For Holmes, knowledge is not something to gain for its own sake. Rather, one must be discriminating, as "the skillful workman [...] will have nothing but the tools which may help him in doing his work" (33–34). In this conception of professionalisation, Holmes echoes the advent of criminology earlier in the century, and his scientific interests suggest the influence of positivism. However, Holmes does not simply employ Lombroso's tools – for instance, criminal photography and the phrenological study of convicted criminals' skulls – but rather develops his "passion for definite and exact knowledge" through the creation of new technologies of detection (19). Other characters complain that Holmes "is a little too scientific" in his approach, a positivist who "approaches to cold-bloodedness", but this was also a criticism of positivist criminology, which opponents found eerily disconnected from the lived experience of crime (19). Holmes's "cold-bloodedness" is precisely the point, as his relationship to humanity is one of professional distance meant to embody the benefits of criminology as well as the ambivalence with which some considered it.

As a representative of criminological thinking, Holmes had an outsized influence on crime fiction well into the twentieth century. His mode of reasoned deduction permeates Golden Age detective fiction, where authors like Margery Allingham, Agatha Christie and Dorothy L. Sayers crafted narratives in which any crime could be solved through the rigorous application of logic, as the constituent parts of those narratives – suspects, clues and so forth – should, theoretically, allow the reader as well as the protagonist to determine who has committed a crime and why. According to Samantha Walton, "[d]espite many examples of scientific nonsense being touted as sense in the crime genre, readers expect the [fictional] world to conform to the same physical laws as their own" (2015: 52). As Walton suggests, while Golden Age crime fiction features its fair share of positivist criminology, it more readily treats the subject of criminality as open to interpretation by all, the quality of those interpretations largely aligning with protagonists who examine cases from a thoughtful, observant perspective alert to material evidence but not necessarily governed by disciplinary rules. Take Lord Peter Wimsey, Sayers's amateur sleuth who views detection as a cultivated hobby comparable to his love of rare books. In *Whose Body?* (1923), Wimsey's frantic patter and cultivated aloofness belie the fact that his is a fiercely observant mind, but one whose amateurism, like Holmes's, distinguishes him from the official police force. Perhaps more importantly, the novel's murderer is a psychiatrist fascinated by the subject of crime, his methods echoing those of positivist criminologists with a decidedly Nietzschean flair. Sir Julian Freke, Wimsey explains, adheres to "an ideal doctrine for the criminal", believing that "conscience is a sort of vermiform appendix" and viewing the mind as dependent upon physiology (136, 170). Upending any notion that the criminologist must be the hero of crime fiction, Sayers posits the dangerous scientific professional whose writings on criminality betray a desire to commit crime in order to dislodge the act from any moral framework. Wimsey's distance from positivist criminology, then, suggests a growing discomfort with the purportedly scientific view of criminality, and a corresponding willingness to abandon the calculated certainties of Holmes.

Sayers's work also shared space with the emerging hardboiled school of crime fiction, in which the amateur detective was replaced with a professional private eye who bore an uneasy resemblance to his criminal counterparts. Here the empiricism of a detective like Holmes and the cool if antic logic of Wimsey gave way to a world-weary moralism that viewed criminality as an inevitable occurrence and the work of the detective as a necessary duty hindered by bureaucratic structures. As Sam Spade explains in Dashiell Hammett's *The Maltese Falcon* (1929):

> At one time or another I've had to tell everybody from the Supreme Court down to go to hell, and I've got away with it. I got away with it because I never let myself forget that a day of reckoning was coming. I never forget that when the day of reckoning comes I want to be all set to march into headquarters pushing a victim in front of me, saying "Here, you chumps, is your criminal!" As long as I can do that I can put my thumb to my nose and wriggle my fingers at all the laws in the book.
>
> *(1992: 176)*

Spade's antipathy to the law ironically colours his successful upholding of its tenets, and his methods serve as an uncompromising version of those of the traditional police force. Much like Raymond Chandler's Philip Marlowe, who "test[s] very high on insubordination" (1992: 10), hardboiled detectives of the period often view the law as an irksome check on their abilities, rather than, as criminologists of the then-contemporary Chicago School claim, one of many limiting factors in the lives of criminals, or those considered as such.

Social disintegration theory, however, infuses hardboiled authors' fascination with urban spaces. In Hammett's *Red Harvest* (1927–1928), the Continental Op becomes frustrated by the lawlessness of Personville, from the gangs that control it to the corrupt police force that shows no sign of maintaining order. A mining town overrun by criminals who formerly served local business interests as strikebreakers, Personville now has no community ties that, according to the principles of social disorganisation theory, are necessary to subvert crime. This is why the Op finds the city so unnerving, as the individual action and personal morality he represents stand in stark contrast to the competing mores of those powerful groups that war against one another and the city itself, making peace achieved through a social contract an impossibility.

Labelling a criminal, making a criminal

Patricia Highsmith's *The Glass Cell* (1964) poses a series of urgent questions informed by then-contemporary criminological thought, including the environmental and psychological causes of criminality as well as incarceration's role in establishing legal definitions of the criminal. Because Highsmith's novel is not a canonical example of criminological thought in crime fiction, its account of the penal system and its effects on the developing criminality of the

Crime fiction and criminology

wrongly convicted protagonist provide a telling instance of how unexpected crime fictions investigate the very same problems as the discipline of criminology.

Like several Highsmith novels, *The Glass Cell* centres on an ostensibly ordinary individual moved to crime by desperate circumstances and irrevocably changed by the experience. The novel follows architect Philip Carter, who, at the narrative's outset, is imprisoned for embezzlement and fraud, framed by his superiors in what was, unbeknownst to him, a crooked construction venture. Dependent on morphine to manage chronic pain – a consequence of his torture at the hands of the prison's guards – Carter must navigate the violent environment in which he finds himself, and for which he initially appears ill-equipped. After Max, his best friend in the prison, dies during a riot, Carter kills another inmate who, while not definitely implicated in Max's murder, nonetheless embodies for Carter the kind of unpunished violence that makes prison a mockery of the American justice system. The experience of killing is strangely banal for Carter, who merely acknowledges that the riot that enabled it "was simply an 'incident' [...] in an existence, a stream of time, that seemed to him one continuous riot" (2004: 110). Despite the brutality of his actions, Carter characterises his crime – the one he has *actually* committed, as opposed to the false accusations that led to his imprisonment – as a form of survival that the prison's conditions demand. He is already a criminal, he reasons, by the fact of his serving out a prison sentence, so this particular crime only meets the expectation that others already have of him. In this sense, he becomes a criminal as a direct result of being labelled as one.

Labelling runs through other aspects of the novel as well, making Highsmith's a narrative that does not follow a "descent" into criminality so much as it traces the effects that a presumption of guilt creates. When, during a visit from his wife Hazel, Carter attempts to describe his friendship with Max, he receives a cold response:

> He's a real criminal, Phil. [...]. He's used to prison. Maybe he wouldn't know what to do if he got out. I've read about people like him. They're incapable of leading an ordinary life with responsibilities and a job and all that.
>
> *(89)*

When Carter explains that Max adopted a criminal career during a difficult period in his life, Hazel responds that "[l]ots of things happen to a lot of people. It doesn't make them criminals" (89). Hazel's dismissal of Max's circumstances seems odd, here, considering that, shortly after this scene, readers learn that Hazel takes courses in sociology at the New School. Thus, one might expect Hazel's response to feature some of the criminological methods of the Chicago School, particularly social disorganisation or labelling theory, yet Highsmith subverts that presumption by having Hazel personify those assumptions regarding criminality that the discipline was actively working to dispel. Consequently, *The Glass Cell* evinces criminological thought not via positive representations of academic approaches to crime, but by illustrating how labelling stereotypes individuals in ways that foreclose possibilities for their futures.

The American court system also comes under attack, as Carter broods on how those who committed the fraud for which he was punished have never faced consequences, protected by economic privilege. "Why wasn't Gawill charged with anything?", Carter wonders.

> Gawill might be guilty, but he was a free man. Wrong was right and right was wrong, and everything was made of paper: sentences, pardons, pleas, bad records, demerits, proof of guilt, but never, it seemed, proof of innocence. If there were no paper, Carter felt, the entire judicial system would collapse and disappear.
>
> *(96)*

Labelled a criminal by a jail sentence he never deserved, Carter comes to view justice – and, by extension, the world – as ephemeral, constructed of documents that accumulate to condemn the innocent without naming the guilty. Guilt, then, becomes a function of a criminal record, separate from an individual's motives, actions or nature.

In keeping with the tenets of labelling theory, Carter becomes a criminal the moment he enters prison, so upon his release there exists no possibility for his re-entry into the social order. While Carter is in prison, his aunt writes him a letter demanding to know of his remorse, despite Carter's proclaimed innocence: "But have you thoroughly examined your conscience *and* your actions? No one is totally innocent. I cannot believe that American courts of justice would sentence a man who is absolutely without guilt" (100). With the presumption of guilt cemented by his conviction, Carter leaves prison changed by the circumstances of incarceration, but also by the assumptions of others that make incarceration a lifelong sentence. "I'm thinking the whole world is like one big prison", he says, "and prisons are just an exaggerated form of it" (143). Whereas Hazel and his aunt view the world as a place of fair opportunity, the prejudices that inform the labels they project ensure that certain individuals never achieve complete equality. What Carter ultimately understands by being labelled a criminal is that the structures of power represented in the prison find their parallels in the social world. In so doing, he personifies Highsmith's attempt to employ criminological thought to demonstrate how the label of "criminal" is attached and strengthened through circumstances outside the control of any individual.

Criminology and contemporary crime fiction

Unlike other conventions that have fallen out of fashion in contemporary crime fiction, criminological thought remains a constant. On the one hand, the positivist emphases of the nineteenth century remain firmly in place, solidified by the recent fascination with DNA evidence, criminal psychology and other facets of the forensic sciences popularised in novels like Thomas Harris's *The Silence of the Lambs* (1988), the protagonist of which is a novice profiler with the FBI's Behavioral Science unit and the antagonist, Hannibal Lecter, a convicted serial killer and psychiatrist who still "responds to serious correspondence from psychiatric students in fields unrelated to his case" (5).

On the other hand, contemporary crime fiction is equally absorbed in sociological approaches that emphasise race, environment and economics. The novels of Richard Price, for example, centre on the economic disparities of New York City, and the Wallander novels of Henning Mankell spend just as much energy tracing the decline of the Swedish welfare state and the tensions that emerge due to increased levels of immigration as they do in following generic formulae. As Andrew Nestingen argues, Mankell's novels "demand consideration of the relationships that underpin socioeconomic and cultural difference in times of globalization, while urging stronger alliances for responding to socioeconomic gaps and cultural miscomprehension" (2008: 226). Throughout these and other contemporary crime fictions echo sociological approaches like those of the Chicago School, as authors point to social disorganisation as plaguing specific, often economically disadvantaged communities.

In her study of British crime fiction of the interwar period, Victoria Stewart argues that "[c]rime is not just of interest as a topic in itself but as a means of exposing, and, potentially, critiquing both historical and contemporary sociocultural attitudes" (2017: 3). This form of exposure is what makes crime fiction such a fertile site for exploring how a culture responds to crime, as authors use criminality as a means for thinking through the legal, psychological and social dimensions of crime at a particular moment. It also explains criminology's longevity

Crime fiction and criminology

as a facet of crime fiction. Whether authors mirror or critique the attitudes of their time, they consistently draw upon criminology to yield fresh perspective on how and why crime exists in a particular fashion. Criminology and crime fiction, then, exist as two versions of the same thing: A thoroughgoing effort to probe the nuances of criminality in ways that make sense of its occurrence while also struggling with the persistent question of what an individual or a society should do to prevent it.

Bibliography

Becker, H.S. (1991) [1963] *Outsiders: Studies in the sociology of deviance*, New York: Free Press.

Becker, P. (2018) "Researching crime and criminals in the 19th century", in R.A. Triplett (ed.), *The Handbook of the History and Philosophy of Criminology*, Oxford: Wiley Blackwell, 32–47.

Chandler, R. (1992) [1939] *The Big Sleep*, New York: Vintage.

Doyle, A.C. (2005) [1887] *A Study in Scarlet*, in L.S. Klinger (ed.), *The New Annotated Sherlock Holmes*, vol. 3, New York & London: W.W. Norton.

Emsley, C. (2007) *Crime, Police, and Penal Policy: European experiences 1750–1940*, Oxford: Oxford University Press.

Hammett, D. (1992) [1929] *The Maltese Falcon*, New York: Vintage.

Harris, T. (1988) *The Silence of the Lambs*, New York: St. Martin's Press.

Highsmith, P. (2004) [1964] *The Glass Cell*, New York & London: W.W. Norton.

Horn, D.G. (2003) *The Criminal Body: Lombroso and the anatomy of deviance*, New York & London: Routledge.

Lombroso, C. (2006) *Criminal Man*, trans. M. Gibson and N.H. Rafter, Durham & London: Duke University Press.

Nestingen, A. (2008) *Crime and Fantasy in Scandinavia: Fiction, film, and social change*, Seattle: University of Washington Press.

Otis, L. (1999) *Membranes: Metaphors of invasion in nineteenth-century literature, science, and politics*, Baltimore & London: Johns Hopkins University Press.

Park, R.E. and Burgess, E.W. (2019) [1925] *The City*, Chicago & London: University of Chicago Press.

Rafter, N.H. (2008) *The Criminal Brain: Understanding biological theories of crime*, New York & London: New York University Press.

Rock, P. (2017) "The foundations of sociological theories of crime", in A. Liebling, S. Maruna and L. McAra (eds), *The Oxford Handbook of Criminology*, 6th edn, Oxford: Oxford University Press, 21–56.

Sayers, D.L. (1995) [1923] *Whose Body?*, New York: HarperCollins.

Scaggs, J. (2005) *Crime Fiction*, London & New York: Routledge.

Stewart, V. (2017) *Crime Writing in Interwar Britain: Fact and fiction in the golden age*, Cambridge: Cambridge University Press.

Thomas, R.R. (2003) *Detective Fiction and the Rise of Forensic Science*, Cambridge: Cambridge University Press.

Walton, S. (2015) *Guilty But Insane: Mind and law in golden age detective fiction*, Oxford: Oxford University Press.

31

CRIME FICTION AND THEORIES OF JUSTICE

Susanna Lee

This chapter examines the relationship between crime fiction and theories of justice. Because both these areas are so vast, it will concentrate on justice as it relates to punishment of the criminal. It will also focus on the sort of crime fiction that most raises the question of justice in punishment.

The rise of crime fiction was contemporaneous with the nineteenth-century emergence of positivist philosophy, which gave precedence to experiential data and excluded metaphysical speculation. If crime was the problem, then identification and removal of the perpetrator was the solution. That was how justice would be achieved. Identifying the criminal was the job of the detective, but the police or the judicial system took care of administering the consequences. Punishment in the "whodunit" model of crime fiction was an essentially unemotional business that involved separating the offender from the social scene. That separation healed the breach that crime had introduced into the social fabric.

In nineteenth- and early twentieth-century works of crime fiction, detention or removal were dispassionate solutions to the social problem of crime. That dispassionate nature belonged to – and was made possible by – a worldview in which social problems *had* solutions, and crime fiction described them. When hardboiled crime fiction emerged on the American scene in the aftermath of World War I, its view on "problem-solving" had become considerably less positivist, and less positive. So too its view on justice. Administrative mechanisms had either receded or become corrupted, and in any case could no longer serve as reliable correctives. As a result, as the twentieth century went on, the individual detective (whether associated with the police or not) began to have more say in whether and how justice would be done. Punishment was not always considered necessary to justice, but nor was it always considered sufficient. The definition and even viability of justice in the detective novel was starting to change.

In recent years, literary and cultural studies scholars have examined crime fiction as it articulates national and transnational ideas of justice. These studies include T.S. Kord on anti-Semitism in German and Austrian crime writing (2018), Alison LaCroix et al. on literary engagement with criminal justice (2017), my own study of crime fiction and moral authority (2016) and Robert Crafton on the African American experience in crime fiction (2015). The parameters of justice – what constitutes a just action and who constitutes a just person – are in numerous ways nationally and even culturally specific. In many cases, notions of justice correspond to dominant national metanarratives. Because intersections between crime fiction and theories of justice abound, legal as well as literary scholars have scrutinised the relationship between legal hermeneutics and narratology. The present chapter continues these lines of questioning to examine what sort of individual stands out as an embodiment of justice at moments of national crisis or moral self-examination.

Hardboiled crime fiction

In most crime novels, whether of the classic "whodunit" variety or the more dystopian models that feature systemic corruption and disillusionment, the detective identifies the perpetrator (usually a murderer). What happens to that perpetrator at the end – incarceration, exile, execution, or nothing – tends to reveal both what society wants and what it realistically expects from punishment. It represents the emotion behind punishment as well as the fallout from that emotion. Through the twentieth century, crime fiction came increasingly to examine that aftermath – to question the broad social and individual consequences of punishment. It also explored ways to mitigate these consequences.

Hardboiled crime fiction launched in the American 1920s, featuring detectives who combined the canny sense of observation and quick mind of Auguste Dupin and Sherlock Holmes with the plainspoken toughness of the American frontier hero and sheriff. In the first hardboiled story, Carroll John Daly's "Three Gun Terry", the titular character announced: "My life is my own, and the opinions of others don't interest me; so don't form any, or if you do, keep them to yourself" (Nolan 1985: 43). When Daly then published *Snarl of the Beast* in 1927, featuring Race Williams, that character made clear that his complete independence was a judicial as well as an existential stance. On the first page Williams announces:

> Right and wrong are not written on the statutes for me, nor do I find my code of morals in the essays of long-winded professors. My ethics are my own. I'm not saying they're good and I'm not admitting they're bad, and what's more I'm not interested in the opinions of others on that subject.
>
> *(1992 [1927]: 1)*

In a sense, this nonconformist stance had to do with the times. The American 1920s were an exciting period for social freedom, music and dancing and daring financial speculation. Those who speak of the "Roaring Twenties" usually think of the bustle of parties and the blare of music on the radio. But the decade also roared with the sounds of police sirens and machine guns, and of newsboys announcing that a Cabinet member had gone to prison. Enacted in 1920, Prohibition blurred the lines between law-abiding citizen and criminal. Though the violent crime surrounding the production and sale of alcohol made criminals more menacing, the mere existence of Prohibition made breaking the law somewhat banal. Blurring the boundary between right and wrong still more, scandal was tainting the lawmakers themselves; the Teapot Dome scandal marked the first time that a Cabinet member had gone to prison.

The maverick freedom that characterised hardboiled fiction and its detectives was a principally American phenomenon, but it did find echoes and descendants in other national traditions. The French hardboiled, or *roman noir*, emerged about twenty years after its American counterpart. Léo Malet introduced Nestor Burma, the first French hardboiled detective, in his 1943 novel *120, rue de la Gare*. In the middle of the Nazi occupation, hope for a national future resided in resistance to the law of the land. When an entire culture comes under assault, the wartime outsider is at the same time a French insider. As Claire Gorrara writes, "The Occupation emerges as a period of dislocation when the everyday is radically altered by the eruption of an alien order" (2003: 25). And as I have argued elsewhere, while other cultures and national traditions had their detective fiction, it is in the American and French traditions in particular that crime fiction character profiles – rooted in nineteenth-century romanticism – translate into national personalities (Lee 2016).

On both sides of the Atlantic, hardboiled novels emerged at historical moments when the establishment was corrupt or incompetent, laws illogical and their application uneven. With official versions automatically suspect and sentencing guidelines irrelevant, punitive justice relied on private initiative. Race Williams's declared "ethics of his own" made sense in this context, as did Nestor Burma's investigative ad-libbing. The idea of rejecting laws on the books in favour of an individual and improvisational version of justice runs through the hardboiled from its beginning to the present day. Sometimes that autonomy seemed welcome, other times it seemed a burden. In Dashiell Hammett's *Red Harvest* (1929), the Continental Op advises a colleague, "don't kid yourself that there's any law in Poisonville except what you make yourself" (1992: 119). The ability to write one's own script and deliver one's own consequences was exciting, but also had the long-term potential to become tiring or corrosive.

Theories of punishment

When detectives are entirely responsible for choosing the punishment, they bear the emotional costs of this decision. Unlike the judicial system, which was an institution and thus not susceptible (at least in theory) to desire and remorse, an individual detective has to live with his or her decisions and actions. Detectives ruminate on punishments meted out and take on the psychic burden of decisions they make. At stake in these ruminations is the individual's ability to conserve cultural ideals in the face of modern obstacles. This is where legal scholarship is useful, as traditional justifications for punishment line up with the detective's social function.

It should be said that when it comes to discussing theories of justice, the hardboiled in some sense resists that discussion. Not only do detectives tend to operate outside the law, but they are usually coming from an anti-idealist (or at least non-idealist) position. Thus the idea of a theory is something to be mocked or dismissed, since this literature has always placed instinctual imperatives above institutional best practices. But even though hardboiled detectives do not have much use for theories, at least in the way that legal scholars discuss them, hardboiled literature does raise questions pertinent to theories of law and justice.

Theories of punishment include such traditional justifications as retribution, deterrence, incapacitation, rehabilitation and restoration. But what matters in most hardboiled novels – individual moral ecosystems unto themselves – is the first of these, what Nora Demleitner et al. describe as "backward-looking theories of punishment, described in terms of retribution or just deserts and based on the notion that punishment is just when it restores the moral balance that criminal behavior upsets" (2018: 2). Crime fiction casts as victim not just the actual individual victim of the crime at hand, but also society at large, the city, moral fibre and even the individual detective. In delivering punishment, the detective represents all those entities, and knows it.

By the middle of the twentieth century, crime fiction focused heavily on retribution. After World War II, Mickey Spillane started publishing his Mike Hammer novels, and they were huge bestsellers. As Hammer announces to his friend, police captain Pat Chambers:

Crime fiction and theories of justice

I hate hard, Pat. When I latch onto the one behind this they're going to wish they hadn't started it. Someday before long I'm going to have my rod in my mitt and the killer in front of me. I'm going to watch the killer's face. I'm going to plunk one right in his gut, and when he's dying on the floor I may kick his teeth out.

(2001, 1: 17)

Whether this has to do with moral anger at the criminal, or respect for "victims' desire for revenge against their offenders" (Boeglin and Shapiro 2017: 1499), the detective serves as both judge and victim in the moral economy of punishment.

Crime fiction is to a significant extent unsuited to non-retributive ideologies of punishment. The reason for this is at least partly commercial. From hardboiled fiction's inception in the cheap pulp magazines of the 1920s, to its publication in 25 cent paperbacks, to weekly television programs, the genre has relied on a serial nature. The offender incarcerated or dispatched in one episode is replaced with another, and the one constant in the world of crime fiction – along with alcohol and clever metaphors – is an endless stream of criminals. In an article about incapacitation as a sentencing principle, Bottoms and Von Hirsch (2012) refer to "offender replacement", taking as example the replacement of incarcerated drug dealers with new sellers. Offender replacement is crime fiction's bread and butter. For this reason, deterrence, wherein potential criminals are cowed by the threat of punishment, does not enter much into the equation. Restoration and rehabilitation of actual criminals are also relatively uncommon, as these can dull the catharsis that readers seek in crime fiction.

On the one hand, on both sides of the Atlantic, the code of justice that the hardboiled character invented was as good or better than the code that the law would have imposed. This was part of the characters' widespread public appeal. When Daly's Race Williams boasted that his ethics were his own, he never seemed dangerous or unethical; his "own" ethics largely reproduced the traditional and even religious principles he claimed to ignore. Even Mike Hammer, that embodiment of unbridled rage, focused his anger on the guilty and so stood largely on the side of right. On the other hand, imposing justice brought the detective's emotions into the game in a way that mere detection – and coolly handing the perpetrator over to the authorities – did not. Dashiell Hammett's Continental Op worried that he was going "blood simple" in the violently corrupt town of Poisonville, where he had essentially free rein (Hammett 1992: 154), and Raymond Chandler's Philip Marlowe allowed that "I was part of the nastiness now" when he agrees to have Carmen Sternwood go to an asylum rather than to prison (Chandler 2002: 197).

Over the decades, the history of crime fiction is one of criminals not deterred, of crimes increased rather than decreased, and of detectives' reactive rage becoming more intense. This increase takes a toll on the person doing the reacting and ends up demanding a rehabilitation of its own. On the one hand, Mike Hammer novels reconcile a celebration of violence with the traditional hardboiled function of moral exemplarity. But even that character reaches the point of wondering if he is fundamentally bad. ("Maybe I was twisted and rotted inside. Maybe I would be washed down the sewer with the rest of all the rottenness sometime" [Spillane 2001, 2: 9]). In fact, the history of twentieth-century hardboiled crime fiction reveals – along with an endless desire for retribution – a correlative need for rehabilitation (see Demleitner et al. 2018: 16). This rehabilitation takes place not in the criminal, but in the detective and in society at large. When it comes to punishment, alternation between wrath and contemplation is founded in the need for crime fiction's fictional universe to retain at once its pathological elements, its emotional tension and its moral steadiness. Avatars of judicial processing, the thoughtful detectives perform a social service by reassuring humanity that it can survive its own shortcomings.

Susanna Lee

Rehabilitating justice

I turn now to two case studies, an American novel, Robert Parker's *Promised Land* (1976) and a French novel, Fred Vargas's *Sous les vents de Neptune* (2004), translated into English as *Wash This Blood Clean From My Hand*. Both feature a detective for whom the criminal investigation blends with a process of introspection. Both represent the act of sentencing – handing out or inflicting punishment – as one that demands its own reckoning and its own rehabilitation. This is distinct from rehabilitation in the usual sense, wherein the criminal is rehabilitated (although Parker's novel contains some of this as well). Rehabilitation takes the form both of self-restraint and of a renewed interest in families, friends and colleagues. In both these novels, ethical responsibility connects to emotional presence in personal relationships. Honesty with oneself and accountability toward others is interwoven with competence as a detective and, in turn, with capacity to represent the nation in times of crisis.

In both novels, the detective's personal inventory stands in for soul-searching on the part of the nation as a whole. Parker's novel was published in 1976, two years after the resignation of President Nixon and three years after America's chaotic exit from direct military involvement in the Vietnam War. *Wash This Blood Clean* was published in 2004, two years after then-leader of France's National Front, Jean-Marie Le Pen, made a surprisingly strong showing in the first round of 2002 presidential voting. These national morality crises pave the way for characters who would orchestrate and also incarnate justice in their respective cultures, much as the turbulence of the post-war period set the scene for American hardboiled pulp fiction.

Both Robert Parker and Fred Vargas were popular authors – and their characters well established – in their respective nations at the time these books were published. *Promised Land* was the fourth novel featuring detective Spenser, and *Wash This Blood Clean* was the sixth book featuring commissioner Adamsberg. Both authors claimed to have been influenced by the American hardboiled.[1] Both novels enact a tension between retributive and rehabilitative modes of punishment, and both make the detective the arbiter and embodiment of these modes. Through their judgement, individual responsibility arises to compensate for nationally compromised political morality.

The character of Spenser – no first name – was raised by his father and brothers after his mother died in childbirth. A private detective, he is a former boxer, Massachusetts State Trooper and serviceman in the Korean War, making him at least forty years old in the first of Parker's novels. Spenser nurses a sardonic nostalgia, but he thrives in the cultural weeds of the early 1970s. He is kind to others, ready to protect the weak and indestructibly strong. Early on in *Promised Land*, a man named Harvey Shepherd hires Detective Spenser to find his wife, Pam. Pam has run away from her husband and children and taken refuge with a pair of violent radical women (essentially a two-woman extremist feminist version of the 1974 Symbionese Liberation Army). Her husband, meanwhile, is a land developer who has gone into debt to loan sharks. One of the lender's enforcers, who threatens Harvey and beats him up, is a friend and associate of Spenser.

The couple's troubles worsen when Pam and her new friends rob a bank and shoot one of the guards. Faced with this multifaceted domestic dispute-turned-crime spree, with bad debt sprinkled in, Spenser manages to separate the consistently venal and brutal criminals from those who are simply hapless or misguided. He finds – almost improvises – just punishments appropriate to each person's actions and motivations. The consequences of criminal actions matter, but so do the perpetrators' intent, background, even emotional capacity. Justice becomes not simply a reparation of the social fabric but a sort of individual therapeutic response, tailored according to each person's willingness to do right by others.

Crime fiction and theories of justice

When Robert Parker was asked in an interview if he was ever tempted to write a political novel, or even to write about national and international political issues, he responded that "the damn subject bores me" (Golsan 2010: 166). Nonetheless, he published his first Spenser novels in the immediate aftermath of Vietnam and the Watergate scandal. Spenser was also one of the earliest detectives to notice and comment on popular culture as a phenomenon – to talk about books and movies and television shows and see that these media created a common American vernacular. And Spenser certainly notices what is going on in politics, mentioning in his first novel, for instance, that he never thought that Nixon would be president, and commenting on Hoover's treatment of radicals (1973: 64).

The main event of *Promised Land* and other Spenser novels is the surprisingly wide range of the detective's salutary influence – his role as a one-man justice machine. As his client Pam puts it:

> I was thinking more about all the conflicts in your character. You reek of machismo, and yet you are a very caring person. You have all these muscles and yet you read all those books. You're sarcastic and a wise guy and you make fun of everything; and yet you were really afraid I'd say no a little while ago and two people you don't even like all that well would get into trouble.
>
> *(1976: 164)*

Justice in this novel is inextricably intertwined with who Spenser is as a person; he functions as modulator and as ballast in conflicts legal and interpersonal. The loan shark, gunrunners and bank-robbery murderers are arrested, the husband is released from his debt and the couple is reconciled. At the end of the novel, Spenser asks his partner, Susan, to marry him, showing the capacity for commitment and emotional presence that he had counselled to his clients.

Crime fiction provides characters who can dole out justice while remaining accountable and exemplary themselves. This accountability is at a premium, particularly at times of political and moral crisis. By the end of the novel, Spenser has taken the time to reconcile a husband and wife, encouraged them to enter counselling, reprimanded a client for using a racial slur, protected those he had promised to protect and ensured that each criminal received a punishment proportional to his or her actions. The police even admire his somewhat unorthodox mode of operating. He shows that in the aftermath of Nixon, a thoughtful individual willing to hold himself accountable could refine or elevate – rather than contaminate – justice and the systems associated with it.

The second case study explores Fred Vargas's 2004 *Wash This Blood Clean From My Hand*. While Vargas's principal character, Jean-Baptiste Adamsberg, is a police commissioner rather than a private detective, the entire process of investigation and pursuit is framed – much more so than in previous Adamsberg novels – as a personal moral inventory. While on a department trip to Quebec incidentally to learn about DNA and forensic technology (a technology that the US Justice Department calls "increasingly vital to ensuring accuracy and fairness in the criminal justice system" and able "to solve crime and protect the innocent", US Department of Justice Archives), Adamsberg is drugged and framed for the murder of a French woman.[2] Adamsberg's framing is foregrounded so that the reader never really doubts his innocence, but Adamsberg himself is deeply troubled by the hours he cannot remember. The person who does the framing is the same psychopathic judge ("the Trident") who had successfully framed Adamsberg's own brother for murder decades before. At the end of the novel, the judge has murdered thirteen people and is threatening Adamsberg's former girlfriend and their child. Adamsberg has the chance to shoot the murderer as he runs out of his apartment, but he does not. "'Target seen from behind, running away', he said. 'It's not self-defense. I've done enough killing as it is, Captain'" (Vargas 2004: 414; translations mine). The novel ends with Adamsberg assured that his girlfriend and child are safe, relieved not to have shot the judge, surrounded by a diverse and oddball group of supportive colleagues, and exonerated in the Quebec murder. It also ends with him coming to terms with being a father.

In this novel, maintaining a clean individual conscience – demanding justice from oneself – is the best protection against precipitous or inconsiderate judgement of others. Vargas has conscience take the form of hesitation and self-doubt, rather than self-assurance. Where Spenser boasts good-naturedly, Adamsberg turns his investigation inward and questions his own abilities. This distinction reflects culturally specific notions of who was best suited as an instrument and arbiter of justice; the brash American and the contemplative Frenchman were established cultural types that came to life in crime fiction. But more than this, *Wash This Blood Clean* came out at a moment of soul-searching for the French. In 2002, Jean-Marie Le Pen had surprisingly come in second in the first round of the presidential election, which led to a second-round run-off between him and Jacques Chirac. The Front National has its roots in collaborationism (its cofounder was a former Waffen-SS officer), which connects it to the era of the original French hardboiled (Shields 2007). Its history also runs through some of the most violent episodes in French colonialism, which was itself much examined in French crime fiction. The results of the 2002 election reminded the country that far-right ideologies were still present and that the government – supposedly the arbiter of justice – could turn into an instrument of destruction. The themes of the novel – a murderous judge who was orphaned in childhood (as was Le Pen) and exploited the confusion of World War II to fabricate a fictitious history – coincide with national alarm at the status of French justice and identity.

Another historical event present to the French public imagination in 2004 was the startling European heatwave that killed thousands of people, most of them elderly, during the summer of 2003. The majority of the dead were women (Bungener 2004). In the course of Vargas's novel, Adamsberg takes particular care to share the credit for his investigation with the colleagues and civilians who had helped him, particularly two elderly women who live alone in Paris. This inclusivity sent the message that it was not enough to bring a murderer to justice; one had to sustain relationships with others. One friend, Clementine, advises him in matters of the heart and another, Josette, an expert hacker, uncovers the information that he needs to pursue the investigation. When Adamsberg, troubled by the holes in his memory and by his lost relationship with Camille, laments that "you can't hack the keyholes of life like those of machines", Josette replies that in fact there is no difference (2004: 398). On one level, these women are stand-ins for France's elderly population, forgotten by the government in their time of need. On another level, they serve as reminders of the nation's abandoned best self. This novel, like Parker's, connects ethical responsibility within an investigation to responsible participation in personal relationships. And like Parker's, it casts compassion for and cooperation with others – particularly with society's most vulnerable – as not just entirely compatible with but actually crucial to the investigation. Adamsberg's diverse investigators take advantage of their invisibility in French society, thus turning a social disadvantage into a practical weapon of justice.

In both of these novels, it is not enough to rid the world of the murderer by retribution or incarceration. The assumption that sentencing alone produces justice – an assumption that undergirded crime fiction in the nineteenth century – no longer holds. The detective has to step in to make decisions and form rehabilitative connections that the judicial system no longer can. Both of these novels draw a connection between honourable behaviour and the paternal role. In *Promised Land*, one of the principal themes is reconciling the ultra-competent alpha male with female autonomy. Initially Spenser's partner complains, "You also can't be everyone's father. It is paternalistic of you to assume that Pam Shepherd with the support of several other women cannot work out her own future without you" (1976: 80). At the end of the novel, though, she calls Spenser "the ultimate man, the ultimate adult in some ways, the great powerful protecting father" (211). Gone are the undesirable associations with fatherhood and paternalism – the powerful protecting father has solved the crime and handed out consequences.[3] Through these rather schematic representations, both novels revive connections between the state and the family and set forth the idealised father as a vehicle of healing. This connection is pertinent to the discussion of the detective as arbiter of justice because the parent-child analogy has been historically much used to support the validity and basic rightness of the state's judgement. Plato's *Crito*, which introduces this highly structured and conservative analogy, does not argue for the state's *de facto* superior understanding and judgement but rather for the practical necessity of submission to state authority (West 1998: 109). In hardboiled crime fiction, published in the midst of political and social upheavals, the idea of the absolute rightness and defensibility of state supremacy has turned into a bad joke. The proverbial father is on his own, detached from the state analogue.

Vargas's novel presents Adamsberg as an actual father, albeit one profoundly uncomfortable with the role. When he first sees his former girlfriend with an infant child, he assumes that the father must be someone else, some new man, "irreproachable, straight, an industrialist with two Labradors [...]" (Vargas 2004: 162). The reader understands that timing makes this unlikely, but Adamsberg is almost wilfully blind to his own fatherhood. In a sense, Adamsberg's uneasiness at being a father stands for an awareness of the immense accountability that comes with representing justice and being a father to the state. Spenser embraces paternalism and Adamsberg retreats from it but for both characters, individual judgement stands in for institutional imperatives. And justice, once a matter of catching the criminal, has become a complicated and multifaceted phenomenon, a series of decisions, a sustained mode of being. Honesty with oneself and accountability toward others is interwoven with competence as a detective and, in turn, with capacity to represent the nation. In the end, personal as much as professional recognition affirms these characters, enabling them to stand for ethical law enforcement and individual responsibility at a moment when political morality has come into question.

Crime novels are not dispassionate essays in ethics and justice. Rather, they walk readers through a living – albeit fictionalised – search for justice, and through the myriad frustrations, ambiguities and epiphanies that come with that search. Contemporary crime fiction increasingly acknowledges that ethical responsibility starts with individual accountability and that in order to dispense justice, one must first be acting, or endeavouring to act, in a just manner. The detectives discussed here consider philosophical imperatives, their own conscience and the constant vicissitudes of real-life circumstances, balancing those elements so as to put theories of justice into the service of society.

Notes

1 Parker had a PhD in English, and wrote his dissertation at Boston University on Chandler, Hammett and Ross MacDonald. He later took the hardboiled step of denouncing his own academic endeavour, noting that he had written the dissertation in two weeks and that that was "about what it's worth" (Leith 2008).

2 www.justice.gov/archives/ag/advancing-justice-through-dna-technology-using-dna-solve-crimes.

3 As Richard Arneson defines paternalism,

> One behaves paternalistically if one treats an adult as though one were a parent dealing with a child. One's behaviour shows concern for the welfare of the person and a presumption that one's judgment about what will promote it is superior. The paradigm of paternalism, and the focus of most philosophical discussion of it, is restriction of people's liberty against their will for their own good.
>
> *(Arneson 1998)*

Bibliography

Arneson, R.J. (1998) "Paternalism", in E. Craig (ed.), *Routledge Encyclopedia of Philosophy*, London: Routledge, 7.

Boeglin, J. and Shapiro, Z. (2017) "A theory of differential punishment", *Vanderbilt Law Review*, 70(5): 1499–559.

Bottoms, A. and Von Hirsch, A. (2012) "The crime-preventative impact of penal sanctions", in P. Cane and H. Kritzer (eds), *The Oxford Handbook of Empirical Legal Research*, Oxford: Oxford University Press, 96–125.

Bungener, M. (2004) "Canicule estivale: la triple vulnérabilité des personnes âgées", *Mouvements*, 32(2): 75–82.

Chandler, R. (2002) *The Big Sleep, Farewell, My Lovely, The High Window*, New York: Everyman's Library.

Crafton, R.E. (2015) *The African American Experience in Crime Fiction*, Jefferson, NC: McFarland.

Daly, C.J. (1992) [1927] *The Snarl of the Beast*, New York: HarperPerennial.

Demleitner, N., Berman, D., Miller, M.L. and Wright, R.F. (2018) *Sentencing Law and Policy: Cases, statutes, and guidelines*, 4th edn, New York: Wolters Kluwer Law & Business.

Golsan, R.J. and Golsan, J. (2010) "Interview with Robert Parker", *South Central Review*, 27(1–2): 163–66.

Gorrara, C. (2003) *The Roman Noir in Post-war French Culture: Dark fictions*, Oxford: Oxford University Press.

Hammett, D. (1992) *Red Harvest*, New York: Vintage.

Kord, T.S. (2018) *Lovable Crooks and Loathsome Jews: Antisemitism in German and Austrian crime writing before the world wars*, Jefferson, NC: McFarland.

LaCroix, A., McAdams, R. and Nussbaum, M. (eds) (2017) *Fatal Fictions: Crime and investigation in law and literature*, New York: Oxford University Press.

Lee, S. (2016) *Hard-boiled Crime Fiction and the Decline of Moral Authority*, Columbus: Ohio State University Press.

Leith, S. (2008) "Robert B. Parker: hard-boiled, old school and y'know, a bit sloppy", *The Telegraph*, 23 February.

Nolan, W. (1985) *The Black Mask Boys: Masters in the hard-boiled school of detective fiction*, New York: The Mysterious Press.

Parker, R. (1973) *The Godwulf Manuscript*, New York: Random House.

———. (1976) *Promised Land*, New York: Random House.

Shields, J. (2007) *The Extreme Right in France: From Pétain to Le Pen*, London: Routledge.

Spillane, M. (2001) *The Mike Hammer Collection*, vols. 1–3, New York: Penguin.

Tyler, T.R. (2006) "Viewing *CSI* and the threshold of guilt: managing truth and justice in reality and fiction", *Yale Law Journal*, 115(5): 1050–85.

The United States Department of Justice Archives, "Using DNA to solve crimes", www.justice.gov/archives/ag/advancing-justice-through-dna-technology-using-dna-solve-crimes (accessed May 2019).

Vargas, F. (2004) *Sous les vents de Neptune*, Paris: Editions Viviane Hamy.

West, T.G. and West, G.S. (eds) (1998) *Four Texts on Socrates: Plato's Euthyphro, Apology, and Crito, and Aristophanes' Clouds*, Ithaca: Cornell University Press.

32

CRIME FICTION AND MODERN SCIENCE

Andrea Goulet

The modern detective genre was born in the nineteenth century, a time when scientific positivism was on the rise, naturalist sciences brought new discoveries about prehistory, and debates on topics ranging from optics to evolution were being popularised through public lectures and periodicals. The entanglement of crime fiction and modern science has been noted at least since 1929, when Régis Messac published his magisterial thesis on "The Detective Novel and the Influence of Scientific Thought". Messac not only traces the appearance in detective fiction of scientific content from fields like physiognomy, phrenology and astronomy; he also argues that the crime genre incorporates a modern, rationalist "scientific spirit" into its very form (1929: 38). Indeed, the deductive and inductive approaches favoured by fictional detectives rely on "conjecture", "calculation" and – most importantly – "observation", a key element of scientific method in an age of rising empiricism.

Each of the early fictional detectives – Poe's Dupin, Gaboriau's Lecoq, Doyle's Holmes – mobilises up-to-date scientific techniques that appear congruent with a broader Cartesian ideology of rational method. Sherlock Holmes in particular embodies the scientific spirit, as when he scolds Watson (in "The Adventure of the Abbey Grange", 1904) for looking at a case "from the point of view of a story instead of as a scientific exercise" (Thomas 1999: 1). Although Holmes's own expertise is variable, he solves mysteries by turning to facts from mathematics, biology, physics, botany, optics, astronomy and especially chemistry; Holmes's active experiments with coal-tar derivatives and dyes, poisons, chloroform, blood tests and phosphorescence make him a "pioneer in forensic science" (O'Brien 2013: 43).

This chapter presents a summary of key overlaps between crime fiction and modern science, with an emphasis on the French and anglophone traditions. Starting with the central analogy between detective work and scientific reconstructions of the past, it moves to the fictional incorporation of late nineteenth-century scientific policing methods and early twentieth-century debates in physics and optics. Rather than propose a uni-directional model of scientific influence, it aims to explore the tensions raised by crime fiction between rationality and mystery, science and superstition. A section on mastery and doubt leads to a historical overview of the mid-twentieth-century noir's critique of scientific authority, followed by a return in the twenty-first century of forensic technology as guarantor of truth. Fred Vargas's contemporary fiction exemplifies the enduring legacy of science in modern stories of crime and investigation.

Cuvier and the reconstructive sciences

In Poe's "The Murders in the Rue Morgue" (1841), the detective Dupin turns to a tome by the French naturalist Georges Cuvier (1769–1832) to lend scientific authority to his identification of the assassin as an orangutan. As famous in the 1830s and 1840s as someone like Stephen Hawking is today, Cuvier was recognised worldwide not only for comparatist anatomical studies, but primarily for his foundational geological work on fossils, which revolutionised ways of understanding the past's relation to the present. In particular, Cuvier's boast in the 1812 "Preliminary Discourse" to his *Recherches sur les ossements fossiles de quadrupèdes* that he could reconstruct an entire lost species from a mere fragment of bone inspired a sustained analogy between paleontologist and fictional detective. In Emile Gaboriau's 1869 *Monsieur Lecoq*, a young detective admires the "astounding investigative faculties of [a senior] agent who could reconstruct drama and truth, just like those naturalists who, upon the mere inspection of two or three bones, were able to draw the animal to which they had belonged" (Goulet 2015: 258). Doyle also describes investigative method in terms of paleontological reconstruction in "The Five Orange Pips" (1891):

> As Cuvier could correctly describe a whole animal by the contemplation of a single bone, so the observer who has thoroughly understood one link in a series of incidents, should be able to accurately state all the other ones, both before and after.
>
> *(1981a: 100)*

The modern crime genre thus partakes epistemologically in what William Whewell in 1837 called the "palaetiological" or "inductive" sciences – those fields like geology and paleontology that move from material clues of shell, fossil or bone to larger deductive conclusions.

In Carlo Ginzburg's classic 1979 essay on scientific method, Sherlock Holmes's investigations similarly reflect a clue-based "evidential paradigm" that moves from detail or fragment to the whole. Although Ginzburg expands this methodological approach to include disciplines like art history and psychoanalysis, its historical aspect is key to the work of the fictional detective, who reconstructs past truths from the physical traces of a crime. The nineteenth-century historical disciplines that sought to recreate the past from fragmentary evidence directly informed the fictions of Poe, Dickens and Doyle; Lawrence Frank (2003) cites these authors' engagement with Laplace's nebular hypothesis, Lyell's geological studies of human prehistory and Darwin's theory of evolution as reinforcing a radically new and secular historical worldview. Cuvier's methods also furnished an evidentiary model for the discovery of truth in forensic science and criminal law (Thomas 1999: 54–55). Beyond the compelling analogy of detective work to fossil reconstruction, Cuvier's work opened the way for modern crime fiction to grapple with the troubling notions of violent human prehistory and subterranean catastrophism through the "catacomb fictions" of the 1860s by novelists like Elie Berthet and Pierre-Léonce Imbert and the archaeological imaginary of early twentieth-century writers like Gaston Leroux and Maurice Leblanc (Goulet 2015).

Forensics and the scientific police

In the final decades of the nineteenth century, new forensic technologies were increasingly used by police and the justice system for criminal identification. In 1881, Alphonse Bertillon established the Bureau of Judicial Identification in Paris, and in the following year, the French capital city's central police department incorporated his biometrics system, consisting of photographic files accompanied by bodily measurement records, into their official law enforcement procedures. The meticulous anthropometrical science of Bertillonage, or "signaletics", represented a move toward a new "*police scientifique*", whose claims to rationalised, professional efficiency made its way quickly into fiction. In *The Hound of the Baskervilles* (1902), Sherlock Holmes is described by a character as the "second highest expert in Europe" after Bertillon, whose work must appeal to "the man of precisely scientific mind" (1981b: 13). Apparently, the influence went both ways, as some claim that the French police consulted the fictional Holmes by reading the 1906 volume *L'Œuvre de Conan Doyle et la police scientifique au vingtième siècle* (O'Brien 2013: 109).

If that is the case, crime fiction may well have contributed to a shift in actual police work from signaletics to fingerprinting, since Holmes favoured the latter, using it in the solutions to seven of his sixty cases (O'Brien 2013: 50). As an emerging technique of identification, fingerprinting's rivalry with Bertillonage followed national lines at first. When the London police began taking the fingerprints of suspected criminals in 1894, their records were understood to complement the established anthropometric system; but "often acrimonious debate among criminologists and legal theorists" led in that decade to the French defence of the superiority of Bertillonage (Thomas 1999: 204). Eventually, fingerprinting won out: In 1914, the International Police Conference officially endorsed dactyloscopy (the forensic analysis of fingerprints) over anthropometry, even among French national police (Thomas 1999: 207).

Italy also played a key role in the development of forensic science, especially through the work of criminal anthropologist Cesare Lombroso. In his 1876 *L'Uomo Delinquente* [Criminal Man], Lombroso called upon degeneration theory and social Darwinism to develop a theory of phrenological indicators of racial and social inferiority. Among the delinquent types he identified was the "atavistic born criminal", recognisable by measurable physical traits like a sloping forehead and protruding jaw. At the turn of the century, Lombroso founded with his disciples the Italian School of Positivist Criminology, which taught up-to-date methods of detection within a scientific framework. His theories contributed to the use in police departments of "mug shots", which were to become a common motif in the fictional crime genre, especially the international *noir*.

Each of these technologies – Bertillonage, fingerprinting, photography and phrenology – contributed to an ideology of scientific and social control over the criminal body. Similarly, the forensic science of lie detection, which had its origins in Lombroso's "sphygmograph" instrument measuring changes in blood pressure and pulse over the course of an interrogation, fulfilled a nineteenth-century dream of technological mastery over violent subjects (Thomas 1999: 21–22). In his book on the anticipation and deployment of forensic technologies in the crime fictions of Poe, Collins, Doyle and Hammett, Ronald Thomas argues that such scientific mechanisms "aimed at achieving in the field of law enforcement the same feat that detective writers sought to produce in the literary imagination: Reading the truth directly inscribed upon the criminal body" (1999: 23). Today's legal procedures of digitised photographic records and DNA "fingerprinting" carry on the hope for the definitive bodily identification of criminal subjects.

Optics and physics

The best-known visual icon of classic crime fiction may well be Sherlock Holmes's magnifying glass. Evoking the scientific gaze of entomological precision, this optical instrument lends authority to the murder detective, rational solver of mystery and consummate "private eye". If the fictional Holmes makes use of optical devices like the magnifying lens, telescope and microscope, it may well be because his creator Doyle had trained as an opthalmologist and was fascinated by the visual techniques of photography as a "scientific subject" (Thomas 1999: 167). And certainly, the myth of rational mastery that undergirds detective fiction by authors from Poe through to Christie and beyond taps into a Cartesian figuration of light as truth, crime as shadow. And yet, just as crime fiction's appeal to science more generally exposes its fault lines and uncertainties, the optical logics of the detective novel are riven with the destabilising epistemology of nineteenth-century empiricist theories of perception. Yes, the fictional detective aims for (and claims) all-seeing mastery above the limited and bumbling confusion of those around him, but the scientific context of physiological optics imbues the genre with a deep scepticism about the evidence of one's eyes; and indeed, the faultiness of physical senses leads authors like Poe, Collins and Doyle to mix their rationalism with affinity for alternative forms of "vision" like clairvoyance and telepathy (Smajic 2010). Similarly, empiricist theories of vision that situate the search for truth not in an abstract "light" of the mind, but in the troubling subjective phenomena of the bodily eye, led to crime stories like Jules Claretie's *L'Accusateur* (1897), which plays with the judicial possibility of retrieving the last image seen by a murder victim's eye (Goulet 2006). By the 1920s, optograms were no longer being attempted in police murder investigations and Maurice Renard relegates them to mere superstition in his 1921 detective novel *Les Mains d'Orlac* (Evans 1993: 341).

Already in Gaston Leroux's *Le Mystère de la chambre jaune* (1907), optical and physical sciences were registering an epistemological ambivalence, an unresolved struggle between abstract deduction and empirical method. My essay on Leroux's novel connects the *camera obscura* of the eye to the story's locked-room motif in order to explore optical tropes – retinal blind spots and presbyopic lenses – that expose methodological concerns underlying judicial and scientific investigation at the fin de siècle (Goulet 2005). And David Platten has analysed *Le Mystère de la chambre jaune* as linking, surprisingly, science to superstition through its opposition of characters: The Stangersons represent a "new breed of scientist, engaged in research on the nature of the universe that would lead to the framing of Heisenberg's 'uncertainty principle' in 1928 and the subsequent discovery of quantum mechanics in the early 1930s"; but rather than celebrate their forward-looking physics, Leroux disparages them in favour of the investigator Rouletabille's faith in Cartesian reasoning (2001: 259). In Leroux's crime novel, then, a nostalgic emphasis on logic and Newtonian physics wrestles with the uncertainties of empiricism, forensic evidence and the destabilising horizon of twentieth-century science.

Mastery and doubt

In *A Study in Scarlet*, Holmes tells Watson that "[d]etection is, or ought to be, an exact science and should be treated in the same cold and unemotional manner". Superstition and story-telling seem to have no place in an investigation based on analytical reasoning, nor in a genre that relies on up-to-date forensic technologies to classify and control the criminal elements of modern society. Indeed, science has often been invoked in the service of a model of the genre as a "purely intellectual experience", excluding coincidence, fantasy and the supernatural; one of S.S.Van Dine's twenty rules for writing detective stories stipulates that "[t]he method of murder, and the means of detecting it, must be rational and scientific" (1928: #14).

But that purified model of rationality exists only in theory. From its very start, the detective genre has blurred boundaries between science and pseudo-science, reason and mystery. The early Dupin stories cannot fully be separated from Poe's fascination with galvanism, Mesmerism, phrenology and Swedenborgian mysticism. And at a time when scientific positivism grappled with its apparent opposite, the occult, nineteenth-century crime writers from Poe through

Crime fiction and modern science

Gaboriau and Doyle could not help but enter "an intermediary zone between mythology and rationalism, on the borders of science" (Messac 1929: 216). In *A Counter-History of Crime Fiction*, Maurizio Ascari provides a genealogical map of the "hybrid zones" between crime fiction and the antirational traditions from which it has classically been distinguished (2007). In a related vein, my 2015 book argues that Poe's "The Murders in the Rue Morgue" was already as counter-rational, gruesome and conflicted as any of the sensational murder narratives that were excised from purified accounts of the detective genre (Goulet 2015: 7).

More specifically, a number of early crime fictions undercut the authority of science even as they seemed to invoke it. While the reconstructive sciences promised an overarching historical mastery over the past, the fiction of Poe, Dickens and Doyle "also pointed to the inadequacies of the various disciplines – philology, geology, paleontology, and evolutionary biology – that informed it, subverting its own claims to the truth" (Frank 2003: 25). Lawrence Frank's readings of *The Mystery of Edwin Drood* and *The Hound of the Baskervilles* emphasise the unreliability of their fragmentary evidence, with the result that confident investigative solutions based on the science of Darwin or Lyell are revealed to be at least ambiguous and perhaps fully illusory (2003). Scientific mastery is put into question differently in L.T. Meade and Robert Eustace's detective series *The Brotherhood of the Seven Kings* (1899) and *The Sorceress of the Strand* (1903). As Rachel Smillie points out, the female criminal masterminds in those fictions are women of science, medical practitioners who function as an uncontainable challenge to male scientific authority; their criminality is directly linked to "the professional threat they pose to their detective counterparts who stand as representatives of male institutional science" (2017: 143). Throughout the nineteenth century and *fin de siècle*, crime fiction's scenes of medical quackery and mystic mumbo-jumbo reveal an underside to detective confidence and its reliance on the exactitude and authority of science.

Twentieth-century noir

For all the doubts lurking under the surface of scientific positivism in nineteenth-century crime fiction, the twentieth century saw a far more explicit and radical undercutting of epistemological certainty. The authority of science was put into question, for example, by G.K. Chesterton, who reacts to a world of "crumbling certainties and increasing complexity" by having his detective, Father Brown, complain that the so-called impartiality of detection as a science is dead and dehumanising (Ascari 2007: 161–62). By the 1930s, Dashiell Hammett's hardboiled private eyes were renouncing forensic technologies like fingerprinting as "forms of quackery" and defining themselves in opposition to the police force's legal authority (Thomas 1999: 91–92). Raymond Chandler's detective stories of the 1930s and 1940s exposed photographic evidence as eminently falsifiable, and Hammett's Sam Spade often failed to discern conclusive proof on criminal bodies, thus undermining "confidence in bourgeois institutions of law and order [...] and in the scientific ideal of objective truth" (Thomas 1999: 91). The noir presents the reader with a realm of shadows and hard-bitten despair: No room here for naïve trust in science and its instruments.

Nor does the noir allow for evolutionist hope in the future. Even when invoking Darwinism, as does Jean-Patrick Manchette in *La Position du tireur couché* (1981), it is to promote a bleak, amoral worldview; Manchette "asks us to face the possibility that we are fundamentally mechanistic creatures, driven solely by the instinct to survive" (Platten 2001: 270). In a postcolonial context, the noir gives a new thrust to the critique of scientific authority by demonstrating the misuses of Western ethnography and the rationalist ideology on which it is founded. Congolese author Bolya Baenga's *La Polyandre* (1995) features a female investigator who is writing a book for the *Centre National de la Recherche Scientifique* (CNRS) but whose perverse corruption exposes the tainted motivations and blind spots of a supposedly neutral scientific field (Higginson 2011: 120–26). When positivistic sciences are adduced in the twentieth-century noir, they are ironised or shot down. Alternatively, in the case of historical detective novels set in the nineteenth century by today's writers like Anne Perry and Caleb Carr, the fascination with forensic science is presented as merely quaintly historical (Thomas 1999: 275).

Science today

And yet the success of contemporary crime writers like Val McDermid, Franck Thilliez and Fred Vargas suggests that science has lost neither its appeal nor its claim to authority. The Scottish author McDermid, who has written a non-fiction book, *Forensics: The Anatomy of a Crime* (2014), uses up-to-date techniques of chemistry and forensic anthropology to add believability to her bestselling crime novels. In French writer Thilliez's thriller *Syndrome E* (2014), advances in neuroscience are harnessed for good and for evil, with the scientific fascination with how the brain works emerging as a double-edged sword. And Vargas, whose crime fiction is explored below, is herself a trained epidemiologist; to research her books, she consults with other scientists, as when she turned to experts on arachnology and toxicology at the actual Muséum d'histoire naturelle for *Quand sort la recluse* (2017) [*This Poison Will Remain*, 2019]. The late twentieth and early twenty-first centuries appear to be witnessing a revival of scientific influence on the fictional crime genre.

For Kerstin Bergman, that revival signals a return to the legitimising function of science. In her essay on the television series *CSI: Crime Scene Investigation* (2000-) and Patricia Cornwell's novel *The Scarpetta Factor* (2009), Bergman proposes that the forensic crime genre in particular sets up science as a reliable key to finding truth; unlike private detectives in the hardboiled genre, forensic examiners like Dr Kay Scarpetta use technology with confidence in the pursuit of justice (2012). If science is today once again presented in forensic narratives as "true and trusted", it may be because fiction allows for "wishful thinking" in an age of postmodern uncertainty; "[p]erhaps the dependability of science is part of what makes [these fictions] so successful; they provide stability, certainty, and truth in times of general indeterminacy" (Bergman 2012: 96). David Platten's reading of Maurice Dantec's *Les Racines du mal* (1995) similarly hypothesises a redemptive function for science, this time in the moral sphere: The novel incorporates theoretical physics, neurology, biology and the science of artificial intelligence into a plot that allows a computer with a conscience to usurp the role of the traditional detective, thus tinging the genre's pessimistic fatalism "with an optimism generated from the laboratory" (2001: 270). The large number of successful contemporary narratives that blur generic boundaries between crime fiction and science fiction (by authors like J.D. Robb or Richard K. Morgan) indicate a future for science in the fighting of crime.

Reconstructive science and Vargas's *The Three Evangelists*

Fred Vargas is the pseudonym of French historian, archaeozoologist and crime writer Frédérique Audoin-Rouzeau. Trained as an archaeologist, Vargas has worked at the CNRS and the Institut Pasteur and in 2003 published a scientific treatise considered definitive in the research area of the epidemiology of the Black Death. Meanwhile, her crime fiction has earned her multiple awards, including an unprecedented three International Dagger Awards from the Crime Writers Association for *The Three Evangelists* (2006; orig. *Debout les morts*, 1995), *The Chalk Circle Man* (2009; orig. *L'Homme aux cercles bleus*, 1991) and *The Ghost Riders of Ordebac* (2013; orig. *L'Armée furieuse*, 2011). Although Vargas's main fictional Detective Inspector Adamsberg employs investigative tactics that are not particularly scientific (he prefers instead to trust in instinct and "flair"), other characters – like the pathologist Ariane Lagarde or the deeply knowledgeable Officer Danglard – corral facts from various scientific disciplines in their search for truth. Throughout her fiction, Vargas intertwines scientific expertise with atmospherics of superstition, folk tales and legendary creatures from werewolves to Icelandic demons. In this way, her work partakes of the hybridity and ambiguities that we have traced from the genre's beginnings and that Ascari emphasises in his *Counter-History of Crime Fiction*.

More specifically, the archaeological thrust of Vargas's novels provides us with a twenty-first-century update of the reconstructive approach employed by early crime writers like Poe, Doyle and Gaboriau. *The Three Evangelists* will serve as a case study of the way in which Vargas combines archaeological history with psychoanalytical "digging" as a way to reflect on the continuing evolution of the science/crime fiction nexus.

While most murder mysteries begin with the discovery of a corpse, *The Three Evangelists* begins with a beech tree that has appeared overnight in the garden of the famous singer Sophia Siméonidis, who is so unsettled by this unexplained entity that she asks her neighbours to dig into the dirt below its roots to find clues to the intruder's provenance. Her neighbours are neither gardeners nor detectives, but historians – the fictional trio known as the "three evangelists": Marc Vandoosler ("Saint Mark"), Mathias Delamarre ("Saint Matthew"), and Lucien Devernois ("Saint Luke"). If their nicknames seem like relics from a faded religious era, it is no coincidence; for the three men are professionally and psychologically invested in reviving the past – and the novel makes direct comparisons between the work of historians and that of detectives (2000: 73, 204).

The historiographical character of the "three evangelists" is evident in the very layout of their crumbling mansion, a five-storey behemoth that the historians inhabit according to the chronological order of their specialisations. On the second floor, we have the prehistorian Mathias; one floor up, Marc the medievalist; then above him, Lucien, a World War I scholar (whose character is based on Vargas's real-life brother); and finally, in the attic, Marc's godfather, an aging lothario and former police detective. Marc, the medievalist, explains this peculiar layout with mock seriousness, saying that it is based on a system of chronological gradation over the millennia that recreates the "stratigraphy of History" (61). From deep time at the bottom to shallow present at the top, the manse's vertical order mimics the geological layers of the earth below – layers that hold weapons and bones, clues to the past for those who dare to dig. Marc twice uses the scientific term "stratigraphy" to describe the house's storeys – and again later to describe the layers of dirt that hold the key to the crime, thus connecting the historians' profession to their amateur investigation of their neighbour's mysterious beech tree. Once that neighbour herself disappears, the three evangelists must apply archaeological methods to a real terrain. At one point in the dig, they find an eighteenth-century earthen pipe and at another, a sixteenth-century ceramic pot; but neither of these apparent clues from the past leads anywhere (52, 227). The dirt outside of Sophia's home seems silent, despite the prehistorian Mathias's attempts "to make the piles of flint and bone speak to him" (226). Flint and bones – the objects of study for Earth scientists, but not so typical for investigators of contemporary crime.

In addition to sifting through the flint and loam of Sophia's property, the historian-detectives consult the reviews and newspaper clippings that have been stored in the singer's family archives. The key to Sophia's murder lies both in those dusty cartons and (quite literally) on earthy matter, since the singer's very identity is aligned with rock: When police find the charred remains of a body in a burning car, they identify it as Sophia because of the presence of a volcanic pebble that she had always kept on her person. As the only material trace to survive the fire, that "volcanic fetish" served as a talismanic reminder of the Greek singer; but since this geological fragment had been planted in the burnt car as a red herring, it simultaneously invokes and undercuts the forensic authority of physical evidence – as we saw happen in the nineteenth-century fictions of Poe, Doyle and Gaboriau.

In a more symbolic sense, the basalt pebble textually links Sophia to her devoted investigators. As Marc tries to unravel the mystery of his neighbour's disappearance, his jumbled thoughts take on the geological traits of volcanic plates:

> His thoughts knocked about, crashing together and bouncing apart. Like plates of the earth's crust [...]. Over the mantle of molten lava. [S]labs that slip and slide all over the Earth's surface. [...] Plate tectonics, that's what it's called. Well, for him, it was thought tectonics. When the plates bounce apart, the volcano erupts.
>
> *(117)*

And if the layers of Marc's mind risk volcanic disruption as they sift through the confusing evidence of Sophia's murder, his solid-as-a-rock friend Mathias is equally vulnerable to the seismic effects of the unknown: Mathias is "a sort of dolmen: a massive, static, and sacred rock, but one that's unknowingly permeated with all sorts of troubling events, orienting its particles of mica toward the direction of the winds" (175). As for Lucien, it is in linguistic form that fragments from the past arise to disrupt the surface of a peacetime present: The historian's speech is peppered with World War I locutions.

Buried trauma leaves scars underground and symptoms above – including on the level of language. In *The Three Evangelists*, "the earth can speak" (228) because it can reveal to a historian's eye, through its loamy textures and gradations of grit, the timing of buried secrets and their disruptive effects. And the past can "speak", whether through Lucien's verbal tics or the discovery that Sophia's name had been written by another murder victim with an "s" in the middle, turning it into *sosie* ("twin") – which leads the investigators to Juliette, the singer's understudy and rivalrous double (271). Marc reconstructs Juliette's movements through a series of underground spaces: The hole under the mysterious beech tree (which she had planted to trouble Sophia), the cellar of *Le Tonneau* (the restaurant under which Juliette had killed her rival), a deep subterranean well (into which Juliette had thrown Marc, out of an archaic impulse to imitate medieval assassins) and back to the hole under the beech tree (in which Juliette had buried Sophia's corpse, knowing that the dirt there had already been deemed free of bones in the initial investigative dig). Though Juliette's motivations are superficially explained by her professional failure fifteen years earlier, the true temporality of criminal investigation in Vargas' work is geological in scope: Explaining the police's inability to solve the crime, Marc tells his companions, "They must not have dug as deeply as we did; someone else had excavated afterwards, deeper, all the way into the black and oily layer of the earth" (273).

In the geological imagination of *The Three Evangelists*, volcanic forces erupt not only on the side of violent crime, but also in the deductive processes of the investigators themselves. If Marc turns to plate tectonics as a figure for the perpetual *glissades* of his mind, he also wonders whether the other historians feel the same subterranean forces at work:

> [W]hat about Lucien? did he eruptify? that's not a word, eruptify. Erupt? Nope. Lucien was more of the chronic seismic smoldering type. And Mathias? Not at all tectonic, that one. Mathias was the [...] ocean that cools lava down. Of course, that doesn't change the fact that in the depths of the ocean, it's never as calm as people might think. There's plenty of crap down there too, [...] Shafts, cracks.
>
> *(117–18)*

In this language of fissures and fractures, tectonic shifts and volcanic eruptions, we may well recognise a Freudian model of the subconscious mind: Digging into the past involves an exposure of deep mental strata as much as of dirt and documents. Indeed, *The Three Evangelists'* climactic resolution takes on the form of a psychoanalytic "talking cure", with the historian/ investigators bringing about a spoken confession from the murderer Nathalie/Juliette, whose eruptive strata of the past emerge as a psychic schism or fissure in the form of split personality.

By the middle of the twentieth century, the geological master trope of nineteenth-century crime fiction had moved inward, through Freud's notion of the psyche as a layered terrain of strata and substrata, fissures and eruptions into violence. By combining the literal underground of a nineteenth-century archaeological imagination with the metaphorical "digging" of twentieth-century psychoanalysis, Vargas's *The Three Evangelists* revives the appeal of modern (but past-oriented) science in fictions of crime and detection. The "archaeological crime fictions" of writers like Didier Daeninckx, Sébastien Japrisot and Fred Vargas explore how buried national traumas (World War I, the Occupation, Algerian repression) continue to haunt the criminal spaces of modernity (Goulet 2015). And more broadly, transnational traditions of crime narrative continue to engage with the complexities of scientific debate in order to expose the rifts in human attempts to master the incomprehensibility of violent death.

Bibliography

Ascari, M. (2007) *A Counter-History of Crime Fiction: Supernatural, Gothic, sensational*, Basingstoke (UK) and New York: Palgrave Macmillan.

Bergman, K. (2012) "Fictional death and scientific truth: the truth-value of science in contemporary forensic crime fiction", *Clues*, 30(1): 88–98.

Doyle, A.C. (1981a) [1891] "The Five Orange Pips", in *The Adventures of Sherlock Holmes*, London: Penguin, 100–119.

Doyle, A.C. (1981b) [1902] *The Hound of the Baskervilles*, London: Penguin.

Evans, A. (1993) "Optograms and fiction: photo in a dead man's eye", *Science Fiction Studies*, 20(3): 341–61.

Frank, L. (2003) *Victorian Detective Fiction and the Nature of Evidence: The scientific investigations of Poe, Dickens, and Doyle*, London: Palgrave Macmillan.

Ginzburg, C. (1989) *Clues, Myths, and the Historical Method*, trans. J. Tedeschi and A.C. Tedeschi, Baltimore: Johns Hopkins University Press.

Goulet, A. (2005) "The yellow spot: ocular pathology and empirical method in Gaston Leroux's *Le Mystère de la chambre jaune*", *SubStance*, 34(2/107): 27–46.

———. (2006) *Optiques: The science of the eye and the birth of modern French fiction*, Philadelphia: University of Pennsylvania Press.

———. (2015) *Legacies of the Rue Morgue: Science, space, and crime fiction in France*, Philadelphia: University of Pennsylvania Press.

Higginson, P. (2011) *The Noir Atlantic: Chester Himes and the birth of the francophone African crime novel*, Liverpool: Liverpool University Press.

Lombroso, C. (2006) [1876] *Criminal Man*, trans. M. Gibson and N. Hahn Rafter, Durham, NC: Duke University Press.

Messac, R. (1929) *Le "Détective Novel" et l'influence de la pensée scientifique*, Paris: Honoré Champion.

O'Brien, J. (2013) *The Scientific Sherlock Holmes: Cracking the case with science and forensics*, Oxford: Oxford University Press.

Platten, D. (2001) "Reading-glasses, guns and robots: a history of science in French crime fiction", *French Cultural Studies*, 12(36): 253–70.

Smajic, S. (2010) *Ghost-Seers, Detectives, and Spiritualists: Theories of vision in Victorian literature and science*, Cambridge: Cambridge University Press.

Smillie, R. (2017) "Criminal genius: constructing women of science in L.T. Meade's detective fiction", *Victoriographies*, 7(2): 143–60.

Thomas, R. (1999) *Detective Fiction and the Rise of Forensic Science*, Cambridge: Cambridge University Press.

Van Dine, S.S. (1928) "Twenty rules for writing detective stories", *The Thrilling Detective Web Site*, www.thrillingdetective.com/trivia/triv288.html (accessed 31 October 2019).

Vargas, F. (2000) [1995] *Debout les morts*, Paris: Éditions J'ai Lu.

Willis, M. (2011) *Vision, Science and Literature, 1870–1920: Ocular horizons*, London: Pickering & Chatto.

33

CRIME FICTION AND THE POLICE

Andrew Nestingen

The representation of the police officer in crime fiction is often divided: Within the officer's character are forces pulling in different directions. Consider, for example, Kurt Wallander as functionary or servant of the Swedish welfare state: A representative figure, then, but someone whose stoic personal suffering generates sympathy and a readerly recognition of his goodness. An instructive manifestation of this tension occurs in the novel *Villospår* (1995) [Sidetracked, 1999]. Wallander is struck by a "very un-policeman like feeling [...] It was as though a dam inside him had burst, and he knew that there were no longer invisible lines dividing Sweden. The violence of the large cities had reached his own police district" (1999: 112–13). Through his work, Wallander seeks to serve the country; he is a public steward. Yet Wallander suffers for it, dams burst inside him, because of the horrible things he observes in his home district. The division in Wallander as seen here is created by the technique of melodrama in which realist narration creates an ugly world for a suffering hero to endure in a way that justifies their efforts to put things right.

The police officer or detective is a typical hero of this kind, for the police officer as a character offers access to emblematic conflicts in late-modern, globalised, capitalist society. The police detective is at once a member of a state institution, working within its rules and laws, but also an emotional subject, who connects with colleagues, victims and their families, suspects, and family, friends and lovers. They see things professionally and suffer things emotionally. Tension set loose by conflicts of gender, class, race and sexuality torment police officers. Jane Tennison (Helen Mirren) in *Prime Suspect* (1991) is a detective who sees the worst of humanity but is also a woman in a man's world and the victim of sexist exclusion and discrimination. There are also class tensions for crime fiction's police detectives to negotiate – the working-class officer, who must investigate members of his own community, for example, in Dennis Lehane's *Mystic River* (2001) or in Tana French's *Faithful Place* (2010). Gender, class and race pull in multiple directions in the HBO crime serial *The Wire* (2002–2008), which is broader than a police narrative, but built around some of the same conflicting identities touched on above.

The list of examples makes it necessary to pause for an important observation about the transmediality of the police story. The genre has a history of interconnection across media since it rose to prominence as a form of crime fiction in the 1950s, the decade in which television also became an influential promulgator of fictional and news narratives, which often featured the police. The majority of police novels that attracted broad readerships were adapted for television or cinema, and in some cases television series were adapted as novels. For example, more than thirty novels were adapted or spun off from the *CSI: Crime Scene Investigation* series (2001–2016). With cable television's production of long-form narratives and police narratives, and their distribution by way of streaming services, the audiovisual police narrative has garnered still greater popularity. For these reasons, this essay uses examples from literature, television and cinema to analyse the broad representation of the police officer, the detective and the police as an institution.

The focus in this genre is the split or divided police officer, pulled in multiple directions by competing discourses, institutions and identities. Analysis of this figure gives us a better understanding of the relationship between the police and crime fiction. Rather than approaching the topic of the police as solely a matter of medium, as noted above, or in terms of genre, the police procedural (Dove 1982) or the police novel (Messent 2010), the chapter looks at crime fiction and the police in order to study the tensions that construct the police officer in fiction and consider how these tensions are organised. What, then, are the key tensions? Elements of gender, class, race and sexuality are entwined within the figure of the officer, typically establishing this figure as a potentially progressive force. But at the same time these progressive elements are set against reactionary institutional cultures and an account of law and justice which emphasise their partial and/or inadequate natures. Peter Messent writes:

> To approach the police novel in terms of its institutional context is to suggest a three-way focus – first, on individual law enforcers and the policing communities to which they belong; second, on the exercise of state power and bureaucracy (the way society is policed); and third, on the general health (or lack of it) of the social system.
>
> *(2010: 178–79)*

This chapter argues that the figure of the police officer becomes a barometer for measuring or assessing this general health by exploring the tensions between the social claims enacted by and on these figures (e.g. the imperatives of social justice) and the capacities of bureaucratic systems to abide by these claims and attendant forms of justice. It argues that the more interesting or, at least, most revealing examples of police officers in crime fiction are those where this tension (e.g. between social justice and the law) is opened up, rather than closed off, and where the general health of a society is brought into question.

Types of police officer

The police officer becomes a pivotal character in crime fiction during the post-World War II period. Earlier, this figure had been an interloper or a dunce, standing in contrast to the Golden Age amateur detective, defined by intellectual acuity and polish. Yet the amateur detective's qualities came to seem contrived. It was difficult to tally this character with World Wars, urbanisation, modernisation, increases and changes in crime, and the rapid growth of modern policing. In Raymond Chandler's words in "The Simple Art of Murder", amateur detective stories

> do not really come off intellectually as problems, and they do not come off artistically as fiction. They are too contrived, and too little aware of what goes on in the world. [...] The poor writer [...] thinks a complicated murder scheme which baffles the lazy reader, who won't be bothered itemizing the details, will also baffle the police, whose business is with details.
>
> *(1995: 985–86)*

Crime fiction and the police

The real world is the world of police, who have the numbers, the methods and the details. Yet Chandler and other hardboiled writers also eschewed the police officer: in "a world where a judge with a cellar full of bootleg liquor can send a man to jail for having a pint in his pocket" (1995: 991), the police are, needless to say, in on the take. Chandler's hardboiled private investigator would also come to seem inauthentic in the post-war period. The police officer emerged as the credible figure for a realist representation of brutal modern life in the city. He was a steward of public resources working in a professional setting, employing novel methods and technology, but also a middle-class citizen with middle-class problems, to which readers could relate.

Scholars writing on the rise of the police procedural or police novel and the figure of the police officer emphasise this figure's status as an agent of the state working in a well-resourced organisation. Stephen Knight writes that after World War II, "the detective [became] a policeman, acting with institutional support, conducting more or less accurately reported police business" (1980: 168). Ernest Mandel makes a similar point, emphasising like Chandler that a shift in the origin and scale of crime required a reinvention of the genre and its *dramatis personae*: "It is not possible for a single genius to solve fifty murders simultaneously, like a chess master against fifty amateurs [...]. What is required is the establishment and growth of ever larger crime-detecting machines, using all the techniques of contemporary science and organized administration", in other words, the police (1984: 54). The early police procedural novel is most often associated with the 87th Precinct novels of Ed McBain – published from 1956 to 2005 – set in a fictionalised New York City. Other landmark texts include the serialised radio program, soon adapted for television, *Dragnet* (1952–1959). The BBC program *Dixon of Dock Green* (1955–1976) is another notable addition to the police procedural (Leishman and Mason 2003: 2). The titles of each of these make evident the police procedural's realist mode of narration. Two of the titles make unglamorous references to the location of action. The other refers to a modern police tactic requiring numbers, coordination and radio communication.

Since the 1990s, the police story, whether in the novel, television series or on film, has mushroomed. Peter Messent writes that "the major figures include Cornwell, Ellroy, Harris, and Wambaugh" (2010: 176). These are just the Americans. Other important Anglophone writers of the police story include Colin Dexter, P.D. James, Val McDermid, Ian Rankin and Ruth Rendell. Noteworthy non-anglophone practitioners include Andrea Camilleri, Vikram Chandra, Kwei Quartey, George Simenon and Fred Vargas. For the purposes of this chapter, I am particularly interested in the ways in which the police novel has been taken up by Nordic writers, from Maj Sjöwall and Per Wahlöö to Karin Fossum, and in turn, Nordic police series such as *Forbrydelsen* (*The Killing*, 2007–2011), *Broen* (*The Bridge*, 2011–2018), *Karppi* (*Deadwind*, 2018-), *Ófærð* (*Trapped*, 2015–2017) and others. Nordic noir has come to characterise a particular kind of socially conscious or critical police procedural form that takes a hard look at the health of society. Looking across this breadth of procedural fiction, we might argue that the combination of realist narration and suspenseful action allows for a great variety of ideological representations of the police, ranging from a conservative shoring-up of hegemonic worldviews to subversion of the epistemological and ontological premises of policing, giving voice to social criticism.

An early example of the socially critical police procedural is the ten-novel series *Roman om ett brott* [*Story of a Crime*] by Maj Sjöwall and Per Wahlöö, published between 1965–1975. As early as 1963, they conceptualised the socially critical crime novel as contributing to a communist critique of the social democratic welfare state. The title of the series suggested that to tell the story of a crime was to relate the symptoms of a capitalist society, whose subjects were repressed by market, state and family. Pressure to conform to these institutions' norms engendered intra- and intersubjective conflict, which erupted in acts of violence (Tapper 2011: 176–77). The notion here is that the crime novel can represent social structures and formations in ways that disclose the underpinning structural contradictions that produce crime, whether the source is the exclusion of the mentally ill or the careerism and corruption of state elites. Even when the police team works to reinstate order, the novels convey fundamental conflicts and injustices subtending the social democratic welfare state. Yet even as these novels gave voice to systemic and class-based critiques, they consciously or otherwise colluded with other conservative ideological formations, for example, patriarchy. It is notable, for example, that women in these novels are primarily victims, not members of the police team, which is made up of men.

The absence of women as police investigators in crime fiction belies readers', and especially young readers', interest in girls and women conducting criminal investigations as protagonists. Authors and audiovisual producers offered them amateur sleuths. The *Nancy Drew* franchise, *Trixie Belden,* and, of course, Agatha Christie's Miss Marple are examples of widely read crime fiction series, in which girls and women figured as protagonists, albeit not police officers. In *Nancy Drew* and *Trixie Belden*, parents are the relevant authority figures, who allow the youngsters to follow their investigations, even as they oversee them – if from a distance. Deborah Jermyn further points out that Dorothy Sayers's Harriet Vane novels and Nora Charles in the *Thin Man* movies indicate "a taste for female sleuths has long been present" (2010: 31).

Women police officers were present in television procedurals prior to the 1980s but this decade saw the emergence of a number of key texts, notably *Cagney and Lacey* (1982–1988), which debuted as a made-for-TV movie in 1981 after being first pitched as a film script in 1974 (D'Acci 1994: 4). In her excellent study of the series, Julie D'Acci points out that between the premiere in 1952 of *Dragnet* and 1990, some sixty television police shows aired on US network TV. In two, a heterosexual couple was featured cooperating to lead police investigations, but the man was the police officer. In seven, women featured as investigators, although often not as police officers, as, for example, in *Charlie's Angels* (1976–1981). Further, in these shows, a white, heterosexual man was typically the women's superior officer or boss. These sixty shows "were dominated by Caucasian male actors and protagonists" (D'Acci 1994: 10). By contrast, *Cagney and Lacey* was the first show in network television history to feature two women as stars (5). Christine Cagney (Sharon Gless) and Mary Beth Lacey (Tyne Daly) differed from each other professionally and personally but worked together as detective partners on complex cases for the New York City Police. As the contrast between *Charlie's Angels* and *Cagney and Lacey* suggests, and D'Acci argues, the emergence of shows featuring women police officers not only changed the representation of women in popular culture, but also contributed to the renegotiation of such categories as "woman, women, and femininity" (7). Women working as authority figures while also leading complex lives away from work was a contrast to "sexy" women being supervised and often objectified by men. The tension between their professional and personal lives generated the show's storylines.

Prime Suspect (1991–1992, 1993–1996, 2003–2006), starring Helen Mirren as Jane Tennison, further broadened the representation of women as police officers. "When the first instalment of *Prime Suspect* aired, the sheer originality of a female cop as driven and yet as nuanced as Tennison took audiences and critics well used to the male heroes of the cop show by surprise", writes Deborah Jermyn (2010: 3). The series deepened the exploration of sexism in the workplace, while situating it within an investigation story driven by strong narrative desire. Further, the emotional life of the protagonist Tennison, in relation to her identity at work and away, was also a significant narrative line over the course of the series. In numerous instances, Tennison's ability to connect with suspects and victims reveals information or produces confessions. Yet at the same time, she struggles with herself, whether in the effort to quit smoking or in her

Crime fiction and the police

relationship with partners and a decision to terminate a pregnancy in the third season (Jermyn 2010: 41–50). Shows such as *Prime Suspect* and *Cagney and Lacey*, as well as Thomas Harris's novel *Silence of the Lambs* (1988) and its film adaptation (1991) starring Jodie Foster as FBI agent Clarice Starling, helped revise the masculine bias in earlier types of police procedural and open up the form to new identities, beyond even the straight, white, middle-class (or lower-middle-class) figures seen in these shows, while not losing sight of relevant questions about the status of "woman, women, and femininity", as D'Acci suggests.

Just as gender and sexuality are key features of the procedural, so too is the representation of race. The representation of women in the history of the genre discloses a problematic but powerful cultural reluctance to make women powerful state insiders. People of colour and representatives of minority populations also feature infrequently as police investigators or authority figures. Walter Mosley, author of the neo-noir hardboiled series about private investigator "Easy" Rawlins, emphasises the extent to which African American characters have not been heroised: "Hardly anybody in America has written about black male heroes. There are black male protagonists and black male supporting characters, but nobody else writes about black male heroes" (qtd. in Neuman 2011). If the dutiful and brave police officer, protecting and serving by investigating and solving crimes, is an archetypical hero in US culture, Mosley offers a compelling description of the problem insofar as African Americans are barred, culturally, from such a role. The detective novels of Chester Himes written between 1957 and 1969, featuring two African American New York City police detectives, were pathbreaking, but also parodic in tone, marking the vulnerable status of these police officers. In a special issue of *African American Review* on Himes's authorship, Jonathan Eburne and Kevin Bell write that the

> detective novels represent the basic conditions of American racial consciousness as fundamentally absurd. Largely because of this, they have been viewed as either the epitome of Himes's conceptual range as an experimental writer, or as the disappointing lapse into pessimism of a writer who had once militated on behalf of New Deal-era collectivism.
>
> *(2009: 226)*

Another writer who draws on humour and the irrational, atypical features of the police novel is Rudolph Fisher and his *The Conjure-Man Dies* (1932): A "landmark" novel "about a black officer in the NYPD investigating a suspected homicide in Harlem" (Leavitt 2017). Fisher's *The Conjure-Man Dies* challenges the notion that investigations into crimes can produce truthful knowledge, especially in the context of race in the US, and does so by probing the relationship between Africans and African Americans during the Harlem Renaissance, so that while "all things African were vanguard and politically laden in the imagination of Harlem Renaissance writers and thinkers [...] ultimately [Fisher] shows that the African is foreign and even 'other' to black Americans" (Mirmotahari 2013: 269). Again, the tense pull between the investigation's aspiration to knowledge and its epistemological limits, as well as the contradictory relation between differing constructions of identity, becomes central to the narrative and its not-always-straightforward claims to the truth.

The complicated representational status of police characters can also be seen in one of the most celebrated crime stories of recent decades, *The Wire*. While *The Wire* is, of course, not simply a police procedural, despite season one focusing on police investigations of drug smuggling, wholesaling and street sales from the police investigators' perspectives, in each season, crime and police investigation of crime is important, but seen from shifting institutional perspectives – the police, the media, the politicians, the schools. The series' showrunner David Simon got his start as a Baltimore journalist and came to write true-crime non-fiction about policing in Baltimore, before moving to fiction and television. His early television works, including *The Corner* (2000) and *Homicide* (1993–1999) combine journalistic writing, true-crime writing and adaptation. They also prepared the way for the fictional invention of the multi-season television serial *The Wire* (Wilson 2000: 130–68; Williams 2014: 1–7). Linda Williams writes that *The Wire* "does not transcend its mass culture bases in city desk journalism and television melodrama; rather, it is woven out of this very cloth" (4). For Williams, the narrative mode of melodrama confronts "new and seemingly intractable social problems to the end of recognizing virtue […] or institutional routes to the social good" (114). Realism is used to convey the intractable social problems, but action and character are used to make virtue visible. In this sense, melodrama is dependent on realism for representing social ills, within which and against which melodrama shows virtue or paths to the social good. A typical way of doing this is by making victimhood – which typically occurs in the realist terrain – connect with virtuous suffering and endurance, that is, suffering that is conveyed in public but also through private actions and displays (114–16).

What a realist-melodrama like *The Wire* does is show the complex, human motives of the many participants in its world, including its police officers, and it does so in a realist mode that combines grittiness with melodramatic recognition of goodness or its possibility (Williams 2014). The police detectives – from "Bunk" Moreland and Jimmy McNulty to Lester Freamon and "Kima" Greggs – are neither good nor bad, though they make constant claims to being "good police", even as their personal and institutional failures (and their claims to progressive political positions as African Americans, Irish Americans, lesbians, etc.) are magnified by or through the lens of melodrama. Rather, their potential to do good – and to function as "good police" – is made possible by the kind of tilting of realism towards melodrama that Williams sees as central to *The Wire*'s success.

Realism, melodrama and the divided detective

The combination of realism and melodrama described by Williams has become popular among producers of police narratives as a means of seeking to comprehend the tumultuous social conflicts of the new millennium, be they connected to war, migration, digital interconnection, the material connections of globalisation or terrorism. Realist depictions of such conflicts are the typical mode of representation, but authors and television- and filmmakers link them to an emotional subject, typically a police officer. The mind and body of the officer becomes a mediating site for representing the tensions between systems, discourses and the individuals within these.

Scholars writing on film and literature of this kind have also labelled it as the "sentimental hardboiled" (Cassuto 2008) or the "introspective realist crime film" (García-Mainar 2016). Cassuto's discussion of the sentimental hardboiled explores how sentimentality, concerned with domestic relationships, serves as a counterpoint to the brutal individualism of the hardboiled novel, the criminal world or system. The sentimental, embodied through some experiences of the investigator, seeks to imagine modes of community which might provide an alternative. García-Mainar's *Introspective Realist Crime Film* is concerned with a cycle of films and television series produced since the millennium, and in particular the way that realist aesthetics work hand-in-hand with melodrama to represent the quandaries of self-reflexive individualism. García-Mainar follows the sociologists Zygmunt Bauman and Alain Tourraine to argue that neoliberalism and digital culture have engendered a new set of predicaments of the self: "Becoming an individual is no longer a process of emancipation, as it was in modernity, but an obligation to accept responsibility for one's self-assertion" (García-Mainar 2016: 10). The idea seems to

Crime fiction and the police

be that finding oneself involves negotiating the forces pulling one in different directions (11). Cassuto and García-Mainar focus on the structural connection between realism and melodrama, but go beyond Knight's ideological critique to argue that the subjective dimension of many crime novels and films is more complicated than an "illusionary" effort of "liberal humanism [seeking] to master the contradictory reality of its world by ideology" (Knight 1980: 177).

The police officer as a type lends itself to realist-melodramatic narration for, as noted above, the figure gives access to topical discourses and institutions as well as a socio-economically situated personal life with a history. Nordic noir is one of the places we find such figures, whether in the stoic Sarah Lund (Sofie Gråbøl) of *The Killing* or Saga Norén (Sofia Helin) of *The Bridge*. Yet since these series are so well known, it is worth examining a less well-known example which shows the pervasiveness of the divided police officer as a figure of melodramatic yet realistic narration.

In the Finnish public broadcasting service's (YLE) procedural series *Karppi* (*Deadwind*, 2018), the protagonist Sofia Karppi (Pihla Viitala) struggles with grief and parental conflict. She has moved her family back to Helsinki from Hamburg, uprooting her husband's teenage daughter. More dramatically, her husband has recently been killed in an accident, leaving her alone with her ten-year-old son, the stepdaughter and her old job as a detective in the Helsinki police. When she ill-advisedly returns to work too soon, a series of conflicts are set in train, which integrate realist and melodramatic modes of narration. When Karppi struggles with her grief in the workplace, creating the appearance of job performance problems, these are interpreted by some colleagues through a gendered lens. One male colleague seeks to have her put on leave as mentally unfit, giving himself the high-profile case Karppi is handling. The theme of grief is also gendered. While Karppi and her children grieve for their late husband and father, Usko Bergdahl (Jani Tolanen), the husband of the central victim Anna Bergdahl (Pamela Tola), struggles with grief, depression and vengeful fantasies, and another character, Andreas Wolf (August Wittgenstein), seeks to avenge his girlfriend with a terrorist act, because she died as a result of criminally improper handling of nuclear waste. The vengeful grief of Bergdahl and Wolf drives the action through a number of crises, thus highlighting the ways in which grief and gender intersect: Grief drives men to violence, while Karppi struggles, but works effectively within the law and the institution of the police, ultimately managing her grief.

Karppi's struggles are given further emphasis by underscoring a parallel between herself and Usko Bergdahl. As Karppi investigates, the details of Usko Bergdahl's late wife's life are forced upon him by police questioning and the tabloid press. Usko becomes the chief suspect when Anna Bergdahl's extramarital affairs are revealed, casting the good-hearted Usko as a suffering, virtuous and grieving parent. The distinctions between these aligned characters are highlighted by their names. Usko means faith in Finnish, and he is a man of emotional commitment who has been pushed too far. In contrast, Sofia Karppi tips and topples, but maintains her rational and emotional balance. Her last name, Karppi, sounds like the Finnish slang for sharp, *skarppi*. The related verb *skarpata* means to get it together or hold it together. Karppi does hold it together, even as her stumbles make her vulnerable. In displaying character traits typically coded male in the police procedural, but also making Karppi a character who raises issues related to "woman, women, and femininity", Karppi is a multivalent melodramatic police officer, whose character creates a social lens on the gendered dimensions of grief and vengeance in a society in which these are heightened by scandal-driven media.

As an investigator, and a character who shows her emotions in a cynically, realistically depicted narrative world, Karppi bears many similarities with other police detectives; Sarah Lund in *The Killing*, Saga Norén and Martin Rohde in *The Bridge*, Alec Hardy and Ellie Miller in *Broadchurch* (2013–2017), Stella Gibson in *The Fall* (2013–2016) and Rust Cole and Marty Hart in the first season of *True Detective* (2014) all oscillate between rational mastery and subjective feelings that give them insight, but tend to bring chaos as well. They all try to hold it together, while looking at brutality with broad vision. We can see a similar pattern in literary police officers such as Henning Mankell's Kurt Wallander, Anne Holt's Hanne Wilhelmsen, Ian Rankin's John Rebus, Arnaldur Indridason's Erlendur Sveinsson, and Vikram Chandra's Sartaj Singh. In each case, the character is a virtuoso investigator, obsessed, difficult, and with a frayed personal life comprised of broken relationships, substance abuse and past traumas, who investigates ugly crimes that show the worst of humanity, but also show the way these characters manage in their criminal investigations to see some goodness and convey it to readers and viewers.

Conclusion

This analysis of the crime novel's police figure sees him or her created through a combination of realism and melodrama, which makes a dystopian late modernity a source of testing and suffering for the virtuous police investigator. Our glance at the history of the police officer figures show that as social Others have gained access to the authoritative role of the police officer, police fiction has experienced an efflorescence. The potential of the police figure to mediate divisive social tensions and conflicts has helped make the police story more popular and more important. The police officer is particularly divided, at once admirably working on gritty streets, while at the same time a pathetic, emotional figure. The contrast between these sides of the police officer is arguably connected to what García-Mainar calls introspection, a continual, shifting engagement with the possibilities and limits of selfhood and its place within conflicting discourses of gender, race, class and sexuality. The divided police officer gives voice to the troubles of late modernity's conflicted discourses, institutions and norms, and in so doing engages readers and viewers in an assessment of society's health.

Bibliography

Cassutto, L. (2008) *Hard-Boiled Sentimentality: The secret history of American crime stories*, New York: Columbia University Press.

Chandler, R. (1995) [1944] "The Simple Art of Murder", in *Later Novels and Other Writings*, New York: Library of America, 977–92.

D'Acci, J. (1994) *Defining Women: Television and the case of Cagney and Lacey*, Chapel Hill, NC: University of North Carolina Press.

Dove, G. (1982) *The Police Procedural*, Bowling Green, OH: Popular Press.

Eburne, J.P., and Bell, K. (2009) "Introduction: A special section on Chester Himes", *African American Review* 43(2–3): 225–31.

Frye, N. (2000) [1957] *The Anatomy of Criticism*, Princeton, NJ: Princeton University Press.

García-Mainar, L.M. (2016) *The Introspective Realist Crime Film*, London: Palgrave Macmillan.

Jermyn, D. (2010) *Prime Suspect*, BFI TV Classics, London: British Film Institute.

Knight, S. (1980) *Form and Ideology in Crime Fiction*, London: Macmillan.

Leavitt, J.B. (2017) "Procedural racism", *Public Books*, 5 September, www.publicbooks.org/procedural-racism/ (accessed 14 November 2019).

Leishman, F. and Mason, P. (2003) *Policing and the Media*, Portland, OR: Willan Publishing.

Mandel, E. (1984) *Delightful Murder: A social history of the crime story*, Minneapolis: University of Minnesota Press.

Mankell, H. (1999) *Sidetracked*, trans. S. Murray, New York: Vintage.

Messent, P. (2010) "The police novel", in C.J. Rzepka and L. Horsley (eds), *A Companion to Crime Fiction*, Chichester, UK; Malden, MA: Wiley-Blackwell, 175–86.

Mirmotahari, E. (2013) "Harlemite, detective, African? The many selves of Rudolph Fisher's *Conjure-Man Dies*", *Callaloo*, 36(2): 268–78.

Neuman, J. (2011) "The curious case of Walter Mosley", *Moment,* 30 November, https://momentmag.com/the-curious-case-of-walter-mosley/4/ (accessed 14 November 2019).

Tapper, M. (2011) *Snuten i skymningslandet: Svenska polisberättelser i roman och film 1965–2019,* Lund: Nordic Academic Press.

Williams, L. (2014) *On The Wire,* Durham, NC: Duke University Press.

Wilson, C.P. (2000) *Cop Knowledge: Police power and cultural narrative in twentieth-century America,* Chicago: University of Chicago Press.

34

CRIME FICTION AND MEMORY

Kate M. Quinn

On the opening page of Astrid Erll's *Memory in Culture*, the blurb attributes the popularity of this field to "a shift from concern with historical knowledge of events to that of memory, from 'what we know' to 'how we remember it'" (2011: i). If we consider this assertion alongside Todorov's (1977) ideas on crime fiction's dual-narrative structure – the story of the investigation in the present revealing the story of the crime committed in the past – we find the crime genre offers particularly fruitful ground to explore the link between "what we know" and "how we remember it".

This chapter will first consider memory and amnesia as evolving tropes and narrative devices in the genre and will then link these ideas to how historical memory specifically is explored by authors in Austria, France and Chile who engage in their own specific national contexts with the memory of the Holocaust, "the very paradigm of a global object of remembrance" (Erll 2011: 62), addressing historical amnesia and hidden or silenced histories of state criminality. These authors are concerned not just with history but with the workings of cultural memory, another form of "how we remember". In this context, Michael Rothberg's suggestion "that we consider memory as multidirectional: as subject to ongoing negotiation, cross-referencing, and borrowing" (2009: 3) is helpful. Thus, the section on "Chilean crime fiction" will illustrate the workings of multidirectional memory in how the Holocaust emerges as a point of reference in crime novels about the Chilean dictatorship, especially in relation to the deliberate state policy of disappearance.

The case study will consider two key novels by Chilean author Ramón Díaz Eterovic, *Nadie sabe más que los muertos* [No One Knows More Than The Dead] (1993) and *La oscura memoria de las armas* [Dark Echoes of the Past] (2008). The earlier novel evokes the paradigm of the Holocaust in negotiating the memory of human rights violations, but this framework is absent in the later novel when the extent of state crimes in Chile under the dictatorship was widely acknowledged both nationally and internationally. After the arrest of General Pinochet in London in 1998, Chile itself became a point of reference for studies on transnational justice, arguably creating conditions for a greater circulation of Chilean crime novels in the global market.

Memory and amnesia

Memory is linked to narrative at the most basic level; what witnesses remember are the elements of "what we know" that assist the detective's reconstruction of criminal events. As we approach "how we remember it", our first consideration is simply whether memories are reliable or unreliable. In courtroom dramas, reliable evidence can help seal a conviction, but fallibility of bystander memory may also undermine cases. Unreliable is not the same as deceptive; witnesses can be sincerely mistaken in what they recall. Investigators too are subject to the flaws of memory, and in texts where theirs is the perspective through which information is mediated for readers, the reliability of that viewpoint must be assessed.

The adaptability of the crime genre and the pressure to develop novel approaches means there is a constant assimilation of new knowledge and ideas which find expression in explorations of all permutations of memory from total recollection to amnesia, as the following examples will illustrate. Doyle's Sherlock Holmes places a premium on the space in his brain-attic in *A Study in Scarlet* (1887) – a device playfully upgraded to a mind-palace in BBC's *Sherlock* – and is selective in the information he stores there. Thus, memory is linked to the organisation of knowledge and a professional premium placed on utility and ease of retrieval. Total indiscriminate recollection is accompanied by an inability to systematise and extrapolate meaning, something that runs counter to detection since interpreting clues and exploring theories are central to investigative work. Holmes's selectivity is a wise precaution as illustrated in Marcus Sedgwick's recent historical crime novel *Mister Memory* (2016) where a murder suspect's inability to forget any detail of his life proves challenging to the investigation. On the opposite end of the spectrum, the trope of amnesia is also a staple of the genre. One classic example is Margery Allingham's *Traitor's Purse* (1941) where Albert Campion awakens in hospital with no idea of who he is and struggles to make sense of his environment until a second blow to the head miraculously restores his memory in time to save Britain from a German plot to undermine the war effort. Although this representation of amnesia would not stand up to modern medical scrutiny, narratively it offered readers a new emotional insight into the detective, stripped of the protection of his customary fatuous persona.

Advances in our understanding of the psychological and physiological processes of memory and popular dissemination of these ideas have led to more nuanced approaches to memory impairment. In season six of CBS's *Elementary* (2018) Sherlock Holmes is contending with the debilitating symptoms of post-concussion syndrome and its effects on his memory. This coincides with mainstream media reporting on the effects of this syndrome on athletes in the USA. In the same season, another mainstream health concern is addressed as Joan Watson's mother is suffering from Alzheimer's disease. Emma Healey's *Elizabeth is Missing* (2014) conveys the unreliable perspective of a woman suffering from Alzheimer's in its first-person narrative. Maud confuses her friend's absence in the present with the events surrounding the disappearance of her sister just after the end of World War II. Failures and gaps in her memories and her confused interpretation of current events present a challenge for readers to decipher what her current reality is and to interpret the clues in the text that link this to her past. The evocation of the broader social history of wartime Britain is also a major part of the novel's appeal. This reflects a wider trend within the genre internationally where the interface between past and present and history and memory proves particularly compelling.

Memory and history

The memory of World War II casts a long shadow over European crime fiction and this section of the chapter considers novels by writers who explore the continuing resonance of this past, and who challenge historical amnesia – a deliberate state policy to bury the truth in Austria and France. Gerhard Roth's *Der See* [The Lake] (1995) and Doron Rabinovici's *Suche nach M.* [The Search for M] (1997) challenge historical amnesia in Austria about the

National Socialist past. Didier Daeninckx's *Meurtres pour mémoire* [Murder in Memoriam] (1984) exposes historical amnesia in France regarding both the Algerian War of Independence and the Holocaust.

Germany is the obvious place to begin an exploration of how crime fiction concerns itself with the history of the Nazi era and the Holocaust. Katharina Hall discusses how engagement with the memory of the war changes over time, establishing that against the backdrop of the Nuremberg trials, crime fiction was already being used as a vehicle to expose the crimes of the Nazi era while it was later used by second-generation writers – those born near or after the end of the war – to "reflect on the actions of their parents under National Socialism" (2016: 13). Hall demonstrates that the relationship with the past, "how we remember" is dynamic and subject to reinterpretation and reimagining through the lens of the present, with its own set of concerns.

Where Germany acknowledges its role in the war and the Holocaust, Austria does not. Second-generation author Gerhard Roth challenges the national denial of responsibility for the Holocaust, a denial based on the official assertion that Austria was the first victim of German aggression, a narrative of victimhood that came under increasing scrutiny after revelations about Kurt Waldheim's wartime service in the German army in Greece and Yugoslavia during the 1986 presidential elections which he won (Krajenbrink 2009: 245). In Roth's unconventional crime narrative, *Der See*, self-medicating pharmaceutical salesman Paul Eck is suspected of involvement in the death of his father from whom he has been long estranged. Eck learns of his father's role in illegally selling arms to parties involved in the Balkan conflict. The resurgence of violent nationalisms in the former Yugoslavia and the attendant ethnic cleansing was at the forefront of European consciousness in 1995, with parallels to Nazi Germany easily drawn. Yet, while the novel is deeply concerned with history and memory, it does not have Todorov's dual structure of present investigation and past crime and it ultimately holds out no hope of clarity or resolution. Arguably, this is a better reflection of the lack of clarity regarding Austria's past and the previous generation's role in Nazi crimes than a conventional crime novel with a reliable narrator and definite sense of closure.

Rabinovici's *Suche nach M.* explores the silence of trauma that informs relationships between victims and their children. According to Daphne Seemann the novel depicts "a society haunted by the ghostly re-emergence of an unmastered past that forces the culture to confront issues of guilt and responsibility" and she locates it within the belated memory work after the Waldheim affair when the nation addressed "the contested historical moment of Austria's Anschluss in 1938, [...] the country's continuing denial of responsibility for Nazi crimes, and the complete neglect of Holocaust victims" (2011: 157). Israeli-born Jewish-Austrian author Rabinovici explores a lack of intergenerational communication of memory between concentration camp survivor Jakob Scheinowiz and Holocaust survivor Moshe Morganthau and their sons, who belong to what Marianne Hirsch describes as the "generation of postmemory", born after the Holocaust but affected by witnessing their parents' trauma. Eventually, one son resolves to find out what he can about his now dead father by connecting with an old friend of his and planning a visit to their former home city of Krakow. He is working through the intergenerationally transmitted trauma in a way that offers some hope for the future. The ethical imperative for Austria is to confront its own "unmastered" past.

France is another nation that recreated its sense of self after the trauma of the war, promoting the image of heroic resistance and taking renewed pride in its place as a colonial power, but Didier Daeninckx's *Meurtres pour mémoire* exposes a criminal reality behind the image. The investigation into the murder of two historians, a father and son killed twenty years apart, uncovers state responsibility for a massacre in 1961 of a group of protesters calling for Algerian independence, and reveals the extent of Vichy collusion in the deportation of French Jews during World War II. The novel opens with a description of the actions of the protesters as they prepare for their march through Paris. History is humanised from the very first page with sympathetic portraits of these very ordinary protagonists, soon to become victims whose deaths and forced detention at the hands of the repressive forces of the state will disappear from public consciousness. The massacre will also offer cover for the assassination of bystander, history teacher, Roger Thiraud. Twenty years later, Thiraud's son Bernard is also murdered and Inspector Cardin doggedly investigates the case. He uncovers the reality of the 1961 massacre and the earlier mass deportation of Jews from Drancy during the Holocaust. Father and son were assassinated to preserve historical amnesia and protect a high-ranking official responsible for both historical crimes.

Claire Gorrara offers a particularly insightful analysis of the novel's engagement with collective memory that builds on ideas explored by Todorov. For Todorov, as Gorrara explains: "Every evocation of the past [...] is predicated on the demands of the present and conforms to selection criteria that are the subject of historically located debate and analysis" and "no representation of the past in the form of memories can escape the inscription of its context" (2005: 133). Clearly these ideas also hold relevance for the Austrian texts already discussed. In the context of historical crimes and crimes of state, Todorov's ideas on literal and exemplary memory can also be usefully deployed. In Gorrara's words: "Literal memory refers to the remembrance of a traumatic past event that can be said to have marked either individuals or groups" while exemplary memory is

> a use of the past built upon the notion that the recall of events, such as the Holocaust, can serve a more general purpose, offering up 'lessons' to help us make sense of and respond to modern-day injustices and atrocities.
>
> *(133)*

Daeninckx's villain is modelled on the real Maurice Papon and the novel was an important contribution to a wider national re-examination of French history in the 1980s and 1990s. More tangibly, it helped focus greater attention on Papon's Vichy career, as well as his role in the repression of protests in Paris in the early 1960s. In the face of mounting evidence, Papon was eventually sentenced for crimes against humanity in 1998. Just like the Waldheim affair in Austria, Papon's trial challenged the French self-image and forced a debate about French responsibility in the deportation of the Jewish population during World War II.

Rothberg analyses the contribution Daeninckx's novel made to recovering the memory of 1961 in *Multidirectional Memory* and comments explicitly on the way in which the novel brings together police thriller and intergenerational historical transmission, finding that "the hard-boiled detective genre [...] bears important implications for thinking about multidirectional memory as it passes across multiple generations" (2009). As many critics of the crime genre have noted, criminal investigations frequently serve as a pretext for a wider exploration of society and Rothberg makes a similar observation about the murder of the Thirauds, concluding "the point of *Meurtres* – the mystery that it stages in order to resolve – is the *connection* between the different eras and the persistence of the unresolved past in the present" (276, emphasis in original).

Memory in Chilean crime fiction

The end of the dictatorship (1973–1989) in Chile saw a minor boom in crime writing, especially novels about the legacy of the recent past and how it marks the present. It is significant that many writers negotiating this legacy turned to the global paradigm of the Holocaust to help frame their concerns. In Jaime Collyer's *El infiltrado* [The Infiltrator] (1989), narrator Simón Fabres recounts the events that led to the death of his employer Raúl Morán in a bombing of an office in Santiago in the early 1980s. Morán works for the military regime drafting documents and reports for them. Fabres's wife Natalia eventually leaves him because of his collaboration with what she considers a propagandistic tool of the state. She works in a resistance cell and dies on a mission that goes wrong. Fabres reveals that he helped plant the bomb that killed Morán. He has become the infiltrator of the title and is revealed as partly responsible for the murder.

Fabres's memories repeatedly draw us back to the time before the rupture of the coup, including to his student readings of sociology and political theory. He engages in a sustained meditation on revolution, violence and totalitarianism in which history is a repetition of a horror story that includes the French Revolution and Pol Pot's Year Zero. The Nazis and the Holocaust feature most prominently as frames of reference. There are references to Eichmann, Goebbels and the Ministry of Propaganda, and Hitler's *Mein Kampf* which Morán considers a horror story. It is easy to draw a parallel between these references to the Nazi regime and the mechanics of the "Final Solution" and the Chilean military regime's deliberate policy of disappearance, the legacy of which continues to mark contemporary Chile. Rothberg's ideas on multidirectional memory, with its historical borrowings and cross-referencing, have clear relevance here too.

Roberto Bolaño's *Estrella distante* [Distant Star] (1996) takes up the idea of history as horror story with a clear focus on state terror and the policy of disappearance. Narrated with the benefit of hindsight from a standpoint in the 1990s, *Estrella distante* opens with the narrator's recollections of 1973 when Allende was still in power and concludes sometime after the restoration of democracy. Thus, the rupture between the youthful engagement with the ideals of social justice of the Popular Unity years and the brutal repression of sixteen years of military dictatorship is very marked. The narrator is obsessed with the career of Carlos Wieder, an Air Force officer he believes responsible for the torture, murder and disappearance of his student friends. In the absence of concrete information, he seeks textual clues to his whereabouts in a variety of outlets. This unconventional method of detection is partly due to the secrecy and obfuscation of the military in covering up human rights violations. Even when Wieder is denounced openly as a torturer in the early 1990s, he fails to appear before the official commission and over time Chile forgets him as the work of justice is sidelined. Some years later again, the narrator is contacted by a former Chilean homicide detective, Abel Romero, who has been hired to locate and execute Wieder. The narrator helps find and identify the target and waits outside while Romero goes off to complete his mission.

Where Collyer inserts references to political theorists, Bolaño turns to literature and among the many literary references in the text a significant number invoke memories of the Holocaust, most significantly the names Bruno Schulz and Georges Perec. Bolaño does not spell out the significance of these authors and it is up to the reader to draw the obvious parallel with Chile. Repeating Todorov's idea, it is the exemplary memory of the Holocaust that invites the comparison. Similarly, Bolaño seems to invite his readership to use the exemplary memory of military violence to reconsider Chile's own colonial history. When Mapuche Amalia Maluenda gives an eyewitness account of Wieder's brutality, she interprets the horror of the recent political violence in a line of continuity with colonial brutality. In this way Bolaño forces his Chilean readers to reconsider their own place as potential perpetrators in a much longer story of terror, and indeed conflict over the status and treatment of the Mapuche has emerged as one of the key unresolved issues facing twenty-first-century Chile. Multidirectional memory is here projected much further back in Chile's history.

Crime fiction and memory

While Chile was not directly involved in World War II, it was still connected to the currents of world history and there were already multiple links with Germany. Chile had witnessed significant migration from Germany in the nineteenth century and had accepted Jewish refugees fleeing the Nazis. However, it later also became a refuge for Nazis like Walter Rauff, and Sergio Gómez's *Patagonia* (2005) engages with this history. The protagonist is an investigative journalist who interviews Abe Barrea, who claims to have met Rauff in his native Poland fifty years before. The narrative alternates between the present of 1998 and World War II, tracing the history of Rauff, Barrea and our journalist, and encompassing Chile, Poland, Germany and Tunisia. We learn about Rauff's participation in the Holocaust, his actions against the Jewish population of German-occupied Tunisia, and his flight to Chile via Ecuador. The novel describes the ghetto of Lodz, and the concentration camps. Gómez also includes a reference to the 1994 bombing of a Jewish centre in Buenos Aires, reminding readers of the continuing threat of anti-Semitism. Chillingly, in the chapter "Berlin 1941" *Patagonia* describes Rauff's development of the technology for mass murder, the gas wagons, and his satisfaction as he considers their efficacy. This is juxtaposed with "Santiago de Chile 1984", which relates how Rauff lived openly in Punta Arenas until his arrest in 1962 after an international arrest warrant was issued in Germany. However, the court ruled that he should not be extradited, and he spent the rest of his life living openly in Chile. He died there in 1984 at a time of renewed attempts to have him extradited to West Germany.

Abe Barrea's life seemingly offers the perspective of a Jewish victim of the Nazis but the journalist learns after his death that he was a Nazi who murdered the real Barrea to assume his identity and escape prosecution after the war. Thus, the novel excludes any final possibility of a redemptive quality in the narrative. The Chilean dictatorship is barely mentioned in the novel but the parallel drawn with the Holocaust and the impunity enjoyed by the perpetrators invites us to refocus on Chile. If a reader is outraged that Rauff escaped prosecution for his role in the Holocaust, they are invited to apply the same standard to Chile's response to its own perpetrators of human rights violations.

Ramón Díaz Eterovic and the Heredia series

Díaz Eterovic is author of the Heredia series, the longest-running detective series in Chile. In *Nadie sabe más que los muertos* (1993), the third novel, the action is set against the backdrop of the 1989 elections, but the very recent past is being evoked as part of a scathing critique of the present and the contemporary discourse surrounding forgetting and national reconciliation. As I have explored in greater detail elsewhere (Quinn 2007), in this novel Heredia investigates the illegal adoption of a child born to a couple who were disappeared by the military, and memory is a central theme. Here the author borrows from the Argentine experience of dictatorship and the widespread policy of illegal adoption of children whose parents had been deemed enemies of the state and executed. In Argentina this continues to be an issue and ongoing efforts to find and reunite such children, now adults, with their biological families are regularly chronicled in the media.

The novel is clearly in dialogue with the response to the Rettig Report (1991), the findings of the Truth and Reconciliation Commission established by President Patricio Aylwin, which included the first systematic attempt to investigate the cases of the disappeared. The former dictator General Pinochet had introduced measures to protect the military from prosecution, among them the 1978 Law of Amnesty. He remained Head of the Armed Forces until 1998 and insisted that forgetting the past was the best way forward. In this context, the idea of forgetting as complicity, an idea voiced by the grandmother of the missing child, carries an important charge and memory becomes a site of resistance as exemplified by Heredia telling a traumatised torture survivor that he needs her memories. The reality of the Holocaust and of political disappearances is that there is a void in the historical record. Memory fails because the victims have been utterly silenced. The state has attempted to erase the very fact of their existence. No one knows more than the dead, but the dead cannot speak. It becomes the duty of survivors and witnesses to address this void and try to achieve some measure of justice for the victims.

Ideas of historical and transnational justice are invoked through Heredia's involvement with journalist Claudia. She is attached to a group of young Jewish activists tracking down Nazis who escaped justice, and their work intersects with Heredia's investigation of the figure of a sinister German doctor who oversaw the illegal placement of the child with a family loyal to the military. This doctor is linked to the notorious Colonia Dignidad (a German community established after World War II and dominated as a cult by Paul Schaefer under whom it was used as a torture centre during the dictatorship).

In 1993 many Pinochet supporters refused to accept there had been widespread human rights violations but by the time *La oscura memoria de las armas* was published fifteen years later, such a position was no longer tenable. Pinochet had been exposed to the international spotlight of transnational justice after his arrest in London in 1998 which created a space for greater scrutiny of the past. President Lagos established a commission of investigation into torture which produced the Valech Report in 2004. *La oscura memoria de las armas* engages with this new report which Heredia even downloads and quotes from. It contains the testimony of 30,000 individuals held at numerous torture centres, among which one of the most notorious was Villa Grimaldi. The investigation uncovers a link between the murders of two torture survivors who had been held at this centre, which is now a site of memory rededicated as a Park for Peace. Lazzara notes, "For a site to have meaning, it must also be narrated" (2006: 30), and Heredia visits Villa Grimaldi accompanied by the daughter of a torture victim who had been held there. While her father survived to give testimony, his brothers were murdered, and she feels a duty to keep their memory alive. The intergenerational transmission of memory is also explored through the participation of young activists in *funas*, protests designed to expose the identities of perpetrators. Fear of exposure lies behind the murders which were committed by former military personnel to cover up their role in the torture at Villa Grimaldi.

The Holocaust is not mentioned in this novel, which focuses on the impact of the Valech Report in Chile. However, by now the national subject matter has gained greater transnational significance. We can appreciate this when one of the foremost scholars on memory, Aleida Assmann, specifically references Pinochet in "Transnational memories" as one of the first military leaders to be prosecuted abroad for crimes which could not be pursued at home (2014: 554).

Memory in the future

The genre is very far from exhausting all potential explorations of how human memory works and as our understanding of this process and its failings deepen, there will be more and more angles to cover. Christopher Nolan's *Memento* (2000) is just one example of a fascinating formal response to the challenge of portraying a specific memory impairment and there is clearly plenty of scope in the genre for more such works. Similarly, in the interplay of "what we know" and "how we know it", the possibilities are relatively unlimited. If the past is constantly being reassessed from the perspective of the concerns of a given present moment, there will always be new explorations. For instance, we can expect to see new perspectives on Latin American historical memory as indigenous voices use the genre to assert their own experiences of national and regional history. Indeed, any marginalised group or minority may find the crime genre offers an ideal vehicle to challenge past assumptions from the perspective not just of the present but even from the standpoint of an imagined future. If an event like the fall of the Berlin Wall in 1989, an "irruption of memory" to borrow the term Wilde (1999) uses in the Chilean context, prompted "intensive re-examination of Germany's twentieth-century history" leading to a "boom in historical crime fiction" (Hall 2016: 20–21), we can reliably predict that more events across the globe will prompt reconsideration of history framed through memory. Planned formal processes of commemoration like the Irish "Decade of centenaries" (covering 1912–1923) also create new possibilities. There have been some historical crime novels dealing with the foundational years of the modern Irish nation but none yet that explicitly deploy the trope of memory. However, in a country currently experiencing a boom in crime writing, it is only a matter of time until such works appear. Again, other national commemorations across the globe will prompt other local responses. Yet, as writers and readers expand their horizons to other linguistic and cultural areas, we see more cross-referencing and borrowing and new configurations and projections of multidirectional memory. While, as King (2014) observed, crime fiction studies are still dominated by analyses of national genre production, the last decade has seen some important publications that take a comparative approach. Just as memory itself has become one of the most significant fields of interdisciplinary investigation in recent decades, the comparative and interdisciplinary route offers new possibilities for academic work on the genre in line with King's call to consider crime fiction as world literature.

Bibliography

Assmann, A. (2014) "Transnational memories", *European Review*, 22(4): 546–56.

Bolaño, R. (1996) *Estrella distante*, Barcelona: Anagrama.

Collyer, J. (1989) *El infiltrado*, Madrid: Mondadori.

Daeninckx, D. (1984) *Meurtres pour mémoire*, Paris: Gallimard.

Díaz Eterovic, R. (1993) *Nadie sabe más que los muertos*, Santiago: Planeta.

———. (2008) *La oscura memoria de las armas*, Santiago: LOM.

Erll, A. (2011) *Memory in Culture*, Basingstoke: Palgrave Macmillan.

Gómez, S. (2005) *Patagonia*, Barcelona: Seix Barral.

Gorrara, C. (2005) "Reflections on crime and punishment. Memories of the Holocaust in recent French crime fiction", *Yale French Studies*, 108: 131–45.

Hall, K. (2016) "Crime fiction in German. Concepts, developments and trends", in K. Hall (ed.), *Crime Fiction in German. Der Krimi*, Cardiff: University of Wales Press, 1–32.

King, S. (2014) "Crime fiction as world literature", *Clues: A Journal of Detection*, 32(2): 8–19.

Krajenbrink, M. (2009) "Unresolved identities in Roth and Rabinovici. Reworking the crime genre in Austrian literature", in M. Krajenbrink and K.M. Quinn (eds), *Investigating Identities. Questions of identity in contemporary international crime fiction*, Amsterdam & New York: Rodopi, 243–60.

Lazzara, M.J. (2006) *Chile in Transition. The poetics and politics of memory*, Gainesville, Florida: University Press of Florida.

Quinn, K.M. (2007) "Detection, dictatorship and democracy. Santiago de Chile in Ramón Díaz Eterovic's 'Heredia series'", *Romance Studies*, 25(2): 147–55.

Rabinovici, D. (1997) *Suche nach M.*, Frankfurt am Main: Suhrkamp.

Roth, G. (1995) *Der See*, Frankfurt am Main: Fischer.

Rothberg, M. (2009) *Multidirectional Memory. Remembering the Holocaust in the age of decolonialization*, Stanford California: Stanford University Press.

Seemann, D. (2011) "Moving beyond post-traumatic memory narratives. Generation, memory and identity in Doron Rabinovici, Robert Menasse and Eva Menasse", *Austrian Studies*, 19: 157–72.

Todorov, T. (1977) *The Poetics of Prose*, trans. R. Howard, Ithaca, NY: Cornell University Press.

Wilde, A. (1999) "Irruptions of memory. Expressive politics in Chile's transition to democracy", *Journal of Latin American Studies*, 31(2): 473–500.

35

CRIME FICTION AND TRAUMA

Cynthia S. Hamilton

Crime fiction critics have generally disregarded trauma theory despite the useful perspective it offers; Sarah Trott's *War Noir* (2016), Mary Ann Gillies's "Trauma and Contemporary Crime Fiction" (2019) and this author's *Sara Paretsky* (2015) stand out as exceptions. Trott uses the medicalised framework of post-traumatic stress disorder (PTSD) to examine Philip Marlowe in relation to Chandler's traumatic experience of trench warfare in World War II. Gillies notes the failure of trauma theorists to use their frameworks to examine popular literatures. She uses Caruth's concept of belatedness to reframe Todorov's two-story model of detective fiction in relation to trauma. Hamilton seeks to reinterpret the conventions of detective fiction in relation to trauma theory, but in a way that enables the connections between trauma theory and crime fiction to extend beyond the medicalisation of individuals and into the realm of the political.

Crime fiction necessarily engages key debates over the meaning and interpretation of traumatic experience, and over who has the right to interpret or assign meaning to evidence. When trauma theory is used as a critical framework, political debates over the plot trajectory of detective fiction – toward re-establishing the *status quo ante* – are relocated at the vortex of controversies in trauma theory over the appropriation of traumatic experience and the politics of healing. A trauma framework thus enables a more nuanced examination of the politics implicit in the formula, most significantly in relation to the vexed question of the formula's support or critique of the status quo. Crime fiction's tendency to privilege realism is re-contextualised through the lens of a trauma framework, which questions the appropriate narrative technique for conveying the impact of trauma and the extent to which traumatic experience is expressible.

Crime fiction and trauma theory

Detective fiction deals with the personal and social trauma caused by murder. The violence ruptures experience, precipitating incomprehension, disorientation and fragmentation; this is the essence of the traumatised reaction as conceptualised within the theories of trauma that emerged in the 1990s. Cathy Caruth's "Unclaimed Experience: Trauma and the Possibility of History" (1991), Shoshana Felman and Dori Laub's *Testimony* (1992) and Judith Lewis Herman's *Trauma and Recovery* (1992) provided the foundation for trauma studies. The definition of trauma presented in Caruth's essay is often cited as authoritative: "In its most general definition,

Crime fiction and trauma

trauma describes an overwhelming experience of sudden, or catastrophic events, in which the response to the event occurs in the often delayed, and uncontrolled repetitive occurrence of hallucinations and other intrusive phenomena" (1991: 181).

Early efforts to formulate and apply trauma theory positioned victims within a medicalised framework heavily dependent on Freud's concepts of repetition compulsion and of mourning and melancholia. This classic trauma theory shapes the approach taken by both Trott and Gillies in their application of trauma theory to detective fiction. When a detective, such as Chandler's Marlowe or Sayers's Lord Peter Wimsey, suffers shell shock or trauma as the result of a single event or series of events, the medicalised model is clearly relevant. Marcia Muller's *Locked In* (2009) provides another useful example. In this novel, Muller's detective, Sharon McCone, receives a traumatic brain injury after being shot and suffers from locked-in syndrome. She retains her keen analytical powers but has no control over her body. In the first-person narration, McCone experiences terrifying flashbacks which she examines for evidence that could identify her assailant. As she recovers and knits together the fragmented images of the attack, she works toward a coherent narrative of the event and is able to identify the perpetrator. But it is not until a large fragment of the bullet moves and is surgically removed that she regains her voice. She can then tell her story and identify her assailant. Healing can begin.

Judith Herman notes that telling the trauma story is central to the recovery process: "Out of the fragmented components of frozen imagery and sensation, patient and therapist slowly reassemble an organized, detailed, verbal account, oriented in time and historical context" (Herman 1998: 177). Talking through the trauma involves many repetitions until "the trauma story no longer arouses quite such intense feelings", at which point "the patient reclaims her own history and feels renewed hope and energy for engagement with life" (195). This is the essence of McCone's story in the evocatively titled *Locked In*.

Acute trauma distorts the way time is experienced, "often with a sense of slow motion", Herman notes, "and the experience may lose its quality of ordinary reality" (43). With recovery, chronological time "starts to move again" (195). Edkins speaks of "trauma time", which "destabilises any production of linearity"; it is experienced as outside linear time but cannot be understood "without recourse to notions of linearity" (Edkins 2003: 16). As Gillies points out, this dynamic is replicated in Todorov's two-story model of crime fiction where the "story of the crime usually occupies one time frame, most often a moment in the past, and the story of its investigation a second, most often the present moment" (2019: 42). Often the detective story ends with the fragmented evidence from the past recovered within a linear narrative that enables closure through the assignment of responsibility. The linearity of time is then restored, enabling progress.

Herman views the trauma victim as a patient who may or may not be capable of recovery. But as Craps points out, the trauma survivor positioned within the therapist-patient model is precluded from speaking "as an expert about his or her own experience, making political claims and actively intervening into power relations" (2015: 42). This perpetuation of victimisation is overcome in *Locked In*, where the detective achieves wholeness through self-healing, reaffirming her agency. Edkins also objects to the talking cure, noting that "the process of re-inscription into linear narratives [...] is a process that generally depoliticises" the trauma (2003: 15). She argues for an alternative strategy, one of "encircling the trauma" (15). This involves "marking the place [of trauma] without narrating it as part of a linear story or national myth" (17). Doing so, she suggests, leaves the disruptive power of the trauma intact. For Edkins, the political takes precedence over personal recovery achieved at the cost of forgetting traumatic revelations of the true nature of coercive power. In Edkins's model, the trauma survivor is seen not as a patient, but as a potential agent for social change.

When the traumatic events have a wider social dimension, the detective may become an agent of social exposure rather than a therapist promoting personal healing. Jenny Edkins relocates trauma in a way that makes its subversive, political potential clearly visible: "What we call trauma takes place when the very powers that we are convinced will protect us and give us security become our tormentors" (2003: 4). For her, trauma involves not only powerlessness, but also betrayal. "Events of the sort we call traumatic are overwhelming but they are also a revelation", Edkins writes; they "strip away the diverse commonly accepted meanings by which we lead our lives in various communities" (5). This is precisely the narrative trajectory of the hardboiled formula as outlined by John G. Cawelti, where the detective's investigation of crime "leads back to the rich and respectable levels of society and exposes the corrupt relationship between the pillars of the community and the criminal underground" (1976: 148–49).

It is at this point that the politics of the detective formula's relationship with the status quo comes into focus. With particular regard to the classical mystery, W.H. Auden argues that the "magic formula" reveals "an innocence which is discovered to contain guilt; then a suspicion of being the guilty one; and finally a real innocence from which the guilty other has been expelled" (1948: 412). When Auden speaks of guilt, he is referring to a "sense of sin", but the projection and transference that characterise his model can also be seen in more secular terms (411). Responsibility and guilt become tangled in life, suggesting the appeal of a ritualistic exoneration within the detective story. The formula offers reassurance that the rupture in experience caused by inexplicable violence is capable of coherent narrative expression; that such experience can be made safe. As Cathy Caruth notes, the threat posed by trauma is directly related to the inability of those who experience it to fully see or comprehend the event experienced (1991: 91–92). Classic trauma theory positions the detective – and by extension the reader – as analyst, the suspects – and by extension the reader – as witnesses.

The absolution available to readers through a classical mystery formula that contains and exorcises guilt would seem to place such detective fiction in opposition to one of the central objectives of trauma literature: Forcing those complicit in socially sanctioned injustice to recognise and take responsibility. Whether actively involved in oppressive actions or implicated through passive, silent acquiescence, trauma demands an appraisal of responsibility. Auden's model equates the social good with existing social institutions and norms; evil must be expelled from society; it is not deeply embedded within it. In so far as detective fiction isolates guilt and restores the status quo, the formula offers an inappropriate vehicle for social criticism. This is the point made, most notably, by Franco Moretti (1988). When the detective re-establishes order by directing blame in ways that serve the interests of the status quo and restrict potential judgements of culpability, this is certainly the case.

Nonetheless, narrative strategies are available that enable conservative messages to be subverted or deconstructed. In Todorov's two-story model, one storyline relates the reconstructed account of the crime itself. This story conceals its constructed, literary nature. The second, that of the investigation, reveals and often acknowledges the story-telling process; it explains how the story of the crime "came to be written" (1977: 45). So, built into the very fabric of the formula is a mechanism that enables discussion of the constructed nature of historical narratives. Because crime novels present a range of competing narratives interpreting evidence and assigning blame, the importance – and implications – of securing definitive status for a particular account is clearly visible. Detective fiction can therefore use the story of the investigation to reveal the gaps, silences and self-serving rationalisations within any totalising narrative of the crime.

Nor is duplicity the only issue. Witnesses to crime are hampered by the limitations of the available language. Their efforts to speak truth can be overwhelmed by competing discourses that misrepresent or negate the individual's experience. "The battle over the meaning of a traumatic experience is fought in the arena of political discourse, popular culture, and scholarly debate", Kalí Tal notes.

> If survivors retain control over the interpretation of their trauma, they can sometimes force a shift in the social and political structure. If the dominant culture manages to appropriate the trauma and can codify it in its own terms the status quo will remain unchanged.
>
> *(1996: 7)*

Three socially sanctioned strategies threaten the integrity of the survivor's experience: Disappearance, medicalisation and mythologisation. Disappearance denies the existence of trauma, while medicalisation labels the victim ill and in need of a cure. Mythologisation reduces a traumatic event to a standardised narrative. "Traumatic events are written and rewritten", Tal writes "until they become codified and narrative form gradually replaces content as the focus of narrative" (6).

Detective fiction can offer just such a codification. It is fully capable of mythologising traumatic experience in ways that serve the interests of the status quo, but this need not be the case. In the story of the investigation, juxtapositions and discontinuities may reveal how responsibility is shifted, exposing the partial, evasive nature of narrative closure. With trauma literature, when the survivor's story is presented for public consumption, decisions are necessarily made, whether consciously or not, about the narrative forms and strategies used. Whitehead argues that "the impact of trauma can only adequately be represented by mimicking its forms and symptoms, so that temporality and chronology collapse, and narratives are characterised by repetition and indirection" (2004: 3). The appropriateness of narrative techniques and strategies most commonly associated with modernism and postmodernism are seen, in Craps's words, as "all but axiomatic" (2015: 39). Such prescriptive judgements of appropriate literary modes could, in themselves, rule out a great portion of crime fiction, which often relies on realism as its narrative mode.

Roger Luckhurst and Michael Rothberg offer a more promising approach that moves beyond the medicalised model, expands the remit of trauma literature and enables the narrative techniques of detective fiction to be discussed in relation to trauma theory. Luckhurst suggests moving away from "privileging narrative rupture as the only proper mark of a trauma aesthetic". He also argues that the range of texts examined as trauma literature should be broadened (2008: 89). Michael Rothberg recommends "traumatic realism" as a workable strategy. Rothberg argues that traumatic realism enables exposure of the apparent transparency of literary representations, with their assumed correspondence between representation and reality (2000: 106). For Rothberg, rather than representing objects, details are an "index" that points to "a necessary absence" (104).

Laurie R. King's *Locked Rooms* (2005) provides a good example. In this novel, King's detective, Mary Russell, is forced by circumstances to face her childhood experience, aged six, of the San Francisco earthquake and fire of 1906 and of the death of her family and her own serious injury, eight years later, in what was originally judged to be an automobile accident. Russell is plagued by a set of three repeating nightmares as she sails from Japan toward San Francisco. In the first, she becomes the target of objects hurled about the room; in the second, she is confronted by a faceless man in a white, featureless room; and in the third, she is unable to access a locked room that she senses would offer comfort. These nightmares are a symptom of Russell's unclaimed experience as it intrudes through vivid, fragmented images. They vividly point to an absence, a locked space within her mind that she can neither remember nor forget. This is traumatic realism at work.

Although the realism associated with detective fiction relies on the norm of a one-to-one correlation between objects and referents, detective fiction also plays with the shifts in meaning that occur when objects and events attract multiple interpretations. The resulting contingencies are fully compatible with the traumatic realism proposed by Rothberg; they undermine straightforward referentiality and draw attention to detail as an index of trauma. Here again, an example from *Locked Rooms* is helpful. The book uses a number of photographs as mementos, signifiers of heart-wrenching absence, aids for identification, and evidence within different witness accounts of events. The meaning of each photograph shifts as it is discussed by those who keep it or to whom it is shown. The meanings accrued circle around the core of anguish. The result is very close to Edkins's concept of "encircling the trauma", with its insistence on "'not forgetting' rather than remembering" (2003: 15).

Both Rothberg and Edkins implicitly affirm the inexpressibility of the traumatic event and recommend forms that do not undermine the revelatory power of the experience. Rothberg insists that traumatic realism is not an act of "passive mimesis" (2000: 103). Instead, it is a project that confronts readers with new knowledge which aims to "program and thus transform its readers so that they are forced to acknowledge their relationship to posttraumatic culture" (103).

Encircling the trauma is more straightforward when it is precipitated by a time-specific event or series of events that stop time, shattering survivors' understanding of their world and destroying their sense of self. Non-specific trauma, including what Craps labels the "insidious trauma" of racism, where traumatisation results "from cumulative micro-aggressions", is more difficult to encircle (2015: 26). Stephen F. Soitos (1996) argues that African American detective fiction incorporates a set of tropes that construct a counter-narrative and signal an alternative worldview, one directly related to the cumulative impact of racism, a form of chronic, non-specific trauma. The time frame of trauma produced by stressors such as the micro-aggressions of racism and sexism, Craps suggests, weaves past and present together in a more complex pattern than is the case with event-precipitated trauma: "past and present are imbricated in one another, as the past continues to structure the present" (2015: 71). To understand such trauma, it is important to remain "hospitable to ghosts" (71). These are not the ghostly imprints of trauma in psychological possession of the victim, such as those of which Ann Whitehead speaks (2004: 7), but the lingering impacts, both institutional and personal, of a long and extensive history of racial oppression that demand to be acknowledged.

Rudolph Fisher's *The Conjure-Man Dies* (1932) configures trauma within both a Eurocentric, rationalistic model of causality and an Africanist worldview that acknowledges alternative ontologies. Fisher displays a complex allegiance both to scientific rationalism and to the African heritage and worldview of the conjure-man. He employs literary realism, a representational strategy associated with notions of social progress, with the importance of evidence-based knowledge, and with the need to gather empirical data for analysis. But he also affirms the existence and importance of a spiritual realm where time is not linear, utilising the metaphysical heritage of detective fiction, often identified with the Gothic. Through this implicit contrast, Fisher exposes the Eurocentric bias behind the formula, a bias that naturalises the imperialistic enterprises, both physical and ontological, that do violence to those marginalised.

Nor is realism the only narrative mode available to writers of detective fiction. In *A Rage in Harlem* (1957), Chester Himes uses surrealism to depict the absurdities produced by racism as well as racism's traumatic impact. His physical descriptions become expressionistic representations of consciousness. An unforgettable metaphor of Harlem as "the voracious churning of millions of hungry cannibal fish. Blind mouths eating their own guts" (1996: 102) captures the way oppression and desperation yield resentment and savagery. Himes's narrative strategies confront the reader with an anger so pure that neither sympathy nor silence seem appropriate responses; one is forced to look at the text itself as an index of trauma.

When Rothberg proposes a multidirectional approach to trauma, he recognises the full range of referentiality available to trauma literature. "Memories are not owned by groups – nor are groups 'owned' by memories", he explains. Memories are shaped by borrowings and adaptations that brings together "now and then, here and there" through a powerfully creative process that builds "new worlds out of the materials of older ones" (2009: 5). Rothberg's multidirectional model suggests the many ways in which literature can use intertextual and historical referencing as well as intra-textual referencing to register and nuance complicity and guilt. This is precisely what Sara Paretsky does in *Total Recall* (2001) (Luckhurst 2008: 116; Hamilton 2015: 140–67). In this novel, slavery and the Holocaust become mutually referential. The relationship between the two is made visually apparent in an early scene where two demonstrations face off with competing grievances outside a conference promoting religious tolerance; one group advocates Holocaust reparations, the other demands economic justice for the descendants of slaves. In *Total Recall*, accounts of personal trauma are interwoven with debates over corporate responsibility, social justice and the importance of recording a history of oppression and injustice that acknowledges the trauma of those who have suffered. As a result, the novel demonstrates the way memories of past injustice frame reactions in the present at a personal level, but also in relation to corporate culture, institutional behaviour and in broader debates within society.

Layers of trauma and the politics of narrative

Paula L. Woods's *Inner City Blues* (1999) brings together multiple layers of traumatic experience: Racism and sexual harassment, the collective trauma of the Rodney King riots and the after-effects of Vietnam. Intersecting instances demonstrate how stressors accumulate, with past trauma conditioning perceptions and responses in the present. In this novel, trauma is not just multidimensional, but also intersectional.

The novel begins with Charlotte Justice, a detective with the Los Angeles Police Department (LAPD), on riot duty during the Rodney King riots in 1992. Using a historically recognisable portrayal of the King riots is a judicious choice, for it enables Woods to give historical resonance to her depiction. She also references other examples of civil unrest precipitated by racism – the Zoot Suit Riots of 1943 and the Watts riot of 1965. Such cross-referencing allows for "multidirectional" analysis, as suggested by Rothberg. Using the riots also allows her to portray her characters' responses under extreme pressure. In this situation, the latent violence of racism surfaces.

Although the plot follows the investigation of the murder of Cinque Lewis, whose body is discovered in the riot area, the central event of the novel is the brutal murder of Charlotte's husband and daughter outside their home in Los Angeles fourteen years before. Because Lewis had murdered her family, his murder marks both the end and beginning of a quest for Justice. As an African American policing the riots, Charlotte is perfectly placed to comment on the racism and sexism she experiences and observes. In the very first chapter, a patrolling officer's racist attitudes and assumptions lead to unprovoked violence against a young black doctor, directly referencing the beating of King. "I don't give a shit about no fuckin' prime directives", Cooper rants, "the first little jungle bunny who looks at me cross-eyed is gonna get a cap in his ass! I *know* how to get this city in order!" (16).

Charlotte's brother Perris is used within the narrative to capture the long-term effects of racism. Shot while serving in the LAPD years earlier, he descends, for a time, into drug and alcohol abuse, a self-destructive coping mechanism linked to the experience of chronic racism. When Charlotte glosses over details of the racist attack, her brother infuriates her by accusing her of "being no better than those cops who covered for Koon and his boys on the Rodney King beating" (37).

Cooper's extreme reaction in the novel is a conditioned, aggressive response linked to his experience of fighting in Vietnam, echoing the hyper-arousal, the "persistent expectation of danger" that Judith Herman identifies as one of the symptoms of undigested and repressed experience (1998: 35). Lewis's killer is a veteran who enjoys using the expertise in garroting acquired in Vietnam. Another character lost his son in Vietnam, precipitating a severe mental breakdown. The responses of the three men differ, but all react to situations that resonate with past trauma, revealing the manifold ways in which old experiences haunt the present.

As Charlotte searches for Lewis's killer, her intrusive flashbacks reflect, in Herman's words, "the indelible imprint of the traumatic moment" recorded in memory, not in a verbal narrative, but in "vivid sensations and images" (1998: 38). In a nightmare image, Charlotte's husband and child lie in a growing puddle of blood, "the bluish-purple trumpets drifting down from the tree in front of my house" and "the gray barrel of a gun glinting at me from the passenger's side of the black car" (2000: 28). The use of first-person narration intensifies the impact of trauma, making Charlotte's narration a witness testimony. Charlotte becomes both victim and detective, witness and analyst.

Her quest for justice is also a pursuit for wholeness and healing. Charlotte has been searching for Lewis for almost fourteen years when she learns that his body has been found. She visits the scene, afraid of "the blue-black nightmares that glowed darky on the other side of the crime tape and threatened to eat me up alive" (66). In the early days after her family's murder, Charlotte was numb and lethargic, a response characteristic of the "constriction" experienced by trauma survivors. This is a response which, in Herman's words, "reflects the numbing response of surrender" (1998: 35). Even after fourteen years, Charlotte cannot move on; she has left her husband's office as a dusty shrine, with the door firmly closed. She cannot bring herself to clear the room: "The last time I tried, six years ago, I was stopped by the smell of Aramis that permeated Keith's sweater and his smudged fingerprints on his glasses", she explains (2000: 166). A still-wrapped present for her baby daughter lies on the end table with its faded pink ribbon; such details are examples of traumatic realism effectively employed.

Woods uses Charlotte to comment directly on the gloss put on the impact of violent death in detective fiction:

> It's so seldom that cops see the long-term consequences of violent death, even when they work homicide. You do the next-of-kin notification, see the disbelief on people's faces when you tell them their loved one is gone, maybe even go to a funeral, but you hardly ever see how that loss can consume a person, year in and year out.
>
> *(280)*

The story of the investigation in *Inner City Blues* traces the prolonged anguish suffered by the survivors of trauma, pointing to the silences and gaps within the neat, chronological account of the murders.

Inner City Blues uses parallel situations to mark progress and difference. The most important of these is a scene near the end of the novel when Charlotte finds herself threatened by Lewis's killer, fourteen years to the day after her family's murder. This time, she is not a helpless witness, but an active participant in the scene. The one-year-old child caught up in the incident is saved, not killed. Her brother arrives in time to provide backup. And Aubrey, her lover, is able to hold her in his arms and comfort her. It is Charlotte herself who fires, in self-defence, the fatal shot. With events brought full circle, she is able to relive the experience with a different outcome, and move on. Before she leaves for a holiday with Aubrey, she stops at the cemetery to put the sweater, glasses and baby booties on her husband's and daughter's grave. It all seems a bit too neat, and it is; the restricted narrative of criminal culpability and of Charlotte's therapeutic recovery leave the chronic racism and sexism exposed in the novel untouched. At the family party to celebrate Charlotte's triumph, her brother worries the family by drinking the celebratory champagne, and her sister and grandmother wear t-shirts that proclaim: "I'm tired. I've been black all day!" (312).

In *Inner City Blues*, Woods shows the interconnected power politics of gender and race that disadvantage black women, compounding the trauma experienced. Charlotte's supervisor tries to exchange professional favours for sex. When she refuses, he attempts to rape her. And when she threatens to complain, he warns her: "Look, we just had a misunderstanding, Charlotte. No harm, no foul. But if you try and make more out of it than it was, it's only going to hurt you, not me" (291). The rule of silence is one that Charlotte understands well. She knows that any complaint will put her pending promotion at risk.

The cumulative impact of the micro-aggressions and coercive force of chronic trauma precipitated by sexism and racism is a potent mix of shame, guilt and rage. When Charlotte attends an LAPD meeting the morning after the attempted rape, she dresses conservatively, not wanting to draw attention to herself. She assumes an inappropriate responsibility for her boss's behaviour, a responsibility conditioned by social messages blaming the victim (221). At community level, the King riots become a confused, self-destructive response, fuelled by multiple injustices and humiliations, to the non-specific trauma of racism.

By the end of the novel, we are presented with a healing narrative, a definitive account that assigns responsibility for the deaths of Charlotte's family, for the young doctor's murder and for the killing of Lewis. There is also a happy ending as Charlotte and Aubrey go away together. But the trauma of chronic racism and sexism remain, with no possibility of closure until responsibility is assigned. The continuing, traumatic heritage of Vietnam also remains. Thus, the mythologisation potentially offered by the ritualistic presentation of guilt, scapegoating and exoneration in detective fiction is dismantled, leaving the question of complicity very much open for the reader's contemplation.

Bibliography

Auden, W.H. (1948) "The guilty vicarage", *Harper's Magazine*, May 1948.
Caruth, C. (1991) "Unclaimed experience: trauma and the possibility of history", *Yale French Studies*, 79: 181–92.
Cawelti, J.G. (1976) *Adventure, Mystery, and Romance*, Chicago: University of Chicago Press.
Craps, S. (2015) *Postcolonial Witnessing: Trauma out of bounds*, Basingstoke: Palgrave Macmillan.
Edkins, J. (2003) *Trauma and the Memory of Politics*, Cambridge: Cambridge University Press.
Felman, S. and Laub, D. (1992) *Testimony: Crises of witnessing in literature, psychoanalysis, and history*, New York: Routledge.
Fisher, R. (1995) *The Conjure Man Dies*, London: The X Press.
Gillies, M.A. (2019) "Trauma and contemporary crime fiction", *Clues*, 37(1): 40–50.
Hamilton, C.S. (2015) *Sara Paretsky: Detective fiction as trauma literature*, Manchester: Manchester University Press.
Herman, J.L. (1998) [1992] *Trauma and Recovery: From domestic abuse to political terror*, London: Pandora.
Himes, C. (1996), *The Harlem Cycle*, vol. 1, Edinburgh: Payback Press.
King, L.R. (2010) *Locked Rooms*, London: Allison & Busby.
Luckhurst, R. (2008) *The Trauma Question*, London: Routledge.
Moretti, F. (1988) "Clues", *Signs Taken for Wonders: Essays in the sociology of literary forms*, London: Verso.

Muller, M. (2009) *Locked In*, New York: Grand Central Publishing.

Rothberg, M. (2000) *Traumatic Realism: The demands of Holocaust representation*, Minneapolis: University of Minnesota Press.

———. (2009) *Multidirectional Memory: Remembering the Holocaust in the age of decolonization*, Stanford: Stanford University Press.

Soitos, S.F. (1996) *The Blues Detective: A study of African American detective fiction*, Amherst: University of Massachusetts Press.

Tal, K. (1996) *Worlds of Hurt: Reading the literatures of trauma*, Cambridge: Cambridge University Press.

Todorov, T. (1977) "The typology of detective fiction", *Poetics of Prose*, trans. R. Howard, Oxford: Basil Blackwell.

Trott, S. (2016) *War Noir: Raymond Chandler and the hard-boiled detective as veteran in American fiction*, Jackson: University Press of Mississippi.

Whitehead, A. (2004) *Trauma Fiction*, Edinburgh: Edinburgh University Press.

Woods, P.L. (2000) *Inner City Blues*, New York: Ballantine Books.

36
CRIME FICTION AND POLITICS

José V. Saval

Crime fiction is an inherently political genre. In the words of Andrew Pepper, it is "the most politically minded of all the literary genres" because of its focus "on the ways in which individual lives are shaped by the push and pull of larger social, political, and economic forces, [...] on the nature and adequacy of the justice system and on the reasons why crimes are committed" (2016: 18). Take Horace McCoy's *They Shoot Horses, Don't They?* (1935), for example. While the novel tells the story of a crime that takes place during a dancing contest, the real crime is perhaps the contest itself. McCoy uses this endurance contest in which the winners are the last couple to remain on the dance floor as a metaphor for the competitive nature of capitalism. Through this contest in which competitors die of exhaustion in a desperate attempt to win the money they need in order to survive, McCoy denounces the ways in which labour, here the dance competition itself, dehumanises individuals, forcing them to compete against each other just to exist.

Mikhail Bakhtin has argued that "images of language are inseparable from images of various world views and from the living beings who are their agents – people who think, talk, and act in a setting that is social and historically concrete" (1981: 49). In crime fiction, the worldview – that is, the political content – espoused in and through the text emerges through both the genre's content and form (Knight 1980: 5). This chapter explores how political messages manifest themselves both through the content and the form. It begins by analysing the scholarly debates about whether the genre is an inherently conservative form that privileges private property and bourgeois notions of law and order or whether it is capable of radical political critique. The chapter then examines some of the ways in which crime fiction responds to the contemporary political fault lines of gender, race and the environment as well as the ongoing consequences of historical injustices. To illustrate the explicit connection between politics and the crime novel, the chapter will analyse Spanish writer Manuel Vázquez Montalbán's *Los mares del sur* (1979) [*Southern Seas*, 1986], which explores class struggle in Barcelona during Spain's momentous transition to democracy following the death of dictator Francisco Franco in 1975.

The politics of form

While critics are divided over whether the genre articulates an inherently conservative or progressive worldview, they agree that its ideology is shaped by both the content and the form. Stephen Knight, for example, argues that

> differences of form between writers are not trivial or arbitrary; they are essential elements in the meaningful innovations which the story offers to its audience, intimately connected with the differences in content between texts such as the setting, the crimes discussed, the nature of the detective.
>
> *(1980: 5)*

For Knight, the genre is in essence conservative:

> [M]ajor examples of crime fiction not only create an idea (or a hope or a dream) about controlling crime, but both realise and validate a whole view of the world, one shared by the people who become the central audience to buy, read and find comfort in a particular variety of crime fiction.
>
> *(2)*

The key concept here is "comforting world-view" (5), as the resolution to the mystery at the novel's end reassures readers about the provision of justice and thus reinforces the legitimacy of the State. Ernest Mandel takes this further, arguing that there is a certain homology between bourgeois society and crime fiction, given its support for, and protection of, the primary capitalist value – that of private property. As Mandel notes, "bourgeois society is, when all is said and done, a criminal society" (1984: 72, 135). Franco Moretti pushes the genre even further into the conservative camp, arguing that in its desire for "a *transparent* society", that is, its desire to reveal what is hidden, the crime genre serves as the literary articulation of Jeremy Bentham's Panopticon, which – as theorised by Michel Foucault – is a means of effective social control through constant supervision (1983: 143).

In contrast to Knight, Mandel and Moretti, others like Sean McCann maintain that the "detective story had always been a liberal genre, centrally concerned with a fundamental premise of liberal theory – the rule of law – and with the tensions fundamental to democratic societies that constantly threw that principle into doubt" (2000: 6). Howard Haycraft also closely aligns the crime genre with democracy and the rule of law. In his essay "Dictators, Democrats, and Detectives", written during World War II, he contrasts the prohibition on the publication of crime stories in Nazi Germany and Fascist Italy with the popularity of the genre in England and the United States to argue that

> the detective story is and always has been essentially a democratic institution; produced on any large scale only in democracies; dramatizing, under the bright cloak of entertainment, many of the precious rights and privileges that have set the dwellers in constitutional lands apart from those less fortunate.
>
> *(1974: 313)*

The debates about the conservative or liberal nature of the genre are most often associated with, or indeed mapped onto, the different subgeneric categories of classic detective fiction and hardboiled fiction. In historical approaches to the detective novel in terms of its political

Crime fiction and politics

values, critics often identify a divide between classic detective fiction and the hardboiled novel – what Julian Symons refers to as "The American Revolution" of the genre (1992: 153–55). This divide manifests in the setting and the manner in which it is represented. While the setting in the former case is often heavily stylised and delineated mainly in terms of its spatial features, the American variant tends to offer detailed descriptions of places and institutions, showing in particular society's dark side with its social issues and dysfunctionalities; as Jameson notes about this latter form, "[t]he detective's journey is episodic because of the fragmentary, atomistic nature of the society he moves through" (Jameson 2016: 11). We can thus talk of tales of realistic violence, set in recognisable surroundings. Symons makes a clear distinction between what he calls the detective novel (Holmes, Christie, and so forth) and, in his words, the crime novel (Hammett, Chandler and others): The social attitude of detective fiction is "conservative" while in the crime novel, it is "varying, but often radical in the sense of questioning some aspect of law, justice or the way society is run" (1992: 203).

Symons and Jameson both clearly adhere to Raymond Chandler's division of the crime novel into two distinct types, as articulated in his 1944 essay, "The Simple Art of Murder". On the one hand, Chandler points to the conservative, rule-bound and "arid" formula of English writers like Arthur Conan Doyle, Agatha Christie and Dorothy L. Sayers, who are claimed only to be interested in intellectual puzzles (1995: 987). On the other hand, he identifies the works of Dashiell Hammett as the epitome of a realistic, gritty and politically critical genre that developed in the United States: "Hammett took murder out of the Venetian vase and dropped it into the alley" (998). Chandler highlights the importance of realist elements in portraying a corrupt society: "The realist in murder writes of a world in which gangsters can rule nations and almost rule cities" (991).

Chandler's distinction between the conservatism of classic detective fiction and the radicalism of the hardboiled novel has become a form of critical orthodoxy and it is only recently that critics have begun to question the assumptions that underlie the argument. Andrew Pepper, for example, argues that Arthur Morrison's 1897 story, "The Affair of the Avalanche Bicycle and Tyre Co. Limited", "offers in many ways a more pointed and bleaker assessment of the effects of finance capital than Dashiell Hammett's *The Maltese Falcon* (1930)" (2016: 7), while Stewart King has shown that sociopolitical elements can appear in all detective novels, even in those traditionally considered to avoid such elements, such as the novels of Agatha Christie. In his study of Christie's *Murder on the Orient Express* (1934), King draws attention to the ways in which the novel questions the failure of the justice system and articulates the more morally ambiguous worldview usually associated with the hardboiled. In so doing, King highlights how the strict taxonomy that separates the supposedly apolitical classic detective novel from the politically charged hardboiled novel is no longer as clear as it was once perceived to be. It is not just the classic detective novel which can move into progressive territory; the hardboiled can express conservative viewpoints, such as in the novels of American writer, James Ellroy, who considers himself a conservative in ideological terms despite using a form that many associate with a politically charged, progressive message.

Studies like Pepper's and King's form part of a growing body of research that argues for generic complexity. For Lee Horsley, for example, "the genre itself is neither inherently conservative nor radical: rather, it is a form that can be co-opted for a variety of purposes" (2005: 158). Scott McCracken provides a concrete example of how this ideological ambiguity can manifest itself in individual novels, arguing that readers are attracted to crime fiction not because they seek reassuring resolutions to mysteries, but because crime fiction texts often raise "more questions" than they answer through "formal closure" (1998: 50).

José V. Saval

The politics of content

According to Fredric Jameson, the figure of the detective is key, because "through him we are able to see, to know, the society as a whole" (2016: 7). In the case of Chandler and the hardboiled novel, the reader will move, with the detective, through a "kind of microcosm and forecast of the country as a whole: a new centerless city, in which the various classes have lost touch with each other because each is isolated in its own geographical compartment" (6–7). In this case, the figure of the detective and the space in which he or she is inserted will produce a particular kind of political reading, mostly via the ways in which the detective understands and negotiates social relations and hierarchies and class differences. This process is always fraught and shot through with contradictions. For example, Philip Marlowe's social conservatism means that he finds common ground with the aristocratic and patriarchal General Sternwood in *The Big Sleep* (1939) even as his distaste of the indolence and moral bankruptcy of the rich produces an equally significant counter-reaction.

The political message of the crime novel is not clear precisely because of these tensions and contradictions. Moreover, we might argue that the crime novel's larger social "imaginary" is necessarily limited by the detective's individualism, at least as he is imagined by Chandler, and the fact that he is isolated from society. The function of the detective is to solve the enigma – the crime – and to restore the broken order of things, and in doing so, and whether this is directly acknowledged or not, he or she seeks to restore the social and political equilibrium. Hence, "the crime novel and the figure of the detective are, to some extent, implicated in the hegemonic ambitions of those who have benefited from the unequal distribution of power" (Pepper 2000: 7). Detection is part of the machinery of the State and a mechanism of political control and while the detective and the crime novel might be opposed to the values of society as a whole, there is a necessary but uneasy push by both towards the re-establishment of the social order, a move which in turn perpetuates relations of domination and subordination. As Pepper argues, "the trajectory of the narrative leads inexorably to a restoration of the *status quo* and thus, a re-affirmation of the existing social order" (2000: 11). This contradiction dissolves any possibility of utopia, beyond pointing to particular social ills, such as racism, sexism and misogyny, though crime fiction can also collude with and reproduce these ills. Still, it is fair to argue that the crime novel, despite these tensions and contradictions, has found ways to expose and confront the problems and abuses of capitalist society, with its attendant hierarchies and divisions. The genre's critique of society is primarily founded on its capacities to lay bare the violence at the heart of this social organisation and on its political vision which is typically aligned with those on the margins of society: The detective himself or herself, the criminal, the victims or witnesses and suspects. While hardboiled crime writers such as Chandler developed a realistic approach to expose corruption in society, whether it be economic, social or political, the very structures of the crime novel – the crime, investigation, solution/punishment – limit the subversive potential of the genre and put pressure on its utopian claims.

If crime fiction has always been "the most politically minded of literary genres", this claim has found additional urgency in the contemporary era, as the breadth and diversity of the genre's politics have become apparent. Hence, it is possible to consider crime fiction's entanglement with the politics of race, gender and sexuality, of postcolonialism and the environment, and of authoritarianism, as this collection as a whole demonstrates. Crime fiction has typically been considered a masculine, male-dominated genre, in spite of the fundamental contribution from women authors such as Agatha Christie, Patricia Highsmith and Sue Grafton, amongst many others. Nevertheless, and according to Stephen Knight, the inherent elasticity and adaptability

Crime fiction and politics

of the form of the crime novel opens up the possibility of sociopolitical transformation at the level of content (1980: 5). Female protagonists, such as Christie's Miss Marple, reinvigorated the genre, offering a new and different perspective to that typically seen in crime fiction up to that point. Subsequent interventions by writers such as Dorothy B. Hughes showed female characters capable and willing to use their sexuality to further their own ambitions. As Jean M. Lutes puts it, in her study about women-authored crime fiction in the mid-twentieth century: "their most surprising feature may be the way they make women's sexuality a narrative force that moves in multiple and unpredictable ways" (2017: 189). In more recent years, crime writers such as Val McDermid and Gillian Flynn have incorporated biting social commentaries on the ills of patriarchy and misogyny into their works (while at the same time showing female characters every bit as capable of violence and manipulation as their male counterparts). Other writers have extended these critiques into the gendered implications of human trafficking and domestic violence.

In the case of racial politics, crime fiction in the UK and the US at the end of the nineteenth century and even into the twentieth century displayed hegemonic notions of law and order that legitimated imperialist ideologies centred on white supremacy and excluding foreign and ethnic "others". By the end of the twentieth century the model had evolved and those previously marginalised were given greater voice and visibility in and by the genre and, in doing so, crime novelists such as Walter Mosley were able to show the effects of implicit and explicit forms of racism previously sanctioned, wittingly or otherwise, by Chandler, Hammett and others. Walter Mosley is an especially interesting figure, not least because of his own complex familial background (he was born in Los Angeles to a Jewish mother of Russian origin and an African American father from Louisiana) and because of his willingness to experiment using different generic forms and archetypes (for example, crime novel, science fiction, Afro-futurism). Mosley is best known for his series of detective novels featuring Ezekiel "Easy" Rawlins, an unlicensed investigator with no experience in law enforcement, who has to confront and negotiate the various forms of racism characteristic of post-World War II Los Angeles. In doing so, and as we see most explicitly in the opening of *Devil in a Blue Dress* (1990), Mosley rewrites the hardboiled novel inherited from Chandler from the perspective of his African American private detective and demonstrates how the (racial) perspective of the protagonist in turn informs the political assumptions of the genre (for example, the extent to which racial prejudice is linked to social inequality).

The potential of the crime fiction genre to expose and lay bare different forms of oppression and abuses of power, as well as its capacities to support existing social and political arrangements, is further evidenced by the sheer diversity of the genre's foci and subject matter, whether looking at the effects of decolonisation or the nature and consequences of environmental crimes, especially those perpetuated by governments in conjunction with multinational corporations. Crime fiction has also engaged with different forms of authoritarianism. As Carlos Uxó demonstrates in Chapter 43, crime fiction under Stalin was banned because it was considered bourgeois entertainment, full of vices. Nevertheless, later on, a particular form of class-conscious detective emerged to try to root out the ills inflicted on Communist societies by decadent forms of Western individualism. An interesting case took place in Cuba where the State actively supported the use of art, including crime fiction, as a weapon to safeguard the Revolution. As Uxó demonstrates, Ignacio Cardenas Acuña became a successful author and contributed to the ideological education of workers by showing through his crime fiction what was "legal" for Cuba's revolutionary state. In other parts of Latin America that suffered periods of dictatorship, novelists such as Osvaldo Soriano and Mempo Giardinelli retrospectively used the conventions of the crime novel to criminalise the dictatorial state for its crimes against the

331

citizenry and indict democratic institutions for their failure to punish state-sanctioned criminals and provide historical justice for the victims.

The politics of Spanish crime fiction: *Southern Seas*

The connection between crime fiction and politics can be clearly seen in the case of detective fiction in Spain, where the *novela negra* – the Spanish variant of the hardboiled – emerged during a time of momentous political change as the country transitioned from an almost 40-year right-wing dictatorship to a modern, liberal democracy following the death of Franco. Crime fiction, of course, existed in Spain prior to the re-establishment of democracy (see the essays in Vosburg 2011), but during the years of the dictatorship, writers set their novels almost exclusively abroad and employed pseudonyms of English inspiration. This was the case with Francisco González Ledesma, a journalist and writer, who in Francoist Spain penned novels under the name of Silver Kane and only later set his novels in contemporary Spain and wrote them under his own moniker. The dominance of pseudo-transnational novels written by Spaniards during the Franco years was, in fact, the result of political pressure, as the regime was uncomfortable with the negative portrayal of crime in Spanish society, in particular the critique of the justice and policing systems that is present in many hardboiled novels. As such, when writers like Mario Lacruz and Maria-Aurèlia Capmany wanted to write about the dictatorship they set their novels abroad in fictitious or real countries that acted as thinly-veiled allegories of Spain. Maria-Aurelia Capmany's *Traduït de l'americà* [Translated from the American, 1959], for example, investigates a mystery primarily in two Albanian cities, the conservative capital Tirana and the progressive coastal city of Valona, which act as metaphors for Madrid and Barcelona respectively (King and Whitmore 2016).

The need to mask criticism of Spanish society in crime fiction disappeared following Franco's death and the subsequent abolition of censorship. Seeing the opportunities that the genre afforded to critique the profound social, political and economic changes that the country was experiencing, writers turned a rather marginal literary form into the most important genre of Spain's Transition. This was the case of Spain's most famous crime writer and public intellectual, Manuel Vázquez Montalbán. A committed communist, anti-Francoist and avant-garde novelist and poet, Vázquez Montalbán largely abandoned the experimental literary forms he had produced in the 1960s to write crime fiction, when he realised that the hardboiled format – with which he was familiar more through the films of Humphrey Bogart and John Huston than the works of Hammett or Chandler – offered him a form that was attractive to readers and which would also allow him to communicate to a broader reading public the social and political commentary he wanted to make. The result was the Carvalho series, named after its private detective and gourmand protagonist, Pepe Carvalho, who appears in eighteen novels, six short story collections and a recipe book. Scott McCracken maintains that "Popular fiction may use simple forms, but if these forms are to win an audience they must be able to address that audience's concerns" (1998: 11). The popularity of the Carvalho series in Spain was thanks to Vázquez Montalbán's articulation of his reading public's concerns about the failure of Spain's Transition to realise the transformations that democracy had promised. The sort of politically charged crime fiction, combined with local cultural and gastronomic elements that Vázquez Montalbán pioneered, not only had an important impact in Spain; it also had a lasting influence on the international development of the genre, particularly among Vázquez Montalbán's fellow Mediterranean writers, Jean-Claude Izzo and Andrea Camilleri, whose protagonists Fabio Montale and Salvo Montalbano are named in homage to the author of the Carvalho series.

Crime fiction and politics

Patricia Hart has argued that Vázquez Montalbán's "books do not really want to be detective novels. Rather, they want to be commentaries about the problems of living in contemporary Spain" (1987: 86). Yet the two cannot really be separated, as is evident in his 1979 novel, *Los mares del sur* [*Southern Seas*], which was awarded Spain's largest literary prize, the Planeta prize. In the novel, Pepe Carvalho is hired by the widow of a wealthy industrialist to investigate the circumstances surrounding the death of her husband, Carlos Stuart Pedrell, who was found stabbed to death at a construction site in a peripheral suburb of Barcelona, after he had abandoned his job and family and supposedly travelled to the southern seas of the novel's title a year earlier in search of spiritual enlightenment. In some ways, Patricia Hart is correct, as Stuart Pedrell's widow is not particularly interested in finding her husband's killer; she is more concerned with ensuring that whatever he was doing during his mysterious sabbatical does not compromise the family's business interests, which she has taken over successfully since her husband's disappearance. Importantly, the novel draws attention to the significance of politics and political choices through the slogans, posters and graffiti in the build-up to the 1979 municipal elections that Carvalho encounters as he wanders around the city in search of answers. The convergence of the investigation and contemporary political events is no accident, according to Mario Santana, who argues that it "reveals a polarity between private and public history – a thematic that permeates the whole narrative" (2000: 547).

Carvalho's encounters with a range of characters from different social backgrounds – from the ultra-rich made up of speculative industrialists, eccentric noblemen and disillusioned daughters of millionaires to the lower classes consisting of prostitutes with a heart of gold, politically committed female unionists, disenchanted, but hopeful communists and misguided knife-carrying thugs – reveal the city's hidden past. In so doing, he exposes the criminality of the ruling class, some of whom made their money through slavery in the early nineteenth century or through dodgy urban development in the 1960s, and their victims, largely the losers of the Spanish Civil War (1936–1939) and those who suffered and continue to suffer economic and social exploitation at the hands of Franco's supporters. At the novel's conclusion, Carvalho provides Stuart Pedrell's widow with an account of what her husband had done since his disappearance and the identity of his murderer, but this crime diminishes in importance, not least because the widow does not want a scandal that could threaten the family's fortune. Indeed, the first crime is only important insofar as it reveals a more damning crime – the enrichment of the upper-class characters through the dodgy construction of a working-class suburb on the city's margins that, in turn, exposes the Franco regime's so-called economic miracle as an illusion. Carvalho's investigation, then, links the city's (and by extension, the nation's) present with its past, calling into question the reluctance of Spain's new democratic class to seek justice for the regime's historical crimes.

Conclusion

At the beginning of *Southern Seas*, Pepe Carvalho tells his assistant that "we private eyes are the barometers of established morality" (1999: 7). While initially Carvalho refers to the loosening of Francoist conservative values being terrible for his business, as very few Spaniards are interested in obtaining proof of their spouse's infidelity, by the end of the novel it pointedly refers to the public discourses that shape what can and cannot be discussed, namely the failure of the Transition to make a meaningful break from the Francoist past. Carvalho does nothing to change this. He simply provides his report and pockets his cheque for the investigation. Such an outcome brings us back to the debate that Horsley identifies "on the question of whether the hard-boiled sub-genre possesses genuinely radical potential or is, in late twentieth-century terms, inherently conservative, imposing in the end a resolution that makes the private eye the instrument of a repressive political order" (2005: 9). What *Southern Seas* shows us is the crime novel's ability to bring any number of political concerns and issues, from transitional justice to environmental crisis, from economic exploitation to domestic violence, to the attention of a crime fiction-reading public who may not necessarily be interested in reading about these concerns in non-fictional analyses, such as histories, political tracts, documentaries, etc. Andrew Pepper argues that

> Detection is a means of social control as well as social revolution. The detective is opposed to dominant values and yet part of machinery through which those values are affirmed. He or she undercuts but also reinscribes relations of domination and subordination.
>
> *(2000: 7)*

As we can see in *Southern Seas*, crime fiction's relationship with politics is complex and multifaceted, challenging readers to take a stance on the contradictions the investigations reveal.

Bibliography

Bakhtin, M. (1981) *The Dialogic Imagination: Four essays*, trans. C. Emerson and M. Holquist, Austin: University of Texas Press.

Chandler, R. (1995) [1944] "The Simple Art of Murder", in *Later Novels and Other Writings*, New York: Library of America, 977–92.

Hart, P. (1987) *The Spanish Sleuth. The detective in Spanish fiction*, Cranbury: Fairleigh Dickinson University Press.

Haycraft, H. (1974) *Murder for Pleasure: The life and times of the detective story*, New York: Biblo and Tannen.

Horsley, L. (2005) *Twentieth-Century Crime Fiction*, New York: Oxford University Press.

King, S. (2018) "*E pluribus unum*: a transnational reading of Agatha Christie's *Murder on the Orient Express*", *Clues*, 36(1): 9–19.

King, S. and Whitmore, A. (2016) "National allegories born(e) in translation: the Catalan case", *The Translator* 22(2): 144–56.

Knight, S. (1980) *Form and Ideology in Crime Fiction*, Houndmills: Macmillan.

Jameson, F. (2016) *Raymond Chandler: The detections of the totality*, London: Verso.

Lutes, J.M. (2017) "Sirens blaring: desire and women-authored crime fiction in the mid-twentieth century", *American Literary History*, 29(1): 179–90.

Mandel, E. (1984) *Delightful Murder: A social history of the crime story*, London: Pluto Press.

McCann, S. (2000) *Gumshoe America: Hard-boiled crime fiction and the rise and fall of new deal liberalism*, Durham, NC: Duke University Press.

McCracken, S. (1998) *Pulp: Reading popular fiction*, Manchester: Manchester University Press.

Moretti, F. (1983) *Signs Taken for Wonders: Essays in the sociology of literary forms*, London: Verso.

Pepper, A. (2000) *The Contemporary American Crime Novel. Race, ethnicity, gender, class*, Edinburgh: Edinburgh University Press.

———. (2016) *Unwilling Executioner: Crime fiction and the state*, Oxford: Oxford University Press.

Santana, M. (2000) "Manuel Vázquez Montalbán's *Los mares del sur* and the incrimination of the Spanish Transition", *Revista de Estudios Hispánicos*, 34: 535–59.

Symons, J. (1992) *Bloody Murder: From the detective story to the crime novel, a history*, London: Pan Books.

Vázquez Montalbán, M. (1999) *Southern Seas*, trans. P. Camiller, London: Serpent's Tail.

Vosburg, N. (ed.) (2011) *Iberian Crime Fiction*, Cardiff: University of Wales Press.

37

CRIME FICTION AND THE CITY

Eric Sandberg

Franco Moretti has described literary forms as "*ortgebunden*" or "place-bound": Each has "its peculiar geometry, its boundaries, its spatial taboos and favorite routes" (1998: 5). To the pastoral, Arcadian fields; to the adventure story, the unexplored wilderness; and to crime fiction, the city. The "unquestionably central place" of urban spaces in crime writing may thus seem inevitable, given the demands of the literary form and the conditions that prevail in the urban environment (Schmid 1995: 244). Our concept of the city encompasses many contradictory notions – extreme poverty and economic opportunity, freedom from traditional social relations and the confinement of close spaces, personal anonymity and the presence of the crowd – but it almost always includes a sense of danger. Take thousands or millions of people from different cultural and religious backgrounds, remove them from their traditional social networks, pack them into a dense, confined and complex space, add extreme disparities of wealth, and you have created not just a city, but the perfect conditions for crime as well. And also, as *homo sapiens* is a story-telling animal, the perfect conditions for stories about crime.

Nonetheless, the link between crime fiction and the city is not ineluctable, but historically contingent. While the city has come to signify, among other things, danger, for much of its history it was understood as a place of relative safety, whose walls, real or figurative, kept danger at bay. It is thus unsurprising that many early narratives of crime take place outside of urban environments. Robin Hood did not rob the rich on the mean streets of Nottingham, but in Sherwood Forest; the blood-curdling tales collected in various editions of *The Newgate Calendar* in the late eighteenth and early nineteenth centuries concerned not just the footpads and murderers of London, but also highwaymen and bandits; and, in a very different cultural context, when a young man travels to the city in the fifteenth-century Chinese *Gong'an*, or court-case tale, "Dragon-Design Bao Sentences the White Weretiger", he encounters danger not at his destination, but in the wilderness he must cross to reach it (Idema 2009). In these stories, and many like them, the countryside or wilderness is a place of danger through which city dwellers must travel at great personal risk, beyond the protection of the justice system and thus vulnerable to crime.

Crime in the city: The degraded mass

It is difficult to locate the exact point at which the city transformed in the collective imagination from a place of safety to a place of danger: The process is only ever partial (the city remains associated with many things besides crime, from cultural sophistication to multicultural cosmopolitanism) and it occurred at different times in different places. But the transformations associated with the intensification of the industrial revolution in nineteenth-century Europe are crucial to the development of the intimate association of crime and the city, and to the rise of the detective novel. In part, this was a response to the astonishing growth of cities during the century. London, for example, already the largest city in the world in 1815, tripled in size to more than three million inhabitants over the next forty-five years, and had doubled again by the early years of the twentieth century (Emsley et al. 2018). These exploding populations frequently lived under conditions which were seen as ideal incubators for criminal behaviour. Consider, for example, Friedrich Engels' 1845 study *The Condition of the Working Class in England* which offers descriptions of Manchester's streets covered in "heaps of refuse, offal and sickening filth", its air darkened by "the thick smoke of a dozen factory chimneys", living conditions which dehumanise – and criminalise – its inhabitants (1999: 72–73).

Also critical to the conceptualisation of the city as a criminal site was the presence of the crowd. Walter Benjamin's influential analysis of the relationship between the urban environment, the figure of the *flâneur*, and the emergence of detective fiction highlights "fear, revulsion, and horror" of the urban mass as central to the form's engagement with the city (qtd. in Salzani 2007: 172).[1] The crowds encountered in the city are seen (from the perspective of the bourgeoisie) as both a threat to order in their own right, and as "an asylum that shields an asocial person from his persecutors" (qtd. in Salzani 2007: 171). The ability of criminals to disappear into the crowd, and the need this implies for someone to track them down, has a direct bearing on the origins of the detective story, as the city is reimagined as wilderness, "a site of danger and adventures" in which the detective acts as a hunter, pursuing and capturing criminals in the urban jungle (Salzani 2007: 169).

The city crowd, the urban detective

This degraded and threatening urban environment appears throughout nineteenth-century fiction. Charles Dickens's *Bleak House* (1852–1853), for example, was instrumental in encouraging public acceptance of policing: A city which contains Tom-All-Alone's, a disreputable street home to "a crowd of foul existence that crawls in and out of gaps in walls and boards" is a city in need of protection (2012: 266). In Fyodor Dostoevsky's 1866 *Crime and Punishment*, Saint Petersburg's squalor and crowding leads to feelings of "deepest revulsion" in Raskolnikov that contribute to his crime (2007: 4). Émile Gaboriau's *Monsieur Lecoq* (1869) opens in a neighbourhood of Paris, "haunt of numerous homeless vagabonds, and escaped criminals and malefactors", and moves on to a triple murder in a drinking den (1975: 3). In these novels, the "urban stress" of poverty, overcrowding and squalid living conditions is countered by the presence of a detective figure (Knight 2016: 772). Gaboriau's Lecoq, like Dickens's Inspector Bucket, and Dostoevsky's Porfiry Petrovich, is the narrative embodiment of what Stephen Knight calls "detection at a disciplinary level of intensity" (Knight 2016: 772). Here Benjamin's *flâneur* is transformed into the detective through an intensification of his – or her, as in the case of the numerous nineteenth-century women detectives who are being reinscribed in literary history – role as an observer: The "eye of the stroller" as Salzani writes, "may be casual, and that of the detective purposeful, but both need to be simultaneously wide-ranging and deeply penetrating" (2007: 175).

The various strands of nineteenth-century urban crime fiction are apparent in Arthur Conan Doyle's Sherlock Holmes stories. Holmes claims that "the lowest and vilest alleys in London do not present a more dreadful record of sin than does the smiling and beautiful countryside", but the novels and short stories in which he appeared over the course of his forty-year career have predominantly urban settings (Doyle 1993: 280). The crimes that occur in this urban environment often rely on the anonymity of the crowd. In "The Engineer's Thumb", Mr Hatherly is particularly vulnerable to Colonel Lysander Stark because he is an "orphan and a bachelor [...] residing alone in London" (203). The colonel – in reality a German forger – is in turn able to carry out his plot due to his own anonymity. Holmes's ability to track down criminals in the urban wilderness relies on his uncanny perceptiveness, his ability to see and understand the signs left by the city, and the passage of the characters through it. Moretti has observed that London is tantamount to an illegible text, or at least one that is "not easy to read", and for most this may well be true (1998: 78). Part of the pleasure of reading Doyle's work arises from observing Holmes's virtuosity in the task of urban decipherment.

Holmes does not (or not just) reflect the reality of the urban environment, however, but is part of what Benjamin describes as a "phantasmagoric" attempt to "escape the fundamental boredom and repetitiveness of capitalist modernity" (qtd. in Salzani 2007: 170–71). This fantasy transforms the city from the site of monotonous and repetitive labour into a site of adventure, confrontation and exaltation. This fantastic city exists, as Moretti points out, in direct counterpoint to the realities of urban crime and poverty: In Doyle's work, for example, crime occurs, is investigated and solved in the wealthy parts of London, while the very real crime of the poor quarters is ignored (Moretti 1998: 136). The narrative demand for mystery, for a puzzle upon which Holmes can demonstrate his ability to decipher the city's palimpsest, excludes the real world of crime. When an unemployed factory worker comes home drunk to a one-room hovel, half a dozen hungry children and an angry wife, murder may well ensue, but there is no mystery to be solved.

Golden Age and hardboiled: The threatening city

The pattern set by Holmes was tremendously influential: Crimes carried out in, and enabled by, urban settings, and unravelled by the detective's logical prowess became almost ubiquitous in crime fiction. A competing pattern, however, is represented by the most prominent exception to this dominant urbanism: Golden Age detective fiction. This is a form of crime fiction that is generally seen as turning its back on the city, relocating crime and detection from the teeming, dangerous metropolis to the deceptively peaceful milieu of isolated rural communities. There are structural reasons for this shift in setting: Golden Age detective fiction relies heavily on the puzzle format, which in turn depends on a controllable space (e.g. a country house) and a limited cast of characters (e.g. the owners, guests and servants) for its particular effects. It also arguably represents an escapist response to physical and social transformations in the urban environment caused by World War I and subsequent economic dislocation.

What is missing here, however, is, as Knight has argued, the extent to which Golden Age detective fiction continues to associate crime and the city (2016: 777). While many Golden Age mysteries are indeed set in rural communities – Agatha Christie's astonishingly violent village of St Mary Mead is a classic example – many others are urban. Of Dorothy L. Sayers's eleven Lord Peter Wimsey novels, five take place largely in London. And even in resolutely rural Golden Age mysteries, the source of the disruption to the social order – generally the murderer – is frequently associated with the city. In E.C. Bentley's *Trent's Last Case* (1913), the rural idyll of White Gables is destroyed by the insane jealousy of New York financier Sigsbee Manderson;

in Sayers's *The Nine Tailors* (1934) the rural order of the nostalgically evoked Fenchurch St Paul is threatened by the actions of butler Geoffrey Deacon – who was brought to the village from London – and his London-based jewel thief accomplice Nobby Cranton. One of the things Golden Age detective fiction does, then, is cauterise the urban wound to protect the (imagined) purity of the countryside.

The interwar period saw the emergence of another, explicitly urban form of crime writing, the hardboiled, which rose to prominence in America, and was from early in its history conceived of in direct opposition to Golden Age detective fiction. Instead of cerebral ratiocination and the logical solution of puzzles, we have direct and at times brutal violence. Instead of the amateur sleuth, we have the professional private eye. Many critics have noted the semantic overlap between the "eye" of the private eye and the "I" of the observing subject, and as Peter Messent points out, this type of embodied "vision and supervision" is closely associated with urban spaces (2013: 62). Thus, instead of the Golden Age's threatened rural paradise, in the hardboiled we find the gritty, compromised modern city. Indeed, Raymond Chandler's early, highly partial and highly influential discussion of the origins of the hardboiled, "The Simple Art of Murder", situates this format as a specifically urban alternative to the rural English tradition, claiming that it takes "murder out of the Venetian vase" – which is to say the stereotypical Golden Age country house – and drops "it into the alley", in other words the famous "mean streets" of the city (1988: 14, 18).

The hardboiled vision of the city has been hugely influential, and while it shares many of the features identified by a theorist like Walter Benjamin as central to early detective fiction, including the importance of the *flâneur*/private-eye figure and the metaphorical identification of the city with the dangers of the wilderness, it possesses a number of special traits. In contrast with the relatively cohesive and legible nineteenth-century European metropolis, the hardboiled city is, as Fredric Jameson argues in his discussion of Chandler, fundamentally fragmented (2016: 6–7). This compartmentalised, stratified and chaotic urban environment is a place in which violence is neither an external threat nor an intermittent interruption of order and decency, but "a secret destiny", an inevitable accompaniment of the fundamental facts of the city: Its wealth, its explosive, unregulated growth and the transient rootlessness of its inhabitants (5). The figure that ties these two phenomena together – the atomisation of the city and its pervasive violence – is the private eye, an "involuntary explorer of the society", whose investigations both bind together individual parts of the fragmented city, and precipitate its violence, inciting a "series of murders and beatings [...] as though they existed already in a latent state" (25).

Jameson's analysis is relevant to the subgenre as a whole. In Dashiell Hammett's novel of urban degeneration, corruption and violence, *Red Harvest* (1929), the Continental Op, a nameless detective based out of San Francisco, unveils the deeply ingrained corruption and violence of the fictitious city of Personville. While the physical degradation of the city – it is "an ugly city of forty thousand people, set in an ugly notch between two ugly mountains" – is clearly symptomatic, this is not the main problem (1974: 5). Nor is the fact that the government, big business and organised crime are more or less indistinguishable here. The real problem – what earns the city its moniker "Poisonville" – is that the various murders investigated by the Continental Op are committed by the few decent people in the town: This is the corrupting influence of the hardboiled city (128). Even the detective himself is tainted: "It's this damned town. Poisonville is right. It poisoned me" (128). In Chandler's work, Los Angeles is figured as less overtly violent, but Marlowe's investigations reveal a reality of crime, vice and degeneration underlying the city's meretricious surface. In *The Big Sleep* (1939), for example, the Sternwoods' façade of wealthy respectability is undermined, first, by their connections to the underworld of organised crime, and, second, by the murderous lunacy of the family's youngest daughter,

Carmen. Metaphors are central to Chandler's work, and his description of Carmen's laughter – it sounds like "rats behind a wainscoting" – is indicative not just of her personal corruption, but of the evil which moves behind the city's veneer (2000: 110). This model of the city has been influential and lasting. While American writers have adapted the form to deal with questions of gender (e.g. Sara Paretsky), race (e.g. Walter Mosely) and history (e.g. James Ellroy), and international writers have adapted the form to local circumstances (e.g. Jakob Arjouni), the vision of the city as an incoherent site of violence and corruption, bound together, and thus made legible by the investigative activity of the private eye, has remained stable.

The police procedural: The multiple city

Despite the legacy of the hardboiled, recent theoretical work has identified its patterns of urban representation as flawed. Philip Howell, for instance, argues that hardboiled is unpersuasive in its representations of the city, largely because it shares the central conceit of classic detective fiction: The activity of the detective figure, and its narration, embody the "rationalist belief that the city is ultimately knowable" (1998: 360). The city may be complex, confusing and threatening, but by narrating the investigators' successful progress through its spaces, hardboiled alleviates urban anxiety. The result is a form of narrative that fails, whatever its overt political alignment, to challenge bourgeoise ideology. Schmid identifies a second problem with the form in its individualism, which both separates crime from the social forces that lie behind it, and the detective from the community through which she moves (1995: 264).

Howell identifies the police procedural, a post-World War II form that developed in America but quickly became international, as a type of crime narrative that is better able to address the particular epistemological challenges presented by the urban environment (1998: 365). It is, Howell argues, more attentive to the detailed particularities of the city; it replaces the conventional individual detective with an ensemble cast of police, suspects, witnesses and bystanders, thus offering multiple perspectives on urban life; and in doing so it recognises the city as a space that is only ever partially knowable (365–67). It thus offers a "formal analogue of the multiple stories, overlapping narratives, partial truths, and sheer contingency of city life" (367). Messent links Howell's theories with Michel de Certeau's work on the city as representable through an accumulation of multiple journeys and narrations: The "formal correlative" for this, he claims, is crime writing – like the police procedural – that offers the diverse viewpoints of a range of individual perspectives (2013: 68). Only thus can the city be adequately and honestly represented.

The rich openness of the form discussed by Howell and Messent may help explain the enormous success of the police procedural, which now represents probably the most successful branch of crime fiction. Ed McBain is often identified as its first major practitioner, and his 87th Precinct novels are, despite their association with the figure of Detective Steve Carella, fine examples of the form's use of multiple, diverse points of view to render the modern city – in this case a fictionalised New York called Isola – legible. Joseph Wambaugh's *Hollywood Station* (2006–2012) dispenses with the central investigative figure altogether. There is a small number of recurring characters in these novels, but Wambaugh is much more interested in the group as a means of representing urban experience. A similar pattern is perceptible in the many international versions of the police procedural that have followed in McBain's footsteps. The ten volumes of Swedish novelists Maj Sjöwall and Per Wahlöö's *The Story of a Crime* (1965–1975) are frequently marketed as the Martin Beck novels, but they deploy a large cast of varied characters to map urban space and experience, and use this diversity as part of their sustained critique of establishment politics. Hideo Yokoyama's Japanese bestseller, *Six-Four* (2012), relies on a huge cast of characters from different groups (the news media, the police administration, the criminal investigation bureau, the government) to explore the ramifications of a re-opened cold case, and the nature of Tokyo as a bureaucratic city.

This approach is even more relevant in the era of globalisation. As Messent argues, it is now fruitless to link crime to a single space or set of spaces. Contemporary criminal activity is no longer geographically contained, and crime fiction frequently reflects this reality (2013: 73). This transformation can be seen in works like Don Winslow's *The Cartel* (2015) and in Hans Rosenfeldt's 2011 Danish-Swedish television series *Broen/Bron* (*The Bridge*), which focus on the role of national borders in crime, but also in works like Vikram Chandra's *Sacred Games* (2006) which embed the modern metropolis in a global context.

Vikram Chandra's *Sacred Games*

First published in 2006, Chandra's *Sacred Games* has earned considerable critical acclaim and, with the release of Netflix's 2018 adaptation, international celebrity. While the novel could be associated with Henry James's pejorative characterisation of nineteenth-century novels as "large, loose, baggy monsters" (1921: xi), blending elements of the political thriller, the domestic family saga and the historical novel across a sprawling set of narratives, it is at heart an urban crime novel. Largely set in early twenty-first-century Mumbai, and the same city (then known as Bombay) in the 1980s and 1990s, the novel employs many of the tropes and patterns of urban detective fiction to represent a threatening yet beloved urban environment through a multitude of narratives which exceed by a long measure the classic quest of the detective to trace and capture the criminal.

Some aspects of the representation of Mumbai in Chandra's novel align very closely with the analysis of the city's relationship to crime writing presented here. It is, in the first instance, a site of squalor and poverty of a sort that has long been remote from the experience of first-world city dwellers, and which is reminiscent of the degraded living conditions of the Victorian city analysed by Engels and used to such effect by writers like Dickens and Dostoevsky. Many of the novel's characters live in "appalling squalor" amidst "the miasma of refuse" from nearby garbage dumps, and these slums are represented as sources of danger and criminality (2006: 912). The "Bengali Bura", home to many of the city's recent immigrants, is a degraded urban space of "dirt and filth and garbage" and the home of one of the novel's many murder victims, Shamsul Shah, hacked to death with cleavers in the doorway of his family's shack (20). Chandra's Mumbai is also defined by the crowd, filled with the "enormous bustle of millions on the move" (72). It is thus a perfect place for criminal figures – and indeed anyone who wishes to remain anonymous – to conceal themselves: It is a "jungle where a man can lose his name and become something else" (111). The main criminal figure of *Sacred Games*, Ganesh Gaitonde, moves from country to city first to escape his family, and then deeper into the city to avoid the consequences of the murder and robbery of his boss, a prime example of the way the urban environment both conceals and nourishes criminal elements. But even Gaitonde must contend with the facelessness of the city-dweller. As he struggles to expand his criminal empire into the territory of other gangs, he comes across an urban cipher, one Vilas Ranande, who remains stubbornly anonymous despite the efforts of a network of informants: "Nobody knew where he lived. Nobody could tell me if he was married, if he had children, if he had a taste for gambling, nothing" (117).

Perhaps most importantly, the Mumbai of *Sacred Games* is a fragmented, chaotic city in which great wealth exists side-by-side with horrendous poverty, and the site of an interconnecting network of corruption and obligation. The venality ranges from bribes accepted by local police – as the novel opens, we see Police Sub Inspector Kamble negotiating what would be called an under-the-table payment if it were not so obvious for a "No Objection Certificate" authorising the release of a body – to the higher echelons of the justice system (6). Deputy Commissioner Parulkar is the central figure here, a grandmaster of the subtle art of contact and double-contact and back-channel, of ministers and corporators cultivated and kept happy, business interests allowed room for profits, backslapping and exchanges with commissioners of police, favours finely weighed and dispensed and remembered, deals made and forgotten", who balances precariously between powerful organised crime groups and the government (9). The primary detective figure of *Sacred Games*, Inspector Sartaj Singh, is not immune to the corrupting influence of the city. He acts as Parulkar's bagman, collecting money from, for example, the Delite nightclub and passing it up the chain of command, and even at times accepting bribes on his own: "Sartaj took cash now, and was grateful for it" (23).

As in much crime fiction, the detective's progress through the city reveals the network of connections that underlie its apparent chaos and fragmentation. This can take the form of corruption, but also of other sorts of obligation, the types of relationships that Gaitonde describes as "the connections that wrap us from head to foot and bind us to each other, as invisible as gravity but as powerful" (264). While Sartaj Singh and Ganesh Gaitonde share the narrative focus of *Sacred Games* (quite literally, with alternating chapters focalised through Singh and narrated by Gaitonde), their experience of the city is expanded on by a host of other perspectives and sub-narratives. The novel is thus the sort of plural text Howell and Messent identify as best suited to representing the modern city. Singh's investigations are aided by a team of other police officers, most notably Constable Katekar, while Gaitonde is surrounded by not just the members of his gang, but also by Jojo Mascarenas, his friend and personal procuress. Characters like these (and many others who are only tangentially connected to the main narrative) offer readers a broad view of Mumbai's many lives, from Jojo's relatively affluent middle-class life to Katekar's respectable but nonetheless straitened working-class existence. The de-centred approach, which moves through Mumbai both geographically and temporally, situating the narrative in both its historical and social context, is an attempt on Chandra's part to do justice to a city that is, as Sartaj Singh recognises "too vast" and thus "impossible to know" from any single perspective (23).

While *Sacred Games* is in some ways a historical novel, tracing its characters' lives back to the 1947 partition of Pakistan and India, it is also very much a novel of the twenty-first century. In part, this is because it recognises that the city does not exist in isolation: It is connected to a complex global network of capital, information and politics. Gaitonde's first fortune is made smuggling gold abroad; the profits of Parulkar's graft are invested in Swiss banks; Mumbai's organised crime is run from Dubai and yachts off the coast of Pataya, well beyond the reach of Sartaj Singh and his colleagues. Even Katekar, a very local figure, is exposed to the international context of his city as he reads his morning paper: "Bomb blast in Israel, four dead. Exchange of fire across Line of Control, situation in Srinagar tense" (71).

As part of this recognition of the globalised context of the modern city, the threat to Mumbai in *Sacred Games* – the risk of nuclear destruction in a terrorist attack – arises not from local criminals, but from abroad. Gaitonde is a gangster, but he loves his city, and has in fact physically built substantial parts of it as he has built his criminal empire, particularly the shanty town of "Gopalmath, the habitation of my heart, the town that I had caused to be built, brick and brick" (386). The nuclear threat to Mumbai arises out of the larger geopolitical context in which the city is situated, and which is largely inaccessible to both detective and criminal. The smaller struggle against crime in the city, against pickpockets, thieves, blackmailers and murderers is dwarfed by the struggle against total destruction. What is particularly interesting here is not the way *Sacred Games* yokes the crime novel to the traditions of the international thriller, but the fact that the potential attack on Mumbai is directed at the very plurality and multiplicity that the form of the novel works so hard to capture. The ultimate criminal figure of the novel, Gaitonde's Guru, is a religious zealot whose goal is to trigger nuclear holocaust to purify the city and the nation as a whole, to wipe away the "resplendent and rotting flesh" (301) of Mumbai and replace it with "perfection [...] symmetry [...] internal consistency" (813). It is only through the personal sacrifice of the policeman Singh (of the loyalty he owes to his mentor and commander Parulkar) and the criminal Gaitonde (of his life) that the catastrophe is averted, and the contemporary city, in all its multifarious splendour, decay and crime is able to survive.

Note

1 Benjamin's comments on detective fiction are scattered widely throughout his body of work, but Carlo Salzani's overview, cited here, collects them and offers a useful analysis of his reading of nineteenth-century crime fiction as a response to the perceived threat of the city.

Bibliography

Chandler, R. (1988) "The simple art of murder: an essay", in *The Simple Art of Murder*, New York: Vintage, 1–18.
———. (2000) *The Big Sleep and Other Novels*, London: Penguin.
Chandra, V. (2006) *Sacred Games*, London: Faber & Faber.
Dickens, C. (2012) *Bleak House*, London: Penguin English Library.
Dostoevsky, F. (2007) *Crime and Punishment*, trans. R. Pevear and L. Volokhonsky, London: Vintage.
Doyle, A.C. (1993) *The Adventures of Sherlock Holmes*, ed. R.L. Green, Oxford: Oxford University Press.
Emsley, C., Hitchcock, T. and Shoemaker, R. (2018) "London history – a population history of London", *Old Bailey Proceedings Online*, March, www.oldbaileyonline.org/static/Population-history-of-london. jsp#a1860-1913 (accessed 10 July 2018).
Engels, F. (1999) *The Condition of the Working Class in England*, ed. D. McLellan, Oxford: Oxford University Press.
Gaboriau, É. (1975) *Monsieur Lecoq*, New York: Dover Publications.
Hammett, D. (1974) *Red Harvest*, London: Casell.
Howell, P. (1998) "Crime and the city solution: crime fiction, urban knowledge, and radical Geography", *Antipode*, 30(4): 357–78.
Idema, W.L. (2009) *Judge Bao and the Rule of Law: Eight ballad-stories from the period 1250–1450*, Singapore: World Scientific Publishing.
James, H. (1921) *The Tragic Muse*, vol. 1, London: Macmillan.
Jameson, F. (2016) *Raymond Chandler: The detections of totality*, London: Verso.
Knight, S. (2016) "The urban connections of crime fiction", in J. Tambling (ed.), *The Palgrave Handbook of Literature and the City*, London: Palgrave Macmillan, 767–84.
Light, A. (1991) *Forever England: Femininity, literature and conservatism between the wars*, London: Routledge.
Messent, P. (2013) *The Crime Fiction Handbook*, Chichester: Wiley-Blackwell.
Moretti, F. (1998) *Atlas of the European Novel 1800–1900*, London: Verso.
Salzani, C. (2007) "The city as crime scene: Walter Benjamin and the traces of the detective", *New German Critique*, 100: 165–87.
Schmid, D. (1995) "Imagining safe urban space: the contribution of detective fiction to radical geography", *Antipode*, 27(3): 242–69.

38

CRIME FICTION AND WAR

Patrick Deer

Crime fiction and war narratives have long been intimately connected, with military conflicts providing material for criminal plots, villainy, victims, mysteries, clues and detectives since the Golden Age of crime fiction that followed World War I. With their emphasis on crime, corruption, detection and policing within the framework of the sovereign nation-state, crime narratives have also proved particularly apt at registering post-war challenges of conflict zones. As literary genres, crime fiction and war narratives also share long-established ties to popular fiction, film and TV adaptations. Yet, as I will discuss here, their relations can be fraught: When these forceful genres collide, they often do so disruptively and agonistically, with powerfully productive results.

Strikingly, the era of seemingly permanent war of the early twenty-first century has seen the ascendancy of crime fiction, most notably in the "Golden Age" of television and streaming video, while war stories occupy a much more uncertain place in contemporary culture. Indeed, with a few exceptions, Iraq and Afghanistan war movies have been deemed "box office poison" for domestic audiences eager to consume the fantasy of lawless cruelty offered by series such as *The Sopranos*, *Breaking Bad* or *Game of Thrones*. Crime fiction reigns supreme in the "Forever War era", where recent war narratives appear to need the crime genre to impose coherence and interpretive order on their fictional worlds.

The uneven relations between crime and war genres were delineated early on in Arthur Conan Doyle's *A Study in Scarlet* (1887). As Sherlock Holmes's hierarchical partnership with the ex-military Dr Watson made clear, when the crime genre and war narrative overlapped, crime fiction would typically have the upper hand. During the interwar years of the Golden Age of detective fiction and hardboiled fiction, the genres consolidated their respective identities and fictional territories. While both detective fiction and hardboiled crime writing often reflected the social fragmentation and ironic disillusion that followed World War I, as in Dorothy Sayers's shell-shocked detective Lord Peter Wimsey or the hardboiled detectives of Chandler or Hammett, their domestic settings tended to be on the home front and feature a civilian cast of characters. Indeed, Alison Light has argued that the whodunit between the wars was consciously constructed by post-World War I writers like Agatha Christie as a feminised "literature of convalescence" (Light 1991: 69–75). World War II saw some further intermingling of the genres, in the wartime noir of Graham Greene's *The Ministry of Fear* (1943) and Michael Curtiz's *Casablanca* (1942), or in the tropes of the returning veterans in Raymond Chandler's *The Long*

343

Goodbye (1953), Dorothy B. Hughes's *In a Lonely Place* (1947), Akira Kurosawa's post-war crime film *Stray Dog* (1949) and Carol Reed and Orson Welles's *The Third Man* (1949). But in post-World War II Victory Culture, war fiction and war films would remain a largely separate and stable genre with crime plots temporarily disrupting the war story's narrative logic, as in the criminal empire of Milo Minderbinder in Joseph Heller's satire *Catch 22* (1962) or the heist plot of *Kelly's Heroes* (1970). In the murky corruptions of the spy thriller, the Cold War saw some intermingling of genres, as in the seeming corruption of John Le Carré's hero Alec Leamas in *The Spy Who Came In From the Cold* (1963) or George Smiley's financial blackmail plot to ensnare the KGB spymaster Karla in *Smiley's People* (1982), yet crime fiction and war stories tended to occupy quite distinct generic terrains.

The era of globalisation that followed the end of the Cold War, by contrast, has seen a highly productive collision of crime and war genres, which has been escalated by the seemingly unending US global war on terror since September 11th, 2001. Recent decades may have seen what Lauren Berlant calls a "waning of genre" under neoliberalism (Berlant specifically targets melodrama and other older realist genres) (2011: 6), but the crime genre has been surging during the post-9/11 US wars in Afghanistan (2001-present) and Iraq (2003–2011). Crime narratives have, for example, been central to the Golden Age of Television, beginning with *The Sopranos* in January 1999, and to representing the American "Homeland" as a wartime home front. Although US global power projection typically disavows the discourse of imperialism and grand narratives, serial TV dramas display the panoramic representational confidence of an empire in a period both of violent military expansionism and domestic national crisis (Deer 2016: 65–70). When elements of war genres appear in recent crime fiction, they often serve as a bridge between seemingly distant war zones and the domestic spaces of crime fiction. By contrast, war narratives often seem to need the elements of the crime genre to render war visible and comprehensible.

Colliding genres

What happens when elements of crime fiction, its tropes, narratives, characters or conventions, collide with those of other genres? Despite its global reach and incorporation into a host of other discourses, crime fiction remains clearly identified with its roots in the protocols, proceduralism and gendered conventions of genre fiction, of noir, detective fiction, or police procedurals (Nilsson et al. 2017: 1–9). The advantage of elements of crime fiction is that they are so strongly identified and identifiable, as they tenaciously disturb and disrupt the genres they come into contact with. That is what makes them so helpful in rendering visible the shifting global spaces, locations, codes and definitions of what is defined as criminality, and the gendered and racialised populations targeted as the objects of criminalisation, in an otherwise extremely unstable representational field. It can also help us locate and represent the struggles of those populations to resist this logic of criminalisation, subjectification and domination.

What makes this generic mingling of crime fiction and war narrative possible, I would contend, is that they share a common structural logic. At the formal level, both crime fiction and war narratives show a strong interest in the metonymic relationships between part and whole. Both genres are powerfully shaped by metonymy (using the name of one thing for that of another with which it is associated) and synechdoche (the part standing in for the whole) (Burke 1969: 503–11; White 1973: 35–36). The historian Hayden White has usefully described metonymy as a rhetorical strategy "of part-part relationships, on the basis of which one can affect a *reduction* of one of the parts to the status of an aspect or function of the other" (35, italics in original). In crime fiction, clues often work metonymically as individual details at crime scenes which lead individual detectives to follow these parts, embedding them within an overall resolution and the larger whole of policing, the criminal justice system or the restoration of social order. War narratives display a similar interest in metonymic relationships between part and whole, where objects and people can become militarised and weaponised into violent forces, and individual protagonists and groups of characters reduced into subordinate parts of a military collective for the purpose of waging war.

But this metonymic logic works differently in crime stories, which explore the individualistic, often antisocial qualities of criminals and those who hunt them, and can display a striking scepticism towards and ironic critique of collective values. By contrast, in an often brutal logic of metonymical reduction, war narratives typically focus on the capacity for action and heroism within individuals but often subordinate them to a collective military discipline that ultimately makes individual troops interchangeable and dispensable. This formal divergence may explain in part why so few of the crime narratives of the current Golden Age of Television refer directly to America's wars in Iraq and Afghanistan, where the audience is often challenged to make indirect connections between domestic crime plots and America's distant war zones in the Global South.

But this powerful divergence in form means that when crime genres and war genres do collide, they often do so in a strikingly disruptive manner that causes problems for conventional narrative structure and narration. States of war can interrupt crime plots and subordinate criminal behaviour to militarised norms of duty, patriotism and discipline. Crime plots often disrupt war narratives by bringing into play individualised, morally corrupt agendas or the civilian procedures of policing and the state. Here we can usefully recover the more conflictual and agonistic side of Mikhail Bakhtin's work, where he represents dialogism (e.g. multiple voices and/or viewpoints) or the incorporation of other discourses in the novel less as a harmonious dialogue and more as a power struggle for generic dominance between intertextual elements saturated by ideological and historical traces that do not necessarily mesh (Bakhtin 1981: 348–49; see also Derrida 1980: 57–58). John Frow has described the way that "much of the logic of genre survives these translations from one context to another [...]. Shifting texts to another generic context [...] suspends the primary generic force of the text, but not its generic structure" (49–50). In the case of particularly forceful genres, like crime or war fiction, I would argue, their "generic force" cannot so easily be suspended and their logic will often collide with and disrupt that of the host genre.

Crime fiction and war stories

The uneven terms of the relationship between the crime and war genres – and the productive collision between them – is clearly visible in Doyle's *A Study in Scarlet* (1887). In the original novella, Sherlock Holmes's loyal companion and amanuensis, Watson, reveals that he is a veteran of Britain's colonial "Little Wars" in Afghanistan (Doyle 2001: 7–8). Agatha Christie readily adopted this formula in her Hercule Poirot mysteries, drawing inspiration from Belgian refugees she met in England during World War I, and giving Poirot his Dr Watson figure in the redoubtable World War I veteran, Captain Hastings.

Doyle's first venture into detective fiction mingles the crime and war genres, even incorporating a western frontier narrative, yet Watson's war stories remain strictly subordinate to Holmes's dogged pursuit of deduction and crime-solving. Indeed, after Holmes successfully deduces that he is a wounded veteran of the Afghan campaign, Watson is constantly disturbed and mystified by the horrors of civilian crime: "My nerves, which were steady enough on the field of battle, tingled as I thought of it" (61). The police also wrongly arrest a young naval officer for the first murder (52). Nevertheless, the intrepid Watson encourages Holmes to investigate the case of the murdered American, Drebber, as Holmes acknowledges:

> I must thank you for it all. I might not have gone but for you, and so have missed the finest study I ever came across: a study in scarlet, eh? Why shouldn't we use a little art jargon. There's the scarlet thread of murder running through the colourless skein of life, and our duty is to unravel it, and isolate it, and expose every inch of it.
>
> *(42)*

Here Holmes makes clear that detecting by "deduction" is a metonymic process of isolating and exposing the various parts of the investigation in order to solve the crime. To the hapless police inspectors, Gregson and Lestrade, he declares, "All this seems strange to you [...]. It is a mistake to confound strangeness with mystery" (64). Of course, Holmes's method is far from scientific and depends on his fin de siècle theatricality and spectacle, for which Watson is the perfect audience. Clearly Holmes needs Watson as his foil; while the ex-military doctor methodically and uncomprehendingly records the details, Holmes will arrange them into a metonymic combinatorial sequence, a "train" or "chain" of clues: "In solving a problem of this sort the grand thing is to be able to reason backward [...]. There are fifty who can reason synthetically for one who can reason analytically" (123). To an admiring Watson, he spells out synechdochically the final links in his chain of reasoning: "You see the whole is a chain of logical sequences without a break or flaw" (126).

The recent BBC/PBS television adaptation of *Sherlock* (2010–2017) featuring Benedict Cumberbatch as Holmes and Martin Freeman as Watson makes powerful use of the tropes of war fiction to complicate the crime narrative. Here Watson's identity as an Afghanistan war veteran is a much more dynamic force in the narrative. In the first episode, "A Study in Pink" (2010), set in post-9/11 London, Holmes rapidly identifies Watson as a veteran suffering from PTSD:

> HOLMES: When I met you for the first time yesterday, I said "Afghanistan or Iraq?" You looked surprised.
>
> WATSON: Yes. How did you know?
>
> HOLMES: I didn't know, I saw. Your haircut, the way you hold yourself, says military. The conversation as you entered the room – said trained at Bart's, so army doctor. Obvious [...]. Wounded in action, suntan – Afghanistan or Iraq.
>
> WATSON: You said I had a therapist.
>
> HOLMES: You've got a psychosomatic limp. Of course you've got a therapist. [...] you're a war hero who can't find a place to live.

Returning from combat trauma in Afghanistan and the homosocial world of the army, Freeman's Watson is an ideal partner for Cumberbatch's kinetic, camp Holmes. Once Watson agrees to join him on the case, Holmes is energised, racing out of 221B Baker Street, declaring "The game is on".

The relations between the crime and war tropes are more equal here, vying for significance. Clearly, this Watson supplies something that Holmes has been lacking. This queering of Holmes, thanks to his teaming up with a traditionally masculine ex-military character, is signalled by the ironic twist on Doyle's original title, renamed "A Study in Pink" instead of "Scarlet", suggesting both the powerfully mimetic desires at stake here and the disruptive force of the war genre within the crime narrative. As a veteran, Watson is also a rogue element, who mirrors and escalates Holmes's maverick behaviour. His unpredictable combination of common sense, duty and love for action also appeals to Inspector Lestrade and to Holmes's brother Mycroft, now a highly-placed figure in the British "Deep State". Mycroft Holmes suggests that Watson fire his therapist as she has wrongly diagnosed him with PTSD; in fact, he is missing the war and, like Holmes, is an adrenaline junkie. Watson saves Holmes from poisoning himself by shooting the villainous serial killer with deadly accuracy, displaying a singular *sang froid* about killing. As Mycroft notes to his subordinate before placing Holmes and Watson under heightened surveillance, "He may be the making of my brother". This fluid interplay of crime and war tropes suggests that while Holmes remains the ideal detective for the post-9/11 world, he must often rely on the masculinity of the military veteran and on the covert power of the national security state.

This collision of genres is abundantly displayed in Henning Mankell's Wallander novels, where the Nordic noir engages with larger transnational structures and there is a loosening of the form to include other kinds of materials. From early in the Wallander series, Mankell's work displays a powerful ethical anxiety, I would argue, about the social force of the crime genre, and the popularisation and internationalisation of forensic tropes in TV and film. By incorporating elements of war and thriller narratives, Mankell is able to bridge the Wallander novels' intensely local Swedish settings with post-Cold War conflict zones in the former Soviet Bloc and in the Global South. This metonymic exploration across genres also allows Mankell to represent the multiple temporalities that haunt even neutral Sweden, whether from repressed histories of fascism in World War II, or the Cold War geopolitical struggles implicated in the assassination of the Swedish Prime Minister Olof Palme in 1986. In *The White Lioness* (1993), Sweden becomes a training ground for a former Soviet KGB agent hired by a pro-apartheid faction of South African intelligence to help assassinate Nelson Mandela, and in *Firewall* (1998) Wallander gets caught up with computer hackers engaging in a cyberwarfare plot to destroy the global financial system. *The Troubled Man* (2009) has Wallander investigating a Cold War cover-up of nuclear submarine incursions into Swedish waters that involves penetration of its government by a CIA mole.

In *The Dogs of Riga* (1992), translated into English in 2001, Mankell disrupts his crime plot by drawing on Cold War genres as Kurt Wallander joins forces with a Latvian policeman, Major Liepva, to investigate the murder of two men who wash up in a life raft on a Swedish beach. After the Major is murdered by a shadowy Colonel, Wallander crosses the Baltic to Riga and plunges into a conspiracy that combines elements of the Cold War spy thriller and transnational drug smuggling. The novel contrasts the Swedish detective's melancholy, humane commitment to the liberal rule of law and police procedure to the disorienting merging of policing with intelligence and crime in the former Soviet Empire. As in other Wallander novels, *The Dogs of Riga* (2004) explores what Slavoj Žižek (2003) calls a "parallax view" of both Third World underdevelopment and First World neoliberal welfare capitalism that "provides an insight into the totality of today's world constellation" (Žižek 2003). But by insisting that there is an irrevocable split between these perspectives and no "common denominator" to link the local and the global, Žižek's reading misses the remarkably productive collision of genres in Mankell's crime fiction, leading him to misread *The Dogs of Riga* as an artistic failure. But the incorporation of elements of the Cold War thriller, I would argue, creates disturbing metonymic connections between Sweden and an underdeveloped Latvia struggling to decolonise while still occupied by Soviet forces.

Where Wallander is typically comfortable at home with the synecdochic decoding of clues, in Latvia he is dogged by a sense of proliferating parts and wholes which he struggles to reduce to a criminal plot, only belatedly assembling the evidence against two police colonels he needs to investigate the conspiracy. He follows the footsteps of the murdered Major Liepva both procedurally and romantically, aided by his widow and a dissident independence movement struggling against Russian mafia and KGB penetration. Wallander is caught in the midst of these competing forces, only to be saved when the corrupt Colonel Putnis, who is smearing the Latvian independence movement by linking it with the burgeoning methamphetamine drug trade in the former Eastern Bloc, is killed by the shadowy Colonel Murniers. The Major's grieving widow, Baiba, refuses to cooperate, ignoring Wallander's advances and injunction not to mourn because it impedes action. He returns to Sweden changed, yet cannot share either his existential epiphanies or Latvian war stories with his colleagues in the Ystad police. Mankell suggests that the collision of crime fiction with the post-Cold War struggle for national independence in the former Soviet empire produces profound disturbances that are dogged by secrecy and silence, challenging Wallander's humane commitment to historical memory and justice.

Wartime crime scenes

Recent war fictions have made frequent use of the crime genre to make sense of the "Forever War" era, to invoke detection, policing and the state in otherwise murky and seemingly lawless war zones. Why do contemporary Iraq and Afghanistan war narratives, like David O. Russell's *Three Kings* (1999), John Connolly's *The Whisperers* (2010), Richard House's *The Kills* (2013), Mary "M.L." Doyle's *The Peacekeeper's Photograph* (2013), John Renehan's *The Valley* (2015), Matt Gallagher's *Youngblood* (2016), Hilary Plum's *Strawberry Fields* (2018), or Nico Walker's controversial novel, *Cherry* (2018), seem to need crime plots and tropes of detection to map and represent their global spaces?

Crime fiction, where typically individual investigations are pursued within a delimited jurisdictional and territorial frame, as we have seen, needs the war and thriller genres in order to open itself up to the ramifications of corporate crime, global securitisation efforts, or terrorism. So in turn does war fiction need crime tropes. Incorporating elements from crime genres allows war writers to raise ethical and political questions by insisting that a crime has taken place in the war zone, that evidence needs to be gathered, and that detection must be pursued. Focusing on an individual crime helps make the horror and violence of war comprehensible, providing readers with answers in the form of the solution to a particular crime when there seem to be few ready answers available about war. This complicates the structure and logic of war narratives, offering war writers ways to represent unlawful behaviour in the war zones of the Global South that challenge the state of exception implied by conventional definitions of "war crimes". Using crime tropes also allows them to contest the privatisation and financialisation of war and the brute force of primitive accumulation that has accompanied globalisation since the end of the Cold War (Harvey 2005). This allows writers to insist on the possibility of detection, documentation and justice when the historical record and archive of the wars have been damaged (Deer 2017), and to explore the increasing militarisation of domestic life in the face of the paramilitary policing of the war on drugs or national security, even as the civilian-military divide widens and hardens. The complex temporal structure of crime fiction is also attractive to contemporary war writers because crime plots often involve a clash of histories and temporalities, where violence is like a palimpsest. Incorporating from crime fiction thus allows writers to invoke the legibility of the sovereign nation-state in the face of increasingly opaque damaged totalities of neoliberal governmentality and transnational war zones (see Pepper 2016: 1–18; Pepper and Schmid 2016: 4–8).

Much of this is at work in David O. Russell's influential film about the 1991 Gulf War, *Three Kings* (1999), whose title echoes Rudyard Kipling's imperial romance *The Man Who Would Be King* (1888). Russell has described the film as a collision of crime and war genres: "It's basically a heist movie, I mean these guys are going off to steal something in this surreal environment; it's like the insanity of consumer culture crashing into contemporary warfare. It's a weird combination" (Russell 1999a), and as a satire of war: "it's got elements of *MASH, Apocalypse Now* and a heist in the middle of it" (Russell 1999c). *Three Kings* opens with the media spectacle and bacchanalia of US troops celebrating their supposed victory in the hundred-hour Gulf War. But the anticlimactic war narrative is interrupted by a criminal plot when three US Army reservists, Troy Barlow (Mark Wahlberg), Chief Elgin (Ice Cube) and the hapless Southerner Private Vig (Spike Jonze) accidentally find a map with the location of Saddam Hussein's bunkers containing looted Kuwaiti gold. To plot the heist, they join forces with a disillusioned special forces soldier, Major Archie Gates played by George Clooney, who has already questioned the American mission in the Gulf War to his commanding officer:

> ARCHIE GATES: Just tell me what we did here, Ron.
> COLONEL HORN: You wanna occupy Iraq and do Vietnam all over again? Is that your brilliant idea?
> ARCHIE GATES: Fuck it, I'm retiring anyway.
> COLONEL HORN: Until you do, you're an Army officer.
>
> *(Russell 1999b)*

When Gates leads the "three kings" to the Iraqi bunkers, they discover not only the looted gold but Kurdish refugees who have responded to the US call to rise up against Saddam Hussein, only to find themselves attacked by the Iraqi army and abandoned by the US military.

The heist plot draws attention both to the racialised violence of American culture and to the cynical motivations of the US effort to liberate oil-rich autocratic Kuwait, under the banner of democratic values, while leaving the Iraqi dictatorship in place. This is made clear in the celebrated torture scene in the bunker complex, where Troy is captured and interrogated by a young Iraqi officer, played by Saïd Taghmaoui, whose family has been killed by American bombing:

> CAPTAIN SA'ID: Your sick fucking country make the black man hate himself. [...] just like you hate the Arab and the children you bomb over here.
> TROY BARLOW: I don't hate children. This is illegal. The war's over.
> SA'ID: That's why you are illegal. You broke the ceasefire, and I think maybe even you steal the gold. So nobody know where you are, right? Your Army don't know. I'm gonna send you to Baghdad for a long time. Nobody found you. Do they care, buddy?
> TROY: Does who care?
> SA'ID: Do your Army care about the children in Iraq? Do they come back to help?
> TROY: No, they're not coming.
>
> *(Russell 1999b)*

This ironic confrontation in the bunker complicates the seemingly clear distinction between war crimes, like torture, the indiscriminate bombing of civilians, or the massacre of civilian refugees, and the wartime criminal adventure and the colonialist military plunder of occupied territory. Ultimately, however, *Three Kings* reverts to imperial romance, as the ironic collision of the heist plot with the postmodern media spectacle of the Gulf War restores Troy, Gates and Elgin's sense of honour, and their Western moral superiority, as they give agency to the confused Iraqi refugees. They bury the gold and lead the convoy of refugees to the border, where Gates reunites with the American TV reporter covering the attempted rescue. But the rescue goes awry when Colonel Horn cuts them off at the pass, arriving in Huey helicopters reminiscent of Colonel Kilgore in *Apocalypse Now* (1979). As military discipline is reasserted, the crime plot collapses. The Colonel tries to shut down the TV crew:

ADRIANA CRUZ: Why aren't you helping them?
COLONEL HORN: Because it's not our policy!

(Russell 1999b)

and orders Gates, Troy and Elgin to be arrested by military police. In the end, though, Gates trades the refugees for the stolen Kuwaiti gold, declaring:

GATES: Get those people over first. They helped us find it, Ron. We made a deal. It's a soldier's honor. You can't fuck them now. Come on. Return the gold. Save some refugees. Get that star.

(Russell 1999b)

Whether he is motivated by retrieving the gold and getting promoted to General, the invocation of "soldier's honor", or the witnessing presence of the TV crew, the Colonel is forced to do the right thing and demand that the Iraqi troops allow the detained refugees across the border.

Three Kings' satirical approach finds strong echoes in the ironic energies of recent Iraq and Afghanistan war films and fiction. Veteran writer Matt Gallagher draws ironically on crime fiction conventions in his 2016 novel, *Youngblood*, as Lieutenant Jack Porter, deployed to wage counterinsurgency warfare during the surge in Iraq, takes on the role of amateur detective. He decides to investigate the murder of an American soldier, Sergeant Rios, during the height of the violent militias war in 2006, motivated by the desire to get rid of his monstrous Sergeant Chambers who Iraqi sources tell him was involved in death squad killings and fabricating evidence. Chambers may also have killed Rios for "going native" in a romance with an Iraqi woman from a powerful local family.

In *Youngblood*, the recovery of Rios's remains does not solve Porter's problems; instead, the breakdown of the relative stability of counterinsurgency warfare draws Porter into the brutalising violence of the US occupation of Iraq, in which he can claim to be no better than his Sergeant. As Porter declares midway through his narrative, "Our grandfathers had pushed back the onslaught of fascism. Just what the fuck were we doing?" (2016: 135). To save the life of Rios's Iraqi lover, Porter goes rogue and steals Army money to pay an insurgent human trafficker, Yousef, to smuggle her across the border to safety. After Yousef is detained and interrogated, Porter nervously sits in his army trailer drinking "a glass of Rip It over ice" (336) and examines the evidence:

I sat down and opened the file. One hundred forty pages of interrogation transcripts awaited. […]
Q: You said earlier that you smuggled things other than weapons.
DETAINEE 2496: Yes.
Q: What?
DETAINEE 2496: Not what. Who.
Q: People.
DETAINEE 2496: People who wanted to get out of the country.
Q: Where did you take them?
DETAINEE 2496: Depends. Syria, usually. Jordan, sometimes. Lebanon.

Crime fiction and war

Q: And you did?

DETAINEE 2496: Of course. It was a business. I'm a businessman.

Q: Who would you do this for?

DETAINEE 2496: Whoever paid. Rich, poor, Sunni, Shi'a. Police, imams. Even worked with an American once.

Q: An American?

DETAINEE 2496: Yes. An officer.

Q: Why would an American officer work with you?

DETAINEE 2496: Business.

(Gallagher 2016: 336–37)

Luckily for Porter, he isn't named in the interrogation transcript. A refugee's life has been traded for American blood money, for "business". But another wartime crime scene is revealed and goes unpunished.

Conclusion

Crime fiction often makes use of the war and thriller genres in order to open itself up as an expansive, global genre, to represent transnational criminal activity and violence and to bridge seemingly distant war zones and the domestic spaces of crime fiction. The advantage of the crime genre for war writers is that, even in its most ironic or sceptical modes, it typically implies legality and discursive boundaries. These are often located in or defined against state sovereignty and the territoriality of the nation-state. This is a stark contrast to the expansionist energies and blurry boundaries of contemporary war discourse which tends to normalise and naturalise a state of permanent global warfare. So it is that crime stories and wartime crime scenes offer an alternative, helping us represent synechdochically both the damaged totalities and global spaces of war zones and to challenge the seemingly endless march of militarisation at home.

Bibliography

Bakhtin, M. (1981) "Discourse in the novel", in *The Dialogical Imagination*, Austin: University of Texas Press, 259–422.

Berlant, L. (2011) *Cruel Optimism*, Durham: Duke University Press.

Burke, K. (1969) *A Grammar of Motives*, Berkeley: University of California Press.

Deer, P. (2016) "Mapping contemporary American war culture", *College Literature*, 43(1): 48–90.

———. (2017) "Beyond recovery: representing history and memory in Iraq war writing", *MFS Modern Fiction Studies*, 63(2): 312–35.

Derrida, J. (1980) "The law of genre", *Critical Inquiry*, 7(1): 55–58.

Doyle, A.C. (2001) [1887] *A Study in Scarlet*, London: Penguin.

———. (2003) *A Study in Scarlet and The Sign of Four*, New York: Dover Thrift.

Gallagher, M. (2016) *Youngblood*, New York: Atria.

Harvey, D. (2005) *The New Imperialism*, Oxford: Oxford University Press.

Mankell, H. (2004) *The Dogs of Riga*, New York: Vintage.

McGuigan, P. (dir.) (2010) "A study in pink", *Sherlock*, television program, BBC, 24 October.

Nilsson, L., Damrosch, D. and d'Haen, T. (eds) (2017) *Crime Fiction as World Literature*, New York: Bloomsbury Academic.

Pepper, A. (2016) *Unwilling Executioner: Crime fiction and the state*, Oxford: Oxford University Press.

Pepper, A. and Schmid, D. (2016) *Globalization and the State in Contemporary Crime Fiction: A world of crime*, London: Palgrave.

Russell, D. (1999a) "Behind the Scenes of *Three Kings* Part 1", https://youtu.be/Eev9S8PyWgc (accessed May 2019).
———. (dir.) (1999b) *Three Kings*, DVD, Warner Home Video.
———. (1999c) "*Three Kings* Video Journal Part 1", https://youtu.be/5wkjGg_pbwU (accessed May 2019).
White, H. (1973) *Metahistory: The historical imagination in nineteenth-century Europe*, Baltimore: Johns Hopkins University Press.
Žižek, S. (2003) "Parallax: review of *The Return of the Dancing Master* by Henning Mankell", www.lrb.co.uk/v25/n22/slavoj-zizek/parallax (accessed May 2019).

39

CRIME FICTION AND GLOBAL CAPITAL

Andrew Pepper

"It's not personal, it's strictly business." So says Michael Corleone (Al Pacino) in *The Godfather* (1972) to justify his planned murder of a mafia rival. The meaning would seem to be clear. The world of crime, seen from the outside as violent and disorderly, in fact operates according to the rational logic of business and hence of capitalism as "a non-violent, civilized mode of material self-enrichment through market exchange" (Streek 2016: 213). In this reading, we can understand and perhaps even relate to Michael, since his proposed act of murder is not personal, but something empirically determined by the laws of marketplace competition. On closer reflection, however, there remains something inadequate about this reading because it lets both Michael and "business" off the hook. By reversing its logic, a different understanding of the relationship between crime and capitalism emerges, one where "business" itself, even when it would appear to be "non-violent", is better understood as a form of violent criminality (and where the violence is only ever thinly masked by reasonable language to make it seem more palatable). From this starting point, my aim is to trace the implications of this formulation both temporally (or historically) and spatially (or geographically), so that crime fiction's long-standing capacity for examining criminality as business and vice versa is opened out to consider the global dimensions of this predicament, i.e. where crime and indeed crime fiction are necessarily understood as a global phenomenon.

My point is not necessarily that capitalism and business are inherently violent, though as Harvey explains below, crime and capitalism both operate through dispossession and by appropriating someone else's wealth (and where the attendant violence is only ever partially abstracted). Capitalism, of course, is typically understood as non-violent in the manner paraphrased by Streek, and Marxist thought has often pointed to the ways in which power is concealed or hidden in language and ideology, requiring careful ideological critique to unmask its hidden logic. However, what distinguishes crime fiction's treatment and interrogation of capital is its insistence upon drawing out the violence which is often hidden by and in other types of fiction and modes of representation. The attendant collapse of any distinction between crime and capitalism is usefully set out and explored by Harvey:

> First, there is the vast array of what we would now consider extra-legal activities, such as robbery, thievery, swindling, corruption, usury, predation, violence and coercion

[...] Second, individuals accumulate wealth by legally sanctioned exchanges under conditions of non-coercive trade in freely functioning markets.

(2015: 53)

Harvey argues that while "theorists of capital circulation and accumulation typically exclude activities of the first sort as excrescences external to the 'normal' and legitimate functioning of the capitalist market", we need to "recognise the symbiotic relation between these two forms of appropriation" since there are "grounds for believing that an economy based on dispossession lies at the heart of what capital is foundationally about" (53–54). Harvey's reference to foundations here is relevant to my argument insofar as I want to suggest that early iterations of crime fiction – even before writing about crime was recognised as a discrete genre with its own codes and readerships – understood the interpenetration of crime and capital and explored its implications. John Gay's *The Beggar's Opera* (1728) is a good example (see Pepper 2016: 41–45). For what, Gay asks, distinguishes the activities of thief/thief-taker, Peachum, who stands at the helm of London's sprawling underworld and who trades the lives of his gang members when they are no longer useful to him, and who assigns these individual members a particular role according to "a particular division of labour" (Ruggiero 2003: 46), and of Macheath, the dashing highwayman who would seem to steal only from those who can afford it? As Matt the Mint puts it, "where is the injury of taking from another, what he hath not the heart to make use of?" (Gay 1986: 69). One reading of the play would be to underscore the latter's status as "social bandit" and as such someone who operates to stymy and oppose the capitalist underpinnings of modern society in a form of "pre-political" rebellion (Hobsbawm 1971: 2). A more persuasive reading, however, would be to point to Macheath's equivalent ruthlessness and capacities for exploitation and to draw attention to Gay's willingness to erode any distinction between crime and business – whereby no one is unco-opted and stands outside of the system and no separation exists between the thief who steals "your goods and plate" and a lawyer who steals "your whole estate" (1986: 60).

If, as Streek argues, "Capitalism is and always was about capital accumulation" (2016: 205), the first part of this chapter explores how the accumulative tendencies intrinsic to capital manifest themselves in crime fiction as criminal violence. In this context, criminality is also figured as an extension of capital production and the everyday activities of commercial exchange. For the proto-capitalist gangsters of Dashiell Hammett's *Red Harvest* (1929), failure "to keep abreast" of the expansionist tendencies of capitalism means, as Luxemburg puts it, "quitting the competitive struggle" and not just "economic death" (1951: 41–42) but perhaps also death quite literally. The relentless accumulation of surplus values, which as Luxemburg tells us, is the key "aim and incentive of capitalist production" (1951: 39), results both in the kind of geographically limited social destruction we see in *Red Harvest*, and also in new models of "accumulation by dispossession" (Harvey 2005: 144) which are global in nature and not contained by city, regional or state borders. The second part of this chapter examines how what Harvey calls the "spatial fix" – where the problems of over-accumulation are "solved" by colonial and neocolonial practices of theft or dispossession (2005) – is interrogated in or by the global turn in crime fiction. Here the capacities of two contemporary crime novels – Alan Glynn's *Bloodland* (2012) and Massimo Carlotto and Marco Videtta's *Nordest* (2005), translated by Antony Shugaar as *Poisonville* (2009) – to confront and lay bare the destructive potentialities of global capitalist expansion, figured as global criminality, are considered. The final section of the chapter examines whether we might identify the system of global capital itself as criminal insofar as it is premised on the violent "appropriation and accumulation" of the "common wealth created by social labour" by private individuals and corporations and their state backers. Alicia Gaspar de Alba's *Desert Blood: The*

Juárez Murders (2005) uses a familiar typical crime fiction set-up – the single dead body and the lone private detective – as its starting point. In light of this move, the chapter asks how well an individualist approach to the structural problem of crime is able to identify and counter not merely the individual criminal(s) but also what is abstracted by what Žižek calls "the smooth functioning of our economic and political systems" (2008: 2).

Primitive accumulation and (economic) death

If the symbiotic relationship between crime and business has been a feature of crime stories from the early 1800s onwards, this thematisation found its fullest initial articulation in the hardboiled US crime stories of the 1920s and 1930s. Novels like *Red Harvest* brought to the surface the era's conjoined anxieties about organised crime, unchecked industrial expansion and monopoly capitalism (i.e. concerns that too much power was concentrated in the hands of one or two key figures). As the "president and majority stockholder of the Personville Mining Corporation, ditto the First National Bank [and] owner of the Morning Herald" Elihu Willsson "was Personville, and he was almost the whole state" (1982: 12). However, following a vicious strike at the mine, where he had to bring in private gunmen to break it up, Willsson temporarily cedes control of the town to the criminal gangs who operate as proto-capitalists, competing with Willsson on albeit disadvantaged terms. For Luxemburg, and indeed for Willsson and the gunmen, who include Max Thaler, Lew Yard and Pete the Finn, the aim of capitalist production is "not a surplus value pure and simple" (i.e. extracting surplus profits from commodities and labour) but "a surplus value ever growing into larger quantities, surplus value ad infinitum" (1951: 39). What we might call "primitive accumulation", then, means staying ahead of the competition, and, as Luxemburg tells us, "failure to keep abreast of this expansion" means (economic) death. In Willsson's case, precisely because he has failed to keep a check on the gunmen's expansion from the realms of bootlegging and gambling into other activities, his pre-eminence is threatened. If Marx understood all too clearly the violence implicit in capital's accumulative tendencies (and famously described how capital "comes dripping from head to toe, from every pore, with blood and dirt" (2004: 926)), these practices are typically masked or abstracted in the social practices of capitalism. What is so instructive about a novel like *Red Harvest*, then, is that violence which is sparked by economic competition between Willsson and the gunmen is not abstracted but rather turned into spectacular excess. In the process, the despoiling of Personville into its alter ego, "Poisonville" – where "[e]verybody's killing everybody" (1982: 130) – spreads to every part of the body politic; as the novel's protagonist, the Continental Op, puts it, with his flair for language, "from Adam's apple to ankles" (61).

The problem, as Willsson and the gangsters discover, is that the violence which the Continental Op sets off in order to try and wipe out Willsson's competition, is "no good for business" (136), where business is understood both as the illegal activities of the gangs (e.g. gambling, bootlegging) and the legal enterprise owned and controlled by Willsson. In this case, the survival of the capitalist economy is paramount and the state – in the guise of the National Guard and the co-opted presence of the Continental Op – intervenes to return the town to Willsson's control; as the Op puts it, "all nice and clean and ready to go to the dogs again" (181). But of course the town was never "nice and clean" for at the start of the novel we are told about the "smelters" and "brick stacks" and that Personville, aka Poisonville, was "an ugly city [...] set in an ugly notch between two ugly mountains that had been all dirtied up by mining" (7). The despoiling of Personville and the destructive violence unleashed by economic competition between Willsson and the gangs, and the willingness of the state to sanction and even underwrite these conditions, are enabled by and indeed are the product of the market liberalisations first identified by post-World War II economist Karl Polanyi, namely "the running of society as an adjunct to the market" (2001: xxiv). Horsley uses the novel's political pessimism and statist solution to question its Marxist credentials, despite "its representation of the greed and exploitation of unrestrained capitalism" (2005: 167), but the particularity of her claim misses the extent to which most if not all crime fiction is better able to point out underlying problems than come up with lasting solutions (a critique one could just as easily redirect at Marx himself). To give Marx his due, he saw, arguably better than Hammett (who remained an *American* crime novelist), the global dimension of the problem of capital accumulation (2010: 164–65). In the next section, I consider how well the globalising imperative of contemporary crime fiction has been able to do what Hammett could not: Lay bare the globalising imperative of capital accumulation which, as Luxemburg tells us, "seen as an historical process, employs force as a permanent weapon, not only at its genesis, but further on down to the present day" (1951: 371).

The globalisation of capital, crime and fiction

The globalisation of crime fiction takes two distinctive forms: The opening up of new national traditions beyond the dominant Anglo-US axis and/or the recognition of hitherto under-examined national traditions; and the move within individual crime stories to examine the consequences of globalisation, especially in relation to the blurred distinction between crime and capitalism – for example, the conjoined domains of multinational corporations and globally networked organised crime groups. The two novels under consideration in this section – Glynn's *Bloodland* and Carlotto and Videtta's *Poisonville* – fall into both of these categories: The former, part of a new vanguard of Irish crime fiction that has really only emerged since the turn of the century, and the latter, part of a longer and more established tradition of Italian crime fiction that has been the focus of renewed critical scrutiny; and both examining what Carlotto calls "the famous locomotive" where "the legal and illegal economies merged in a single system" which is global or at least transnational in scope (2006: 108).

Carlotto and Videtta originally published their joint novel under the title *Nordest*, a reference to the Veneto region of Italy where Carlotto has set most or all of his novels. But the decision, taken by his translator, Antony Shugaar, in conjunction with his English-language publisher, Europa, to rename it *Poisonville* speaks to or about the ongoing influence of Hammett's *Red Harvest* as an exemplary work of political crime fiction and the notion, expressed by Walter Mosley, that we all now "live in a hardboiled world, a corrupt world, a kind of global Poisonville" (2009: 601). There are two crime scenes at the start of the novel, which Carlotto and Videtta attempt to reconcile. The first, more typically, because this is a crime novel, is the site where the corpse of Giovanna Barovier, fiancée to Francesco Visentin, the novel's first-person narrator and scion of a well-to-do Veneto family, is discovered. The second is a more general and indeed normal "scene" – "A winter Wednesday in northeastern Italy" where "four more companies had gone out of business" and "There were four more now-empty industrial sheds with 'For Rent' signs, posted in Italian and in Chinese". In this milieu where de-industrialisation, environmental degradation, people-smuggling and drug trafficking go hand-in-hand with the globalisation of finance and crime, we see two specific markers: The ubiquity of Chinese finance and the growing presence of "criminal cultures from Eastern Europe and the third world" (2009: 12–13). Here, then, the particular crime that sets the investigation in motion, the murder of Giovanna Barovier, is part of a much larger manoeuvre by the town's business and political elite, under the umbrella of the Torrefranchi Foundation, to shore up its position by moving its operations from the Veneto, with its high-cost base, to "an industrial site just outside Timisoara,

Crime fiction and global capital

in Romania" in order to be able to better compete with the Chinese who, we are told, "are eating our lunch on a daily basis" (96). With its position threatened by the influx of Chinese capital, the Foundation – in effect a privately-owned multinational corporation – led by the formidable Contessa Selvaggia in consort with Francesco's father Antonio, willingly sanctions arson, fraud and toxic waste dumping, and hires in "muscle" from the Romanian mafia in order to kill off those like Giovanna who threaten to expose the connections between legal and illegal domains.

What Harvey calls "accumulation by dispossession" (2005) takes multiple forms in the novel and is tied to the expropriation of the common wealth by the Torrefranchi Foundation for its own enrichment, the use of extra-legal means including violence to further this process, and the move to exploit lower wage costs in other parts of the globe (for example, Romania). In doing so, the line between crime and finance dissolves spectacularly as both allow capital to expand "more intensively (reaching ever deeper into social life and commodifying ever more human relations) and expansively (spreading globally, taking command of the production capacity and reproduction of whole populations)" (Haiven 2014: 38). The move by the Foundation to relocate its production to Timisoara in Romania is intended to bring down "[h]igh operating costs" (2009: 96) in Italy and exploit a lax regulatory regime in order to create "a free-market network […] that not even the most reactionary and pompous apparatus of government could hobble" (64). But insofar as this network and its financial benefits cannot be realised without violence, predation, theft and murder suggests that the global intensification and expansion of capital, described by Haiven and thematised in the novel, are characterised by Carlotto and Videtta as criminal. Hence, the novel's original crime scene is not a single dead body but rather the "Wednesday like any other". The role or function of crime fiction is not merely to thematise criminality but also to intervene and punish. Here, *Poisonville*'s far-reaching social and economic insights retreat into something more familiar, where, following Hammett's hardboiled original, individual solutions have to suffice. Francesco's private enquiries, together with the public ministrations of the quietly dogged Inspector Mele, publicly expose the guilt of the Foundation up to a point, but it is left to Francesco, as individual, to exact private justice for the murder of his fiancée, while the wider crimes of waste dumping and pollution go unpunished. If *Red Harvest* concludes with the return of Personville to Willsson "all nice and clean and ready to go to the dogs again", *Poisonville* ends with Contessa Selvaggia safely ensconced in the Foundation's new HQ in Romania using the language of "competition" and a "flexible labor market" (2009: 222) to abstract the violence which the novel has shown to be central to the company's successful global expansion.

The violence and destruction implicit and explicit in the social and territorial expansion of capital is again figured in Glynn's *Bloodland*, where the initial "crime" – the "accidental" death of Irish socialite-celebrity Susie Monaghan in a helicopter crash along with five others – is gradually linked to a wider political-corporate conspiracy premised on the convergence of crime and finance and on the criminality implicit in the capitalist practices of acquisition and accumulation (imagined as a global phenomenon). The conspiracy revolves around attempts by US corporate bigwig, Chuck Rundle, chairman and CEO of BRX, a privately-owned engineering and mining conglomerate, and Jimmy Vaughn, chairman of the private equity firm Oberon Capital Group, to exploit and murder in the present in order to speculate on and appropriate the future. Their plan is to acquire a mining concession in Congo (from under the noses of the Chinese) in order to stockpile a rare metallic ore, thanaxite, by exploiting local workers. The rare metal is then to be used in the development of new automated technologies of warfare. Here, then, the lofty language of risk management, tied to the mapping out of multiple possible futures ("You can only ever have access to the tiniest, slimmest portion of it" [2012: 355]), is underwritten by neocolonial exploitation and the aggressive cornering of the arms market. As such, the novel's individual "crimes" (for example, the staged helicopter "crash" and the exploitation of mine workers in the Congo) help to service the wider corporate power grab. Here, a nexus of multinational corporations, private security and equity firms and national governments (for example, in Ireland and the US) coalesce to produce what Wendy Brown calls a "neoliberal political rationality" (2015: 47) which requires the orientation of politics (for example, the decision of Rundle's brother to run for the US Presidency) towards the demands of capital and the usurpation of judicial principles by the logic of accumulation.

If this is the consummation of a process first identified by Polanyi and described by Streek: "Now states were located in markets, rather than markets in states" (2016: 22), it has implications both for our consideration of crime fiction *and* global capital. For just as an "Irish" crime novel like *Bloodland* no longer takes place predominantly in Ireland or deals with exclusively Irish concerns, the capacity of crime fiction, tied as it has been to the state's security agenda, to expose the ill-effects and indeed criminality of global capital flows must have its limits. But nor is it the case that states, at least ones as powerful as the US, wither away in the face of corporate expansionism. In *Bloodland*, Vaughn's ambitions, as chairman of Oberon and a sitting member on the Council for Foreign Relations, are linked to the accumulation of profit *and* enhancing the US's military capabilities: In this instance, by developing, in conjunction with the Pentagon, a fully automated battlefield management system with "lasers, sensors, antitank rockets, thousands of rounds of ammunition" (2012: 328) and with no scope for human error or "sentiment" (329). Typically, crime fiction has maintained and enacted an uneasy relationship with authority and *Bloodland* is no exception. As such, a set of corresponding (but equally uneasy) anti-corporate or anti-capitalist sentiments, also typically present in the genre, require that this kind of power grab be thwarted. Hence, in *Bloodland*, the conspiracy is exposed by Jimmy Gilroy, an Irish investigative journalist, and the fallout exposes Chuck Rundle and ruins his brother's tilt at the Presidency. But it is pertinent that the prime mover in the plot, Jimmy Vaughn, who best analogises capital accumulation under neoliberalism, is allowed to walk away unscathed. In doing so, Glynn suggests that he is untouchable precisely because he epitomises the logic of the free market, free trade and entrepreneurial rationality (even as this logic is shown to be founded upon greed, exploitation and violence).

Individual crimes, global systems: Or the human consequences of accumulation

The crime novel, by and large, tells individual stories and in the cases of, for example, *Red Harvest, Poisonville* or *Bloodland*, uses these individual stories to dramatise or at least bring into partial focus "structural violence" (Žižek 2008: 2) so that we see criminality not merely as individualised but more importantly as systemic. In this final section, I want to think about the capacities of one particular crime novel, Alicia Gaspar de Alba's *Desert Blood*, which tells the story of an individual murder, to lay bare the ills of an entire system: "a new, complex, interconnected spectrum of procedures for exploiting material and human resources" (Rodríguez 2012: 9–10) where the human resources in question comprise the hundreds of thousands of mostly poor, mostly dark-skinned and mostly female workers employed at the maquiladoras or assembly plants on the Cuidad Juárez side of the US-Mexico border. It is not strictly true that *Desert Blood* tells the story of a single murder, that of Cecilia, a pregnant woman whose baby the novel's protagonist, Ivon Villa, is going to adopt; rather, this murder is itself part of a series of murders also known as the femicides or feminicides – "the longest epidemic of femicidal violence in modern history" accounting for "over five hundred women

Crime fiction and global capital

[…] found brutally murdered on the El Paso/Juárez border" since 1993, with "thousands more […] reported missing and […] unaccounted for" (Gaspar de Alba 2010: 1). These murders were ineptly investigated by the Mexican authorities and routinely ignored, for a long while, by the local, national and international media. At the same time, they have been the subject of intense critical scrutiny by feminist and anti-capitalist scholars for the ways they connect the exploitation and disposability of precarious labour and a culture of uninhibited misogyny to the post-NAFTA (North American Free Trade Agreement) emergence of a particular kind of extreme capitalism: "corporate, monopolistic, global, speculative, wealth-concentrating, and predatory" (Rodríguez 2012: 12).

The challenge for *Desert Blood*, then, is twofold. First, it is to find a way of using the single murder of Cecilia, and Ivon Villa's private investigation into it, and subsequently the disappearance of her sister, to explain "how the threat of violent death continues to prevail as a technique of governance in contemporary settings" and where "a patriarchal state ideology" permits the violence to continue unimpeded (Wright 2011: 709, 726). And second, it is to dramatise these murders and their consequences for ordinary families in order to mobilise state and civic forces to shine a light at the multiple killers who remain hidden in plain sight. As we shall see, the fact that the novel is more successful in the latter task speaks to a larger problem for the genre, which I will try to address, briefly, in the conclusion. So when Cecilia is found murdered – "Stabbed to death and with a rope around her neck" (2005: 41) – the novel lets us see the grief and anger of her friends and family and their determination, together with civic organisations such as Contra el Silencio, to expose and punish the "Sick fucks running loose in this city" (42). And when Ivon visits the mortuary and actually sees the horrifically mutilated body "of the girl who was going to be her mother" (50), the effect is not merely shock and bewilderment but a desire to act, in consort with other predominantly female community figures, in contrast to the masculinist, individualising tendencies of hardboiled crime novels like *Red Harvest*. If *Desert Blood* manages to bear witness to the horrors of the femicides in order to inform and educate readers (especially Anglophone ones) and expose "the social, political, economic, and cultural infrastructure of the U.S.-Mexico border that makes it possible for such crimes to take place with impunity" (Gaspar de Alba 2005: v), it is arguably less successful in its efforts to implicate the wider practices and operations of global capital. In the end, Gaspar de Alba points to the "bilateral assembly line of perpetrators" (335) on both sides of the border who have made possible the production of violence: "Pornographers, gang members, serial killers, corrupt police men, foreign nationals with a taste for hurting women" (333). And while the novel ostensibly dismisses the "whodunit" aspect of many traditional crime stories, asking instead "Who was profiting from the deaths of all these women?" (333), it does, at the same time, give us a culprit or culprits and a solution which includes the safe return of Ivon Villa's sister, a move that reassures insofar as it suggests that individual action in the face of global capital's abstracted violence will and can produce good outcomes.

Conclusion

It is perhaps unfair to single out *Desert Blood* for this kind of criticism and for, effectively, doing what crime fiction has typically done, i.e. find individual solutions to problems that have been produced by wider systems (e.g. capitalism, colonialism, patriarchy) and where structural solutions or transformations do not appear to be possible. Therefore, rather than condemning specific crime novels for their depoliticising endings (whereby, as Moretti puts it, individuals are punished and yet the factory, as synecdoche of an entire system of social organisation under capitalism, "is innocent, and thus free to carry on" (1983: 139)), we should think about crime fiction in general outside or beyond the logic of their endings or redirect "attention away from the finality of the solution towards the dynamics of the investigation" (Gulddal, King and Rolls 2019: 6). In the case of *Desert Blood*, what endures longest in our minds is not the pat resolution, but the horrors of the murders and the difficulties faced in bringing the multiple parties responsible to account. But insofar as global capital is also mobile, elusive, crosses borders and cannot be easily discerned or indeed corralled, we might also argue that serial crime narratives are better equipped to lay bare its essential features and violences – rather than those like *Red Harvest, Poisonville, Bloodland* and *Desert Blood*, where some kind of definitive ending is attempted, and even where the solution is presented as a temporary sticking plaster. A TV series like *The Wire* (2002–2009) springs to mind, whereby the "narrative loops connecting the different dramatic scenes" across episodes and even series might be seen as "narrative cycles" which in turn are implicated in the various cycles of capital accumulation (Kraniauskas 2012: 181). And yet even here there are limits because, as Kraniauskas also argues, "the narrative pursuit of money through the cycle (or loop) of accumulation from the street into finance only goes so far" (181). Which is another way of saying that insofar as crime narratives are always located somewhere, for example, Northeastern Italy, El Paso-Juárez or indeed Baltimore, their abilities to track the flows and effects of global crime will always be somewhat circumscribed.

Bibliography

Brown, W. (2015) *Undoing the Demos: Neoliberalism's stealth revolution*, New York: Zone Books.
Carlotto, M. (2006) *The Goodbye Kiss*, trans. L. Venuti, New York: Europa.
Carlotto, M. and Videtta, M. (2009) *Poisonville*, trans. A. Shugaar, New York: Europa.
Gaspar de Alba, A. (2005) *Desert Blood: The Juárez murders*, Houston, TX: Arte Público Press.
———. (2010) *Making a Killing: Femicide, free trade and la frontera*, with G. Guzmán, Austin: University of Texas Press.
Gay, J. (1986) *The Beggar's Opera*, London: Penguin.
Glynn A. (2012) *Bloodland*, London: Faber and Faber.
Gulddal, J., King, S. and Rolls, A. (2019) "Criminal moves: towards a theory of crime fiction mobility", in J. Gulddal, S. King and A. Rolls (eds), *Criminal Moves: Modes of mobility in crime fiction*, Liverpool: Liverpool University Press, 1–24.
Haiven, M. (2014) *Cultures of Financialization: Fictitious capital in popular culture and everyday life*, Basingstoke: Palgrave Macmillan.
Hammett, D. (1982) *The Four Great Novels*, London: Picador.
Harvey, D. (2005) *The New Imperialism*, Oxford: Oxford University Press.
———. (2015) *Seventeen Contradictions and the End of Capitalism*, London: Profile.
Hobsbawm, E. (1971) *Primitive Rebels: Studies in archaic forms of social movement in the 19th and 20th centuries*, Manchester: Manchester University Press.
Horsley, L. (2005) *Twentieth-Century Crime Fiction*, Oxford: Oxford University Press.
Kraniauskas, J. (2012) "Elasticity of demand: reflections on *The Wire*", in L. Kennedy and S. Shapiro (eds), *The Wire: Race, class, gender*, Ann Arbor: University Press of Michigan, 170–92.
Luxemburg, R. (1951) *The Accumulation of Capital*, trans. A. Schwarzschild, London: Routledge and Kegan Paul.
Marx, K. (2004) *Capital: A critique of political economy, volume 1*, trans. B. Fowkes, London: Penguin.
———. (2010) *Essential Writings of Karl Marx*, St Petersburg, FL: Red and Black.
Moretti F. (1983) *Signs Taken for Wonder: Essays in the sociology of literary form*, trans. S. Fischer, D. Forgacs and D. Miller, London and New York: Verso.
Mosley, W. (2009) "1926 Poisonville", in G. Marcus and W. Sollors (eds), *A New Literary History of America*, Cambridge, MA: Belknap Press of Harvard University Press, 598–602.
Pepper, A. (2016) *Unwilling Executioner: Crime fiction and the state*, Oxford: Oxford University Press.
Polanyi, K. (2001) *The Great Transformation: The political and economic origins of our times*, Boston: Beacon Press.

Rodríguez, S.G. (2012) *The Femicide Machine*, trans. M. Parker-Stainback, Los Angeles: Semiotext(e).

Ruggiero, V. (2003) *Crime in Literature: Sociology of deviance and fiction*, London and New York: Verso.

Streek, W. (2016) *How Will Capitalism End?: Essays on a failing system*, London and New York: Verso.

Wright, M. (2011) "Necropolitics, narcopolitics, and femicide: gendered violence on the Mexico-U.S. Border", *Signs: Journal of Women in Culture and Society*, 36(3): 707–31.

Žižek, S. (2008) *Violence: Six sideways reflections*, London: Profile.

40
CRIME FICTION AND THE ENVIRONMENT

Marta Puxan-Oliva

Given the ability of crime fiction to engage critically with issues of racial and sexual discrimination, terrorism and drug trafficking, it is no surprise that crime writers should also use the genre to reflect on one of the most pressing concerns in the contemporary world: The environment. This chapter argues that the genre is especially well-equipped to mark environmental problems as a result of crime, which makes it a unique tool not only for depicting and discussing ecological crises and abuses, but also for directly exposing the criminal acts they involve and their violent effects on people and the environment. It is perhaps for this reason that crime novels have lately been increasingly interested in addressing environmental issues and using them to revisit and experiment with some of the genre's conventions. This trend contributes to the current blurring and challenging of the genre's limits, moving crime fiction towards a hybridised form better suited to representing environmental crises. It also encourages other genres to use crime fiction's narrative conventions to highlight criminality in environmental conflicts. Nevertheless, scholarship on the relationship between crime fiction and the environment is just beginning to emerge, as indicated by the special "Crime Fiction and Ecology" issue of *Green Letters* (Walton and Walton 2018).

Not all crime novels dealing with environment use it for the same ends. Distinctions should be made to clarify the specific uses that this chapter targets. In line with Abhra Paul's suggestion (2018: 80), in several crime novels environmental issues are marginal to the story's focus, while in others a crime related to the environment is the fictional core problem. Furthermore, the interest of some novels in environmental concerns challenges genre conventions and drives crime fiction towards hybridisation. This chapter addresses the ways in which crime fiction authors engage with the environment in novels where environmental crime is a central theme and/or a means of interrogating genre boundaries. By combining crime fiction studies and ecocriticism, the chapter describes this incipient field of criticism and gestures towards a number of potentially fruitful issues for future debate. In particular, it highlights the use of crime fiction to reveal the criminal activity contained in environmental degradation; the move of crime fiction and fiction dealing with environmental crime towards genre hybridisation; the global nature of environmental crime displayed in fiction and the systemic working of crime against the environment. These issues will also be analysed further through a case study of the Chilean novel *El alemán de Atacama* [The German of Atacama, 1996], by Roberto Ampuero.

Ecocritical approaches to crime fiction and the environment

Since the 1990s, the ways in which literature engages with the environment has been the subject of ecocriticism. While many novels written before the 1990s expressed environmental concerns, the emergence of this disciplinary approach has opened new, fruitful lines of research within crime fiction studies that may, in turn, enrich ecocritical perspectives on literature more broadly. For this reason, those few literary critics who have addressed the relationship between crime fiction and environment have adopted ecocritical approaches, which provide tools, concepts and nuanced discussions that expand previous understandings of the environment and highlight their most problematic literary uses. In recent decades, ecocritics have reformulated the notion of "environment". While in the early to mid-1990s, they thought of it as closer to "natural environment", applying the nature/culture distinction, today they have moved to consider both natural and built environments (Buell 2005: 22). The new definition of "environment" therefore includes cities and populated spaces as well as the wilderness.

Crime novels may be helpful in updating discussion of the "wilderness", or the "environmental imagination" of the wilderness, as Lawrence Buell (1995) puts it, by situating crimes within places such as forests, rivers, oceans, deserts or mountains. The wilderness has long had an acknowledged place in crime fiction: By imagining isolated places such as these, where crimes remain hidden from human sight and outside social frameworks, narratives can induce fear, produce a sense of mystery and highlight the violation of legal frameworks, since those frameworks are mostly based in built environments. Crime novels, however, have long emphasised what William Cronon (2015) refers to as "the trouble with wilderness": What we have imagined as untouched, isolated natural spaces are in fact part of a human space where natural resources, animal and plant life, and human beings interrelate in a complicated manner. This is precisely where the problem originates – in short, wilderness cannot be thought of in opposition to civilised space anymore.

Several novels address specific ecocritical issues that arise when humans interact with wilderness. Novels such as Peter Bowen's *Wolf, No Wolf* (1997), Deon Meyer's *Blood Safari* (2007), Nevada Barr's *Track of the Cat* (1993) and *Blood Lure* (2001), for example, comment on the environmental damage caused by ecotourism and environmental activism. Paradoxically, the "green" enthusiasm for wildlife has become a significant part of the tourism industry, affecting accommodation and new infrastructure that changes the lifestyle and economy of the territory with serious effects on the land and its inhabitants. Operating in the space that Karen Thornber (2012) defines as "ecoambiguity", ecotourism contributes to the retreat of native communities, the construction of excessive infrastructure and the lucrative use of preserved space for profit. In his chapter "Mysteries of Nature and Environmental Justice", Patrick Murphy examines the abuse of wildlife, particularly as it affects animals who are endangered today because of the "violent" behaviour towards livestock or human beings that is attributed to them (2009: 119–43). Positions on environmental actions to protect wildlife do not always coincide. Bowen's *Wolf, No Wolf* tells of the assassination of activists who want to reintroduce wolves into an area of Montana where ranchers and Native Americans would have to be removed to create a national park. In this case, the proposed reintroduction of wolves clashes with a prosperous cattle-based economy that was made possible by the historic hunt that drove wolves to extinction. While engaging with the wildlife controversy, the novel ambiguously tends to back capitalism and local ways of life over broader environmental concerns.

Toxic dumping and extractivism have also been targeted as a set of crimes that damage the environment and/or the local community and its labour force (Mezquita Fernández 2017). Toxic industrial waste dumping – not only the consequence of extractivism – results in the death of bees in the Venice lagoon in Donna Leon's *Earthly Remains* (2017) and Catalan villagers in Pau Vidal's *Aigua bruta* [Dirty Water, 2007]. Addressing extractivism specifically, John Grisham's legal thriller *Gray Mountain* (2014) portrays the criminal practices of strip-mining companies that use explosives on mountain summits in order to reach the layers of coal beneath, releasing a dust that, when inhaled, produces black lung disease and, ultimately, the indirect, long-term murder of the population. Even if Grisham's novel also includes an investigation into a lawyer's murder, the novel exemplifies how legal thrillers are marking extractivism as an environmental crime that destroys the environment and the more disadvantaged sectors of society, which for this very reason demands urgent prosecution. Indeed, as in Grisham's novel, on many occasions the effects of industrialisation and extractivism include what Rob Nixon has called the "environmentalism of the poor" (2011); that is, they provide evidence that environmental destruction mostly affects the poorest segments of the population. This is another way in which these novels demonstrate crime fiction's commitment to social and ecojustice and a potential call for social activism and engagement.

Ecocriticism has also concerned itself with animals and plants, which operate in some novels as vehicles that signal an ecological concern involved in crime. This phenomenon occurs – as Alicia Carroll (2018) notes – in Agatha Christie's discussion of herbalism in texts such as *Five Little Pigs* (1942), in which Christie dismisses knowledge and use of plants as a form of female knowledge, and in Fred Vargas's *Quand sort la recluse* (2017) [*This Poison will Remain*, 2019] in its focus on a recluse and venomous spider. Furthermore, animals and plants can serve to decentre the anthropocentric perception of crime and move it towards a perspective akin to that of animal and posthuman studies, as Katherine Bishop (2018) explains with regards to the presence of the vegetal in crime fiction. In Wajdi Mouawad's *Anima* (2012), this move to the posthuman perspective is especially successful. In Mouawad's novel – another genre-hybrid *tour de force* – the partner of a woman who has been horribly murdered becomes the case's private investigator, but the novel does not privilege his point of view. Instead, it is narrated through the eyes of multiple animals that witness the scenes, creating an estranging distance that challenges the traditional narrative perspective of the detective. *Anima*, therefore, provides a sense that the reality of a crime does not reside with human perspectives. Rather, it develops a posthuman approach as a tool to question both the criminal interpretation and involvement of those who produce the crime narrative.

In the process of revising the notion of environment to include spaces that were not traditionally thought of as part of it, ecocritics have revisited earlier discussions on the opposition between rural and urban spaces, using as a point of departure Raymond Williams's *The Country and the City* in which he debunks the long-standing separation of a rural idyll that preserves morality and a city associated with crime and transgression of the law. Crime fiction can also be understood as contributing to this revision, insofar as the genre may help us interrogate the borders between countryside and city, and between the ways each is traditionally imagined. These new discussions include examination of the ways in which crime novels interrogate the rural idyll (N. Bishop 2018) and depict the environmental effects of massive urbanisation projects on the countryside (Murphy 2009). The reimagining of narratives about the country and the city is also developed in Ricardo Piglia's brilliant *Blanco nocturno* (2010), where old ideas of isolation, life and justice in the Argentinian Pampa are challenged when the murder of a foreigner is falsely resolved because the agents of the crime belong to powerful local authorities and business families linked to global finance networks. The murder is motivated by illegal land speculation for the construction of a massive mall that would revolutionise the local economy. However, the involvement of local authorities in collaboration with much larger urban and global networks blocks the investigation. In Piglia's novel, the idea of an untraceable murder in the isolated countryside is reinscribed onto an impenetrable net of conflicting versions, unreliable informants and witnesses whose implication in the crime equates the countryside with corrupted urban settings and its juridical practices.

In these novels, most local environmental crimes relate to wider problems, and they are frequently tied to international networks. Recent discussions in both ecocriticism and crime fiction studies have noted fiction's tendency to address conflicts from a global perspective. Heise, for example, has claimed that local, specific environmental problems must be linked to global concerns without losing their local specificity (2008: 2013). Similarly, critics like Stewart King (2014) and Louise Nilsson et al. (2017) have insisted on the worldly dimensions of crime fiction and its potential to speak to transnational audiences and foster developments in the global novel, and that crime fiction should therefore be added to the body of work examined within the field of World Literature. In conjunction with crime fiction's focus on narrating the global environmental crisis, this line of inquiry holds significant potential. The fact that specific environmental problems are immediately identifiable within a general global crisis that is defined by planetary phenomena concerning human beings as a species – climate change and the Anthropocene Era – makes the global novel especially suitable as a form, even if the form is still very loosely defined (Beecroft 2016; Hoyos 2015). While other criminal acts such as drug trafficking, smuggling, war and financial crimes also have a clear global dimension that demands an equally international narrative form, environmental crises may have interesting particularities that challenge genre boundaries even further. Global environmental crime requires one to think about the planet at large, and about temporal dimensions beyond the individual – and even the national – histories that crime fiction has most frequently addressed. According to Heise's argument (2008), which was also espoused by Milner, Burgmann, Davidson and Cousin (2015), Murphy (2009) and King (2018), science fiction might be the genre best suited to solving the scale problem of thinking at a planetary level and from a geological time frame, since the genre itself directly draws on those narrative principles. King (2018) examines the hybridisation of speculative fiction and crime fiction in Jordi de Manuel's *L'olor de la pluja* [The Smell of the Rain, 2006,] and Antti Tuomainen's *The Healer* (2013). These productive inquiries may also be pursued in Rosa Montero's *Lágrimas de lluvia* [Tears in Rain, 2011] and Frank Schätzing's *Der Schwarm* [The Swarm, 2004]. As an ecothriller, *Der Schwarm* shows that the conventions of different genres can be freely combined to suit narrative purposes. Gulddal et al.'s *Criminal Moves* (2019) point out that this renders discussions about closed genres less productive than discussions about their flexible uses and what they call "mobility of genre".

Schätzing's novel forces us to reconsider crime in terms of global ecocrime. While this ambitious novel contains actual killings of people and animals, those killings occur on a massive, planetary scale. In a tribute to Stanislaw Lem's *Solaris*, the global abuse of the planet through oil drilling and toxic waste dumping into the sea results in speculation that the chemical substances in oceans have been manipulated and are acting independently of human intelligence, which would ultimately destroy the human species. The novel borrows extensively from the investigation plot to narrate a human environmental crime with devastating effects at global and geological levels. By bringing crime novel conventions onto a planetary spatial and temporal scale through science fiction narrative strategies, the novel is able to narrate the crimes of the Anthropocene in a temporal dimension that is uncommon to crime fiction and elevate the criminals and victims to represent global human communities, multiplying the stories, narrative perspectives and settings. Through these conventions, it becomes a truly global novel.

Arguably, this movement to address the global dimension of environmental crime in literature has endeavoured to search for alternative ways in which human beings might improve environmental relations and avoid catastrophe. Crime fiction participates in this movement by engaging with alternative understandings through the depiction of controversially named "indigenous cosmologies". Bowen's *Wolf, No Wolf* depicts a United States in which the ecological balance partially achieved by Native Americans has been ambiguously recuperated, as do Tony Hillerman's *The Blessing Way* (1970) and Craig Johnson's *The Cold Dish* (2004). Crime novels also represent indigenous groups, such as the Atacameños in *El alemán de Atacama* or the Jarawas in Gangopadhyay's *The King of the Verdant Island* (2010). Harshly repressed, reduced to reservations or absorbed by capitalism into often-illegal businesses, these communities are used in the novels to establish a contrast with a conception of the environment that fosters and justifies environmental crime. As the proponents of Latin American ecocriticism insist, decolonial epistemologies reveal that environmental crime is grounded in the colonisation of thought imposed by old and new imperial powers, and that alternative epistemologies might contribute to more balanced understandings of environment.

Roberto Ampuero's *El alemán de Atacama*

Roberto Ampuero's *El alemán de Atacama* is an illustrative example of the productive confluence between crime fiction and the aforementioned ecocritical nodes. In this Chilean novel, Cayetano Brulé, a Cuban detective living in Chile, investigates the murder of the German activist Willi Balsen in the small village of San Pedro de Atacama. The indigenous community of Atacameños had accepted Balsen's project of constructing water wells to help with cultivation and improve the desert's access to water. The subsequent investigation into the murder reveals that Balsen, Bárbara Schuster and a parliamentarian Mariano Patiño were killed because Schuster and Balsen discovered that a German mineral extraction company was illegally trafficking toxic waste in the desert and poisoning the subterranean waters and the village's environment, with deadly short- and long-term effects.

Mostly subscribing to a realist crime novel form, *El alemán de Atacama* explores a multilayered environmental conflict that interweaves a revision of the idea of "wilderness" with ecotourism and environmental activism, global toxic waste disposal and profit and indigenous perspectives on ecological balance. Interestingly, Ampuero's novel does not provide easy solutions to the environmental conflict; instead, it interrogates its most paradoxical aspects.

As discussed above, the introduction of environmental concerns into crime fiction offers the possibility of a richer interrogation of the "wilderness" as a troubled concept. Following the tradition of desert literature, the Atacama Desert functions in Ampuero's novel as a millenarian and isolated space where nature is preserved and pristine, yet also one where secret activities like the illegal trafficking and burial of toxic waste are deemed possible. Nevertheless, the fact that tourism sustains the village economically; Brulé's constant feeling that he is under surveillance in a place where, in fact, "nunca sucede nada, aquí nos conocemos todos" [nothing ever happens, here we know each other well] (74); and the rather smooth and conventionally-solved investigation that takes place in that space bring to mind Cronon's trouble with the imagined wild desert.

The novel portrays a triple conflict that reflects the local/international dimensions of a global crisis while simultaneously questioning their paradoxical aspects. San Pedro de Atacama's inhabitants take economic advantage of the Atacama Desert's international reputation as an ecotouristic site, which has fostered such greed that hotel owners have disastrously started to dig new water wells, following Balsen's irrigation plan. These uncontrolled perforations damage the phreatic surface (80) and leave the village to suffer from endless drought. Ecotourism, therefore, becomes one of the central causes of the novel's unbalanced ecosystem, disrupting the already precarious functioning of the village's water supply. The idea for the wells comes, however, from

Crime fiction and the environment

the failed NGO SOSDritteWelt project led by Balsen, who argued that the water supply could be improved for agricultural purposes. As detective Brulé's investigation discovers, Balsen, in desperation, had resorted to falsifying indigenous ceramics and selling them on the black market to collect money to fund water pumps, an effort that would have presumably fixed the village's dry well problem, albeit unconvincingly.

The novel criticises well-intended causes and efforts that are ultimately unaware of their ecological – even Anthropocenic – damage through the desolate perspective of the native Ayllu de Solor people. In accepting the "foreign" project, the Atacameño community has enabled the breaking of the fragile environmental equilibrium they had shaped through years of desert living. The novel emphasises its divergent critique of global capitalism as responsible even for well-intended activist and tourist development through indigenous cosmologies. As seen above, these cosmologies have been established as a starting point for decolonial thought, which is prominent in Latin American thinking, including ecocriticism. As the Atacameño Saúl Puca tells Brulé:

> Dicen los achaques que don Willi, como era extranjero, no supo interpretar a la Pachamama. [...] Un oasis descansa en el equilibrio más delicado que existe. Ni siquiera las selvas tropicales son tan delicadas. Aquí basta con que alguien roce un pelo del equilibrio para que todo se venga abajo y nos arruine.

> [The Achaques say that Mr. Willi, since he was a foreigner, did not understand the Pachamama well. [...] An oasis rests on the most fragile balance. Not even the tropical jungles are as fragile. If anyone touches a hair of that balance, it will all fall apart and we will be ruined.]

> *(85, translation mine)*

El alemán de Atacama resists the urge to make idealistic statements and conclusions. The novel suggests that while traditional knowledge may not be able to resolve the community's water supply problem, it ultimately proves far less harmful to the environment and the inhabitants' survival in the inhospitable Atacama Desert than the activists' approaches, however well-intended.

Balsen's foreign misunderstanding of the local problem and its causes does not create any solutions for local water management, but it highlights the problematic entanglement of local context with the global environmental crisis and the environmentalism of the poor. It also emphasises the failure of international – in this case, as usual, Anglo-European – intervention. These themes are reiterated in the main motive for the murder, which is not inspired by the victim's hydraulic project, but rather by his discovery that the German-led company Antares deals not only in oil and mineral extraction (another target of the novel's criticism against the corruption and speculation of global capitalism) but in burying the deadly toxic waste from a failed European scientific experiment that aimed to create a new substance to replace the toxic chlorofluorocarbon used in refrigeration systems. Illegal disposal thus becomes big business for the Antares company. In these terms, the already international murder of a German activist, which is being investigated by a Cuban detective in Chile for a German journalist who works for the *Frankfurter Allgemeine Zeitung*, reaches a truly global scale within the hull of the Liberian-flagged *Sierra Leone*, the merchant ship that transports the toxic waste from Germany to Colombia, Panamá, then Peru, before docking at the Chilean port of Antofagasta. The local environmental project of digging wells resonates with and is infiltrated by the global toxic waste deposits beneath the desert, which are buried away from the world's gaze, under the surface of a spectacular wilderness.

367

Through these plot entanglements, the crime novel's genre conventions suggest that while the codified crime for which there is an investigation and a legal path is the murder of Willi Balsen and, collaterally, the murders of Mariano Patiño and Bárbara Schuster, there are two other local/international crimes that have more severe consequences and contain true-crime elements (Marún 2004). In this sense, the novel follows the genre's tendency to engage with social causes: The murder is only the tip of the iceberg of our corrupt, globalised capitalist world. However, in its attempt to represent the bleaker aspects of the situation, this novel can also be seen as problematising the genre through the conventional, fully fleshed and explicit resolution of the murder. In other words, the crime is solved at the individual level: The German head of the Antares Company and his immediate criminal collaborators are arrested, and the reader might reasonably expect that the disposal of toxic waste in the Atacama Desert will stop. However, what remains unsolved is the environmental crime. The global toxic waste problem may only be displaced; the waste still exists, and its disposal may merely be redirected somewhere else. In a subtler way, the novel goes even further with this conclusion by ending with a melancholy, yet relaxed Cayetano Brulé, who is focused on the individuals involved in the murder (crime) but remains oblivious to the greater, invisible crime: That the Atacama Desert is left with permanently damaged aquifers and poisoned lands, the slow violent effects of which will not be immediately perceived or demand urgent legal and punitive solutions or any conceivable justice on the detective's part, since he has done his job with regards to the legal framework in which he acts and the crime he has been commissioned to solve. In this sense, the novel's subscription to crime fiction's formal conventions highlights the environmental crime even as it overshadows its non-resolution by drawing on the easy solution of the murder. The novel does not necessarily accept this as a quick resolution of the multilayered crime; rather, it offers a critical gaze on the genre and its possible limitations. Through a subtle metafictional reference in the heterodiegetic use of journals/reports in the narrative – which, as Gina Canepa (2007: 9) observes, anticipates Ampuero's later auto-reflexive crime fiction – the novel indicates the genre's complacency: In the process of resolving the target, usually a bloody crime, the greater, less structured and more pervasive crimes are usually left unsolved. Roberto Ampuero's *El alemán de Atacama*, therefore, demonstrates both the possibilities and the limitations of the crime fiction genre as a means of discussing, challenging and encompassing environmental crime and the main critical concerns of ecocriticism.

Environmental crime: Crime fiction in the spotlight

As detailed above, crime fiction's engagement with ecocritical issues and the analysis of *El alemán de Atacama* demonstrate that crime fiction is indeed especially well-equipped to mark environmental problems as criminal. The genre is singularly fruitful in the effort to revise the prevailing idea of "crime" as an individual act that has immediate, visible and usually bloody/violent consequences. It helps expand the definition of crime to include areas such as the environment, which have historically been less sensitive to the label of criminality and consequently less explored as criminal. Through its portrayal of other global crimes such as drug trafficking and terrorism, crime fiction has already developed the capacity to encompass environmental crime at a global scale, to represent its perpetrators as part of an international network, and to depict its victims and other criminal, damaging consequences at various levels that range from the local to the global. When environmental crime fiction's narrative strategies intersect with those of the global novel, it can use its already existent transnational capacity to reach popular audiences all over the world and raise environmental awareness in readers who might not be directly concerned about environmental problems. Therefore, the genre serves as a powerful tool, not only for activist purposes, but also, as *El alemán de Atacama* makes clear, as a means of exploring the contradictions and complexities of ecological conflicts. By representing environmental crime through the narrative conventions of crime fiction, the novels reveal the collective responsibility of the perpetrators. At the same time, however, crime fiction that fully addresses environmental issues inherently pushes the limits of its own genre conventions, because it destabilises the idea that crime is always aligned with murder, challenges the genre's traditional use of geographical and temporal scale and questions its tendency to conform to realist conventions. More remarkably, most of the examples provided here interrogate our understanding of criminal violence. In their engagement with environmental crime, they interlace spectacular, immediate violence with a "slow violence" that, as Rob Nixon puts it, "occurs gradually and out of sight, a violence of delayed destruction that is dispersed across time and space, an attritional violence that is typically not viewed as violence at all" (2011: 2). How might a crime whose real criminal dimensions transcend our current understandings of violence instigate a reformulation of previous understandings of crime and violence, which are at the core of current definitions of crime fiction? How does the fact that most environmental crimes cannot be solved in one case, by one individual, or within one legal framework play into the pressure for a final resolution? The successful indexing and exposure of environmental crimes, therefore, simultaneously nurtures ecocritical discussion and contributes to renewed reflection on and understanding of the potentialities of crime fiction's conventions and the ways we might challenge them.

Bibliography

Ampuero, R. (2012) [1996] *El alemán de Atacama*, Madrid: Debosillo.

Beecroft, A. (2016) "On the tropes of literary ecology: the plot of globalization", in J. Habjan and F. Imlinger (eds), *Globalizing Literary Genres: Literature, history, modernity*, New York and London: Routledge, 195–212.

Bishop, K.E. (2018) "'When 'tis night, death is green': vegetal time in nineteenth-century econoir", *Green Letters*, 22(1): 7–19.

Bishop, N. (2018) "Rural nostalgia: revisiting the lost idyll in British Library Crime Classics detective fiction", *Green Letters*, 22(1): 31–42.

Buell, L. (1995) *The Environmental Imagination: Thoreau, nature writing, and the formation of American culture*, Cambridge, MA: Belknap Press of Harvard University Press.

———. (2005) *The Future of Environmental Criticism: Environmental crisis and literary imagination*, Malden, MA: Blackwell.

Canepa, G. (2007) "El desierto como basurero en *El alemán de Atacama* de Roberto Ampuero: ecoliteratura en los tiempos de globalización", *Polis: Revista Latinoamericana*, 17 http://polis.revues.org/4264 (accessed 31 October 2019).

Carroll, A. (2018) "'Leaves and berries': Agatha Christie and the herbal revival", *Green Letters*, 22(1): 20–30.

Cronon, W. (2015) "The trouble with wilderness; or, getting back to the wrong nature", in K. Hiltner (ed.), *Ecocriticism: The essential reader*, London and New York: Routledge, 102–19.

Gulddal, J., King, S. and Rolls, A. (2019) "Criminal Moves. Towards a Theory of Crime Fiction Mobility", in J. Gulddal, S. King and A. Rolls (eds), *Criminal Moves: Modes of mobility in crime fiction*, Liverpool: Liverpool University Press, 1–24.

Heise, U.K. (2008) *Sense of Place and Sense of Planet: The environmental imagination of the global*, Oxford: Oxford University Press.

———. (2013) "Globality, difference, and the international turn in ecocriticism", *PMLA*, 128(3): 636–43.

Hoyos, H. (2015) *Beyond Bolaño: The global Latin American novel*, New York: Columbia University Press.

King, S. (2014) "Crime fiction as world literature", *Clues*, 32(2): 8–19.

———. (2018) "Environmental crimes in world crime fiction: towards a global reading practice", unpublished paper presented at ACLA 2018 conference.

Marún, G. (2004) "Una denuncia ecológica: *El alemán de Atacama* de Roberto Ampuero", in S. Godsland and J. Collins (eds), *Latin American Detective Fiction: New readings*, Manchester: Manchester Metropolitan University Press, 112–21.

Mezquita Fernández, M.A. (2017) "Ecocrítica en la ficción criminal: terrorismo medioambiental en *Zia Summer* y *Jemez Spring* de Rudolfo Anaya", in J. Sánchez Zapatero and A. Martín Escribà (eds), *La globalización del crimen: Literatura, cine y otros medios*, Santiago de Compostela: Andavira, 349–46.

Milner, A., Burgmann, J.R., Davidson, R. and Cousin, S. (eds) (2015) "Ice, fire and flood: science fiction and the Anthropocene", *Thesis Eleven*, 13(1): 12–27.

Murphy, P.D. (2009) *Ecocritical Explorations in Literary and Cultural Studies: Fences, boundaries, and fields*, Lanham: Lexington Books.

Nilsson, L., Damrosch, D. and D'Haen, T. (eds) (2017) *Crime Fiction as World Literature*, New York: Bloomsbury Academic.

Nixon, R. (2011) *Slow Violence and the Environmentalism of the Poor*, Cambridge, MA: Harvard University Press.

Paul, A. (2018) "Nature, hunter and the hunted: Eco-consciousness in Samares Mazumdar's selected Bengali crime fictions", *Green Letters*, 22(1): 78–88.

Thornber, K. (2012) *Ecoambiguity: Environmental crises and East Asian literatures*, Ann Arbor: University of Michigan Press.

Walton, J.L. and Walton, S. (2018) "Introduction: crime fiction and ecology", *Green Letters*, 22(1): 2–6.

41

CRIME FICTION AND NARCOTICS

Andrew Pepper

Narcotics – or what are colloquially called "drugs" – enter the realm of the crime story in a number of instructive ways. First and most importantly, they are a commodity, to be bought and sold for profit, and where the profit margins to be accrued are enhanced by a set of moral and political decisions taken around the issue of prohibition. The mind-altering properties of drugs, whether illegal or otherwise (for example, the way they work on "the chemical messengers in the neurophysiological system" [Herlinghaus 2013: 2]) are also a factor in determining demand and hence price but the categorical definition of what constitutes "drugs" is not at all clear. As Derrida notes, "the concept of drugs is not a scientific concept, but is rather instituted on the basis of moral or political evaluations" (qtd. in Herlinghaus 2013: 8). As such, we could argue that "the existing moral and legal separations between alcohol and sugar, on the one hand, and hashish and cocaine, on the other are nothing less than arbitrary" (Herlinghaus 2013: 3). Nonetheless, prohibition measures produce a whole machinery of state interdiction and a set of attendant moves to close supply routes and arrest drug traffickers. This, in turn, produces the kind of "good" cops versus "bad" traffickers narrative that has been a genre staple since as far back as Robin Moore's *The French Connection* (1969). The drug trade is also a commercial enterprise and therefore the thematisation of the drug trade as a business in crime fiction allows for critical reflection on the proximity of the legal and illegal and organised crime and capitalism; a point underscored by Roberto Saviano's astute claim that "[t]he rules of drug trafficking [...] are also the rules of capitalism" (2013: viii). The drug trade also has a long history that dates at least as far back as the Opium Wars (1839–1842 and 1856–1860) in which the British army, in consort with the East India Company, sought to forcibly compel China to open its border to opium cultivated in India – an early conflagration of commerce and imperial force in order to establish new territories for state-sanctioned capitalism (see Paley 2014: 6).

If the intricacies of these events were not directly captured by crime fiction of the era, their effects were explored in more oblique ways as drugs entered the public and private spaces of the Victorian crime story. Narcotics, of course, became a plot staple of the crime story from *The Moonstone* (1868) onwards, either where the mind-altering properties of drugs are key to the working out of the narrative, as in Collins's novel, or where the protagonist's drug-taking habits allude to a darker, unsettling aspect of their character, e.g. Sherlock Holmes's cocaine binges (*The Sign of Four*, 1890). The thematisation of drug taking in this crime fiction and the references in Doyle's stories to opium dens (e.g. "The Man with the Twisted Lip") also work to situate the metropolitan "centre" as a nodal point in a wider network of colonial routes and actors (Mukherjee 2003). This places the emerging crime story in a necessarily global context, where the material presence and effects of drugs requires or presupposes an interpretative framework that is capable of moving between local, national and global spaces and where this presence in turn situates the crime story within an expansive network of affiliations and transactions that link Western consumption habits to (exploitative) growing and production cycles in the Global South. Another consequence of this move is that the Western body that consumes drugs becomes effectively Orientalised. In a contemporary context, the representation of the global drugs trade and the globally focused efforts of state enforcement practices allow crime writers to push their interrogations into further-reaching critical terrain; e.g. to explore the nature and limits of sovereignty, the role of borders in an era of so-called "free trade" and the causes and contexts of the violence which is now so central to our understanding of the "war on drugs".

In my chapter, I consider three aspects of this brief outline of the relationship between crime fiction and drugs. First, I look in more detail at the early representations of drug taking, e.g. in what we might call (English) classical and (US) hardboiled examples. Rather than setting up an unhelpful division between these two modes of writing, my focus is on the ways that both sets of writers use the mind-bending properties of drugs to put pressure on assumptions about their detectives' rationality and capacity to bring order to the narrative and their worlds. In these novels, emphasis is placed on the particularities and consequences of individual drug taking, without any explicit acknowledgement of the "role that narcotic plants from the New World" and indeed the Global South "have played, across the centuries, in the transatlantic formation of Western modernity" (Herlinghaus 2013: 2). In the second section, and following Herlinghaus's concept of "narcoepics" or "new, transnational, epics of sobriety" (29), I look briefly at two crime novels by Mexican authors – Juan Pablo Villalobos's *Fiesta en la madriguera* (2010) [*Down The Rabbit Hole*, 2011] and Yuri Herrera's *La Transmigración de los cuerpos* (2013) [*The Transmigration of Bodies*, 2016] – where the violence and exploitation of the narco economy is figured obliquely and where an ethical imperative to show us something of this world is set alongside a countermove that refuses to directly address "the socio-economic forms of violence that generate from informal labor and illicit drug trafficking across the Western hemisphere" (Herlinghaus 2013: 35). In the final section, I offer a more detailed discussion of Don Winslow's *The Power of the Dog* (2006), which adopts an alternative ethical stance; namely to represent as much as possible and to try and connect different global spaces via an expansive account of violence and exploitation. Here the corporatisation or "neo-liberalisation" of the drugs business ("catching the drug business up with the times" (2006: 310)) is tied to the actions and behaviours of "endriago" (translated as monster) figures who are the "ultraviolent, destructive subjects of gore capitalism" and use "violence as a tool of empowerment and capital acquisition" (Valencia 2018: 134). In order to complicate the master narrative of the "war on drugs", the ("bad") drug cartels and the ("good") state interdiction machinery come together as a single "cartel" to further "the territorial and social expansion of capitalism" (Paley 2014: 6). It is here, as I will argue in the conclusion, that the critical potential of crime fiction about drugs is most self-evident.

Drugs, colonialism and addiction

The central mystery of *The Moonstone* hinges on two related items: Opium and a stolen diamond. They are related insofar as both have their origins in India and were acquired, forcibly or through colonial trade (i.e. violent dispossession), by figures from the English ruling classes. In Collins's novel, the question of how Rachel Verinder could have seen her suitor, the otherwise upstanding Franklin Blake, steal the priceless diamond from her is cleared up by Ezra Jennings, an aspiring doctor and opium addict, who proposes that Blake acquired the stone unknowingly, while under the "spiritualised intoxication of opium" (1986: 443). Opium and the appropriated diamond – an example of what Harvey has called "accumulation by dispossession" (2005: 144) – are implicated in practices of colonial trade which, while not entirely condemned by Collins, contribute to the fraying or unravelling of society and self. The pursuit of the diamond and the "eating" of opium are both threats to the social norms of Victorian society and the belief in the rational capacities of individual actors – and both must be exposed and marginalised in order for these norms to be restored. If this manoeuvre does not entirely banish anxieties about the iniquities of colonial theft or about the mind-altering capacities of imported drugs like opium, it allays them to some extent. Some of this ambivalence can also be found in the early Sherlock Holmes stories such as *A Study in Scarlet* (1887) where Watson's concerns about the effects of drug taking and addiction, prompted by noticing the "dreamy, vacant expression" in his friend's eyes, are a little at odds with the values of "cleanliness and temperance" that Holmes purports to live by (1992: 14). In *The Sign of Four*, meanwhile, the presence of a "hypodermic syringe" filled with a "seven percent solution" of cocaine and the sight of Holmes's "wrist all dotted and scarred with innumerable puncture-marks" (64) raises, for Watson and hence the reader, the troubling spectre of addiction and the "potential loss of those great powers with which [he has] been endowed" (64).

In the end, the threat posed by narcotics (which were legally available in late nineteenth-century London) to both narrative coherence and the sanctity and rationality of character is managed. Just as in *The Moonstone*, where the seemingly unanswerable question of why Blake "stole" the diamond is resolved in such a way that his name is cleared and he is free to marry Rachel Verinder, Holmes's predilection for cocaine does not damage his mental faculties, and in the stories collected as *The Adventures of Sherlock Holmes* (1892) onward, we hear little or nothing more about his drug taking – a move usually tied to Doyle's association with *The Strand* (Pittard 2011). As such, drugs, like the colonial trade which brought them to England in the first place, and the crimes which Holmes and Blake investigate, are banished to the social margins or occluded from our view.

The same occlusion occurs in the novels of Dashiell Hammett, where drugs constitute part of the fabric of endemic criminality – e.g. the "chalk-white and eyeless" face of a drugged-up Rhea Gutman reflect a more general baseness and venality (1982: 518) – but are not visible as one of the commodities (e.g. gold, money, the falcon itself) which circulate as part of a global network of exchange linking Europe, the US and East Asia (see Pepper, forthcoming). The difference vis-à-vis the earlier stories of Collins and Doyle is one of degree: While Franklin Blake has no notion that he "stole" the diamond under the influence of opium, until it is raised as a possibility later on in the narrative by Ezra Jennings, Hammett's Continental Op is roused from a gin and laudanum-induced slumber, and strange, mixed-up dreams, to find an ice pick driven into the chest of his drinking partner and sometimes admirer, Dinah Brand. At the time, he has no idea whether he might have done the deed, given his "right hand held the round blue and white handle of Dinah Brand's ice-pick" (1982: 147). Here, the mind-altering capacities of laudanum are stitched more directly into a realm of violence and lawlessness of which the detective is very much a part; as the Op admits, when he says, in a chapter entitled "Laudanum", "this is the first time I've ever got the fever. It's this damned burg. You can't go straight here. I got myself tangled at the beginning" (139). The Op is not an addict but *Red Harvest* (1929) looks ahead to other crime-related stories like Robert Stone's *Dog Soldiers* (1975) where trafficking and violence are brought into explosive conflagration and where the consequences of addiction and the proximity of the drug trade as business to the wider logic of capitalism and imperialism are easily visible.

Narcoepics and the ethics of not seeing

On one level, it makes good sense to look at "the worldwide drug industry [...] as if it were a business like any other" (Wainwright 2016: 3) and crime fiction has enthusiastically contributed to this task, notably in relation to the Pablo Escobar-inspired, and post-Escobar, global expansion of the cocaine business, as depicted in the Netflix TV series *Narcos* (2015-). But the revolution of the drug business, first in Colombia and then in Mexico, has also resulted in a cataclysmic upsurge in violence, which in turn has required crime writers to address the knotty issue of what and how to represent and the ethics implicit in these decisions. Winslow's *The Power of the Dog*, as we shall see, is very much motivated by an ethics of full disclosure – showing us the visceral horrors and brutalities of the drug trade in order to illuminate the same violent logic at the heart of contemporary capitalism. However, the refusal of two so-called "narcoepics" from Mexico to do likewise is motivated by an alternative ethical position premised on evasion, elision and partial disclosure, one where we can never fully see the folds between capitalism, globalisation and the emergence of new constellations of power and violence.

The challenge of perspective is central to Villalobos's *Down the Rabbit Hole* where we see the operations of the nameless Mexican cartel from the perspective of Tochtli, a young boy, who sees but does not fully understand what is at stake when bodies are made. "The most normal thing to do is to cut off the head", he declares, "although, actually, you can cut anything" (2011: 10). With little or no understanding of the logic of supply and demand which drives capitalism and indeed the drug trade, Tochtli's consumption demands become increasingly outlandish to us, rather than to him, and reach their apotheosis in the form of a Liberian pygmy hippopotamus. To Tochtli, who own hats "from all around the world", a hippo is the logical next step: "I've already written it down on the list of things I want and given it to Miztli" (5). In one sense, of course, given the ubiquity of violence and the global nature of consumer capitalism, it is neither absurd to see death as normal nor outlandish to make such niche consumption demands. But when, having travelled with his father and other members of the cartel to Liberia, and secured two pygmy hippos from traders, with "ears [...] just how I imagined them: miniscule like bullets from a tiny little gun" (42), the animals fall ill after they've been sedated and packed into crates, requiring one of the cartel to shoot them. At this point the horror of the situation becomes apparent even to Tochtli: "I squealed horribly as if I was a Liberian pygmy hippopotamus who wanted the people listening to want to be dead so they didn't have to hear me" (49). Or does it? Because what kind of work, metaphorical or otherwise, is being enacted by the hippos and their harrowing deaths? And what is the significance of the novel's move from Mexico to Liberia and back to Mexico? In a moment, Villalobos allows us to see the senseless violence of the global drugs trade by showing us the needless slaughter of two hippos, but the moment passes and after the hippos' heads have been shipped to Mexico and hung on the wall as adornments, we are left to ask what if anything has been learnt and what is the place of the hippos, dead and/ or alive, in the wider systems of trade and violence that Tochtli and we as readers cannot fully see or understand.

In this slim novel, Villalobos asks us what can and, more importantly, what cannot be seen and understood about the drug business as a global business and about the nature of the violence it enacts and perpetuates. In *The Transmigration of Bodies*, Herrera places a character known as The Redeemer in the middle of a terse stand-off between two rival narco-gangs and where

Crime fiction and narcotics

the narco-violence may or may not be connected to, but nonetheless finds an analogy with, a plague which has afflicted and laid waste to the poorer parts of a nameless Mexican city "overtaken by sinister insects" (2016: 15): "The disease came from a bug and the bug only hung around in squalid areas" (9). The speed and arbitrariness of infection and death – "two men in a restaurant, total strangers, started spitting blood almost simultaneously and collapsed over their tables" (10) – produces an epidemic of death and surplus of bodies that finds an equivalent in the "destructive potentiality" of narco-accumulation and violence whereby "[l]iving people are raw materials for the work of the sicarios, and dead bodies are the product" (Biron 2012: 820). But how exactly is a malarial disease equivalent to a man-made feud – between the Castros and Fonsecas who are described as "[p]oor as dirt a couple of decades ago, now too big for their boots, and neither had moved out of the barrio" (2016: 33)? In the same way that we cannot see the bugs that infect the blood of the living, the drugs which fuel and perpetuate the competition between the Castros and the Fonsecas remain hidden from view, as do the bodies (of the narco violence and/or the plague?) which may or may not be on board "a convoy of eight sealed cars advancing slowly along the tracks" (31). The exchange of bodies is complicated by the revelation that Baby Girl – one of the hostages – has contracted the disease and so it is a body rather than a person that is handed back to the family and it is Baby Girl's inability to speak, her silence, which requires our attention: "What name can you give to something that doesn't exist yet exists for that reason precisely?" (94). In the same way, Herrera names his world and the bodies, living and dead, that inhabit it but refuses to make it fully cohere and in doing so the epidemic of death which the novel also names but obfuscates remains just out of sight; a move that I want to tie back to Herlinghaus's ethics of sobriety insofar as what we are confronted with is not a world of rational decisions and actors but a more inchoate one characterised by montage and collision – "an increasing sense of hazardous or catastrophic images, an alleged ubiquity of violence, together with unforeseen scenarios of either exhaustion or crisis" (2013: 27).

The drugs trade and the social and territorial expansion of capitalism

If Villalobos and Herrera are keen to move the violence of the narco-economy off the page, so to speak, in order not to sensationalise it and to distance us from its effects, Winslow has no such compunction, but we should be careful about making a virtue of the former and condemning the latter. For Winslow's practice of openness and full disclosure – i.e. showing us everything – and the expansiveness of his novelistic lens (encompassing, as it does, the whole of the Americas) have a strong ethical strain too. "The accumulation of capital has always been a profoundly geographical affair", Harvey tells us (2000: 23), drawing on Luxemburg's framework whereby the "aim and incentive of capitalist production" is the pursuit of "a surplus value growing into larger quantities" so that "[e]xpansion becomes a condition of existence" (1951: 40). What *The Power of the Dog* gives us is the demystified truth of this formulation; namely that "Force is the only solution open to capital: the accumulation of capital [...] employs force as a permanent weapon" (Luxemburg 1951: 371). And so the production of dead bodies that Winslow depicts with such vim are not anathema to capitalism but should be understood as the logical realisation of its fundamental processes. In what remains of my chapter I will expand upon this point.

There are two examples from Winslow's *The Power of the Dog* that underscore the relationship between the "war on drugs" and the social and territorial expansion of capitalism. Both take place in Colombia, which is both the source of the drug business's raw material (e.g. cocaine) and the site of covert US foreign policy, partly funded by the Mexican cartels, aimed at suppressing left-wing guerrilla activities. The pretence for US involvement in Colombia may be drugs but it is in actuality "ground zero in the war against the Communist guerrillas"

(2006: 492). Both examples involve Adán Barrera, described as a "young accountant" rather than a larger-than-life narco-lord – so that "[i]f you didn't know what business he was really in, you would never guess" (205). As someone who is modest, thrifty and sober, he would appear to be the model "enlightened" capitalist who is seeking to take advantage of the opening up of markets in the aftermath of NAFTA (North American Free Trade Agreement), which is described as "the essential key to Mexican modernisation" (248). NAFTA is also key to the modernisation or neoliberalisation of the drug trade because one of its effects is a "smooth flow of traffic between Mexico and the United States" and with this "a smooth flow of drug traffic" (401). As cheerleader for a new kind of cartel, Barrera is trying to reconfigure the drug business to free up entrepreneurs to enter the market as business start-ups by lowering the "taxes" he charges for services (309). In a more traditional sense, he must secure the surplus values that would otherwise be claimed by his competitors. One of his rivals is Güerro Méndez and what takes Barrera to Colombia is a meeting with the Orejuela brothers to convince them to sell their drugs to him, rather than Méndez. To be enlightened here means being compliant to the law of finance, which in the demystified world of drug trafficking where capitalism's predatory aspects are very much not abstracted, also means exercising violence in pursuit of accumulation. As such, Barrera arranges to have Méndez's two children thrown from the Santa Ysabel bridge – to weaken Méndez and to underscore his own "business" prowess (295).

In a more conventional genre novel, this would be the moment in which Barrera's status as "bad" is confirmed and where our allegiances shift unequivocally to his rival, Art Keller, of the Drug Enforcement Agency (DEA), who has sworn to bring Barrera to justice for his role in the torture of another DEA agent. But alliances in Winslow's novels are transitory and if here and elsewhere Barrera is public enemy number one, he also works with the CIA to procure weapons for the Nicaraguan Contras and is a financial backer of Plan Colombia which ostensibly targets drug production but actually is intended to "'neutralise' left-wing movements across Latin America" (318). This ambivalence can be seen in the second example, where Barrera's search for a secure supply of cocaine again takes him to Colombia; this time to the Amazonian jungle of southwest Colombia and territory held by the left-wing guerrilla fighters of the Revolutionary Armed Forces of Colombia (FARC). There, he encounters Tirofino, who asks him about his political sympathies and alleged support for the aforementioned "neutralisation" of leftist movements. Barrera's answer is not unexpected – he tells Tirofino that it was "not political" and "just business" – and in doing so he underscores capitalism's capacities for appropriating support from the state. Responding, Tirofino describes being a woodcutter in 1948 when he witnessed a right-wing militia murder all the men in his village: "Because you may say you have no politics, but the day you see your friends and family lying in the dirt, you will have politics" (410).

The exchange is so instructive not merely because of Barrera's halfhearted disavowal of the connection between politics and business but also due to the acknowledgement that the story prompts from Barrera: "There's money and the lack of money, and there's power and the lack of power. And that's all there is." To which Tirofino wryly remarks, "You're half a Marxist already" (410). What Harvey calls "the spatial fix" (2005) is one solution to the problem of over-production and over-accumulation insofar as surplus capital has to seek out new markets and territories; a process described by Streek, following Luxemburg, as "land-grabbing through market expansion" which is "accompanied by a deep transformation of social structures" (2016: 208). This is exactly what Tirofino has witnessed in his small corner of Colombia and this is what has occasioned his transformation into a left-wing guerrilla. As such, the violence that we see in the novel, especially in Colombia where "headless bodies are washed up on the shore like fish waiting to be cleaned" (2006: 491), is directly tied to what Paley calls "drug war

Crime fiction and narcotics

capitalism"; not the efforts of state agencies to limit the flow of illegal narcotics across the US's southern border but the explicit convergence of state and cartel interests in order to open up "social worlds and territories once unavailable to global capitalism" (2014: 5). In the case of Tirofino and many thousands of others in Colombia and across Latin America, the violence unleashed by the US in pursuit of its hemispheric ambitions and occasioned by anxieties about perceived left-wing challenges to capitalism's hegemony, "disproportionately impacts poor working people and migrants" (Paley 2014: 34).

If Tirofino describes Barrera as "half a Marxist already" (2006: 410), the same label could also be applied to Winslow himself. As an example of crime fiction, *The Power of the Dog* operates according to a set of recognisable generic norms; i.e. whereby the narrative is structured around the long struggle between DEA agent and Mexican drug trafficker. But insofar as Keller and Barrera are also uneasy bedfellows in the "free trade" agenda unleashed by NAFTA and the attendant emergence of neoliberalism premised on "the virtues of privatisation, the free market and free trade" (Harvey 2011: 10), the political ambitions of the novel are never far from the surface. Barrera's "reinvention" of the drug trade, premised on a "horizontal" model where "a growing pool of highly motivated, richly rewarded independent businessmen [...] paid 12 per-cent of their gross to the Barreras and took [their] own risk, reaped [their] own rewards" (2006: 309), may be successful in one sense. As Barrera remarks, "we are building a network that is fast, efficient and entrepreneurial, using the newest and best technology and financial mechanisms" (311). But as *The Power of the Dog* and the two sequel novels – *The Cartel* (2015) and *The Border* (2019) – show us, the result is not a virtuous circle of risk-taking and rewards but rather the freeing up of entrepreneurs to commit acts of ever more grotesque violence whose "logical end point" is the turning of living people into dead bodies or "raw materials for the work of the *sicarios*" (Biron 2012: 820). As such, the freedoms promised by the cheerleaders of neoliberalism do not bring greater prosperity to the poorest parts of the American hemi-sphere, e.g. south-west Colombia or Ciudad Juárez, but exactly the opposite: Levels of violence and acts of creatively twisted barbarism that speak to the emergence of a new "necropolitical" order where, as Julián Cardona puts it, "some become very rich [and] most go to the trash" (see Vulliamy 2010: 130). Moreover, the US is no honest broker or virtuous bringer of rights and freedoms but rather an active participant in the violence unleashed against the poor. And it is Winslow's understanding of this complicity which gives his novels their political significance.

Conclusion

It is fair to say that Winslow's "drug war" novels are more overtly politicised than a more typ-ical narco-novel which might uncritically detail, and maybe even sensationalise, the violence of the key protagonists. Still, since there is an obvious affinity between the world of drugs and of capitalism – to the point where we might say that the determining characteristics of the drug trade are also the determining characteristics of the global economy: Privatisation, deregulation, franchising, financialisation, de-risking and of course accumulation, which has always been what capitalism is fundamentally "about" (Streek 2016: 205) – it is not surprising that fiction about the drugs trade tells us a lot about the state of modern capitalism. And in depicting the violent dynamics of modern capitalism, they inevitably further a political argument; i.e. that there is no real distinction between crime, for example, where individuals steal and kill one another, and business, where entrepreneurs competitively chase after surplus values. In my conclusion, I want to examine two further aspects of the depiction of narcotics in crime fiction: One to do with gender and the other with transnationality. Insofar as Winslow shows the disposability of the poor, we might ask or wonder whether more could be done to depict the effects of drug war violence or the violence which accrues from narco-accumulation specifically on women. Here it is worth paying attention to the interventions by Latin American novelists like Alicia Gaspar de Alba in *Desert Blood* (2005) and Roberto Bolaño in *2666* (2004) which map "a fatal encounter of industrial *maquiladora* production and narco-accumulation [...] on the one hand, and the 'free' labour power of migrant women (abstract labour to exploit and kill), on the other" (Kraniauskas 2016). In both novels the issue of gendered violence and exploitation is tied to Ciudad Juárez's position on the frontline of an aggressively pursued "free trade" agenda where low-paid menial jobs for a disposable labour force are created by shifts in global finance patterns. Drugs, like money, flow smoothly and without drawing attention to themselves across borders and so it also stands to reason that fiction about the flows of drugs and money across borders will be inherently transnational in their outlook. As such, any attempt to examine the role of drugs in crime fiction must first eschew the kind of nation-centred approach to crime and crime prevention which this volume is seeking to contest. *The Power of the Dog* offers one of the most geographically expansive accounts of the drugs trade, whereby an emphasis on supply routes and networks of demands, and on the transnational affiliations and hostilities between the related domains of crime, business and politics, expose the limits of a nation-centred approach for understanding the crime novel.

Bibliography

Biron, R. (2012) "It's a living: hit men in the Mexican narco war", *PMLA*, 126(2): 820–34.

Collins, W. (1986) [1868] *The Moonstone*, London: Penguin.

Doyle, A.C. (1992) *The Adventures of Sherlock Holmes*, Ware, Hert.: Wordsworth.

Hammett, D. (1982) *Dashiell Hammett: The four great novels*, London: Picador.

Harvey, D. (2000) *Spaces of Hope*, Edinburgh: Edinburgh University Press.

———. (2005) *The New Imperialism*, Oxford: Oxford University Press.

———. (2011) *The Enigma of Capital and the Crises of Capitalism*, London: Profile.

Herlinghaus, H. (2013) *Narcoepics: A global aesthetics of sobriety*, London and New York: Bloomsbury.

Herrera, Y. (2016) *The Transmigration of Bodies*, trans. Lisa Dillman, High Wycombe: And Other Stories.

Kraniauskas, J. (2016) "A monument to the unknown worker: Roberto Bolaño's *2666*", *Radical Philosophy*, 200, www.radicalphilosophyarchive.com/article/a-monument-to-the-unknown-worker (accessed 3 July 2019).

Luxemburg, R. (1951) *The Accumulation of Capital*, trans. A. Schwarzschild, London: Routledge and Kegan Paul.

Mukherjee, U.P. (2003) *Crime and Empire: The colony in nineteenth-century fictions of crime*, Oxford: Oxford University Press.

Paley, D. (2014) *Drug War Capitalism*, Oakland: AK Press.

Pepper, A. (forthcoming) "Dashiell Hammett's *The Maltese Falcon* as world literature: global circuits of translation, money, and exchange", *Modern Fiction Studies*.

Pittard, C. (2011) *Purity and Contamination in Late Victorian Detective Fiction*, Farnham: Ashgate.

Rodríguez, S.G. (2012) *The Femicide Machine*, trans. M. Parker-Stainback, Los Angeles: Semiotext(e).

Saviano, R. (2013) "Foreword", trans. P. Mossetti, in A. Hernández, *Narcoland: The Mexican drug lords and their godfathers*, trans. Iain Bruce, London and New York: Verso, vii–x.

Streek, W. (2016) *How Will Capitalism End?: Essays on a failing system*, London and New York: Verso.

Valencia, S. (2018) *Gore Capitalism*, trans. J. Pluecker, Los Angeles: Semiotext(e).

Villalobos, J.P. (2011) *Down the Rabbit Hole*, trans. R. Harvey, High Wycombe: And Other Stories.

Vulliamy, E. (2010) *Amexica: War along the borderline*, New York: Farrar, Straus and Giroux.

Wainwright, T. (2016) *Narconomics: How to run a drug cartel*, New York: PublicAffairs.

Winslow, D. (2006) *The Power of the Dog*, New York: Vintage.

42

CRIME FICTION AND MIGRATION

Charlotte Beyer

Migration is a vital theme in crime fiction, because it draws attention to certain issues which are central to our understanding of what the crime genre is and what it does. The theme of migration shows crime fiction's capacity to provide more than entertainment, and to educate readers and deliver social and cultural critique on compelling and urgent topical issues of its time. Migration has become an increasingly controversial political and cultural issue, because it is perceived and represented in discourses across the political spectrum as a national and international security issue, and frequently associated with terrorism and political extremism (Papademitriou and Banulescu-Bogdan 2016). Migration is regarded as being at odds with nationalism and the nation-state, a perception evident in cultural and political discourses in, for example, President Trump's America and Brexit Britain (Eaglestone 2018). Due to the moral panic surrounding illegal migration in general and human trafficking in particular, these crimes have gained much attention in the news media and crime fiction (Beyer 2018). Writing as a migrant in a second language, and as a crime fiction specialist, I am inevitably tangled up in the subject of crime fiction and migration in complex ways. Crime fiction features prominent characters who are migrants, including such well-known detectives as Agatha Christie's Hercule Poirot. However, relatively few critical discussions have investigated crime fiction and migration in depth, and it is to this issue that I turn my attention.

Crime fiction has always had the capacity to interrogate social and political issues; however, a recent focus on the global flows of people and goods in crime fiction and on crime fiction itself as a genre in global circulation has enhanced the focus on the impact of migration on societies and cultures. Karen Seago argues that crime fiction "is about the transgression of a country's legal, moral and social values, about understanding how and why this transgression occurred and […] returning to the normative centre of that society" (2014: 2). Migration in crime fiction questions or disrupts these values, highlighting the oppression at the "normative centre" of society as well as interrogating the meanings of mobility and agency by promoting a transnational outlook. Rather than following one specific body of theory or critical approach, my discussion therefore draws on a range of theoretical discourses, including feminism, postcolonialism, criminology, sociology, cultural studies and crime fiction criticism, in order to unpack the topic of migration in crime fiction. This chapter discusses the politics of representing migration in crime fiction and examines the ways in which authors use the genre's conventions to investigate various kinds of migration, crime and illegality. I then move on to analyse the British author Eva Dolan's 2014 crime novel, *Long Way Home*. Set in the British town of Peterborough, Dolan's novel presents a compelling study of the ways in which crime fiction represents and investigates migration and criminality. Through these discussions, the chapter demonstrates that crime fiction uses the theme of migration to engage critically with the complex and fast-moving social and cultural conflicts unfolding in our contemporary world.

Migration in crime fiction: The politics of representation

The theme of migration illustrates crime fiction's central functions, namely making visible that which was previously hidden or concealed and achieving justice for victims. Alexander Betts argues that human migration is "the defining issue of this century" (Betts 2015). Goldin et al. state that migration entails "moving across a national border, often with the purpose of settling for a period of time" (2011: 1). The term "migration" is used here to cover a wide range of mobilities and crossing of borders, criminal or non-criminal. Commenting on the role and function of migration, Bowling and Westenra argue that,

> Mobility and fluidity are notable features of contemporary global society. Mass border crossing is an essential feature of this society, accelerated by neoliberal globalization and the global capitalist economy, which require people to be free to move with trans-national flows of money.

> *(2018: 3)*

However, Goldin et al. also draw attention to negative political connotations associated with migration, noting how, "[o]ur governments and societies retain an antiquated suspicion of outsiders, who were born in one nation-state and seek to make their life in another one" (2011: 1). The West's concern with migration is linked to other related issues, such as crime and detection across borders and mobility. The West views migration as disruptive and as a threat to its affluence and privilege, leading to increasingly strict forms of migration management. In overcoming these forms of migration management, opportunistic criminals take advantage of migrants, turning them into a lucrative, illegal business. It is these hidden forms of exploitation behind the media portrayals of migration which crime fiction probes. Recent scholarly assessments of migration in crime fiction are influenced by developments in postcolonial theory and transnationalism in literature and culture (Allen and Møllegaard 2018). Others (Gregoriou 2018; Beyer 2018) examine representations in contemporary media, true crime and crime fiction of interrelated themes such as human trafficking, modern slavery, transnationality and glocal inequality. These developments in critical approaches to transnationality, crime fiction and representation are significant. They highlight gaps in knowledge production which are reflected in the continued neglect of the topic of migration in crime fiction. As we shall see in the analysis of Dolan's *Long Way Home*, the causes of migration combine with the genre's focus on criminality to generate a unique focus on society, highlighting the complex position of migrants and migration within it. As Dolan explains regarding *Long Way Home*, "[e]verything in this book is based in reality […] the brutality and corruption, the poor living conditions and violence and exploitation" (Nette 2014). Crime fiction achieves this unique focus primarily by shining a light on migrants as victims of crime and opportunist uses of migration in crime, and by interrogating issues about national identity and who has the right to belong in a place.

Migration in crime fiction has become a highly politicised subject as a result of right-wing political developments during the 2010s. Dolan comments on the significance of these political developments in establishing the context for *Long Way Home*, referencing "[t]he under reporting of Hate Crimes and the establishment of dedicated units in the UK" (Nette 2014). Crime fiction authors employ the genre's conventions to explore migration, using different prisms such as historical crime fiction, detective stories and police procedural novels; themes such as gender and migration, migration and national identities; and specific migration-related crimes. Crime fiction uses the theme of migration to interrogate identity and its definition for detectives, criminals and victims through its generic conventions. In America, migration is seen as essential to the "melting pot", and the discourse of the uniquely blended American identity is fundamentally based on migrant contributions. The effects of migration on American crime narratives can be seen in American-Italian author Mario Puzo's influential classic *The Godfather* (1969) detailing the way in which Puzo's Sicilian migrants use crime as a ladder to social mobility in the way initially recognised by Daniel Bell (1970), while a more contemporary example is Alex Segura, who draws on his cultural heritage as a Cuban-American to diversify the American genre in his Pete Fernandez series (2013-). Critical of contemporary immigration policies in America, crime fiction author, activist and academic Aya de Leon traces the impact of restrictive and pernicious immigration laws which disenfranchise migrants and deprive them of citizenship and rights. In her crime series, *Justice Hustlers* (2016-), de Leon produces feminist heist novels which carve out a space for urban black female characters confronting race- and gender-based crimes. De Leon argues that, "Our xenophobic society holds many negative myths and stereotypes about immigrants, creating pressure on immigrant communities to prove that they're 'good'. To be 'good' is to assimilate […] and separate from the culture of their homelands" (2018). She further argues that anti-immigrant rhetoric and political campaigns are used by repressive political forces looking for scapegoats in order to gain or remain in power. Crime fiction can be used to combat the xenophobia and racism engendered by anti-migration discourses. Although writing from an American perspective of migration, de Leon's critique is valid in terms of looking at migration in relation to global crime literatures which interrogate hostile negative attitudes towards migrants and expose migration-related crimes. Using crime fiction conventions to question constructions of national identity and the apparent inclusivity of the American melting pot such novels have a crucial role to play in contesting anti-migration and racist discourses and in demonstrating the complexity of migrant contributions to society.

Similarly in Britain, Black and Asian diaspora writers produce hard-hitting crime narratives concerned with violence, racism and assimilation problems experienced by ethnic communities in Britain and, in so doing, interrogate exclusionary notions of national identity. Examples of such novels include M.Y. Alam's *Annie Potts Is Dead* (1998), which focuses on crime and racial tension in deprived Asian diaspora communities in Bradford, and Mike Phillips's crime novels featuring investigative journalist Sam Dean exploring criminality and black British experience (1989-). Migration is a global issue which affects the wider world, not merely the western hemisphere, and this is reflected in crime fiction. Australian crime author Peter Temple, himself a migrant from South Africa, explores issues of immigration, identity and belonging in his crime fiction (Phillips 2014). South African crime author Mike Nicol's *Revenge* trilogy (2008–2011) explores the representation of migration, race and crime (Fasselt 2016). In addition to interrogating issues of identity and crime, these writers use the crime genre to show how migration is being criminalised in various ways, demonstrating that migration is a rising issue in the western world and beyond. Using the conventions of historical crime fiction, crime writers portray migration to challenge national discourses around history and origin. Margaret Atwood's postmodernist historical crime novel *Alias Grace* (1998) challenges Canada's self-image as a non-violent and peaceful nation. In the novel, the nation's fears about female agency and the impact of migration on nineteenth-century colonial Canada are projected onto Irish migrant domestic servant Grace Marks. Barbara Vine's (Ruth Rendell) *Asta's Book* (1993) uses Edwardian East London as its setting for a crime plot concerning Danish female migrants and domestic noir secrecy told through a diary format. In these texts, migration is not itself the crime; however, migrant characters are used to problematise national difference and marginalisation. Here, authors utilise crime fiction conventions to write back to official historical accounts, drawing compelling connections between migration and crime in earlier times and society today.

Crime fiction often focuses on criminal dimensions of migration, also known as "crimmigration", such as people smuggling, human trafficking, illicit mobility and modern slavery. Forced migration in crime fiction may be shown to be caused by political issues, such as those experienced by refugees, asylum seekers, war victims or global disruptions. Far from being exclusive to Europe, migration-related crimes are an issue around the world, and crime fiction reflects this global phenomenon. British and European novels portray contemporary migration as a contentious and politicised topic, using non-professional detective figures to expose the exploitation of migrants. This weaponising of migration can be seen in Ruth Dugdall's *Nowhere Girl* (2014) and Danish authors Lene Kaaberbøl and Agnete Friis's *The Boy in the Suitcase* (2011). In both texts, the central crime plot revolves around the illegal transnational trade in children and illegal migration from the Global South and former Eastern Bloc countries and their illegal migration or trafficking to the west (Beyer 2018). Human trafficking presents a particularly complex variant of illegal migration explored in crime fiction from recent decades, in plots involving organ trafficking, child soldiering, transnational sex trafficking, drug mules and more (Beyer 2018). These novels employ the crime fiction convention of the unofficial detective working outside the establishment to draw attention to the often horrific forms of migrant exploitation. However, for the victims of crimmigration in these novels, justice is frequently portrayed as partial and/or elusive. The limited impact that the outsider detective can have on the establishment implicitly contributes to these complications with regards to providing justice for victims. Many recent police procedural novels examine transnational female sex trafficking, thus connecting illegal migration with prostitution and the sexual exploitation of women. Such works include British author Matt Johnson's novel *Deadly Game* (2015) and Irish author Stuart Neville's 2011 *Stolen Souls*. Both these novels focus on illegal aspects of migration, through plots which examine the trafficking and sexual exploitation of Eastern European women. Through their use of police procedural conventions, Johnson's and Neville's novels explore the difficulties faced by the police in tackling the organised gangs which are behind the scourge of transnational sex trafficking, and the problems authorities face in assisting the female victims of sex trafficking amidst lack of funding and adequate victim rehabilitation, thus highlighting the issue of the unfair treatment of migrants.

One of crime fiction's primary functions is to make visible what has previously been obscured. Importantly, crime fiction's preoccupation with secrecy and concealment extends to its treatment of the theme of migration. Through its portrayal of migration, crime fiction digs below the surface of our outwardly multicultural society in order to reveal the experiences of migrants. Crime fiction highlights and exposes the often appalling circumstances that migrants encounter and which are hidden from view or masked by one-dimensional political discourses and negative representations of migrants in the media. Through representations of transnational migration, crime fiction explores the effects of racism and xenophobia through its depiction of marginalised migrant communities. In revealing the reality of migration, crime fiction concerns itself with justice for the victims of crime, particularly migrant victims. Eva Dolan's novel *Long Way Home* explicitly links crime and migration in this way, by making the treatment of vulnerable migrant workers and trafficking victims part of a broader social critique based on real-life events. Dolan commented on the factual basis for her novel, highlighting specifically the exploitative aspect of crimmigration and modern slavery, explaining that she heard about "the methods of a local gangmaster who conducted his business like a latter-day slave owner, keeping order with threats and beatings, withholding wages" (Nette 2014). Angered by this, Dolan wondered "how was this happening in a country with supposedly rigorous employment and human rights laws? How common was it?" (Nette 2014).

Migrants in the popular media are more generally represented in terms of one-dimensional stereotypes. Crime fiction, however, questions those stereotypes by extending its preoccupation with different categories of migration and through portrayals of migrants involved in or affected by crime (Beyer 2018). These innovative and creative uses of the crime genre's conventions extend the thematic and narrative range of the genre in significant and compelling ways. Crime fiction is a genre that concerns itself with investigating criminality and advocating justice for the victims; however, increasingly the genre also indicates that justice for victims is at best partial and compromised. On the one hand, there are populist discourses about migrants as criminals; on the other, the crime novel often subverts these discourses by drawing attention to the criminal behaviour displayed by the citizens of the host country or the criminal gangs and networks which exploit migrants. This ability of crime fiction to utilise its generic conventions to cut through simplistic political and media discourses around migration, and instead reveal the complex and often horrendous realities behind the stereotypes, demonstrates why the crime genre is so important to the representation of migration.

Eva Dolan's *Long Way Home*

Set in the Eastern English town of Peterborough, Dolan's police procedural novel *Long Way Home* uses the crime genre's conventions to foreground the politicised and increasingly anti-immigration context of early 2010s austerity Britain. In the novel, the remains of the body of a migrant are found in a burned-down shed, leading to a police investigation which uncovers human trafficking, modern slavery and murder. The murder is investigated by DI Zigic and DS Ferreira from the local Hate Crimes Unit, who are themselves from diaspora migrant backgrounds. The police characters in *Long Way Home* are depicted as a successful example of migration, because despite suffering racism they now represent the State. The strength of Dolan's novel lies in its representation of several migrant characters and their experiences, including migrant workers forced to accept slave-like conditions, trafficked Chinese illegal migrants, and Eastern European women sold to sex traffickers. Dolan explains in an interview with Nette that she "wanted to explore how the roots of a murder based on race or ethnicity are different to ones arising out of crime fiction's usual holy trinity of sex, money and power" (Nette 2014). By triangulating migration, criminality and social and political critique, *Long Way Home* demonstrates crime fiction's capacity to actively participate in and shape current debates. The novel's depiction of negative public attitudes to migrants and migration, and its scathing depiction of austerity Britain and the devastating impact on individuals and communities, illustrate the important role crime fiction can play in investigating criminality and seeking justice for victims.

Long Way Home's provincial setting allows a close investigation of the impact of migration and crime on local communities rather than the larger city settings typically featured in contemporary hardboiled crime fiction. The novel's opening chapter introduces the main police characters and illustrates the different types of migrants who co-exist in local communities, some recent, some from several generations ago, and the tensions this causes with local communities in times of austerity and politicised anti-migrant sentiment. The opening scene illustrates the shift in focus in crime fiction that results from a centring of migration in the plot. When the reader is encouraged to identify with the migrant as a victim of crime, an emotional identification and response of empathy can be generated in the reader through their affective engagement with the text's conventions. This engagement is significant as it shows crime fiction's capacity to interrogate topics which are otherwise frequently depicted in stereotypical terms in popular media discourses. *Long Way Home* portrays migrants in Britain as marginalised, deprived of basic rights and regularly threatened by violence. This predicament is illustrated effectively from the beginning, through the novel's powerful prologue. The prologue presents a suspense-filled scene in which an unnamed man flees a barn in a deserted countryside where some men had held him captive and are coming to kill him, setting their dogs on him as he flees. Alone, wounded and terrified, the man runs for his life to escape the murderers. The reader later learns that the man is Paolo, one of the novel's main migrant characters.

A young Portuguese migrant, Paolo has come to Britain to earn money in order to set himself and his girlfriend up for the future. His dreams soon turn sour, however, as he is forced to live in cramped unhealthy conditions and coerced into slave-like work: "The unfairness burned him. They worked hard, they did everything they were told to, and yet they were treated with such disrespect" (2014: 162). Migrants are made to do the jobs the British themselves reject: "They wanted their old and their sick looking after, their offices cleaned and their factories building, but they wouldn't work like this" (162). Paolo's life as a migrant reflects de Leon's assertion that, "the loss of self and the loss of connection to their home community" are key challenges migrants experience in attempting to assimilate to other cultures (2018). Paolo watches a Chinese migrant worker murdered and buried in cement on a building site by unscrupulous British bosses who attach no value to migrants' lives. Because Paolo witnessed the murder, the thugs later try to kill him too, as depicted in the novel's prologue. The fate of the murdered Chinese migrant worker illustrates the callous exploitation and objectification of migrants in a society which reduces people to financial units. Paolo wonders why none of his fellow workers on the building site do anything to prevent the Chinese worker being murdered, but finally admits to himself that, "they were broken" (163). Dolan thus exposes an inhumane and unregulated economy which treats migrant workers as commodities with no rights or access to advice or legal protection, whose safety and dignity do not matter, and who can swiftly be replaced with new supplies of migrant workers. This plot line depicts a neoliberal austerity-ravaged society in freefall. The crimes against, and sometimes committed by, migrants portrayed in the novel are products of this criminally negligent society. The prologue establishes the idea that migrants live precariously in their host countries, that they are exploited, intimidated and terrorised, and their lives are regarded as insignificant to the point of murder. The novel exposes the chasm between the terrible and undignified living conditions of the working migrants, and the cheap inadequate housing of the working-class white British, in contrast to the grandiose Olympic stadiums and facilities being built to show off British dominance and affluence to the world. Through the twin themes of migration and crime, the novel delivers a devastating critique of British austerity and the weaponising of anti-migrant sentiment in everyday life. Paolo's terrifying experience as a victim is important in producing a sympathetic representation of migrants. Using the genre's convention of sympathetic victim portrayal, Dolan helps the reader to see the migrant characters as victims who deserve justice rather than opportunist criminals who deserve punishment.

Migration in *Long Way Home* is depicted as a divisive factor which produces and is produced by disruption and chaotic change and widening social divisions, which threaten the cohesion of local communities already ravaged by inequality, lack of opportunities and austerity. The novel implies that migration-related crimes are an increasing problem for the local police force. *Long Way Home* thus politicises the theme of migration and migrant characters through its plot, which focuses on the crimes committed by and against migrants. The novel contrasts the myth of migration and travel as a privileged expression of agency, contrasting "the vapour trails of aeroplanes heading north, people flying away to new lives or maybe back to their old ones, freshly rich and full of plans" (27) with the harsh reality of assimilation, marginalisation and tension: "fresh graffiti on the gates of the bed and breakfast opposite, Nigga and Paki in uneven black spray paint" (43). Foregrounding problems of inequality and xenophobia, the novel's unrelenting descriptions of the brutality of migrants' lives make visible the systemic social, political and economic discrimination they encounter in modern Britain. Dolan uses the novel's closure to expose the lack of real justice for migrant victims. Despite the criminals being charged with murder, *Long Way Home*'s closing scenes suggest that there is no assimilation or integration for the exploited economic migrants who are either killed by the system or return to their homeland. The novel closes with the cremation ceremony of the murdered Chinese worker, where he is portrayed as a stereotypical anonymous migrant who has seemingly made no lasting impact on the society he worked in, and who is regarded as an isolated individual torn away from his original social fabric. In contrast, Paolo, the survivor, is afforded a more positive closure. However, the novel's bleak ending suggests the impossibility of permanently integrating migrants into the host culture and the inevitable continuation of criminal exploitation of migrants. The seemingly positive conclusion to the novel that culminates in the arrest of the criminals is thus undermined and subverted by the ultimately harsh message of the ending. The novel's conclusion is illustrative of Scott McCracken's argument that in crime fiction "more questions are raised in the narrative than are answered by formal closure" (1998: 50). *Long Way Home* illustrates the challenges crime fiction faces in going beyond negative media portrayals of migrants, and instead producing complex and realistic portrayals of migration. Dolan's novel, however, also illustrates a highly effective embedding of migration as a central theme in crime fiction. *Long Way Home* demonstrates how crime fiction uses the genre's conventions to take creative risks by incorporating politically controversial themes such as migration and contributing to wider cultural debates about national identity and crime.

Extending the genre

Migration in crime fiction reflects the cultural ambivalence surrounding representation of migrants and migration and highlights the political debates and weaponisation of migration in the media and popular culture. Crime writers use the genre's conventions to harness the themes of crime and migration and to offer compelling and realistic representations of crime and social justice issues, in a generic literary format which appeals to wide audiences. The popular media's stoking of moral panic surrounding illegal migration and human trafficking crimes means that crime fiction authors treating these themes as part of their novels' crime plots have to walk a fine line between perpetuating damaging and one-dimensional stereotypes and offering fresh, more complex representations of migrants and their social and cultural contexts. The outcome of this balancing act is central to the genre's ability to offer social and cultural critique, and to explore and expose contemporary forms of criminality. The chapter has explored how crime fiction engages with complex and rapidly evolving political and cultural situations such as Trump's America and Brexit Britain, by using migration as the critical lens through which to explore and portray crime. By interrogating and challenging notions of home, agency and national identity, Dolan's novel uses its crime plot to uncover and reveal the darker sides of a society rife with inequality and exploitation caused by austerity and social inequality. As Dolan explains, in *Long Way Home*, her preoccupation with migration revealed "a kind of hierarchy of victims – who gets lost within British society, whose suffering gets ignored – and an exploration of an isolated, self-policing sub culture" (Nette 2014). These themes are highlighted and exposed in *Long Way Home* through the text's police procedural conventions, which problematise the role and function of the police force and its detectives in dealing with complex migration crimes such as modern slavery, in difficult social conditions of rising inequity and racially-motivated violence. Although some aspects of *Long Way Home* are specific to British contexts, the novel's concern with different types of migrants, migration and criminality is echoed in crime novels around the western world. The theme of migration in crime fiction contributes to generating innovative and challenging plots which ask uncomfortable but necessary questions about representations of politics in crime fiction and the marginalisation of individuals and groups due to race/ethnicity and nationality. Migration in crime fiction thus questions those vital values and generic conventions associated with crime fiction, such as the restoration of order and the insistence on justice for victims.

Bibliography

Allen, S. and Møllegaard, K. (eds) (2018) *Narratives of Place in Literature and Film*, Abingdon: Routledge.

Atwood, M. (2017) "Margaret Atwood Interview Alias Grace Premiere", *Red Carpet News TV*, 23 October, www.youtube.com/watch?v=WSLQp0UbTPs (accessed 27 October 2019).

Barnett, D. (2018) "Unusual suspects: the writers diversifying crime fiction", *The Guardian*, 15 June, www.theguardian.com/books/2018/jun/15/unusual-suspects-the-writers-diversifying-detective-fiction (accessed 9 May 2019).

Bell, D. (1970) "Crime and mobility among Italian-Americans", in A.J. Heidenheimer (ed.), *Political Corruption: Readings in comparative analysis*, New Brunswick, NJ: Transaction Books, 159–66.

Betts, A. (2015) "Human migration will be a defining issue of this century. How best to cope?", *The Guardian*, 20 September, www.theguardian.com/commentisfree/2015/sep/20/migrants-refugees-asylum-seekers-21st-century-trend (accessed 31 October 2019).

Beyer, C. (2018) "'In the suitcase was a boy': representing transnational child trafficking in contemporary crime fiction", in Gregoriou, 89–115.

Bowling, B. and Westenra, S. (2018) "'A really hostile environment': adiaphorization, global policing and the crimmigration control system", *Theoretical Criminology*, 1 June, https://doi.org/10.1177/1362480618774034 (accessed 31 October 2019).

Dolan, E. (2014) *Long Way Home*, Kindle edition, New York: Random House.

Eaglestone, R. (2018) "Introduction: Brexit and literature", *Brexit and Literature*, Abingdon: Routledge.

Evans, M., Moore, S. and Johnstone, H. (eds) (2018) *Detecting the Social: Order and disorder in post-1970s detective fiction*, New York: Springer.

Fasselt, R. (2016) "Making and unmaking 'African foreignness': African settings, African migrants and the migrant detective in contemporary South African crime fiction", *Journal of Southern African Studies*, 42(6): 1109–24.

Goldin, I., Cameron, G. and Balarajan, M. (2011) *Exceptional People: How migration shaped our world and will define our future*, Princeton, NJ: Princeton University Press.

Gregoriou, C. (ed.) (2018) *Representations of Transnational Human Trafficking: Present-day news media, true crime, and fiction*, Cham: Palgrave Pivot.

Leon, A. de (2018) "Immigration narratives in crime fiction", *CrimeReads*, 21 September, https://crimereads.com/immigration-narratives-in-crime-fiction/ (accessed 9 May 2019).

McCracken, S. (1998) *Pulp: Reading popular fiction*, Manchester University Press.

Nette, A. (2014) "Interview: Eva Dolan, author of Long Way Home", *Pulp Curry*, 17 February, www.pulpcurry.com/2014/02/interview-eva-dolan-author-of-long-way-home/ (accessed 12 October 2019).

Nilsson, L., Damrosch, D. and D'haen, T. (eds) (2017) *Crime Fiction as World Literature*, New York: Bloomsbury Academic.

Nowicka, M. and Krzyżowski, Ł. (2017) "The social distance of Poles to other minorities: a study of four cities in Germany and Britain", *Journal of Ethnic and Migration Studies*, 43(3): 359–78.

Crime fiction and migration

Papademetriou, D.G. and Banulescu-Bogdan, N. (2016) *Understanding and Addressing Public Anxiety about Immigration*, The 14th Plenary Meeting of the Transatlantic Council on Migration, Migration Policy Institute.

Phillips, B. (2014) "The representation of migrants in Australian detective fiction", *Anuari de filologia. Literatures contemporànies*, 4: 75–87.

Plunkett, J. (2011) "Midsomer Murders producer suspended over diversity remarks", *The Guardian*, 15 March, www.theguardian.com/media/2011/mar/15/midsomer-murders-producer-race-row (accessed 9 May 2019).

Rolls, A., Vuaille-Barcan, M.L. and West-Sooby, J., (eds) (2016) *Translating National Allegories: The case of crime fiction*, New York: Routledge.

Rutter, J. (2015) *Moving up and Getting on: Migration, integration and social cohesion in the UK*, Cambridge: Policy Press.

Seago, K. (2014) "Introduction and overview: crime (fiction) in translation", *Journal of Specialised Translation*, 22: 2–14.

43

CRIME FICTION AND AUTHORITARIANISM

Carlos Uxó

Can crime fiction only thrive in democratic settings? Is Haycraft right when he asserts that detective stories are only produced on a large scale in democracies, as they are a "democratic institution" that dramatise the kind of rights enjoyed only in "constitutional lands" (1974: 313)? Or McCann when he links American hardboiled with the "pursuit of a [...] democratic culture" (2000: 5), and describes the detective story as "a liberal genre" (6)? Ultimately, is a regulated, accountable and fair process of upholding the law and fighting the transgressions of its authority necessary for the development of crime fiction? I answer these questions in the negative and argue instead that liberal democracy is not a *sine qua non* for crime fiction: While it is true that many authoritarian leaders loathed crime fiction (Franco, Mao, Stalin, Hitler and the Latin American dictators of the 1970s and 1980s), the genre enjoyed immense popularity in post-Mao China, the Soviet Union after Stalin, Cuba and many countries in the Eastern Bloc.

My intention in this chapter is to ponder the tridimensional relationship between crime fiction, authoritarian regimes and world literature, exploring the extent to which it is possible to understand "the circulation and translation of ideas, themes, and concerns about crime and policing across and between national traditions, while attempting to pay due attention to specific sociocultural and institutional contexts" (Pepper 2016: 10–11). To this end, I will focus on two groups of authoritarian regimes: Communist (mostly Eastern Bloc, but also Cuba), and Latin American military dictatorships.

Katharina Hall analyses the moral implications, problems and opportunities resulting from featuring a police officer as the investigator in crime narratives set in a dictatorship (2013: 288). Focusing on novels featuring a Nazi detective, Hall sees a shift from the traditional role of "villain" afforded to Nazi officers, to a more morally complex investigative agent through which, Hall argues, writers can examine the problem of "reconciling the genre's dominant depiction of the detective as a representative of truth, morality, and justice with that of a detective working for a corrupt, fascist regime" (290). It is by focusing on this moral complexity that writers avoid the textual crisis they can generate if the reader cannot identify with the detective. Taking this problem as point of departure, Stewart King's "La novela criminal de dictaduras y la justicia universal" [Crime Fiction, Dictatorships and Universal Justice, 2018] is to the best of my knowledge and at the time of writing the only study to have used a world literature approach to analyse the relationship between crime fiction and dictatorships. King examines four novels set in dictatorships with a twofold aim: To rethink in a multinational context Katharina Hall's examination of novels in which the investigator is a police officer working for an authoritarian regime, and to consider whether it is possible to identify in those four novels a sense of shared justice that goes beyond their respective national borders. Referring to Max Weber and Alison Young (who, in turn, refers the reader to Benedict Anderson), King urges us to consider crime fiction as a global phenomenon in which texts produced in specific national settings can be read as part of a "transnational dialogue" (2018: 51). Here, the imagined community is no longer bound by national borders and instead places itself under the jurisdiction of a universal justice that supersedes local laws. King illustrates this by reading four novels as examples of world literature, in which all the authors appeal to a shared universal sense of justice, thus delegitimising the legal system imposed by the dictatorships in which their novels are set.

As will be demonstrated in relation to the two chosen international cases, it is possible to argue that crime novels set in dictatorships can speak to a transnational imagined community, which shares interpretations of the role of the state in relation to justice, legal process, or the fight against transgressions of the law. This circulation of ideas results in a transnational dialogue in which crime authors and readers from different countries engage. While the crime novels mentioned can be read in relation to a national-specific context, a transnational approach, which considers the broader function or significance of these texts, truly expands our understanding.

Crime fiction and Latin American dictatorships

In the 1970s and 1980s, authoritarian regimes mushroomed in Latin America, where crime fiction had been a popular genre for some time (mainly in Mexico and Argentina, but also in Chile). As right-wing dictatorships became the norm, the left leanings of many crime writers hindered the development of the genre, sometimes with tragic consequences, as in the case of Argentinian writer Rodolfo Walsh's "disappearance" after writing an "Open letter to the Military Junta" (1977). Others, like Chilean Roberto Ampuero, or Argentinians Mempo Giardinelli and Sergio Sinay, went into exile.[1] Those who stayed were forced to publish overseas or under pseudonyms, or produced metaphorical texts such as Ricardo Piglia's *Respiración artificial* [Artificial Respiration, 1980], a thought-provoking text that borders crime fiction. The initials of *Respiración artificial* (RA) are also those of República Argentina (Argentinian Republic); the allegorical intention of the novel is clear. In most cases, it was only after the return to democracy that crime fiction resurfaced, and when it did, crime writers turned to other sources for inspiration, such as the works of Spanish writer Vázquez Montalbán, who also represented the transition from dictatorship to democracy, or the French *néo-polar*, with its highly violent, socially conscious take on the genre that challenges hegemonic narratives of power, with the occasional nod to postmodernist trends *à la* Jean-Patrick Manchette. Most importantly, in the context of this chapter, many crime writers shared an awareness of being part of a transnational phenomenon that eventually led to what is known as *neopolicial*.[2]

As Argentinian José Pablo Feinman puts it, the question crime writers asked themselves, not dissimilar to the one Katharina Hall analysed in her above-mentioned article on Nazi detectives, was:

> What happens to police fiction when crime is not simply in the streets, but it is there, in the streets, because the State is responsible for the existence of the crime? What happens when the police, far from representing the image of Justice, represents the image of terror?
>
> *(2011: 215)*

The typical answer was to feature what King calls "ethical outsiders" (2018: 56) as investigators, or to leave the crimes unpunished, justice being considered an impossibility: "The purpose of the investigation may be to know the truth and, at its best, make it public; never to obtain justice" (Gamerro 2011: 329).

Since the novels abandon the belief in the possibility of justice, the emphasis shifts from the crime to the surrounding context, where the novels explore the limits between fiction and reality, and position at the centre of the text discussions on power, and who holds it (Fraser 2006: 199), echoing what Hammett or Sciacia, among others, had already done in other settings. In Giardinelli's *Luna caliente* [Sultry Moon, 1983], for example, there is no mystery to solve, as the focus is on the dictatorship's ability to control and, ultimately, force the killer to work for the regime. In Feinman's *Últimos días de la víctima* [Last Days of the Victim, 1979] the investigator is in fact a contract killer who decides to find out more about the person he has been paid to kill, Külpe – a name Spanish speakers associate with *culpa*, guilt, and with a Kafkaesque K (Simpson 1990: 142). Ultimately, this decision leads the investigator into a trap in which he is murdered: The searcher of the truth becomes the victim. In Saer's *Nadie nada nunca* [Nobody Nothing Never, 1979], Inspector Caballo Leyva, who has to investigate the killing of a number of horses (*caballos* in Spanish), is ready to torture where necessary. At the end of the novel, the mystery remains unsolved, although there is a suggestion that the army may have used the horses for shooting practice. In Brazilian Rubem Fonseca's *High Art* (1983) investigator Mandrake decides to learn *Percor* (literally "perforate and cut", a combat knife-fighting technique developed by the police) after he is attacked and his wife is raped. While the murderer behind the first (of many) killings is found, his suicide and the violence encountered in the investigation leaves no doubt: Justice is nowhere to be seen.

When dictatorships gave way to democratic regimes, crime writers grappled with the collective trauma and tried to make sense of their new realities, often still wary of the judicial processes in place. Thus, Argentinian Eduardo Sacheri's *La pregunta de sus ojos* [The Secret in their Eyes, 2005], Chilean Ramón Díaz Eterovic's *La oscura memoria de las armas* [Dark Echoes of the Past, 2008] and Guatemalan Dante Liano's *El hombre de Montserrat* [The Man from Montserrat, 2005] examine not only the haunting atrocities of their respective dictatorships, but the challenges faced by the new democratic regimes in search of an elusive justice. To this end, in crime novels written after the dictatorships, events in the plot often begin during the dictatorial regime and conclude in democracy, thus emphasising the continuities between governments.

In the context of this chapter, it is important to emphasise the self-perception of crime fiction authors, readers and critics from Latin America as a transnational community trying to cope in similar ways with the trauma of their respective dictatorships and their transition to democracy, topics further developed in the chapters on memory and trauma in this volume.

Crime fiction in communist countries

In the following paragraphs, crime fiction written in communist countries will be analysed, in order to show that the genre shared similar traits with some Eastern Bloc countries and in Cuba – what I term crime fiction *Internationale*. The profuse circulation of novels in translation and theoretical readings of the genre throughout these countries clearly demonstrates the development of a transnational take on the genre. Sharing analogous aims and rules, this *Internationale* developed a distinct crime fiction model, in direct opposition to those produced in capitalist countries.

Crime fiction and authoritarianism

For decades, the Soviet Union under Stalin (1922–1952) banned the publication of crime fiction, considering it "the most naked expression of bourgeois society's fundamental ideas on property" and a mere market-driven product whose main goal is "maximum money-making" (Eisenstein 1988: 91). In 1938, however, the Central Committee of the Komsomol, the Union of Communist Youth, foresaw what they believed to be the genre's potential as a tool to foster revolutionary education for the Eastern Bloc and began to promote detective films. The conditions for crime fiction's emergence were facilitated when Nikita Khrushchev, Stalin's successor, denounced in 1956 Stalin's cult of personality, and the newly elected Central Committee of the Soviet Union Communist Party felt the need to distance itself from past mistakes. This, coupled with the continuing urge for patriotic exaltation in the midst of the Cold War, reinforced the educational role afforded to crime fiction.

That same year, the magazine *Yunost'* [Youth] published the first crime novel of the post-Stalin era: Arkady Adamov's *Delo Pestrykh* [The Motley Case, 1956]. The 1962 German edition of the novel included a telling prologue by the translator, Valerian P. Lebedew, who stated: "This is not a simple confrontation of policemen and criminals, but of the embodiment of the class-conscious man who watches over the morality of the State, and the parasite of society, the anti-Communist type infected by Western individualism" (Adamov, quoted in ana 2013).[3] Adamov's aim, therefore, was not only to provide an example of the success of Soviet security forces in their fight against crime in a specific case, but to make readers aware of the confrontation between Communism and Western individualism. While at one level the intended readership is Russian, this and similar novels are not bound by national borders, but aim to speak to a larger, transnational imagined community that, from the authors' point of view, shares their views on justice, morality and social duties.

The KGB played a significant role in the development of crime fiction in the Soviet Union and in the broader Eastern Bloc, where Soviet guidelines on how to adapt the genre to a communist setting were applied. KGB director Vladimir Semichastny (1961–1967), keen to improve the agency's reputation and to respond to the growing popularity of Ian Fleming's James Bond series, supported "positive fictional portrayals" of Soviet intelligence agents, with officials ultimately turning to Bulgarian author Andrei Gulyashki to create a Bond-like character (Jens 2017: 34). In Gulyashki's *The Zakhov Mission* (1963), however, the protagonist is closer to Sherlock Holmes than James Bond, and dishes out long explanations on the virtues of a simple life while investigating the theft of military information (Nette 2014). After Gulyashki, during a trip to London apparently financed by the KGB, failed to get permission from Ian Fleming to use 007 as a character for his novels, the author published *Срещу 07* in 1966 (literally "Against 07", but translated and published in Australia as *Zakhov vs 07*). In the novel, British agent 07 kidnaps a Russian scientist attending a conference in Bulgaria, killing a few people in the process. An international persecution ensues, taking the characters to Paris, Tangier (where 07 is helped by an ex-Auschwitz doctor) and Antarctica, culminating in the rescue of the scientist, and the escape of 07, thus making possible the continuation of the novel in the series that would follow. The international pursuit, the diverse nationalities of the characters, the Nazi link (which, by extension, criminalises the West as a whole, portrayed as a continuation of the Nazi regime), as well as the almost simultaneous publication of the novel in Bulgaria and the Soviet Union, all point to an understanding of criminality and a readership that goes well beyond the domestic limits, and which would spawn a number of similar products in other countries in the Eastern Bloc, as well as in Cuba.

Perhaps the most successful of these was *Seventeen Moments of Spring* (1969), by Iulian Semyonov, who had already gained recognition with *Petrovka, 38* (1963), a novel about Moscow police. Yuri Andropov, who succeeded Semichastny as the head of the KGB, commissioned

Semyonov to write "a follow-up novel about a Soviet agent in Germany during the Great Patriotic War", for which he received considerable support from the agency, including access to secret archives (Rosenberg 1987; Jens 2017: 34). Andropov had been First Secretary of the Yaroslavl Komsomol Regional Committee at the time the Komsomol was promoting detective films in 1938, and he must have been very familiar with this policy. In this case, however, he stressed the need "to write a novel in which the most important thing [would be] the constitution and the law". The result was a text in which "the KGB major-general and lieutenant-general concern themselves with legality [and] worry [...] about what is morally the right thing to do", an approach that widened the reach of a novel no longer limited to national events, and was without a doubt one of the keys to its success outside the Soviet Union (Rosenberg 1987).[4]

In the novel, Soviet agent Maxim Isaiev infiltrates the SS under the name of Max Otto von Stierlitz, and plays a crucial role in the demise of the Nazi regime. Historical events are altered, when not rewritten, in a careful attempt to reclaim the Soviet Union's role in the German defeat, while maintaining a safe distance from Stalin's excesses. This bending of historical events would be furthered in the ensuing television series, based on the novel and scripted by Semyonov, which convinced many Soviet citizens that Maxim Isaiev was a real agent, and that it was thanks to him that the Third Reich was defeated. The success of *Seventeen Moments of Spring* led to a series of novels in which Stierlitz travelled to the Far East, Spain (during the Civil War), Belgrade, Zagreb, Paris, Krakow and post-war West Germany, pointing again to the internationalisation of the conflict (and the safe setting of criminal activities outside the Soviet Union).

Adamov, Gulyashki and Semyonov, together with the brothers Arkady and Georgy Weiner, Leonid Slovin, and Vil Lipatov made crime fiction one of the most popular genres in the Soviet Union (Brine 1985: 415–16). Their readership, however, was not exclusively Soviet, as translations of their books (and TV series based on them) were readily available in many of the Eastern Bloc countries. In Romania, for example, the "Enigma" collection published translations of Soviet, Polish, Bulgarian, Czechoslovakian and Hungarian authors, with the "Aventura" collection publishing Romanian writers. As these examples show, the Eastern Bloc developed its own crime fiction publishing structures, with a fluid circulation kept outside the western model. Such circulation, however, was not limited to books in translation, as the Soviet formula itself was reproduced domestically, with recurrent features like the setting of criminal activities in foreign countries, the emphasis on collective work and austerity, the complete absence of investigators outside the organs of state security, the bipolar view of the world, or the conception of any crime as an attack on the state. This was the case of East Germany, Bulgaria and Poland, as well as Cuba, where "revolutionary crime fiction" appeared in the 1970s. Given the unprecedented extent of the support given by Cuban cultural (and army) officials to the development of the genre, which by the 1980s would be the most widely published and read on the island, it is a case worth examining in closer detail.[5]

Crime fiction in Cuba emerged in the wake of the First Congress of Education and Culture held in Havana in April 1971, at which Cuban cultural officials decided to implement new policies based on three main principles: The consideration of art as a weapon of the Revolution; the need for a political assessment of artistic manifestations; and the call to intensify the control of literary awards, which were perceived, in essence, as political acts. The Congress also reiterated that Cuba was at war with Capitalism, and demanded, as a consequence, that all cultural manifestations openly support revolutionary processes. Cuban cultural officials imposed strict censorship and a tight control over every cultural activity, coupled with the promotion of cultural manifestations or specific genres perceived as especially useful in the war against Capitalism.

In March of that same year Cuban writer Ignacio Cárdenas Acuña had published *Enigma para un domingo*, the first Cuban crime novel since the 1959 Revolution. Although the genre, until then, occupied a negligible position in Cuban literature, Acuña's novel was an immediate and unexpected success both in Cuba and within the Communist Bloc with translations into Russian, German, Romanian, Hungarian and Ukrainian. As a consequence of its success, the University of Havana convened a panel towards the end of 1971 which concluded that crime fiction could be used within a communist context, and the Ministry of Interior announced the creation of the Anniversary of the Triumph of the Revolution Crime Fiction Award. Thanks in part to this award, crime fiction became the most important genre of the 1970s with a staggering thirty-eight per cent of novels published in Cuba between 1979 and 1983 being crime fiction (Braham 2004: 126). As one critic notes, it is impossible "to find another cultural area that enjoyed the support and incentives" that the crime genre did during this period (Fernández Pequeño 1994: 14).

Aware of the apparent contradiction of fostering what they perceived as a capitalist genre in a communist setting, parallel to the publication of crime novels, collections of short stories and even theatre plays, an impressive number of programmatic texts were published, insisting almost obsessively that Cuban crime fiction was a new phenomenon, a genre with few connections to its capitalist origins. For intellectual heavyweight José Antonio Portuondo, the crux was the understanding of the role afforded to the concepts of justice and legality in revolutionary crime fiction as opposed to other crime fiction models. The British model, he argued, was based on the idea that "what is legal is therefore just" (that is, crime fiction is written to support a legal body that, according to Communism, is unjust by nature); in hardboiled crime fiction, the detectives are forced to act outside the sanctioned legality to defend what is considered just; and in spy novels intelligence agents constantly resort to illegal activities in defence of a system that is unjust. Revolutionary crime fiction, on the contrary, was based on the idea that "what is just is legal", and therefore justice and legality coincide completely. In this setting, crime fiction acquires "a political and literary dimension" impossible to place "outside the confrontation between Capitalism and Socialism". Therefore, whereas in a capitalist context crime fiction was considered to be an ideologically rotten genre, in the context of the Revolution it becomes a weapon, contributing to the ideological education of workers (Portuondo 1973: 133), and helping to establish the opposition "state security organs + citizenry vs delinquents", considered to be the beating heart of revolutionary crime fiction (Cristóbal Pérez 1979: 11).

While it is interesting to note that these programmatic texts seem quite reluctant to mention similar developments in other Eastern Bloc countries, translations of communist crime fiction were readily available, together with Bogomil Rainov's 400-page essay on crime fiction.

As occurred in the Eastern Bloc, Semyonov's novel *Seventeen Moments of Spring* and its television adaptation were also an extraordinary success in Cuba. While watching the series, a young Uruguayan living in Cuba, Daniel Chavarría, decided to write a Cuban version, entitled *Joy*, that won the Anniversary of the Triumph of the Revolution Award in 1977 as well as the award for the best Cuban crime fiction novel, 1971–1981. It would also become a bestseller in the socialist world.

Daniel Chavarría's *Joy*

Joy is what many Cubans insist on calling counterespionage or counterintelligence fiction (emphasis on "counter", or defence against an attack), in an attempt to distance this model from James Bond's actions. The novel tells of a plot that is discovered to introduce a virus in Cuba that can eventually destroy the national citrus fruit production. This discovery leads the intelligence service to open an investigation that successfully derails the attempt and allows Cuba to produce a documentary, to be shown all over the world, detailing the CIA involvement in the affair.

Unlike similar novels, *Joy* is not based on a real case. As López Calvo has shown in relation to another Cuban crime novel, Juan Ángel Cardi's *El American Way of Death* (1980), it is possible to see in *Joy* "the influence of Soviet 'factography' on Cuban writing" (2012: 32). Rather than aiming to reflect reality, factography was concerned with transforming reality through what was known as "operativity", "a situational aesthetics that conceptualized representation not as an objective reflection of a static world, but as an operation that by definition intervenes in the context of the aesthetic act" (Fore 2006: 105). Factography, therefore, disregards objectivism and emphasises the performative role of literature. Accordingly, *Joy*'s approach is more subjective than objective, disregarding the mimetic in favour of the operational. Real events and people mix with fictional characters and situations in order to achieve the books' main goal: To present what might be called a collectivised view of crime, victims and investigator, thus transforming the readers' views and, ultimately, reality.

In line with what programmatic texts demanded from crime fiction novels, *Joy* does not depict a confrontation between a private eye and a criminal, but instead, it broadens its reach by collectivising the crime (the spread of the bacteria in Cuba is a trial for future attacks on other communist countries), the investigating team (the protagonist flies to the USSR to consult with colleagues; a network of spies from different nationalities investigate in a number of countries to help Cuban officials), and the victim (Cubans at the outset, extending to all of humankind).

Thus, *Joy*, like the many crime novels from the Eastern Bloc and Cuba that were translated and published in other communist countries, appealed to a large imagined community, who read them in a transnational rather than exclusively domestic context.

One can only hope that transnationality becomes one of the foci of future studies on the relationship between crime fiction and authoritarianism, paying due attention to King's concept of "transnational dialogue", mentioned earlier. To date, for example, an almost exclusively national approach has been applied to the study of crime fiction in the Eastern Bloc. While these studies are certainly useful, a deeper analysis of what I have termed the crime fiction *Internationale* seems crucial to fully understand an intrinsically international phenomenon. This should be done without imposing our views from the West and, by incorporating other perspectives, we can hopefully develop a more complex appreciation of the role of crime fiction in authoritarian regimes. Thus, research on the extent to which, for example, Romanian readers and writers knew about Cuban or Bulgarian crime fiction, or on the international commonalities of the criteria applied for translation and publication of crime fiction novels in the Eastern Bloc would undoubtedly help us better understand the development of the genre in communist countries.

Future research on crime fiction and authoritarian regimes should also analyse the evolving relationship between genre and state power. Recent criticism (Pepper 2016) argues that crime fiction displays a sceptical and ambivalent relationship with the state, a move that seems to also take place in countries under authoritarian regimes. In Cuba, for example, revolutionary crime fiction has given way to a more openly critical *neopolicial*, which often reflects on anxieties about the efficacy and reach of the state power. Whether a similar evolution can be traced in other authoritarian contexts is certainly worth investigating.

Crime fiction and authoritarianism

Notes

1 Ampuero lived in Cuba between 1974 and 1979 at the time the aforementioned series *Seventeen Moments of Spring* was broadcast. The protagonist of his crime fiction is a Cuban detective living in Chile. Political divergences with the Cuban authorities, though, have hampered the circulation of his books on the island.
2 The term *neopolicial* was coined by Mexican writer Paco Ignacio Taibo II but was made popular by Cuban writer Leonardo Padura. In this and many similar articles on the topic, critics tend to study *neopolicial* as a continental rather than a domestic development.
3 The quote is a translation of the 1964 Spanish edition of the novel (Editorial Molino), which in turn appears to be a translation of the 1962 German edition (*Die Bunte Bande von Moskau*, Goldmann, 1962). In the context of this chapter, it is interesting to note the international circulation of the novel, as well as the irony of having a communist book published in a fascist dictatorship, for which I have no explanation. It has also been translated into Chinese and Ukrainian.
4 Placing crime in foreign countries was also a common occurrence in crime fiction written in Spain and Italy during their respective fascist dictatorships.
5 Not all crime fiction written in Eastern Bloc countries should be seen as identical, though. In each country, literary traditions and the sociopolitical context combined to create a national specific flavour. In Poland, for example, finance crime received an attention absent in other countries.

Bibliography

Adamov, A.G. (1962) *Die Bunte Bande von Moskau*, Munich: Goldmann.
ana. (2013) "La terrible banda de Moscú: Primera novela policíaca de la Rusia soviética", www.bibliotecanegra.com/curiosidades/la-terrible-banda-de-moscu-primera-novela-policiaca-de-la-rusia-sovietica-14328 (accessed 22 December 2018).
Braham, P. (2004) *Crimes Against the State, Crimes Against Persons. Detective fiction in Cuba and Mexico*, Minneapolis: University of Minnesota Press.
Brine, J.J. (1985) *Adult readers in the Soviet Union*, PhD thesis, University of Birmingham, etheses.bham.ac.uk/1398/1/Brine86PhD.pdf (accessed 22 December 2018).
Cristóbal Pérez, A. (1979) "Prólogo", in D. Chavarría, *Joy*, Havana: Arte y Literatura: 5–13.
De Rosso, E. (2011) *Retóricas del crimen. Reflexiones latinoamericanas sobre el género policial*, Alcalá la Real: Alcalá Grupo Editorial.
Eisenstein, S. (1988) "The detective story", in *The Psychology of Composition*, London: Methuen, 91–94.
Feinman, J.P. (2011) "Estado policial y novela negra argentina", in De Rosso, 213–33.
Fernández Pequeño, J.M. (1994) *Cuba: la narrativa policial entre el querer y el poder (1973–1988)*, Havana: Instituto Cubano del Libro.
Fore, D. (2006) "The operative word in Soviet factography", *October*, 118: 95–131.
Fraser, B.R. (2006) "Narradores contra la ficción: La narración detectivesca como estrategia política", *Studies in Latin American Popular Culture*, 25: 199–219.
Gamerro, C. (2011) "Para una reformulacion del género policial argentino", in De Rosso, 319–29.
Hall, K. (2013) "The 'Nazi detective' as provider of justice in post-1990 British and German crime fiction: Philip Kerr's *The Pale Criminal*, Robert Harris's *Fatherland*, and Richard Birkefeld and Göran Hachmeister's *Wer Übrig Bleibt, Hat Recht*", *Comparative Literature Studies*, 50(2): 288–313.
Haycraft, H. (1974) "Dictators, democrats, and detectives", in *Murder for Pleasure. The life and times of the detective story*, New York: Biblo and Tannen, 312–18.
Jens, E. (2017) "Cold War spy fiction in Russian popular culture: from suspicion to acceptance via *Seventeen Moments of Spring*", *Studies in Intelligence*, 61(2): 31–41. www.cia.gov/library/center-for-the-study-of-intelligence/csi-publications/csi-studies/studies/vol-61-no-2/cold-war-spy-fiction.html (accessed 20 December 2018).
King, S. (2018) "La novela criminal de dictaduras y la justicia universal", in G. Forero Quintero (ed.), *Justicia y paz en la novela de crímenes*, Antioquia: Siglo del Hombre Editores S.A.
López Calvo, I. (2012) "Factography and Cold War ideology in the Cuban detective novel", in A. Hammond (ed.), *Global Cold War Literature. Western, Eastern and postcolonial perspectives*, London: Routledge, 30–42.
McCann, S. (2000) *Gumshoe America: Hard-boiled crime fiction and the rise and fall of new deal liberalism*, Durham: Duke University Press.

Nette, A. (2014) "A proletarian James Bond?", *Overland*, 214, https://overland.org.au/previous-issues/issue-214/feature-andrew-nette/ (accessed 23 December 2018).

Pepper, A. (2016) *Unwilling Executioner: Crime fiction and the state*, Oxford: Oxford University Press.

Portuondo, J.A. (1973) "La novela policial revolucionaria", *Astrolabio*, Havana: Arte y Literatura, 127–33.

Rosenberg, K. (1987) "The law-abiding Soviet secret agents", *New Statesman*, 18: 20.

Simpson, A.S. (1990) *Detective Fiction from Latin America*, London: Associated University Press.

44
CRIME FICTION AND DIGITAL MEDIA

Tanja Välisalo, Maarit Piipponen, Helen Mäntymäki and
Aino-Kaisa Koistinen

In 2012, twenty-one fiction writers were challenged by *The Guardian* to write a Twitter story. Crime writer Ian Rankin's narrative consisted of typical elements of the crime genre – a crime, criminal and victim: "I opened the door to our flat and you were standing there, cleaver raised. Somehow you'd found out about the photos. My jaw hit the floor" ("Twitter fiction"). Rankin's story is an example of Twitterfiction known as "shorty" or "Twister", in which an individual tweet forms a narrative (Thomas 2014: 95), or of flash fiction, which is fiction with fewer than 1,500 words (Galef 2016: ix), often shared through online sites.

Rankin's shorty explores the compatibility of a specific popular genre and digital media, which is also the aim in this chapter. In addressing this issue, we first distinguish between distributing texts in a digitised form and digital fiction/digital textual forms; all these are products of the digital revolution, which has its roots in the recent development of communication and information technologies. In the so-called convergence culture created by the digital age, digitalisation has not only offered new publication platforms but also facilitated the interaction between text and audience through such platforms. This chapter addresses the ways in which crime fiction has generally adapted to digital media environments, but we propose that it is especially in the spaces of production, interaction and engagement that digital forms of crime fiction seem to flourish.

The chapter adds to the so far very limited number of studies on crime texts in digital environments; the few studies that exist focus on fandom (e.g. Stein and Busse 2012) and video game adaptations (e.g. Walker 2015). We understand this lack as deriving from the novelty of digital crime fiction formats. As our case study concerns transmedia storytelling, we first briefly explore the effects of the digital revolution on the publishing industry and offer a theoretical discussion of transmedia storytelling; second, we reflect on the crime genre's adoption of digital forms and transmedia storytelling as well as the scholarly assessment of these forms; and third, we analyse the digital game *Miss Fisher and the Deathly Maze* (2017) as transmedial digital crime fiction. The game is analysed by close playing (cf. close reading): This method uses the "implied player" model not only to examine the intended gameplay (cf. "implied reader") but also to study the possibilities and instances of transgressive play, actions not intended by the game designers but nevertheless possible in the game (Aarseth 2007: 131–32).

The digital age and transmedia storytelling

With the digital revolution, large technology companies have invaded the area previously occupied by traditional media and publishing companies. Digitisation and digital distribution have widely replaced conventional channels of distribution and they now exist alongside bookstores, movie theatres and traditional television channels. Crime narratives are read as ebooks through digital devices like Kindle or consumed as audiobooks through Audible or Storytel; DVD and Blu-ray have been replaced with on-demand TV and streaming platforms that offer access to digital services at an increasing rate. Distribution channels and content producers have lately converged (cf. Birkinbine et al. 2017), as companies like Netflix and Amazon now produce content instead of only delivering it.

Besides creating new distribution channels, the digital age has transformed the existing print culture tradition by developing new modes of narration based on the digital tools available; this invites us to consider what counts as digital fiction in general. Maria Engberg refers to digital fiction as an umbrella term, under which such "specific writing practices" as hypertext and network fiction, interactive fiction, email, cell phone or multimedia novels, and locative media fiction can be included (2014: 138–39); she also notes that the term's definition is not stable. Alice Bell, Astrid Ensslin and Hans Kristian Rustad define digital fiction more strictly as "fiction whose structure, form, and meaning are dictated by, and in dialogue with, the digital context in which it is produced and received" (2014: 4; cf. Hayles 2008: 3 on electronic literature). Digital fiction thus refers to texts that are produced in and for digital platforms, using digital technologies. In this chapter, we embrace this definition for digital fiction but extend it to include narratives that have transmedially expanded to digital platforms, such as the Miss Fisher storyworld.

Taking into account Bell, Ensslin and Rustad's definition, Rankin's shorty can be classified as digital crime fiction because it is born-digital. In contrast, a single Miss Fisher crime novel by author Kerry Greenwood would not count as digital crime fiction if it were simply digitised, because the same novel could be read as a print book and the content would be identical in the two formats. However, digital technologies have enabled new ways to expand a given narrative world, offering different, medium-specific experiences to audiences (cf. Jenkins 2006: 95–96). These technologies allow a print novel to be expanded transmedially to, for example, games, as with Miss Fisher. Moreover, digital expansions of crime fiction resonate with the phenomenon of participatory culture: Its advent has resulted in a proliferation of interactive digital crime fan fiction, the creation of online fandom and fan fiction sites that cater for specific interest groups (e.g. gay or feminist stories).

Our case study, the transmedial Miss Fisher storyworld, illustrates the expansion of creative and commercial media production that utilises the opportunities offered by digital environments. Miss Fisher first appeared as the detective protagonist in Australian writer Kerry Greenwood's twenty-volume historical crime novel series (1989–2014) set in Melbourne in the 1920s. The first novel, *The Cocaine Mystery*, introduces the Honourable Phryne Fisher, an amateur detective with a flashy lifestyle, sharp intelligence and forward-looking values. The novels rewrite the classic puzzle story into a cosy epoque story that borrows lavishly from other crime story formulas including the hardboiled and police procedural (Ryan-Fazilleau 2007). Despite the popularity of the novels, many crime fiction fans know Miss Fisher from the ABC Australia television series, first broadcast in 2012, and soon after available on streaming services such as Netflix. In 2017, a digital game titled *Miss Fisher and the Deathly Maze* was published, and in 2019, a film, *Miss Fisher & The Crypt of Tears* and a spin-off series, *Miss Fisher's Modern Murder Mysteries*, were released. The pleasure of this storyworld strongly lies in its nature as historical fiction, as a heroine created in the twenty-first century has landed in the past to show her contemporaries a glimpse of future worlds. The readers and viewers as well as the players of the digital game are transported to a historical setting to play a game of detection.

On the phrynefisher.com home page by publisher Allen & Unwin, fans have access to Miss Fisher's favourite recipes and are able to download screensavers and wallpapers. The home page offers a glossary of terms used in the novels and advertises twelve TV tie-in editions with photos of actress Essie Davis on the covers. The publisher has also released *A Question of Death: An Illustrated Phryne Fisher Treasury* (2015) containing short stories with images from the TV series and a cover image of Miss Fisher with the text "As seen on ABC 1". Moreover, a rich production of material by fans – fan fiction, blogs, vlogs and other social media inserts – has expanded around the storyworld. Such production of digital media paratexts in the form of user-created content can be described as rhizomatic because of the unpredictability of the connections between the semiotic chains through which they are produced (cf. Deleuze and Guattari 2004: 8–13). Seriality, a traditional component of the crime genre, undoubtedly facilitates the stories' crossover to other media where the "original" stories are then expanded upon (cf. Mittell 2015: 292–318). This production questions the autonomy of individual texts or series and perhaps also the crime genre's traditional focus on resolution, since a text's resolution might be challenged in a chain of other texts. Transmediality and the mobility of texts invite crime fiction scholarship to evaluate its theoretical approaches, because they are currently based on a more static understanding of texts.

The Miss Fisher storyworld negotiates the boundaries of several different media intertextually, multimodally and transmedially. It exemplifies how digital developments have changed the distribution of crime texts and series and also the modes of consumer engagement when they allow for (transnational) audience interaction. Ultimately, these developments create a complex intertextual web, blurring the boundary between producer and audience and questioning the idea of textual containment, the relationship between text and paratext. As such, the Miss Fisher storyworld is representative of what Henry Jenkins (2006) calls "convergence culture" in which old and new media meet in different areas of culture.

In *Convergence Culture*, Jenkins also coined the concept of transmedia storytelling, when referring to the ways in which a fictional storyworld can unfold in different mediums. Ideally, each medium contributes to the storytelling in a unique manner (2006: 97–98). In transmedia storytelling, a story is told, for instance, on television, yet expanded online or in tie-in novels and games, which all add something to the storyworld. The difference between adaptations and transmedia expansions roughly lies in how they contribute to the broader storyworld; that said, the boundary between these two concepts often remains fluid (cf. Harvey 2015: 9, 79–92). Even though transmedia storytelling does not necessarily have to include expansions in *digital* media, it is clear that the rise of digital media platforms has enabled transmedia producers and users to create more and more expansions to varied storyworlds.

Since Jenkins's theorisation of the concept, understandings of transmedia have become more diverse. Theorists have adapted and expanded Jenkins's theory to include, for example, the features by which both audiences and creators recognise and define a specific "transmedial world" (Klastrup and Tosca 2004), the design and production of transmedia projects (Dena 2009) as well as users and user practices (Koistinen et al. 2016).

Digital crime texts and transmediality

It has become commonplace to argue in crime fiction scholarship that the genre is flexible, malleable and mobile: It both "reflects the evolution of modern society" (Gruesser 2013: 7) and revitalises itself through changing generic conventions (Horsley 2005: 16). Christiana Gregoriou writes that the genre's "migrations" into different communication channels such as film, theatre or television in the form of adaptations, translations or remakings ensure its survival and revitalise the source texts (2017: 2–3).

A look into the Miss Fisher storyworld and the history of crime narratives proves Gregoriou's point. Adaptations and remakings of Arthur Conan Doyle's detective Sherlock Holmes have existed in different media since the nineteenth century, and American author Earl Derr Biggers's Charlie Chan series (1925–1932) was soon adapted into film and radio, and later into television and comics. It was not necessary for the audiences to have firsthand knowledge of the Chan novels in order to enjoy the radio drama or comics; and readers first familiar with the novels were given a new, broadening experience with the audiovisual texts. With fan fiction and other digital expansions, these series illustrate the malleability, cultural reproduction and expansion of crime narratives across time and different media.

While fan fiction is one of the most visible forms of digital crime fiction today, it is only one example of how digitalisation enables consumer engagement with crime texts. Today's media companies deliberately create space for consumer interaction and digital-only experiences: The publisher of Stieg Larsson's *Millennium* trilogy introduced an iPhone app in 2011, which expands on the Millennium world and allows users to visit the series' locations (Martin 2011), thereby creating space for crime fiction tourism and inviting consumers to interact with real spaces.

Other apps for mobile devices offer different kinds of pleasures associated with engaging and reading crime texts (see crimefictionlover.com). The reading app Hooked (launched in 2015) delivers messages called "hoots" that form chat fiction (horror and crime) stories that can be shared and commented on. An app called The Pigeonhole offers "disappearing" books, the first of which was Stefan Ahnhem's thriller *Victim Without a Face* (2015). Readers receive "staves" – instalments – that they can comment on and are encouraged to share their reading experience with others; they are rewarded with some "fun extras" and the staves disappear after a certain period of time.[1] The staves are a digital development of the nineteenth-century serial story. In addition, audiobook player apps such as Bound have designed audiobooks that variously combine a crime narrative with sound effects, music and artwork, thereby creating a multisensory immersive environment. Besides apps, this kind of digital, multisensory engagement is available in the iClassics Collection that combines famous stories with soundtracks, illustrations, animations and interaction, for instance "iDoyle".

As the above examples show, the crime genre has harnessed new technologies to engage the interest of its audiences. Yet, unlike fantasy and science fiction which have embraced the possibilities of the digital when it comes to production, reception and formats, crime fiction has more cautiously adopted transmediality (however, it is simultaneously true that these other genres often smuggle crime fiction conventions into their transmedial worlds). The crime genre's relatively slow adaptation into the digital environment also explains the scarcity of scholarship on digital crime texts: Since very few digital crime fictions seem to exist, the material to explore is limited.

Several reasons for the apparent lack of digital crime fiction can be identified. First, according to a survey done on crime and mystery fiction readership in the US in 2015, crime is the genre of older generations, with sixty-three per cent of the readers being over forty-five ("Distribution" 2019). This may partly explain the publishing industry's slow engagement with digital technologies compared to other popular genres such as fantasy and science fiction that cater for crossover audiences. Second, while writers may want to experiment with new forms and media or attempt to interact with audiences through digital narratives and platforms, not all forms of digital crime fiction might allow for the kind of (immersive reading) experience that readers of non-digital crime fiction are argued to long for (cf. Gregoriou 2009: 49–52 and 101–02 on reading crime texts and the pleasures of escapism, relaxation, suspense, fear and deviance).

In 2008, Matt Richtel announced in *The New York Times* that he would write "Twiller", a "real-time thriller" (Richtel 2008). In her assessment of Twiller, Bronwen Thomas contends that "there was very little explicit continuity between or across tweets, resulting in a reading experience that offered little possibility of immersion or absorption in the narrative" (2014: 95).[2] In contrast to Twiller, the true-crime podcast *Serial* (2014) engaged its audience in a completely different manner. The podcast was "received [...] with great dissatisfaction", not because of its digital form but because of its narrative resolution: Listeners were unhappy with the creator's investigation of the crime, which paved the way for "the participation of so many audiences to engage, as amateurs, either through asserting opinions or even physically seeking answers" (Ora 2018: 119). This audience engagement and also the digital materials – paratexts – on *Serial*'s website distinguish *Serial* from traditional crime radio dramas, marking it as (transmedial) digital crime fiction. A further example of audience engagement with digital crime fiction was offered in 2004 by Kate Pullinger, Stefan Schemat and Chris Joseph with their story *The Breathing Wall* that uses text, sound and image. Reading the narrative is only possible with a headset and a microphone, and the software used "works by monitoring your rate of breathing".[3] The murder case can only be solved through this interaction between the text and the reader's body (see Ensslin 2011). The crime apps, Twitter shorties, flash fiction and *The Breathing Wall* highlight the question of whether we (still) approach digital works "with expectations formed by print" (Hayles 2008: 4) and whether new digital forms call for a redefinition of readerly engagement, pleasure and immersion.

Third, the commercial interests of the media industry might favour some forms of digital crime fiction and ignore others: Compared to the commercial expansions of transmedia storytelling in the form of tie-in crime games, it might be more challenging to generate money with Twillers or crime flash fictions produced by individual writers. Also, the complexity of the reading experience of a text like *The Breathing Wall* undoubtedly poses a challenge to the economically motivated media industry. In contrast, the consumption of digital games is a prominent part of today's commercial digital culture: Examples range from Sherlock Holmes video games to such police procedural games as *Her Story* (2015), which combines video clips of fictional police interviews with player interaction, and crime/adventure games like *Look Right* (2017), which joins multimedia content with interactive websites and the player's active participation.

Fourth, the crime genre and its settings are typically realistic – or mimetic – and the genre is often teleologically oriented, focusing on crime, investigation and resolution. In mimetically oriented genres, "dense world-building" is not quite as necessary (Harvey 2018: 161) as in fantasy and science fiction: Transmediality is typically utilised in fantastic fiction, because parallel worlds and other narrative structures allow for the creation of narratives in different media (e.g. Harvey 2015: 38, 94–95). As a realistic genre, crime fiction would not seem to be equally suitable for transmedial world-building and narrative expansions. For example, Tom Dowd et al.'s *Storytelling Across Worlds* (2013) lists only a couple of transmedia crime text examples (e.g. the Sherlock Holmes, Nancy Drew and *CSI* textual worlds). However, Harvey (2018: 162) recently suggested that detective fiction and its subgenres might become "dominant formations within the transmedia sphere", basing his claim on the commercial success of the crime and thriller genres' tie-in games and the transmedial expansion of BBC's *Sherlock* series. Considering the Miss Fisher storyworld consisting of novels, a television series, fan fiction, social media texts, apps for mobile devices and a tie-in game, it appears that the crime genre is moving towards transmedia storytelling. Such a transmedial and multi-platform storyworld is what the younger generations now expect (cf. Jenkins 2006: 129–30).[4]

Miss Fisher in the digital maze

In his "Twenty Rules for Writing Detective Stories" from 1928, S.S. Van Dine famously characterised the classic detective story as a "game" where the writer has to play fair with the reader (see also Suits 1985). Defining detective stories as games has also been criticised because, compared to games, there is a lack of choices offered to the reader: Readers can only decide whether to read the story or not, but in order to participate, they must read (Aarseth 2004: 366). Yet, this "gaming" aspect partly explains why critics have juxtaposed crime puzzles and computer games, to the extent that the crime genre is claimed to be "an obvious genre for adaptation into computer games" (Walker 2015: 226). While the classic detective story that Van Dine discusses invites the reader to solve the crime alongside the detective, in the digital game *Miss Fisher and the Deathly Maze*, the player is the detective. This game consists of separate episodes, each telling their own independent story, similar to the television series. The first episode was published as a mobile game for Apple and Android devices in 2017, and for PC on Steam in 2018. The second episode, "Cleopatra's Curse", was published in 2017, but Tin Man Games has cancelled the third episode because of the poor sales of the game.

The Deathly Maze has three levels of game mechanics: The core mechanics are dialogue and exploring the game environment, which can both be used to find clues (a secondary mechanic). The player has to combine these clues to make deductions (third level mechanics) and solve the crime. Dialogue functions as a tool for reaching the goal, but the player can find pleasure also in uncovering all the possible dialogue threads by restarting dialogue with the same character in the same scene and choosing different dialogue options each time. Rereading books and rewatching television episodes are typical pleasures for fans and audiences, but the crime genre does not yield to this practice quite as easily once the mystery has been solved. However, the abundance of optional dialogue in *The Deathly Maze* facilitates the replaying of the game: New playthroughs can reveal information the player previously failed to obtain. While this information might not be crucial to solving the crime – since the player was earlier able to finish the game without it – it provides additional information about the characters and their relationships (e.g. Miss Fisher flirting with Inspector Robinson or being berated by Aunt Prudence). Thus, solving the mystery might be only one of the pleasures of digital gaming: The game (playthroughs) also offers a pleasure deriving from the active agency of the player in exploring the game world and making decisions.[5]

The player's progression in *The Deathly Maze* is, however, fairly controlled, with plenty of instructions given through dialogue with the other game characters. There is unlimited time for exploring the environment, which also makes for one of the pleasures of the game. In some points, progression depends on the player realising the proper course of action, for example, where to find the speakeasy, or to go to a certain place in order to advance. Deduction, a typical crime genre convention, is the only game mechanic constantly available in *The Deathly Maze*; deducting is also essential to progression, and its importance grows as the game advances. Here also lies the weakness of the game and perhaps detective and crime games in general: As the game progresses, the deductions become more unsatisfactory because, although the player can make independent deductions based on the clues, the game mechanics might not enable them. Furthermore, the deductions based on the clues are not always correct, which leaves the player feeling that information is being withheld. These problems might disrupt player immersion and/or autonomy.

Crime fiction and digital media

With the novels and television series, the reader/viewer follows the detective character, while in the game they play as the detective. The connection to the detective character is broken in those game sections where other characters conduct investigations. These sections are highly directed and there are very few choices available to the player. This could be understood as an attempt to emphasise Miss Fisher's role as the protagonist, but while these sections function to tie the story into the first episode and the larger story arc of the transmedial world, they are not satisfactory from the perspective of the player. Thus, the player's experience of and immersion into detective work is disrupted by changes in the player character and dysfunctional deduction mechanics.

Transmedial connections in the game are established through several means. In the game episodes, strong connections to the events in the novels and television series exist: There are references to the capture and seeming execution of the killer of Miss Fisher's sister, and the story of episode one is very similar to the novel *Ruddy Gore*, also adapted for television. More subtle references are also made to the extended transmedial world: On Miss Fisher's dressing table there is a letter from Jane, Miss Fisher's adoptive daughter, who also appears in the novels and the television series. This reference rewards a player familiar with the transmedial world, but it is not a prerequisite to understanding the story of the game.

Based on the reviews from different mobile app marketplaces,[6] transmedia audiences, in particular, find playing the game rewarding, even though they find the game lacking in mechanics. Reviewers make repeated positive references to the characters, dialogue and music familiar from the television series, and they also mention the "spirit" or "feeling" of the series being present in the game. These reviewers can clearly be identified as transmedial players who, despite their positive experiences, do comment on the problems of the deduction mechanics. On the basis of the reviews, the expectations of the players who are fans of the television series differ from those of the players who have no knowledge of the wider Miss Fisher storyworld and have a different set of expectations of digital games in general. Still, the obvious deficiencies of the game design affect both groups of players.

Concluding thoughts

This chapter has discussed how the developments in digital technologies and new platforms that allow stories to spread multimodally and transmedially have impacted crime fiction and its forms. The crime genre and its production, distribution and reception are now characterised by constant change in digital contexts because of the rapid developments in the digital environment itself. The production of "crime texts" is no longer in the hands of publishing companies, but anyone with the necessary skills is free to participate in the digital creation and distribution of content from their individual starting points.

The new possibilities for creating, distributing and, above all, engaging with stories through transmedia storytelling – (digital) expansions of familiar fictional worlds – provide the pleasure of recognition similar to those evoked by adaptations. Adaptations are at times interpreted and critiqued on the basis of their so-called "fidelity" to the "source text" (see Hutcheon 2006: 2–7). In a similar manner, transmedia expansions are often expected to fit in the broader storyworld and remain faithful to, for example, the norms, laws of physics, values and social structures of a given fictional world (Klastrup and Tosca 2004). Thus, it can be argued that narrative expansions in the digital age tap into the pleasure of interpreting and evaluating how stories shape and change when they are retold via different mediums (cf. Hutcheon 2006: 2). The digital evolution nevertheless makes these stories more accessible to broader audiences, making it easier for them to create their own adaptations, or transmedia expansions, and to share them online in fan communities. That said, while the digital age would appear to give endless opportunities to change, expand and experience the crime genre, these opportunities seem to wait to be fully utilised beyond fan fiction and social media texts, true-crime podcasts, digital games and occasional Twitter shorties.

Notes

1 See https://thepigeonhole.com/faq.
2 The cell-phone novel that predates Twitterature and is mostly written by amateurs has proved extremely popular (Goodyear 2008).
3 See www.thebreathingwall.com/.
4 Different media attract and create demographically different audiences. Audience demographics was a central reason why ABC deliberated in 2013 upon whether to release a third Miss Fisher series: Of all the TV networks in Australia, ABC 1 had the oldest audience (Vickery 2013), and the network wanted to attract a younger one. Since 2014, Australians have embraced streaming platforms, which has changed the audience demographics of the series: It was one of the most popular TV dramas in a 2017 study (*Online & On Demand* 2017).
5 In general, the different pleasures offered by transmedia storytelling compared to non-digital texts perhaps culminate in the transition from reader/viewer to co-creator/collaborator in participatory practices (cf. Dowd et al. 2013: 30).
6 Apple App Store, 3 reviews (18 August 2018); Google Play, 172 reviews (19 August 2018); Steam, 12 reviews (11 August 2018).

Bibliography

Aarseth, E. (2004) "Quest games as post-narrative discourse", in M-L. Ryan et al. (eds), *Narratives across Media. The languages of storytelling*, University of Nebraska Press, 361–76.

———. (2007) "I fought the law: transgressive play and the implied player", DiGRA '07 – *Proceedings of DiGRA 2007 Conference: Situated Play,* The University of Tokyo, 4: 130–33, www.digra.org/digital-library/publications/i-fought-the-law-transgressive-play-and-the-implied-player/ (accessed 14 November 2019).

Bell, A., Ensslin, A. and Rustad, H.K. (2014) "From theorizing to analyzing digital fiction", in A. Bell, A. Ensslin and H.K. Rustad (eds), *Analyzing Digital Fiction*, New York: Routledge, 3–17.

Birkinbine, B.J., Gómez, R. and Wasko, J. (eds) (2017) "Introduction", in *Global Media Giants*, New York: Routledge, 1–7.

Deleuze, G. and Guattari, F. (2004) *A Thousand Plateaus*, trans. B. Massumi, London and New York: Continuum.

Dena, C. (2009) *Transmedia Practice. Theorising the practice of expressing a fictional world across distinct media and environments*, PhD thesis, University of Sydney, www.scribd.com/doc/35951341/Transmedia-Practice (accessed March 2019).

"Distribution of mystery/crime book readers in the United States as of 1st quarter 2014, by age" (2019) *The Statistics Portal*, www.statista.com/statistics/327441/mystery-crime-book-readers- by-age-usa/ (accessed February 2019).

Dowd, T., Fry, M., Niederman, M. and Steiff, J. (eds) (2013) *Storytelling Across Worlds. Transmedia for creatives and producers*, New York: Focal Press.

Engberg, M. (2014) "Digital fiction", in M-L. Ryan, L. Emerson and B.J. Robertson (eds), *The Johns Hopkins Guide to Digital Media*, Baltimore: Johns Hopkins University Press, 138–43.

Ensslin, A. (2011) "From (w)reader to breather: cybertextual de-intentionalization and Kate Pullinger's *Breathing Wall*", in R.E. Page and B. Thomas (eds), *New Narratives, Stories and Storytelling in the Digital Age*, Lincoln and London: University of Nebraska Press, 138–52.

Galef, D. (2016) *Brevity. A flash fiction handbook*, New York: Columbia University Press.

Goodyear, D. (2008) "I ♥ novels: young women develop a genre for the cellular age", *New Yorker*, 22 December, www.newyorker.com/magazine/2008/12/22/i-love-novels (accessed March 2019).

Gregoriou, C. (2009) *Deviance in Contemporary Crime Fiction*, Basingstoke: Palgrave Macmillan.

———. (2017) *Crime Fiction Migration: Crossing languages, cultures and media*, London: Bloomsbury.

Gruesser, J.C. (2013) *Race, Gender and Empire in American Detective Fiction*, Jefferson, NC, and London: McFarland.

Harvey, C.B. (2015) *Fantastic Transmedia: Narrative, play and memory across science fiction and fantasy storyworlds*, Basingstoke: Palgrave Macmillan.

———. (2018) "Transmedia genres: form, content, and the centrality of memory", in M. Freeman and R.R. Gambarato (eds), *The Routledge Companion to Transmedia Studies*, New York and London: Routledge, 157–64.

Hayles, K.N. (2008) *Electronic Literature: New horizons for the literary*, Notre Dame, Indiana: University of Notre Dame Press.

Horsley, L. (2005) *Twentieth-Century Crime Fiction*, Oxford: Oxford University Press.

Hutcheon, L. (2006) *A Theory of Adaptation*, New York and London: Routledge.

Jenkins, H. (2006) *Convergence Culture: Where old and new media meet*, New York and London: New York University Press.

Klastrup, L. and Tosca, S. (2004) "Transmedial worlds – rethinking cyberworld design", in M. Nakajima, Y. Hatori and A. Sourin (eds), *Proceedings of the 2004 International Conference on Cyberworlds*, Los Alamitos, CA: IEEE Computer Society, 409–16.

Koistinen, A-K., Ruotsalainen, M. and Välisalo, T. (2016) "The world hobbit project in Finland: audience responses and transmedial user practices", *P@rticipations*, 13(2): 356–79.

Martin, R. (2011) "Millennium publisher launches Salander app", *The Local*, 13 December, www.thelocal. se/20111213/37920 (accessed March 2019).

Miss Fisher and the Deathly Maze (2017) Melbourne, Australia: Tin Man Games, iOS, Android.

Mittell, J. (2015) *Complex TV: The poetics of contemporary television storytelling*, New York and London: New York University Press.

Online & On Demand 2017: Trends in Australian online viewing habits (2017) www.screenaustralia.gov.au/getmedia/f06697b8-07be-4a27-aa8b-bc3ad365238c/online-on-demand-2017 (accessed May 2019).

Ora, R. (2018) "Invisible evidence: *Serial* and the new unknowability of documentary", in D. Llinares, N. Fox and R. Berry (eds), *Podcasting: New aural cultures and digital media*, Palgrave Macmillan, 107–22.

Pullinger, K., Schemat, S. and Joseph, C. (2004) *The Breathing Wall*, www.thebreathingwall.com/ (accessed February 2018).

Richtel, M. (2008) "Introducing the twiller", *The New York Times*, 29 August, https://bits.blogs.nytimes.com/2008/08/29/introducing-the-twiller/ (accessed February 2019).

Ryan-Fazilleau, S. (2007) "Kerry Greenwood's 'rewriting' of Agatha Christie", *JASAL – Journal of the Association for the Study of Australian Literature*, 7(3): 59–70.

Stein, L.E. and Busse, K. (eds) (2012) "Introduction: the literary, televisual and digital adventures of the beloved detective", *Sherlock and Transmedia Fandom: Essays on the BBC series*, Jefferson, NC, and London: McFarland, 9–24.

Suits, B. (1985) "The detective story: a case study of games in literature", *Canadian Review of Comparative Literature*, 12(2): 200–19.

Thomas, B. (2014) "140 characters in search of a story: twitterfiction as an emerging narrative form", in Bell et al., 94–108.

"Twitter fiction: 21 authors try their hand at 140-character novels" (2012) *The Guardian*, 13 October, www.theguardian.com/books/2012/oct/12/twitter-fiction-140-character-novels (accessed February 2019).

Vickery, C. (2013) "Miss Fisher's Murder Mysteries under a cloud as ABC tries to broaden audience", News.com.au, 16 December, www.news.com.au/entertainment/tv/miss-fishers-murder-mysteries-under-a-cloud-as-abc-tries-to-broaden-audience/news-story/aebeb956f38e24ac3f4cae7db1395b01 (accessed May 2019).

Walker, B. (2015) "The mystery of the missing formula: adapting the world's most popular girl detective to multimedia platforms", in C.A. Cothran and M. Cannon (eds), *New Perspectives on Detective Fiction: Mystery magnified*, New York and London: Routledge, 225–42.

45

CRIME FICTION AND THE FUTURE

Nicoletta Vallorani

A discussion of crime fiction and the future may be approached through two different, though closely related, perspectives. The first concerns the developments of the genre in the face of changes in society and culture. The second investigates the network of contacts, contaminations, hybridisations and cross-relations that have evolved over time between two kinds of narratives – crime fiction and science fiction – that appear to be connected in many ways. In keeping with the tendency of popular narratives to produce mash-ups, crime fiction has often combined with the spy story, the adventure story, the historical novel and the true-crime genre, so this contiguity with science fiction is no surprise. My contention is that in recent times the tendency towards "intermarriage" has become more visible, and crime fiction has gained much from intermittent cross-fertilisations, acquiring more flexibility, appeal and ability to build successful plots. I suggest that the increased permeability of the borders between crime fiction and science fiction – in their multiple inflections – have evolved from a shared tendency to address social issues, which became more visible from the mid-twentieth century and onwards (Scholes and Rabkin 1977; Pepper 2000).

The 1930s represented a key moment for the two genres. Both crime fiction and science fiction were originally defined by a specific and quite strict thematic and stylistic "grammar", a code that was expected to be honoured by the authors and understood by the public. However, with time, they have become more and more flexible and have increasingly incorporated a number of variations on their original formulaic structure. In some cases and in a sparse though identifiable pattern, the elements of social commentary that produced some of the formulae of both genres (Delany 2009: 17–28) have developed into new forms of political, cultural and social commitment, responding more or less at the same time and in similar ways (Pepper 2000: 170–75). In following related trajectories, the two genres have articulated a fruitful interchange, exploiting the notion of the genre as a fluid entity, revised and reshaped in its "rules" in response to a specific culture in a particular space and time (Cawelti 1997: 5–35)

I will build my analysis precisely on this foundation. Basic analogies and a parallel development marked by frequent exchanges between science fiction and crime fiction – in all respects mutual – concern their potential as social narratives, that is, as genres which, from a particular moment, begin privileging a reflection on political and cultural issues. The "particular moment" I refer to (and start out from) is the 1970s, when – especially in anglophone countries but later

406

rapidly spreading across the Western world – both crime and science fiction seem to flourish and introduce new formulae that highlight the genres' ability to develop speculative approaches to their social contexts. In authors like Philip K. Dick, John Brunner, James G. Ballard as well as Jim Thompson, Chester Himes and Patricia Highsmith, speculation is a key word, albeit differently inflected in their building of the plot, and the shaping of characters and setting.

It is tempting to distinguish between the two genres according to the way speculation is oriented temporally: Respectively, towards the past and its present consequences in crime fiction, and towards the future and its present possibilities in science fiction. However, this simplifies the complexity of the two genres for the sake of critical taxonomy, leaving aside the unsettling dynamism of time in current narratives of science fiction, where "speculation" is a relevant, if highly ambiguous, resource. The much-cited debate between Ursula K. Le Guin and Margaret Atwood called into play this very ambiguity, the former insisting on the need to keep the label "dystopian science fiction" to encompass reflections on possible futures or alternative human societies (Le Guin and Wood 1979), and the latter claiming that "speculative fiction" is more suitable because none of the usual devices of science fiction normally appear in such narratives (Atwood 2012). Darko Suvin suggests, instead, the notion of "extrapolation", a process whose direction does not always follow an ordinary timeline (2016: 40–45), but which may become warped and tangled, as opposed to orderly or rational. In crime fiction, on the other hand, the more traditional stories – and formulae – rely on a notion of a linear and stable timeline that allows the reader (and the author) to think of the plot in terms of the speculative process required for the detective to "read" past events in order to explain the present and secure the future. A slightly different perspective has developed over time to the point that, as Todorov points out, "prospection" has replaced the traditional "retrospection" in current thrillers (1995: 47), producing texts where the stability and coherence of the category starts to unravel and become more fluid.

In this way, from the 1970s onwards, science fiction and crime fiction have drawn closer together in the way they re-examine the notion of speculation. The increased permeability between the two genres and their cross-fertilisation has multiplied the narrative, thematic and stylistic approaches, added new devices and led to the sharing and bending of traditional formulae to serve a reshaped cognitive horizon, born precisely out of the increased permeability and cross-fertilisation between the two genres, which in some cases has given rise to hybrid subgenres, such as noir science fiction and cyberpunk thrillers.

Crime fiction and science fiction: The contact zones

In his chapter on formula fiction, Cawelti suggests that formulae are culturally specific: Though at the same time identifying "larger plot types" and working independently of space and time, they are supposedly flexible enough as to follow the evolution of the social and cultural contexts to which they refer (1997: 5–7). Considering that both science fiction and crime fiction tend to reflect on the status of the community, the need to revise certain formulaic structures so as to increase contamination between the two genres is significant. The original stable organisation of each of them progressively gives way to more mobility and mutability, a process that is pushed forward by moments of convergence breaking down the traditional parallel development before the 1970s.

In any case, in both genres, the author/reader nexus – besides defining the "language" to be used – appears to be grounded in the double purpose of entertaining the public and producing some sort of social commentary. The two genres are "social" in the sense that they tend to reflect on the status of the community, and privilege speculation rather than mere action.

The dialogue between addresser and addressee serves as a bridge for communicating new ideas, making new discoveries in science easily understandable, or reflecting on ecological, economic or political crises. From its origin in the nineteenth century, the scientific romance was deeply indebted to new discoveries in the field of science that were popularised through fiction, as the "twin" works of Jules Verne and H.G. Wells on voyages to the moon show. In a general perspective, though rooted in what is pragmatically achievable, if not yet achieved (Sanders 1980: 157), science fiction entertains the public by proposing a notion of "science" that easily merges with hypotheses, unverified theories, mere anticipations and magic.

Crime fiction pursues the same kind of balance between information, popularisation and entertainment. Born as a tool for representing the complexities of evil and the ways in which it ought to be punished by the law (Ascari 1998: 21), it originally served to underline and possibly redeem the individual's anonymity within the complex machinery of the institutions (Oliva 2003: 10–12). In some respects, crime fiction explains the functioning of the state in the same way as science fiction gives popular currency to science. In the 1920s (one of the moments of convergence) its methods were influenced by scientific discoveries when the inductive paradigm – the orderly progression from the detail to the general frame – inspired by a scientific spirit entered the practice of investigation (Ascari 1998: 22). In the 1940s, the hardboiled novel had already gained popularity through its direct and provocative engagement with social issues. A decade later, Jim Thompson exploited the crime narrative in order to reflect on the political and cultural crisis of the American way of life: *Nothing More than Murder* (1959) revealed the dreariness and the lack of ethics of a middle-class provincial couple through a close psychological analysis of characters. Around the 1970s, a period of political and social unrest fuelled by politically traumatic events surrounding the Vietnam War seemed to reinforce the "genetic" blood tie between science fiction and crime fiction, acting as a vehicle for the introduction of new paradigms and opening fruitful paths for the future. James Crumley, for example, switched from the analysis of the implications of the Vietnam crisis (*One to Count Cadence*, 1969) to merciless representations of a desolated and ruthless social reality, where the crisis of the subject combines with the inability of the community to overcome the trauma of murders and war (*The Wrong Case*, 1975; *The Last Good Kiss*, 1978). In the 1980s and 1990s, the process of solving crimes became a tool to reflect on suffering, frustration, the inability to improve one's own social condition, ethnic and gender discrimination, class conflicts, etc. Ellroy and other authors revealed a double narrative drive: Crime is evil but it is also exploited to emphasise the pressure that a dysfunctional community may exercise on a weak and unstable personality, turning him/her into a killer (Pfeil 1995: 3–36).

The sharp focus on asymmetric power relations through issues like class, race and gender also opened up new territories for both crime and science fiction, both of which became more complex. While the latter moves beyond a stereotyped vision of both characters and traditional topics, the dominant trends of hardboiled fiction still appear extremely relevant to the sociological dystopia developing in the 1960s. In science fiction, moreover, what might be called a "terminal crisis" of science as the rational hub of the genre occurs more or less when Philip K. Dick produces some extremely successful sci-fi stories based on quite unlikely scientific principles (Warrick 1987). In a very short time, a deep change in the grammar of the genre occurred, and scientific plausibility was no longer the basic formula as long as scientific "mistakes" produced wonder and new visions. Technology also took on an unsettling dynamism and an ambiguity that suited the narrative trends developing from the 1970s onward. A proliferation of science fiction authors who cross over into the utopian/dystopian tradition moves the focus of the genre towards issues previously considered peripheral. The enormous success of such authors as Philip K. Dick, Theodore Sturgeon, Ursula K. Le Guin and, later, Octavia

Butler legitimised the introduction of technical devices lacking any plausibility as long as they contributed to breaking down traditional forms. At the same time the failure of technology to produce a better world became one of the most powerful topics tackled, from Le Guin (*The Word for World is Forest*, 1984) to Nora K. Jemisin (*The Fifth Season*, 2015), as science that fails was considered more interesting than the achievements of human knowledge.

The speed with which science fiction has branched out into different directions (including utopia, dystopia, social speculation, etc.) increases hybridisation and reinforces the clear affinities between crime and science fiction, encouraging more contamination. Speculation as a method for constructing the plot and providing the characters with new complexity tends to coalesce around topical social issues. Moreover, the accessibility of new technologies, real or fictional, in investigations breaks down the wall between the two genres, also adding suspense, variety and interest to the methods of detection. Faithful to Cawelti's statement that "the detective must use his unique investigative skills" (2004: 300) to mend the rip produced in the community by the criminal act, the many new forms of crime fiction – mostly in its TV and film versions – enjoy a range of new technologies that prove fascinating in themselves as prodigies of science, regardless of the importance for the plot (307). In this respect, science fiction may to some extent be a key factor in helping to reshape contemporary crime fiction, in that what first appears as a technological or scientific hypothesis in one genre soon becomes a reality and a resource to be exploited in the other.

Through this process of mutual fertilisation, both crime and science fiction develop their basic chronotopes, moving towards new geographies – both physical and symbolic – so as to develop "a new narrative potential, born from hybridity and the multiplication of contact zones" (Moretti 2010: 4).

Speculating the city: China Miéville detecting the future

China Miéville's *The City & The City* (2009) inhabits a genre contact zone. It also exploits – in its unique urban setting as well as in the plot development – the very notion of contact zone, hybridising the narrative at several levels. The novel itself is the result of cross-fertilisation between crime and science fiction and reflects its author's insistence that critical theories on a popular genre like science fiction desperately require revision in light of current cultural and political contexts. A Marxist activist, Miéville clearly rejects the Suvinian paradigm that privileges utopian science fiction over science fantasy and, instead, calls for a "Marxist critique of fantastic fiction" that addresses the "unreality function" of this brand of narrative (2009, 233–35). *The City & The City* seems to be literally built on the crossing of borders: Between genres and between two separate yet geographically overlapping cities, Besźel and Ul Qoma. In Robinson's words, the novel

> takes us very quickly from a conventional detective scene to seek out (detect) the strange but achingly familiar truth of a city juxtaposed/superimposed on its other, whose buildings and inhabitants are routinely 'unseen' day by day as two coexistent and tightly imbricated realities are firmly kept apart.
>
> *(2013: 24)*

Though the temporal and spatial settings respect the protocols of science fiction, the novel is constructed as a noir police procedural. The dynamics of the story are triggered by a murder – a PhD student of American origin, whose corpse is found in a dilapidated neighbourhood – and the plot follows the investigation of Inspector Tyador Borlu of the Extreme Crime Squad, who later collaborates with Lisbyet Corwi, a former cop in that very neighbourhood. The opening pages of the novel seem to reproduce the purest hardboiled narrative, albeit in an unfamiliar environment. Progressively, the personal and the professional blend in a speculative journey that, in reconstructing the victim's story, also provides hints on the very unusual setting and the relationship the main characters have with it.

This environment is in fact rather special. Dave McKean, who has collaborated with Miéville on at least one occasion, is a key influence, as he introduced the notion of "double city" in his short film [N]eon (2002), which begins with the words "There are two cities" as images conjure up a cityscape composed of different famous European cities. Seven years later, Miéville produces a noir setting by combining and partially overlapping two bordering cities: Besźel and Ul Qoma, both located somewhere in Europe but separated because of some unspecified political conflict. They play out the paradigm of "Split Cities [...] Budapest and Jerusalem and Berlin, and Besźel and Ul Qoma" (Miéville 2011: 90). Though the twin cities exist in the same space, the citizens of each are obliged to "unsee" each other under penalty of severe punishment. The Breach that connects them is a transitional space through two universes, recalling the idea of a supranational power capable of supervising the strictures of law in both cities while reinforcing the separation between them:

> But pass through Copula Hall and she or he might leave Besźel, and at the end of the hall come back to exactly (corporeally) where they had just been, but in another country, a tourist, a marvelling visitor, to a street that shared the latitude-longitude of their own address, a street they had never visited before, whose architecture they had always unseen, to the Ul Qoman house sitting next to and a whole city away from their own building, unvisible there now they had come through, all the way across the Breach, back home.
>
> *(80)*

The act of selective seeing requires specific training to preserve the space occupied by each city. Though crosshatched, the two communities have different histories, cultures and deeply different political organisations. The structure of their urban spaces – as happens in any community – is shaped according to their symbolic universes, moulded by different allegiances, political choices, economic needs, etc. Again, this aspect of setting evokes both the science fiction dystopian tradition and recent tendencies in international noir, such as Derek Raymond's *Factory Series* and the novels by Jean-Patrick Manchette.

Moreover, the story contains useful clues that highlight the outdated notion that the two genres thematise the past and the future in different ways, instead directing their speculations respectively towards multiple pasts and multiple futures. Time – "the chaos of our material history, an anarchy of chronology" (Miéville 2011: 62) – is a mess that impacts spatial organisation.

In Miéville as well as in other contemporary science fiction authors, time and space within the narrative is less tightly bound: It has no specific connection to a timeline or to a space and can therefore develop detection in several unpredictable directions. In *The City & The City*, for example, space and time are drastically reshuffled and interfere with each other, creating the rhizomatic image of a city containing an intricate web of different, overlapping maps, not all of which are "real" or "realistic". Rejecting Suvin's stringent demands for "cognition", which would exclude the majority of existing science fiction, and, in so doing, providing one of the most relevant features of the so-called New Weird (VanderMeer and VanderMeer 2008: 1113–16), Miéville also refuses to comply with the genre's traditional boundaries, crossbreeding both his two cities and the two genres of crime and science fiction. In breaking moulds, Miéville exploits their full potential to make the resulting narrative "a viable subject for political critique" (Williams 2014: 617). *The City & The City* is constructed as a police procedural in a noir setting, slightly switched towards the future and only lightly tweaked in comparison with the current European urban environment.

In this respect, the construction of the two interrelated spaces is a symbol of hidden geographies of power. The creation of a border that is not to be crossed, the rule of "unseeing" and the obligation imposed on citizens to voluntarily and consciously deny their own perceptions reveal a control over individual freedom that surfaces in many noir novels where both victims and criminals are reduced to mere cogs in the state machinery, conforming to the status quo.

The implications of the act of "unseeing" add new complexities to the investigation: Sight is a tool for gathering evidence and advancing the investigation. If the very possibility of seeing is denied – albeit with some exceptions – detection becomes flawed. Indeed, Miéville consciously exploits the endless changes implied in perceiving the post-postmodern metropolis as constituting a double-sided – and often multilayered – "object":

> It's not just us keeping them apart. It's everyone in Besźel and everyone in Ul Qoma. Every minute, every day. We're only the last ditch: it's everyone in the cities who does most of the work. It works because you don't blink. That's why unseeing and unsensing are so vital. No one can admit it doesn't work. So if you don't admit it, it does. But if you breach, even if it's not your fault, for more than the shortest time [...] you can't come back from that.
>
> *(2011: 170)*

The instability of Besźel and Ul Qoma's overlapping geographies produces different urban alphabets. In these cityscapes, ideography and ideology interweave and often clash, in a fusion of time/space, continuity/discontinuity, visibility/invisibility, memory/amnesia. The citizens of the two cities are like ghosts without bodies, histories or places to stay. They crop up in the urban landscape, moving in and out of the present, the future and the past, producing no more than ripples in their environment. This results in a mutual reverberation between the space of the city and the bodies inhabiting it, in a process affecting their individual identities and their membership of the community to which they belong.

Going global: Science fiction and crime fiction in troubled times

"The body" has become a keyword for the future in both crime and science fiction. The increasing instability of a physical frame that we used to consider as something we were born with and bound to keep from birth until death has become one of the favourite topics in science fiction and also affects crime fiction. In *Lagoon* (2014) by the African American Nnedi Okorafor, the enemy is a shapeshifting alien who lacks a stable body but can take any form it wants. The impossibility of identifying the alien by sight as an evil being creates the same kind of difficulty that emerges in Western colonial assumptions about the visible difference of the Other's body. The origin of this line of thought hosts a "process of ambivalence" that is "central to the stereotype" (Bhabha 1994: 18). Since identity, even when alien, is an entity-in-progress (24), the stereotype changes over time and becomes more flexible in order to survive. For example, while the alien is cruel and destructive in Wells's *The War of the Worlds* (1897), in *Lagoon* it becomes a benign entity. Quite unexpectedly, in contrast to the traditional formulae of crime and science fiction, visible difference is not necessarily evil, and may instead become the ambiguous hero of a new kind of detection, from the crippled protagonist of Minette Walters's

The Chameleon's Shadow (2007) to the addicted protagonist and his war-traumatised friend in the BBC version of Sherlock Holmes, *Sherlock* (2010–2017).

The issue of the body acquires further complexities when framed within the current, multifaceted debate on globalisation, in which these two popular genres have demonstrated an unexpected ability to respond to contemporary cultural and political challenges sooner and better than other kinds of narratives. Through their focus on heteronormative bodies – weak, marginal, sick, disabled, migrant, etc. – that are often incapable of overcoming their differences and integrating into the community, crime and science fictions seem to speak the language of the poorest, weakest members of the community, giving new currency to the "petits récits" that were lost in the grand narratives of official histories.

Though the growing emphasis on cogent social issues has sometimes resulted in the tendency to "market the margins" (Huggan 2001: 228–64), this has also produced the need to rethink the binary stereotypes of hero/villain to encompass a broader spectrum of subjectivities. This process becomes evident when women are involved both as subjects of narration (authors) and as narrated "objects" (characters). This has been a major change in recent years that is likely to produce enormous revisions in the features of the two genres in the future.

When Derek Raymond in 1990 published the postmortem story of Dora Suarez, the protagonist of the fourth novel in his *Factory Series*, he introduced significant innovations to the hardboiled framework. The female character is a prostitute leading a "sinful" life, but she is also a migrant with a Spanish father and a Polish mother of Jewish origins, a dropout and one of the first literary characters to die of AIDS. Indeed, she is dead at the beginning of the story, and her voice is heard through her diary, which is found by the nameless detective on the crime scene. In the late 1980s, Pat Cadigan successfully introduced a similar, though luckier, female character. "Deadpan" Allie has no family, she survives by scavenging for food, does drugs and is constantly looking for work, but she is also a technological genius, and this makes her the focus of the engaging cyberpunk novel *Mindplayers* (1987).

The change that heralds the introduction of new female representations and new spaces for women as authors has been brought about, quite obviously, by the hardboiled hero, whose multifaceted form provides convincing psychological analysis, facilitates the introduction of more "active" female characters who were absent in the traditional formulae of science and crime fiction, and offers very promising future developments for both genres. Often, these unusual female characters appear in novels written by women. While P.D. James suggests that detection is an "unsuitable job for a woman" (1972), James Tiptree Jr. exploits science fiction to show that many women act in unexpected ways and undertake unpredictable jobs ("The Women Men Don't See", 1973). In the late 1980s, the collection *The Hidden Side of the Moon* (1987) presented Joanna Russ's most feminist science fiction, and in the late 1990s Ann Cleeves shaped a strong, feminist and icy protagonist, Detective Chief Inspector Vera Stanhope (1999–2017), who appears to be cut from the same cloth. The paradigm of "Deadpan" Allie also reappeared in Lisbeth Salander, the protagonist of Stieg Larsson's bestselling Swedish *Millennium Trilogy* (2005–2007).

The new protagonism of women has further developed through women's increasing success in the many fields of science. In this respect, too, contiguities between science and crime fiction have emerged and are becoming more evident in recent times. Kathy Reichs's forensic scientist and archaeologist Temperance Brennan, for example, successfully reinvents the model of the apparently frosty woman of science through her very complex personality (1997–2005), while in the disturbing first episode of the *Area X Trilogy, Annihilation* (2014), four women scientists face the alien threat that has defeated the members of eleven previous expeditions. All these women, though tough and often unemotional, help to frame what Caroline Reitz calls the

Crime fiction and the future

"ethics of care" (2014: 19–46), which could be described as the defining feature of women as protagonists in both science and crime fiction. These new female heroes of new, hybridised narratives close the circle, so to speak, by evoking the twin notions of intermarriage and cross-fertilisation as a tool for survival, in literature as well as in life.

Bibliography

Ascari, M. (1998) *La leggibilità del male: genealogia del romanzo poliziesco e del romanzo anarchico inglese*, Bologna: Pàtron.

Atwood, M. (2012) *In Other Worlds: SF and the human imagination*, New York, NY: Anchor Books.

Bhabha, H.K. (1994) *The Location of Culture*, London; New York: Routledge.

Cawelti, J.G. (1997) *Adventure, Mystery, and Romance: Formula stories as art and popular culture*, Chicago: University of Chicago Press.

———. (2004) *Mystery, Violence, and Popular Culture*, Madison, Wis.: University of Wisconsin Press/Popular Press.

Delany, S.R. (2009) [1977] *The Jewel-Hinged Jaw: Notes on the language of science fiction*, Middletown, Conn.: Wesleyan University Press.

Huggan, G. (2001) *The Postcolonial Exotic: Marketing the margins*, London; New York: Routledge.

Jemisin, N.K. (2018) *The Broken Earth Trilogy*, New York, NY: Orbit.

Le Guin, U.K. (2011) [1974] *The Dispossessed: An ambiguous utopia*, New York, NY: Harper Voyager.

Le Guin, U.K. and Wood, S. (1979) *The Language of the Night: Essays on fantasy and science fiction*, New York: Putnam.

Miéville, C. (2011) [2009] *The City & The City*, London: Pan Books.

Moretti, F. (2010) "History of the novel, theory of the novel", *Novel: A Forum on Fiction*, 43(1): 1–10.

Okorafor, N. (2014) *Lagoon*, London: Hodder & Stoughton.

Oliva, C. (2003) *Storia sociale del giallo*, Lugano: Todaro.

Pepper, A. (2000) *The Contemporary American Crime Novel: Race, ethnicity, gender, class*, Chicago: Fitzroy Dearborn Publishers.

Pfeil, F. (1995) *White Guys: Studies in postmodern domination and difference*, London; New York: Verso.

Reitz, C. (2014) "Nancy Drew, dragon tattoo: female detective fiction and the ethics of care", *Textus. English Studies in Italy*, XXVII(2): 19–46.

Robinson, J. (2013) "Making London, through other cities", in S. Bell and J. Paskins (eds), *Imagining the Future City. London 2062*, London: Ubiquity Press, 23–26.

Sanders, J. (1980) "Science fiction and detective fiction: the case of John D. Macdonald", *Science Fiction Studies*, 7(2): 157–65.

Scholes, R. and Rabkin, E.S. (1977) *Science Fiction: History, science, vision*, New York: Oxford University Press.

Suvin, D. (2016) [1979] *Metamorphoses of Science Fiction: On the poetics and history of a literary genre*, Oxford: Peter Lang.

James, P.D. (1972) *An Unsuitable Job for a Woman*, London: Faber & Faber.

Todorov, T. (1995) *The Poetics of Prose*, Ithaca, NY: Cornell University Press.

VanderMeer, A. and VanderMeer, J. (eds) (2008) *The New Weird*, San Francisco: Tachyon Publications.

Warrick, P.S. (1987) *Mind in Motion: The fiction of Philip K. Dick*, Carbondale: Southern Illinois University Press.

Williams, R. (2014) "Recognizing cognition: on Suvin, Miéville, and the utopian impulse in the contemporary fantastic", *Science Fiction Studies*, 41(3): 617–63.

INDEX

Abbott, Megan 108, 154, 245, 246
Acuña, Ignatio Cárdenas 331, 393, 394
Adair, Gilbert 233
Adamov, Arkady 391, 392
Adams, Frank 33
adaptations 31, 44, 48–56, 77, 81–83, 89–90, 136–37
Adenle, Leye 113
affect, in crime fiction 244–51
African American crime fiction 113, 163, 305–6, 322–23, 323–25, 331
Agnew, John 212
Ahnhem, Stefan 400
Alba, Alicia Gaspar de 354–55, 358–59, 378
Alienist, The (Carr) 241–43
Allingham, Margery 103, 112, 277, 311
alterity (other) 68, 82, 88, 98, 104, 112, 120–21, 154, 170–71, 172, 173, 252–59
Ampuero, Roberto 362, 365–68, 389
Anderson, Benedict 34
Anderson, Miranda, Pezzotti 78, 96, 98, 112
Anglo-American, dominant tradition 2, 4, 7, 18, 76, 78, 85, 86, 94, 96, 122, 142, 143
A Not So Perfect Crime (Solana) 215–16
anthropocene 365, 367; also see climate change
Appadurai, Arjun 236, 239, 242
Aristotle 204
Arjouni, Jakob 256, 339
Arnold, Jane 112
Ascari, Maurizio 15, 102, 143, 295, 297
Atwood, Margaret 381, 407
Auden, D.H. 157, 161, 320
Augé, Mark 248
Auguirre, Eugenio 245
Auster, Paul 233–24
austerity, in Britain 383–85

Australia, crime fiction in 44, 88, 124–25
Austria, in crime fiction 310, 311–13
authoritarianism (totalitarianism) (*also see* state crimes) 331–32, 388–94

Bacon, Francis 28, 29
Baenga, Bolya 295–96
Bakhtin, Mikhail 50, 327, 345
Ballard, J.G. 407
Bandyopadhyay, Sharadindu 51–55; Bryomkesh Bakshi stories 51–55; *Detective Bryomkesh Bakshi* (film) 51–55
Barcelona (Catalonia), crime fiction in 88, 213–14, 215–16
Barnard, Robert 187–88
Barr, Nevada 363
Barthes, Roland 51, 178, 179, 204
Bassnett, Susan 85
Baudelaire, Charles 85
Bayard, Pierre 14, 130, 133–35, 178–79, 183, 188, 189, 190–91, 195, 197
Beccaria, Cesare 274
Becker, Howard 276
Becker, Peter 274
beginnings and endings, in crime fiction 177–84, 198, 219–20
Bell, Daniel 381
Bell, Ensslin and Rustad 398
Bell, Joseph 129
Bengali and Hindi film and television 51–52
Bengali crime fiction 125–27
Bengtsdotter, Lina 41
Benjamin, Walter 217, 336, 337, 338
Bentham, Jeremy 274, 338
Bentley, Edward 186–87, 190, 337–38
Berglund, Karl 78

Index

Bergman, Kerstin 76–77, 296
Berkeley, Anthony 25, 190
Berlant, Lauren 246, 248, 344
Bernard, Robert 187
Bernthal, J.C. 108, 153
Berthet, Elie 292
Bertillon, Alphonse 292–93
Betts, Alexander 380
Beyer, Charlotte 98
Big Little Lies 44
Bishop, Katherine 364
Bjork-James, Sophie Statzel 263
Black Mask magazine 33, 161
Blacksad 69
Blakstad, Matthew 263–64
Bloch, Robert 24
Blumenberg, Hans 194, 197
Bodyguard (TV) 207–9
Bolaño, Roberto 314, 378
Bolin, Alice 154, 155
book trade, international 39–42, 45–46; *also see* markets
Borges, Jorge Luis 18, 200, 233
Bottoms and Von Hirsch 285
Bowen, Peter 363, 366
Bradford, Richard 18
Breaking Bad 343
Brennan, Teresa 246
Breu, Christopher 63, 154, 156
Brown, Andrew 114, 118
Brown, Charles Brockden 171
Brown, Fredric 190
Bridge, The [*Broen/Bron*] 303, 307, 340
Brooks, Peter 62, 136, 185, 219, 220
Brunner, John 407
Buell, Lawrence 363
Bundy, Ted 252
Burdett, John 264
Burke, James Lee 253, 256–59
Burke, Seán 177
Butler, Octavia 408–9

Cadigan, Pat 412
Cagney and Lacey 304, 305
Caillous, Roger 150
Cain, James M. 245
Calcutta, in crime fiction 125–27
Camilleri, Andrea 90, 98–101, 254, 302, 332
Canalez, Juan Diaz 69
capitalism (global capitalism) 7, 49, 80, 82, 98, 109, 147, 248, 250, 327, 347, 353–60, 363, 366, 367, 371, 372, 374, 375–77, 392–93
capital accumulation and expansion 354–56, 357, 358–59, 372–73, 375–78
Capmany, Maria-Aurèlia 332
Cardi, Juan Ángel 394

Carlotto, Massimo (and Marco Videtta) 354, 356–57, 358
Carr, Caleb 241, 296
Carr, John Dickson 160, 229, 233
Caruth, Cathy 318, 320
Casablanca 343
Cassuto, Leonard 306, 307
Castells, Manuel 221
Cawelti, John 14–15, 142, 320, 407, 409
Chabon, Michael 32
Chambers, Ross 181
Chandler, Raymond 2, 24, 50, 58, 76, 80, 96, 102, 104, 112, 142, 150, 152, 153, 154, 162, 163, 185, 197, 206–7, 245, 256, 278, 285, 295, 302, 303, 318, 319, 329, 330, 331, 332, 338–39, 343; *Big Sleep, The* 162, 220, 223–24, 330, 338; *Farewell My Lovely* 213; *Long Goodbye, The* 343–44; 'Simple Art of Murder, The' 24, 102–3, 142, 150, 162, 206, 302, 329, 338
Chandra, Vikram 97, 303, 308, 340–42
Chaney, Jen 37–38
Chang, Henry 224–26
Charlie Chan (Biggers, Earl Derr) 255, 400
Charlie's Angels 304
Chavarría, Daniel 393–94
Chesney, Marion 256
Chesterton, G.K. 22–23, 189, 212, 295
Child, Lee 192
Chile, in crime fiction 310, 313–16, 317, 362, 366–68, 389, 390
China, crime fiction in 3, 18, 41, 88–90, 145–47
Chinatown Beat (Chang) 224–26
Christie, Agatha 2, 3, 4, 5–6, 23, 35, 60, 76, 85, 103, 112, 122, 134, 151–52, 153, 157, 159, 160, 162, 171, 178, 178, 179, 180–83, 187–90, 192, 195, 197, 205, 277, 294, 304, 329, 330, 331, 337, 343, 345, 364, 379, 364, 379; *ABC Murders, The* 188–90, 192; *After the Funeral* 188; *Appointment with Death* 151; *Body in the Library, The* 180, 231–33; *Dead Man's Folly* 180, 182, 183, 229; *Endless Night* 152, 188; *Evil Under the Sun* 151, 153; *Hallowe'en Party* 180–83; *Murder at the Vicarage* 160; *Murder in Mesopotamia* 153; *Murder of Roger Ackroyd, The* 2, 178, 179, 181, 187–88, 189, 190, 192, 195, 253; *Murder on the Links* 153; *Murder on the Orient Express* 5–6, 178, 329; *Mysterious Affairs at Styles, The* 23, 151, 160, 188; *Peril at End House* 151, 152, 190; *Three-Act Tragedy* 188
Christie, Nils 168
city, in crime fiction 212, 213, 214, 215, 222, 223, 224–26, 246, 275, 278, 280, 303, 305, 335–43, 364, 409–11
City & The City (Miéville) 409–11
Ciudad Juárez (femicides) 358–59, 378
Cixin, Liu 41
Claretie, Jules 294

Index

classical allusions, in crime fiction 27–28, 134, 159, 177, 194
Claverton, Rosie 263
Cleeves, Ann 412
climate fiction 16, 19–20, 217, 365; *also see* anthropocene
Close, Glen S. 149, 155–56
close reading 5, 52
Clough, Patricia Ticineto 248
clue-puzzle 14, 23, 24, 36, 80, 85, 102, 103, 104, 141, 144, 149, 150–52, 160–61, 186, 196–97, 198, 200
clues, in crime fiction 149, 178, 186, 194–201, 292, 297, 344–45, 402
Cobra (Meyer) 115–18
Collins, Wilkie 2, 24, 58, 120–21, 150, 171, 185, 186, 191, 293, 294, 371, 372–73
Collyer, Jaime 314
Colombia, in crime fiction 374, 375–77
colonial attitudes 112, 120–22, 125–27, 143, 288, 312, 314, 345, 349, 354, 372–73, 411; *also see* postcolonial; colonialism and decolonialism 52, 58, 120–28, 295, 366, 367, 371, 372–73, 388
Communist/Soviet Bloc, and crime fiction 388, 390–92
confessional literature 61, 62
Connelly, Michael 240
Connolly, John 348
convergence culture 397, 399
Cooper, James Fennimore 163
Cornell and Hartmann 111
Cornwell, Patricia 152, 154, 171, 204, 265, 266, 296, 303
cosmopolitanism 7, 94, 95, 98, 217, 336
covers (book jacket designs) 98, 238–39, 241–42
Crafton, Robert 282
Craig and Cadogen 26
Craps, Stef 319, 321, 322
Crawford, Norlisha 113
Creswell, Tim 211
criminals, in crime fiction 168–76, 383–85, 408
criminology and crime fiction 240, 273–81, 293, 379; positvist 274–74; Chicago School 275, 278, 279, 280
Crispin, Edmund 230
Croft, Freeman Willis 205
Cronon, William 363
Crumley, James 408
CSI 296, 302, 401
Cuba, in crime fiction 331, 366, 367, 381, 390, 392–94
Curran, John 190
Curtis Brown, literary agents 42
Cuvier, Georges 292

Daeninckx, Didier 299, 312
Daly, Carroll John 255, 283, 285

Damrosch, David 76, 78, 79, 80, 81
Darwin, Charles (Darwinism) 196, 292, 293, 295
DC (comics) 65, 71, 74
Deadwind 303, 307
Deaver, Jeffrey 262, 265, 266, 267–68
De Certeau, Michel 339
Defoe, Daniel 3
Deleuze, Gilles 51, 246, 399
Demleitner, Nora 284
democracy, and crime fiction 388
Derrida, Jacques 15, 135–36, 371
detection, detective fiction 2, 14, 22–24, 26, 27–30, 31, 35, 97, 100, 102, 107–8, 121, 127, 152, 161, 178–79, 196, 285, 293, 295, 311, 314, 330, 334, 336, 337, 348, 402, 409, 410, 411, 412
detection and psychoanalysis 24, 129–37, 195, 246–47, 248, 292, 299
Detection Club 24, 151, 190, 196
Detective Dee and the Mystery of the Phantom Flame 89, 90
detectives 23, 24, 36, 71, 81, 105–6, 159–67, 168–69, 198–99, 205, 213, 262–63, 283, 284, 285, 291, 296, 297, 345, 372, 381
Dexter, Colin 136–37, 303
Dey, Panchkori 52
Dick, Philip K. 16, 407, 408
Dickens, Charles 185, 186, 231, 292, 295, 336, 340
digital (cyber) crime 60, 141, 262–69
digital gaming and crime fiction 397, 400, 401
digital media (transmedia storytelling), and crime fiction 397–404
dime novel, US 23, 24, 32
Dimock, Wai Chee 80
disability 171
distant reading 5, 17, 79–80
Dixon of Dock Green 303
Dolan, Eva 380, 382–83, 383–85, 386
Dontsova, Daria 253
Döring, Tobias 112
Dostoyevsky, Fyodor 14, 50, 336, 340
Double Indemnity 248
Dowd, Tom 401
Doyle, Arthur Conan / Sherlock Holmes 2, 16, 22, 23, 28, 32–33, 35, 36, 48, 49, 50, 52, 53, 54, 58, 76, 77, 79, 85, 88–89, 103, 112, 118, 121, 125, 126, 129, 130–37, 141, 150, 159–60, 162, 163, 186, 187, 187, 195, 196, 197, 200, 227, 230, 233, 277, 291, 292, 293, 294, 295, 297, 298, 311, 329, 337, 343, 345–46, 372–73, 400; adaption by Norbu 49–50, 79; 'Adventure of Abbey Grange, The' 291; 'Adventure of the Devil's Foot, The' 121; 'Adventure of the Speckled Band, The' 121; 'Adventure of the Six Napoleons, The' 54; 'Adventure of the Yellow Face, The' 112; 'Blue Carbuncle, The' 159–60; 'Case of Identity, A' 89, 129, 130–37; 'Charles

Index

Augustus Milverton' 53; 'Engineer's Thumb, The' 337; 'Five Orange Pips, The' 292; *Hound of the Baskervilles, The* 293, 295; 'Man with the Twisted Lip, The' 53, 372; 'Scandal in Bohemia, A' 134–36; *Sherlock/Elementary* 311, 346–47, 401, 412; *Sign of Four, The* 121, 371, 373; *Study in Scarlet, A* 121, 197, 277, 294, 311, 343, 373
Dragnet 238, 303, 304
Driscoll, Beth 43
Driscoll, Fletcher, Wilkins and Carter 41
drug addiction 372–74
Dry, The 39 (Harper) 42–45, 46
Dugdale, Ruth 382
Duhamel, Marcel (Gallimard) 86, 87, 88
Durkheim, Émile 275

Ebersohn, Wessel 123
Eburne and Bell 305
Eco, Umberto 16, 32, 195, 233
Edkins, Jenny 319, 320, 322
Effron, Malcah 230
Eisner, Will 67–68
El alemán de Atacama (Ampuero) 366–68
Eliot, T.S. 24, 120
Elliot, Kamilla 50
Ellroy, James 303, 329, 408
Emsley, Clive 274
Engberg, Maria 398
Engels, Freidrich 336, 340
environment, and crime fiction (eco-criticism) 362–69
Erdmann, Eva 214, 216
Erll, Astrid 310
Eterovic, Ramón Díaz 310, 315, 390
European crime fiction 19, 78, 85, 86–87, 254, 288, 311–12, 410–11
Evanovich, Janet 255, 256

fair play 14, 23, 24, 187, 189, 196, 198, 199
Fantômas 33, 35
Featherstone, Mike 59
Feinman, José Pablo 389, 390
Felman, Shoshana 132–33, 134, 318
Felski, Rita 195
feminist crime fiction, readings of 63, 90, 102–10, 153, 163, 381, 412
Femme Fatale 15, 69, 104, 109, 245
Feuilleton (French) 32
Finnish crime fiction 19–20, 217, 307
Fisher, Randolph 305, 322
Fitzgerald, Helen 263
Flanders, Judith 141
Fleming, Ian 32, 58, 391
Flynn, Gillian 152, 154, 245, 331
Fonseca, Rubem 390
formula, crime fiction as 3, 14–15, 22, 25, 30, 32, 58, 62–64, 67–68, 85, 97, 123, 141, 144, 147,

152, 160, 162, 168, 204, 320, 322, 329, 345, 398, 406–8
Forrest, Katherine V. 109
Forster, E.M. 185, 192
Fortsetzungsroman (German) 32
Foucault, Michel 6, 248, 328
Four Just Men, The (Wallace) 31, 34–36
Fowler, Roger 171
Frankfurt Book Fair 43, 46
Frank, Lawrence 292, 295
French crime fiction 2, 85–88, 97, 164, 283–84, 287–88, 296–99, 313
French, Tana 154, 301
Freud, Sigmund [Freudian readings] 104, 129, 132, 144, 246, 249, 299, 319
Frow, John 345
Fu Manchu (Sax Rohmer) 33, 35, 122, 225, 255
Futrelle, Jacques 230
future, in crime fiction 264, 316–17, 357–58, 362, 406–13

Gaboriau, Émile 23, 35, 36, 48, 85, 164, 227, 291, 292, 295, 297, 298, 336
Gabriel, Cohen 222
Gallagher, Matt 348, 350–51
Game of Thrones 343
García-Mainar 306, 307, 308
Gass, William 228
Gay, John 354
gender and detection 26, 60, 81, 90, 102–10, 149, 163–64, 169, 173–75, 214, 301–2, 307–8, 325, 327, 330, 331, 344, 377, 412–13; gender, sexuality and death 150, 154–57, 170, 173–74, 175, 219
Genette, Gérard 236, 237
genre, and crime fiction 13–21, 23–28, 45, 57–58, 59, 79, 80, 122, 129, 144–45, 146, 147, 178, 182, 195, 196, 199, 202, 204, 209, 212–13, 214, 217, 219–20, 221–22, 223, 224, 227, 229, 233, 236, 240, 242, 244, 273, 291–92, 294, 295, 296, 302–3, 311, 327, 328–33, 344–47, 354–55, 362–63, 368–69, 381, 398, 403, 406–7
geology (unearthing) in crime fiction 149, 292, 295
Ghosh, Kshetramohan 126–27
Giardinelli, Mempo 390
Gibson, William 262
Gillies, Mary Ann 318, 319
Ginzburg, Carlo 129, 195, 292
Glass Cell, The (Highsmith) 278–80
globalisation/glocalisation/glocal 3, 51, 52, 55, 58, 62–63, 77, 80, 82, 94, 97, 216, 239, 267, 306, 340, 344, 347–48, 356–58, 359, 362, 365, 366–68, 372, 374–75, 380, 412
Glynn, Alan 354, 356–58
Godfather, The 353, 381

Index

Godsland, Shelley 156
Godwin, William 3, 27
Goethe, Johann Wolfgang von 77, 78
Golden Age 5, 6, 14, 22, 23, 24, 25, 26, 36, 103–4, 108, 112, 142, 145, 150, 151, 152, 153, 160–61, 185, 186, 191, 192, 196–97, 205, 207, 219, 221, 228–34, 276, 277, 337–38, 343
Gómez, Sergio 315
Gong-An (China) 88–90, 335
Goodis, David 245, 249
Gorrara, Claire 284, 313
Gothic 2, 16, 24, 26, 27, 102, 143, 154, 169, 322
Goyenda (detective) fiction (India) 125–27
Grafton, Sue 105, 163, 265, 330
graphic novels, and crime fiction 50, 65–75
Green, Anna Katharine 230
Greenblatt, Stephen 29
Greene, Graham 253, 343
Greenwood, Kerry 398–99
Gregoriou, Christiana 50, 58, 94, 96, 154, 400
Gresham, William Lindsay 246, 249–50
Grisham, John 364
Grossberg, Lawrence 246
Gulddal, Jesper 178, 204, 238
Gulddal, King and Rolls 17, 26, 179, 365
Gulf War, 348–50
Gulik, Robert van 89–90
Gulynshki, Andrei 391, 392
Guy, Rosa 105

hacking 165–66, 262–63, 266, 268
Haiven, Max 357
Hall, Katharina 312, 388, 389
Hamilton, Bruce 192
Hamlet (Shakespeare) 14, 28–30
Hammett, Dashiell 2, 3, 5–6, 76, 102–3, 104, 112, 150, 154, 161, 162, 199–200, 205–6, 222–23, 256, 278, 284, 285, 293, 295, 329, 331, 332, 338, 343, 354, 355–56, 357, 373, 390; *Glass Key, The* 104; *Maltese Falcon, The* 5–6, 104, 161, 199–200, 278, 329; *Red Harvest* 223, 278, 284, 354, 355–57, 359, 373
Hanley, Jane 69
Hannah, Sophie 192–93
Hansen, Joseph 108
hard-boiled 5, 6, 24, 76, 80, 85, 86, 97, 102, 103, 104, 105, 109, 112, 116, 117, 152, 161, 163, 164, 192, 199–200, 206–7, 215, 219, 221, 222, 230, 233, 244, 245, 250, 255, 265, 276, 278, 282, 283–86, 289, 295–96, 303, 305, 306, 313, 320, 328–33, 337–39, 343, 355, 372, 383, 388, 398
Harper, Jane 39, 42–45, 46
Harris, Thomas 152, 242, 280, 305
Harrod, Mary Beth 62
Hart, Patricia 333
Harvey, David 353–54, 357, 373, 375, 376

Haugtvedt, Erika 37
Hausladen, Gary 212, 213, 216
Hawking, Stephen 292
Hawkins, Paula 192
Haycraft, Howard 141, 143, 204, 222, 328, 388
Healer, The (Tuomainen) 19–20
Healey, Emma 311
Heller, Jason 61–62
Hererra, Yuri 372, 374–75
Herlinghaus, Hermann 371
Herman, Judith Lewis 318, 319, 324
Heyns, Michiel 124
Hiassen, Carl 217
Higashino, Keigo 40, 41, 239
Higginson, Pim 69
Highsmith, Patricia 245, 278–80, 330, 407
high/low, debates 4, 5, 13, 15, 16, 26, 27, 34, 37, 57, 86, 87, 107, 179, 180, 185, 228
Hillerman, Tony 114, 115, 366
Himes, Chester 97, 113, 116, 245, 305, 322–23, 407
history/counter-history, of crime fiction 2, 16, 22–30, 102, 141, 143, 159, 196, 205, 276, 285, 291–92, 295, 297, 338
Hitchcock, Alfred 24, 203
Hogg, James 171
Holocaust 310, 312, 313, 314, 315, 316, 323
Homicide 306
homophobia 109, 173, 175
Horkheimer and Adorno 33
Horn, David 275
Hornung, E. W. 255
Horowitz, Anthony 192, 233
Horsley, Lee 104, 107, 151–52, 210, 228, 229, 230, 329, 333, 356
Howell, Philip 213, 339, 341
Hughes, Dorothy B 150, 154–57, 245, 249, 331, 344
human trafficking, in crime fiction 379, 380, 382, 383–85
humour, in crime fiction 25, 162, 255–56, 305
Hutcheon, Linda 49, 228
Hutchinson, Dave 264
hybridisation, of genre 3, 6, 13, 14, 16, 18, 19–20, 24–26, 57–64, 79, 96, 113, 264, 295, 297, 344–47, 348, 357–58, 362–63, 406–11

identity 52, 55, 68–71, 96, 97, 106, 109, 125, 127, 169, 214, 252, 305, 380–81
Identity Crisis 70–74
Imbert, Pierre-Léonce 292
In a Lonely Place (Hughes) 150, 154–57
India, crime fiction of 51–55, 125–27, 340–42
Indridason, Arnaldur 308
Inner City Blues (Woods) 323–25
intertextuality 4–5, 22, 49–50, 51, 52–53, 58, 77, 86, 87

Index

Irwin, John T. 205
Izzo, Jean Claude 332

Jakobson, Roman 204, 209
James, E.L. 40
James, Henry 340
James, P.D. 212, 232, 303, 412
Jameson, Fredric 64, 94–95, 222, 223, 329, 330, 338
Jane Eyre 120
Japan, in crime fiction 41, 59, 63, 69, 239, 339
Jemissin, Nora K. 409
Jenkins, Henry 399
Jermyn, Deborah 304
Johnson, Craig 366
Johnson, Matt 382
Joy (Chavarría) 393–94
Judge Dee stories (China) 86, 88–90
justice/injustice in crime fiction 6, 53, 61, 65, 70, 80–81, 105, 106, 111, 112, 116, 122–23, 125, 127, 147, 149, 150, 160, 161, 163, 233, 236, 253, 255, 258, 280, 282–89, 292, 296, 302, 310, 314, 316, 323–25, 327–28, 329, 390, 393
Juul, Pia 87

Kaaberol and Friis 382
Kaemmel, Ernst 144
Kant, Immanuel 95
Kayman, Martin 16, 25
Kerr, Philip 163
King, Laurie 321
King, Rodney (34:6)
King, Stewart 76, 77, 78, 79, 80, 81, 98, 141, 145, 317, 329, 365, 388, 389, 394
King and Whitmore 88
Killing, The 49, 206–7, 303, 307
Kirino, Natsuo 59, 62, 63, 245, 248
Knight, Stephen 25, 103, 143, 144, 303, 307, 328, 330, 336, 337
Knox, Ronald 24, 25, 150, 196
Kord, JS 282
Kotwasińka, Agnieszka 26
Kracauer, Siegfried 31, 32
Kraniauskas, John 360
Kristeva, Julia 149, 156, 252, 254, 255, 259
Kurnaiwan, Eka 18

Lacan, Jacques 130, 131–33, 135–36, 144, 248
LaCroix, Alison 282
Lafferty, Mur 59, 61–62
Langford, Barry 58
Larsson, Stieg 41, 59–61, 78, 90, 109, 152–53, 154, 165–66, 239, 262–63, 400, 412
Latin America, in crime fiction 310, 313–17, 366–68, 374–77, 388, 389–90
Latsis and Henissart (Emma Lathen) 187

Laub, Dori 318
Leblanc, Maurice 86, 255, 292
Le Carré, John 344
Le Guin, Ursula K. 407, 408, 409
Ledesma, Francisco González 332
Lefebvre, Henri 220–21
Lehane, Dennis 245, 301
Lem, Stanislav 365
Leon, Aya de 381
Leon, Donna 364
Leroux, Gaston 292, 294
lesbian crime fiction 105, 107, 108, 109
Liano, Dante 390
Light, Alison 103, 343
Lindsay, Jeff 171, 172, 175, 253, 256
Lippard, Laura 212, 217
Lombroso, Cesare 274, 275, 277, 293
London, in crime fiction 23, 24, 77, 95, 336, 337, 338, 354, 373
Long Way Home (Dolan) 383–85
Lorde, Audre 59
Louisiana, in crime fiction 256–59
Lovecraft, H.P. 26
Lucarelli, Carlo 59, 62–63
Luckhurst, Roger 321
Lutes, Jean 331
Luxemburg, Rosa 354, 355, 356, 375, 376
Lyell, Charles 292, 295

Macdonald, Ross 162
McAlpine, Gordon 233
McBain, Ed 164, 192, 200, 303, 339
McCabe, Cameron 229, 231
McCall Smith, Alexander 105
McCann, Sean 328, 388
McCloud, Scott 66, 74
McCoy, Horace 245, 327
McCracken, Scott 329, 332, 385
McDermid, Val 91, 108, 168, 171, 173–75, 192, 296, 303, 331
McKean, Dave 410
McLaren, Philip 88, 124–25
Mabuse, Dr 32
Maccarone, Angelina 254
Makholwa, Angela 114
Makinen, Merja 178
Malet, Léo 91, 283
Malmgren, Carl 151, 230
Manchette, Jean-Patrick 295, 389, 410
Mandel, Ernest 303, 328
Manga (comic) 50, 66, 69–70
Mankell, Henning 48, 76, 81–83, 227, 280, 308, 347–48; *Dogs of Riga, The* 347; *Firewall* 347; *Sidetracked* 301; *Wallander* (BBC adaptation) 48, 81; *White Lioness, The* 76, 82–83, 347
maps, and crime fiction 221–22

419

marketing/publishing, of crime fiction 13, 16, 31, 34, 37, 39–47, 77, 78, 79, 85, 86–87, 98, 236–42, 398–99, 403
Markowitz, Judith 108
Marling, William 245
Marvel (comics) 65
Marxist readings, of crime fiction 144, 247, 353–54, 356, 376, 409
Marx, Karl 355, 356
masculinity 102–4, 107, 108, 112, 125–26, 169, 347; male violence 44, 123–24, 152–53, 154–57
Massey, Doreen 95
Massumi, Brian 246
Matzke and Mühleisen 96, 113, 122
Meade and Eustace 295
melting pot (US) 381
Meltzer, Brad 71–74
memory, and crime fiction 310–17, 323–25
Mencken, H.L. and George Mason 33
Mercurio, Jed (*Bodyguard*) 207–8
Mermaids Singing (McDermid) 173–75
Messac, Régis 24, 291
Messent, Peter 164, 252, 302, 303, 338, 339, 340, 341
Metress, Christopher 245
Mexico, in crime fiction 77, 80, 163, 216, 245, 358–59, 374–75, 375–77, 389
Meyer, Deon 82–83, 114, 115–18, 124, 125, 363
Midsomer Murders 85
Miéville, China 16, 409–11
migration/immigration, in crime fiction 99, 100, 225, 280, 379–86
Miller, D.A. 246
Miller, J. Hillis 180
Mina, Denise 105
Miss Fisher and the Deathly Gaze (game) 397, 398–99, 400, 401, 402–3
Mitchell, Gladys 103–4
mobility, of crime fiction/border crossing 3–4, 6, 13, 15–17, 18, 25, 26, 76, 85, 87, 94, 96, 100, 365, 379–86, 399–400, 407
Montero, Rosa 365
Moonstone, The 2, 120–21, 150, 185, 186, 187, 191
Moore, Robin 371
Moretti, Franco 5, 17–18, 76, 79–80, 142, 195, 196, 320, 328, 335, 337, 359
Morgan, Richard 246
Morrison, Arthur 329
Mosley, Walter 113, 163, 213, 214, 305, 331, 356
mothers 106, 170, 174, 175
Mouawad, Wajdi 364
Mukherjee, Pablo 143
Mukhoopadhyay, Bhuban Chandra 52
Muller, Marcia 163, 319
Mumbai, in crime fiction 340–42
Munt, Sally 105

Murch, Alma 24–25
murder, in crime fiction 14, 15, 61, 62, 67, 103, 104, 105, 106, 141–48, 149, 150, 151, 152, 153–57, 159, 171–73, 180–83, 188–90, 195, 198, 205, 206, 207, 215, 219, 234, 245, 248, 249, 253, 297, 302, 303, 312, 318, 324, 329, 358–59
Murphy, Patrick 363
Murray, Simone 43
Mystery of a Hansom Cab 49

NAFTA (North American Free Trade Agreement) 359, 376, 377
Name of the Rose, The 16
Nancy Drew 304, 401
Narcos 374
narcotics (drugs), in crime fiction 371–78
Naremore, James 245
Naremore and Fay 249
national traditions, of crime fiction 2, 3–5, 18, 76, 79–80, 85, 86–87, 276, 283, 284, 299, 356, 388
Native American crime fiction 114–15, 363, 366
Nava, Michael 109
Nazi Germany 163, 283, 312–15, 328, 388, 389, 391, 392
Neely, Barbara 105
Nesbø, Jo 80
Nestingen, Andrew 82, 280
Neville, Stuart 382
Newgate Calendar 144, 227, 355
New York, in crime fiction 164, 198, 224–26, 241–42, 280, 304, 305, 339
Ngai, Sianie 246
Ngũgĩ, Mũkoma wa 59, 62, 63, 80, 113; *Black Star Nairobi* 113; *Nairobi Heat* 62, 63, 80
Nichol, Bran 202
Nichol, Mike 381
Nicol, Pulham, McNulty 68, 71, 74
Nieland, Justus 249
Nielsen BookScan 39, 40
Nightmare Alley (Gresham) 249–50
Nilsson, Damrosch, D'haen 76, 81, 82, 98, 145, 365
Nixon, Rob 145, 364, 369
noir 5, 45, 60, 63, 69, 103, 104, 113, 152, 154–57, 206, 222, 244–51, 283, 291, 293, 295–96, 318, 344, 407, 410
Nolan, Christopher 316
Norbu, Jamyang 49–50, 79
Nordic noir 2, 17, 41, 44, 49, 59–61, 87, 94, 96, 98, 206–7, 239, 303, 307–8, 347; Scandinoir 87, 206
novela negra (hard-boiled) 332
Nussbaum, Martha 177, 178, 179, 181, 183
Nuttall, Sarah 115

Ó'Cuilleanàin, Cormac 156
Oedipus Rex 27, 134, 159

Index

Okorafor, Nnedi 411
Oliver, Maria-Antònia 213
Oliver and Trigos 248
Ondaatje, Michael 233
Opium Wars 371
Orczy, Baroness 104–5
Orford, Margie 114, 117, 123–24, 125
Otis, Laura 276

Palmer, Jerry 205
Panek, Leroy 258
paratexts, in crime fiction 215, 236–42,
   399, 401
Paretsky, Sara 90, 105, 163, 318, 323, 339
Park and Burgess 275
Parker, Robert 163, 286–89
Patterson, James 171, 172, 175
Paul, Abhra 362
Peach, Linden 169, 170
Peacock, Steven 60
Pearson and Singer 96–97, 100, 122
Peirce, Charles 195
Pepper, Andrew 25, 77, 80–81, 112, 145, 147, 163,
   327, 329, 330, 334, 394
Pepper and Schmid 25, 77, 94, 95, 96, 97, 98,
   100, 224
Perry, Anne 296
Petersen, Robert 66
Pezzotti, Barbara 173
Philips and Strobl 65, 70
Phillips, Mike 381
Piglia, Ricardo 364–65, 389
Pinkerton Detective Agency 161
Pinter, Jason 63
place (and space), crime fiction and 18, 80, 82,
   88, 94–96, 100–1, 211–17, 221–23, 224–26,
   236, 239, 241, 245–46, 248–49, 275, 335–38
Plain, Gill 25, 68, 149, 153, 154, 178,
   219, 252
Plato 289
Platten, David 294, 296
plots and plotting 14–15, 31, 32, 33, 62, 108–9,
   159–60, 183, 185–93, 194, 198, 199, 203–4, 205,
   219–21, 222, 223–24, 228, 344, 345, 348–50,
   385–86, 407
Poe, Edgar Allan 2, 3, 16, 18, 23, 24, 27, 28, 76, 85,
   97, 123, 125, 129, 130, 131–33, 135–36, 141,
   150, 159, 160, 163, 171, 195, 197, 204–5, 216,
   227, 230, 233, 291, 292, 293, 294, 295, 297, 298;
   'Murders in the Rue Morgue, The' 2, 18, 28,
   120, 159, 195, 292, 295; 'Purloined Letter, The'
   28, 130, 131–33, 135–36, 144
Polanyi, Karl 356, 357
police, in crime fiction 25, 27, 36–37, 63, 71, 77,
   81–83, 97, 99, 104–5, 113, 116–17, 125–27,
   144, 146, 160, 163–65, 192, 200, 207–8, 222,
   227, 231, 238, 274, 278, 282, 287, 292–95,

301–8, 323–25, 339–42, 347–48, 383–85,
   388–89, 411
politics, in crime fiction (*also see* social criticism) 5,
   61, 63, 82–83, 98, 100, 120, 122, 127, 145,
   147–48, 169, 192, 215, 221–22, 320, 323–25,
   327–34, 353–60, 375–78, 379–83
Porter, Dennis 58, 220
Portuondo, José Antonio 393
postcolonialism 3, 52, 58, 63, 83, 94, 96–97, 100,
   113–18, 120, 122–23, 145, 214, 233–34, 295,
   330, 379–80
postmodernism, and crime fiction 16, 25, 26,
   37, 57, 58–59, 61, 63, 105, 179, 200,
   215–16, 223, 228, 229, 233, 296, 321, 349,
   381, 389, 411
Power of the Dog, The (Winslow) 375–77
Pratt, Mary Louise 95
Prendergast, Christopher 196
Pretty Little Liars 154
Price, Richard 280
Priestman, Martin 18, 25
Prime Suspect 301, 304, 305
privacy 67–68
Private Eye, The 67, 68
prizes, literary prizes 17, 42, 240, 333
professional/professionalisation 27, 31,
   126, 200
prohibition (US) 161, 283, 328, 371
Promised Land (Parker) 286–89
Promoda (Ghosh) 126–27
Propp, Vladimir 253
psychoanalysis 24, 103–4, 105, 129–37, 195,
   246–48, 292, 299
psychological insights 24, 27, 29, 30, 103, 129,
   142, 144, 160, 173–75, 192–93, 196–97,
   203–9, 242, 264, 274, 278–80, 311, 322,
   408, 412
Pullinger, Schemat and Joseph 401
Puzo, Mario 381
Pyrhönen, Heta 149, 150–51, 217

Quartey, Kwei 303
Queen, Ellery 186, 198–99
queer detection, readings of 108–9, 149, 153, 346
Quinn, Anthony 242

Rabinovici, Doron 311
race and ethnicity 2, 26, 81–82, 96–97, 100, 105,
   111–19, 127, 163, 213–14, 224–26, 256–58, 280,
   301, 302, 305, 323–25, 327, 330, 339, 381–82,
   383, 408
radical geography 213
Rafter, Nicole Hahn 274
Rand, Lou 108
Rankin, Ian 80, 303, 308, 397, 398
Raymond, Derek 410, 412
Rayner, Jay 87–88

Index

reading and reading strategies 66–69, 71, 74, 80, 91, 98, 129, 134–35, 150, 177, 178–79, 180, 183, 195, 196, 200, 211, 216–17, 221, 228, 229, 233, 236, 237, 239, 240, 241, 242, 253, 296, 334, 389, 400–1, 402
realism 22–23, 150, 152, 153, 160, 161, 162, 164, 202–9, 306–8, 318, 321–22, 324
Reddy, Maureen 112, 118
Reed, Sarah 88
Reeve, Arthur 22, 23, 33
Reichs, Kathy 152, 154, 265, 266, 412
Reitz, Caroline 112, 412
Ressler, Robert 242
Reynolds, Barbara 191
Richtel, Matt 401
Ricoeur, Paul 129
Riley, Brenden 261
Ritzer and Schutzel 57
Robertson, Roland 51
Rock, Paul 274
Rolls, Alistair 17
Rolls, West-Sooby and Vuaille-Barcan 86, 88
Rolls and Sitbon 86
Roman Hat Mystery, The (Queen) 198–99
Roth, Gerhard 311–12
Rothberg, Michael 310, 313, 314, 321, 322, 323
Rowland, Susan 152, 230
Roy, Dinendra Kumar 52
Russ, Joanna 412
Rymer, J.M. 49
Rzepka, Charles 25

Sacheri, Eduardo 390
Sacred Games (Chandra) 340–42
Saer, Juan José 390
Sallis, James 16
Salzani, Carlo 336
Saviano, Roberto 371
Sayers, Dorothy B. 23, 26, 35, 106–8, 112, 151, 152–53, 157, 160, 186–87, 190, 191–92, 205, 215, 222, 228, 229, 231, 234, 277–78, 304, 319, 329, 337–38, 343; *Busman's Honeymoon* 108; *Documents in the Case, The* 191; *Gaudy Night* 108; *Great Short Stories of Detection, Mystery and Horror* 26; *Strong Poison* 106–8, 151; *Whose Body?* 23, 106, 277
Scaggs, John 25, 65, 150, 151, 273
Schmid, David 80, 169–70, 173, 211, 213, 216, 339
Sciascia, Leonardo 390
science fiction, and crime fiction 16, 41, 61–62, 264, 365, 400, 401, 406–12
science, forensic science 26, 53, 91, 121, 154, 156, 196, 200, 203, 232, 261–69, 280, 287, 291, 292, 293, 294, 347, 412; science, scientific development 8, 23, 23, 26, 28, 102, 121, 159–160, 195, 197, 274–75, 277, 280, 291–99, 303

Seago, Karen 50, 94, 96, 379
Sedgwick, Eve Kosofsky 246
Sedgwick, Marcus 311
Seeman, Daphne 312
Segura, Alex 381
self-referentiality (metafiction) 181–82, 227–34; *also see* postmodernism
semiotics 203
Semyonov, Iulian 391–92, 393
sensation fiction/sensationalism 2, 16, 23, 24, 27, 34, 35, 37, 102, 141, 142, 143, 144, 146, 147, 154, 233, 277, 295, 319, 324
September 11 (9/11) 344
seriality, in crime fiction 7, 23, 31–38, 106, 303, 306, 344, 399
Serial 37, 401
serial killers 2, 62, 155, 166, 169–72, 174, 175, 190, 241–42, 248, 253, 276, 280, 347, 359
Série Noire (imprint) 86, 87, 88, 245
Southern Seas
Shakespeare, William 23, 28–30
Shaw, Bruce 25, 253, 256
Sherez, Stav 264, 265, 267
'Shoe, The' (Xiaoqing) 145–47
Sicily 90, 98–101
Simenon, Georges 5, 6, 58, 87, 164, 303
Simon, David 37, 305
Six Wakes 61–62
Sjöwall, Maj and Per Wahlöö 77, 87, 90, 164, 303, 339
Škvorecký, Josef 233
Smillie, Rachel 295
Smith, Roger 123
Snack Thief, The (Camilleri) 98–101
Sobchack, Vivian 249
social criticism/critique; *also see* politics 58, 59, 60–61, 63, 77, 86, 91, 98, 105, 109, 122–23, 145, 146, 147, 148, 163, 164, 224, 236, 256, 265, 303, 320, 332, 359, 362–64, 365, 368, 379, 382
social media 1, 37, 42, 43, 44, 48, 49, 68, 208, 262–64, 269, 399, 401, 404
Soitos, Stephen 322
Soja, Ed 221
Solana, Teresa 211, 214, 215–16
Sophocles 27
Sopranos, The 343
South Africa, in crime fiction 82–83, 114–18, 121, 123–24, 347, 381
Southern Seas (Montalbán 332–33
Spain, in crime fiction 156, 215, 327, 332–33
Spillane, Mickey 154, 284, 285
Spinoza, Baruch 246, 247
Spiral 254
Squires, Claire 45
Stalin, Josef 391
state crimes (totalitarianism) 310, 314, 391
Steel Kiss, The (Deaver) 267–68

Index

Stewart, Victoria 280
Stillman, Sarah 155
Stolarek, Joanne 229
Stone, Nick 204
Stone, Robert 373–74
Streek, Wolfgang 358, 376
Sturgeon, Theodore 409
Sturm, Brian 66
stylistic analysis 171–75
Sunset Boulevard 249
Superman 32, 74
supernatural 2, 26, 27, 29–30, 88, 89, 90,
 102, 294
surveillance (visual technology) 164, 221, 262, 263,
 266, 294, 347, 366
Sutcliffe, Peter 253
Suvin, Darko 407
Swedish crime fiction 76–77, 78, 81–83,
 347–48
Sylvain, Dominique 255
Symons, Julian 14, 17, 25, 141, 144, 185, 329

Taibo II, Paco Ignacio 163, 216, 245
Taken 254
Tal, Kalí 321
Tan, Yi-Fu 216, 217
Tatort (German TV) 254
technology (digital technology) 90, 164, 237,
 261–69, 408, 409
Temple, Peter 381
Tey, Josephine 234
Tharoor, Tilottama 62–63
Thilliez, Franck 296
Thomas, Bronwen 61, 401
Thomas, Ronald 261, 266, 276, 293
Thompson, H. Douglas 26
Thompson, Jim 171, 245, 407, 408
Thompson, John B. 40, 42, 43, 44
Thornber, Karen 363
Three Evangelists, The (Vargas) 296–99
Three Kings 348–50
Tiptree, James Jr 412
Tithecott, Richard 172
Tlholwe, Diale 118
Todorov, Tzevtan 5, 15, 17, 18, 142, 186, 228,
 229, 253, 310, 312, 313, 314, 318, 319,
 320, 407
Tomkins, Sylvan 246
tourism, and/in crime fiction 85, 86, 92, 94, 213,
 215, 217, 363, 366, 367, 400
Tracy, Dick 65
transgenderism 173, 174
transgression, sexual 102, 104, 106–7, 108, 169,
 170, 180
translation 22, 40, 43, 45, 48, 77, 78, 79, 81, 85–93,
 95, 144, 164, 214, 215, 239, 240, 262, 345, 390,
 392, 393, 394, 400

transnationalism 2, 3, 4, 6, 7, 18, 19, 20, 22, 23,
 25, 32–33, 37, 48, 50, 51, 57, 58, 59, 62–63, 65,
 76–77, 78, 80, 82, 85, 94–101, 113, 143–45,
 165, 166, 214–17, 224–26, 236, 239, 249, 282,
 299, 310, 316, 332, 347–48, 351, 356–60, 365,
 368, 372, 375–78, 379, 380, 382, 388, 389,
 394, 411–13
Trapped 303
trauma, in crime fiction 85, 103, 108, 115, 118,
 124, 149, 169, 192, 207, 208, 246, 247,
 248–49, 298, 299, 308, 312, 313, 316, 318–25,
 346, 390, 408, 412
Trenter, Stieg 76–77
Trollope, Anthony 185
Trott, Sarah 318
Trousdale, Rachel 94, 95
true crime 16, 34, 37–38, 143, 144, 306, 368, 380,
 401, 404
True Detective 26, 154, 308
Truffaut, François 249
Tuomainen, Antti 13, 16, 19–20, 217, 365
Turton, Stuart 192, 234
Twin Peaks 154

Upfield, Arthur 124
Uxó, Carlos 331

Van Dine, S.S. 14, 24, 141, 143–44, 150, 196, 222,
 294, 402
Vargas, Fred 286–89, 291, 296–99, 303, 364
Vaughan, Brian K. 67–68
Vázquez Montalbán, Manuel 215, 327, 322–33,
 381, 389
verisimilitude 34, 91, 209
Verne, Jules 408
veterans 106, 108, 156, 207, 208, 324, 343–44,
 345–47, 350
Vian, Boris 245
victims and scapegoats (others) 149–58, 169, 170,
 175, 252–59, 264, 284, 285, 304, 306, 312–13,
 315, 316, 319, 321, 322, 323–25, 330, 332, 333,
 368, 380–86, 390, 394
Vidal, Pau 364
Vidocq 3, 125, 244
Vietnam (war, in US imagination) 256, 286, 287,
 323, 324, 325, 349, 408
Villalobos, Juan Pablo 372, 374
Vine, Barbara 382

Wallace, Edgar 31, 34–36, 37
Walpole, Horace 27
Walters, Minette 411–12
Walton, Samantha 277
Walton and Jones 105
Wambaugh, Joseph 240, 303, 339
war, and crime fiction 343–51
war on terror 344, 346

Wash This Blood Clean From My Hands
  (Vargas) 286–89
Watson, Kate 171, 173
Weber, Max 388
Wells, Carolyn 23
Wells, H.G. 408, 411
West, Fred and Rosemary 253
Western tradition, of crime fiction/ethnocentrism
  3, 13, 17, 18, 30, 78, 79, 89, 90, 113, 120, 122,
  125, 143, 145, 199, 233, 253, 295, 331, 349, 372,
  381, 386, 391, 392, 407, 411
Whewell, William 292
White, Hayden 344
Williams, Linda 306
Williams, Raymond 247, 364
Wilson, Barbara 105, 108
Wilson, Colin 242
Wing, Mary 108
Winn, Dilys 26
Winslow, Don 340, 372, 375–77
Wire, The 37, 301, 305, 306, 360
Wittgenstein 21

Woods, Paula 323–25
Woolrich, Cornell 245, 248
world literature, crime fiction as 4, 7, 17, 76–84,
  144–45, 214, 216–17, 317, 365, 388, 389
World War I 23, 103, 153, 160, 161, 186, 199, 298,
  299, 318, 337, 343, 345
World War II, 24, 49, 53, 86, 106, 232, 284, 288,
  302, 303, 311, 313, 315, 316, 328, 331, 339, 343,
  344, 347
Worthington, Heather 25, 104, 143

xenophobia 117, 122, 381, 382, 385
Xiaoqing, Cheng 145–47

Yokoyama, Hideo 339
Yoshida, Shuichi 245
Young, Alison 388
Young Detective Dee: Rise of the Sea Dragon 89

Zaremba, Eve 108
Zigomar (French) 33
Žižek, Slavoj 82, 130–31, 246, 347, 355